The Professional
Pastry Chef

Charts, cake decorating designs, chocolate figurines, marzipan designs, and templates designed and drawn by Bo Friberg

Chapter opening art drawn by Lisa Johnson

All other illustrations drawn by Joyce Hasselbeck

Photography by Bo Friberg

The Professional Pastry Chef

SECOND EDITION

Bo Friberg

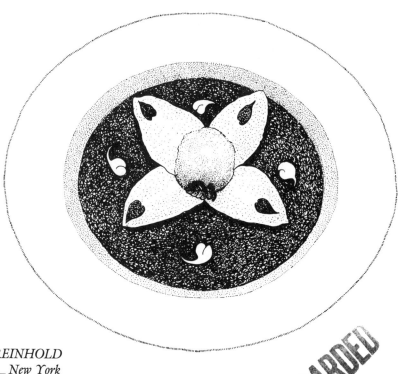

VNR *VAN NOSTRAND REINHOLD*
_____ *New York*

To two great Swedish confectioners-John Håkanson and Curt Anderson-who not only had the patience and craft to teach me what they knew about their profession, but also taught me a l about life!
To the students of the California Culinary Academy for your help in testing these recipes in the course of your learning.
To Amy for all of your help, hard work, patience, and understanding.

Printed in the United States of America
For more information, contact:

Van Nostrand Reinhold
115 Fifth Avenue
New York, NY 10003

International Thomson Publishing GmbH
Konigswinterer Strasse 418
53227 Bonn
Germany

International Thomson Publishing
Berkshire House 168-173
High Holborn
London WCIV 7AA
England

International Thomson Publishing Asia
221 Henderson Road #05-10
Henderson Building
Singapore 0315

Thomas Nelson Australia
102 Dodds Street
South Melbourne, 3205
Victoria, Australia

International Thomson Publishing Japan
Hirakawacho Kyowa Building, 3F
2-2-1 Hirakawacho
Chiyoda-ku, 102 Tokyo
Japan

Nelson Canada
1120 Birchmount Road
Scarborough, Ontario
Canada M1K 5G4

International Thomson Editores Mexico
Campos Eliseos 385, Piso 7
Col. Polanco
11560 Mexico D.F. Mexico

RRDHB 16 15 14 13 12 11 10 9 8 7

Library of Congress Cataloging-in-Publication Data

Friberg, Bo, 1940-
The professional pastry chef / Bo Friberg; charts, cake decorating designs, chocolate figurines, marzipan designs, and templates drawn by Bo Friberg; chapter opening art drawn by Lisa Johnson; all other illustrations by Joyce Hasselbeck.
  p. cm.
ISBN 0-442-31893-6
1. Pastry. I. Title.
TX773.F75 1989   *89-16556*
641.8'65-dc20   *CIP*

Contents

Foreword by Thomas A. Bloom   *vii*

Foreword by Jeremiah Tower   *viii*

Preface   *ix*

Introduction   *xi*

1   Mise en Place   2

2   Basic Doughs   12

3   Breads and Rolls   44

4   Breakfast Breads and Pastries   80

5   Cookies   120

6   Tarts   142

7   Sponge and Tea Cakes   158

8   Decorated Cakes   172

9   Individual Pastries   222

10   Desserts for Restaurant Presentation   270

11   Charlottes and Bavarois, Custards,
     Mousses, and Soufflés   304

12   Meringues   330

13   Ice Cream and Frozen Desserts   352

14   Light Desserts   380

15   Holiday Breads and Desserts   402

16   Chocolate and Chocolate Candies   438

17 Sugar Work 466

18 Decorations 498

19 Sauces and Fillings 554

Appendix A: Ingredients 571
    Alcoholic Flavorings
    Butter, Lard, and Margarine
    Chocolate and Chocolate Products
    Cream and Milk
    Eggs
    Flour
    Fruit
    Jellying Agents
    Leavening Agents
    Nuts
    Sweeteners
    Tartaric Acid
    Thickeners
    Vanilla

Appendix B: Equipment 598

Appendix C: Conversion and Equivalency Tables 606

Index 617

Foreword

The revised *Professional Pastry Chef* provides an excellent source of international recipes as well as a basic guide for apprentices who want to make baking their occupation. Master Pastry Chef Friberg presents a broad scope of baking and pastry, and touches on each department in the world of sweets.

The Professional Pastry Chef is a must for all pastry and hotel chefs. It represents the knowledge Chef Friberg has gained throughout his training and experience in his native country, Sweden. This revision offers an extensive collection of pastry and dessert recipes. Chef Friberg also explains in full the whys and the wherefores behind his recipes. The formulas are easy to follow and have been tested in the pastry shops and classrooms of the California Culinary Academy.

Eleven years ago Bo Friberg joined the California Culinary Academy as an instructor, and throughout his career he has continued to strive for excellence in his teaching as well as his work as a chef. Chef Friberg's extensive research along with his creative talents allows him to offer new and innovative approaches.

The faculty, staff, and graduates of the California Culinary Academy join me in congratulating "Chef Bo" on this book.

Thomas A. Bloom, Ph.D.
President
California Culinary Academy
Professional School for Chef Training

Foreword

I never went to school to be trained as a professional chef, because my career as a chef began by accident. So as I ran the kitchen at *Chez Panisse* in Berkeley in the early seventies, I knew my knowledge of the art of pastry making was minimal. Fortunately, I was backed up by Lindsey Shere and her superb pastry skills.

Nevertheless, I read many dessert and pastry books. The ones "for the housewife" were mainly recipe books, so I bought some professional tomes, which were usually a thousand pages long and absolutely frightening. So I was left a bit in the lurch.

I met Bo Friberg at the California Culinary Academy some years later when I introduced the evening dinner classes and slowly wormed my way into his kitchen, out of which emerged effortlessly each day large quantities of superb pastries, all made by students who theoretically had very limited knowledge and expertise.

I quickly became friends with Bo and admired his talent for explaining and producing pastries, from the simplest cakes to the most complicated sugar baskets, all with no worry or panic.

The first edition of this successful book seemed geared to professionals. This wonderful new edition has a broader range and appeal, because recipes both simple and complex, from Peach Cobbler with Cinnamon to Individual Baked Alaskas or Triple Chocolate Terrine, are totally accessible. It will further the knowledge and skill of a professional pastry chef, but most of all, it is a book for every cook to work with and enjoy. *The Professional Pastry Chef* will lead you as far as you want to go with pastries, breads, ice creams, candies, and anything to do with sugar.

I salute Bo on his new creation and know that every reader will be eager to use it.

Jeremiah Tower, chef/owner
Stars and 690 restaurants, San Francisco

Preface

This second edition of *The Professional Pastry Chef* began two years ago as a simple revision of the first edition. I was very pleased and honored that the popularity and use of my book was high enough to warrant a revised and expanded edition. What ultimately came out of that revision process is a totally new book. This edition has grown to nearly 650 pages with more than 400 recipes, 250 illustrations, 50 new color photographs, and a new format that will make it much easier to use whether you are a student, an experienced pastry chef, a pastry teacher at the professional level, or a serious home baker.

All of the classic desserts and pastries from the first book have been included along with new ideas for modern variations and impressive plate presentations. The yield of the original recipes has been reduced to better suit the smaller restaurant or a restaurant with a large menu producing small quantities of many different items.

Another format change is the inclusion of step-by-step illustrations. These can be of great help to the student and instructor alike. A student can much more easily comprehend a recipe by following the illustrations along with the text. The teacher can refer to the illustrations in many cases without having to physically demonstrate each project.

I have expanded the nonrecipe portion of the book to include information on ingredients and equipment, high-altitude baking and conversions, and information on the metric system. There are also new chapters on chocolate, sugar work, decorating, light desserts, and holiday baked goods.

Instructions in all of the recipes have been rewritten and reformatted into shorter, numbered steps that are easier to follow.

This book differs from many other textbooks in some very

important ways. My background allows me to approach the subject matter from several different angles. This book is written by a Master Pastry Chef with over thirty years of professional experience in the industry. I have worked in both small shops and large retail and wholesale operations in the United States and in Europe. I worked for the Swedish American Cruise Ship Line, and I have spent the last eleven years teaching all levels of students at one of the most prestigious cooking schools in the country, the California Culinary Academy. In writing this book I called upon all of these experiences to try and make the book as useful as I could for the largest possible audience.

Both instructors and students will be pleased to note that all of the recipes and procedures in this book have been tested by literally thousands of students in my classes and have been changed and improved as needed. In the instructions, I point out typical pitfalls and explain why certain steps must be completed in a particular order or manner.

Upon leaving any school, students must be able not just to perform but also to produce at a reasonable speed in order to make a good living in this field. Although there are many fine cooking schools that are not set up to actually serve food to the public, these recipes are not in any sense designed just for practice or for all-day student projects where labor cost is not an issue. These are workable, practical recipes to be used in the real world of pastry and baking production. Students will certainly want to carry this text with them out into the industry after graduation.

Depending on the type of institution and its curriculum, an instructor may want to use this book in different ways. Although the order of the chapters follows a logical sequence of procedures that is in keeping with students' skill development, it is not necessary to follow this format. It is, however, important that students first learn how to work with basic doughs and ingredients. While the illustrations will be of great help showing the student the particular steps for a given item, it is still very important that the instructor follow up a lecture on puff paste, for example, by showing the students how the turns are made, how to roll and cut the dough, how to make bouchées, and so on. While these techniques are explained in this book the way I do them (and I do from time to time explain a variation), instructors are encouraged to give the students their own input.

I wish every reader—professional, nonprofessional, student, instructor, beginner, or experienced master—great success.

Introduction

All of these recipes have two things in common: They have been written so that anyone with a basic knowledge of cooking will be able to understand them, and they have all been thoroughly tested, by myself and by my students. I started the first edition of this book eight years ago when I came back from a trip to Europe, full of inspirations and new ideas, and began to catalog the new recipes along with other recipes I was teaching. This edition, like the first, is a little different from some other cookbooks in that it tells you not only what you should do, but also what not to do, based on common mistakes I have observed in working with students.

Some of the selections are classic recipes made my way. Some date back to when I was an apprentice. A few I have "borrowed" from restaurants and pastry shops around Europe, where I would order something that looked interesting, pick it apart, literally and mentally, and then try to duplicate or even improve it. Many of the recipes I developed through knowing what goes well together and what the American customer likes. In addition to the classics, this second edition contains recipes and techniques that are in keeping with current trends in the industry, such as lighter or reduced-calorie desserts and more artistic presentations.

Many changes in the pastry field during the last ten years have been influenced by the increased availability of reasonably priced imported specialty produce, such as tropical fruits, and excellent quality "halfway" products from European manufacturers, such as gianduja, florentina mix, chocolate shells, praline paste, and truffle fillings. Being able to order passion fruit, for example, at a price that makes it economically feasible to use it, and having plums, peaches, and raspberries, once strictly seasonal, available almost all year round, can allow the pastry chef much more creativity.

Pastry is distinct from other types of cooking because you cannot just stick your finger in for a taste and then add a pinch of this and a pinch of that as you might when making a pot of soup; most ingredients must be measured precisely, and many formulas work on scientific principles. For this reason the pastry chef must learn how different ingredients react with others, and how and why ingredients respond to temperature, friction, and storage. To create new recipes (or sometimes to figure out what you did wrong) you need to know, for example, that baking soda must be mixed with some type of acid to make it react, that gelatin will not work in the presence of an enzyme found in certain fresh fruits, and that yeast does not multiply successfully without sugar. You should also know at what temperature sugar will caramelize, how hot yeast can get before it is killed, what causes air to become trapped in cake batters, and what storage temperatures will destroy the appearance of chocolate products.

To be a first-rate pastry chef, you must have some artistic talent, a good sense of coordination and taste, and a steady hand. You must also earn the respect of the people working with you. You must be able to solve problems and hire the right people. A good chef must be born with a little of these talents, but keen interest and a lot of practice will improve these skills over the years. A competent chef's most important asset is common sense. It is the one thing that cannot be taught. When you believe in yourself and believe that you can do the job, you will give everything your best effort. If the result is less than perfect, at least you will have learned something, and the next time you will try a little harder.

My first experiment with cooking happened in my mother's kitchen when I was 11 years old. Coming home from school and finding the house empty, I attempted some kind of candy. I don't remember exactly what it was supposed to be, but I do remember that my poor mother had great difficulty cleaning up the sticky pots and pans. We both learned something from this: my mom, to time her trips to the grocery store better; and I, to clean up my messes.

After graduating from school at 14, I started as an apprentice at one of the local bakeries. It was quite small, just three bakers and myself. I was lucky, without knowing it, to happen to pick the best: my master and teacher for the next five years was a dedicated and skilled craftsman. He slowly and surely taught me the tricks of the trade, as well as a lot about life. When I began I was, of course, a young boy who knew everything already. However, I soon found out about the real world, and especially how to take constructive criticism and learn from my mistakes. I remember his words: "One mistake is no mistake. But two mistakes are two mistakes too many." I also began to develop my own tricks of the trade.

I spent my first six months of training practicing the three Ls: listening, looking, and learning. While I was helping a little here and cleaning up a little there, I had helped in making the dough for rye bread, but I had not done it on my own from start to finish. One morning when I arrived at work, my master said "Bo! We are shorthanded today. Make up the rye bread!" I was startled and said, "I can't do that!" My master angrily replied, "Do not ever use that word here again! You can do anything you want to do if you want to do it badly enough. The least you can do is give it your very best try." I have always remembered and tried to live by those words. It is one of the philosophies that I try to instill in all of my students.

After I had become a regular on the rye bread, the retired owner of the bakery used to come down to check me out. (Bakeries in Sweden were always in the cellar with small windows level with the street, so when the bakers looked out all they could see were shoes.) After a few lectures about "loaves that were not perfectly formed," I learned that he would always walk straight from the door to the shelves where the breads cooled and pick up a loaf in the center of one shelf to examine. After I started placing the almost-perfect loaves in this place, I could practice and improve in peace. But if I happened to pay too much attention to those shoes outside the windows, I used to hear from across the room, "Bo, throw some sheet pans on the floor. I don't see you doing anything, so at least let me hear you!" In the end my "yes-I-know-that" attitude must have improved too, for my master named his first and only son Bo, which I claimed as the ultimate victory. He assured me, however, that naming his son had nothing to do with a certain apprentice.

Unfortunately very few restaurants today can afford to completely train an apprentice; it costs too much in both time and materials. Schools such as the California Culinary Academy now provide the training that small businesses cannot. Now an employer can hire a graduate with at least sixteen months of basic training.

Once you master the basic methods, you can start to create, improve, and put a little bit of yourself and your own style into the dishes you prepare. In our industry today, I am pleased to see more creativity and that "bit of self" going into dessert menus. Even so, too often you still find restaurants where, even though the food coming out of the main kitchen is unusual and carefully prepared, the dessert menu offers only a basic chocolate cake with too much sponge and not enough filling, a basic custard, and an overbaked cheesecake. Or the worst offender: plain vanilla or chocolate ice cream, sometimes "creatively" put together in one dish. Most of the time these desserts are not even made on the premises, and are a few days old and dry as well as boring.

The first and last impressions of a meal are very important. I do not expect anything of a meal if the kitchen cannot make a decent salad or serve the soup hot. However, even if the meal is mediocre, a dessert that looks and tastes terrific will leave the guest with a positive last impression. I have noted with pleasure a rebirth of interest in great desserts. It is especially rewarding for me when I realize, glancing at a restaurant menu or tasting a dessert, that one of my former students has been in the kitchen.

This book is about making pastries and cakes that are good and exciting. It is not meant to impress or to set any particular standards. The methods described and used in the recipes are not the only or necessarily the best methods. There are different ways to form a loaf of bread, frost a cake, or hold a decorating bag. One way is good for one person, another way better for someone else.

In this book I offer the best of my knowledge and experience, as I give it to my students. It is my hope that this knowledge will be useful to you as you seek to better yourself in our creative and honorable profession.

Before You Use This Book

Certain ingredient information is standard throughout the book. Please note the following conventions:

- "Butter" always refers to sweet butter. Salted butter can be substituted if the salt in the recipe is reduced by about ⅕ ounce (6 g) for every pound (455 g) of butter. You cannot substitute salted butter, however, if the recipe contains little salt or if the main ingredient is butter.
- The number of eggs specified in each recipe is based on 2-ounce (55-g) eggs (graded large). If you use eggs of a different size, adjust the number accordingly.
- Yeast is always specified as "fresh compressed yeast." To substitute dry yeast for fresh, reduce the amount called for by half.
- Gelatin is available in both sheet and powdered form; the same measure of either can be used. Sheet gelatin is more expensive but more convenient. To prepare the gelatin, place it in enough cold water to cover the sheets. Within a few minutes it will absorb enough liquid to become soft and spongy. Then remove the sheet without squeezing it out. Sheet gelatin will always absorb the same amount of liquid, so you do not need to soak it in a specified amount of water as you do powdered gelatin.
- Both metric and U.S. units are given throughout. However, to avoid unmeasurable fractions, metric amounts have been rounded to the nearest even number. The equivalent for 1 ounce, for instance, is given as 30 grams rather than 28.35 grams.

The Professional
Pastry Chef

— O N E —

Mise en Place

Almond Paste
Butter and Flour Mixture
Cinnamon Sugar
Coffee Reduction
Egg Wash
Hazelnut Paste
Poaching Syrups I and II
Praline and Praline Paste
Simple Syrup
Streusel Topping

Vanilla Extract
Vanilla Sugar
Savory Recipe Variations
   Cheese Soufflé
   Cheese Straws
   Gougères
   Ham and/or Cheese
     Croissants
   Quiche Lorraine

*T*he *literal translation* of *mise en place* is to "put things in place." In the professional kitchen the term means the things we need to get done ahead of time, or prep work. Preparation is an important factor for the professional pastry chef. In the pastry kitchen, many things should be done at the end of the day so they will be ready the next morning, such as making pastry cream and other fillings or removing butter from the freezer so it can thaw and soften.

Before starting any project the professional will make a "plan of attack," first going through the recipe mentally and making sure all of the ingredients needed to complete it smoothly are at hand, then thinking of how to accomplish the tasks most efficiently. If roasted sliced almonds are needed for German Poppy Seed Cake, they should be prepared first thing so they are cold by the time they are used. If melted chocolate is needed to finish Vanilla Macaroons, it can be placed over hot water and stirred from time to time while the buttercream is being formed on the macaroons.

Items that are used regularly should always be accessible. If you make croissants every morning, you don't need to make fresh egg wash each day. Instead, make enough to last three or four days and store

it covered in the refrigerator (in fact, it actually works better if it is a day or more old). When going to the refrigerator for milk to make pastry cream, think about what you are making next, and if, for example, that happens to be apple filling, get the apples at the same time instead of making two trips. If you can think one or two steps ahead you will get a lot more done in less time, or, as my master used to tell me when I was an apprentice, "What you do not have in your head, you have to make up for with your feet."

Almond Paste

1 pound, 14 ounces (855 g) paste

10 ounces (285 g) blanched
*   almonds*
10 ounces (285 g) powdered sugar
1¼ cups (300 ml) Simple Syrup,
*   approximately (page 7)*

1. Place the almonds in a high-speed food processor and process until they are finely ground.

2. Add the powdered sugar, then gradually add the simple syrup until the mixture forms a paste. The amount of syrup needed will vary depending on how dry the almonds are. Freshly blanched almonds will need less syrup. Store the almond paste tightly covered. If kept for more than one week, store in the refrigerator.

Butter and Flour Mixture

Using a butter and flour mixture is a quick and easy way to prepare cake pans, forms, or molds in a recipe that says to grease and flour the pan. Rather than apply the two separately, brush on the flour at the same time you grease the pan. This method can save a great deal of time when the task is done over and over throughout the day.

1. Combine four parts melted butter or margarine with one part bread flour by volume.

2. Apply the mixture with a brush.

The combination can be left at room temperature for up to one week. If the mixture is refrigerated, warm it before using (but do not boil) and stir to combine.

Cinnamon Sugar

Combine one part ground cinnamon with five parts granulated sugar by volume.

Coffee Reduction

1. Make coffee 10 times the normal strength.
2. Bring to a boil in a saucepan and reduce by half.
3. Let cool and use as needed. Coffee reduction can be stored at room temperature for a few weeks; it should be refrigerated if it is to be kept any longer.

Egg Wash

Egg wash gives a shine to soft breads and rolls, croissants, puff paste items, and cookies. It can also be used as a "glue" to hold pieces of dough together, or to make almonds or sugar adhere when sprinkled on a pastry before baking.

Make egg wash for general use by beating whole eggs with a pinch of salt. If you want maximum shine from the egg wash, make egg yolk wash by using egg yolks only; add a pinch of salt and thin to an easy-to-brush consistency with milk or water. You will need approximately 2 tablespoons (30 ml) milk or water for every eight yolks. This yolk wash will be too strong, however, for any item that is baked at a high heat or needs to spend more than 15 minutes in the oven, as do bread and croissants. For these products use regular egg wash or thin the yolk wash further.

Egg Wash for Spraying
1 cup (240 ml) egg wash

3 eggs
2 egg yolks
½ teaspoon (2.5 g) salt

Applying egg wash with a spray bottle instead of a brush (the more typical and time-consuming method) has been common in European bakeries since the early sixties. The spray technique makes a lot of sense. Not only is it faster, but it also produces a smooth, even application. Moreover, since you do not actually touch the product, you do not risk damaging the soft dough. The only disadvantage is that you will, of course, be applying egg wash to the baking paper around the items you are spraying, but this small amount of waste is offset by the advantages. It is a good idea to designate an easy-to-clean area in the kitchen to use for spraying, or be sure to place a few sheets of baking paper around your work area to aid in clean-up.

1. Combine eggs, egg yolks, and salt. Process for 10 to 15 seconds in a food processor. Strain through a *chinois*.
2. Cover the mixture and refrigerate for a minimum of 2 to 3 hours, or preferably overnight.
3. Pour the egg wash into a hand-operated spray bottle set to fine mist.
4. Spray the item to be baked, holding the bottle about 10 inches (25 cm) above, and turning the sheet pan as necessary to ensure even coverage on all sides.
5. To achieve the maximum amount of shine, let the egg wash dry for a few minutes and apply a second coat.

Hazelnut Paste

1 cup (240 ml) paste

8 ounces (225 g) hazelnuts, toasted
  and skins removed (page 592)
3 ounces (90 ml) Simple Syrup,
  approximately (page 7)

1. Process the hazelnuts and simple syrup together in a food processor until the mixture becomes a thick paste.

2. Store in airtight containers to use as needed.

NOTE: As with the praline paste, this product is typically purchased rather than made by most professional operations. The commercial product is more concentrated, so you may need to decrease the amount specified in the recipes if you substitute purchased paste.

Poaching Syrup I

5 cups (720 ml) syrup

1 quart (960 ml) water
1 pound (455 g) granulated sugar
½ lemon, cut into wedges
1 teaspoon (5 ml) vanilla extract
6 whole cloves
1 cinnamon stick

Combine all ingredients in a saucepan. Bring to a boil and add fruit.

To poach pears or apples

1. Place a lid or plate that fits down inside the saucepan on top of the fruit to keep it submerged; otherwise the fruit will bob on top of the syrup and the exposed part will oxidize, turn brown, and will not cook.

2. Boil gently for about 5 minutes.

3. Lower the heat and simmer very slowly until the fruit is tender and cooked all the way through. Do not poach the fruit too rapidly or it will be overcooked on the outside and still raw inside. Worse yet, the uncooked part will turn brown.

4. To check if pears or apples are done, pinch gently with your fingers. They should feel soft but not mushy, having about the same amount of resistance as the fleshy part of your hand.

To poach plums, peaches, apricots, cherries, and other fragile fruits

1. Bring the syrup to a boil, add fruit, and lower the heat immediately to simmer very gently; do not boil.

2. Cook the fruit until it is tender.

NOTE: Remove peaches after they have cooked for a few minutes, peel off the skin using a small pointed knife, then return them to the syrup and continue cooking until soft.

Variation: Poaching Syrup II

Follow the preceding recipe but omit whole cloves and cinnamon stick.

Praline

1 pound (455 g) praline

4 ounces (115 g) hazelnuts
4 ounces (115 g) almonds
corn oil, or other bland oil
8 ounces (225 g) granulated sugar
1 teaspoon (5 ml) lemon juice

1. Remove the skin from the almonds and hazelnuts (see page 489). Toast the nuts lightly and reserve.
2. Lightly oil a marble slab or sheet pan.
3. Caramelize the sugar with the lemon juice to a light golden color (see page 488).
4. Immediately add the toasted nuts, stir to combine, and pour onto the oiled marble.
5. Let the praline cool completely, then crush with a dowel or rolling pin to the desired consistency.

Praline Paste

Pass the crushed praline through a grinding machine until a paste-like consistency is reached. Since making praline paste is time-consuming, most professionals purchase it ready-made. The commercial product can be used in the recipes in this book.

Simple Syrup

(28° Baumé)
3 quarts (2 l, 880 ml) syrup

2 quarts (1 l, 920 ml) water
2 pounds, 8 ounces (1 kg, 135 g) granulated sugar
1 pound, 8 ounces (680 g) glucose or light corn syrup (see note 1)

1. Place water, sugar, and glucose or corn syrup in a saucepan; stir to combine.
2. Heat to boiling and let boil for a few seconds.
3. Set aside to cool. If any scum has developed on the surface, skim it off before pouring the syrup into bottles. Simple syrup should be refrigerated if kept for more than two to three weeks.

NOTE 1: To avoid any mess when measuring glucose or corn syrup, first weigh the sugar and leave it on the scale, then make a well in the sugar and pour the corn syrup into the well until you have the right amount. Glucose or heavy corn syrup is too thick to pour but can easily be scooped up using your hand if you wet your hand first. (The corn syrup is added to prevent the syrup from crystallizing when stored.) If you are using a small amount of corn syrup in a recipe that does not have sugar, it may be easier to measure the syrup by volume. Converting dry to liquid ounces is simple: Fluid ounces are two-thirds of dry ounces (e.g., 6 ounces by weight = 4 fluid ounces).

NOTE 2: Since it is impossible to know exactly when the syrup will come to a boil, and hopefully you do not have the time to stand there watching it, do not be concerned about boiling the syrup just a little longer than called for in the recipe; it will not adversely affect the viscosity of the syrup. However, boiling the syrup for as much as five minutes longer than specified will increase the Baumé to 30°; 10 minutes of boiling will bring it to 34°. Should this happen, let the syrup cool to approximately 60°F (16°C), check the sugar content using the Baumé thermometer, and replace the evaporated water as needed. The water that you add should first be boiled, then cooled to 60°F (16°C) to get an accurate reading and also to sterilize the water so that the syrup can be stored.

Streusel Topping

2 pounds, 10 ounces (1 kg, 195 g)

6 ounces (170 g) brown sugar
6 ounces (170 g) granulated sugar
11 ounces (310 g) butter
*1 tablespoon (5 g) ground
   cinnamon*
2 teaspoons (10 g) salt
1 teaspoon (5 ml) vanilla extract
*1 pound, 2 ounces (510 g) bread
   flour, approximately*

1. Mix brown sugar, granulated sugar, butter, cinnamon, salt, and vanilla.
2. Stir in flour. The mixture should be crumbly and not come together like a dough; you may need to add extra flour.
3. Store covered in the refrigerator to prevent the topping from drying out.

Variation:
Hazelnut Streusel

Add 10 ounces (285 g) chopped or coarsely crushed, unroasted hazelnuts when you add the flour.

Vanilla Extract

6 long, soft, whole vanilla beans
*1 quart (960 ml) good quality
   vodka*
2 whole vanilla beans

1. Split six of the beans open and cut into small pieces.
2. Put the pieces and the vodka in a jar and seal tightly.
3. Let stand in a dark cool place for about one month, shaking the bottle from time to time.
4. Sieve the liquid through a strainer lined with cheesecloth.
5. Clean the bottle and return the vanilla extract to the bottle.
6. Add two whole vanilla beans. Store tightly sealed.

Vanilla Sugar

There are a number of recipes for making vanilla sugar. A simple way, which protects the beans from drying out when stored, is to place split or whole beans in a jar of granulated sugar. The jar should be tall enough to hold the beans standing up and allow room for plenty of sugar around them. Make sure the jar is tightly sealed. Shake it once a day to circulate the sugar and increase the fragrance. After one week the vanilla sugar is ready to use. As you use up the vanilla sugar and the beans, keep adding to the jar. Naturally, the more beans you store in the jar in relation to the amount of sugar, the stronger the flavor or fragrance.

Savory Recipe Variations

It may seem strange to find savory treats in a dessert book, but in my experience the pastry department is usually called upon to help with the preparation and baking of items such as quiches, cheese puffs, and puff pastries like ham or cheese croissants and cheese straws. This of course does make sense since these items are all variations on basic pastry doughs and products, and we have much better ovens in which to bake them. I have included some of the most frequently used versions.

Ham and/or Cheese Croissants

50 hors d'oeuvres

10 ounces (285 g) ham and/or Swiss cheese
milk
2 pounds (910 g) Classic Puff Paste (page 21)
Egg Wash (page 5)

1. Process the ham in a food processor to make a purée (this makes it easier to roll up the croissants). If using cheese and ham, finely dice or grate the cheese and mix with the ham. If using cheese alone, grate it and mix in enough milk to make a paste or the cheese will just fall off when you roll up the croissants.

2. Roll out puff paste to a 16- by 36-inch (40- × 90-cm) rectangle, which should be slightly thinner than ⅛ inch (3 mm). Let rest, then cut into three 4-inch-wide (10-cm) strips. Cut 3-inch (7.5-cm) triangles from the strips.

3. Place a small amount of filling on top of the puff paste at the wide end of each triangle. Roll up tightly, stretching and pinching the ends underneath to prevent them from unrolling, and place on sheet pans lined with baking paper. Shape each one into a crescent as you place them.

4. Brush with egg wash. Bake at 400°F (205°C) for about 20 minutes, or until baked through. Serve the same day they are baked.

NOTE: These hors d'oeuvres can be made in advance, frozen, and baked as needed, as long as they are kept well covered in the freezer.

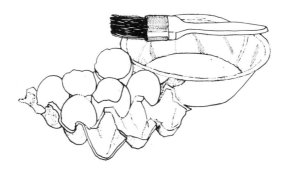

Quiche Lorraine

two 11-inch (27.5-cm) quiches

1 recipe Pie Dough (page 17)
3 cups (720 ml) heavy cream
½ teaspoon (2.5 g) salt (see note)
pinch white pepper
pinch ground nutmeg
12 egg yolks
14 ounces (400 g) bacon, cut in
*   small pieces, cooked and drained*
14 ounces (400 g) diced
*   Gruyère cheese*

1. Roll out pie dough ⅛ inch (3 mm) thick and line two 11-inch (27.5-cm) false-bottom tart pans (see Figure 2–11, page 33). Prick the bottom of the shells lightly and let rest for at least 30 minutes.

2. Combine cream, salt, pepper, nutmeg, and egg yolks; blend thoroughly. Distribute the bacon and cheese evenly over the bottom of the shells. Pour the custard on top, dividing it evenly between the two pans.

3. Bake at 375°F (190°C) directly on the bottom of the oven (do not use a sheet pan) for approximately 30 minutes, or until the custard is set. Serve warm.

NOTE: You can substitute diced ham for the bacon. Adjust the amount of salt according to the saltiness of the ham or bacon.

Cheese Soufflé

8 servings

melted butter
5 ounces (145 g) grated Parmesan
*   cheese*
3 ounces (85 g) bread flour
3 ounces (85 g) softened butter
2 cups (480 ml) milk
7 eggs, separated
2 ounces (55 g) grated
*   Gruyère cheese*
¼ teaspoon (1 g) cayenne pepper
½ teaspoon (1 g) ground nutmeg
2 teaspoons (10 g) salt

1. Brush melted butter over the insides of eight 5-ounce (150 ml) soufflé molds. Coat with Parmesan cheese; reserve the remaining cheese for the batter. Set the forms aside.

2. Combine the flour and butter.

3. Heat the milk in a saucepan to the scalding point.

4. Whisk in the flour mixture and bring to a boil, stirring constantly.

5. Add the egg yolks a few at a time and return the mixture to boiling, continuing to stir constantly.

6. Remove from heat. Add the remaining Parmesan, the Gruyère cheese, cayenne, nutmeg, and salt.

7. Whip the egg whites to stiff peaks (be careful not to whip them dry). Gently fold egg whites into the batter.

8. Fill the prepared forms three-fourths full.

9. Bake immediately at 400°F (205°C) for approximately 15 minutes. Serve at once.

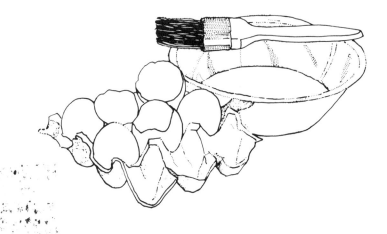

Cheese Straws

sixty-four 3½-inch (8.7-cm)
hors d'oeuvres

3½ ounces (100 g) grated
  Parmesan cheese
1 teaspoon (2 g) paprika
1 pound (455 g) Classic Puff
  Paste (page 21)
Egg Wash (page 5)

1. Combine the Parmesan and paprika; reserve.
2. Roll out the puff paste ⅛ inch (3 mm) thick in a rectangle 14 by 10 inches (35 × 25 cm).
3. Brush the entire surface of the dough heavily with egg wash.
4. Sprinkle the cheese mixture over half of the dough, starting from one of the long sides.
5. Fold the plain half of the dough over the cheese. Roll the dough to 6 inches (15 cm) in width, sealing and pressing the cheese into the dough.
6. Place dough in the refrigerator to relax and firm up for 30 minutes.
7. Cut the dough lengthwise into sixteen strips ⅜ inch (9 mm) wide. Twist each strip into a spiral as shown in Pretzels (Figure 9–17, page 254) stretching the strips to 16 inches (40 cm) at the same time.
8. Place on sheet pans lined with baking paper, securing both ends of each twisted strip to the paper by pressing hard with your thumbs. This will help to keep them straight; they still tend to curl and twist somewhat, but can easily be straightened before they are completely baked through. Let rest for at least 30 minutes before baking.
9. Bake at 400°F (205°C) for approximately 15 minutes, or until golden brown and done.
10. Immediately cut each strip into four 3½-inch (8.7-cm) lengths. Cheese straws should be served the same day they are baked.

Gougères (Cheese Puffs)

80 hors d'oeuvres

¼ recipe Pâte à Choux (page 15)
7 ounces (200 g) Gruyère cheese,
  finely diced or grated

1. Mix the cheese into the pâte à choux. Place in a pastry bag with a no. 6 (12-mm) plain tip.
2. Pipe out in small mounds, about the size of cherries, onto sheet pans lined with baking paper.
3. Bake immediately, following the instructions for pâte à choux.

Basic Doughs

Linzer Dough
Pâte à Choux
Pie Dough
Pizza Dough
Puff Paste
    Classic Puff Paste
    Quick Puff Paste
Salt Dough

Unbaked Salt Dough
Short Dough
    Cocoa Short Dough
    Hazelnut Short Dough
Weaver's Dough
Whole Wheat Weaver's Dough
Bread Basket

A *mastery of dough making* is obviously critical to the success of a professional pastry kitchen. Different techniques are required to create short dough, puff pastry, choux paste, and perfect pie dough. However, in making any basic dough, it is most important to use a good, workable recipe and follow the proper procedures for preparation.

Short dough along with its many variations, such as linzer dough, is without question the dough used most frequently in the majority of pastry shops. A proficient pastry chef will always keep a supply of short dough in the refrigerator ready to use as a base for cakes and pastries or to line forms and tart pans. Short dough is also irreplaceable for preparing what I call "nothing-left-in-the-showcase" cookies. With one basic dough, you can make a variety of cookies and pastries quickly and efficiently.

Another basic dough used continually in the pastry kitchen is puff pastry. It is one of the most exciting, and also one of the most challenging, doughs to work with. The use of puff pastry dates back many centuries, and one can find numerous theories as to its origin in cookbooks and food reference books. It is impossible to say which story is accurate, but one I particularly like tells of a pastry apprentice in France. The young man was given the responsibility of making up all of the pastry doughs for use the next day. When he was finished, he realized that he had forgotten to add the butter in one of the recipes. Knowing the master would certainly find out, but not wanting to start over, he quickly mixed in the missing butter, flattening and turning the dough over several times to try and hide his mistake. The next day the master let it be known that he intended to have a few words with the apprentice. The apprentice, fearing he was to be scolded for ruining the dough, ran away. When he was found at last and brought trembling before the master, he was astonished to find out that rather than intending to punish him, the master wanted to praise him and learn the secret of the wonderful new flaky dough he had invented!

Pâte à choux, also known as eclair paste, is a basic and versatile paste used to make many items in the pastry kitchen, including cream puffs or profiteroles, swans, *croquembouche*, and of course, eclairs. Pâte à choux (like short dough) is also used in combination with puff pastry to make delicious sweets such as Gâteau Saint-Honoré and Choux Surprise. The translation of pâte à choux is "cabbage paste," referring to the baked cream puff's resemblance to a small cabbage head.

Pie dough, pizza dough, and linzer dough are much quicker and less complicated to master than puff pastry or pâte à choux. This chapter also contains four recipes for decorative doughs. Of these, only the whole wheat weaver's dough is intended for consumption. The salt doughs and the weaver's dough are used for purely decorative purposes (although technically they are completely edible, you would have to be pretty hungry, or uninformed, to give them a try).

Linzer Dough

1 pound, 14 ounces (855 g) dough

6 ounces (170 g) granulated sugar
8 ounces (225 g) softened butter
3 egg yolks
8 ounces (225 g) bread flour
2 teaspoons (3 g) ground cinnamon
½ teaspoon (1 g) ground cloves
6 ounces (170 g) finely ground hazelnuts
2 teaspoons (2 g) grated lemon peel

1. Combine sugar, butter, and yolks in a mixer bowl on low speed.
2. Sift flour with cinnamon and cloves.
3. Add flour, hazelnuts, and lemon peel to the butter mixture; mix just until all ingredients are incorporated and smooth. Overmixing will make this dough very hard to work with.
4. Refrigerate the dough on a paper-lined sheet pan.

Pâte à Choux

2 pounds, 10 ounces (1 kg, 195 g) paste

8 ounces (225 g) cake flour
11 ounces (310 g) bread flour
1 quart (960 ml) water
8 ounces (225 g) sweet butter
1½ teaspoons (7.5 g) salt
1 quart (960 ml) eggs,
*   approximately*

One-Half Recipe
1 pound, 5 ounces (595 g) paste

4 ounces (115 g) cake flour
5½ ounces (155 g) bread flour
1 pint (480 ml) water
4 ounces (115 g) sweet butter
½ teaspoon (2.5 g) salt
1 pint (480 ml) eggs,
*   approximately*

Pâte à choux or choux paste, as the name suggests, is not really a dough in the strictest sense, but rather a thick paste that could be described as a roux with the addition of eggs. There are many different recipes and philosophies to choose from when it comes to making this classic pastry. However, the one factor that holds true in each case is that the more eggs you add to the base mixture, the higher and lighter your finished pastries will be, ideally becoming just hollow shells.

Pâte à choux begins as a cooked mixture of water or milk, fat (usually butter), and flour, with a small amount of salt added if sweet butter is used. The sifted flour is added to the boiling water and fat, and stirred in quickly. The resulting roux is then cooked for a few minutes and stirred constantly to allow as much liquid as possible to evaporate so that the maximum number of eggs can be incorporated. Although some chefs use a slightly different formula that incorporates a stronger flour (especially for larger items such as Paris Brest as opposed to profiteroles), I find it quite satisfactory to compromise and use a combination of bread and cake flours. You should add as many eggs as the paste can absorb and still stay in a precise shape once it is piped out; the paste will have a slightly shiny appearance if the correct number of eggs has been added. On the other hand, if not enough eggs have been added, the baked pastries will be low and heavy, and filled with a gluey mass that must be removed before the pastries can be filled. Add the eggs in a few at a time; you can then mix them in more easily and avoid accidentally adding too many. Sometimes a small amount of ammonium carbonate is added with the eggs to give an extra lift. The ammonium gas released during baking helps to increase the volume; the strong-smelling gas quickly dissipates as the pastry cools.

It isn't necessary to brush the pâte à choux pastries with egg wash before baking; in fact, it is just a waste of time. The egg wash usually dries before the pastries have finished expanding, which gives them an unattractive cracked appearance (resembling a dry riverbed!). In most cases the pastries are to be finished with a glaze or powdered sugar on top anyway.

Pâte à choux is never prepared ahead of time and refrigerated or frozen in a batter or dough form before being shaped, as you would, for example, with puff paste. It must be piped out first, then either baked or frozen immediately, before the paste develops a skin. The formed paste is then put into a hot (425°F/219°C) oven (directly from the freezer without thawing, if frozen) to produce the maximum amount of steam, which rapidly expands the paste and leaves a large empty space in the center. The heat coagulates the gluten and proteins, which set the structure and make a firm shell. After approximately 10 minutes the heat is reduced (375°F/190°C) to finish baking and allow the shells to become firm and dry, without getting too dark. As long as you do not let it become too brown, you cannot overbake pâte à choux, so make sure that the shells have been baked long enough to hold their shape and not fall. The baked shells for eclairs and profiteroles can be stored covered for a day or so before being filled, but once filled, they must be served the same day.

1. Sift the flours together on a sheet of baking paper and reserve.

2. Heat water, butter, and salt to a full rolling boil, so that the fat is not just floating on the top, but is dispersed throughout the liquid.

3. Form the ends of the baking paper into a pouring spout. Then, using a heavy wooden spoon, stir the flour into the liquid, adding it as fast as it can be absorbed. Avoid adding all of the flour at once as this can make the paste lumpy.

4. Cook, stirring constantly until the mixture comes away from the sides of the pan, about 3 to 5 minutes.

5. Let the paste cool slightly, so the eggs will not cook when added. Transfer the paste to a mixer bowl (or, if you are adding the eggs by hand, use the spoon and leave the paste in the saucepan).

6. Mix in the eggs, two at a time, using the paddle attachment. Add as many eggs as the paste can absorb and still hold its shape when piped.

7. Pipe the paste into the desired shape according to the individual recipe.

8. Bake at 425°F (219°C) until fully puffed and starting to show some color, about 10 minutes. Reduce heat to 375°F (190°C) and bake about 10 to 12 minutes longer depending on size.

9. Let the pastries cool at room temperature. Speeding up the process by placing them in the refrigerator or freezer can cause the pastries to collapse.

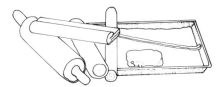

Pie Dough

four 10-inch (25-cm) shells

*1 pound, 9 ounces (710 g)
  bread flour
4 teaspoons (20 g) salt
1 pound (455 g) cold butter
5 ounces (140 g) cold lard
⅔ cup (160 ml) ice water,
  approximately*

Making pie dough is a quick and easy task as long as the ingredients are kept cold and they are only mixed until just combined. In a good pie dough, most of the fat should still be visible in separate small lumps. Overmixing or using soft fat will make the dough hard to work with and the baked crust will be crumbly and mealy instead of flaky. While some chefs insist on the exclusive use of lard in their pie crust, I feel that even though it unquestionably produces a beautiful, flaky crust, the flavor of the lard can be overwhelming, especially if the pie uses a sweet fruit filling. In my opinion, a compromise using both lard and butter gives the best overall result. Also, the flakiness of the pie crust depends a great deal on the flour-to-fat ratio. As in short dough, the more flour in the dough, the harder the finished shell. A pie dough should therefore be rolled out using the smallest amount of flour possible. Scraps from rolled pie dough should be treated with the same care as puff paste. They should be layered on top of each other to roll out a second time; never knead the scraps together. This will help to keep the dough from becoming rubbery and hard to work with.

1. Combine the flour and salt in a bowl.
2. Add the firm butter and lard, and pinch them down with your fingertips to the size of hazelnuts.
3. Add the ice water and mix just until the dough comes together; the butter should still be lumpy.
4. Flatten the dough to help it chill faster.
5. Let it rest in the refrigerator, covered, for at least 30 minutes before using. The pie dough should rest for an additional 30 minutes after it has been rolled out to prevent it from shrinking when baked.

NOTE: Unless you are making a large amount, always mix pie dough by hand because it is very easy to overmix the dough by machine.

To make a decorative fluted edge

Roll the dough out ⅛ inch (3 mm) thick, large enough so that it will extend about 1 inch (2.5 cm) beyond the edge of the pie pan. Roll the dough up on a dowel and unroll it over the pan (see Figure 2–11, page 33). Fold the edge under, and form it into a ½-inch (1.2-cm) lip standing up around the edge of the pan.

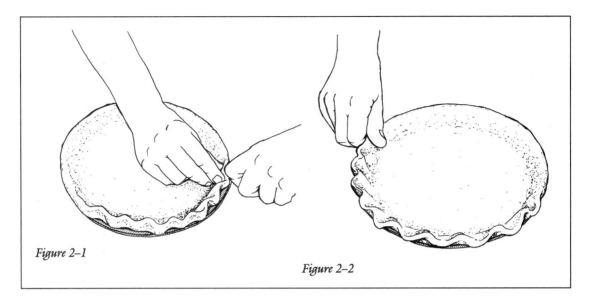

Figure 2–1

Figure 2–2

Method I: Use the knuckle of your right index finger and the tips of your left thumb and index finger to bend the lip of dough into an evenly spaced fluted design (Figure 2–1).

Method II: Pinch the lip of dough between your thumb and the side of your bent index finger to make the fluted pattern (Figure 2–2).

Pizza Dough

two 10- to 12-inch (25- to 30-cm) pizza crusts

½ ounce (15 g) fresh compressed yeast
¾ cup (180 ml) water, at room temperature
1 teaspoon (5 g) granulated sugar
2 tablespoons (30 ml) olive oil
1 teaspoon (5 g) salt
1 tablespoon (15 ml) honey
10 ounces (285 g) bread flour

1. Dissolve the yeast in water (help it along by squeezing it with your fingers).

2. Mix in sugar, olive oil, salt, and honey.

3. Add the flour and knead with the dough hook until the dough has a smooth elastic consistency, about 10 minutes.

4. Place the dough in an oiled bowl, cover, and let rise until half-doubled in volume.

5. Place the dough, covered, in the refrigerator for at least two hours. Bring the dough to room temperature before proceeding.

6. Divide the dough in half. On a floured board, roll and stretch the dough with your hands to make each piece into a 10- to 12-inch (25- to 30-cm) circle.

7. Top as desired and bake at 450°F (230°C) on a heated pizza stone or a thin sheet pan placed in the bottom of the oven to allow the crust to brown on the bottom.

Puff Paste

The preparation of puff paste demands great care. To produce a light and flaky puff paste, everything must be done correctly, start to finish, or the results will be disappointing. Making the basic dough (the flour and water mixture) correctly is extremely important. If you add too much flour, or you do not work the dough long enough, it does not matter how carefuly you roll in the butter; the paste will be glutenous and rubbery, hard to work with, and will shrink when baked.

Great care must also be taken when rolling in the butter and turning the dough to get the optimum rise, or puff. If rolled in properly, there will be a layer of butter between each layer of dough. In a hot oven, the moisture in the dough layers produces steam that, if properly sealed in by the butter, will push up as it evaporates. This is how puff paste rises without the addition of a leavening agent.

Creating an even layer structure can be accomplished only if the butter and dough have the same consistency, which is why some flour must first be worked into the butter. As in short dough, gluten is formed when flour and water (here, the water in the butter) are combined. Although not necessary, adding a small amount of acid (lemon juice, for example) to the butter strengthens the gluten and also gives the butter an extra measure of pliability to ensure that the butter will stretch with the dough.

There are many specially made fats on the market designed for puff pastry, but none quite stands up to butter when it comes to taste. Also, because butter has a much lower melting point, it will not leave an unappetizing film in one's mouth the way some shortening products do.

There are actually close to two thousand layers of butter and dough in a puff paste made with four double turns. The French word for puff paste is *feuilletage* from *feuilles*, meaning leaves; the pastry we call a napoleon is known as *mille feuilles* or "a thousand leaves."

Even after you have made perfect puff paste there are many things to watch out for as you work with it:

- Be very careful not to damage the layer structure when rolling the dough. Never let your rolling pin roll over the edge of the dough, which mashes down the sides, and always apply even pressure as you are rolling so that the butter is evenly distributed.
- As a general rule, let the puff paste rest 5 to 10 minutes between rolling it out and cutting it. It should then rest an additional 15 minutes after it has been made up (for example,

into turnovers) before baking to eliminate shrinkage. (If the dough seems particularly rubbery and shrinks back a lot as you roll it, it will need to rest a bit longer.)

- As you cut the dough, hold the knife at a sharp 90° angle so the edges of the dough are perfectly straight. This way the dough will rise straight up in the oven.
- When using egg wash on a product made with puff paste, take care not to let any drip on the sides. This can seal the paste to the pan and prevent it from rising.
- Start baking puff paste in a hot oven; if the oven is not hot enough you will lose the effect of the steam, and the butter will run out of the dough instead.

Puff paste freezes very well both as a dough and made up, ready to be baked. However, it should not be stored in the refrigerator for more than three days. Longer than that the flour and water mixture in the dough will start to ferment, causing the dough to turn gray. It will gradually become darker and both taste and appearance will suffer. The ideal way to use puff paste (providing you have the freezer space) is to make up all of the dough the day after the dough is made. You can then freeze your apple turnovers, fleurons, or whatever recipes you need. If this is not practical, freeze the dough, divided into suitably sized pieces, to take out when needed. Puff paste must be kept well covered at all times, especially in the freezer, to prevent the top from drying and forming a skin (freezer burn).

Scraps from rolled puff paste dough (as with any other dough such as Danish, pie, and croissant) will not be as good rolled out the second time, but can be used successfully in some recipes. Puff paste scraps are preferable to fresh dough for pastries that should not puff up as much. Scrap pieces can be frozen until needed, or combined with a fresh dough. Never knead the scraps together to form a larger piece; lay them on top of each other and then roll to retain the layered structure. Scraps from puff paste can also be used for Butter Wheat Bread (see page 59).

Classic (French) Puff Paste

11 pounds (5 kg) dough

Butter Block

4 pounds, 6 ounces (1 kg, 990 g)
    cold butter
juice of 1 lemon
1 tablespoon (15 g) salt
17½ ounces (500 g) bread flour

Dough

1 quart (960 ml) cold water
4 tablespoons (60 g) salt
14 ounces (400 g) cake flour
7 ounces (200 g) softened butter
2 pounds, 10 ounces (1 kg, 195 g)
    bread flour, approximately

One-Quarter Recipe

2 pounds, 12 ounces (1 kg, 250 g)
    dough

Butter Block

17½ ounces (500 g) cold butter
juice of ¼ lemon
pinch of salt
4½ ounces (130 g) bread flour

Dough

1 cup (240 ml) cold water
1 tablespoon (15 g) salt
3½ ounces (100 g) cake flour
2 ounces (55 g) softened butter
11 ounces (310 g) bread flour,
    approximately

To make the butter block

1. Work cold butter into the proper consistency with the warmth of your hand, adding lemon juice, salt, and bread flour.

2. Shape into a 12-inch (30-cm) square (6-inch/15-cm for ¼ recipe) and refrigerate until firm.

The butter should not be so soft that it is hard to handle; you should be able to transfer the finished block from one hand to the other without breaking it. It should not be so firm that it cracks or breaks if you press on it. Ideally, the dough and the butter block should have the same consistency. A dough that is softer than the butter will be forced to the sides by the firmer butter; a dough that is too firm will force the butter out on the sides. Either will result in poor quality puff paste. Do not make the dough before the butter block is ready.

To make the dough

1. Mix water, salt, cake flour, soft butter, and enough of the second measurement of bread flour to make a soft, elastic dough. If you add too much flour the dough will be too glutenous and rubbery. Keep mixing until the dough is elastic enough to be pulled easily (about 6 to 8 minutes at medium speed).

2. Shape the dough into a tight ball. With a sharp knife, cut a cross halfway into the ball. Let rest for 5 minutes, covered.

To assemble

1. Pull the corners of the cuts out to make the dough square-shaped (Figure 2–3).

2. Roll the opened dough out to a square slightly larger than the butter block.

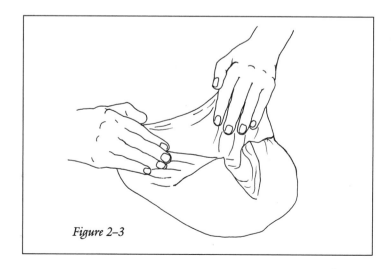

Figure 2–3

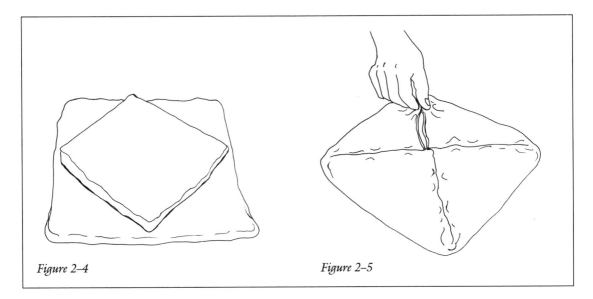

Figure 2–4   *Figure 2–5*

3. Place the butter block diagonally within the square so there are four triangles around the sides (Figure 2–4). Fold these dough triangles in so they meet in the center. Pinch the edges together to seal in the butter block (Figure 2–5).

4. Roll the dough into a rectangle ½ inch (1.2 cm) thick. Do not roll the dough wider than a sheet pan is long.

5. Give the dough four double turns (instructions follow), refrigerating it for a minimum of 30 minutes between each turn. Be sure the dough is well-covered at all times.

6. After the last turn, roll the puff paste out ½ inch (1.2 cm) thick, cut into halves, place the two pieces on a sheet pan with paper between them, and cover. Refrigerate or freeze. Remember that puff paste should not be kept in the refrigerator more than a few days.

To make a double turn

1. Roll the dough into a rectangle 30 by 20 inches (75 × 50 cm) or 15 by 10 inches (37.5 × 25 cm) for ¼ recipe, as carefully and evenly as possible. Arrange the dough with a long side closest to you.

2. Make a vertical mark in the center of the rectangle. Fold both ends of the dough in to this mark (Figure 2–6).

3. Brush away excess flour from the top of the dough, and bring the two short sides together to fold once more as if you were closing a book (Figure 2–7). You will now have a dough with one double turn.

4. Carefully place the dough on a sheet pan, cover, and refrigerate for 30 minutes.

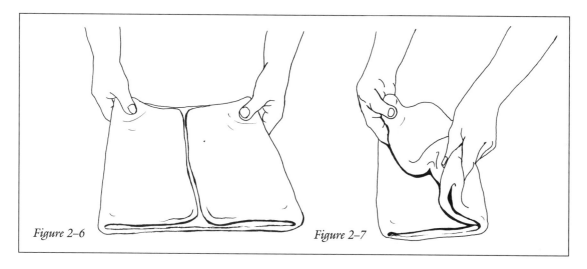

Figure 2–6   Figure 2–7

5. When you begin the second double turn, place the dough in front of you so that the short ends of the rectangle are on your left and right, opposite to the way the dough lay when you "closed the book" with the first turn. Roll out and turn as above; repeat as you make the remaining turns.

Quick Puff Paste

11 pounds, 2 ounces (5 kg, 60 g) dough

5 pounds (2 kg, 275 g) bread flour
4 tablespoons (60 g) salt
5 pounds (2 kg, 275 g) cold butter
1 pint (480 ml) cold water, approximately

One-Quarter Recipe
2 pounds, 12 ounces (1 kg, 250 g) dough

1 pound, 4 ounces (570 g) bread flour
1 tablespoon (15 g) salt
1 pound, 4 ounces (570 g) cold butter
½ cup (120 ml) cold water, approximately

If you do not have time to make classic puff paste, quick puff paste is a fast compromise. You will not get the height of the French version, but this one can easily be made, from scaled to baked, in 2 hours. It is perfect for lining tarts and making fleurons and napoleons, when the dough must not puff up too much.

1. Combine flour and salt.
2. Cut the butter (it should be firm but not hard) into 2-inch (5-cm) pieces; add to flour mixture, being careful not to knead.
3. Mix in just enough water so the dough can be handled. Mix carefully so the lumps of butter remain whole; the dough should look like well-made pie dough.
4. Shape the dough into a square. Roll two single and two double turns alternately (see pages 96 and 97).
5. Cover and refrigerate.
NOTE: This dough does not rest between turns; it is ready to use immediately after the last turn. However, after the dough has been rolled, it must rest 20 to 30 minutes before baking to prevent it from shrinking.

Fleurons

28 pieces

1 pound (455 g) Classic Puff
*   Paste (page 21)*
Egg Wash (page 5)
vegetable oil

Fleurons are small, crescent-shaped puff pastry garnishes. They are used in classic French cooking, usually as a garnish with seafood.

1. Roll out puff paste to a 12-by-12-inch (27.5- × 27.5-cm) square about ⅛ inch (3 mm) thick (see note). Prick the dough lightly.

2. Place the dough on cardboard or an inverted sheet pan. Brush with egg wash.

3. Using the back of a chef's knife, mark a diamond pattern in the egg wash.

4. Refrigerate or freeze until firm (the egg wash will dry slightly). It is much easier to brush on the egg wash and mark the dough before you cut, than to try and do each fleuron individually.

5. Starting from the bottom edge of the square on the left side, cut away a little less than a half circle of dough using a 3-inch (7.5-cm) fluted cookie cutter dipped occasionally in oil. Cut straight down without twisting the cutter. Make a second cut parallel to the first and 1½ inches (3.7 cm) higher to form a crescent (Figure 2–8). The cut that makes the top of one crescent becomes the bottom of the next one. Continue cutting until you have made the first row of seven fleurons. Make three additional rows of seven fleurons each in the same way. The only scraps of dough will be at the beginning and at the end.

6. Bake at 400°F (205°C) about 10 minutes. You may need to lower the heat and leave them in a few minutes longer to finish drying (Figure 2–9). Fleurons can be frozen before baking; bake directly from the freezer for about 12 minutes, following the same procedure. If you are making a great many fleurons and you are not sure about the quality of the dough, make a few samples so you can adjust the thickness as necessary.

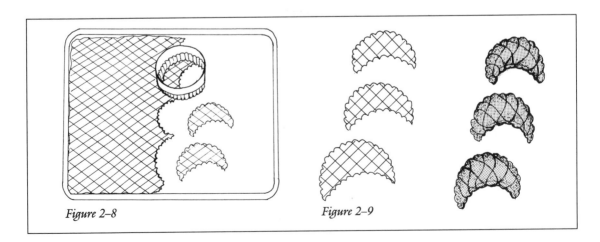

Figure 2–8   *Figure 2–9*

NOTE: In the recipes for fleurons, vol-au-vent, and bouchées, the amount of dough required and the thickness specified for rolling it out assume you are using properly layered, freshly made puff paste following the recipe in this book. If you are using another recipe or a dough that you know (or suspect) is getting old (more than four days in the refrigerator), you may need to adjust the thickness of the dough when rolling it out. Bake a few samples before making a large batch. A good puff paste should rise four times its original height.

Vol-au-Vent
one 10-inch (25-cm) pastry shell

1 pound, 8 ounces (680 g)
  Classic Puff Paste (page 21)
Egg Wash (page 5)

You could say that a vol-au-vent is a big bouchée or, conversely, that a bouchée is a small vol-au-vent; in principle they are the same thing. A vol-au-vent is a large pastry shell, from 5 to 10 inches (12.5 to 25 cm) in diameter, that serves 4 to 12 people. Ten inches is the largest size shell that is practical to make. If this is not large enough for the number of servings needed, it is best to make two smaller shells.

1. Roll the puff paste to a square slightly larger than 10 inches (25 cm) and approximately ½ inch (1.2 cm) thick (see note above).

2. Refrigerate the dough first if it has become soft; then, using a 10-inch (25-cm) template as a guide (a cake pan is a good choice), cut out a circle of dough. Be sure to cut at a 90° angle to prevent the vol-au-vent from falling to one side as it puffs up in the oven.

3. Place an 8½-inch (21.2-cm) template in the center of the circle and cut again. Carefully transfer the ring-shaped piece of dough to a sheet pan, cover, and place in the refrigerator.

4. Roll the remaining circle of dough ⅛ inch (3 mm) thick and in a shape that will allow you to cut from it one 10-inch (25-cm) circle which will be the bottom, and one 8-inch (21.2-cm) circle to use for the lid of the vol-au-vent. Cut out the circles, prick the dough thoroughly, and refrigerate for approximately 30 minutes. (If you have enough scrap dough on hand you can roll and cut these two circles first, then allow them to rest in the refrigerator while you are making the ring.)

5. Take out the 10-inch (25-cm) circle and place it on an even sheet pan.

6. Brush the outer 1 inch (2.5 cm) with egg wash and place the chilled ring on top so it sticks to the egg wash. Adjust to make the vol-au-vent perfectly round.

7. With the back side of a knife, mark the vol-au-vent every 1½ inches (3.7 cm) around the outside, holding the knife vertically, marking from the bottom to the top, and pushing in just a little

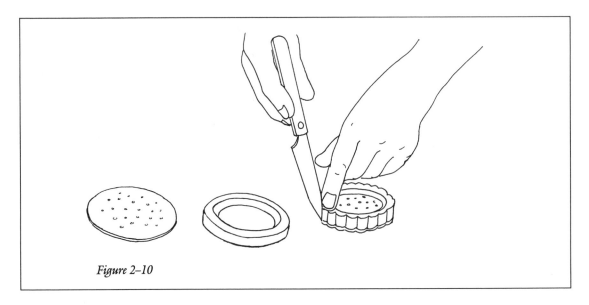

Figure 2–10

to create a scallop pattern (Figure 2–10).

8. Prick the top of the ring and brush lightly with egg wash (do not let any egg wash drip down the sides).

9. Using an 8½-inch (21.2-cm) template, cut a lid out of the remainder of the thin sheet. Place it on the pan next to the vol-au-vent. Brush the lid with egg wash and mark it with a diamond pattern using the back of a chef's knife.

10. Bake at 400°F (205°C), double-panned to prevent the bottom from getting too dark, for about 15 minutes or until puffed. Then reduce the temperature to 375°F (190°C) and continue baking until dry and golden, 30 to 35 minutes. If the top gets too dark before it is dried through, cover it with a piece of paper or aluminum foil. The lid will, of course, be finished baking long before the case of the vol-au-vent; remove it carefully.

One of the best ways to keep the sides of a vol-au-vent from falling in as it puffs up is to arrange a cake cooling rack above the vol-au-vent on baking forms or coffee cups set at the edges of the baking pan. Place them at a height slightly below the point you expect, or want, the dough to puff. This acts as a mold, preventing the vol-au-vent from puffing too high and helping to keep the edges straight.

To make a smaller vol-au-vent, follow the directions using whatever size is required for the outside template; just use a ring 1 inch (2.5 cm) smaller to create the frame.

Bouchées

fifteen 3¼-inch (8.1-cm) pastry shells

2 pounds (910 g) Classic Puff Paste (page 21)
vegetable oil
Egg Wash (page 5)

Although bouchée means "mouth-size," bouchées are individual patty shells. They are usually 1½ to 3½ inches (3.7 to 8.7 cm) across. There are two basic ways to make them: the production method and the classic method. Using the production method they won't get quite as high, but they can be made very quickly and you can be sure that the sides will not fall as they bake. The classic method produces higher and more elegant bouchées, but they take a little longer to finish.

Classic method

1. Roll out puff paste to a rectangle measuring 7 by 10 inches (17.5 × 25 cm) slightly less than ½ inch (1.2 cm) thick (see note following recipe for fleurons, page 25). Place the dough in the refrigerator for a few minutes to relax and firm up.

2. Using a 3¼-inch (8.1-cm) plain or fluted cutter, cut out fifteen circles of dough. Dip the edge of the cutter in oil periodically and push the cutter straight down without twisting.

3. Using a 2-inch (5-cm) cutter, cut a circle out of each round to form rings. Carefully place the rings on a sheet pan and refrigerate.

4. Layer the scrap dough, including the circles cut out of the centers, and roll it out ⅛ inch (3 mm) thick. Prick the dough and place in the refrigerator to firm and relax.

5. Cut out fifteen 3¼-inch (8.1-cm) circles (not rings) from the sheet of dough plus fifteen 2-inch (5-cm) circles to use as lids as desired.

6. Brush egg wash on the larger circles and place the reserved rings on top. If you wish, brush the top of the rings with egg wash, but be very careful not to let any run down the sides.

7. Bake at 400°F (205°C) until puffed, about 10 minutes. Reduce heat to 375°F (190°C) and bake until they are dry enough to hold their shapes, about 30 minutes. (You might have to use a second pan underneath to prevent the bottoms from becoming too dark, and you may need to remove the bouchées on the edges of the pan if they are done before those in the middle.)

8. When the bouchées have cooled somewhat, lift off the lids and scrape out the unbaked puff paste with a fork. If necessary, put them back in the oven to dry further.

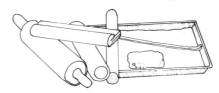

Production method

Follow steps 1 and 2 as in the classic method.

3. Rather than cutting all the way through the dough and removing the 2-inch (5-cm) center, cut only two-thirds of the way through the dough. Do not forget to continue dipping the cutter in oil as you work to produce a clean cut.

4. Thoroughly prick the 2-inch center of the circles. Place on sheet pans about ¾ inch (2 cm) apart.

5. Bake as directed in step 7 for classic bouchées, increasing the time slightly.

6. When the bouchées have cooled slightly, lift off the lids and use a fork to scrape out the unbaked paste inside. If necessary, put the shells back in the oven to dry further.

Salt Dough

4 pounds, 6 ounces (1 kg, 990 g) dough

2 pounds (910 g) bread flour
1 pound (455 g) salt
1 pint (480 ml) water,
    approximately
Egg Wash (page 5)

This is an inexpensive and easy-to-make dough used to make bread ornaments or to practice braiding. Try to keep the dough as firm as possible as there is no gluten structure, and the dough will therefore stretch and fall apart easily should the consistency be too soft. Because of the nonexistent gluten structure, salt dough is excellent for patterns that are assembled after they are baked. The pieces will not shrink or change shape.

1. Combine flour and salt.

2. Add just enough water for a fairly stiff dough.

3. Roll out to desired thickness — ¼ inch (6 mm) for most uses. Should the dough seem to drag as you cut around your templates, refrigerate the dough until it is firm. Dipping the tip of the knife in oil from time to time will also help prevent a ragged finish.

4. Brush the pieces with egg wash.

5. Bake at 375°F (190°C) until the pieces have a pleasant, light brown color.

When making large pieces, check to be sure they are dry enough not to break. Keep the douth covered at all times while working. Store dough covered in the refrigerator no longer than three days. For a sturdier dough, use up to a 1:1 ratio of flour and salt.

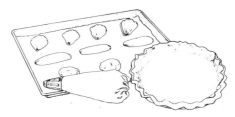

Unbaked Salt Dough

4 pounds, 5 ounces (1 kg, 960 g) dough

9 ounces (255 g) cornstarch
2 cups (480 ml) water
2 pounds, 12 ounces (1 kg, 250 g) popcorn salt (see note 1)

This dough is ideal for small intricate showpieces as it is very pliable and easy to work with. Figures made with this dough are not baked; they are left to air dry instead. Typically pieces take up to three days to dry completely, so you will have to allow more time than usual to complete your project. If the figure you are making is more than ¼ inch (6 mm) thick, it should be made in layers, letting each layer dry before adding the next, or the dough will shrivel from the moisture trapped inside. The drying process may be accelerated by placing the finished pieces in a gas oven using the heat from the pilot light only, or by placing the pieces outside to dry in the sun.

1. Mix the cornstarch and the water in a saucepan. Heat the mixture over medium heat, stirring constantly with a heavy spoon, until it starts to gelatinize, approximately 10 minutes. As the mixture thickens it will be rather difficult to stir and you may need to have some help during the last few minutes.

2. Remove the mixture from the heat and transfer the paste to a mixing bowl. Incorporate the salt, plus 1 or 2 tablespoons of additional water as needed to make a stiff but pliable dough. Store the salt dough covered in the refrigerator.

NOTE 1: Popcorn salt is a very finely ground salt. If it is not available use a coffee grinder to grind table salt to a very fine consistency.

NOTE 2: You can add food coloring to the dough or apply color to the finished pieces using a brush or a fixative syringe. If coloring the dough, try to use natural sources as much as possible. Ground cinnamon, nutmeg, or cocoa powder make nice shades of brown; cayenne pepper or paprika are good for creating russet tones. Avoid harsh or bright colors.

NOTE 3: The ingredients in this recipe can alternatively be measured by volume, using one part each of cornstarch and water and two parts of salt.

Short Dough

The name short dough makes more sense if you realize that "short" refers to its crumbly quality, produced by the shortening. Although butter produces the best flavor, it makes the dough hard to manage. The butter is just the right consistency for a very brief span of time; the butter in the dough will be rock-hard if the dough is stored in the refrigerator and too soft if the dough is left at room temperature. Another disadvantage to using butter is that, if too much flour is worked into the dough while it is being rolled out, the dough will become rubbery and shrink when it is baked. A short dough made with a high-quality vegetable margarine may not be as tasty, but it is less complicated to handle. By comparison, if you work too much flour into a short dough made with margarine, the dough will crumble and be hard to work with, but it will not shrink during baking. In cold climates all or part butter can be used more successfully.

If short dough has been overmixed, mixed using the wrong tool, mixed at the wrong speed, or any combination of these, too much air will be incorporated into the dough. This will result in a very soft product that could very well be piped out using a pastry bag. When this happens, you can imagine the problems and frustrations the baker has attempting the roll the "dough" into a thin sheet, for example, to line tartlet pans. However, adding too much flour to the short dough, either when making the dough or while rolling it out, will make the baked crust tough, hard, and unpleasant rather than crumbly.

Being cautious about working in excess flour is especially important when working with a short dough made with butter. The toughness that can occur is the result of hydration and the development of insoluble proteins in a gluten-rich flour. The water contained in the butter, together with that in the eggs, forms a gluten structure when combined with flour. The strength of the gluten structure is proportionate to the amount of flour used and the amount of time the dough is worked. A short dough in which the gluten structure has been allowed to develop will also shrink when baked. When used properly, the butter (or other fat) will insulate the insoluble proteins and keep them from coming in contact with the water. But, if the dough is overmixed, or handled in a rough manner, the water is forced through the fat instead.

To work at a reasonable production speed, you need a dough that is somewhat elastic, so that it will not break as it is molded and fit into pans, but it should not be too soft. Use the dough hook at low speed and mix just until combined. Remember, overmixing will incorporate too much air, making the dough difficult to work with. Before you roll short dough, knead it with your hands until it is smooth. This will minimize cracking around the edges when you roll it out, and help to prevent it from breaking as it is shaped. Use bread flour to roll out the dough, but only the minimum amount needed to prevent the dough from sticking to the table. Add new dough, cold and firm from the refrigerator, to the scraps from the batch you are working with, as needed.

Short dough, before or after it is shaped, can be stored covered in the refrigerator for up to two weeks and can be frozen for many months. Short dough can be baked at any temperature between 325° and 425°F (163° and 219°C), but 375°F (190°C) is ideal. When the dough starts to show a golden brown color, it is done.

Short Dough

4 pounds, 14 ounces (2 kg, 220 g) dough, enough to line about ninety-five 2½-inch (6.2-cm) tartlet pans or seven 11-inch (27.5-cm) tart pans

12 ounces (340 g) granulated sugar
1 pound, 12 ounces (795 g) butter or margarine
2 eggs
1 teaspoon (5 ml) vanilla extract
2 pounds, 2 ounces (970 g) bread flour

1. Place sugar, butter or margarine, eggs, and vanilla in a mixing bowl; mix at low speed with the dough hook just until combined.
2. Add the flour and mix only until the dough is smooth.
3. Place the dough on a paper-lined sheet pan; press out as flat as possible so that the dough takes up less space and cools down quickly.
4. Cover and refrigerate.
NOTE: If overmixed, the dough will be much harder to roll out. If you use all butter or a large percentage of butter, you must take care that the dough is not too soft.

Cocoa Short Dough

3 pounds, 12 ounces (1 kg, 705 g) dough

8 ounces (225 g) granulated sugar
1 pound, 12 ounces (795 g) butter or margarine
2 eggs
1 teaspoon (5 ml) vanilla extract
2 pounds, 4 ounces (1 kg, 25 g) bread flour
1 ounce (30 g) cocoa powder

1. Place sugar, butter or margarine, eggs, and vanilla in mixing bowl. Mix on low speed using the dough hook, just until the ingredients are combined.
2. Sift flour with cocoa powder; add to the dough, and mix only until smooth.
3. Place dough on a paper-lined sheet pan; press the dough as flat as possible.
4. Cover and refrigerate.

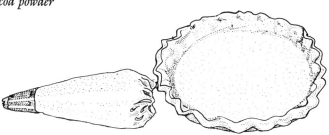

Hazelnut Short Dough

3 pounds (1 kg, 365 g) dough

8 ounces (225 g) granulated sugar
1 pound (455 g) butter or
*   margarine*
1 egg
½ teaspoon (2.5 ml) vanilla
*   extract*
1 pound, 2 ounces (510 g)
*   bread flour*
4 ounces (115 g) finely ground
*   hazelnuts*

1. Place sugar, butter or margarine, egg, and vanilla in a mixing bowl; mix on low speed using the dough hook, just long enough to incorporate the ingredients.
2. Add flour and hazelnuts, and mix just until the dough is smooth.
3. Cover and refrigerate.

Short Dough Cake-Bottoms

one 10-inch (25-cm) cake-bottom

9 ounces (225 g) Short Dough
*   (page 31)*

1. Work the short dough smooth with your hands, shaping it to a thick circle in the process.
2. Start to roll it out to ⅛ inch (3 mm) thick and slightly larger than 10 inches (25 cm). Sprinkle just enough bread flour on the board to keep it from sticking. Keep moving and turning the dough over as you roll it, first with your hands and then, as the dough gets thinner, by rolling it up on a dowel. Look closely at the dough as you roll it out. If only the edge of the dough is moving and not the middle, the middle is sticking to the table. Try to roll the dough into the general shape of what you plan to make. Trim off the ragged edge that always develops when the dough starts to get thin; this edge often tears away from the dough when you are picking it up or rolling it.
3. When the short dough is ⅛ inch (3 mm) thick, roll it up on a dowel (never a rolling pin) and place it on a sheet pan lined with baking paper.
4. Place a 10-inch (25-cm) adjustable ring or template on top of the short dough, and cut around the outside edge; remove the leftover dough. If you cut the dough circle before transferring it to the pan, you will probably stretch the dough as you move it, resulting in an oval rather than a circle.
5. Prick the dough lightly so that any trapped air can escape.
6. Bake at 375°F (190°C) for about 10 minutes.

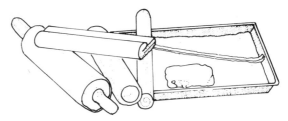

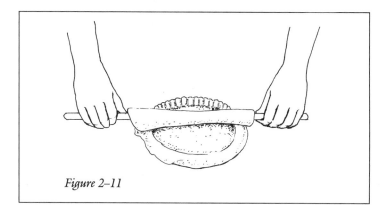

Figure 2–11

Lining Large Tart Shells

1. Prepare and roll the dough ⅛ inch (3 mm) thick as directed for short dough cake-bottoms, making a circle 1 to 2 inches (2.5 to 5 cm) larger than the tart pan.

2. Roll the dough up on a dowel (not a rolling pin), place the tart pan in front of the dough, and, working as quickly as possible, unroll the dough over the pan (Figure 2–11).

3. Pick up the edges of the dough all around to allow the dough to fall into the pan where the sides meet the bottom. Gently press the dough against the sides and bottom of the pan. Take care not to stretch the dough; it should still be ⅛ inch (3 mm) thick when you have finished.

4. Roll your rolling pin over the top edge of the pan to trim away the excess dough.

5. Prick the dough lightly to allow trapped air to escape.

If the tart shell is to be prebaked (baked blind), line the bottom with a circle of paper and fill it with dried beans or pie weights; bake as indicated in the recipe. It is not necessary to use pie weights if it does not matter that the sides will settle (not shrink) slightly as the crust bakes. The dough settles because it is so thin and the sides of the form are completely straight. Lining the forms with a thicker layer of dough will prevent settling, but a thicker crust detracts from the taste. A short dough that has been made correctly does not need to rest before it is baked, and it should not shrink or puff up during baking as long as the dough has been pricked.

Lining Small Individual Forms

1. Prepare the dough and roll out as instructed for short dough cake-bottoms, rolling the dough into a rectangle ⅛ inch (3 mm) thick. If you are lining forms that are very small, roll the dough slightly thinner so that there will be room in the forms for the filling.

2. Stagger the forms, 1 to 2 inches (2.5 to 5 cm) apart, in the approximate shape of the dough. The taller the forms, the more space you need to leave between them, so the dough will line the sides.

3. Roll the dough up on a dowel, and unroll it over the forms (Figure 2–12).

4. Push the forms together with your hands to create enough slack for the dough to fall into the forms without overstretching and breaking (Figure 2–13).

5. Dust the dough lightly with bread flour and, using a ball of dough about the same size as the inside of the forms, gently pound the dough in place (Figure 2–14).

6. When all the air pockets are eliminated, roll the rolling pin over the forms to trim away the excess dough (Figure 2–15). (You can also press down on the forms with the palm of your hand to do the same thing.)

7. Place the finished forms on a sheet pan. Bake as directed in individual recipes.

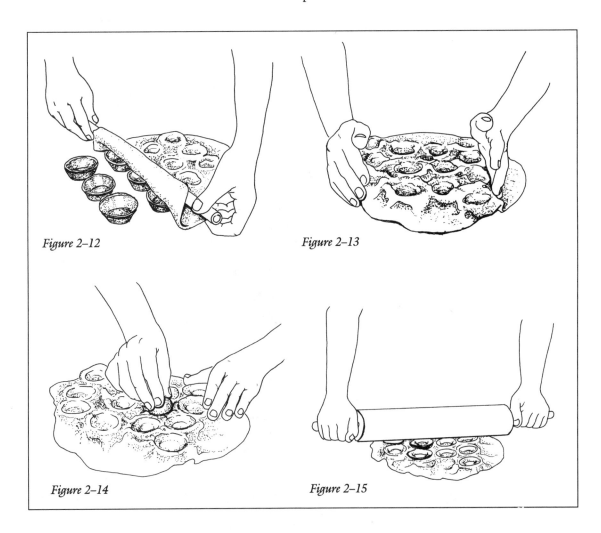

Figure 2–12

Figure 2–13

Figure 2–14

Figure 2–15

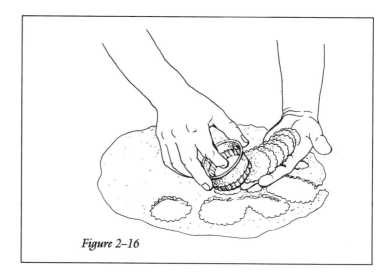

Figure 2–16

Short Dough Cookies

1. Prepare the short dough as for short dough cake-bottoms and roll it into a rectangle ⅛ inch (3 mm) thick. Make sure the dough does not stick to the table.

2. Cut the cookies with a plain or fluted cutter, holding your other hand next to where you are cutting.

3. As you cut each cookie, flip the dough in one smooth motion into your waiting palm (Figure 2–16). Smaller cookies are the easiest to flip, but with a little practice this method works well with sizes up to 3½ inches (8.7 cm). If you are doing this for a living you simply have to learn this technique to save time.

4. When you have about six cookies in your hand, place them on a sheet pan lined with baking paper. Continue to cut the remaining cookies in the same manner. Stagger the cutting and placing of the cookies for the least amount of wasted dough and space.

5. Bake the cookies at 375°F (190°C) until golden brown, 10 to 12 minutes depending on size.

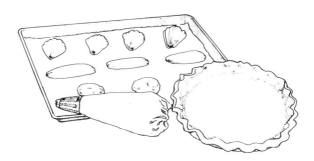

Weaver's Dough

7 pounds, 6 ounces (3 kg, 355 g)
dough

¼ cup (60 ml) vegetable oil
2 eggs
4 tablespoons (60 g) salt
2 ounces (55 g) granulated sugar
1 quart (960 ml) cold water
5 pounds, 4 ounces (2 kg, 390 g)
   bread flour
Egg Wash (page 5)

Like salt dough, weaver's dough is used to make ornaments and decorations. But, because weaver's dough has some elasticity, it is better suited to long pieces—in making a bread basket for example. Since the dough contains no yeast, ornaments that are made from it will look exactly as you shaped them. For the same reason, the ornaments will be quite hard and not very appetizing, and are intended for purely decorative purposes.

1. Add the oil, eggs, salt, and sugar to the water.
2. Incorporate the flour. Knead to make a smooth, elastic and firm dough.
3. Cover the dough and let rest for about 1 hour before using. Weaver's dough can be stored covered in the refrigerator for up to four days without deteriorating and can be kept frozen for months.
4. Shape dough as desired.
5. Before baking ornaments, brush with egg wash (if you let the first layer dry and then brush a second time you will get the maximum amount of shine on the finished pieces).
6. Bake at 350°F (175°C) until the ornaments have a nice deep-golden color.

Whole Wheat Weaver's Dough

6 pounds, 2 ounces (2 kg, 785 g)
dough

½ ounce (15 g) fresh
   compressed yeast
1 quart (960 ml) cold water
½ ounce (15 g) malt sugar
2 ounces (55 g) granulated sugar
2 tablespoons (30 g) salt
3 pounds, 8 ounces (1 kg, 590 g)
   finely ground whole wheat flour
6 ounces (170 g) softened butter
Egg Wash (page 5)

This is another dough intended for ornaments and decorating pieces, but because it contains a small amount of yeast, the baked goods are soft enough to be pleasant to eat. Whole wheat weaver's dough is especially suitable for rolled, cut-out, flat pieces. To make nice clean edges, place the rolled dough in the freezer for a few minutes to harden so that it won't drag as you cut it.

1. Dissolve the yeast in the water.
2. Add malt sugar, sugar, and salt.
3. Incorporate about half of the flour.
4. Add the soft butter, then the remaining flour.
5. Knead until you have a smooth, elastic dough. Adjust with additional flour as necessary. Do not overknead the dough because it will become too soft to work with.
6. Cover the dough and let rest for 1 hour in the refrigerator.
7. Punch dough down, and form as desired. If the pieces are to be eaten, allow them to proof until half-doubled in volume before baking.
8. Brush the pieces with egg wash and bake at 375°F (190°C) until they are golden brown.

Bread Basket

one basket measuring 15 inches long, 12 inches wide, and 15 inches high (37.5 × 30 × 37.5 cm)

1 recipe Weaver's Dough (page 36)
Egg Wash (page 5)
½ recipe Boiled Sugar Basic Recipe (page 469) (see note 3)

Before you can make this decorative woven bread basket, you must first become a carpenter and make the guide that is used to weave the dough. While making the form does take a little work, and requires some special equipment, once you have made (or purchased) it, the form will last forever. These instructions will make a medium-sized oval basket with slanted sides. If you wish to make another design, keep in mind that you must have an even number of dowels, and they should be spaced approximately 1½ inches (3.7 cm) apart. If you want to keep the oval shape, but would like to make a smaller or larger basket, modify the template to the size desired and increase or decrease the weight and thickness of the dough strings accordingly.

1. Cut a 14½- × 9½-inch (36.2- × 23.7-cm) rectangle from ¾-inch (2-cm) particle board.

2. Copy and enlarge the template (Figure 2–17) to make a 12- × 8½-inch (30- × 21.2-cm) oval.

3. Center the drawing on top of the particle board and mark the position of the holes. Remove the paper.

4. Make a pilot hole using a small bit, then drill the holes using a ⁵⁄₁₆-inch (8-mm) drill bit, drilling the holes at a slight outward angle. If you do not have a drill guide to ensure the same angle for all twenty holes, cut a piece of wood to the proper angle and hold this in front of the drill bit. If you try to approximate the angle freehand, you are sure to end up with an uneven circumference in your finished basket.

5. Cut twenty ⁵⁄₁₆-inch (8-mm) wooden dowels to 6 inches (15 cm) in length.

6. Divide the weaver's dough as follows:

- Eight 7-ounce (200-g) pieces for the sides of the basket.
- One 12-ounce (340-g) piece for the bottom. (Form into an oval shape before refrigerating.)
- Two 1-pound (455-g) pieces for the handle.
- Two 10-ounce (285-g) pieces for the border (see note).
- Four 1-ounce (30-g) pieces for the dowels.

Leave the eight 7-ounce (200-g) pieces out to work with and refrigerate the remaining pieces covered.

7. Pound and roll each of the 7-ounce (200-g) pieces into strings using the technique described in Braided Bread (see pages 49–50 and Figures 3–3 to 3–5); do not use any flour as you are rolling. As the dough is (and must be) very firm and rubbery (glutenous), the strings can only be rolled out a little at a time, left to relax for a few minutes, then rolled and stretched a bit further.

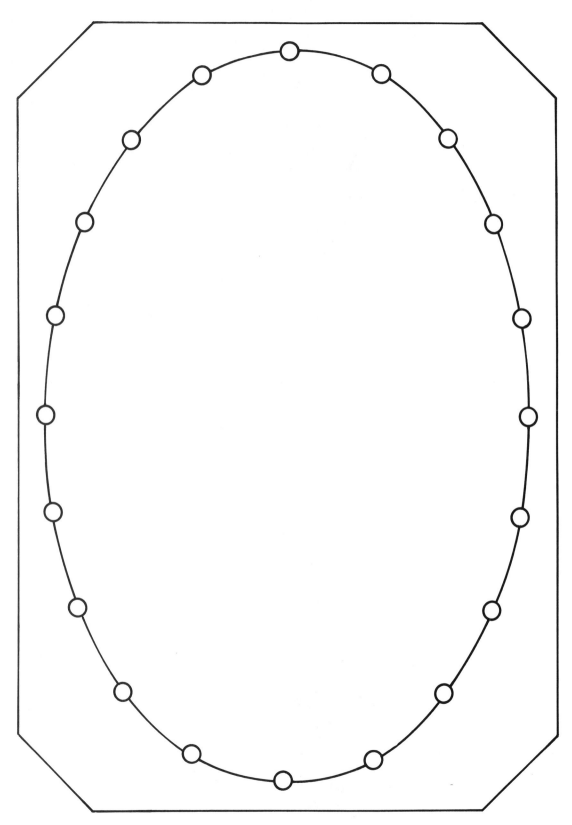

Figure 2–17

Work on the strings alternately in this way, moistening the palm of your hand with water as needed to prevent the strings from sliding instead of rolling (have a plate with a small amount of water nearby to use as you are working). Keep the strings uniform in thickness and continue rolling until they are 3 feet (90 cm) long. Keep the strings covered with a damp towel during this process.

8. While you are rolling the strings and waiting for them to relax, cover the particle board base with aluminum foil. Press the foil on top of the holes so you can see their location, then push the wooden dowels through the foil and into the holes. Cover the dowels with aluminum foil. Set the form aside.

9. Use some flour to prevent the dough from sticking, and roll out the 12-ounce (340-g) piece of dough into an oval slightly larger than the base of the basket. Reserve covered in the refrigerator.

10. Weave the first string of dough in and out around the dowels on the foil (Figure 2–18). Weave a second string on top of the first, alternating the sequence in front of and behind the dowels. Stretch the strings slightly as you weave (see note 2). Add the remaining strings in the same manner, starting and finishing each of the strings staggered along one long side. Cut the strings to fit where the ends meet and press them together using a little egg wash as glue. Because the sides of the basket are slanted, you will have some extra dough left from the lower strings. However, making all of the strings the same length to begin with is the simplest way of ensuring that they all have the same thickness, and that the ones for the top (wider part) of the basket will be long enough. Adjust the strings as you weave them to be sure the height of the basket is even all around.

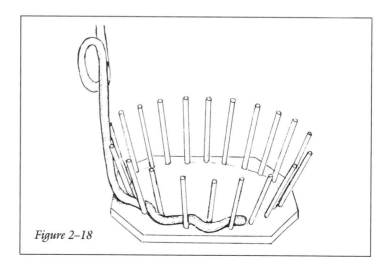

Figure 2–18

11. Brush egg wash over the bottom ½ inch (1.2 cm) of the inside of the basket. Place the reserved oval piece of dough inside the basket, stretching the dough slightly and pressing it against the egg wash. Prick the dough on the bottom of the basket thoroughly.

12. Brush egg wash on the inside base and on both the inside and outside of the basket. Place the particle board on a sheet pan.

13. Bake the basket at 350°F (175°C) until golden brown, approximately 1 hour and 30 minutes. Let the basket cool completely.

14. Remove the wooden dowels by twisting as you pull them out.

15. Cover the outside of the basket with aluminum foil. Remove from the particle board and place upside down on a sheet pan.

16. Return the basket to the oven and bake until the bottom is golden brown, about 30 minutes. Let cool.

17. While the basket is baking, make the handle (see note 3): Roll each of the two 1-pound (455-g) pieces of dough to 7 feet (2 meters, 10 cm) long, using the same method used to roll the strings for the sides. If you do not have a table long enough to allow for the full length, loosely curl one end of the string as you are working on the other.

18. Braid the strings together in a 2-braid (see instructions on page 51). Since it would take a great deal of room to braid the strings at their full length, curl the ends loosely as needed as you place one on top of the other to form the X. The finished braid should be 36 inches (90 cm) long; stretch if necessary.

19. Place the braid on a sheet pan lined with baking paper and form it into a softly curved half-circle measuring 14 inches (35 cm) across the bottom. Bend the lower 5 inches (12.5 cm) of each side inward slightly to conform with the angle of the slanted sides of the basket (Figure 2–19).

20. Brush the handle with egg wash. Bake at 350°F (175°C) until golden brown, approximately 1 hour (it is important to bake the handle and the basket to the same color or the handle will not look as attractive on the finished basket). Let cool.

21. To make the border: Using the same method as to braid the handle, roll out the two 10-ounce (285-g) pieces of dough to 8 feet (2 meters, 40 cm). Braid the pieces together in a 2-braid. Stretch the finished braid to 38 inches (95 cm) long (allow the dough to relax first as needed). Carefully transfer the braid to a sheet pan lined with baking paper and shape into an oval the same size as the top of the baked basket. Press the ends together using a little egg wash to make them stick.

22. Brush the oval with egg wash. Bake at 350°F (175°C) until golden brown, approximately 35 minutes.

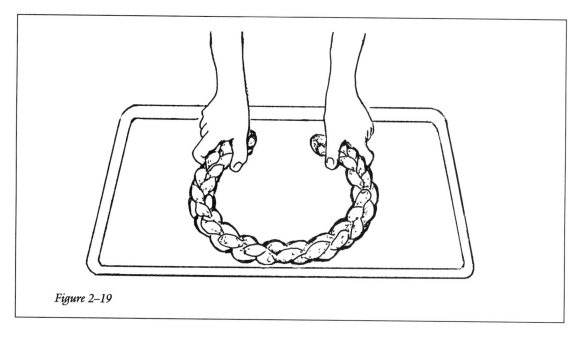

Figure 2–19

23. Roll each of the remaining four 1-ounce (30-g) pieces of dough to 25 inches (62.5 cm) long. These pieces must be perfectly even in diameter. Let the dough relax, then cut each rope into five 5-inch (12.5-cm) pieces. Place the pieces on a sheet pan lined with baking paper and keep them perfectly straight.

24. Brush the dough with egg wash. Bake at 350°F (175°C) until golden brown, approximately 15 minutes. Let cool.

25. Using a serrated knife, trim both ends of the basket handle flat so they can sit against the bottom of the basket. The dough is very hard so this will take some patience. Trim the sides of the lower part of the handle as needed so they will fit snugly inside. (If the handle does not fit correctly, heat it in the oven and then bend it into the proper shape.) Plan to place the handle so that the flat side (the side that was against the sheet pan) is facing the side of the basket where the strings were joined.

26. Insert the bread dough dowels into the holes around the rim of the basket; you may need to trim them a bit to fit using a file or coarse sandpaper.

27. Trim the top of the basket as necessary, using a serrated knife or a file, so that the border will lie flat and even on top. Also trim the inside of the border if needed where the handle will be placed inside.

28. Follow the boiled sugar recipe cooking the syrup to 310°F (155°C); do not add any acid. Let the syrup cool until it is thick enough to be applied with a metal spatula.

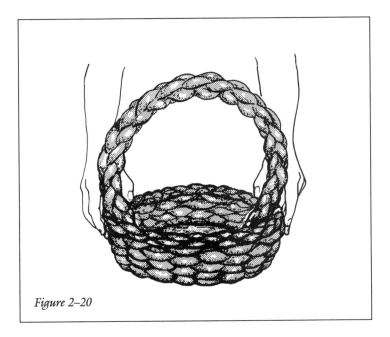

Figure 2–20

29. When the sugar has reached the proper consistency, spread a thin layer in four or five places on the bottom of the border. Immediately press the border in place, placing the seam in the border on the side of the basket where the ends of the strings meet.

30. Quickly and carefully apply sugar to the inside of the basket where the handle will sit and to the outside of the handle where it will touch the inside of the basket. Position the handle in the basket and press in place (Figure 2–20). Hold the handle straight for a few minutes until the sugar is hard.

All that is required now is to bake some rolls and bread knots to fill up the basket. Tying a satin ribbon to the top of the basket handle adds a great deal to the appearance.

NOTE 1: If you don't have time to make a border, use the extra dough for two additional strings. Your basket will look just fine.

NOTE 2: Although the weaver's dough is very firm, the weight of the top strings tends to flatten and compress the bottom two or three strings as you weave the sides of the basket. To avoid this, place the basket in the refrigerator or freezer after weaving the first two strings long enough to allow them to firm up. Repeat after weaving two more, and so on. The strings are intentionally rolled out too short. By stretching them and making them stick to the dowels as you weave, they will remain in place. After they are baked, the dowels are easy to pull out because of the aluminum foil.

NOTE 3: Unfortunately, it is impossible to bake the basket handle standing up. Therefore, the side that is against the sheet pan will be flat after baking, and is not very attractive. This is fine if the basket is to be displayed in a corner or against a wall, but doesn't look good if visible from all sides. If this is the case, you can make two thinner handles and glue them together after baking for a more three-dimensional effect. In steps 17 and 18, divide the 1-pound pieces of dough into four pieces each. Roll the pieces out evenly to the same length given, but braid the eight pieces into two 4-braids instead (see instructions on page 52). Glue the flat sides of the two handles together with boiled sugar or royal icing after they have cooled. Attach the handle to the basket as directed.

NOTE 4: While the bread dough portion of the basket will last practically forever without breaking down, the sugar glue will absorb moisture from the air and will soften and fall apart fairly quickly. To prevent this from occurring, spray or brush the basket with marzipan lacquer and store the basket in an airtight plastic bag. The handle can alternatively be attached with royal icing. This will last forever like the bread dough, but the icing will take approximately 24 hours to harden completely. If time permits, this is the practical way of assembling the basket. Hold the handle in place while the icing dries by wrapping plastic wrap over the handle and securing it underneath the basket.

THREE

Breads and Rolls

Breads
  Baguettes
  Braided White Bread
  Butter Wheat Bread
  Farmer's Rye Rings
  Garlic Bread
  Italian Easter Bread
  Joggar Bread
  Onion-Walnut Bread
  Potato Bread
  Raisin Bread
  Rosemary Bread
  Russian Rolled-Wheat Bread
  Sourdough Starter

San Francisco
  Sourdough Loaves
Swedish Orange Rye Bread
Swedish Peasant Bread
Swedish Thin Bread
Rolls
  Bread Sticks
  Kaiser Rolls
  Pre-dough
  Rustica
  Swedish Whole-Grain
    Crisp Rolls
  Tessiner Rolls

The baking of bread dates back to the Stone Age, when people first learned to grind seeds, probably barley and millet, in mills made from stone. It was not a great step from the first porridge to bread. Early bread, heavy and unleavened, was cooked on heated stones (it was not called the Stone Age for nothing). Over the centuries the process of milling the grain was improved. The early Egyptians, with the aid of wind-powered fans and sieves, developed a way to remove parts of the chaff and bran. The Romans and Greeks further advanced cultivation and milling methods and produced different kinds of flour in various stages of refinement.

Baking bread has always had an important place in the European home. Different regions of various countries produce breads that differ not only in flavor, but also in shape. Although today most bread baking is commercial, it is still a favorite hobby of many.

Basically, there are three types of bread products: loaf breads in many shapes; breakfast items, such as croissants and Danish; and soft cakes such as muffins and doughnuts. Some of these are leavened with baking powder or soda, but most are leavened with yeast.

Baking with yeast demands that the ingredients be in proper proportion. Yeast needs sugar to grow, but too much sugar can slow the process to the point where it stops altogether. Sugar also colors and flavors the bread. Salt is used in a yeast dough to add color and flavor and to retard the yeast just a little. When I see a loaf of baked bread that is pale instead of a healthy brown color, I know that the loaf was

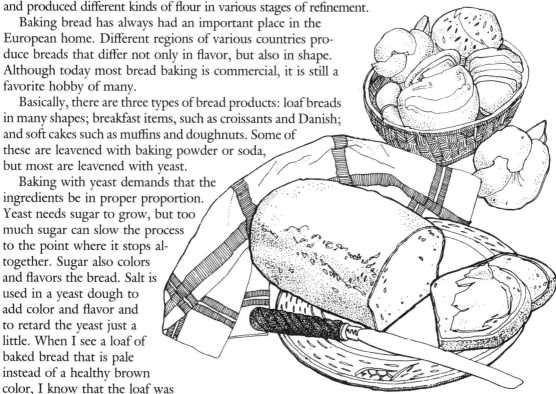

either baked at too low a temperature or that the salt was left out.

Yeast fermentation is damaged at temperatures above 115°F (46°C), and the yeast is killed at 145°F (63°C). At the other end of the scale, yeast fermentation is slowed but not damaged at temperatures below 65°F (19°C) and is nonexistent at 40°F (4°C) or lower. In certain types of yeast dough, such as for Danish pastry, braided white bread, and croissants, it is essential that the yeast be kept cold to prevent fermentation while the dough is being shaped.

The easiest bread to make is plain white bread, which has all white glutenous flour and only the amount of sugar that is healthy for the yeast. White bread can therefore be made with cold milk, which slows the fermentation long enough to give you time to braid it into different kinds of loaves. In a bread with a higher proportion of sugar, with a sweet flour such as rye, or with flours that have little or no gluten structure, such as whole wheat, it is very important to keep the dough from getting too cold.

The ideal temperature for the yeast to develop is from 78° to 82°F (25° to 27°C), with 85 percent humidity. The dough should be kept as close to this temperature as possible by starting with a warm liquid, 105° to 115°F (40° to 46°C). However, if the liquid is too hot, the yeast will be damaged or killed. Use a thermometer until you know your judgment is accurate. Take care to keep the dough covered and away from drafts at all times.

There are two methods of fermenting the yeast. In the sponge method a very soft dough is made using a small amount of flour, water, sugar (although sugar is not necessary if milk is used because milk is naturally sweet), and, most of the time, all of the yeast. This "sponge" rises in a warm place, covered, until doubled in volume. The sponge is then mixed with all the remaining ingredients to make the dough. This method allows the yeast to ferment in peace, without interference from other ingredients. In breads with a high sugar content, such as Swedish Orange Rye or Italian Triestine bread, the sponge method is essential for a satisfactory result.

In the straight-dough method, all the ingredients are mixed together at the beginning and, in most cases, kneaded to form a gluten structure. The dough is then given one or two periods to rise before being punched down and made into loaves or rolls.

A pre-dough is sometimes used to develop flavor, which comes from the acids and alcohol produced during the rising period, and to soften the gluten giving the final product increased volume. To make the pre-dough, a small percentage of yeast is mixed with water and flour to form a stiff, smooth dough. The mixture is then covered and left to rise for 12 to 24 hours.

Danish pastry and croissants depend on thin layers of butter or margarine to "help" the yeast. The fat particles produce steam when the Danish or croissants are baked, and that, together with the trapped air and the yeast, gives them their light, flaky consistency.

Most bread doughs should rise to double in volume, but this includes the rising that will occur in the oven before the bread reaches 145°F (63°C), when the yeast is killed. Therefore, prior to baking, the bread should rise to just about half of its double-in-volume potential to allow for the final rise in the oven (there are some exceptions in individual recipes). A loaf that has risen too much is very crumbly, dries out faster because of the extra air, and has less flavor because the flavor does not increase with the dough's volume. On the other hand, if the bread is not allowed to rise long enough, the gluten will not have formed all the elasticity it needs to expand and, as a result, the loaf will crack (usually on the side) and will be compact and heavy. Not enough rising time for Danish pastry and croissants will make some of the butter run out on the pan and result in a drier and heavier pastry. Last, but certainly not least, it is very important that the proof box (the box where the yeast ferments in a dough in industrial baking) or other rising area is not too hot. Ideally it should be about 82°F (27°C) with 85 percent humidity.

Some of the recipes in this chapter give baking instructions for ovens with steam injectors. If your oven is not equipped with steam read the directions that follow the recipe for Baguettes (page 48), which offer an alternative method of creating steam. Steam creates a moist environment that prevents the dough from forming a crust too soon. After a specified length of time a damper is opened to let the steam out, and the bread finishes baking. The resulting crust is much thinner and crisper, fragile enough to crack and break. The steam also helps the bread brown on top: the moisture in the air melts the sugar in the dough on the surface, which caramelizes as it bakes. For this reason you generally don't need egg wash when baking with steam. It takes some experimenting with a steam oven to determine the proper length of time for the steam period. If too much steam is used, almost no crust will form at all. If the steam is not left in the oven long enough you will not achieve the desired effect either. The trick is to use exactly enough steam so that the crust is just thick enough to crack.

If you keep to all of these rules and guidelines, I can assure you that you will be very satisfied with the results of the following recipes.

Breads

To Form Loaves of Bread

To make round or oval loaves of bread, put the required weight of dough on the table and cup your hand around it. Using primarily the section of your palm at the base of the thumb, knead and move the dough around counter-clockwise as you lift one section at a time from the outside, and press it down in the center, forming a tight skin around the dough (Figure 3–1). When you have worked all the way around the circle a few times and the dough is tight, gradually turn it upside down using the same movements, so that the seam is on the bottom. Hold the side of your hand against the table and form the loaf round or oval as desired (Figure 3–2).

Baguettes

five 13-ounce (370-g) loaves

1½ ounces (40 g) fresh
   compressed yeast
3 cups (720 ml) warm water
   (105°–115°F, 40°–46°C)
4 teaspoons (20 g) salt
2 ounces (55 g) malt (or
   granulated) sugar
2 pounds, 7 ounces (1 kg, 110 g)
   bread flour, approximately
cornmeal

One-Half Recipe
three 11-ounce (310-g) loaves

¾ ounce (23 g) fresh
   compressed yeast
1½ cups (360 ml) warm water
   (105°–115°F, 40°–46°C)
2 teaspoons (10 g) salt
1 ounce (30 g) malt (or
   granulated) sugar
1 pound, 3 ounces (540 g)
   bread flour, approximately
cornmeal

If you are halving the recipe, follow instructions as given, but scale the dough into 11-ounce (310-g) pieces and roll each piece to 20 inches (50 cm) in length.

1. Dissolve the yeast in warm water. Stir in salt, malt, and enough of the bread flour to make a fairly firm dough. Knead until the dough is smooth and elastic. Place dough in oiled bowl, cover, and let rise until doubled in volume.

2. Punch down the dough. Scale the dough into 13-ounce (370-g) pieces. Roll and pound each piece into a 23-inch (57.5-cm) baguette (as you would form bread strings, Figures 3–3, 3–4, and 3–5, pages 49–50).

3. Place the baguettes on a sheet pan lined with baking paper. Dust with cornmeal. Let rise until half-doubled in volume.

4. With a razor blade or a very sharp knife cut deep slits 4 to 5 inches (10 to 12.5 cm) long, at a sharp angle, on top of each baguette.

5. Bake at 400°F (205°C) with steam, leaving the damper closed for the first 10 minutes. Open the damper and continue to bake approximately 20 minutes longer or until the loaves are golden brown and feel light. Cool on racks. Freeze if not to be used the same day.

NOTE: If your oven does not have steam injectors, place a pan containing four or five ice cubes in the oven, and add ice cubes, a few at a time, to create steam during the first 10 minutes of baking. After 10 minutes remove the pan and continue baking as directed.

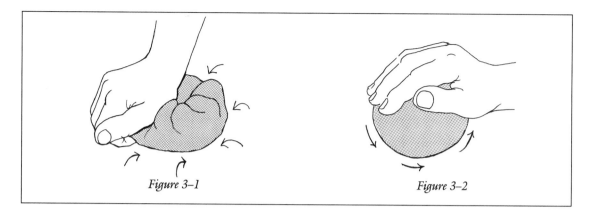

Figure 3–1   Figure 3–2

Braided White Bread

six 18-ounce (510-g) loaves, or
fifty-five 2-ounce (55 g) knots,
double loops, or twists

4 ounces (115 g) fresh compressed
*   yeast*
1 quart (960 ml) cold milk
3 tablespoons (45 g) salt
2 pounds (910 g) bread flour
2 pounds (910 g) cake flour
4 ounces (115 g) granulated sugar
8 ounces (225 g) softened butter
Egg Wash (page 5)
poppy or sesame seeds, optional

1. Dissolve yeast in milk. Add salt, both flours, and sugar. Mix using dough hook until dough forms a ball. Mix in butter.

2. Knead until a fine gluten structure develops, 8 to 10 minutes. Test by pulling off a small piece of dough and stretching it lightly: if it forms an almost translucent membrane the dough has been kneaded enough. Do not overknead. If the dough is overkneaded the gluten structure will be permanently damaged, resulting in a loose and hard-to-work dough that will not rise properly (if at all) because the damaged gluten cannot trap enough air.

3. Place the dough in an oiled bowl, cover, and let rise until doubled in volume.

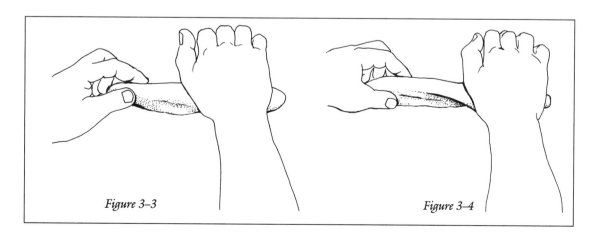

Figure 3–3   Figure 3–4

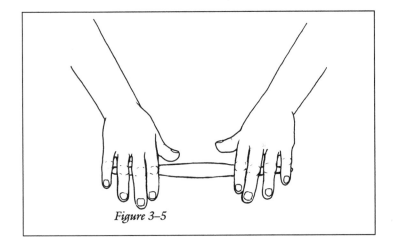

Figure 3–5

One-Half Recipe
three 18-ounce (510-g) loaves, or
twenty-seven 2-ounce (55 g)
knots, double loops, or twists

2 ounces (55 g) fresh
compressed yeast
1 pint (480 ml) cold milk
1½ tablespoons (22 g) salt
1 pound (455 g) bread flour
1 pound (455 g) cake flour
2 ounces (55g) granulated sugar
4 ounces (115 g) softened butter
Egg Wash (page 5)
poppy or sesame seeds, optional

Braided Loaves

1. Punch down dough and divide into pieces for braiding. The total weight of each braided loaf should be about 18 ounces (510 g). The weight of the pieces depends on how many strings are used. For example, if you want three strings per braid, make each piece 6 ounces (170 g); if you want six strings, make each piece 3 ounces (85 g). Weights of the strings for each braid are specified in the instructions that follow. Keep the pieces covered to prevent a skin from forming.

2. Form the pieces into strings by repeatedly folding the dough and pounding it with the heel of your hand to remove air bubbles or pockets (Figures 3–3 and 3–4). Then gently roll the string between your hands and the table until you have reached the desired length (Figure 3–5).

3. Pound and roll enough pieces for one loaf into tapered strings, thicker at the centers and thinner on the ends. It is better not to roll all the dough into strings at once, but to braid each loaf after rolling out one set of strings.

4. Lay the strings in front of you and join them at the top. Braid according to the instructions that follow. Take care not to braid too tightly, and try not to stretch the strings any more than is necessary. This is usually only a problem if the dough has been overkneaded.

5. In following the instructions for the different braids, count from left to right; when you move string number 1 in a 5-string braid over numbers 2 and 3, number 1 becomes number 3 and number 2 becomes number 1 (Figure 3–6). In Figure 3–7, string number 5 is being moved over numbers 4 and 3; number 5

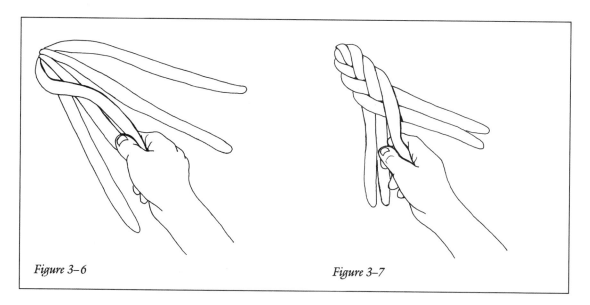

Figure 3–6

Figure 3–7

becomes 3, and number 4 becomes number 5. Doing this is not as complicated as reading about it—give it a try!

6. As you come to the end of the braid, pinch the strings together and tuck them underneath.

7. Place the braided loaves four to a sheet pan. If they have shrunk during the braiding, which will happen in a six- or eight-string braid, gently stretch them to about 14 inches (35 cm) as you put them on the pan. This will give you more attractive, uniform loaves.

8. Brush the loaves with egg wash, and let rise until half-doubled in volume. For extra shine, brush the braids with egg wash again prior to baking. Sprinkle with poppy or sesame seeds if desired.

9. Bake at 400°F (205°C) for about 25 minutes. Cool on racks.

Two-string braid

1. Weigh the dough into 9-ounce (255-g) pieces.

2. Pound and roll the pieces out to 20-inch (50 cm) strings.

3. Place the strings in a wide *X* shape in front of you.

4. Pick up the two ends of the bottom string, and move the two ends straight across the other string so they change sides, but do not cross over each other.

5. Repeat the procedure with the other string and repeat, until the braid is finished.

Three-string braid

1. Weigh the dough into 6-ounce (170-g) pieces.
2. Pound and roll out to 12-inch (30-cm) strings.
3. Braid 1 over 2. Braid 3 over 2.
4. Repeat braiding sequence.

Four-string braid

1. Weigh the dough into 4½-ounce (130-g) pieces.
2. Pound and roll out to 12-inch (30-cm) strings.
3. Braid 2 over 3.
4. Braid 4 over 3 and 2.
5. Braid 1 over 2 and 3.
6. Repeat braiding sequence.

Five-string braid

1. Weigh the dough into 3½-ounce (100-g) pieces.
2. Pound and roll out to 12-inch (30-cm) strings.
3. Braid 2 over 3.
4. Braid 5 over 4, 3, and 2.
5. Braid 1 over 2 and 3.
6. Repeat braiding sequence.
7. When the braid is finished, roll the whole loaf one-quarter turn to the left (on its side) before proofing and baking.

Six-string braid

1. Weigh the dough into 3-ounce (85-g) pieces.
2. Pound and roll out to 14-inch (35-cm) strings.
3. Braid 1 over 2, 3, 4, 5, and 6.
4. Braid 5 over 4, 3, 2, and 1.
5. Braid 2 over 3, 4, 5, and 6.
6. Braid 5 over 4, 3, 2, and 1.
7. Braid 2 over 3 and 4.
8. Repeat from step 4.

Seven-string braid

1. Weigh the dough into 2½-ounce (70-g) pieces.
2. Pound and roll out to 12-inch (30-cm) strings.
3. Braid 7 over 6, 5, and 4.
4. Braid 1 over 2, 3, and 4.
5. Repeat braiding sequence. This is the same general procedure as is used for the three-string braid, and can be used for any odd number of strings (5, 7, 9, etc.). Always place the odd string in the center (over half of the remainder), alternating between left and right.

Eight-string braid

1. Weigh the dough into 2-ounce (55-g) pieces.
2. Pound and roll out to 14-inch (35-cm) strings.
3. Braid 2 under 3 and over 8.
4. Braid 1 over 2, 3, and 4.
5. Braid 7 under 6 and over 1.
6. Braid 8 over 7, 6, and 5.
7. Repeat braiding sequence.

Knots

1. Punch dough down and divide into 2-ounce (55 g) pieces. Keep the pieces you are not using covered to prevent a skin from forming.
2. Working with one piece at a time, roll into a 9-inch (22.5-cm) rope and tie the rope into a loose knot so that the ends protrude out just slightly beyond the body of the roll (Figure 3–8).
3. Place the rolls on a sheet pan lined with baking paper.
4. Let the rolls rise until half-doubled in volume.
5. Brush with egg wash and bake at 400°F (205°C) for approximately 15 minutes.

Double Loops

1. Punch dough down and divide into 2-ounce (55-g) pieces. Keep the pieces you are not using covered to prevent a skin from forming.
2. Working with one piece at a time, roll into an 11-inch (27.5-cm) rope and place it in front of you vertically.
3. Pick up the end closest to you and, forming a loop on the right, cross it over the top of the rope just below the tip, so that one-third of the length is now in a straight line pointing to the left.

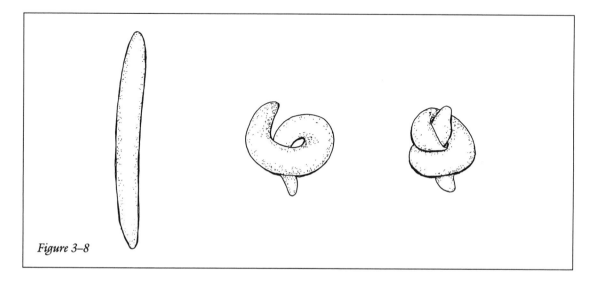

Figure 3–8

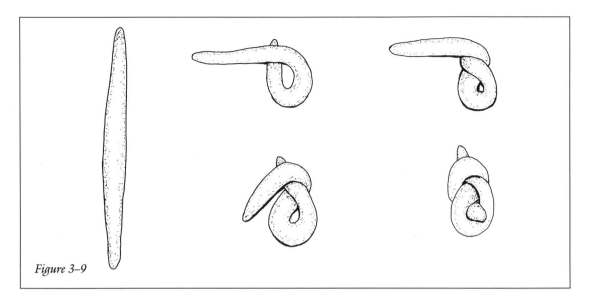

Figure 3–9

4. In one continuous motion, twist the bottom of the loop one-half turn to the right and tuck the top end underneath and up through the opening (Figure 3–9).

5. Place the rolls on a sheet pan lined with baking paper.

6. Let the rolls rise until half-doubled in volume.

7. Brush with egg wash and bake at 400°F (205°C) for about 15 minutes.

Twists

1. Punch dough down and divide into 2-ounce (55-g) pieces. Keep the pieces you are not using covered to prevent a skin from forming.

2. Working with one piece at a time, roll into a 16-inch (40-cm) rope and place it in front of you in a U shape, with inner edges touching.

3. Fold the bottom up to about ¾ inch (2 cm) from the top.

4. Using both hands, twist the sides in opposite directions as if you were opening a book. Repeat this motion (Figure 3–10).

5. Place the rolls on a sheet pan lined with baking paper.

6. Let the rolls rise until half-doubled in volume.

7. Brush with egg wash and bake at 400°F (205°C) for approximately 15 minutes.

Variation: Milk Rolls
fifty-five 2-ounce (55-g) rolls

1. Follow directions for the full recipe of Braided White Bread substituting 1 pound, 10 ounces (740 g) of bread flour for the 2 pounds (910 g) of cake flour.

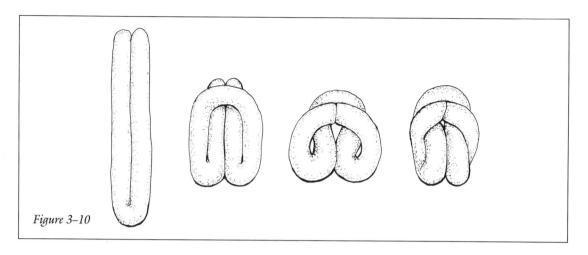

Figure 3–10

2. Knead the dough for 10 to 12 minutes until it is smooth and elastic.

3. Place the dough, covered, in a warm place and let rise until doubled in volume.

4. Punch the dough down, and let rise until doubled a second time.

5. Punch dough down and divide into 2-ounce (55-g) pieces. Form the pieces into oval rolls (see instructions, page 75).

6. Place on sheet pans lined with baking paper. Let the rolls rise until half-doubled in volume.

7. Brush with egg wash, and sprinkle with poppy seeds if desired. Cut four "shark's teeth" on the top of each roll using a pair of scissors (Figure 3–11).

8. Bake the rolls at 425°F (220°C) for approximately 12 minutes.

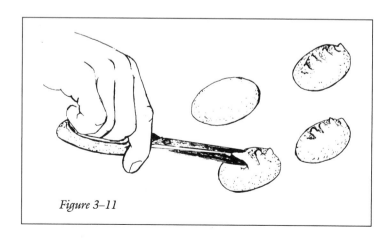

Figure 3–11

Star Braid

one loaf

*1 recipe Braided White Bread
   dough (page 49)*
Egg Wash (page 5)
poppy and sunflower seeds, optional

This bread makes a striking centerpiece for any festive table. The recipe makes a star 15 inches (37.5 cm) in diameter. If you want a smaller star reduce the weight and length of the pieces. Although you need only know how to make a four-string braid to make this loaf, you should not attempt it before you are fairly successful in rolling out and forming the strings. If you take too long, the first string will have risen while you are still shaping the last one. If you are slow you should keep the dough in the refrigerator as you are forming the strings.

1. Make the bread dough and weigh out sixteen 2-ounce (55-g) pieces (12 pieces for the points and 4 pieces for the center of the star). Keep the pieces you are not working with covered to prevent a skin from forming.

2. Pound and roll 12 pieces into 12-inch (30-cm) strings that are tapered at both ends (see Figures 3–3, 3–4, and 3–5, pages 49–50).

3. Bend each string in an upside-down *U*-shape and place them, overlapped, on a paper-lined sheet pan (I find it easier to use an inverted pan) in a wreath with the ends pointing out.

4. Space each string one-third of the distance between the two halves of the previous string; when you add the last one, place one side under the first string (Figure 3–12).

5. Place the strings so that you leave a 5-inch (12.5-cm) opening in the center. An easy way to do this is to arrange the strings around a cookie cutter or other round object of the proper size.

6. Divide into six sections of four strings (Figure 3–13), and form each section into a four-string braid (Figure 3–14): Braid 4

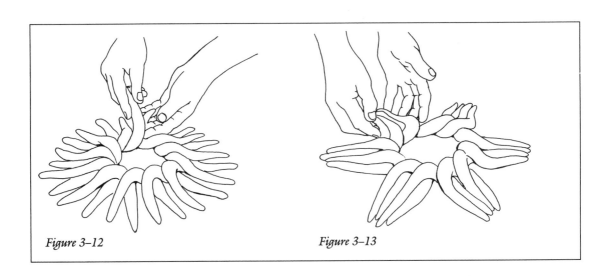

Figure 3–12   *Figure 3–13*

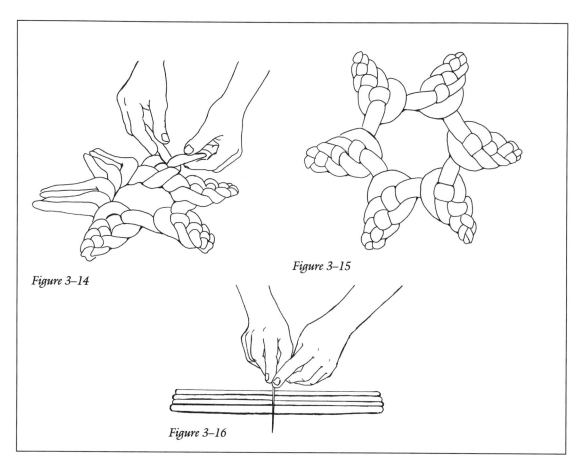

Figure 3–14

Figure 3–15

Figure 3–16

over 3, braid 2 over 3, braid 1 under 2, and repeat from the beginning. (For more information on braiding see pages 50–51.)

7. As you come to the end of each braid pinch the ends together and tuck them under. (Figure 3–15). If the opening in the center is becoming too large, move the sections closer together after you have finished braiding.

8. Pound and roll the remaining four pieces into 28-inch (70-cm) strings.

9. Place them next to each other and cut in half (Figure 3–16).

10. Cut both pieces in half again. The strings will shrink as you do this and probably end up different lengths, but it will not show in the finished shape. You should now have four pieces, each consisting of four strings, approximately 7 inches (17.5 cm) long.

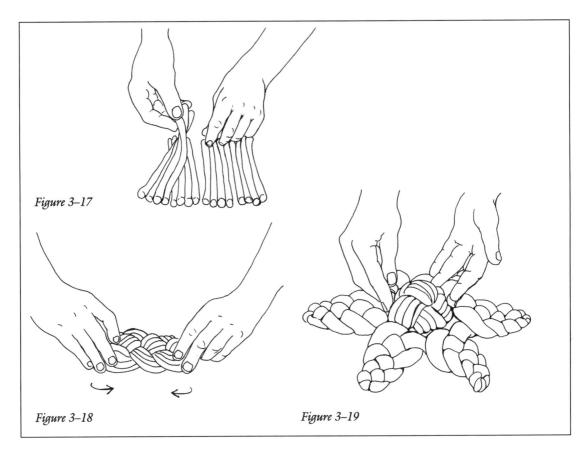

Figure 3–17

Figure 3–18

Figure 3–19

11. Place the strings next to each other and braid, following the preceding directions for the four-braid, braiding from the center out to one end (Figure 3–17).

12. Turn the pieces around so the opposite side is facing you and braid from the center again, making sure that the pieces in each group remain together. Leave both ends of the braid open.

13. Pick up the braid with both hands and push the two ends under so that you form a round loaf (Figure 3–18).

14. Place the loaf in the center opening of the star (Figure 3–19). Brush with egg wash.

15. Let rise until half-doubled in volume.

16. For a good shine, brush a second time with egg wash; sprinkle with poppy and/or sunflower seeds if you wish.

17. Bake at 375°F (190°C) until golden brown, about 40 minutes.

NOTE: You can use the method for forming the center to make a normal-sized loaf: Start with four 4-ounce (115-g) strings for a 1-pound (455-g) loaf. It takes a little extra time, but the finished loaf looks very unusual and few people will know it is only a four-string braid.

Butter Wheat Bread

seven 18-ounce (510-g) loaves

3 ounces (85 g) fresh
   compressed yeast
1 quart (960 ml) warm water
   (105°–115°F, 40°–46°C)
1 pound (455 g) whole wheat flour
2 pounds, 8 ounces (1 kg, 135 g)
   bread flour, approximately
3 tablespoons (45 g) salt
2 pounds (910 g) puff paste
   or croissant scraps
whole wheat flour
Egg Wash (page 5)

One-Third Recipe
two 21-ounce (595-g) loaves

1¼ ounces (35 g) fresh
   compressed yeast
1⅓ cups (320 ml) warm water
   (105°–115°F, 40°–46°C)
5 ounces (140 g) whole wheat flour
13 ounces (370 g) bread flour,
   approximately
1 tablespoon (15 g) salt
11 ounces (310 g) puff paste
   or croissant scraps
Egg Wash (page 5)
whole wheat flour

This is a great way to use up puff paste or croissant scraps that otherwise might go to waste. If you are making a third of the recipe, follow the directions as given but divide the dough into 21-ounce (595-g) pieces.

1. Dissolve the yeast in the warm water. Add the flours and mix for 5 minutes on medium speed.

2. Add salt and dough scraps and mix until the dough is smooth, about 3 minutes. Add more bread flour if needed to make a medium-firm dough.

3. Place the dough on a sheet pan and let rise in a warm place, covered, until the dough starts to fall, about 45 minutes.

4. Divide the dough into 18-ounce (510-g) pieces, keeping the pieces covered as you weigh them to prevent a skin from forming.

5. Knead each piece between your palm and the table until the loaf is tight and round, and the dough has enough tension to spring back when pressed (see Figures 3–1, and 3–2, page 49). If kneaded too much, the skin will break, giving the loaf a ragged look.

6. Immediately after kneading each loaf, flatten it slightly with your hand, brush with egg wash, and invert it in whole wheat flour. Shake off excess.

7. Place the loaves, flour-side up, on sheet pans, four to a pan.

8. Using a sharp paring knife, cut a flower baguette pattern ⅛ inch (3 mm) deep by first making one vertical cut in the center and then three fanned cuts on either side, all joining at the bottom.

9. Let the loaves rise until half-doubled in volume.

10. Bake at 400°F (205°C) until the loaves have a healthy brown color and test done (they should feel light when you pick them up and sound hollow when tapped), about 50 minutes. Place on racks to cool.

Farmer's Rye Rings

four 1-pound, 3-ounce (540-g) loaves

2 ounces (55 g) fresh
    compressed yeast
1 quart (960 ml) warm milk
    (105°–115°F, 40°–46°C)
1 teaspoon (5 ml) vinegar
3 tablespoons (45 ml) honey
2 tablespoons (30 g) salt
1 pound (455 g) medium rye flour
8 ounces (225 g) whole wheat flour
1 pound, 2 ounces (510 g)
    bread flour, approximately
water
medium rye flour

1. Dissolve the yeast in the milk. Add vinegar, honey, and salt. Mix in rye and whole wheat flours.

2. Reserve one handful of the bread flour. Mix in the remainder and knead for four to five minutes until you have a smooth, elastic dough. Adjust the consistency, if required, with the reserved flour. Place the dough in an oiled bowl, cover, and let rise in a warm place until doubled.

3. Punch down the dough. Divide into four 1-pound, 3-ounce (540-g) pieces. Form the pieces into tight round loaves (see Figures 3–1 and 3–2, page 49). Flatten the loaves.

4. Using a thick dowel, make a hole in the center of each loaf, cutting all the way through the dough. (The original technique for making the holes was to use your bare elbow; try it if it seems appropriate.) Let the rings relax for a few minutes, then widen the holes by stretching the dough until the opening is approximately 6 inches (15 cm) in diameter.

5. Place the rings on sheet pans lined with baking paper. Spray or brush with water. Dust the top of the rings with enough rye flour to cover. Let rise until doubled in volume. Using a sharp knife, make three evenly spaced slashes on top of each ring.

6. Bake at 425°F (219°C) with steam leaving the damper closed for the first 10 minutes. Open the damper and bake approximately 20 minutes longer or until baked through.

NOTE: If your oven does not have steam injectors, follow the directions given in the recipe for Baguettes on page 48.

Garlic Bread

six 18-ounce (510-g) loaves

2 ounces (55 g) minced garlic
olive oil
2 ounces (55 g) fresh
    compressed yeast
1 quart (960 ml) warm water
    (105°–115°F, 40°–46°C)
2 egg whites
2 ounces (55 g) softened butter
2 ounces (55 g) granulated sugar
4 tablespoons (60 g) salt
2½ tablespoons (15 g) ground,
    dried oregano

This is one of the most popular breads we make at the California Culinary Academy. Everyone loves the wonderful aroma and flavor of garlic.

California produces 80 percent of the garlic grown in the United States. The annual garlic festival held in Gilroy, California (just south of San Francisco), draws tens of thousands of garlic worshipers eager to sample not only savory dishes but such oddities as garlic ice cream and garlic-flavored chocolate mousse as well!

The history of the bulb dates back to ancient times when it was treasured as a medicine and antidote. Garlic was introduced to Europe during the Crusades. Today it is popular all over the world with the major exceptions of Japan, Scandinavia, and, to some degree, England.

Fresh garlic is available all year round. A bulb consists of twelve to sixteen smaller bulbs, called cloves, each wrapped in a papery skin. Fresh garlic should be stored in a cool, dry place.

2½ *tablespoons (15 g) ground,*
    dried basil
4 *pounds, 4 ounces (1 kg, 935 g)*
    bread flour, approximately
water
whole wheat flour

One-Half Recipe
three 18-ounce (510 g) loaves

1 *ounce (30 g) minced garlic*
olive oil
1¼ *ounces (35 g) fresh*
    compressed yeast
1 *pint (480 ml) warm water*
    (105°–115°F, 40°–46°C)
1 *egg white*
1 *ounce (30 g) softened butter*
1 *ounce (30 g) granulated sugar*
2 *tablespoons (30 g) salt*
4 *teaspoons (8 g) ground,*
    dried oregano
4 *teaspoons (8 g) ground,*
    dried basil
2 *pounds, 2 ounces (970 g)*
    bread flour, approximately
water
whole wheat flour

1. Sauté the garlic in olive oil to remove some of the sting. If the garlic is very strong, reduce the amount.

2. Dissolve the yeast in the warm water. Stir in the egg whites, butter, sugar, salt, oregano, basil, and all but a few ounces of the bread flour. Knead the dough, adding the reserved bread flour, until the dough is fairly stiff and smooth. Place the dough in an oiled bowl, cover, and let rise for one hour.

3. Punch down the dough and divide into 18-ounce (510-g) pieces. Shape each piece into a round loaf. Starting with the loaf formed first, shape each into a tight oval loaf (see Figures 3–1 and 3–2, page 49). The loaves should spring back when pressed lightly.

4. Place the loaves seam side down on sheet pans lined with baking paper. Brush with water and sprinkle lightly with whole wheat flour. Make diagonal slashes across each loaf, about ¼ inch (6 mm) deep. Let rise until doubled in volume.

5. Bake at 375°F (190°C) for about 30 minutes. Cool on racks.

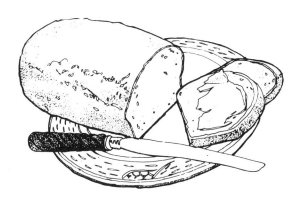

Italian Easter Bread
(Colomba Pasquale: Easter Doves)
four 1-pound, 2-ounce (510-g) loaves

14 ounces (400 g)
   blanched almonds
2 ounces (55 g) fresh
   compressed yeast
1¼ cups (300 ml) warm milk
   (105°–115°F, 43°–46°C)
1½ tablespoons (22 g) salt
1 pound, 10 ounces (740 g)
   bread flour
7 ounces (200 g) softened butter
10 egg yolks
½ teaspoon (2.5 ml) flori de sicilia
   or orange flower water
3 ounces (85 g) granulated sugar
grated zest of one lemon
6 ounces (170 g) Candied Orange
   Peel (page 520)
Simple Syrup (page 7)
granulated sugar
powdered sugar

Italian Easter Bread, also called *Colomba Pasquale* or Easter Doves, is the panettone bread made in Italy at Easter time. Veiled with crystallized sugar and studded with whole almonds, the loaves are shaped to resemble a dove in flight. It is important that the bread be allowed to proof long enough to be light and airy; compared to a standard bread it would actually be considered overproofed.

1. Reserve 32 almonds to use for decoration. Lightly toast the remaining almonds and crush coarsely, reserve.

2. Dissolve yeast in warm milk (be sure the milk is not too hot). Add salt, flour, and butter. Knead dough to a smooth, elastic consistency, approximately 10 minutes.

3. Mix egg yolks, *flori de sicilia* or orange flower water, and sugar. Incorporate this mixture into the dough in four portions, letting the dough completely absorb each portion before adding the next.

4. Combine the lemon zest and orange peel with the reserved chopped almonds. Mix into the dough. Place the dough in an oiled bowl, cover, and let rise in a warm place for one hour, punching the dough down twice during that period.

5. Divide the dough into eight 9-ounce (255-g) pieces. Working with two pieces at a time, pound and roll them into 8-inch (20-cm) ropes (see Figures 3–3, 3–4, and 3–5, pages 49–50), not tapered on the ends, but shaped instead like sausages.

6. Place one piece on a sheet pan lined with baking paper and make an indentation in the center. Place the second piece in the indentation, across the first, to form the wings of the dove. Repeat with the remaining pieces to form three more loaves. Let the loaves rise until doubled in volume.

7. Brush the top and sides of the loaves with simple syrup. Sprinkle with granulated sugar, then dust heavily with powdered sugar. Place eight almonds, evenly spaced, on the top of each loaf, pressing them in so they adhere tightly.

8. Bake at 375°F (190°C) for about 20 minutes, or until baked through. Remove the loaves from the pans and allow them to cool on racks.

Joggar Bread

four 1-pound, 4-ounce (570-g) loaves

1 cup (240 ml) warm water
  (105°–115°F, 40°–46°C)
1 pint (480 ml) warm milk
  (105°–115°F, 40°–46°C)
2 ounces (55 g) fresh
  compresssed yeast
2 eggs
¼ cup (60 ml) honey
¼ cup (60 ml) molasses
2 tablespoons (30 g) salt
3 ounces (85 g) unprocessed
  wheat bran
6 ounces (170 g) cornmeal
4 ounces (115 g) rolled wheat
1 pound (455 g) whole wheat flour
3 ounces (85 g) softened butter
1 pound, 8 ounces (680 g)
  bread flour, approximately
water
whole wheat flour

This is a great-tasting, wholesome bread that is rich in fiber. "Joggar" is the Swedish spelling of "jogger."

1. Combine water and milk in a mixer bowl. Add the yeast and mix to dissolve.

2. Mix eggs, honey, and molasses, and add to the liquid together with the salt, bran, cornmeal, rolled wheat, and whole wheat flour.

3. Knead in the butter and the bread flour, adjusting the amount of bread flour as necessary for a fairly stiff dough. Continue kneading until the dough is smooth and elastic, approximately 8 minutes. Place the dough in an oiled bowl, cover, and let rise until doubled in volume.

4. Punch the dough down, then cover and let rise a second time until doubled in volume again.

5. Punch the dough down, and divide into four 1-pound, 4-ounce (570-g) pieces. Form the pieces into round loaves (see Figures 3–1 and 3–2, page 49) and flatten the loaves lightly. Spray or brush the loaves with water, then sprinkle enough whole wheat flour over the loaves to cover the tops.

6. Place the loaves on sheet pans lined with baking paper. Slash the top of the loaves, cutting just deep enough to penetrate the skin, making a series of parallel lines approximately ¾ inch (2 cm) apart, first in one direction, then at a 45° angle to create a diamond pattern. Let the loaves rise until half-doubled in volume.

7. Bake at 400°F (205°C) with steam, leaving the damper closed for the first 10 minutes. Open the damper and bake approximately 30 minutes longer or until baked through.

NOTE: If your oven does not have steam injectors, follow the directions given in the recipe for Baguettes on page 48.

Onion-Walnut Bread

eight 17-ounce (485-g) loaves

*8 ounces (225 g) peeled white
    onions, minced*
butter or olive oil to sauté onions
*2 ounces (55 g) fresh
    compressed yeast*
*5 cups (1 l, 200 ml) warm milk
    (105°–115°F, 40°–46°C)*
2 ounces (55 g) granulated sugar
4 tablespoons (60 g) salt
1 cup (240 ml) olive oil
*4 pounds, 12 ounces (2 kg, 160 g)
    bread flour, approximately*
*8 ounces (225 g) finely
    chopped walnuts*
Egg Wash (page 5)
whole wheat flour

One-Quarter Recipe

two 17-ounce (485-g) loaves

*2 ounces (55 g) peeled white
    onions, minced*
butter or olive oil to sauté onions
*¾ ounce (25 g) fresh
    compressed yeast*
*1¼ cups (300 ml) warm milk
    (105°–115°F, 40°–46°C)*
*1 tablespoon (15 g) granulated
    sugar*
1 tablespoon (15 g) salt
¼ cup (60 ml) olive oil
*1 pound, 3 ounces (540 g)
    bread flour, approximately*
*2 ounces (55 g) finely
    chopped walnuts*
Egg Wash (page 5)
whole wheat flour

1. Sauté the onions in butter or olive oil until golden.

2. Use a stainless steel or other noncorrosive bowl to mix the dough. The oil from the walnuts, in contact with bare metal, will color the dough grey. Dissolve yeast in warm milk. Stir in sugar, salt, and olive oil.

3. Mix in half of the flour. Mix in walnuts and onions. Mix in enough of the remaining flour to make a quite-firm dough. Knead until smooth. Place the dough in an oiled bowl, cover, and let rise until doubled in volume.

4. Divide dough into 17-ounce (485-g) pieces, and knead the pieces into firm, round loaves (see Figures 3–1 and 3–2, page 49). Brush loaves with egg wash. Invert in whole wheat flour, completely covering the tops of the loaves with flour.

5. Turn right-side up, and immediately mark the top with three plain cookie cutters, using the back of the cutters so you can press firmly and leave a distinct mark without cutting the skin of the loaf. Start with a 4½-inch (11.2-cm) cutter for the outside ring, mark the next ring inside, leaving ½ inch (1.2 cm) between them, and finish with a small ring in the center, spaced ½ inch (1.2 cm) from the middle one.

6. Let the loaves rise until doubled in volume.

7. Bake at 400°F (205°C) about 35 minutes. Cool on racks.

To form rolls

Although in principle all bread doughs can be made into rolls, this dough works particularly well.

1. Divide each 17-ounce (485-g) piece into eight equal pieces.

2. Shape into rolls (see Figure 3–20, page 75) and finish as instructed for the loaves, using smaller cutters to mark the tops.

3. Bake at 400°F (205°C) about 20 minutes.

Potato Bread

four 17-ounce (485-g) loaves

Sponge

*1 cup (240 ml) warm water
   (105°–115°F, 40°–46°C)*
*2 tablespoons (30 ml) light
   corn syrup*
*½ ounce (15 g) fresh
   compressed yeast*
8 ounces (225 g) bread flour

Dough

6 ounces (170 g) potatoes
*2 ounces (55 g) fresh
   compressed yeast*
*1 pint (480 ml) warm milk
   (105°–115°F, 40°–46°C)*
1½ tablespoons (22 g) salt
1 ounce (30 g) malt sugar
6 ounces (170 g) whole wheat flour
*1 pound, 10 ounces (740 g)
   bread flour, approximately*
Egg Wash (page 5)
whole wheat flour

To make the sponge

1. Combine water and corn syrup; dissolve yeast in the mixture.
2. Add bread flour and mix until you have a very soft smooth sponge.
3. Cover and let rise in a warm place until the sponge starts to fall.

To make the dough

1. Peel, cook, and mash the potatoes. Set aside to cool.
2. Dissolve yeast in milk. Add salt, malt sugar, and whole wheat flour.
3. Mix the mashed potatoes and the sponge into the dough.
4. Reserve a handful of the bread flour, then mix in the remainder. Knead for about eight minutes, then adjust with the reserved flour if necessary. The dough should be smooth and elastic, but not sticky.
5. Cover the dough and let rest for 60 minutes in a warm place, punching the dough down once halfway through.
6. Divide the dough into 17-ounce (485-g) pieces. Pound each piece into a tapered oval loaf about 10 inches (25 cm) long. They should be thicker in the center and thinner on the ends.
7. Brush the loaves with egg wash and invert in whole wheat flour. Place right-side up on sheet pans lined with baking paper and let the loaves rise until half-doubled in volume.
8. With a sharp knife, make three slashes at a 45° angle across each loaf. Cut only deep enough to go through the skin.
9. Bake at 400°F (205°C) with steam, leaving the damper closed for the first 10 minutes. Open the damper and continue baking approximately 20 minutes longer.

NOTE: If your oven does not have steam injectors follow the instructions given after the recipe for Baguettes on page 48.

Raisin Bread

six 18-ounce (510-g) loaves

*1 quart (960 ml) warm milk
    (105°–115°F, 40°–46°C)*
*2 ounces (55 g) fresh
    compressed yeast*
2 tablespoons (30 g) salt
3½ ounces (100 g) sugar
¼ cup (60 ml) honey
*3 pounds (1 kg, 365 g)
    bread flour, approximately*
2 ounces (55 g) softened butter
*1 pound, 4 ounces (570 g)
    dark raisins*
Egg Wash (page 5)
Cinnamon Sugar (page 4)

One-Quarter Recipe
two 1-pound (455-g) loaves

*1 cup (240 ml) warm milk
    (105°–115°F, 40°–46°C)*
*¾ ounce (23 g) fresh
    compressed yeast*
1½ teaspoons (8 g) salt
1 ounce (30 g) sugar
1 tablespoon (15 ml) honey
*12 ounces (340 g) bread flour,
    approximately*
½ ounce (15 g) softened butter
5 ounces (140 g) dark raisins
Egg Wash (page 5)
Cinnamon Sugar (page 4)

1. Dissolve the yeast in the warm milk. Stir in salt, sugar, and honey.

2. Reserve a few ounces of the bread flour, and add the remainder. Mix in the butter.

3. Knead to make a soft, smooth dough. Adjust with the reserved bread flour if necessary. Do not overknead the dough as this will make it harder to knead in the raisins later.

4. Place the dough, covered, in a warm place and let rise until doubled in volume, about one hour.

5. Knead in the raisins by hand, at the same time developing the necessary gluten structure. Let the dough rest, covered, for 10 minutes.

6. Divide the dough into 9-ounce (255-g) pieces. (See note.) Keep them covered. Starting with the first one weighed, pound and roll each piece into a 10-inch (25-cm) string.

7. Twist two strings together loosely, and place them in rectangular bread pans, 8 × 4 × 2½ inches (20 × 10 × 6.2 cm).

8. Brush with egg wash and sprinkle with cinnamon sugar. Let the loaves rise until half-doubled in volume.

9. Bake at 375°F (190°C) for about 40 minutes. Unmold and cool on racks.

NOTE: When making the quarter recipe, follow the instructions as given but divide the dough into 8-ounce (225-g) pieces. Due to the large amount of sugar in this bread, you must protect the dough from cooling below 75°F (25°C) or the yeast action will be severely reduced.

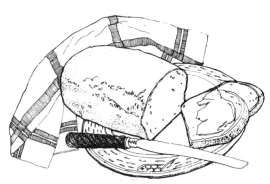

Variation: Hot Cross Buns

fifty-five 2-ounce (55-g) buns

1 full recipe Raisin Bread dough
2 teaspoons (3 g) ground cinnamon
1½ teaspoons (3 g) ground nutmeg
½ teaspoon (1 g) ground cloves
12 ounces (340 g) currants
finely chopped peel from 2 lemons
Egg Wash (page 5)
12 ounces (340 g) Pastry Cream
   (page 569)
vanilla extract
8 ounces (225 g) Simple Icing
   (page 529)

1. Prepare the bread dough as described above, incorporating the cinnamon, nutmeg, and cloves with the flour, and substituting the currants and lemon peel for the raisins.

2. Divide the dough into fifty-five 2-ounce (55-g) pieces. Roll into round buns (see Figure 3–20, page 75). Place on sheet pans lined with baking paper.

3. Cut a cross on top of each bun using a sharp knife or razor blade. Cut just deep enough to penetrate the skin. Let the buns rise until half-doubled in volume.

4. Brush with egg wash. Place the pastry cream in a pastry bag with a no. 4 (8-mm) plain tip. Pipe a cherry-sized dot of the cream in the center of the cross, pushing the tip into the dough so that most of the cream is inside the bun.

5. Bake at 400°F (205°C) for approximately 20 minutes or until done. Let cool.

6. Add a few drops of vanilla to the simple icing. Add some powdered sugar if necessary to firm up the icing so that it can be piped. (It should still be slightly runny.) Place icing in a disposable pastry bag made from baking paper. Pipe the icing on the buns, following the outline of the cross.

Rosemary Bread

six 1-pound (470-g) loaves

2 ounces (55 g) fresh
   compressed yeast
3 cups (720 ml) warm water
   (105°–115°F, 40°–46°C)
2 ounces (55 g) granulated sugar
1 cup (240 ml) olive oil
3 tablespoons (45 g) salt
6 tablespoons (30 g) fresh rosemary,
   finely chopped
3 pounds, 12 ounces (1 kg, 705 g)
   bread flour, approximately
Egg Wash (page 5)

This recipe can easily be divided by three should you wish to make only two loaves. Increase the amount of yeast slightly to ¾ ounce (23 g).

1. Dissolve the yeast in warm water. Stir in sugar, oil, salt, rosemary, and enough of the flour to make a smooth, non-sticky dough.

2. Knead 6 to 8 minutes to develop the gluten structure. The dough will get a little looser as it becomes smoother.

3. Place the dough in an oiled bowl, cover, and let rise for 30 minutes.

4. Punch down and let dough rise an additional 30 minutes.

5. Punch the dough down again and divide into six 1-pound (470-g) pieces. Shape pieces into tight oval loaves (see Figures 3–1 and 3–2, page 49). The loaves should be tight enough to spring back when lightly pressed, but not so tight that the skin on the dough breaks. Place loaves on sheet pans lined with baking paper.

6. Brush with egg wash. Let rise until half-doubled in volume.

7. Using a serrated knife, cut halfway into each loaf at a 45° angle, starting in the center.

8. Bake at 400°F (205°C) until the loaves sound hollow when tapped, about 35 minutes. Place the loaves on racks to cool.

Variation: Crisp Bread
12 pieces

1. Measure the dough into 8-ounce (225-g) pieces and form into round loaves. Let stand a few minutes to relax the loaves.

2. Starting with the loaf you formed first, roll each out to a 10-inch (25-cm) circle.

3. If the dough is still rubbery, let it rest some more by rolling all the circles halfway, then coming back to finish.

4. Cut a 3-inch (7.5-cm) hole from the center of each circle. Place the rings and the cutouts on sheet pans, rub with olive oil, and sprinkle lightly with kosher salt. Let rise until one quarter larger in size.

5. Bake at 375°F (190°C) for about 30 minutes.

Russian Rolled-Wheat Bread
five 17-ounce (485-g) loaves

1¼ cups (300 ml) water
½ cup (120 ml) light corn syrup
9 ounces (255 g) rolled wheat
    (see page 579)
2 cups (480 ml) warm water
    (105°–115°F, 40°–46°C)
2½ ounces (70 g) fresh
    compressed yeast
2½ tablespoons (38 g) salt
2 ounces (55 g) softened butter
8 ounces (225 g) whole wheat flour
2 pounds, 4 ounces (1 kg, 25 g)
    bread flour, approximately
Egg Wash (page 5)
rolled wheat

This robust Russian peasant bread is one of my personal favorites, probably because it is one of the breads I ate while I was growing up. We called it *Ryskt Matbröd* and it was very popular in Sweden at that time. Try serving Russian Rolled-Wheat Bread spread with sweet butter and topped with Swedish *herrgårdsost* (roughly translated, "estate or mansion cheese") or with Swedish fontina cheese. Add a glass of milk and you have a fast, delicious, and filling snack.

1. Heat the first measurement of water and the corn syrup to boiling. Pour over the first measurement of rolled wheat. Do not stir. Let stand overnight.

2. Pour the warm water into a mixer bowl, add the yeast, and mix to dissolve. Add the rolled-wheat mixture, salt, butter, whole wheat flour, and all but a handful of the bread flour. Knead the mixture for 6 to 8 minutes, adding the reserved bread flour if needed to make a smooth, elastic dough. Let rest, covered, in a warm place for 30 minutes.

Two-Loaf Recipe
two 17-ounce (485-g) loaves

½ cup (120 ml) water
¼ cup (60 ml) light corn syrup
3½ ounces (100 g) rolled wheat
¾ cup (180 ml) warm water
  (105°–115°F/40°–46°C)
1 ounce (30 g) fresh
  compressed yeast
1 tablespoon (15 g) salt
1 ounce (30 g) softened butter
4 ounces (115 g) whole wheat flour
12 ounces (340 g) bread flour,
  approximately
Egg Wash (page 5)
rolled wheat

3. Divide the dough into 17-ounce (485-g) pieces. Shape each piece into a smooth, round loaf (see Figures 3–1 and 3–2, page 49). Flatten lightly with your hand. Brush with egg wash and sprinkle with rolled wheat.

4. Using a 3-inch (7.5-cm) plain cookie cutter, cut a circle ⅛ inch (3 mm) deep in the center of each loaf. Cut about 10 slashes to the same depth radiating out from the circle. Let rise until half-doubled in volume.

5. Bake at 400°F (205°C) for approximately 35 minutes. Cool on racks.

NOTE: This bread can be made with very good results even if the resting time for step 1 is reduced to three or four hours. The loaves will just not be as moist as they will be if the rolled wheat is given the full length of time to absorb the maximum amount of liquid.

Sourdough Starter
approximately 3 pounds
(1 kg, 365 g) starter

1½ ounces (40 g) fresh
  compressed yeast
3 cups (720 ml) water,
  at body temperature
1 ounce (30 g) granulated sugar
1 pound, 8 ounces (680 g)
  bread flour

Although it is a lengthy and sometimes frustrating procedure to make sourdough bread using your own starter, it can be all the more rewarding to sample the finished product when you have been successful. If you are one of those purists who refuse to use anything other than natural wild yeast in your sourdough, then this is the one recipe in this book that I cannot promise will work, even if you follow the directions precisely. Due to the fickle temperament of Mother Nature, the performance of natural (wild) yeast varies tremendously. If you have the inclination, time, and patience and you are up for a real challenge, you may want to try making your own sourdough bread the way it was done many years ago—just don't say I didn't warn you if it doesn't work!

The reason for making a sour dough is to provide leavening and flavor for the bread using the natural yeast organisms in the air. These organisms are plentiful in a kitchen or bakery where bread has been baked for many years. If this is not the case in your kitchen, it is a good idea to add a small amount of fresh or dry yeast to the starter to assure success. Using only the starter to leaven the bread will produce a reasonably good but fairly dense product, and this takes such a long time to proof that it isn't really practical. Therefore, we again help the starter along by including a small amount of fresh or dry yeast to guarantee a light and flavorful bread.

Making bread with sourdough starter, as you will see, is not done in a few hours like most other types of bread. Instead, it requires several days and a great deal of patience, as the starter (affectionately referred to as the mother) must be tended to with care. Should you not have the time or patience for this method, use a commercial starter to make life a little easier; just follow the directions on the package.

1. In a plastic or crockery container with a large opening and plenty of room for expansion, dissolve yeast in water, then add sugar. Stir in flour using a wooden spoon; keep stirring until you have a smooth paste.

2. Cover loosely to allow gases to escape, and let stand at approximately 80°F (26°C) for at least two to three days, preferably a little longer. The mixture should bubble and have a strong sour smell. Stir the starter down once a day during the time it is fermenting, also stirring in any crust that forms on the top.

3. When the starter is ready to use, remove the 1 pound, 4 ounces (570 g) needed for the sourdough bread, and replenish the remaining starter by adding 2 cups (480 ml) warm water and 1 pound (455 g) bread flour. Again, let stand loosely covered in a warm place for 24 hours before using. After that the starter should be stored in the refrigerator (see note). The starter, or part of it, may also be frozen; before using allow it to slowly thaw and start to bubble again at room temperature.

NOTE: Care of your starter: In addition to stirring the starter down once a day, if the starter is not used (and therefore not replenished), 1 cup (240 ml) warm water and 8 ounces (225 g) bread flour should be added once a week. If more than 3 to 4 weeks goes by without using the starter, remove it from the container, discard half (or give it to a friend who will appreciate it and not think it is a bad joke!), wash and rinse the container, and place the remaining starter inside. Replenish with water and flour as described in step 3. If the starter is left alone too long without adding fresh water and flour, it will slowly die in its own residue.

San Francisco Sourdough Loaves

four 18-ounce (510-g) loaves

1 ounce (30 g) fresh
    compressed yeast
2 cups (480 ml) warm water
    (105°–115°F, 41°–46°C)
2 tablespoons (30 g) salt
1 ounce (30 g) malt sugar or
    granulated sugar
1 pound, 4 ounces (570 g)
    Sourdough Starter
2 pounds, 6 ounces (1 kg, 80 g)
    bread flour, approximately
cornmeal

1. Dissolve yeast in water; add salt, sugar, and starter. Incorporate enough flour for a quite-firm, not-sticky dough. Continue to knead for about 8 minutes until the dough is elastic and pliable.

2. Place in a lightly oiled bowl and turn the dough so that the top will be oiled as well. Cover and let rise in a warm place for 2 hours.

3. Punch the dough down and scale into 18-ounce (510-g) pieces.

4. Pound and roll each piece into a 16-inch (40-cm) long loaf (see Figures 3–3 to 3–5, pages 49–50; also see note). Let rise until half-doubled in volume. Be patient here; the loaves will take quite a bit longer to rise than regular bread. While proofing, spray the loaves with water to prevent a crust from forming on the top.

5. Before baking, spray the loaves again, then dust with cornmeal. Slash the tops of the loaves using a sharp serrated knife or a razor blade, cutting lengthwise at a slight angle as for Baguettes.

6. Bake at 425°F (219°C) using steam for the first 10 minutes and baking for a total of approximately 40 minutes, or until done (if your oven is not equipped with steam injectors, follow the instructions given following the recipe for Baguettes on page 48). Allow the bread to cool on a rack.

NOTE: Sour bread is also typically made in a flat round shape in San Francisco. Scale into 2-pound (910-g) pieces, then form the pieces into tight round loaves. Let relax for a few minutes, then flatten them to approximately 9 inches (22.5 cm) in diameter. Proof and spray as for the long loaves. Dust with bread flour (quite heavily so that it shows after baking). Slash the tops of the loaves first in a series of parallel lines, then with additional parallel lines at a 45° angle to the first set to form a diamond pattern. Bake as directed in step 6, but approximately 5 minutes longer.

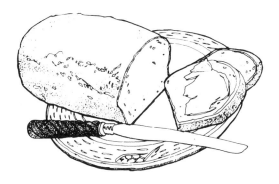

Swedish Orange Rye Bread

eight 17-ounce (485-g) loaves

2 cups (480 ml) molasses
5 cups (1 l, 200 ml) hot water
  (130°F, 54°C)
3 ounces (85 g) fresh
  compressed yeast
4 ounces (115 g) medium rye flour
2 pounds (910 g) bread flour
10 ounces (285 g) Candied
  Orange Peel (page 529)
1 pound (455 g) medium rye flour
1 pound, 10 ounces (740 g)
  bread flour, approximately
3 tablespoons (45 g) salt
1½ ounces (40 g) butter
vegetable oil

One-Quarter Recipe
two 17-ounce (485-g) loaves

½ cup (120 ml) molasses
1¼ cups (300 ml) hot water
  (130°F, 54°C)
1 ounce (30 g) fresh
  compressed yeast
1 ounce (30 g) medium rye flour
8 ounces (225 g) bread flour
2½ ounces (70 g) Candied
  Orange Peel (page 529)
4 ounces (115 g) medium rye flour
7 ounces (200 g) bread flour,
  approximately
2 teaspoons (10 g) salt
½ ounce (15 g) butter
vegetable oil

It is very important that the temperature of this dough does not fall below 75°F (24°C). Because of the high amount of sugar in the recipe, the yeast needs a warm dough in order to work properly.

1. Stir molasses into the hot water. Add yeast, first measurement of rye flour, and first measurement of bread flour. Mix to a smooth sponge. Let rise, covered, in a warm place until the sponge just starts to fall, about 1 hour.

2. Chop peel to the size of currants.

3. Add the peel to the sponge along with all the remaining ingredients except the oil, but do not add more bread flour than is necessary to be able to form the dough into a loaf. Do not overmix. The dough should be sticky and will not come away from the side of the bowl. Let dough rest, covered, for 10 minutes.

4. Divide the dough into 17-ounce (485-g) pieces. Roll each piece into a tight circle and form into an oval loaf (see Figures 3–1 and 3–2, page 49). The dough should spring back lightly when pressed down. Place the loaves in greased bread pans. Let rise until doubled in volume.

5. Bake at 375°F (190°C) for about 45 minutes. You may have to protect the loaves from overbrowning by placing a second pan underneath, or by covering the tops with baking paper. Brush the loaves with vegetable oil as soon as they come out of the oven. Unmold and cool on racks.

Swedish Peasant Bread

six 18-ounce (510-g) loaves

3 cups (720 ml) water
1½ tablespoons (22 g) salt
9 ounces (255 g) medium rye flour
2½ cups (600 ml) warm water
  (105°–115°F, 40–46°C)
2 tablespoons (30 ml)
  white vinegar
1 cup (240 ml) light corn syrup
2½ ounces (70 g) fresh
  compressed yeast
1 ounce (30 g) malt sugar
6 ounces (170 g) softened butter
2 tablespoons (12 g) ground cumin
2 tablespoons (12 g) ground fennel
3 pounds (1 kg, 365 g)
  bread flour, approximately
Egg Wash (page 5)
whole wheat flour, optional

One-Third Recipe
two 18-ounce (510-g) loaves

1 cup (240 ml) water
1½ teaspoons (8 g) salt
3 ounces (85 g) whole wheat flour
3 ounces (85 g) medium rye flour
¾ cup (180 ml) warm water
  (105°–115°F, 40°–46°C)
2 teaspoons (10 ml) white vinegar
⅓ cup (80 ml) light corn syrup
1 ounce (30 g) fresh
  compressed yeast
1 tablespoon (9 g) malt sugar
2 ounces (55 g) softened butter
2 teaspoons (4 g) ground cumin
2 teaspoons (4 g) ground fennel
1 pound (455 g) bread flour,
  approximately
Egg Wash (page 5)
whole wheat flour, optional

This type of bread has been made for centuries by peasant farmers all over Europe. The shape, texture, and taste of the bread would differ within as well as between countries, making the breads representative of a particular region. However, the peasant breads were always robust multigrain loaves made to last for two weeks or longer. These breads were made using the scalding method: Boiling water is poured over the grain and the mixture is left to sit overnight. This allows the grain to absorb the maximum amount of moisture possible and ensures that the bread will stay moist longer. The peasant bread was stored in the bread chest that was central to every farmer's kitchen. Swedish Peasant Rings were threaded onto sticks and stored hung from the rafters.

1. Heat first measurement of water to boiling. Add salt, whole wheat flour, and rye flour. Mix until smooth and let stand, covered, for 1 hour.

2. Stir vinegar and corn syrup into the remaining warm water. Add yeast and mix to dissolve. Stir in the flour-water mixture, malt, butter, and spices.

3. Reserve a few ounces of the bread flour, add the remainder, and knead about two minutes. Adjust with the reserved bread flour as needed to make a dough that is not sticky. Knead until smooth, two to four minutes longer.

4. Turn the dough onto a floured table and let rest, covered, for 10 minutes.

5. Divide the dough into 18-ounce (510-g) pieces. Roll each piece into a firm round loaf (see Figures 3–1 and 3–2, page 49). The bread should spring back immediately when you press it lightly.

6. Using the side of your hand, press down on the center of each loaf and roll the loaf back and forth until you have almost severed the two halves.

7. Brush with egg wash. Invert the loaves in whole wheat flour. Place the loaves flour-side up on sheet pans. Slash a few lines across the top of each loaf using a sharp knife. Let the loaves rise until doubled in volume.

8. Bake at 375°F (190°C) for about 35 minutes. Cool on racks. As a variation, make Swedish Peasant Rings by scaling the full recipe into eight 1-pound (455-g) pieces, flattening the round loaves by rolling them to 9-inch (22.5-cm) circles, and cutting a 3-inch (7.5-cm) opening in the centers. Brush the rings with egg wash, invert them in flour, and prick the rings all over with a docker. Proof and bake as above.

Swedish Thin Bread
(Knäckebröd)
*one hundred and sixty-eight 2-inch
(5-cm) crackers*

*4 ounces (115 g) vegetable
    shortening*
2 ounces (55 g) soft butter
2 ounces (55 g) granulated sugar
6 ounces (170 g) oat flakes
*1 pound, 5 ounces (595 g)
    bread flour, approximately*
1 teaspoon (5 g) salt
1 teaspoon (4 g) baking soda
1½ cups (360 ml) buttermilk

This type of bread or cracker—hard, crisp, and healthy—is included in the daily diet of the majority of Scandinavians. The crackers are delicious eaten plain as a quick snack, or they can be cut into a larger size before baking and served topped with cheese or pâté as an appetizer.

1. Cream shortening, butter, and sugar until light and fluffy.
2. Combine oat flakes, flour, salt, and baking soda.
3. Incorporate the dry ingredients into the butter mixture in two additions, alternating with the buttermilk. The dough will be fairly sticky. Adjust with a little additional flour if necessary to be able to roll the dough out very thin; however, keep in mind that the softer the dough, the crisper the finished product.
4. Divide the dough into four 12-ounce (340-g) pieces. Place three pieces in the refrigerator.
5. Roll the remaining piece into a 14- by 12-inch (35- × 30-cm) rectangle, using flour to prevent the dough from sticking. The dough will be very thin.
6. Mark the top of the rolled sheet with a waffle roller or, if not available, prick well.
7. Roll the dough up on a dowel and transfer to a sheet pan lined with baking paper. Score the top, cutting halfway through, marking forty-two 2-inch (5-cm) squares.
8. Repeat steps 5, 6, and 7 with the remaining three pieces of dough.
9. Bake at 325°F (163°C) for approximately 30 minutes or until completely dry. Let the crackers cool on the pan. Break apart on the scored lines. Stored in airtight containers, the crackers will stay fresh and crisp for several weeks.

Rolls

With a few exceptions, virtually any bread dough can be made into rolls or knots, and conversely, the opposite is also true. Rolls can be defined simply as bread dough that is portioned into individual servings, usually around two ounces (55 g) each, before it is baked. Rolls (especially knots) take much longer to form than loaves, but fortunately the results are worthwhile. Rolls look much more elegant served in a bread basket on the lunch or dinner table than do slices of bread, and rolls do not become stale as quickly. In most European countries a Kaiser roll or other type of crusty roll is considered an absolute must at the breakfast table.

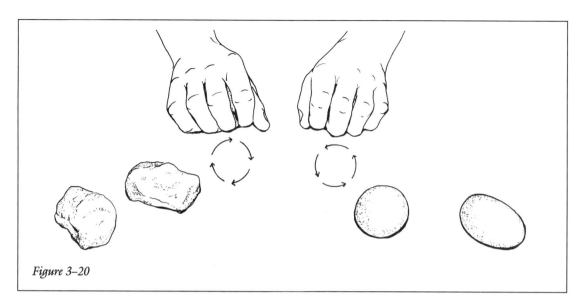

Figure 3–20

To Form Rolls

Forming a perfectly round, smooth, tight roll with the palm of your hand is very easy if you use the right technique. As when forming bread loaves, you want to form a tight skin around the mass of dough. Place two balls of dough on the table with your cupped hands on top, fingers clenched like claws. Press down fairly hard on the dough as you move both hands simultaneously in tight circles. Move your left hand counter-clockwise, and your right clockwise, so both are moving toward the outside (Figure 3–20). As you press down, forming the dough into a tight round ball, let the dough stick to the table just a little or it will not form a skin. For this reason, use as little flour as possible and, if the dough just slides and doesn't stick at all, try rubbing the table with a wet towel. If you are making oval rolls, such as Milk Rolls, first roll the dough round. Then, without lifting your hands (keeping them cupped around the dough), move them away and back toward you a few times in a straight line.

An easier instructional method is to practice with just one hand: Use your left hand (if you are right-handed) as the table top, holding it flat, and work the dough into a round ball by cupping your right hand on top and moving it in a circle.

Bread Sticks

twenty-four 16-inch (40-cm)
bread sticks

1 ounce (30 g) fresh
* compressed yeast*
2½ cups (600 ml) warm water
* 105° to 115°F (40° to 46°C)*
1 ounce (30 g) malt sugar
1 tablespoon (15 g) salt
2 pounds, 4 ounces (1 kg, 25 g)
* bread flour, approximately*
¼ cup (60 ml) olive oil
sesame seeds or semolina flour

Bread Sticks are essentially Swedish Crisp Rolls made in a different shape. They are known as *grissini* in Italy where they seem to be included in the bread basket at every meal. Bread Sticks are great for snacks and are more nutritious than many other popular snack foods.

1. Dissolve the yeast in the warm water. Add malt sugar and salt. Incorporate about three-quarters of the flour. Add the olive oil and knead the dough for 6 to 8 minutes, adding as much of the reserved flour as required to make a smooth and elastic dough.

2. Place the dough in a bowl oiled with olive oil and turn the dough to coat both sides with oil. Cover and let rise in a warm place until doubled in volume.

3. Punch the dough down and form into a rectangle 10 × 6 inches (25 × 15 cm) using your hands. Cover the dough and let it relax for 30 minutes.

4. Cut the dough in half lengthwise. Cut each half, lengthwise, into 12 equal pieces.

5. Pound and roll the pieces into strings (see Figures 3–3 to 3–5 on pages 49–50) without using any flour. Roll and stretch the strings to make them 16 inches (40 cm) long.

6. Line the pieces up and spray them lightly with water. Sprinkle sesame seeds or semolina flour on top, then roll each piece a half turn and sprinkle again to cover them on all sides.

7. Place the Bread Sticks on sheet pans lined with baking paper, spacing them a few inches apart.

8. Bake immediately (without allowing the Bread Sticks to rise first) at 425°F (219°C) for approximately 10 minutes or until golden brown. They will still be soft inside. To dry them completely, reduce the oven temperature to 300°F (149°C) and bake them about 20 more minutes. Stored in airtight containers, the Bread Sticks will stay fresh and dry for several weeks.

Kaiser Rolls

approximately sixty-five 2-ounce
(55-g) rolls

1 quart (960 ml) warm water
* (105°–115°F, 40°–46°C)*
1 ounce (30 g) fresh
* compressed yeast*
4 tablespoons (60 g) salt

1. Dissolve yeast in water. Mix in salt and sugar. Add butter and pre-dough. Mix in enough bread flour to form a dough. Knead dough until smooth and elastic, 10 to 15 minutes. Place dough in an oiled bowl, cover, and let rise for 30 minutes.

2. Punch down the dough to remove all air, cover, and let rise an additional 30 minutes.

3. Divide the dough into 2-ounce (55 g) pieces and form into round rolls (see Figure 3–20, page 75). Place on sheet pans lined with baking paper.

3 ounces (85 g) malt (or
  granulated) sugar
3 ounces (85 g) softened butter
1 full recipe Pre-dough
3 pounds, 5 ounces (1 kg, 505 g)
  bread flour, approximately

4. Mark the rolls with a Kaiser cutter, or cut an X on the tops with a razor blade. Let the rolls rise until half doubled in volume.

5. Bake the rolls at 400°F (205°C) with steam, leaving the damper closed during the first 10 minutes. Open the damper and continue baking approximately 10 minutes longer or until done.

NOTE: If your oven does not have steam injectors, follow the instructions given for Baguettes on page 48.

Pre-dough

1 pint (480 ml) warm water
  (105°–115°F, 40°–46°C)
2 ounces (55 g) fresh
  compressed yeast
1 pound (455 g) bread flour

1. Dissolve the yeast in the water (see note).

2. Add all the bread flour at once, mixing with the dough hook on low speed. Mix until the dough has developed a smooth consistency, about 10 minutes. It will be quite a soft dough, which, in turn, makes the yeast react faster.

3. Place the dough, covered, in a warm place and let rise until it begins to bubble and fall.

NOTE: For best results, start with cold water and leave pre-dough to rise (covered) overnight.

Rustica

approximately thirty-three 2-ounce
(55-g) rolls

2 cups (480 ml) warm water
  (105°–115°F, 40°–46°C)
1/2 ounce (15 g) fresh
  compressed yeast
2 tablespoons (30 g) salt
1 1/2 ounces (40 g) malt (or
  granulated) sugar
1/2 recipe Pre-dough (above)
1 pound, 14 ounces (855 g)
  bread flour, approximately
3 tablespoons (45 ml) olive oil
olive oil
water
bread flour

This is a half recipe of Tessiner Rolls formed in a different way. Shaping these rolls is a little more time-consuming, but the dough can be altered to the basic oval tessiner, or any other shape desired.

1. Follow the directions for Tessiner Rolls (page 79) through step 2.

2. Lightly oil the area of the work table where you are forming (rolling) the rolls. Roll them into round rolls (see Figure 3–20, page 75). Keep oiling the table as needed so that the rolls are not completely closed on the bottom.

3. Place the rolls, bottom (wrinkled) side up, on a sheet pan (you can crowd them) and spray the rolls lightly with water.

4. Fill more sheet pans almost to the top with bread flour. Invert the rolls into the flour, leaving enough room around them for them to expand. Let the rolls rise in the flour until half-doubled in volume.

5. Gently transfer the rolls, inverting each one flour-side up, to a sheet pan. Bake as directed for Tessiner Rolls.

Swedish Whole-Grain Crisp Rolls

115 crackers

1 cup (240 ml) boiling water
8 ounces (225 g) cracked wheat
1½ ounces (40 g) fresh
   compressed yeast
1 pint (480 ml) warm milk
   (105°–115°F, 40°–46°C)
2 tablespoons (30 ml) honey
1 tablespoon (15 g) salt
4 ounces (115 g) bread flour
1 pound (455 g) whole wheat
   flour, approximately
3 ounces (85 g) soft lard

Crisp rolls, or *skorpor* as they are called in Scandinavia, are a delicious and hearty snack eaten plain, dipped in coffee or tea, or topped with butter, cheese, or marmalade. They are a type of cracker and should not be mistaken for dried, leftover rolls. The characteristic fragile and crunchy texture, which is the trademark of a real crisp roll, is only obtained by making sure the dough has been prepared and proofed properly.

1. Pour boiling water over cracked wheat; stir to combine. Cover and set aside until soft: 2 to 3 hours or, preferably, overnight.

2. Dissolve yeast in milk. Add honey and salt, then incorporate the bread flour, half of the whole wheat flour, and the reserved cracked wheat. Add lard and knead for 6 to 8 minutes, adding enough of the remaining whole wheat flour as required to make a fairly firm and elastic dough.

3. Place the dough in an oiled bowl and let rise in a warm place until doubled in volume.

4. Punch dough down and repeat step 3 twice.

5. After the third rising, punch the dough down and divide it into 1-ounce (30-g) pieces. Form the pieces into 3-inch (7.5-cm) ovals, slightly tapered at the ends (see Figure 3–20, page 75).

6. Place on sheet pans lined with baking paper, and let rise until doubled in volume.

7. Bake at 400°F (205°C) until light brown and baked through, approximately 15 minutes. Let cool.

8. Cut the rolls in half horizontally using a serrated knife or, in the traditional way, by breaking the two halves apart with a large fork. Return the pieces to the sheet pans, cut sides up.

9. Toast the halves at 400°F (205°C) until they have browned lightly. Reduce the oven temperature and leave the rolls in the oven until they are completely dried through. If stored in airtight containers, these rolls will keep fresh for many weeks.

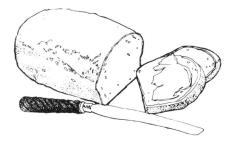

Wheat Crisp Rolls

64 crackers

1½ ounces (40 g) fresh
   compressed yeast
1 pint (480 ml) warm milk
   (105°–115°F, 40°–46°C)
4 ounces (115 g) granulated sugar
2 tablespoons (30 g) salt
1 tablespoon (6 g) ground
   cardamom
1 pound, 14 ounces (855 g)
   bread flour
2 ounces (55 g) lard

1. Dissolve yeast in milk. Add sugar, salt, and cardamom.
2. Incorporate about two-thirds of the flour.
3. Add lard and knead for approximately 6 minutes, adding enough additional flour to make a smooth and elastic dough.
4. Proceed with directions for Swedish Whole-Grain Crisp Rolls, steps 3 through 9, but make the rolls round instead of oval.

Tessiner Rolls

*approximately sixty-five 2-ounce
(55-g) rolls*

1 quart (960 ml) warm water
   (105°–115°F, 40°–46°C)
1 ounce (30 g) fresh
   compressed yeast
4 tablespoons (60 g) salt
3 ounces (85 g) malt (or
   granulated) sugar
1 recipe Pre-dough (page 77)
3 pounds, 12 ounces (1 kg, 705 g)
   bread flour, approximately
6 tablespoons (90 ml) olive oil

1. Dissolve the yeast in water. Add salt, sugar, and pre-dough. Mix in approximately three-quarters of the flour. Incorporate the olive oil together with most of the remaining flour and knead for 8 to 10 minutes, adjusting the amount of flour as needed for a smooth, elastic dough. Place the dough in an oiled bowl, cover, and let rise in a warm place for 30 minutes.
2. Punch the dough down to remove all air, then let rise again for 30 minutes.
3. Punch the dough down and divide into 1¾-ounce (50-g) pieces. Form into round balls, then roll into tapered ovals 3 inches (7.5 cm) long (see Figure 3–20, page 75).
4. Place six per row, with the long sides touching, on sheet pans lined with baking paper. Let rise until half-doubled in volume.
5. Use a sharp, thin knife or a razor blade to make a cut down the full length of each loaf (six rolls). Start the cut at one-third of the width of the rolls, cutting at an angle ½ inch (1.2 cm) deep toward the center of each loaf.
6. Bake at 400°F (205°C) with steam, leaving the damper closed for 10 minutes. Open the damper and continue baking approximately 10 minutes longer or until done.

NOTE: If your oven does not have steam injectors, follow the instructions given in baking Baguettes on page 48.

Breakfast Breads and Pastries

Apple Turnovers
Berliners
Brioche
Butter Gipfels
Cherry Cross-over Strip
Choux Surprise
Cinnamon Swirls
Croissants
English Muffins
Gugelhupf
Hungarian Chocolate Twists
Puff Paste Diamonds
Swedish Breakfast Spirals
Danish Pastries
   Danish Pastry Dough
   Bear Claws
   Butterhorns
   Danish Cinnamon Wreath

Danish Twists
Envelopes
Mayor's Wreath
Raisin Snails
Sister's Pull-Apart
   Coffee Cake
Sugar Buns
Muffins
   Apple-Pecan Buttermilk
      Muffins
   Blueberry Ginger Muffins
   Chocolate Chip Muffins
   Chocolate Honey Muffins
   Honey-Bran Muffins
   Oat Bran–Yogurt Muffins
   Pumpkin Muffins
   Zucchini-Walnut Muffins

*U*nfortunately, *breakfast for a lot of us* simply means a cup or two of coffee, gulped down while we dress, or shave, or drive to work. This habit really is a shame because a good breakfast is the most important meal of the day. Because our bodies have been without food for 10 hours or so our brains need sugar. Breakfast can be a welcome opportunity to enjoy sweets, whether they be in the form of fruits, oat-bran muffins for the health-conscious, or the delicious indulgence of a pastry.

I grew up eating a big breakfast. There were always two or three different types of home-baked bread on the table: rye, a whole grain, and white bread to toast (try toasting the Raisin Bread on page 66!). We spread the bread with fresh, sweet butter and piled on an abundance of other wonderful things like ham, cheeses, and smoked fish.

Even though an old-fashioned breakfast can still be had in many countries, travelers often get stuck with the so-called continental breakfast, which does not provide much opportunity to try the local specialties. The typical restaurant breakfast in Scandinavia is served on a large buffet and contains almost everything, from scrambled eggs to herring, caviar and pâtés. It also includes, of course, the famous *Winerbrod,* known in this country as Danish pastries (the actual translation is "bread from Vienna," but it has come to mean any fine or delicate bread). In Germany you can have a breakfast sweet very familiar to Americans: doughnuts. Called Berliners, German doughnuts have a different round shape and no hole, but basically they are the same thing. While traveling in Switzerland, don't miss having coffee and gipfels (what we call croissants) at a *konditorei*, or cafe — a delicious experience. And in France you will naturally want to try the baguettes. Fresh out of the oven, their taste and crispness are found nowhere else, and when topped with sweet butter and marmalade they are a wonderful breakfast treat.

In the United States, the muffin has been gaining in popularity as people have become more concerned about nutrition. Many types of muffins are both lower in calories and higher in fiber than Danish pastries or croissants, and the aroma of a freshly baked bran or zucchini muffin is just as good as the muffin is good for you.

Apple Turnovers
20 pastries

2½ pounds (1 kg, 135 g) Classic
  Puff Paste (page 21)
Egg Wash (page 5)
1 pound (455 g) Chunky Apple
  Filling (page 566)
Cinnamon Sugar (page 4)
AA confectioners' sugar
crushed, sliced almonds
Simple Syrup (page 7)

1. Roll out puff paste to ⅛ inch (3 mm) thick, 22½ inches (56.2 cm) long, and 18 inches (45 cm) wide. Let it rest 5 to 10 minutes to relax.

2. Cut the pastry into five rows of four squares each, making twenty 4½-inch (11.2-cm) squares.

3. Brush two adjoining edges of each square with egg wash.

4. Pipe a mound of apple filling in the center of each, dividing it evenly, and sprinkle cinnamon sugar on the apple filling.

5. Fold the upper part of the squares onto the part brushed with egg wash to make triangles (make sure no apple filling gets on the egg wash). Press the edges together with your fingers.

6. Mix equal amounts of sugar and almonds. Brush the tops of the triangles with egg wash, invert into the sugar mixture, then place the turnovers sugar-side up on sheet pans, no more than 16 to a full-sized pan, 24 × 16 inches (60 × 40 cm).

7. Make a small cut in the center of each turnover.

8. Bake at 375°F (190°C) until golden and completely baked through, about 25 minutes. You may need a second pan underneath and/or baking paper on the top to prevent the turnovers from overbrowning.

9. Brush lightly with simple syrup as soon as the pastries come out of the oven.

NOTE: Apple Turnovers are excellent to make up ahead and freeze. When needed, bake them directly from the freezer. Cherry Filling (see page 565) can be substituted for the apple filling.

Berliners

about 45 buns

Sponge

*1½ cups (360 ml) warm milk
   (105°–115°F, 40°–46°C)
2 ounces (55 g) fresh
   compressed yeast
12 ounces (340 g) bread flour*

Dough

*½ cup (120 ml) warm milk
   (105°–115°F, 40°–46°C)
1½ ounces (40 g) fresh
   compressed yeast
4 ounces (115 g) granulated sugar
1 teaspoon (5 g) salt
grated rind of ½ lemon
6 egg yolks
4 ounces (115 g) softened butter
1 pound, 2 ounces (510 g)
   bread flour, approximately
vegetable oil for frying
Cinnamon Sugar (page 4)
½ recipe Chunky Apple or Cherry
   Filling (pages 565–566), puréed*

1. Make the sponge by dissolving the yeast in the milk and adding the flour. Mix to a smooth consistency and let the sponge rise, covered, in a warm place until it starts to fall.

2. Make the dough by dissolving the yeast in the milk in a mixer bowl. Add the sponge and start kneading.

3. Continue to knead the dough as you add the sugar, salt, lemon rind, egg yolks, and butter.

4. Add enough of the flour to make a medium-soft dough. The dough should not be too firm, so do not add all the flour at once.

5. Refrigerate the dough, covered, for 1 hour to relax it.

6. Divide the dough into 14-ounce (400-g) pieces. Roll each piece into a rope, then cut each rope into 10 equal pieces.

7. Roll the small pieces into smooth round buns (see Figure 3–20, page 75). Place them on a sheet pan covered with a cloth or towel. Do not use any flour when working with Berliners because it will burn in the frying oil, making the outside too dark.

8. Let the buns rise in a warm place, around 80°F (26°C), until half-doubled in size (this will happen fairly quickly due to the softness of the dough).

9. Preheat the frying oil to 350°F (175°C). Use a frying thermometer to test the temperature, and try to time it so the oil is ready when the Berliners have risen. You should have 5 to 6 inches of oil. Use a good quality vegetable oil, or better yet, an oil specifically made for deep-frying. It is very important that the oil be at the correct temperature. If it is not hot enough, the buns will absorb too much oil and be heavy and unappetizing. If the oil is hotter than it should be, the Berliners will brown before they are cooked through, the flavor will not be as good, and the oil will darken and you will not be able to use it a second time.

10. Pick the Berliners up one at a time and quickly add them to the oil, seam side up. Do not fill up the pan completely because the Berliners will increase in volume as they cook.

11. When they are golden brown, about 5 minutes, turn the buns over and cook about 4 minutes longer on the other side. Try to turn them all over at about the same time so they are uniform in color. The Berliners should have a lighter colored ring on the top where they were not in the oil as long. This is considered the trademark for a perfectly prepared Berliner—it shows that it has risen enough to swell up high in cooking, and that the fat was hot enough not to be absorbed.

12. As you remove the Berliners from the oil, place them on a rack for a few seconds to drain.

13. While they are still hot, roll them in cinnamon sugar.

14. After the Berliners have cooled down a bit, inject them with apple or cherry filling using a special plain tip made for that

purpose, pushing the sharp end of the tip halfway into the side of the Berliner. If you do not have a tip made for filling, use a no. 3 (6-mm) plain tip and be careful not to make the opening in the bun any larger than necessary. Berliners should be served the day they are made.

Variation: Klenäter

thirty-nine 1¼- × 4-inch (3.1- × 10-cm) pastries

Known as *schüferli* in Germany and Switzerland, these pastries are very popular there, and are considered a must at Christmas time in Sweden. They are traditionally leavened with baking powder rather than yeast, but are even better made with the Berliner dough.

1. Make a half recipe of Berliners, preparing the dough through step 5 with the following changes:

   - Replace the ¼ cup (60 ml) of milk in the dough (not the sponge) with an equal amount of brandy.
   - Add ½ teaspoon (1 g) of cardamom to the flour.
   - Omit apple or cherry filling.

2. Roll the dough into a rectangle 12 × 16 inches (30 × 40 cm), using as little flour as possible. (Let the dough relax for a few minutes as needed to keep it from shrinking.) Brush off any excess flour from the top and the bottom.

3. Preheat frying oil to 350°F (175°C).

4. Cut the dough into three 4-inch (10-cm) strips using a fluted cookie wheel. Leave the strips in place. Using the same tool, cut crosswise to make thirteen 1¼-inch (3.1-cm) wide pieces out of each strip. Cut a 2-inch (5-cm) slit, lengthwise, in the center of each piece.

5. Pick up one piece and pull one end of the strip through the slit. Then, holding the rectangle by two diagonal corners, stretch lightly so it takes on a slight diamond shape (Figure 4–1).

6. Repeat with the remaining pieces and place them on a sheet pan covered with a cloth or towel (they are ready to cook immediately and do not require additional proofing).

7. Pick up the pieces one at a time and drop them carefully into the hot frying oil. Cook approximately 2 minutes or until nicely browned, then turn and cook about 1 minute longer on the other side.

8. Remove from the oil with a slotted spoon or skimmer and place on paper towels or napkins for a few seconds to drain.

9. While still warm, turn in cinnamon sugar to coat thoroughly.

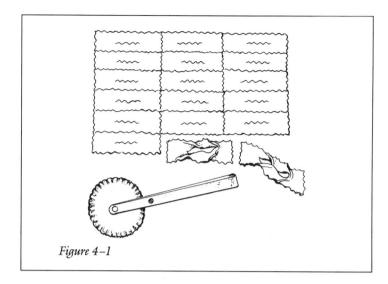

Figure 4–1

Brioche

*about thirty-five 2-ounce (55 g)
brioche or four 1-pound, 3-ounce
(540 g) loaves*

2 ounces (55 g) fresh
    compressed yeast
6 tablespoons (90 ml) cold milk
1 ounce (30 g) malt sugar
4 teaspoons (20 g) salt
4 ounces (115 g) granulated sugar
8 eggs
1 pound, 2 ounces (510 g)
    bread flour, approximately
1 pound (455 g) cake flour
10 ounces (285 g) softened butter
Egg Wash (page 5)

1. Dissolve the yeast in the milk. Add malt sugar, salt, sugar, and eggs. Reserve about 3 ounces (85 g) of the bread flour; then add the remainder, with the cake flour, to the egg mixture. Gradually mix in the butter, adding it in small pieces.

2. Knead until the dough forms a ball. Adjust the dough with the reserved bread flour if necessary. The dough should not stick to the sides of the bowl and should have a slightly shiny appearance. Cover the dough and refrigerate for 5 to 6 hours. During this time the dough should double in size. If you are not going to make up the dough within a few hours, freeze it so that the large amount of yeast does not make the dough sour.

3. Punch down the dough.

4. To make loaves, divide the dough into 1-pound, 3-ounce (540-g) pieces. Pound the pieces into tight loaves (see Figures 3–3 and 3–4, page 49) and place in buttered loaf pans. Let rise until doubled in volume. Bake the loaves at 375°F (190°C) until they have a healthy brown color and are baked through, about 35 minutes. Unmold and let cool on racks.

5. To make brioche, divide the dough into 2-ounce (55-g) pieces and roll each piece into a firm ball (see Figure 3–20, page 75); set the balls to the side in order, so you can form them in the same order they were rolled.

6. Starting with the ball of dough you rolled first, place it in front of you and hold your hand above it with your fingers held tightly together and your hand completely vertical. Press down on the ball at one-third of the width, and move your hand backward

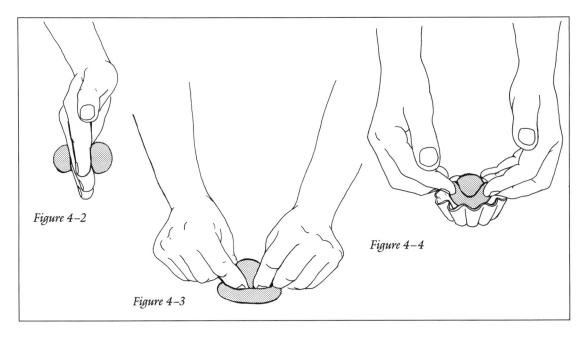

Figure 4–2

Figure 4–3

Figure 4–4

and forward in a sawing motion until you almost sever the ball (Figure 4–2).

7. You should now have two round balls of dough, one twice the size of the other, connected by a very thin string of dough. Gently pinch the connecting string between the thumbs and index fingers of both hands and, still holding on to it, force your thumbs and fingers straight down into the top of the larger ball, all the way to the bottom. Open your fingers slightly to create a hole, and let the smaller ball drop into it (Figure 4–3). Be sure the smaller ball of dough sits well inside the larger, or it can fall off as the dough expands in the proof box, and later in the oven. Form the remaining brioche in the same way.

8. Place the brioche into buttered forms (Figure 4–4) and let them rise until half-doubled in volume. Brush with egg wash, being careful not to let any egg wash drip between the dough and the form, as this will make it difficult to remove the brioche after baking.

9. Bake at 400°F (205°C) for about 18 minutes. Unmold before completely cool, and finish cooling on racks. A faster cooling method, and one more typically used in the industry, is to quickly turn the brioche on its side, leaving it in the form; this allows air to circulate underneath.

Butter Gipfels

about sixty 2-ounce (55-g) gipfels

8 ounces (225 g) butter
1 pound, 12 ounces (795 g)
  softened butter
5 ounces (140 g) lard
4 ounces (115 g) bread flour
juice from ½ lemon
3 ounces (85 g) fresh
  compressed yeast
3 cups (720 ml) cold water
2 ounces (55 g) malt sugar
3 tablespoons (45 g) salt
4 ounces (115 g) granulated sugar
4 eggs
3 pounds, 6 ounces (1 kg, 535 g)
  bread flour, approximately
Egg Wash (page 5)

A version of croissants made in Germany and Switzerland, Butter Gipfels have a more pronounced crescent shape (almost circular), which requires using a different, slightly slower, rolling technique. Although the fat content is almost the same as croissants, gipfels are lighter in texture.

1. Heat the 8 ounces (225 g) of butter and brown lightly (*beurre noisette*). Remove from the heat and set aside to cool to room temperature.

2. Combine the remaining softened butter, lard, 4 ounces (115 g) bread flour, and lemon juice.

3. Shape the mixture into a rectangle, 14 × 12 inches (35 × 30 cm), on a sheet of baking paper and reserve (place in refrigerator if necessary).

4. Dissolve the yeast in the water. Add malt, salt, sugar, eggs, and browned butter.

5. Reserve a handful of the 3 pounds, 6 ounces (1 kg, 535 g) bread flour, and add the rest. Mix for approximately 1 minute until you have a smooth, soft dough. Adjust with the reserved flour as needed.

6. Cover the dough and place in the refrigerator for 30 minutes.

7. Roll the dough out into a 14- × 18-inch (35- × 45-cm) rectangle.

8. Place the butter block on top of the dough, covering two-thirds of the rectangle. The butter block should have the same consistency as the dough.

9. Fold the uncovered third of the dough over half of the butter block. Fold the remaining butter-covered piece on top of the dough.

10. Roll the dough out to a rectangle ½ inch (1.2 cm) thick. Give the dough one single turn (see Figures 4–14 and 4–15, page 96).

11. Cover and refrigerate for 30 minutes.

12. Make two more single turns, refrigerating the dough for 30 minutes between them.

13. After completing the third turn, roll the dough out to the size of a full sheet pan, 16 × 24 inches (40 × 60 cm) (refrigerate to relax the dough first if necessary).

14. Cover the dough and place in the refrigerator or freezer for at least 2 to 3 hours or, preferably, overnight.

15. Cut the dough in half crosswise. Roll one piece at a time to a rectangle 16 × 40 inches (40 cm × 1 m), about ¹⁄₁₆ inch (2 mm) thick.

16. Let the dough relax for a few minutes (roll the second piece

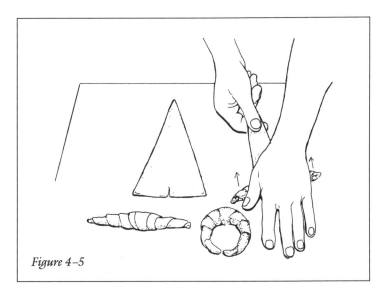

Figure 4–5

in the meantime), then cut the dough lengthwise into two strips, each 8 inches (20 cm) wide.

17. Cut each strip into 14 triangles, 6 inches (15 cm) across the base.

18. Cut a slit in the center of the base of each triangle as for croissants (see Figure 4–13, page 95).

19. Roll the triangles tightly by holding the pointed end still with one hand while using the palm of the other hand to curl up the dough, lightly stretching it as you roll (Figure 4–5).

20. Roll each piece between your palms and the table to make it about 9 inches (22.5 cm) long and very tapered at the ends.

21. Place on sheet pans lined with baking paper and curl each gipfel into a full circle so that the ends meet. Pinch the ends together. Let the gipfels rise until half-doubled in volume.

22. Brush with egg wash.

23. Bake at 400°F (205°C) with steam leaving the damper closed for 5 minutes. Open the damper and continue baking approximately 10 minutes longer, or until baked through.

NOTE: If your oven does not have steam injectors, follow the directions for baking Baguettes on page 48.

Cherry Cross-over Strip

two 24-inch (60-cm) strips or 16 pastries

2 pounds (910 g) Classic Puff Paste (page 21)
2 pounds (910 g) Cherry Filling (page 566)
AA confectioners' sugar
sliced almonds, crushed
Egg Wash (page 5)
Simple Syrup (page 7)
Simple Icing (page 529)

1. Roll out puff paste to ⅛ inch (3 mm) thick, 23 inches (57.5 cm) long, and 16 inches (40 cm) wide. Cut the dough in half to make two strips 23 inches × 8 inches (57.5 × 20 cm) each.

2. Fold each strip lengthwise over a 1-inch-wide (2.5-cm) dowel so that the long cut edges meet and are closest to you. (The dough should be firm for easy handling. Reserve the second strip in the refrigerator if needed while you are working.)

3. Using the back of a chef's knife, lightly mark, but do not cut, a line about 2 inches (5 cm) away from and parallel to the cut edges.

4. With the sharp edge of the knife, cut ¼-inch (6-mm) strips, up to the mark, along the entire length of the dough, leaving the folded edge uncut (Figure 4–6).

5. Use the dowel to lift the strip and place on an inverted sheet pan lined with baking paper (two strips will fit on one pan). Remove the dowel carefully and separate the fringed edges so that the dough lies flat and open. Repeat with the second strip.

6. Place the cherry filling in a pastry bag with a no. 8 (16-mm) plain tip. Pipe the filling down the uncut center of the strips. If needed, spread it out with a spatula to the edge of the cuts.

7. Fold the left and right strips alternately over the filling, using both of your hands in an even rhythm (Figure 4–7). Make sure each left strip is folded on top of the right, and each right is folded on top of the left, and so on so that they lock each other in place.

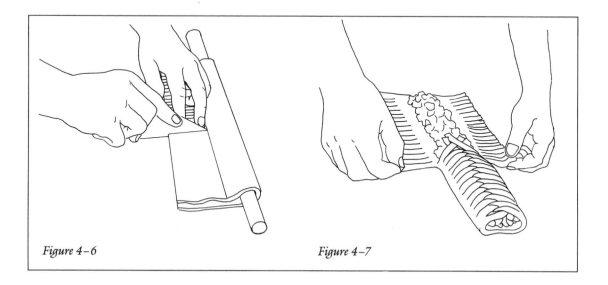

Figure 4–6   *Figure 4–7*

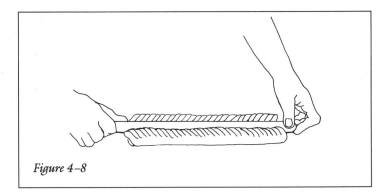

Figure 4–8

8. Place the dowel in the middle and press down hard enough to be sure the strips will not unfold in the oven (Figure 4–8). You will leave a small indentation, but you do not want to press the filling out.

9. Mix equal amounts of sugar and sliced almonds. Brush the pastry lightly with egg wash, then sprinkle the sugar and almond mixture on top.

10. Bake double-panned at 375°F (190°C) for about 35 minutes. You may need to protect the top with baking paper to give the dough time to bake through completely.

11. Brush the pastry with simple syrup as soon as it comes out of the oven. When cool, ice with simple icing. Slice each strip into eight pieces at an angle.

NOTE: Cross-over strips freeze very well; bake as needed directly from the freezer. This pastry is also delicious with Chunky Apple Filling (see page 567); sprinkle some cinnamon sugar (see page 4) on the filling before braiding the top.

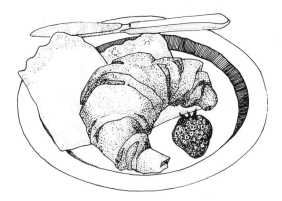

Choux Surprise

24 pastries

2 pounds, 4 ounces (1 kg, 25 g)
Classic Puff Paste (page 21)
10 ounces (285 g) Pâte à Choux
(page 15)
AA confectioners' sugar
crushed, sliced almonds
Egg Wash (page 5)
6 ounces (170 g) Pastry Cream
(page 569)
Simple Syrup (page 7)
Simple Icing (page 529)

1. Roll out puff paste to a rectangle measuring 22½ × 15 inches (56.2 × 37.5 cm) and ⅛ inch (3 mm) thick. Cut into twenty-four 3¾-inch (9.3-cm) squares (four strips cut into six pieces each).

2. Pipe a small mound of pâte à choux, about the size of a prune, in the center of each square. Brush the sides of each square with egg wash. Fold the points in to meet in the center like an envelope. With your thumb, press firmly, all the way down to the pan, in the spot where the points come together (see note).

3. Mix equal amounts of sugar and almonds. Brush the squares with egg wash, invert onto the sugar mixture, then place right-side up on a sheet pan lined with baking paper.

4. Pipe a small amount of pastry cream in the impression left by your thumb.

5. Bake double-panned at 375°F (190°C) for about 40 minutes. Be certain that the pastries are done. If the choux are not thoroughly baked they will fall.

6. Brush the pastries with simple syrup as soon as they come out of the oven. When cool, spread simple icing on top.

NOTE: It is important that you press firmly when you make the indentation for the pastry cream. You want to push all the pâte à choux underneath out of the way. Otherwise, as it bakes, the pâte à choux will puff up and force the pastry cream off the pastry and onto the pan.

Variation: Wales Surprise

two 24- × 4-inch (60- × 10-cm)
strips

1 pound (455 g) Puff Paste
(page 21)
10 ounces (285 g) Pastry Cream
(page 569)
1 pound (455 g) Pâte à Choux
(page 15)
4 ounces (115 g) raspberry jam
AA confectioners' sugar
crushed, sliced almonds
Simple Syrup (page 7)
Simple Icing (page 529)

Here is an excellent opportunity to use up any leftover scrap dough. If you are using fresh puff paste, be sure to prick the dough well or it will puff too high.

1. Roll out puff paste to a 24- × 8-inch (60- × 20-cm) strip. Let the puff paste rest for a few minutes to avoid shrinkage, then cut into two 4-inch (10-cm) wide strips.

2. Place the strips on sheet pans lined with baking paper. Spread the pastry cream out evenly on top of the strips, spreading almost all the way to the edges.

3. Put the pâte à choux in a pastry bag with a no. 3 (6-mm) plain tip. Pipe the pâte à choux in a figure-eight pattern, with the loops of the eights touching the long sides, to cover each strip.

4. Place the jam in a pastry bag with a no. 3 (6-mm) plain tip. Pipe the jam in one line, lengthwise, down the center of each strip. Sprinkle crushed almonds on top.

5. Bake and finish as directed in Choux Surprise. Cut into desired number of pieces when cold.

Cinnamon Swirls

thirty 2½-ounce (70-g) pastries

*2 ounces (55 g) fresh
    compressed yeast*
*1 pint (480 ml) warm milk
    (105°–115°F, 40°–46°C)*
3 ounces (85 g) granulated sugar
1 tablespoon (15 g) salt
*2 tablespoons (12 g)
    ground cardamom*
4 eggs
*2 pounds, 10 ounces (1 kg, 195 g)
    bread flour, approximately*
7 ounces (200 g) softened butter
*1 pound, 8 ounces (680 g)
    Danish Filling II (page 106)*
Cinnamon Sugar (page 4)
Egg Wash (page 5)
AA confectioners' sugar
sliced almonds

1. Dissolve the yeast in the warm milk. Add sugar, salt, cardamom, and eggs. Reserve a few ounces of the flour, and mix in the remainder. Mix in the butter (it is important that the butter not come in contact with the yeast before the yeast has had a chance to start expanding).

2. Knead the dough for a few minutes, then adjust with the reserved flour, if required, to make the dough firm enough to roll out. Continue to knead until the dough is smooth and elastic. Cover and let rest 10 minutes.

3. Roll the dough into a rectangle 14 × 36 inches (35 × 90 cm). Spread the Danish filling over the dough, leaving a 1-inch (2.5-cm) strip uncovered along the bottom (long) edge. Sprinkle cinnamon sugar heavily over the filling. Roll up the rectangle, from the top toward you, to make a tight rope.

4. Cut the rope into thirty slices. Place on paper-lined sheet pans, cut side up, tucking the ends underneath to prevent the swirls from unrolling as they expand. Let rise until half-doubled in volume.

5. Brush the swirls with egg wash. Sprinkle with a mixture of equal parts AA confectioners' sugar and sliced almonds.

6. Bake at 410°F (210°C) for approximately 15 minutes or until golden brown and baked through. Use a second pan underneath to prevent overbrowning on the bottom.

Variation I: Cinnamon Knots

1. Roll the dough out to the same size but spread the filling over the left half only. Sprinkle cinnamon sugar over the filling.

2. Brush egg wash on the other side of the dough and fold over the filling. The dough should now measure 14 × 18 inches (35 × 45 cm).

3. Roll out to a 16- × 24-inch (40- × 60-cm) rectangle (dust with flour underneath to prevent sticking). Cut into thirty 16-inch (40-cm) strips. Place each strip in front of you horizontally.

4. With one hand on top of each end of the strip, quickly move one hand up and the other hand down simultaneously to twist the strip (Figure 4–9). Wind the twists into a knot shape in the same way you would roll up a ball of yarn; each turn should cross over the previous one and hold it in place (Figure 4–10). As you finish each knot, tuck the end underneath (Figure 4–11), and place it on a sheet pan. Let the knots rise until half-doubled in volume.

5. Brush with egg wash and sprinkle with the sugar and almond mixture.

6. Follow the baking instructions above, increasing the time a few minutes.

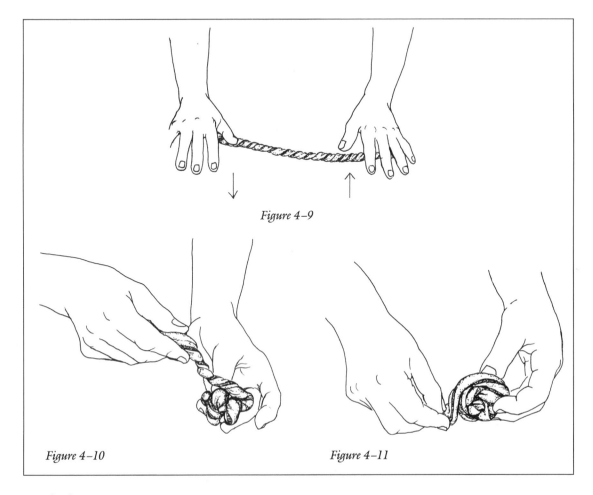

Figure 4–9

Figure 4–10

Figure 4–11

Variation II:
Twisted Loaves and Wreaths

1. Increase Danish Filling II to 2 pounds, 10 ounces (1 kg, 295 g).

2. To make loaves, divide the dough into six pieces and roll each piece into a 12- × 12-inch (30- × 30-cm) square. To make wreaths, divide the dough into four pieces and roll each piece into an 8- × 22-inch (20- × 55-cm) rectangle.

3. Spread the filling on the dough, sprinkle with cinnamon sugar, and brush egg wash on the uncovered, bottom portion of each rectangle. Roll the dough as directed for swirls.

4. Place the rope seam-side down, then cut in half lengthwise using a knife or pastry wheel. Turn the pieces so the cut sides face up.

5. Twist the two pieces together by alternating one on top of the other, keeping the cut sides facing up the entire time. Pinch the ends together. If making wreaths, join the ends together. Try to disguise the seam as well as possible. Let the loaves or wreaths rise until half-doubled in volume.

6. Brush with egg wash and sprinkle with the sugar and almond mixture.

7. Bake at 375°F (190°C) for approximately 25 minutes, or until light brown and baked through, using a second pan underneath to protect the bottom of the pastries.

Croissants

forty-four 3-ounce (85-g) croissants

2 pounds, 8 ounces (1 kg, 135 g) chilled butter
juice of ¼ lemon
3 pounds, 8 ounces (1 kg, 590 g) bread flour
3 ounces (85 g) fresh compressed yeast
1 quart (960 ml) cold milk
3 ounces (85 g) granulated sugar
1 ounce (30 g) malt sugar
3 tablespoons (45 g) salt
Egg Wash (page 5) or milk

One-Quarter Recipe
about fifteen 2-ounce (55-g) croissants

10 ounces (285 g) chilled butter
few drops of lemon juice
18 ounces (510 g) bread flour
1 ounce (30 g) fresh compressed yeast
1 cup (240 ml) cold milk
4 teaspoons (20 g) granulated sugar
2¼ teaspoons (7 g) malt sugar
2 teaspoons (10 g) salt
Egg Wash (page 5) or milk

Croissant dough is easier to work with if it is allowed to rest several hours between giving the dough three single turns and forming the croissants. Because you generally want to bake croissants early in the morning, you can make the dough the morning before, leave it to rest until the afternoon, form the croissants in the afternoon, leave them overnight in the refrigerator, and proof and bake the next morning. An even better method is to prepare the dough in the afternoon, let the dough rest overnight in the refrigerator, then form, proof, and bake the croissants in the morning. If your refrigerator does not keep a consistent temperature below 40°F (4°C), store the dough in the freezer instead. This is important to keep the yeast dormant; otherwise the dough will start to proof in the refrigerator, lowering the quality of the finished product and possibly making the dough taste sour.

1. Work the lemon juice and 4 ounces (115 g) of the flour (1 ounce/30 g for ¼ recipe) into the chilled butter by kneading it against the table, or in a bowl, with your hand. Do not use a mixer.

2. Shape the butter into a 10-inch (25-cm) square (5-inch/12.5-cm for ¼ recipe). Place the butter on a piece of paper and set aside. If the room is warm, place it in the refrigerator, but do not let it get too firm. If this happens, rework and reshape the butter back to the original consistency.

3. Dissolve the yeast in the cold milk. Add sugar, malt, and salt. Mix for a few seconds using the dough hook, then start adding the remaining flour. Mix in enough flour to make a dough that is slightly firm but not rubbery. Take care not to mix any longer than necessary.

4. Place the dough on a table dusted lightly with flour. Roll it out to a 14-inch (35-cm) square (7-inch/17.5-cm for ¼ recipe).

5. Check the butter to be sure that it is smooth and at the same consistency as the dough, adjusting if necessary. Place the butter square on the dough diagonally so that there are four triangles on the sides, fold in the sides, and seal in the butter (see Figures 2–4, and 2–5, page 22).

6. Give the dough three single turns (directions follow). After

the last turn, roll the dough out ½ inch (1.2 cm) thick. Refrigerate, covered, at least 2 hours.

7. Roll dough into a rectangle 49½ × 20 inches (123.7 × 50 cm), slightly thinner than ¼ inch (6 mm) and as even as possible. *(If you are making the ¼ recipe, roll out dough following instructions given after step 14.)* Let the dough rest 5 minutes so that it will not shrink when you cut it, then cut it lengthwise into two 10-inch- (25-cm) wide strips.

8. On the bottom edge of the strip closest to you, start at left edge and make a mark every 4½ inches (11.2 cm). Do the same on the bottom edge of the top strip.

9. Place a ruler from the first mark on the bottom strip (the lower left corner) up to the second mark on the top strip (4½ inches/11.2 cm from the left edge) and cut the dough, using a knife or pastry wheel, following the ruler through the top strip. Then cut from the second mark on the bottom strip to the third mark on the middle strip and across the top. Repeat for the length of the dough.

10. Beginning on the opposite end, follow the same pattern and cut from right to left (Figure 4–12). Pick away the scrap dough and save for the next batch of Butter Wheat Bread (see page 59).

11. Make a ½-inch (1.2-cm) cut in the center of the short side on each croissant (Figure 4–13). Pull the cuts apart a little, then form the croissants by rolling the triangles toward you. Roll them up tightly, but do not stretch the dough too much.

12. Shape the triangles into crescent shapes; the point of the triangle should be inside the center curve and tucked underneath the roll. Place on sheet pans; do not put more than 16 to 18 on

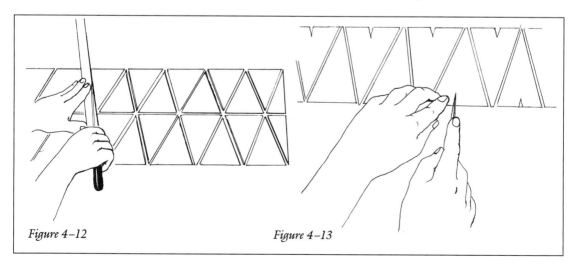

Figure 4–12   Figure 4–13

a full-sized pan to ensure that they bake evenly. If too crowded, they will get overdone on the ends before they are fully baked in the middle.

13. Let the croissants rise until half-doubled in volume in a 78° to 82°F (25°–28°C) proof box with 80 percent humidity. If the proof box gets too hot the butter will start to leak out. This can also happen while they are baking if they have not proofed enough.

14. Brush the croissants with egg wash (or use milk, which is typical in France). Bake at 425°F (219°C) until golden and baked through, about 25 minutes.

To form croissants using the one-quarter recipe

1. Roll the dough out to 18 × 31½ inches (45 × 78.7 cm) and ⅛ inch (3 mm) thick. Let the dough relax for a few minutes, then cut in half lengthwise to make two strips 9 inches (22.5 cm) wide.

2. Continue as directed in main recipe.

Instructions for a single turn

1. Roll the dough into a rectangle ½ inch (1.2 cm) thick, as carefully and evenly as possible.

2. Divide the rectangle crosswise into thirds by sight alone, or mark the dough lightly with the edge of your hand.

3. Fold one-third of the dough over the middle section (Figure 4–14), then fold the remaining one-third over both of them

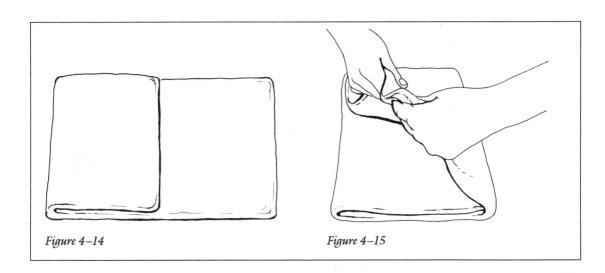

Figure 4–14   Figure 4–15

(Figure 4–15), brushing away the excess flour from the inside as you fold. The dough now has one single turn.

4. Refrigerate, covered, for 30 minutes.

5. Position the dough so that the long sides run horizontally, roll the dough to the same size rectangle as before, and make the second single turn.

6. Chill the dough, covered, for 30 minutes; then make the last single turn.

English Muffins

twenty-five 3½-inch (8.7-cm) muffins

1 ounce (30 g) fresh
   compressed yeast
1½ cups (360 ml) warm water,
   105° to 115°F (43° to 46°C)
2 ounces (55 g) granulated sugar
2 teaspoons (10 g) salt
1 egg
1½ pounds (680 g) bread flour,
   approximately
3 ounces (85 g) soft butter
cornmeal

1. Dissolve yeast in warm water. Add sugar, salt, and egg. Incorporate about two-thirds of the flour and mix to a smooth paste.

2. Cover and let rise in a warm place until the sponge has risen to its maximum size and starts to fall. Mix in the butter and the remaining flour. Adjust with additional flour if needed; the dough should be soft, smooth, and slightly sticky.

3. Cover the dough and let rise in a warm place until doubled in volume.

4. Punch down the dough and let it rest for 10 minutes.

5. Roll the dough out ¼ inch (6 mm) thick, using flour to prevent it from sticking.

6. Cut out 3½-inch (8.7-cm) circles using a plain cookie cutter. If necessary, let the dough relax for a few minutes before you cut to prevent the circles from shrinking into ovals.

7. Line a sheet pan with baking paper. Sprinkle cornmeal lightly over the paper. Grease the inside of 3½-inch (8.7-cm) crumpet rings (see note 1) and place the rings on the cornmeal. Place the dough rounds inside the rings.

8. Stack the dough scraps, then roll out and cut more rounds until all of the dough is used.

9. Let the muffins rise until doubled.

10. Use a metal spatula to transfer the muffins (including the rings) to a hot, lightly greased griddle (see note 2). Remove the rings and cook the muffins for 2 minutes. Turn the muffins and cook for 2 minutes longer on the second side. Lower the heat and continue cooking for approximately 12 minutes or until done, turning the muffins again halfway through cooking. Carefully transfer muffins to a cake rack to cool.

11. To split the muffins, pierce them horizontally all around the sides with a fork, then break the two halves apart. You should never cut an English Muffin in half. Not only will they no longer look the way they are supposed to, but they will not be as crisp after they are toasted.

12. Store leftover muffins in the freezer. The muffins will start to taste like the store-bought variety after a few days in the refrigerator.

NOTE 1: If you do not have crumpet rings or other suitable rings, you can make the muffins without them. They will not be quite as high nor will they be perfectly round.

NOTE 2: Although English Muffins should be baked on a griddle, they can, if necessary, be baked in the oven. Leave the muffins on the sheet pan they were proofed on. Bake at 450°F (230°C) for 2 minutes on each side. Remove the rings and lower the oven temperature to 400°F (205°C). Bake approximately 14 minutes longer or until done, turning the muffins once halfway through baking.

Gugelhupf

four 15-ounce (430-g) loaves

6 ounces (170 g) dark raisins
¼ cup (60 ml) dark rum
¾ ounce (20 g) fresh
    compressed yeast
1 cup (240 ml) warm water
    (105°–115°F, 41°–46°C)
½ ounce (15 g) malt sugar
8 ounces (225 g) bread flour
40 whole blanched almonds
¾ cup (180 ml) warm milk
    (105°–115°F, 41°–46°C)
1 tablespoon (15 g) salt
4 ounces (115 g) granulated sugar
4 ounces (115 g) softened butter
2 eggs
finely diced zest of 1 lemon
1 pound (455 g) bread flour,
    approximately
powdered sugar

1. Macerate (soak) raisins in rum.

2. Dissolve the yeast in the warm water. Add the malt sugar and 8 ounces (225 g) of flour and mix to a smooth sponge. Cover and let rise in a warm place until doubled in volume.

3. Grease four 1-quart (960-ml) gugelhupf forms or similar molds. Place the whole almonds in the bottoms of the forms, spacing them evenly around the rings, using 10 per form.

4. Incorporate the milk, salt, and sugar into the sponge. Add the butter, eggs, and lemon zest.

5. Hold back a handful of the bread flour, mix the remainder into the dough, then adjust the consistency as needed with the reserved flour to make a smooth soft dough.

6. Cover and let rise in a warm place for 1 hour, punching the dough down once in that time.

7. Knead in the raisin and rum mixture.

8. Divide the dough into four 15-ounce (430-g) pieces. Form the pieces into round loaves.

9. Let the loaves relax for a few seconds, then use a thick dowel to punch a hole in the center of each loaf.

10. Place the loaves in the reserved pans, pressing the dough firmly into the forms. Let rise until half-doubled in volume.

11. Bake at 375°F (190°C) for approximately 20 minutes or until baked through. Invert immediately onto a cake cooler and remove the forms. When cool, dust very lightly with powdered sugar.

NOTE: In addition to being good as a snack or with a coffee break, gugelhupf slices are excellent toasted.

Hungarian Chocolate Twists

four 1-pound (455-g) loaves

2 ounces (55 g) fresh
    compressed yeast
1 pint (480 ml) cold milk
1 ounce (30 g) malt sugar
3 ounces (85 g) granulated sugar
2 pounds, 4 ounces (1 kg, 25 g)
    bread flour, approximately
2 tablespoons (30 g) salt
grated rind of 1 lemon
1 teaspoon (5 ml) vanilla extract
2 eggs
5 ounces (140 g) butter
1 ounce (30 g) cocoa powder
⅓ cup (85 ml) water
Orange Almond Filling
    (recipe follows)
Egg Wash (page 5)
sliced almonds

1. Dissolve the yeast in the cold milk. Add malt and sugar. Reserve a few ounces of the flour and mix the remainder into the milk mixture.

2. Combine the salt, lemon rind, vanilla, and eggs. Add to the dough. Mix in the butter.

3. Knead the dough 8 to 10 minutes; halfway through the kneading, add more flour if necessary to make a fairly soft and elastic dough.

4. Divide the dough into two parts, with one part 4 ounces (115 g) lighter than the other.

5. Combine the cocoa powder and the water and add to the lighter piece of dough, mixing well so it is uniform in color.

6. Cover both pieces of dough and let them rest for approximately 10 minutes.

7. Divide the chocolate dough and the light dough into four pieces each. Form each piece into a rectangle without kneading or overworking it. Cover the pieces.

8. Starting with the first piece you formed, roll each piece out to approximately 15 × 4 inches (37.5 × 10 cm).

9. Spread the filling evenly over the eight rectangles, leaving a ½-inch (1.2-cm) border on the bottom long sides.

10. Brush the borders with egg wash and roll the dough toward you (starting from the top long side) in a very tight spiral.

11. Press the egg-washed border on the outside to seal the rolls. Roll each rope between your hands and the table to make it 20 inches (50 cm) long.

12. Place a plain and a chocolate rope next to each other in an upside-down *U* shape, with the light piece on the inside. "Braid" by twisting each side of the *U* four times toward the outside (Figure 4–16). (Hold the pair of ropes on each side of the *U* in

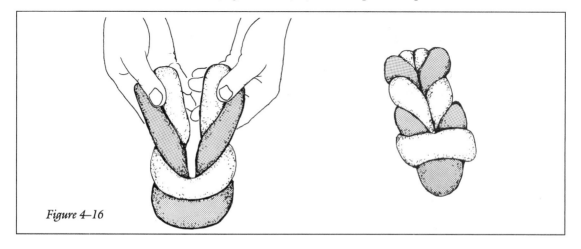

Figure 4–16

your hands and turn your hands as if you are opening a book.) Make sure the chocolate and the light dough lines up evenly in the finished twist.

13. Place the twists on sheet pans, brush with egg wash, and sprinkle lightly with sliced almonds.

14. Bake double-panned at 375°F (190°C) for about 40 minutes.

Orange Almond Filling

5 ounces (140 g) Almond Paste
    (page 4)
4 egg whites
1 pound, 11 ounces (765 g)
    blanched almonds or hazelnuts,
    finely ground
8 ounces (225 g) granulated sugar
5 ounces (140 g) Candied Orange
    Peel (page 520), chopped fine
additional egg whites as needed

1. Incorporate the egg whites into the almond paste, adding them gradually so you do not get lumps.

2. Add nuts, sugar, and orange peel.

3. If the filling feels too firm to spread (this will usually be the case if it is left overnight since nuts absorb moisture), add enough additional egg whites to give it a spreadable consistency.

Puff Paste Diamonds

20 pastries

2 pounds (910 g) Classic Puff
    Paste (page 21)
Egg Wash (page 5)
14 ounces (400 g) Pastry Cream
    (page 569)
fresh fruit
1 recipe Apricot Glaze (page 526)

1. Roll out puff paste to ⅛ inch (3 mm) thick and to a rectangle measuring 16 × 20 inches (40 × 50 cm). Refrigerate covered for a few minutes to firm and relax the dough.

2. Cut into four 4-inch (10-cm) wide strips lengthwise, then cut across the strips every 4 inches (10 cm), making twenty 4- × 4-inch (10- × 10-cm) squares. Refrigerate the dough again if necessary. Do not attempt to cut and fold the squares when the dough is soft.

3. Fold the firm squares into triangles with the folded side toward you. Cut through ¼ inch (6 mm) from the edge on both the left and right sides, ending the cuts ¼ inch (6 mm) from the top (Figure 4–17). Do not cut all the way to the top so you cut the sides off: The dough should still be in one piece.

4. Unfold the triangles; the square will now have an L shape on each side (Figure 4–18). Brush with egg wash. Prick the center of the squares.

5. Cross the left L to the right side and the right L to the left side to form a frame (Figure 4–19). Brush lightly with egg wash, being careful not to get any on the sides.

6. Using a no. 4 (8-mm) plain tip, pipe an even layer of pastry cream on the inside of the frame.

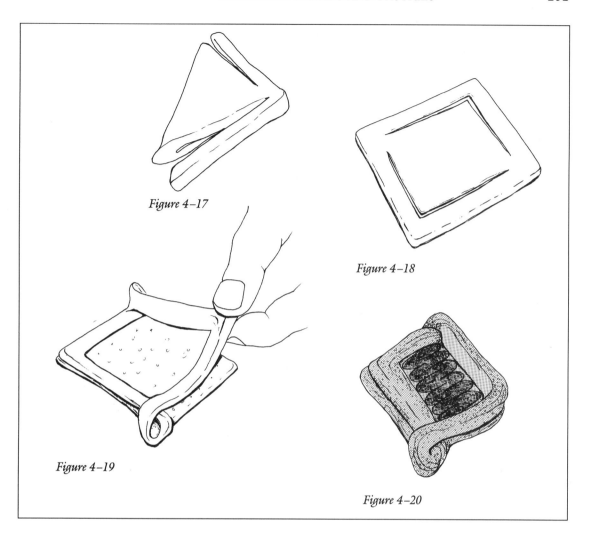

Figure 4–17

Figure 4–18

Figure 4–19

Figure 4–20

7. Bake at 400°F (205°C) for about 20 minutes, or until baked through and golden brown (Figure 4–20). Let the diamonds cool completely.

8. Decorate the pastry cream, staying inside the frame, with fresh fruit (see Fruit Tartlets, page 234). Brush entire pastry with apricot glaze.

NOTE: Puff Paste Diamonds can be prepared up to the point of baking, then frozen to bake and decorate as needed. Bake directly from the freezer.

The pastries can also be baked topped with apples or pears (follow the directions in Fruit Waffles, page 235, to prepare the fruit; top with cinnamon sugar before baking). Or bake the pastries with fresh apricots or plums. Cut the fruit in halves, remove pits, slice and fan the fruit over the pastry cream. Bake and glaze as directed above.

Swedish Breakfast Spirals
about 70 pastries

Dough
3 ounces (85 g) fresh
    compressed yeast
1 pint (480 ml) cold milk
6 eggs
5 ounces (140 g) granulated sugar
4 teaspoons (20 g) salt
3 pounds (1 kg, 365 g) bread flour
1 pound, 5 ounces (595 g)
    softened butter

Filling
1 pound, 5 ounces (595 g)
    softened butter
12 ounces (340 g) brown sugar
12 ounces (340 g)
    granulated sugar
7 ounces (200 g) roasted hazelnuts,
    finely ground
3 tablespoons (15 g)
    ground cinnamon

Topping
9 ounces (255 g) butter
¼ cup (60 ml) heavy cream
7 ounces (200 g) granulated sugar
3 tablespoons (45 ml) light
    corn syrup
4 ounces (115 g) sliced almonds,
    slightly crushed

To make the dough
1. Dissolve yeast in the milk; stir in the eggs, sugar, and salt.
2. Mix in enough of the flour to make a sponge with the consistency of soft butter, then mix in the remaining flour and the butter. This method ensures that you will not get lumps of butter from adding it to a cold dough. Mix the dough until smooth.
3. Spread the dough out evenly on a sheet pan and refrigerate (or freeze if necessary) until the dough is firm.

To make the filling
1. Cream butter with both sugars.
2. Add hazelnuts and cinnamon.
3. If the filling is left overnight, the nuts will absorb much of the moisture and it may be necessary to soften the filling to a spreadable consistency by adding some pastry cream or an egg.

To make the topping
1. Place the butter and cream in a saucepan over low heat. When the butter starts to melt, add the sugar and corn syrup.
2. Boil to 215°F (102°C), then add the almonds.
3. Boil 5 minutes longer over medium heat. The hotter the sugar mixture gets (as it is being reduced), the smaller and slower the bubbles will become. With some experience you will be able to judge the temperature by the appearance.
4. Remove the topping from the heat and let cool until it is firm enough to be spread with a spatula. If the topping becomes too hard, or if it is made ahead, you will need to reheat it. When you reheat it, the butter will separate; stir in 1 tablespoon (15 ml) of heavy cream to bring it back together.

To assemble

1. Roll the dough to 14 inches (35 cm) wide, 6 ft (1 m, 80 cm) long, and ⅛ inch (3 mm) thick.

2. Spread the filling evenly over the dough. If you are not making the spirals in paper cups, leave a ½-inch (1.2-cm) strip at the bottom without filling, and brush it with egg wash (page 5). This will prevent the spirals from unrolling as they rise.

3. Roll the strip up tightly, starting at the top edge.

4. Cut the roll into 2-ounce (55-g) pieces. An easy way to do this is to cut the roll into four equal sections and then cut each section into 18 pieces.

5. Place the spirals level in muffin-size paper cups; you can place the paper cups in muffin pans to keep the spirals from spreading too flat if desired.

6. Let the spirals rise until almost half-doubled in volume. Be careful not to let them rise too long or, when they expand in the oven, a lot of the topping will fall off onto the sheet pan and be lost.

7. Spread the topping onto the spirals using a small spatula.

8. Bake at 375°F (190°C) until golden brown, about 40 minutes.

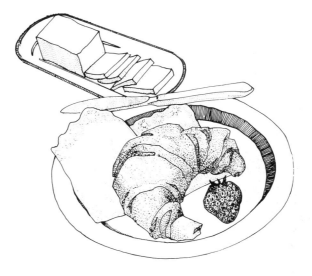

Danish Pastries

Danish Pastry Dough

12 pounds, 8 ounces (5 kg, 680 g)
dough or about ninety 3-ounce
(85-g) pastries

1 quart (960 ml) cold water
8 eggs
4 pounds (1 kg, 820 g)
*   cold margarine*
4 ounces (115 g) fresh
*   compressed yeast*
8 ounces (225 g) granulated sugar
1 tablespoon (15 g) salt
4 pounds, 8 ounces (2 kg, 45 g)
*   bread flour, approximately*
4 ounces (115 g)
*   softened margarine*
1 tablespoon (6 g)
*   ground cardamom*

One-Third Recipe

4 pounds, 3 ounces (1 kg, 905 g)
*   dough or about thirty 3-ounce*
*   (85-g) pastries*

1⅓ cups (320 ml) cold water
3 eggs
1 pound, 5 ounces (595 g)
*   cold margarine*
1½ ounces (40 g) fresh
*   compressed yeast*
3 ounces (85 g) granulated sugar
1 teaspoon (5 g) salt
1 pound, 8 ounces (680 g)
*   bread flour, approximately*
1 ounce (30 g) softened margarine
1 teaspoon (2 g) ground cardamom

All of the ingredients except the softened margarine must be cold. On really hot days you may want to decrease the amount of yeast slightly so that the dough does not rise too fast. Due to the limited amounts of sugar and butter in the dough, and the soft consistency, these precautions keep the yeast from "taking over" before you have a chance to roll in the fat. Margarine is used for this dough because the light and flaky texture is more important than the butter flavor. Because the fat and the dough need to be at the same consistency to give the best layered structure, and margarine has a higher melting point than butter, margarine is preferable with such a soft dough. You may need to adjust the amount of salt called for in the recipe, depending on the salt content of the margarine you are using.

1. Mix the water and eggs, then refrigerate the mixture and the flour, for at least one hour before making the dough.

2. Shape the cold margarine into a 10-inch (25-cm) square (5-inch/12.5-cm for ⅓ recipe) and place in refrigerator. It should be firm and cold, but not hard, when the dough is ready.

3. Dissolve the yeast in the water and egg mixture (use your hand to speed this up since yeast dissolves slowly in cold liquid). Stir in salt and sugar.

4. Reserve a handful of the flour and mix in the remainder. Add the softened margarine and enough of the reserved flour to make a soft, sticky dough.

5. Place the dough on a floured table and shape into a 14-inch (35-cm) square (7-inch/17.5-cm for ⅓ recipe).

6. Place the chilled margarine square diagonally on the dough so that there are four dough triangles showing. Fold the triangles in toward the center and seal in the margarine (see Figures 2–4 and 2–5, page 22).

7. Roll the dough as carefully and evenly as possible into a rectangle, 30 × 20 inches (75 × 50 cm) (12 × 8 inches/30 × 20 cm for ⅓ recipe). Use plenty of flour to prevent the dough from sticking to the table and the rolling pin.

8. Give the dough two single turns in succession (see Figures 4–14 and 4–15, page 96). (The dough does not need to rest between the turns because such a soft dough has less gluten structure and is therefore more pliable.)

9. Cover and refrigerate for 30 minutes.

10. Roll the dough to the same size as before and make two additional single turns. Carefully place the dough on a sheet pan and refrigerate, covered, for 30 minutes.

11. Roll the dough out to about ½ inch (1.2 cm) thick, cover with plastic wrap, and place it in the refrigerator or freezer, depending on how hot the room is where you are working and when you are going to make up the Danish. In either case the dough should chill for at least 30 minutes.

12. Make up the Danish according to the individual recipes and let the pieces rise until half-doubled in volume. Watch carefully to check on their rising: if they rise too long they will lose their flakiness and get spongy; if they do not rise enough, the fat will run out when they are baked. Individual pieces of formed Danish and Danish dough can be prepared ahead and stored in the freezer (unbaked) with excellent results. However, the pieces should never be frozen after baking. To use frozen Danish made up in individual pieces, let them thaw slowly, preferably in the refrigerator, before placing them in the proof box to rise. Use frozen dough as soon as it has thawed enough, in the refrigerator or at room temperature, to be workable.

13. Do not brush the Danish with egg wash before baking unless you are covering them with an almond or streusel topping. Instead, brush the pastries with simple syrup as soon as they are out of the oven, then let them cool completely and ice lightly with white fondant or simple icing.

Danish Filling I

5 pounds (2 kg, 275 g) filling

1 pound, 4 ounces (570 g) cake or cookie scraps (no chocolate)
¾ cup (180 ml) water, approximately
2 pounds (910 g) Almond Paste (page 4)
8 ounces (225 g) granulated sugar
1 pound (455 g) softened butter

1. Mix the scraps with just enough water to make a firm paste. Keep mixing until smooth.

2. Add the almond paste and sugar.

3. Incorporate the butter gradually, and beat until smooth.

NOTE: This filling will keep fresh at room temperature for several days. If it is to be stored longer, it should be refrigerated.

Danish Filling II

3 pounds (1 kg, 365 g) filling

10 ounces (285 g) softened butter
2 pounds (910 g) Almond Paste
  (page 4)
4 ounces (115 g) finely ground
  hazelnuts
6 ounces (170 g) Pastry Cream,
  approximately (page 569)

1. Mix the butter into the almond paste, adding it gradually to avoid lumps. Mix in hazelnuts.

2. Stir in enough pastry cream to reach the desired consistency. If the filling is to be piped onto the dough, it needs to be a little firmer than if it is to be spread; for spreading you want the filling loose enough that you can apply it easily.

3. Store in the refrigerator.

Cream Cheese Filling for Danish

2 pounds, 9 ounces (1 kg, 165 g) filling

1 pound, 6 ounces (625 g)
  cream cheese
3½ ounces (100 g) sugar
3½ ounces (100 g) softened butter
3 eggs
1½ ounces (40 g) bread flour
½ teaspoon (2.5 ml)
  vanilla extract
4 ounces (115 g) dark raisins
¼ cup (60 ml) milk, approximately

1. Place the cream cheese and sugar in mixer bowl. Add the butter gradually at medium speed, and mix until smooth.

2. Mix in the eggs and flour; then add the vanilla extract, raisins, and enough milk so that the mixture can be piped.

3. Store in the refrigerator.

Bear Claws

30 pastries

4 pounds, 3 ounces (1 kg, 905 g)
  Danish Pastry Dough, or
  ⅓ recipe (page 104)
1 pound (455 g) Danish Filling I,
  approximately (page 105)
Egg Wash (page 5)
12 ounces (340 g) sliced almonds
  (see note 2)
Simple Syrup (page 7)
Simple Icing (page 529)

1. Roll the dough into a rectangle measuring 55 × 12 inches (1 m, 37.5 × 30 cm) and approximately ⅛ inch (3 mm) thick. Allow the dough to relax for a minute or so, then cut lengthwise into three 4-inch (10-cm) strips.

2. Place Danish Filling I in a pastry bag with a no. 6 (12-mm) plain tip. Pipe a ribbon of filling ¼ inch (6 mm) down from the top edge, and along the complete length of each strip.

3. Brush egg wash on the entire lower part of each strip under the filling. Fold the top edges down, over and past the filling, and press the ¼-inch (6-mm) borders into the egg wash, just below the filling, to seal.

4. Fold the lower part of each strip up past the sealed point and under the filling, and press again to secure (Figure 4–21). Lightly flatten and shape the strips with your palm.

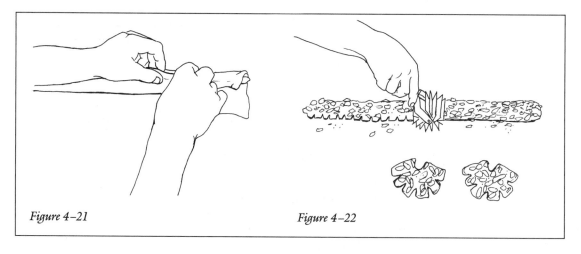

Figure 4–21   *Figure 4–22*

5. Roll a bear-claw cutter (see note 1), which looks like a miniature water wheel with a handle, along the unfilled edge to create the typical claw pattern. Be careful not to cut into the filling or it will leak out. Turn the filled strips over so that the seams are underneath.

6. Push the strips together next to each other with a ruler or a dowel.

7. Brush the strips with egg wash and sprinkle generously with sliced almonds. If you are making only one strip, it is more convenient to do this before cutting the claws (Figure 4–22).

8. Cut each strip into 10 pieces 5½ inches (13.7 cm) long. The pieces will weigh approximately 3 ounces (85 g) each.

9. Pick up the Bear Claws and shake off any almonds that are not sticking. Stretch the pastries slightly, and place them on paper-lined sheet pans, bending each strip into a half-circle so that the cuts open up. Let rise until half-doubled in volume.

10. Bake at 410°F (210°C) for about 15 minutes. Brush the pastries with simple syrup as soon as you remove them from the oven. Let cool completely, then ice lightly with simple icing.

NOTE 1: If you do not have a bear-claw cutter, use a multiple pastry wheel, with the wheels pushed together. If you do not have either of these tools, a chef's knife will do; it just takes a little longer. Make cuts ¾ inch (2 cm) long and ¼ inch (6 mm) apart along the length of the strip.

NOTE 2: The quantity of sliced almonds is specified because it is a fairly large amount. However, a faster and more practical method in a professional kitchen is to work with a greater amount of almonds, sprinkle them on top, and simply return the leftovers to the almond supply.

Butterhorns

about 30 pastries

4 pounds, 3 ounces (1 kg, 905 g)
Danish Pastry Dough, or 1/3
recipe (page 104)
Egg Wash (page 5)
6 ounces (170 g) Cinnamon Sugar
(page 4)
1 pound, 5 ounces (595 g) Streusel
Topping, or 1/2 recipe (page 8)
Simple Icing (page 529)

1. Roll the dough into a rectangle measuring 24 × 14 inches (60 × 35 cm) and approximately 1/4 inch (6 mm) thick. If necessary, trim the edges of the strip to make them even.

2. Brush the entire surface of the dough with egg wash. Generously sprinkle cinnamon sugar over the dough.

3. Fold the long sides in to meet in the center; brush again with egg wash, then fold in half in the same direction (double turn). Even the top by gently rolling with a rolling pin.

4. Cut the folded strip into pieces 3/4 inch (2 cm) wide, and at the same time use the knife to turn them over a quarter-turn so that the cut sides are up.

5. Brush the top (cut sides) of the pieces with egg wash and sprinkle a 1/2-inch (1.2-cm) thick layer of streusel over them. Press the streusel with the palm of your hand to help keep it in place.

6. Carefully place the pieces on sheet pans and let rise until half-doubled in volume.

7. Bake at 425°F (219°C) until golden brown, about 15 minutes. Let the pastries cool completely, then spread a small amount of simple icing on top.

Danish Cinnamon Wreath

one 12-inch (30-cm) wreath

1 pound (455 g) Danish Pastry
Dough (page 104)
6 ounces (170 g) Danish Filling
I or II (pages 105–106)
4 tablespoons (48 g) Cinnamon
Sugar (page 4)
Egg Wash (page 5)
sliced almonds
Simple Syrup (page 7)
Simple Icing (page 529)

1. Roll the dough into a strip 22 inches (55 cm) long, 7 inches (17.5 cm) wide, and approximately 1/8 inch (3 mm) thick.

2. Spread the Danish filling over the dough. (It is a common misconception that spreading on a little extra filling will make the wreath especially tasty, but this is not so! The filling will overpower the dough and it will be like eating filling flavored with some dough. In addition, part of the filling will run out and burn on the sheet pan.)

3. Sprinkle cinnamon sugar over the filling, and roll the strip into a tight string, starting from the top.

4. Roll the coiled string between your palms and the table to make it even, and about 24 inches (60 cm) in length.

5. Place the string on a sheet pan lined with baking paper and shape it into a wreath 10 inches (25 cm) in diameter, making sure the seam is on the bottom. Seal the ends by pushing one inside the other.

6. Holding scissors at a 45° angle from the wreath, make cuts 1/2 inch (12 mm) wide almost to the bottom of the wreath. As you cut, use your free hand to turn these cuts to the side (Figure 4–23), alternating between left and right.

7. Brush with egg wash, and sprinkle lightly with sliced almonds. Let the wreath rise until half-doubled in volume.

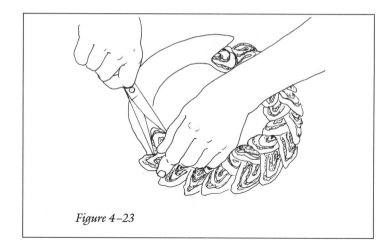

Figure 4–23

8. Bake at 400°F (205°C) for about 30 minutes. Brush with simple syrup immediately after removing the wreath from the oven. Let the wreath cool completely, then lightly spread simple icing over the top.

Danish Twists

about 30 pastries

4 pounds, 3 ounces (1 kg, 905 g) Danish Pastry Dough or ⅓ recipe (page 104)
1 pound (455 g) Pastry Cream (page 569)
or
1 pound (455 g) apricot jam
or
1 pound (455 g) Cherry Filling (page 565)
Simple Syrup (page 7)
Simple Icing (page 529)

This is a very simple and quickly made Danish pastry. It does, however, require a carefully rolled and well-chilled dough to achieve the characteristic crispness around the topping. The crispness is also lost if the dough is rolled too thin, if the strips are cut too wide, or if the Danish is left to rise too long before baking. Choose a good piece of dough (avoid end pieces). If you accidentally roll the dough too thin, make envelopes or turnovers from that piece and start over with a fresh piece of dough.

1. Roll the dough into a rectangle measuring 14 × 12 inches (35 × 30 cm) and approximately ⅜ inch (9 mm) thick.
2. Chill the dough if needed. It should still be firm before you go on to the next step.
3. Cut the dough lengthwise into ⅜-inch (9-mm) strips using a sharp knife or pastry wheel and a ruler as a guide.
4. Twist the strips tight, stretching them slightly at the same time (see Figure 4–9, page 93).

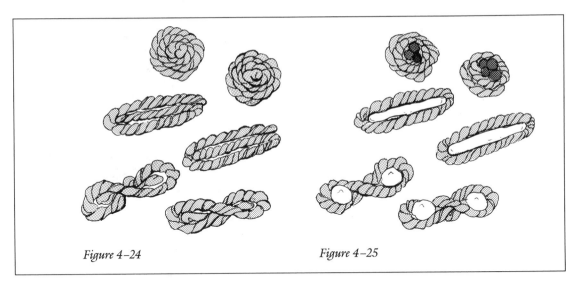

Figure 4–24   *Figure 4–25*

5. Shape into singles, figure eights, or cherry twists (Figures 4–24 and 4–25). Instructions follow. Check to make sure the pieces weigh about 2½ ounces (70 g), which will make the finished pastries 3 ounces (85 g) each. If any are too heavy, cut a piece off the end before you shape it; if too light, conceal a scrap piece under the pastry after forming it.

6. Let the pastries rise until half-doubled in volume.

7. Bake at 425°F (219°C) until golden brown, about 15 minutes. Brush the pastries with simple syrup as soon as they are out of the oven. Let them cool completely, then ice with a small amount of simple icing.

Singles

Twist the strips and fold them in thirds as in a single-turn. Place them on paper-lined sheet pans and, at the same time, tuck the end piece underneath. Pipe a ribbon of pastry cream lengthwise in the center of each Danish.

Figure Eights

Twist the strips and form into figure-eight shapes. Overlap both end pieces enough to protrude into the center and cover the openings in the eight. Invert onto paper-lined sheet pans. Pipe a dot of apricot jam into both indentations on the eight.

Cherry Twists

Twist the strips and shape into loose spirals. Secure the end piece underneath as you place each on paper-lined sheet pans. Pipe a small amount of cherry filling (a generous tablespoon/15 ml) onto the center of each twist.

Envelopes
30 pastries

*4 pounds, 3 ounces (1 kg, 905 g)
    Danish Pastry Dough, or ⅓
    recipe (page 104)*
Egg Wash (page 5)
*8 ounces (225 g) Danish Filling I,
    II, or Cream Cheese Filling for
    Danish (pages 105–106)*
*8 ounces (225 g) Pastry Cream
    (page 569) or apricot jam*
sliced almonds
Simple Syrup (page 7)
Simple Icing (page 529)

1. Roll the dough into a rectangle measuring 21 × 17.5 inches (52.5 × 43.7 cm) and approximately 1¼ inches (6 mm) thick.

2. Let the dough rest for a few minutes before you cut the squares so that they will not shrink and become rectangles. Mark and cut the dough into 3½- × 3½-inch (8.7- × 8.7-cm) squares using a ruler as a guide, or use a multiple pastry wheel adjusted to 3½ inches (8.7 cm). The pieces will weigh approximately 3 ounces (85 g) apiece.

3. Lightly brush egg wash along the cuts to cover all four edges of each square.

4. Place Danish or cream cheese filling in a pastry bag. Pipe a dot of filling the size of a cherry in the center of each square.

5. Fold the four corners of each square in to meet in the center. Press the center down firmly with your thumb to prevent the dough from unfolding.

6. Place the Envelopes on sheet pans lined with baking paper. Pipe a dot of either pastry cream or jam, the size of a cherry, on top of the pastries in the indentation created by your thumb. Or, if you used cream cheese filling inside the Envelopes, you can also use it for the top, to indicate what is inside.

7. Lightly sprinkle sliced almonds on the pastries; they will stick to the topping. Let rise until half-doubled in volume.

8. Bake at 425°F (219°C) until golden brown, about 15 minutes. Brush the pastries with simple syrup immediately after removing them from the oven. When the Envelopes have cooled, spread a small amount of simple icing on the top.

Mayor's Wreath

one 12-inch (30-cm) wreath

1 pound (455 g) Danish Pastry
    Dough (page 104)
6 ounces (170 g) Danish Filling II
    (page 106)
Egg Wash (page 5)
sliced almonds
Simple Syrup (page 7)
Simple Icing (page 529)

1. Roll the dough out to a strip 8 inches (20 cm) wide, 18 inches (45 cm) long, and ⅛ inch (3 mm) thick. Cut this strip lengthwise into three equal pieces.

2. Check the Danish filling to be sure it is not too soft, as the strips will be braided later; adjust if needed. Place the filling in a pastry bag with a no. 3 (6-mm) plain tip. Pipe a ribbon of filling along the entire length of each strip approximately ½ inch (1.2 cm) from the top.

3. Brush egg wash along the bottom of the strips, and then roll each one into a spiral, rolling from the top to the bottom.

4. Roll each coiled strip out to 20 inches (50 cm) in length by rolling it between your palms and the table.

5. Place the three strings, seam side down, next to each other on the table. Braid them as a three-braid loaf (see page 52), starting from the middle and working to each end.

6. Carefully place the braided loaf on a sheet pan lined with baking paper. If necessary, stretch the braid slightly to make it 24 inches (60 cm) in length.

7. Shape into a wreath that is 10 inches (25 cm) in diameter. Fold the ends together so that the seam shows as little as possible.

8. Brush with egg wash, and sprinkle lightly with sliced almonds. Let rise until half-doubled in volume.

9. Bake at 375°F (190°C) for about 30 minutes. Brush with simple syrup immediately after removing the wreath from the oven. Let cool completely, then lightly spread simple icing over the top.

Raisin Snails

30 pastries

4 pounds, 3 ounces (1 kg, 905 g)
    Danish Pastry Dough, or ⅓
    recipe (page 104)
Egg Wash (page 5)
2 pounds (910 g) dark raisins,
    soaked in water, then well
    drained
6 ounces (170 g) Cinnamon Sugar
    (page 4)
Simple Syrup (page 7)
Simple Icing (page 529)

1. Roll the dough into a rectangle measuring 48 × 14 inches (1 m, 20 cm × 35 cm) and approximately ⅛ inch (3 mm) thick.

2. Brush the surface of the dough with egg wash leaving a 1-inch (2.5-cm) strip along the bottom long edge uncovered. Generously distribute the soft raisins over the egg-washed part of the dough, then sprinkle the cinnamon sugar quite heavily on top. Roll over the top with a rolling pin to make the raisins stick to the dough.

3. Starting at the top, roll the dough up evenly, stretching it if necessary, to make a tight rope. Place the rope at the edge of the table with the seam underneath.

4. With a sharp knife, cut into 30 pieces weighing approximately 3 ounces (85 g) each.

5. Place the snails on paper-lined sheet pans, cut sides up, tucking the ends underneath so they will not unroll while baking. Let rise until half-doubled in volume.

6. Bake at 425°F (219°C) until golden brown, about 15 minutes. Brush the pastries with simple syrup immediately after removing them from the oven. When the snails have cooled, spread a small amount of simple icing on the top of each one.

NOTE: Although you can use regular dry raisins in the snails, the soaked raisins provide additional moisture for the pastries, which lack any filling. Also, soaking the raisins makes the snails easier to slice.

Sister's Pull-Apart Coffee Cake
one 10-inch (25-cm) cake

1 pound, 4 ounces (570 g) Danish Pastry Dough (page 104)
6 ounces (170 g) Danish Filling I or II (pages 105–106)
6 ounces (170 g) Pastry Cream (page 569)
sliced almonds
Simple Syrup (page 7)
Simple Icing (page 529)

1. Roll the dough into a strip 22 inches (55 cm) long, 7 inches (17.5 cm) wide, and ⅛ inch (3 mm) thick. Allow the dough to relax for 1 minute to avoid shrinkage. Cut a 7-inch (17.5-cm) square from one end, and set this piece aside.

2. Spread the Danish filling over the larger piece of dough.

3. Roll up the strip into a tight string, starting from the top. Roll the string between your palms and the table to make it even. Cut the strip into 12 equal pieces.

4. Roll and shape the reserved square of dough into a 10-inch (25-cm) circle. Place it on a sheet pan lined with paper.

5. Put about one-third of the pastry cream in a pastry bag with a no. 3 (6-mm) plain tip. Set aside. Using a metal spatula, spread the remainder of the pastry cream over the dough, covering the entire surface. Place a 10-inch (25-cm) adjustable cake ring around the dough (or use the ring from a springform pan).

6. Arrange the 12 pieces, cut-side up, on the cream. Press them in lightly with your knuckles. Pipe a dot of pastry cream, about the size of a hazelnut, on top and partially inside each piece. Sprinkle with sliced almonds. Let the cake rise until half-doubled in volume.

7. Bake at 375°F (190°C) for about 35 minutes. Brush the cake with simple syrup as soon as you remove it from the oven. Remove the ring and ice the cake lightly with simple icing once it has cooled.

Sugar Buns
30 pastries

4 pounds, 3 ounces (1 kg, 905 g)
    Danish Pastry Dough, or ⅓
    recipe (page 104)
Egg Wash (page 5)
1 pound (455 g) Pastry Cream
    (page 569)
melted butter
granulated sugar

1. Roll the dough into a rectangle measuring 24 × 20 inches (60 × 50 cm) and approximately ⅛ inch (3 mm) thick.

2. Mark and cut the dough into 4-inch (10-cm) squares using a ruler as a guide, or use a multiple pastry wheel adjusted to 4 inches (10 cm). The pieces will weigh approximately 3 ounces (85 g) each.

3. Lightly brush egg wash along the cuts to cover all four edges of each square.

4. Pipe a mound of pastry cream about the size of an unshelled walnut in the middle of each square. (If you use too much pastry cream it will be difficult to seal the pastries; if you use too little filling, it will be absorbed by the dough, leaving the inside dry.)

5. Pick up the corners, stretch them if necessary to cover the filling, and fold in to meet in the center. Pinch the seams closed so the pastry cream will not leak out.

6. Place the buns, seam-side down, on paper-lined sheet pans. Let rise in a warm place until half-doubled in volume.

7. Bake at 400°F (205°C) until golden brown, about 20 minutes. Because of the pastry cream inside, the buns will puff up as high as a large profiterole, so they must bake long enough to hold their shape once removed from the oven. Let the buns cool completely.

8. Brush the tops and sides of the buns with melted butter. Fill a bowl with enough sugar to make a well in it deep enough to fit a bun without flattening it. Dip each bun into the sugar well; the sugar should stick to the melted butter.

Muffins

Apple-Pecan Buttermilk Muffins
thirty 4-ounce (115-g) muffins

Butter and Flour Mixture
    (page 4)
6 medium-sized Granny Smith
    apples
1 pound (455 g) softened butter
1 pound (455 g) brown sugar
1 cup (240 ml) honey

1. Line muffin pans with paper cups, skipping every other space because this amount of batter will make the muffins "mushroom" out on top of the pan as they bake. Grease the top of the pan around each cup with butter and flour mixture; set aside (see note).

2. Peel, core, and cut apples in half. Poach in water for about 5 minutes to soften; drain and set aside to cool.

3. Cream the softened butter with the sugar and honey to a light and fluffy consistency. Mix in eggs and vanilla.

6 eggs
1 teaspoon (5 ml) vanilla extract
1 teaspoon (5 g) salt
4 teaspoons (16 g) baking powder
4 teaspoons (16 g) baking soda
1 pound, 8 ounces (680 g)
 cake flour
6 ounces (170 g) whole wheat flour
1 tablespoon (5 g)
 ground cinnamon
1 teaspoon (2 g) ground nutmeg
1¼ cups (300 ml) buttermilk
¾ cup (180 ml) light cream
8 ounces (225 g) pecans,
 coarsely chopped
Streusel Topping (page 8)

4. Sift together salt, baking powder, baking soda, cake flour, whole-wheat flour, cinnamon, and nutmeg. Add to the batter in three segments, alternating with the buttermilk and light cream.

5. Chop the reserved apples into ½-inch (1.2-cm) cubes and add to the batter together with the pecans.

6. Use an ice cream scoop to portion 4 ounces (115 g) batter into each muffin cup. Sprinkle streusel topping lightly on top of the batter.

7. Bake at 400°F (205°C) for about 30 minutes or until the muffins spring back when pressed lightly in the middle. Remove from the pans as soon as they are cool enough to handle to prevent the muffins from becoming wet on the bottom.

NOTE: If you want the batter to stay within the paper cups, use 3 ounces (85 g) of batter per muffin (it is not necessary in that case to skip any spaces or to grease the tops).

Blueberry Ginger Muffins

thirty 4-ounce (115-g) muffins

Butter and Flour Mixture
 (page 4)
14 ounces (400 g) brown sugar
14 ounces (400 g) softened butter
½ cup (120 ml) molasses
⅔ cup (160 ml) honey
6 eggs
1 teaspoon (5 ml) vanilla extract
2 teaspoons (10 g) salt
1 tablespoon (12 g) baking powder
1 tablespoon (12 g) baking soda
1 teaspoon (2 g) ground ginger
1 pound (455 g) cake flour
14 ounces (400 g) bread flour
1 cup (240 ml) buttermilk
1 pound, 8 ounces (680 g) fresh or
 frozen blueberries (if frozen,
 do not thaw)

1. Line muffin pans with paper cups, skipping every other space because the muffins will "mushroom" out on top as they bake. Grease the top of the pan around each cup with butter and flour mixture; set aside.

2. Cream together the brown sugar and butter until light and fluffy. Mix in molasses, honey, eggs, and vanilla.

3. Combine the dry ingredients, and mix into the sugar mixture, alternating with the buttermilk in three segments.

4. Stir in the blueberries gently so that the berries do not break and turn the batter blue.

5. Place the batter in a pastry bag with a large, plain tip. Pipe the batter in a dome shape slightly above the rim of each cup, using 4 ounces (115 g) of batter per muffin. If the batter is firm enough to allow you to do so, use an ice cream scoop to portion it out instead.

6. Bake at 375°F (190°C) until brown and baked through, about 35 minutes.

NOTE: If you use frozen berries, you will have no choice but to use an ice cream scoop. Do not fold in the frozen berries until you are ready to portion the muffins; if left to stand, the batter will "set up," making it very difficult to work with.

Variation: Banana Muffins

Replace the blueberries with bananas chopped into ½-inch (1.2-cm) cubes. Increase bread flour by 2 ounces (55 g) and omit the ground ginger.

Chocolate Chip Muffins

twenty-eight 4-ounce (115-g) muffins

Butter and Flour Mixture
  (page 4)
14 ounces (400 g) dark chocolate
8 ounces (225 g) walnuts
10 ounces (285 g) softened butter
10 ounces (285 g) brown sugar
¾ cup (180 ml) honey
4 eggs
1 teaspoon (5 ml) vanilla extract
1 tablespoon (12 g) baking powder
4 teaspoons (16 g) baking soda
1 pound, 12 ounces (795 g)
  bread flour
2 ounces (55 g) unprocessed
  wheat bran
1¼ cups (300 ml) buttermilk
1½ cups (360 ml) half-and-half
8 ounces (225 g) dark raisins

1. Line muffin pans with paper cups, skipping every other space because the muffins will "mushroom" out on top as they bake. Grease the top of the pan around each cup with butter and flour mixture; set aside (see note).

2. Chop the chocolate and walnuts into raisin-sized pieces; set aside.

3. Beat the butter and sugar until fluffy. Add the honey, eggs, and vanilla.

4. Sift baking powder, baking soda, and flour together. Add the bran.

5. Add the dry ingredients to the butter mixture in three parts, alternating with the buttermilk and half-and-half. Stir in raisins, chocolate, and walnuts.

6. Use an ice cream scoop to portion 4 ounces (115 g) of batter into each muffin cup.

7. Bake at 375°F (190°C) for about 25 minutes or until brown and baked through. To check if the muffins are done, press down in the center; they should spring back. As soon as they can be handled, either remove the muffins from the pan or tilt them in the pan to allow air underneath; this will keep them from getting wet on the bottom.

NOTE: If you want the batter to stay within the paper cups, use 3 ounces (85 g) of batter per muffin. It is not necessary in that case to skip any spaces or to grease the tops.

Chocolate Honey Muffins

thirty 4-ounce (115-g) muffins

Butter and Flour Mixture
  (page 4)
6 ounces (170 g) walnuts
7 ounces (200 g) dark chocolate
7 ounces (200 g) white chocolate
10 ounces (285 g) softened butter
10 ounces (285 g) brown sugar
1 cup (240 ml) honey
¼ cup (60 ml) molasses
6 eggs
1 teaspoon (5 ml) vanilla extract

1. Line muffin pans with paper cups, skipping every other space because the muffins will "mushroom" out on top of the pan as they bake. Grease the top of the pan around each cup with butter and flour mixture; set aside (see note).

2. Chop the walnuts, dark chocolate, and white chocolate to raisin-sized pieces; set aside.

3. Cream together the butter and sugar until light and fluffy. Add the honey, molasses, eggs, and vanilla.

4. Sift together the salt, baking powder, baking soda, bread flour, cake flour, and cocoa powder. Add to the butter mixture in three parts, alternating with the buttermilk and half-and-half. Add the raisins, walnuts, and chocolate.

5. Use an ice cream scoop to portion 4 ounces (115 g) of batter into each muffin cup.

1 teaspoon (5 g) salt
4 teaspoons (16 g) baking powder
2 teaspoons (8 g) baking soda
14 ounces (400 g) bread flour
10 ounces (285 g) cake flour
2 ounces (55 g) cocoa powder
1¼ cups (300 ml) buttermilk
1¼ cups (300 ml) half-and-half
6 ounces (170 g) dark raisins

6. Bake at 400°F (205°C) for about 30 minutes or until the muffins spring back when pressed lightly in the center. Remove from the pans as soon as they are cool enough to handle to prevent the muffins from becoming wet on the bottom.

NOTE: If you prefer a smaller muffin, use 3 ounces (85 g) of batter per muffin. It is not necessary in that case to skip any spaces or to grease the tops.

Honey-Bran Muffins
thirty-five 4-ounce (115-g) muffins

1¾ cups (420 ml) water
1 pound, 3 ounces (540 g)
*   unprocessed wheat bran*
4 ounces (115 g) wheat germ
Butter and Flour Mixture
*   (page 4)*
12 ounces (340 g) softened butter
1 pound, 5 ounces (595 g)
*   brown sugar*
1 cup (240 ml) molasses
1 cup (240 ml) honey
6 eggs
1 teaspoon (5 ml) vanilla extract
1 pound, 12 ounces (795 g)
*   bread flour*
2½ teaspoons (10g) baking powder
2 tablespoons (24 g) baking soda
1 teaspoon (5 g) salt
1¾ cups (420 ml) half-and-half
2¼ cups (540 ml) buttermilk
6 ounces (170 g) dark raisins

1. Bring the water to a boil and pour over bran and wheat germ. Mix to combine and set aside to cool.

2. Line muffin pans with paper cups, skipping every other space because this amount of batter will make the muffins "mushroom" out on top of the pan as they bake. Grease the top of the pans around each cup with butter and flour mixture; set aside (see note).

3. Cream together butter and brown sugar until fluffy. Combine molasses, honey, eggs, and vanilla; add to the butter mixture. Fold in the soaked bran and wheat germ.

4. Sift together the dry ingredients. Add to the batter in three parts, alternating with half-and-half and buttermilk. Stir in the raisins.

5. Use an ice cream scoop to portion 4 ounces (115 g) of batter into each muffin cup.

6. Bake at 375°F (190°C) for about 25 minutes or until dark brown and baked through. To check if the muffins are done, press down in the center, they should spring back. As soon as they can be handled, either remove the muffins from the pan, or tilt them in the pan to allow air underneath; this will keep them from getting wet on the bottom.

NOTE: If you want the batter to stay within the paper cups, use 3 ounces (85 g) of batter per muffin. It is not necessary in that case to skip any spaces or to grease the tops.

Oat Bran–Yogurt Muffins

thirty-five 4-ounce (115-g) muffins

Butter and Flour Mixture
*   (page 4)*
12 ounces (340 g) softened butter
1 pound, 6 ounces (625 g)
*   brown sugar*
1 cup (240 ml) molasses
1 cup (240 ml) honey
12 eggs
2 teaspoons (10 ml) vanilla extract
1 pound, 12 ounces (795 g)
*   bread flour*
2 tablespoons (24 g) baking powder
4 teaspoons (16 g) baking soda
1 teaspoon (5 g) salt
1 pound, 10 ounces (740 g)
*   unprocessed oat bran*
1½ cups (360 ml) half-and-half
2¼ cups (540 ml) plain,
*   low-fat yogurt*
8 ounces (225 g) dark raisins

1. Line muffin pans with paper cups, skipping every other space because this amount of batter will make the muffins "mushroom" out on top of the pans as they bake. Grease the top of the pans around each cup with butter and flour mixture; set aside.

2. Cream butter and sugar until fluffy. Combine molasses, honey, eggs, and vanilla; add to butter mixture.

3. Sift together flour, baking powder, baking soda, and salt. Stir in oat bran and reserve.

4. Stir the half-and-half into the yogurt. Add the dry ingredients to the batter in three parts, alternating with the yogurt mixture.

5. Portion 4 ounces (115 g) of batter per muffin into the prepared pans using an ice cream scoop.

6. Bake at 375°F (190°C) for about 25 minutes, or until brown and baked through (the muffins should spring back when pressed lightly in the center). As soon as they can be handled, either remove the muffins from the pans, or tilt them in the pans to allow air underneath and prevent the muffins from getting wet on the bottom as they cool.

NOTE: For a smaller muffin, use 3 ounces (85 g) of batter per muffin. It is not necessary in that case to skip any spaces or to grease the tops.

Pumpkin Muffins

twenty-five 4-ounce (115-g)
muffins

Butter and Flour Mixture
*   (page 4)*
1 pound (455 g) softened butter
13 ounces (370 g) brown sugar
4 eggs
½ cup (120 ml) molasses
½ cup (120 ml) honey
1 teaspoon (5 g) salt
1 teaspoon (2 g) ground ginger
1 teaspoon (1.5 g) ground cinnamon
1 teaspoon (2 g) ground allspice
½ teaspoon (1 g) grated nutmeg
1 tablespoon (12 g) baking powder
1 tablespoon (12 g) baking soda

1. Line muffin pans with paper cups, skipping every other space because this amount of batter will make the muffins "mushroom" out on top of the pans as they bake. Grease the tops of the pans around each cup with butter and flour mixture; set aside.

2. Cream together the butter and brown sugar. Mix in eggs, molasses, and honey; reserve.

3. Sift together the salt, ginger, cinnamon, allspice, nutmeg, baking powder, baking soda, and flour. Mix in the raisins, coating them with flour to prevent them from sinking to the bottom of the batter. Reserve.

4. Combine the vanilla, buttermilk, and pumpkin. Add the pumpkin mixture to the butter mixture in two sections, alternating with the dry ingredients.

5. Place the batter in a pastry bag with a no. 8 (16-mm) plain tip. Pipe the batter into the prepared pans, slightly above the rim of each cup, using 4 ounces (115 g) of batter per muffin. Or, use an ice cream scoop to fill the pans.

2 pounds (910 g) bread flour
8 ounces (225 g) dark raisins
1 teaspoon (5 ml) vanilla extract
1½ cups (360 ml) buttermilk
1½ cups (360 ml) pumpkin purée

6. Bake at 375°F (190°C) until the crust is brown, about 35 minutes.

NOTE: For a smaller muffin, use 3 ounces (85 g) of batter per muffin. It is not necessary in that case to skip any spaces or to grease the tops.

Variation: Persimmon Muffins

Delete raisins and pumpkin purée. Add instead 8 ounces (225 g) of dates chopped to the size of raisins, 1¼ cups (300 ml) persimmon purée, and 8 ounces (225 g) persimmon chunks, also chopped into raisin-sized pieces.

Zucchini-Walnut Muffins

thirty 4-ounce (115-g) muffins

Butter and Flour Mixture
    (page 4)
8 eggs
1 pound, 12 ounces (795 g)
    granulated sugar
1 pound, 4 ounces (570 g) grated
    zucchini (skin on)
10 ounces (285 g) grated carrots
2 cups (480 ml) vegetable oil
1 teaspoon (5 g) salt
1 pound, 12 ounces (795 g)
    bread flour
4 teaspoons (16 g) baking powder
3 teaspoons (12 g) baking soda
1 tablespoon (5 g) cinnamon
2 teaspoons (4 g) allspice
1 teaspoon (2 g) nutmeg
8 ounces (225 g) unprocessed
    wheat bran
10 ounces (285 g) chopped walnuts
walnuts, finely chopped
brown sugar

1. Line muffin pans with paper cups, skipping every other space as the muffins will "mushroom" out on top as they bake. Grease the top of the pan around each cup with butter and flour mixture; set aside.

2. Beat eggs and sugar just to combine. Stir in zucchini, carrots, oil, and salt.

3. Sift flour with baking powder, baking soda, and spices. Add to the egg mixture.

4. Stir in the bran and the 10 ounces (285 g) of walnuts.

5. Scoop 4 ounces (115 g) of the batter into each of the prepared cups.

6. Mix equal parts of finely chopped walnuts and brown sugar and sprinkle on top of the muffins.

7. Bake at 400°F (205°C) for approximately 35 minutes. Remove the muffins from the pans as soon as they are cool enough to touch to prevent them from becoming wet on the bottom.

NOTE: For a smaller muffin, use 3 ounces (85 g) of batter per muffin. It is not necessary in that case to skip any spaces or to grease the tops.

— F I V E —

Cookies

Almond Macaroon Cookies
Biscotti
Brysselkex Cookies
Chocolate Chip Cookies
Chunky White-Chocolate-
  Chip Cookies
Cocoa Cuts
Coconut Macaroons
Double-Chocolate Indulgence
Florentinas
Gingersnaps
Hazelnut Butter Cookies
Hazelnut Squares

Heide Sand Cookies
Ladyfingers
Macadamia Nut Cookies
Oat Flakes
Orange Macaroons
Palm Leaves
Peanut Butter Cookies
Pirouettes
Raisin Brownies
Raisin Oatmeal Cookies
Raspberry Turnovers
Spritz Rings
Strassburger Cookies

*I*t is a tradition in Sweden to serve cookies and coffee at 3 o'clock each afternoon: the Swedish equivalent of English afternoon tea. Traditionally there should be seven kinds of cookies, neatly lined up on trays. If it is not possible to have seven different types, the custom is to serve an odd number of varieties. When someone dropped by our house to visit during the day, we always served coffee and cookies automatically. Cookies are also great for after-dinner treats. At the California Culinary Academy we use a special mirror to display cookies each time we have a buffet. And I always make sure we serve at least seven kinds.

Cookies should look as good as they taste. You want to create petite, bite-sized morsels that your guests just can't resist, even if they are not hungry! Besides being small, cookies should be uniform in size and thickness. Not only will they bake more evenly, your cookies will create an elegant presentation when displayed on a tray or mirror. Pay special attention when the following recipes call for chilling the dough at various stages in the preparation; skipping this important step will result in misshapen, unprofessional-looking cookies.

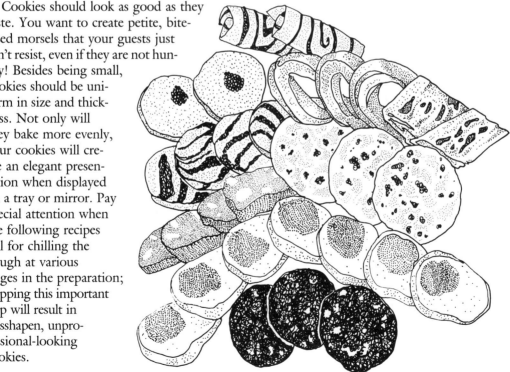

Cookies can be decorated, and made more delicious, with jam piped on top, dipped in chocolate (completely or in part), sandwiched together with jam or buttercream, dipped in fondant, or topped with sifted, powdered sugar.

Shaping the cookie dough is done in several ways. Some cookies, such as Coconut Macaroons and Spritz Rings, are piped out into shapes using a pastry bag with a specific tip. In other recipes the dough is divided into equal portions; each portion is then rolled into a rope of uniform thickness and cut into cookies. This technique is used with Macadamia Nut, Hazelnut, and all variations of Brysselkex cookies. This production method not only gives you cookies of uniform size, but also makes storage easier: If well wrapped, the logs can be kept in the refrigerator for days or in the freezer for weeks. The cookies can be baked and finished as needed, allowing you to produce fresh cookies with a minimum of effort. A third way of forming cookies is to spread the dough in sheets on a pan, or roll it into ropes and press these on the pan. The cookies can be cut to size as soon as the baked dough comes out of the oven. This procedure is used for Cocoa Cuts and Hazelnut Squares.

There is no reason to use anything but butter in cookie doughs. Cookies baked with butter will taste fresh at least three to four days if they are stored properly. Cookies baked with jam stay at their best for the shortest amount of time, as the jam tends to become rubbery. To keep cookies crisp, store them in a jar with a little air for circulation, or keep the cover on loosely (although this might be taken as an invitation for munching by your coworkers or friends). If cookies become soft anyway due to high humidity or rain, dry them in a cool 200°F (94°C) oven, providing they are not dipped or filled. Other cookies, such as macaroons, need to be kept soft; store these in an airtight container. If they get a little dry, take them out of the container and place them on a sheet pan in the refrigerator overnight. The old-fashioned method of putting a few apple slices in the jar with macaroons is also helpful.

Most cookies have a high sugar content, which makes them susceptible to overbrowning. It is usually a good idea to bake them double-panned to prevent them from becoming too dark on the bottom before they have a chance to reach an appetizing golden brown color on the top. Generally cookies should be baked at around 375°F (190°C), except macaroons, which need high heat, 425°F (219°C), to ensure softness.

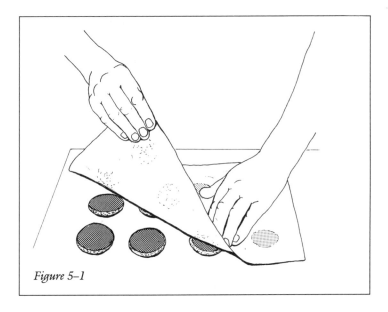

Figure 5–1

Almond Macaroon Cookies

about sixty 2-inch (5-cm) cookies

2 pounds (910 g) Almond Paste (page 4)
1 pound (455 g) granulated sugar
5 to 10 egg whites

1. Place the almond paste and sugar in a mixing bowl. Blend in one egg white at a time, being careful not to get any lumps in the batter. Add as many egg whites as the batter will absorb without getting runny; this will vary depending on the firmness of the almond paste and, to some degree, the size of the egg whites.

2. Beat for a few minutes at high speed to a creamy consistency.

3. Place the batter in a pastry bag with a no. 6 (12-mm) plain tip. Pipe the batter in 1½-inch (3.7-cm) mounds onto sheet pans lined with baking paper. They will spread slightly, so do not pipe them too close together.

4. Bake the cookies, double-panned, at 410°F (210°C) for about 10 minutes, or until light brown.

5. Let the macaroons cool and then store them in the refrigerator still attached to the baking paper. To remove them from the paper, turn them upside-down and peel the paper away from the cookies, rather than the cookies off the paper (Figure 5–1). If they are difficult to remove, brush water on the back of the papers, turn them right-side up, and wait a few minutes; then try again. The cookies can be served as is or dipped in melted baker's chocolate.

Macaroon Decorating Paste

Make the recipe above using two or three fewer egg whites. The paste should be soft enough that you can pipe it out without a monumental effort, but it should not change shape at all when it is baked. Always bake it in a hot oven; follow directions for the individual recipe in which the paste is used.

Biscotti

(see photograph in color insert)
about 120 cookies

1 pound, 4 ounces (570 g)
    bread flour
4 teaspoons (16 g) baking powder
12 ounces (340 g) granulated
    sugar
6 ounces (170 g) bread crumbs
8 ounces (225 g) whole almonds
    with skins
8 ounces (225 g) whole hazelnuts
    with skins
1 teaspoon (5 ml) orange
    flower water
1 teaspoon (5 ml) vanilla extract
¼ cup (60 ml) orange juice
5 eggs
Egg Wash (page 5)
AA confectioners' sugar
dark baker's chocolate, melted

1. Sift the flour with baking powder. Add sugar and bread crumbs, and combine using low speed. Mix in almonds and hazelnuts.

2. Combine the orange flower water, vanilla, orange juice, and eggs. Gradually add the liquid to the dry ingredients and mix for approximately 1 minute, until you achieve a firm dough.

3. Divide the dough into four equal pieces. Roll each piece into a uniform rope 16 inches (40 cm) long. Place the ropes on sheet pans lined with baking paper. Brush egg wash on top of the ropes, then sprinkle with confectioners' sugar.

4. Bake at 350°F (175°C) for about 25 minutes, or until golden brown. Let cool for at least one hour or, preferably, overnight.

5. Slice ropes diagonally into cookies ⅜ inch (9 mm) thick. Place the slices cut-side down on sheet pans lined with baking paper.

6. Bake at 375°F (190°C) until the cookies start to turn golden brown around the edges, approximately 15 minutes.

7. When the cookies have cooled completely, dip them halfway into melted dark baker's chocolate. Store in airtight containers.

NOTE: If making more cookies than you will use within one week, store some of the uncut baked ropes in the refrigerator (covered) to slice and dry as needed.

Brysselkex Cookies

Brysselkex Dough

1 pound, 11 ounces (765 g) butter
1 teaspoon (5 ml) vanilla extract
10 ounces (285 g) powdered sugar
2 pounds, 3 ounces (1 kg)
    bread flour
1 ounce (30 g) cocoa powder

Many varieties of cookies can be made from this one basic dough; the most common are vanilla, marble, and checkerboard.

1. Mix butter, vanilla, sugar, and flour until smooth.
2. Divide the dough in half. Add cocoa powder to one half.
3. Refrigerate the dough if necessary until it has a workable consistency.

Vanilla Brysselkex
about 100 cookies

1 recipe Brysselkex Dough
    (omit cocoa powder)
AA confectioners' sugar

1. Divide the dough into three equal pieces. Refrigerate if needed.
2. Roll each piece into a rope 2 inches (5 cm) in diameter.
3. Brush excess flour from the ropes and roll in sugar to coat.
4. Transfer the ropes to a sheet pan; roll them so they are even and just slightly thinner. Refrigerate until firm.
5. Cut the ropes into ¼-inch (6-mm) slices. Place the cookies on sheet pans lined with baking paper.
6. Bake at 375°F (190°C) until golden brown, about 15 minutes.

Marble Brysselkex
(see photograph in color insert)
about 100 cookies

1 recipe Brysselkex Dough

1. Divide plain and chocolate doughs into three portions each; this can be done by eye, as the pieces need not be exactly equal.

2. Roll all six pieces, separately, into ropes about 10 inches (25 cm) long.

3. Arrange the ropes in three groups with one plain and one chocolate rope in each (Figure 5–2). Cut each pair into thirds so you now have three small chocolate and three small plain in each group (Figure 5–3).

4. Working with one group at a time, gently press the six pieces on top of one another, alternating plain and chocolate; keep each group separate (Figure 5–4).

5. Roll each group of stacked dough into a rope 1¾ inches (4.5 cm) in diameter (Figure 5–5), twisting the ropes as you form them to create a marbled effect (Figure 5–6).

6. Carefully transfer the logs to a sheet pan and refrigerate until firm.

7. Slice and bake as directed for Vanilla Brysselkex.

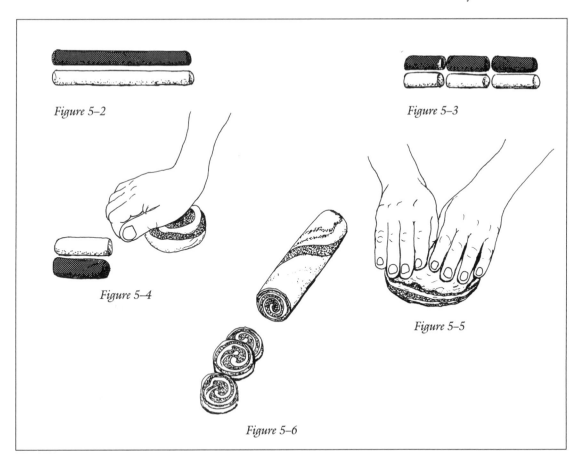

Figure 5–2

Figure 5–3

Figure 5–4

Figure 5–5

Figure 5–6

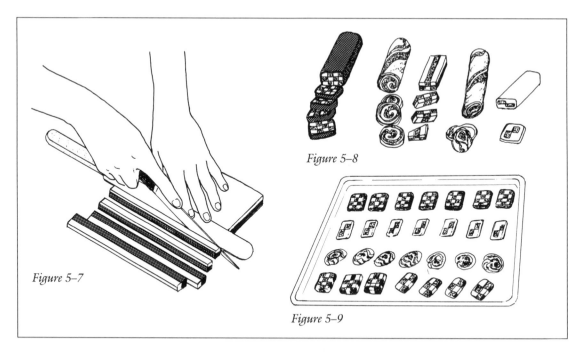

Figure 5–7

Figure 5–8

Figure 5–9

Checkerboard Brysselkex

(see photograph in color insert)
about 150 cookies

1 recipe Brysselkex Dough
2 pounds, 10 ounces (1 kg, 195 g)
*   Short Dough or Cocoa Short*
*   Dough (page 31)*
Egg Wash (page 5)

1. Roll the plain and chocolate doughs into rectangles of equal size, ⅝ inch (1.5 cm) thick.

2. Brush egg wash on the chocolate dough and place the plain dough on top.

3. Refrigerate until firm.

4. Cut the rectangle into ⅝-inch (1.5-cm) strips (Figure 5–7). Lay half of the strips on their sides. Brush with egg wash.

5. Arrange the remaining strips on top of the egg-washed strips, stacking them so that the chocolate dough is on top of the plain dough, and vice-versa, to create the checkerboard effect.

6. Roll out the short dough ⅛ inch (3 mm) thick and the same length as the strips.

7. Brush the short dough with egg wash.

8. Place one of the stacked cookie strips on top, and roll to enclose all four sides in short dough. Cut away the excess dough. Repeat with the remaining strips. You can omit wrapping the logs in short dough, or stack three or four strips together to create different patterns and sizes (Figures 5–8 and 5–9).

9. Refrigerate the logs until firm.

10. Slice and bake as instructed in Vanilla Brysselkex. Like most cookies that are divided into pieces from ropes, these can be refrigerated or frozen, well wrapped, then sliced and baked as needed.

Chocolate Chip Cookies

(see photograph in color insert)
about 60 cookies

6 ounces (170 g) brown sugar
6 ounces (170 g) granulated sugar
9 ounces (255 g) softened butter
2 eggs
1 teaspoon (5 ml) vanilla extract
13 ounces (370 g) bread flour
1 teaspoon (5 g) salt
1 teaspoon (4 g) baking soda
6 ounces (170 g) chopped walnuts
12 ounces (340 g) large
   chocolate chips

1. Beat the butter and sugars together. Add the eggs and vanilla.

2. Sift the flour, salt, and baking soda together; mix into batter. Stir in walnuts and chocolate chips.

3. Divide the dough into 1-pound (455-g) pieces. Roll the pieces into ropes and cut each rope into 20 equal pieces.

4. Place the pieces, cut-side up (it is not necessary to roll the pieces round), on sheet pans lined with baking paper; stagger the cookies so they do not bake together.

5. Bake the cookies at 375°F (190°C) until just done, about 10 minutes. The cookies should still be a bit sticky in the middle and just slightly brown on the edges.

Chunky White-Chocolate-Chip Cookies

about 100 cookies

1 pound (455 g) white chocolate
14 ounces (400 g) walnuts
10 ounces (285 g) granulated
   sugar
10 ounces (285 g) brown sugar
11 ounces (310 g) softened butter
1 teaspoon (5 g) salt
4 eggs
2 teaspoons (10 ml) vanilla extract
1 pound (455 g) bread flour
1 teaspoon (4 g) baking soda

1. Chop the white chocolate and the walnuts into raisin-sized pieces and set aside.

2. Mix together the sugars, butter, and salt until well combined. Add the eggs and vanilla.

3. Sift together the flour and baking soda. Add to the butter mixture. Stir in the walnuts and white chocolate. Chill the dough if too soft to form.

4. Divide the dough into 1-pound (455-g) pieces. Roll each piece into a 20-inch (50-cm) rope; use flour as needed to prevent the dough from sticking.

5. Cut each rope into 20 pieces and place them, staggered, on sheet pans lined with baking paper.

6. Bake the cookies at 375°F (190°C) until they just start to turn color, about 10 minutes. They taste best if still somewhat soft in the center.

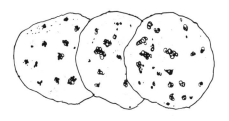

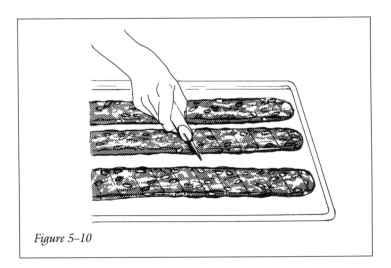

Figure 5–10

Cocoa Cuts

(see photograph in color insert)
about 60 cookies

12 ounces (340 g) softened butter
8 ounces (225 g) granulated sugar
14 ounces (400 g) bread flour
2 tablespoons (16 g) cocoa powder
¼ teaspoon (1 g) ammonium
carbonate
or
1 teaspoon (4 g) baking soda
Egg Wash (page 5)
AA confectioners' sugar
sliced almonds

1. Beat the butter and sugar until well combined.
2. Sift the flour, cocoa powder, and ammonium carbonate or baking soda together and blend into butter mixture. Mix until smooth.
3. Divide the dough into four equal pieces, about 8 ounces (225 g) each. Refrigerate the dough if necessary to make it easier to handle.
4. Roll each piece of dough into a 20-inch (50-cm) rope. Transfer the ropes to full-sized sheet pans lined with baking paper (the cookies will bake out slightly, so do not put more than three ropes on a pan if you increase the recipe).
5. Roll the ropes on the pans to make them the full length of the pan, 24 inches (60 cm). Flatten the ropes slightly using the palm of your hand.
6. Brush egg wash over the dough. Combine equal parts of confectioners' sugar and sliced almonds. Sprinkle the mixture over the cookie dough.
7. Bake at 375°F (190°C) for about 12 minutes or until baked through. Since it is harder to judge when chocolate dough is baked (because of the color), look at the almonds: when they start to turn light brown the cookies should be almost done.
8. As soon as the cookies come out of the oven, cut them, at a slight angle, into 1¼-inch (3.1-cm) strips using a metal table scraper (Figure 5–10). If you are making several pans of these cookies, stagger the baking so you will have time to cut each pan before the cookies become crisp.

Coconut Macaroons

forty 2-inch (5-cm) cookies

6 ounces (170 g) Almond Paste
  (page 4)
2 egg whites
5 ounces (140 g) butter
7 ounces (200 g) granulated sugar
12 ounces (340 g) ground coconut
  (see note 2)
3 eggs
1 pound (455 g) Short Dough
  (page 31)
6 ounces (170 g) raspberry jam
Simple Syrup (page 7)
dark baker's chocolate, melted

1. Soften the almond paste by gradually mixing in the egg whites; reserve.

2. Melt the butter in a saucepan. Add the sugar and bring to a boil.

3. Transfer to a mixing bowl and combine with the coconut. Gradually blend in the eggs and the almond paste mixture; stir until smooth. Let the batter rest for a few minutes.

4. Roll out the short dough ⅛ inch (3 mm) thick. Cut out 40 cookies using a 2-inch (5-cm) fluted cookie cutter. Place the cookies on a sheet pan lined with baking paper.

5. Place the reserved coconut mixture in a pastry bag with a no. 8 (16-mm) star tip. Pipe the coconut batter onto the short dough, holding the bag straight up above the cookies to make a star design. If the batter seems difficult to pipe or is too runny, adjust with an additional egg or extra ground coconut.

6. Make a small indentation in the top of the coconut batter. Put the raspberry jam into a piping bag and pipe it into the indentations.

7. Bake the cookies at 400°F (205°C) until the top of the coconut batter starts to brown and the short dough is golden, about 15 minutes.

8. Brush simple syrup over the pastries as soon as they come out of the oven, take care not to soak them. Let cool completely.

9. Hold on to the baked coconut topping and dip the short dough, including the top of the short dough cookie, into melted dark baker's chocolate. Allow the excess to drip back into the bowl, and place the pastries on baking paper.

10. Move the cookies on the paper once or twice before the chocolate sets up completely to remove excess chocolate. If you have trouble with this dipping method, set the cookie on top of a dipping fork as you immerse it in the chocolate to prevent it from breaking and falling in the chocolate. Store Coconut Macaroons, covered, in a cool, dry place.

NOTE 1: For a simpler version, omit dipping the cookies in chocolate and serve plain.

NOTE 2: Ground coconut, also known as macaroon coconut, is available from baking suppliers. The coconut is dried and processed to a texture similar to that of coarse polenta. If substituting flaked or shredded coconut, dry it by spreading a thin layer on a sheet pan and leaving it at room temperature for a few days. Or, dry the coconut in a very low oven, but be sure not to toast (brown) the coconut. Chop the dried coconut very fine or grind it in a food processor.

Double-Chocolate Indulgence

(see photograph in color insert)
about 80 cookies

6 ounces (170 g) cocoa block
    (bitter chocolate)
1 pound (455 g) dark chocolate
3 ounces (85 g) butter
5 eggs
14 ounces (400 g) granulated
    sugar
½ teaspoon (3 g) mocha paste
    or
2 tablespoons (30 ml)
    Coffee Reduction (page 5)
1 teaspoon (5 ml) vanilla extract
3 ounces (85 g) cake flour
2 teaspoons (8 g) baking powder
1 teaspoon (5 g) salt
1 pound (455 g) chocolate chips
6 ounces (170 g) walnuts, chopped
powdered sugar

1. Place the cocoa block and dark chocolate in a bowl with the butter. Melt together over simmering water. Reserve.

2. Whip the eggs and granulated sugar until fluffy. Add mocha paste or coffee reduction and vanilla. Mix the egg mixture into the melted chocolate.

3. Combine the flour, baking powder, salt, chocolate chips, and walnuts. Add to the chocolate and egg mixture and stir just until combined. Refrigerate the dough until it is firm enough to be handled.

4. Divide the dough into 18-ounce (510-g) pieces. Roll each piece into a rope 16 inches (40 cm) long, using powdered sugar to prevent the dough from sticking. Refrigerate the ropes until they are firm.

5. Cut each rope into 20 equal pieces. Place the cookies, cut-side down, on sheet pans lined with baking paper.

6. Bake the cookies, double-panned, at 400°F (205°C) for about 10 minutes.

Florentinas

45 cookies

Florentina Batter (recipe follows)
dark baker's chocolate, melted

1. Draw forty-five 3-inch (7.5-cm) circles on baking papers using a plain cookie cutter as a guide. Invert the papers, place them on sheet pans, and set aside while you make the batter.

2. Using two spoons, divide the batter between the circles, flattening and spreading it to within a ¼ inch (6 mm) of the drawn lines. Wet the spoons to keep the batter from sticking.

3. Bake at 375°F (190°C) for about 8 minutes, or until light brown. Stagger the baking so you will have time to trim the edges of the cookies as soon as you take each pan from the oven.

4. If the cookies are just a little uneven, place a cookie cutter that is slightly larger than the baked cookie around the cookie (not on top). Using a circular motion, push the soft cookie into a nice even round shape. If the cookies are very uneven or have spread too far beyond the lines, transfer the baking paper, with the baked cookies on it, to a piece of cardboard or an even table top. Use a 4¾-inch (11.8-cm) cookie cutter to cut out the center of the cookie to the correct size. Pull the baking paper back on the pan, let the cookies cool, then break off the excess from the outside (Figure 5–11).

Figure 5–11

5. When the cookies are cold, brush a thick layer of dark baker's chocolate on the bottom (flat) side. For the classic Florentina look, comb the chocolate into a wavy pattern using a cake-decorating comb, just before it hardens. Do not refrigerate Florentinas.

Florentina Batter

7 ounces (200 g) butter
6 ounces (170 g) granulated sugar
3 tablespoons (45 ml) glucose or
  light corn syrup
¼ cup (60 ml) heavy cream
7 ounces (200 g) sliced almonds,
  lightly crushed
2 ounces (55 g) rolled oat flakes

1. Combine the butter, sugar, glucose (or corn syrup), and cream in a saucepan; bring to a boil.

2. Add the almonds and oats and cook over medium heat for 2 to 3 minutes. Remove the batter from the heat.

3. Try baking a small piece of batter as a test. If the batter spreads out too thin, cook the batter in the saucepan a little longer. Conversely, if the batter does not spread enough, add a little more cream and test again; you will need to warm the batter to mix in the cream. Although Florentina Batter does not have to be baked immediately, it is easier to work with if spread into the desired shape as soon as possible.

Gingersnaps

120 cookies

8 ounces (225 g) softened butter
1 pound, 6 ounces (625 g)
    granulated sugar
3 eggs
1 cup (240 ml) molasses
2 tablespoons (30 ml) vinegar
1 pound, 12 ounces (795 g)
    bread flour
2 tablespoons (24 g) baking soda
4 teaspoons (8 g) ground ginger
1 teaspoon (1.5 g) ground
    cinnamon
1 teaspoon (2 g) ground cloves
1 teaspoon (2 g) ground cardamom
granulated sugar

1. Beat butter and measured sugar until well combined. Incorporate eggs, molasses, and vinegar.

2. Sift together the flour, baking soda, ginger, cinnamon, cloves, and cardamom. Add to the butter mixture and mix just until combined. Refrigerate.

3. Divide dough into four 18-ounce (510-g) pieces. Roll each piece into a rope and cut each rope into 30 pieces.

4. Form the pieces into round balls, and roll the balls in granulated sugar to cover. Place the cookies on sheet pans lined with baking paper.

5. Bake at 375°F (190°C) until light brown on top but still soft in the center, approximately 10 minutes.

NOTE: These cookies freeze well. Bake the formed cookies directly from the freezer without thawing.

Hazelnut Butter Cookies

(see photograph in color insert)
110 cookies

1 pound, 5 ounces (595 g)
    softened butter
11 ounces (310 g) granulated
    sugar
12 ounces (340 g) hazelnuts,
    finely ground
1 pound, 5 ounces (595 g)
    bread flour
½ teaspoon (2 g) baking soda
whole hazelnuts, lightly roasted,
    skins removed

1. Mix the butter and sugar. Add the nuts.

2. Sift the flour with the baking soda. Blend it into the butter mixture, mixing only until just combined. Refrigerate the dough if necessary.

3. Divide the dough into three pieces (this can be done by eye; it need not be exact), and roll each piece into a rope 1½ inches (3.7 cm) in diameter. Refrigerate the ropes until firm.

4. Slice the ropes into ⅜-inch (9-mm) cookies. Place the cookies, staggered, on sheet pans lined with baking paper. Leave the cookies until they are fairly soft.

5. Push a hazelnut, point up, into the center of each cookie. Push the nut all the way to the sheet pan so it will not fall off after the cookies are baked (if you try to do this while the dough is still firm the cookies will crack).

6. Bake at 375°F (190°C) for about 12 minutes, or until the cookies are golden brown. Store the cookies in airtight containers to prevent softening.

NOTE 1: Be sure to press the hazelnuts all the way to the bottom of the pan or they will bake loose in the oven and the nuts will fall off. I got into a little trouble with these cookies myself as an apprentice. My boss told me that half of the cookies in the showcase had just an empty hole. He told me to "push the nuts down firmly," so I did. A few days later it was the same story all over again, except this time, naturally, my boss was a bit angry. Since I knew for certain that I pressed those nuts down all the way to the metal (yes, I'm afraid there was no baking paper way back then), I got a little suspicious and decided to conduct an investigation. The next time I made the cookies I walked up to the shop a few moments after the prep girl had picked up the tray and peeked around the corner. Sure enough, she was picking the nuts off the cookies and eating them as fast as she could chew!

NOTE 2: This recipe can be made with walnuts, cashews, or pecans; you can also combine different types of nuts.

Hazelnut Squares

(see photograph in color insert)
ninety-six 2-inch (5-cm) cookies

15 ounces (430 g) granulated
    sugar
10 ounces (285 g) softened butter
3 eggs
1 teaspoon (5 ml) vanilla extract
8 ounces (225 g) bread flour
2 tablespoons (16 g) cocoa powder
1 tablespoon (12 g) baking powder
6 ounces (170 g) roasted hazelnuts,
    skins removed
1½ ounces (40 g) unroasted
    hazelnuts, coarsely crushed

1. Beat the sugar and butter until light and creamy. Add the eggs and vanilla.

2. Sift the flour, cocoa powder, and baking powder together. Mix into the batter.

3. Coarsely crush the roasted hazelnuts and add them to the batter.

4. Spread the batter evenly over a 24- × 16-inch (60- × 40-cm) baking paper. You will have to spread back and forth a few extra times to fill in the lines made by the crushed nuts as you drag them across: Sprinkle the unroasted hazelnuts over the batter.

5. Drag the baking paper onto a sheet pan (see Figure 15–3, page 422).

6. Bake at 375°F (190°C) for about 20 minutes. When the hazelnuts start to brown the cookies are done.

7. Cut the sheet into 2-inch (5-cm) squares as soon as it comes out of the oven. Store the cookies in airtight containers so that they remain crisp.

Heide Sand Cookies

(see photograph in color insert)
about 75 cookies

1 pound, 10 ounces (740 g)
    bread flour
7 ounces (200 g) powdered sugar
1 pound, 5 ounces (595 g)
    softened butter
a few drops of lemon juice
½ teaspoon (2.5 ml)
    vanilla extract
pale pink decorating sugar
8 ounces (225 g) smooth
    apricot jam

1. Sift the bread flour with the powdered sugar. Place in a mixing bowl with the butter, lemon juice, and vanilla. Mix at low speed until smooth. Refrigerate the dough if necessary to make it easier to handle.

2. Divide the dough into three pieces, about 17 ounces (485 g) each. Roll the pieces into ropes 2½ inches (6.2 cm) thick, pressing the dough together to compact it. Do not use any flour as you roll because it will prevent the colored sugar from sticking.

3. Place the ropes in the colored sugar and roll them to 2 inches (5 cm) in diameter. Remove ropes from the sugar.

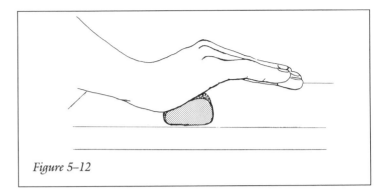

Figure 5–12

4. Using the palm of your hand, flatten the side nearest you to form a smooth teardrop shape (Figure 5–12). Refrigerate the ropes until firm.

5. Cut the ropes into ⅜-inch (9-mm) slices. Arrange the pieces on sheet pans lined with baking paper. Let the cookie slices sit until softened.

6. Make an indentation in the wider part of the cookies and fill it with apricot jam.

7. Bake at 375°F (190°C) for about 15 minutes or until the cookies are golden brown. Store the baked cookies in airtight containers to keep them crisp. You can store the dough, formed into ropes, in the freezer, or for 1 week in the refrigerator to bake as needed; but do not roll in decorating sugar before they are to be made up.

Ladyfingers

about one hundred and eighty 2-inch (5-cm) cookies

3 ounces (85 g) cornstarch
4 ounces (115 g) bread flour
6 eggs, separated
6 ounces (170 g) granulated sugar
a few drops of Tartaric Acid Solution (page 596) or lemon juice

1. Sift together the cornstarch and bread flour (with cocoa powder if used), and reserve.

2. Whip the egg yolks with 2 ounces (55 g) of the sugar until they are light and creamy; reserve.

3. Add 2 ounces (55 g) of the remaining sugar, along with the tartaric acid or lemon juice, to the egg whites. Whip the egg white mixture until foamy and tripled in volume, about 2 minutes.

4. Gradually add the last 2 ounces (55 g) of sugar and whip to stiff peaks.

5. Fold in the reserved egg yolk and sugar mixture, and then fold in the flour and cornstarch mixture.

6. Place the batter in a pastry bag with a no. 5 (10-mm) plain tip. Pipe 2-inch-long (5-cm) cookies onto sheet pans lined with baking paper.

7. Bake at 425°F (219°C) for about 8 minutes or until golden brown. Ladyfingers will keep for weeks if stored in a dry place.

Variation:
Chocolate Ladyfingers

Delete 1 ounce (30 g) of the cornstarch and replace with 1 ounce (30 g) of cocoa powder.

Macadamia Nut Cookies

96 cookies

14 ounces (400 g) granulated
   sugar
3 ounces (85 g) brown sugar
12 ounces (340 g) softened butter
3 eggs
1 teaspoon (5 ml) vanilla extract
1 pound, 3 ounces (540 g)
   bread flour
½ teaspoon (2 g) baking soda
9 ounces (255 g) chopped
   macadamia nuts
9 ounces (255 g) shredded coconut

1. Cream the granulated sugar, brown sugar, and butter until light and fluffy. Mix in eggs and vanilla.

2. Sift the flour with baking soda and incorporate into the batter together with the nuts and coconut.

3. Divide the dough into four equal pieces. Roll each piece into a rope 2 inches (5 cm) thick.

4. Cut each rope into 24 equal pieces. Stagger the pieces on sheet pans lined with baking paper.

5. Bake at 375°F (190°C) until the cookies are just starting to color at the edges, about 12 minutes. Like Chocolate Chip Cookies, these cookies taste best if they are a little chewy.

Variation: Pine Nut Cookies

Replace the macadamia nuts with whole roasted pine nuts.

Oat Flakes

one hundred 2½-inch (6.2-cm) cookies

9 ounces (255 g) melted butter
8 ounces (225 g) rolled oats
3 eggs
12 ounces (340 g) granulated
   sugar
1 ounce (30 g) bread flour
3 tablespoons (36 g) baking powder
dark baker's chocolate, melted

This cookie batter should be made the day before it is used to allow the oats time to absorb moisture.

1. Combine the butter and oats. Blend in the eggs and sugar. Mix the flour and baking soda together; then incorporate into the batter. Refrigerate overnight.

2. Place the batter in a pastry bag with a no. 6 (12-mm) plain tip. Pipe into cherry-sized cookies on sheet pans lined with baking paper. Do not crowd the cookies because they will spread out quite a bit.

3. Bake at 375°F (190°C) for about 8 minutes. The whole surface of the cookies should be golden brown, not just the edges.

4. When the cookies have cooled completely, brush melted dark baker's chocolate on the back. For a variation, you can sandwich two cookies together before the chocolate hardens. Store the cookies in an airtight container; they become soft easily.

Orange Macaroons

96 cookies

1 pound, 8 ounces (680 g)
    blanched almonds, skins removed
1 pound, 6 ounces (625 g)
    granulated sugar
11 ounces (310 g) Candied
    Orange Peel (page 520)
1 pound, 6 ounces (625 g)
    powdered sugar
4 ounces (115 g) bread flour
½ teaspoon (2.5 ml) orange
    flower water
8 egg whites
powdered sugar
whole almonds with skin

1. Grind the blanched almonds and granulated sugar to a coarse consistency. Add orange peel and continue grinding to a very fine consistency; transfer to a mixing bowl.

2. Add the measured powdered sugar, flour, orange water, and egg whites; blend until all ingredients are incorporated.

3. Divide the dough into six equal pieces. Roll each piece into a rope 16 inches (40 cm) long, using powdered sugar to prevent the dough from sticking.

4. Cut each rope into 16 pieces. Roll the small pieces into balls, then roll the balls in powdered sugar to coat them completely. Place on sheet pans lined with baking paper.

5. Flatten the cookies just enough so that they do not roll. Press a whole almond on top, in the center of each cookie.

6. Bake at 325°F (163°C) for approximately 12 minutes, or until very lightly browned. When cold, store covered to prevent the macaroons from drying out.

NOTE: It is a good idea to bake a few test cookies to make sure they spread out properly before rolling all of the dough. They should spread out flat like Chocolate Chip Cookies. If the cookies do not spread out enough, add more egg white; if they spread too thin, add a small amount of flour.

Palm Leaves

forty-five 3-inch (7.5-cm) cookies

2 pounds (910 g) Classic Puff
    Paste (page 21)
8 ounces (225 g) granulated
    sugar, approximately
dark baker's chocolate, optional
Vanilla Buttercream, optional
    (page 501)

1. Roll out puff paste in the granulated sugar to a 24- × 12-inch (60- × 30-cm) rectangle about ⅛ inch (3 mm) thick. If the dough is uneven or too large on any side, trim it to the proper dimensions. Keep turning and moving the dough as you roll it out, spreading the sugar evenly underneath and on top of the puff paste at the same time. The sugar is not only taking the place of flour to prevent the dough from sticking, but also makes the Palm Leaves crisp, shiny, and sweet, as the sugar caramelizes while the cookies are baking. You may not use up all the sugar in the recipe, but the more sugar you can roll into the puff paste, the better.

2. Place the dough in front of you horizontally. Fold the long sides of the rectangle in to meet in the center.

3. Fold the dough in half in the opposite direction (crosswise) to bring the two short sides together at the right side.

4. Using a dowel about 1 inch (2.5 cm) in diameter, make a deep indentation horizontally down the center of the folded dough; fold in half again on this line (the indentation makes it possible to fold the dough again and still have the edges line up squarely). Refrigerate the strip until firm.

5. Cut the folded strip into slices ⅛ inch (3 mm) thick (Figure 5–13) and place the slices, cut-side up, on sheet pans lined with

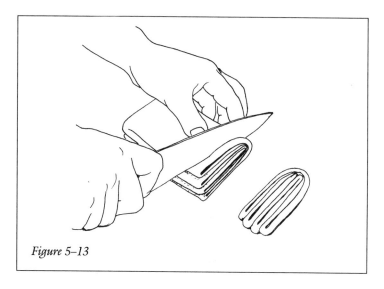

Figure 5–13

baking paper. Keep in mind as you place them on the pans that they will spread to about three times as wide while baking.

6. Bake at 425°F (219°C) until the sugar starts to caramelize and turn golden on the bottoms, about 8 minutes.

7. Remove the pan from the oven and quickly turn each cookie over on the pan using a spatula or metal scraper. Return the cookies to the oven and bake for a few minutes longer or until as much sugar as possible has caramelized on the tops. Let the cookies cool.

NOTE: Palm Leaves can be served as is, or you can dip the tip of each cookie into melted dark baker's chocolate. Two cookies (with or without chocolate) can also be sandwiched together with buttercream.

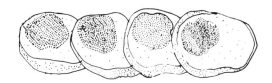

Peanut Butter Cookies

60 cookies

8 ounces (225 g) softened butter
8 ounces (225 g) granulated sugar
6 ounces (170 g) brown sugar
9 ounces (255 g) chunky
*　　peanut butter*
2 eggs
2 teaspoons (10 ml) vanilla extract
13 ounces (370 g) bread flour
4 teaspoons (16 g) baking powder
½ teaspoon (3 g) salt
2 ounces (55 g) dark chocolate,
*　　grated*
4 ounces (115 g) roasted peanuts,
*　　coarsely chopped*

1. Cream the butter, both sugars, and the peanut butter until fluffy. Add the eggs and vanilla extract.
2. Sift together the bread flour, baking powder, and salt. Add to the butter mixture along with the chocolate and peanuts. Chill the dough until firm.
3. Divide the dough into three equal pieces, about 18 ounces (510 g) each. Roll each piece into a rope and cut the ropes into 20 pieces each.
4. Place the small pieces on sheet pans lined with baking paper. Flatten each cookie with a fork.
5. Bake at 375°F (190°C) for about 10 minutes.

Pirouettes

(see photograph in color insert)
about eighty 3-inch (7.5-cm)
cookies

8 ounces (225 g) granulated sugar
3½ ounces (100 g) cake flour
½ cup (120 ml) heavy cream
½ teaspoon (2.5 ml) vanilla
*　　extract*
4 egg whites, at room temperature
4 ounces (115 g) melted butter
cocoa powder, optional

1. Combine 2 ounces (55 g) of the sugar with the flour. Gradually add the cream and vanilla, and mix until smooth. Set aside to rest for about 30 minutes.
2. While the batter is resting, make a round 3-inch (7.5-cm) template from paper that is ⅟₁₆ inch (2 mm) thick. Grease and flour the back of (inverted) even sheet pans.
3. Whip the egg whites to a foam. Gradually add the remaining 6 ounces (170 g) of sugar and whip to soft peaks. Fold the reserved batter into the egg whites. Fold in the melted butter.
4. Using the template, spread out thin wafers on the prepared sheet pans (see method shown for Figures 18–47 and 18–48, page 548).
5. Bake at 400°F (205°C) until light brown in a few spots (this will ensure that the cookies are cooked enough to become crisp when cold), about 5 minutes.
6. Immediately roll the hot wafers around a dowel just large enough in diameter to allow the ends of the wafer to meet and overlap very slightly. Press the edges together to make them stick.
7. Push each finished Pirouette to the opposite end of the dowel and leave it there until firm. Continue forming the remaining wafers in the same way. If the cookies become too brittle to bend easily, reheat until soft. Store the Pirouettes in airtight containers so they do not become soft.

NOTE: Pirouettes can be served either plain or with the ends dipped in melted baker's chocolate. They also can be filled and served as a pastry. Also, a portion of the batter may be colored with cocoa powder at the rate of ½ teaspoon (2 g) per 1 ounce (30 g) of batter. Use a piping bag to decorate the cookies with spirals or parallel lines. Bake as directed. Roll the striped cookies so the parallel lines run diagonally rather than horizontally or vertically.

Raisin Brownies

one 16- × 12-inch (40- × 30-cm) sheet

14 ounces (400 g) walnuts
1 pound, 8 ounces (680 g) dark chocolate
1 pound (455 g) butter
1 pound, 12 ounces (795 g) granulated sugar
8 eggs
1 teaspoon (5 ml) vanilla extract
1 pound (455 g) bread flour
½ teaspoon (2 g) baking powder
6 ounces (170 g) dark raisins

1. Chop the walnuts into raisin-sized pieces. Set aside.
2. Cut the chocolate into chunks, place in a bowl with the butter, and melt together over simmering water. Set aside to cool.
3. Line the bottom of a half-sheet-pan (16 × 12 inches/ 40 × 30 cm) with baking paper.
4. Whip sugar, eggs, and vanilla until light and fluffy. Fold into cooled chocolate mixture.
5. Sift the flour with baking powder and add to the chocolate. Add 12 ounces (340 g) of the walnuts and the raisins.
6. Spread the batter evenly in the prepared pan. Sprinkle the remaining 2 ounces (55 g) of walnuts over the top.
7. Bake at 400°F (205°C) for about 30 minutes or until the cake is completely set, but still slightly soft. Cool and slice into pieces of the desired size.

Raisin Oatmeal Cookies

100 cookies

1 pound, 3 ounces (540 g) softened butter
12 ounces (340 g) granulated sugar
9 ounces (255 g) dark raisins
8 ounces (225 g) rolled oats
1 teaspoon (5 ml) vanilla extract
1 teaspoon (4 g) baking soda
1 pound, 5 ounces (595 g) bread flour

1. Beat the butter and sugar together lightly. Add the raisins, rolled oats, and vanilla; mix until combined.
2. Sift the baking soda with flour; mix into the batter. Refrigerate the dough if necessary.
3. Divide the dough into four equal pieces, about 17 ounces (485 g) each. Roll each piece into a rope 16 inches (40 cm) long. Refrigerate the ropes until firm.
4. Cut each rope into 25 pieces. To save time, place all the ropes together and cut them simultaneously.
5. Place the slices, cut side down, on sheet pans lined with baking paper. Stagger the pieces so that the cookies do not bake together. Use a fork to flatten and mark the cookies.
6. Bake at 375°F (190°C) until golden brown, about 15 minutes. Keep the baked cookies in airtight containers to prevent them from getting soft.

Raspberry Turnovers

24 cookies

1 pound, 2 ounces (510 g)
   Short Dough (page 31)
5 ounces (140 g) raspberry jam
Egg Wash (page 5)
AA confectioners' sugar
sliced almonds, crushed

1. Roll out the short dough ⅛ inch (3 mm) thick. Cut out twenty-four cookies using a 3-inch (7.5-cm) fluted cookie cutter.

2. Place the jam in a disposable pastry bag made from a half sheet of baking paper (see page 505). Pipe raspberry jam onto each circle, slightly off center and toward you, dividing it evenly between the cookies. Brush egg wash on the lower edge. Fold the top over the jam and onto the lower half. Press the edges together with your fingers.

3. Combine equal parts of sugar and almonds. Brush the tops of the turnovers with egg wash, then invert them into the almond and sugar mixture. Be sure not to get any egg wash or sugar on the bottoms of the turnovers or it will burn. Place the turnovers right-side up, on sheet pans lined with baking paper.

4. Bake at 375°F (190°C) until golden brown, about 10 minutes.

NOTE: Use short dough that has not been rolled out too many times before; the dough will break if too much flour has been mixed into it. The jam should be fairly thick so it will not run out when you pipe it. Because raspberry jam gets rubbery after one day, the turnovers should be served the same day they are baked. Raspberry Turnovers can be made up in large batches and stored in the refrigerator or freezer. Bake as needed directly from the freezer.

Spritz Rings

(see photograph in color insert)
about 110 cookies

1 pound, 5 ounces (595 g) butter,
   at room temperature
10 ounces (285 g) powdered sugar
3 egg yolks
1 teaspoon (5 ml) vanilla extract
1 pound, 11 ounces (765 g)
   bread flour
raspberry jam, optional

1. The butter must be quite soft or you will have trouble piping out the dough. Beat butter with sugar for a few minutes. Mix in yolks and vanilla. Add flour and mix until you have a smooth, pliable dough.

2. Place the dough in a pastry bag with a no. 4 (8-mm) star tip. Do not put too much dough in the bag at one time or it will be much more difficult to pipe out. Pipe out 2-inch (5-cm) rings, or 2½-inch (6.2-cm) S shapes, on sheet pans lined with baking paper. If you make S shapes, the ends should curl in and close.

3. Make an indentation in the curled parts of the S and pipe in a small amount of raspberry jam.

4. Bake at 375°F (190°C) until golden brown, about 15 minutes. Store Spritz Rings in airtight containers to keep them crisp.

Strassburger Cookies

about 80 cookies

1 pound, 8 ounces (680 g)
  softened butter
1 pound (455 g) powdered sugar
6 eggs
3 egg yolks
2 teaspoons (10 ml) vanilla extract
2 pounds, 8 ounces (1 kg, 135 g)
  cake flour
2 teaspoons (4 g) ground
  cardamom
melted dark baker's chocolate

This is one of the most common cookies found in Europe, and also one of the most versatile. Strassburger Cookies can be piped out in an array of different shapes, and two cookies may be sandwiched together with jam or another filling before they are dipped in chocolate.

1. Beat butter and sugar until light and creamy, approximately 5 minutes. Mix in eggs and egg yolks a few at a time. Add vanilla extract. Add flour and cardamom and stir until well combined.

2. Place the cookie dough (a portion at a time) in a pastry bag with a no. 6 (12-mm) star tip. Pipe out in one of the following shapes onto sheet pans lined with baking paper. (Attach the baking paper to the sheet pan using a pea-size piece of dough in each corner to keep the paper from moving as you pipe.)

3. Bake at 375°F (190°C) for approximately 12 minutes.

Pleated ribbons

Pipe the cookies in 3½-inch (8.7-cm) flattened ribbons, holding the pastry bag close to the sheet pan so that the width of the dough is piped out flatter than the width of the tip. As you pipe, wiggle the tip back and forth a little so the dough forms pleats, or gathers. Bake and cool the cookies, then dip one half into melted chocolate.

Horseshoes

Pipe 3-inch (7.5-cm) lengths bent in a half circle. Bake and cool, then dip both ends into melted chocolate.

Cones

Pipe out 2½-inch (6.2-cm) long cone-shaped cookies (wider at the top and narrowing down to a point at the bottom), following the example in Figure 9–23 on page 261. Bake and cool, then dip the tips of the cookies into melted chocolate.

Variation: Cocoa Strassburger Cookies

Replace 2 ounces (55 g) of cake flour with cocoa powder.

Tarts

Apple Tart Parisienne

Chocolate Pine Nut Tart

Clafoutis with Cherries

Cointreau Tart with Apple,
   Pear, or Rhubarb

Kiwi Tart

Mandarin Tart with Armagnac

Pecan-Whiskey Tart

Raspberry-Lemon Tart

Strawberry-Rhubarb Tart

Swedish Hazelnut Tart

Tart Hollandaise

Tart Tatin

Walnut-Caramel Tart

*I*t *is a common misconception* that a tart is a European type of pie, or nothing more than a pie with a fancy name. Pies and tarts do have some similarities: they are both made of a crust and a filling, and they are usually baked in a metal tin. However, the baking pan itself sets the two apart: Tart pans are not as deep as pie pans, so they hold less, they have almost straight sides, the sides are usually fluted, and the pans have no lip. A tart is removed in one piece from the baking pan. A pie, on the other hand, is cut and served from the baking pan; it cannot be unmolded because of its fragile crust and large, mounded filling. Since a pie will fall apart if you try to take it out of the pan whole, pie pans have slanted sides to make serving easier. In most cases a pie is made with a double crust, and a tart with a single, but actually both can be made either way.

The tart pan most often used professionally is an 11-inch (27.5-cm) round, but tarts are also made in square or rectangular shapes. Tart pans can be one solid piece or two-piece "false-bottom" pans; the latter make removing the baked tart easy. The tart pan is usually lined with a short-type dough (pie dough or puff paste is used for some recipes).

Since a tart pan is only about 1 inch (2.5 cm) deep, the dough should not be rolled out any thicker than ⅛ inch (3 mm) to allow sufficient space for the filling. The shells are sometimes "baked blind," which means that the shell is lined with baking paper or aluminum foil, filled with dried beans or pie weights to prevent the dough from puffing or distorting, and fully or partially baked, depending on the filling used. As a rule, the less time it takes to bake the filling, the longer the shells need to be prebaked.

In the case of a custard filling, the shells must be completely baked through before the custard is added, even though they will go back in the oven later, since the custard is baked at such a low temperature. For tarts that are assembled and finished in a completely baked crust, you may want to "waterproof" the crust by coating the inside with a thin film of apricot glaze or melted baker's chocolate. A thin layer of sponge cake or some leftover ladyfingers can also be placed in the bottom to absorb excess juices from fruits or moisture from the filling.

When making tarts with pie dough or puff paste allow a sufficient amount of resting time before baking the shells to keep the crust from shrinking. With short dough the beans or weights are not used to prevent puffing, but to keep the sides straight. If you want the sides absolutely straight, do not use any baking paper so the beans will come in contact with the dough (you can put a circle of paper in the bottom only). However, the beans tend to stick to the crust, so you must carefully pick them out with a fork.

If you need to freeze unbaked tart shells, you can either store them frozen in the pans, or freeze them in the pans and then remove the shells once they are solid. In either case, if they are properly covered, they can be frozen for 4 to 6 weeks.

To remove a tart from a false-bottom tart pan, first make sure the sides are not stuck anywhere. Use the tip of a pairing knife, if needed, to loosen the edge, but never run the knife around the sides. Remove the fluted ring. Run a thin knife all around between the crust and the metal bottom, then slide the tart onto a serving platter or piece of cardboard; do not attempt to lift it. If you use a one-piece pan, treat the sides in the same manner, then place a piece of cardboard over the top, hold the tart with both hands, invert it to unmold, place your serving platter or more cardboard on top (which is the bottom of the tart), and invert it again. With either type of pan the dough has a tendency to stick when cold, and the butter acts as a sort of glue. To remedy this, place a hot sheet pan, or hot damp towels, on the outside of the pan to warm it up and help loosen the crust.

In addition to being delicious, a freshly made tart looks beautiful, arranged perhaps with colorful, glazed fruit shining on top. A tart is elegant, which makes it appropriate for almost any occasion: as a luncheon dessert, as one of the selections on a buffet (where a fruit tart not only adds color but offers a choice for the customer who wants something light), or even after dinner, perhaps dressed up with a sauce and decoration. With the exception of custard fillings, which should be chilled, a tart may be served warm or at room temperature, but should never be served cold.

Apple Tart Parisienne

two 11-inch (27.5-cm) tarts

1 pound, 2 ounces (510 g)
*   Short Dough (page 31)*
8 medium-sized apples (Granny
*   Smith or pippin)*
2 ounces (55 g) butter
3 ounces (85 g) granulated sugar
4 ounces (115 g) smooth
*   apricot jam*
Calvados Custard (recipe follows)
Cinnamon Sugar (page 4)
powdered sugar
Crème Fraîche (page 559)
fanned strawberry halves

1. Roll short dough to ⅛ inch (3 mm) thick, and use it to line two 11-inch (27.5-cm) tart pans (see Figure 2–11, page 33). Line with baking paper, then fill with dried beans or pie weights (see note).

2. Bake at 400°F (205°C) for about 12 minutes or until dough is set, but not colored; do not use a double pan. Set the shells aside to cool.

3. Peel, core, and cut the apples into 10 wedges each. Sauté the apples in a skillet with the sugar and butter over medium heat, until they begin to soften. Reserve.

4. Remove the dried beans or pie weights from the cooled tart shells.

5. Divide the apricot jam between the shells and spread over the bottom. Arrange the apple wedges in concentric circles on top of the jam. Pour Calvados Custard over the apples. Sprinkle lightly with cinnamon sugar.

6. Bake the tarts at 350°F (175°C) for about 35 minutes or until custard is set.

7. Let the tarts cool, then sift powdered sugar over the tops. Place the tarts under a salamander or hot broiler just long enough to caramelize the sugar on the apples. Be careful not to over-brown. Cut the tarts into the desired number of servings.

8. Presentation: Place a slice of tart, off center, on a dessert plate. Spoon a small amount of crème fraîche in front of the slice, and place a fanned strawberry on the plate behind the tart.

NOTE: Although it usually is not necessary to use dried beans or pie weights with short dough, in this recipe you want to make sure the sides do not settle during the prebaking, or you will risk having the custard run between the crust and the pan.

Calvados Custard

about 5 cups (1 l, 200 ml) custard

3 ounces (85 g) bread flour
7 ounces (200 g) granulated sugar
6 eggs
2½ cups (600 ml) half-and-half
1 vanilla bean, split
*   or*
1 teaspoon (5 ml) vanilla extract
2 ounces (60 ml) calvados

1. Combine the flour and sugar. Mix in the eggs and stir to a smooth paste.

2. Scald the half-and-half with vanilla bean, if used. Remove the bean and add calvados and vanilla extract, if used.

3. Gradually whisk half-and-half into the egg mixture.

Chocolate Pine Nut Tart

two 11-inch (27.5-cm) tarts

1 pound, 2 ounces (510 g)
   Short Dough (page 31)
12 ounces (340 g) dark chocolate
3 ounces (85 g) cocoa block
   (bitter chocolate)
8 ounces (225 g) butter
grated rind of 2 oranges
6 ounces (170 g) roasted pine nuts
6 ounces (170 g) granulated sugar
6 egg yolks
¼ cup (60 ml) orange liqueur
5 egg whites
1 teaspoon (5 g) salt
4 ounces (115 g) apricot jam
8 ounces (225 g) Ganache
   (page 567)
1 cup (240 ml) heavy cream
2 teaspoons (10 g) granulated
   sugar
Orange Sauce (page 561)
Chocolate Sauce for Piping
   (page 560)

1. Roll out the short dough ⅛ inch (3 mm) thick and use it to line two 11-inch (27.5-cm) tart pans (see Figure 2–11, page 33). Reserve in the refrigerator.

2. Place dark chocolate, cocoa block, butter, and orange rind in a bowl. Melt together over simmering water. Set aside but keep warm.

3. Reserve 2 ounces (55 g) of the pine nuts for garnish. Grind the remainder with 3 ounces (85 g) of the sugar to a fine flour-like consistency (be careful not to grind beyond this point or you will get an oily paste).

4. Whip the yolks to the ribbon stage. Add the orange liqueur.

5. Whip the egg whites and the salt to a foam. Gradually add the remaining 3 ounces (85 g) of sugar and whip to soft peaks. Do not overwhip or the additional air will cause the tart to crack while baking.

6. Combine the nut mixture with the chocolate. Add the egg yolks, then carefully fold in the egg whites.

7. Spread the apricot jam over the bottom of the two lined pans. Divide the chocolate filling between them.

8. Bake at 350°F (175°C) for approximately 35 minutes. Let the tarts cool.

9. Carefully remove the tarts from the pans. Warm the ganache until it is melted and liquid, then spread it quickly over the top of the tarts. Before it starts to set up, sprinkle the reserved pine nuts on top. Chill briefly to set the ganache.

10. Slice the tarts into the desired number of pieces. Whip the heavy cream with the 2 teaspoons (10 g) of sugar to stiff peaks. Place in a pastry bag with a no. 7 (14-mm) star tip and reserve in the refrigerator.

11. Presentation: Pour a round pool of Orange Sauce on one side of a dessert plate. Pipe a pea-sized dot of whipped cream on the opposite side of the plate, and set a tart slice on the whipped cream (to prevent it from sliding) so the tip is in the sauce. Pipe a large rosette of whipped cream at the wide end of the tart. Decorate the Orange Sauce with the Chocolate Sauce for Piping as shown on pages 518 and 519.

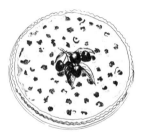

Clafoutis with Cherries

(see photograph in color insert)
two 11-inch (27.5-cm) tarts

1 pound, 2 ounces (510 g)
  Short Dough (page 31)
1 ounce (30 g) flour
12 ounces (340 g) granulated
  sugar
8 eggs
1 cup (240 ml) heavy cream
12 ounces (360 ml) milk
1 pound, 4 ounces (570 g) cherries,
  pitted and halved
Romanoff Sauce (page 563)
whole cherries with stems

Clafoutis is actually a type of fruit pancake and does not normally have a short dough crust. I have added a crust to make it more practical to cut and serve, and to improve the taste. While cherries are the most commonly used fruit for clafoutis, other fruits that are suitable for baking, such as apricots, blueberries, or plums, can be substituted.

1. Roll out the short dough ⅛ inch (3 mm) thick and use it to line two 11-inch (27.5-cm) tart pans (see Figure 2–11, page 33). Prick the dough lightly and place a piece of baking paper over the pastry.

2. Fill with dried beans or pie weights, and prebake at 375°F (190°C) for approximately 10 minutes. Remove the paper and the dried beans or pie weights and continue to bake about 2 minutes longer. The dough should be set and golden, but not browned.

3. Combine the flour and sugar, then add the eggs and cream.

4. Scald the milk, then gradually whisk the hot milk into the first mixture. Reserve.

5. Divide the cherries between the two tarts, arranging them cut-side up on top of the crust. Pour the custard over the cherries. (See note.)

6. Bake the tarts at 350°F (175°C) for approximately 30 minutes or until the custard is set. Cool at room temperature.

7. Remove the tarts from the pans and cut into the desired number of serving pieces, using a serrated knife to cut through the cherries.

8. Presentation: Place a slice of clafoutis on a dessert plate. Pour Romanoff Sauce over one-third of the tart on the narrow end. Set two or three whole cherries next to the slice. Serve at room temperature.

NOTE: It is best to place the tart shells next to the oven before you pour in the custard, so you will be moving them as little as possible. If the custard runs between the crust and the pan, the tarts will be difficult to remove later. One method that works well is to fill the shells only part way with custard, set them in the oven, then "top off" with the remaining custard. Since all custards shrink as they are baked, the tarts should be filled as close to the top as practical without overflowing.

Cointreau Tart with Apple, Pear, or Rhubarb

two 11-inch (27.5-cm) tarts

1 pound, 2 ounces (510 g)
* Short Dough (page 31)*
apples, pears, or rhubarb
1 recipe Cointreau Custard
* (recipe follows)*
Cinnamon Sugar (page 4), for
* apples and pears; granulated*
* sugar for rhubarb*
Apricot or Pectin Glaze (page 526)
whipped cream, optional

For the crust

1. Line two 11-inch (27.5-cm) false-bottom tart pans with short dough, rolled ⅛ inch (3 mm) thick (see Figure 2–11, page 33). Prick the dough lightly with a fork, place a piece of baking paper in the bottom, and fill with dried beans or pie weights.

2. Bake at 375°F (190°C) just until golden, about 12 minutes. Let cool, then remove the paper and the weights.

For an apple or pear tart

1. Peel and core the apples or pears; place them in acidulated water. If they are not quite ripe enough, poach for a few minutes to soften them up (use Poaching Syrup II, page 6).

2. When you are ready to assemble the tarts, cut each apple or pear in half lengthwise, then cut crosswise into thin slices. Divide the Cointreau Custard evenly between the two shells; it should fill each halfway. Arrange the sliced fruit in concentric circles over the custard, starting at the outside edge. Sprinkle cinnamon sugar on top over two or three circles of the fruit.

3. Bake at 350°F (175°C) until the custard is set, about 30 minutes.

4. When the tarts have cooled enough so that they will not break when you handle them, remove them from the pans and glaze with apricot or pectin glaze. Slice and serve at room temperature. If you like, pipe whipped cream at the edge of each slice.

For a rhubarb tart

1. Cut the stalks into 2-inch × ½-inch (5-cm × 1.2-cm) pieces. Place them in a stainless steel or other noncorrosive pan, and sprinkle granulated sugar on top to draw out some of the juice.

2. Steam covered at 375°F (190°C) until slightly softened, about 8 minutes. If overcooked, the rhubarb will turn into a purée.

3. Place the rhubarb on the custard and proceed as in apple or pear tart, but use granulated sugar instead of cinnamon sugar on top.

Cointreau Custard

3¼ cups (780 ml) custard

10 egg yolks
6½ ounces (185 g) granulated
* sugar*
3⅓ cups (800 ml) heavy cream
3 tablespoons (45 ml) Cointreau

1. Beat egg yolks and sugar by hand for a few seconds, just enough to combine.

2. Add cream and Cointreau, and blend thoroughly.

Kiwi Tart

two 11-inch (27.5-cm) tarts

1 pound, 2 ounces (510 g)
Short Dough (page 31)
1 recipe Cointreau Custard
(page 148)
4 kiwis, peeled and sliced crosswise
20 strawberries, approximately,
cut in half lengthwise
Apricot Glaze (page 526)

1. Line two 11-inch (27.5-cm) false-bottom tart pans with short dough rolled ⅛ inch (3 mm) thick (see Figure 2–11, page 33). Line with baking paper, then fill with dried beans or pie weights.

2. Bake at 375°F (190°C) to a light golden color, about 12 minutes. Cool at room temperature, then remove paper and weights.

3. Divide the Cointreau Custard equally between the two tart shells. Bake at 350°F (175°C) until the custard is set, 30 to 35 minutes.

4. When the tarts are cool to the touch, remove them from the pans. Arrange sliced kiwis in the center and the strawberries around the edge. Brush with apricot glaze. Cut the tarts into the desired number of slices.

Mandarin Tart with Armagnac

two 11-inch (27.5-cm) tarts

⅓ recipe Almond Sponge batter
(page 162)
1 pound, 8 ounces (680 g)
Hazelnut Short Dough
(page 31)
1 recipe Red Currant Glaze
(page 527)
1 pound, 8 ounces (680 g)
Pastry Cream (page 569)
¼ cup (60 ml) Armagnac
6 tablespoons (90 ml) mandarin
or orange juice
10 seedless mandarins,
approximately
Raspberry Sauce (page 563)
Sour Cream Mixture for Piping
(page 564)

1. Draw two 10½-inch (26.2-cm) circles on a sheet of baking paper. Invert the paper on a sheet pan and divide the Almond Sponge batter between the circles, spreading it out evenly. (Or pour the batter into an adjustable cake ring of the same size.)

2. Bake at 400°F (205°C) for about 10 minutes. Reserve.

3. Roll out hazelnut short dough to ⅛ inch (3 mm) thick and use it to line two 11-inch (27.5-cm) tart pans (see Figure 2–11, page 33). Cover the dough with baking paper and fill with dried beans or pie weights.

4. Bake at 375°F (190°C) for approximately 18 minutes, or until the edges are golden brown. Immediately remove the paper and weights, then return to the oven to finish baking the bottom, if necessary. Let the shells cool.

5. Brush red currant glaze over the base, and slightly up the sides, of the cooled shells. Reserve the remaining glaze.

6. Place one-fourth of the pastry cream in each of the shells, and spread it over the glaze, covering the bottom of the shells.

7. Trim the sponge circles to fit inside the tart, if needed (slice the cake into two layers horizontally if baked in the ring). Place one sponge in each tart shell on top of the pastry cream.

8. Combine the Armagnac with the mandarin juice; brush over the sponges. Evenly spread the remaining pastry cream on top.

9. Using your hands, peel and section the mandarins. Arrange the sections on top of the pastry cream, making concentric circles starting from the edge.

10. Warm the reserved currant glaze, and brush on top of the mandarin wedges. Cut the tarts into the desired number of slices.

11. Presentation: Place a tart slice off-center on a dessert plate. Pour a pool of Raspberry Sauce in front of the slice, and decorate the sauce with the Sour Cream Mixture for Piping (see pages 518–519).

NOTE: If mandarins are not available, substitute oranges; you will need about eight.

Variation

For a quick and colorful fruit tart, arrange other assorted fresh fruits (including some mandarins as desired) in concentric circles on top of the pastry cream. Brush with glaze as directed. Take into consideration whether you will be cutting the tarts into buffet or restaurant slices as you arrange the fruit, so that your pattern does not fall apart when sliced.

Pecan-Whiskey Tart

two 11-inch (27.5-cm) tarts

1 pound, 2 ounces (510 g)
  Short Dough (page 31)
Pecan Filling (recipe follows)
dark baker's chocolate, melted
1 pint (480 ml) heavy cream
1 tablespoon (15 g) granulated
  sugar
2 tablespoons (30 ml) whiskey
pecan halves
mint sprigs

1. Line two 11-inch (27.5-cm) tart pans with short dough rolled ⅛ inch (3 mm) thick (see Figure 2–11, page 33). Reserve in the refrigerator while you make the filling.

2. Divide the pecan filling between the shells.

3. Bake at 350°F (175°C) for approximately 35 minutes, or until the filling is firmly set. Let cool completely.

4. Unmold the tarts. Place the melted baker's chocolate in a piping bag (see page 505) and cut a very small opening. Decorate the tarts by streaking the chocolate across the tart in thin parallel lines. Turn the tart 90° and repeat the procedure to create lines going in the opposite direction (Figure 6–1). As you streak the chocolate across the tarts, move quickly, alternating left to right and right to left, overlapping the edge of the tart on both sides. Cut the tarts into the desired number of pieces.

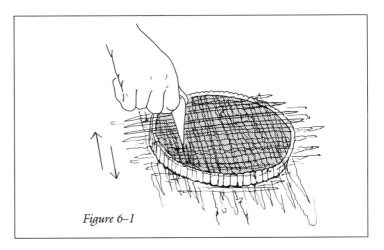

Figure 6–1

5. Whip the cream, sugar, and whiskey to very soft peaks; reserve in the refrigerator.

6. Presentation: Place a slice of tart on a dessert plate. Spoon a small mound of cream onto the plate next to the slice. Stand a pecan half in the cream, and place a mint sprig next to it.

Pecan Filling

8 eggs
13 ounces (370 g) brown sugar
½ cup (120 ml) light corn syrup
½ cup (120 ml) molasses
1 teaspoon (5 g) salt
1 teaspoon (5 ml) vanilla extract
¼ cup (60 ml) whiskey
3 ounces (85 g) melted butter
1 pound, 4 ounces (570 g) pecans,
    roughly chopped

1. Whisk the eggs just to break them up, about 1 minute.
2. Mix in sugar, corn syrup, molasses, salt, vanilla, and whiskey.
3. Stir in melted butter and pecans.
NOTE: If you wish to leave out the whiskey, add an additional 2 ounces (55 g) of melted butter.

Raspberry-Lemon Tart

two 11-inch (27.5-cm) tarts

1 pound, 2 ounces (510 g)
    Short Dough (page 31)
1 recipe Lemon Cream (page 568)
1 dry pint (480 ml) fresh
    raspberries
softly whipped cream
mint sprigs

1. Line two 11-inch (27.5-cm) false-bottom tart pans with short dough, rolled ⅛ inch (3 mm) thick (see Figure 2–11, page 33). Place a piece of baking paper in the bottom, and fill with dried beans or pie weights.

2. Bake at 375°F (190°C) to a light golden, not brown, color, about 12 minutes. Cool to room temperature.

3. Remove the paper and weights from the cooled tart shells. Divide the lemon cream evenly between the shells.

4. Bake at 375°F (190°C) until the filling is just set, about 15 minutes (the filling will set a little more as it cools).

5. Let the tarts cool completely, then remove them from the pans and slide onto cake cardboards. Cut (or mark if presenting whole) into the desired number of pieces.

6. Arrange the raspberries on the surface of each slice, placing them within the markings for each piece so that they will not be cut when the tart is sliced. To preserve the natural satin look of the raspberries, do not rinse or glaze them.

7. Presentation: Place a slice in the center of a dessert plate. Spoon softly whipped cream over the tip of the slice and onto the plate. Place a mint sprig next to the cream.

Variation: Fig Tart

(see photograph in color insert)

1 pound, 2 ounces (510 g)
Short Dough (page 31)
¾ recipe Lemon Cream (page 568)
or
1 recipe Cointreau Custard
(page 148)
24 fresh figs, cut in quarters,
lengthwise
softly whipped cream
mint sprigs

1. Follow the preceding directions in steps 1, 2, and 3.
2. Arrange the figs on top of the lemon cream or Cointreau Custard, cut side up, making concentric circles and spacing the fig quarters about ¼ inch (6 mm) apart.
3. Bake as instructed for Raspberry-Lemon Tart.
4. Presentation: Place a slice in the center of a dessert plate. Spoon softly whipped cream over the tip of the slice and onto the plate. Place a mint sprig next to the cream.

Strawberry-Rhubarb Tart

two 11-inch (27.5-cm) tarts

4 pounds (1 kg, 820 g) rhubarb
2 tablespoons (16 g) cornstarch
1 pound (455 g) granulated sugar
2 pounds, 14 ounces (1 kg, 310 g)
Short Dough (page 31)
Egg Wash (page 5)
20 medium-sized strawberries
Apricot Glaze (page 526)
Romanoff Sauce or Crème Fraîche
(pages 563 and 559)
mint sprigs

1. Trim off the tops and bottoms of the rhubarb stalks and discard. Cut the stalks into ½-inch (1.2-cm) cubes.
2. Stir the cornstarch into the sugar, add the rhubarb cubes, and mix well. Set aside for about half an hour to draw some of the juice out of the rhubarb.
3. Cook the rhubarb mixture over low heat until soft, but not falling apart. Strain off the liquid; you may save the liquid to make the sauce for a variation of this recipe (instructions follow), or discard it.
4. Roll out 1 pound, 2 ounces (510 g) of the short dough ⅛ inch (3 mm) thick and use it to line two 11-inch (27.5-cm) tart pans (see Figure 2–11, page 33). Line the pans with baking paper and fill with dried beans or pie weights.
5. Bake at 375°F (190°C) until the short dough is set but has not yet started to brown, approximately 8 minutes.
6. Remove the paper and the weights. You may need to return the shells to the oven and bake a little longer if the bottom is not set. Divide the rhubarb evenly between the two tart shells and continue baking until the shells begin to turn golden brown, approximately 10 minutes. Do not overbake. Cool slightly.
7. Roll the remaining short dough into a rectangle 11 inches (27.5 cm) wide and ⅛ inch (3 mm) thick. Cut sixteen ⅜-inch (9-mm) strips using a fluted pastry wheel. It is usually a good idea to transfer the dough to a sheet pan or a sheet of cardboard and chill it before cutting the strips.
8. Brush egg wash lightly around the edge of the baked tarts.
9. Twist the short dough strips one at a time (see Figure 9–17, page 254) into a corkscrew shape, then arrange them 1 inch (2.5 cm) apart on top of the tarts, placing them first in one

direction, then across at a 45° angle to form a diamond pattern (see Figure 9–25, page 265). Brush egg wash on the first layer of strips before placing the second layer on top. Then brush additional egg wash on the second layer.

10. Return the tarts to the oven and bake at 375°F (190°C) until the short dough strips are golden brown, approximately 10 minutes. Let the tarts cool to room temperature.

11. Rinse the strawberries, trim off the tops (a melon baller is excellent for this), and slice them lengthwise into six pieces each. Place the strawberry slices in the diamonds between the short dough strips.

12. Brush the tops of the tarts with apricot glaze to preserve the fresh look of the berries. Cut the tarts into the desired number of serving pieces.

13. Presentation: Place a tart slice in the center of a dessert plate. Spoon Romanoff Sauce or crème fraîche over the tip of the slice, and let some run onto the plate. Place a large mint sprig next to the sauce.

Variation: Rhubarb Meringue Tart

(see photograph in color insert)

1. Follow the directions for Strawberry-Rhubarb Tart through step 6.

2. Make one-quarter recipe of Italian Meringue (see page 333).

3. Cut or mark the tarts into serving pieces.

4. Using a pastry bag with a no. 3 (6-mm) star tip, pipe the meringue on top of the rhubarb, within the markings for each slice, starting at the tip of the slice and piping the strips of meringue next to each other in a zig-zag design (piping left to right then right to left) to the edge.

5. Caramelize (brown) the meringue in a salamander or very hot oven (450°F/230°C). (See note.)

6. Adjust the sweetness of the reserved rhubarb juice by adding either sugar or water as necessary. Thicken with 1 tablespoon (8 g) cornstarch per pint (480 ml) of liquid.

7. Presentation: Place the tart slice off center on a desert plate. Pour a pool of sauce on the larger exposed part of the plate. Decorate the sauce with Chocolate Sauce for Piping (recipe page 560, decorating instructions pages 518–519).

NOTE 1: Do not pipe out and brown the meringue more than two to three hours before serving. Serve Rhubarb Meringue Tart warm or at room temperature.

NOTE 2: If you will be presenting the tarts whole, pipe rosettes of meringue around the outer edge only, to allow the rhubarb to be seen.

Swedish Hazelnut Tart

(see photograph in color insert)
two 11-inch (27.5-cm) tarts

1 pound, 2 ounces (510 g)
   Short Dough (page 31)
5 ounces (140 g) apricot jam,
   softened
12 ounces (340 g) hazelnuts
5 ounces (130 g) Candied
   Orange Peel (page 520)
12 ounces (340 g) granulated
   sugar
12 ounces (340 g) softened butter
3 eggs
4 egg yolks
1½ teaspoons (7.5 ml) vanilla
   extract
powdered sugar
Ganache (page 567)
fresh orange slices for decoration

1. Line two 11-inch (27.5-cm) tart pans (false-bottom or solid) with short dough rolled ⅛ inch (3 mm) thick. Place the lined pans in the refrigerator to firm the dough.

2. Soften the jam by working it in a bowl with a spoon until smooth. (You may add a small amount of water if the jam is too firm.) Divide the jam between the tarts and spread it out in a thin film on the bottom of each tart. Return the pans to the refrigerator.

3. Grind the hazelnuts, orange peel, and 6 ounces (170 g) of the sugar very finely, until almost a paste.

4. Cream the butter with the remaining 6 ounces (170 g) of sugar. Gradually mix in whole eggs, egg yolks, vanilla, and the nut mixture. Be careful not to overmix; if too much air is incorporated the tarts will puff up while baking and then fall in the center, giving them an unattractive appearance.

5. Divide the filling between the lined pans and spread it out, mounding it just slightly higher in the center.

6. Bake the tarts at 350°F (175°C) until the filling is firm in the middle and the shells are golden brown, about 50 minutes. Let the tarts cool completely, then unmold.

7. Make a template that is ½ inch (1.2 cm) smaller than the tarts and has a 4-inch (10-cm) circle cut out of the center. Place the template on the tarts, one at a time, and sift powdered sugar on top. Slice the tarts.

8. Warm the ganache until it develops a slight shine. Place in a pastry bag with a no. 4 (8-mm) plain tip. Pipe the ganache in a heart design near the crust edge of each slice; decorate with a small slice of fresh orange. (Unfortunately, the oranges will look fresh for only 6 to 8 hours, but they are very easy to replace.)

NOTE: To get a precise and sharp contrast, use a plain cookie cutter as a guide for the center circle when you cut your template, then place the cutter in the opening to act as a seal while you sift the powdered sugar.

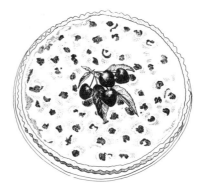

Tart Hollandaise

two 11-inch (27.5-cm) tarts

1 pound, 8 ounces (680 g) Classic or Quick Puff Paste (page 21)
5 ounces (140 g) apricot jam, softened
3 pounds (1 kg, 365 g) Mazarin Filling (page 569)
2 ounces (55 g) sliced almonds
1 pound (455 g) Short Dough (page 31)
Egg Wash (page 5)
powdered sugar

1. Line two 11-inch (27.5-cm) tart pans (false-bottom or solid) with puff paste rolled ⅛ inch (3 mm) thick. Place baking paper in the bottoms, fill with dried beans or pie weights, and let rest for at least 30 minutes in the refrigerator.

2. Bake the shells at 375°F (190°C) for about 10 minutes. Let them cool until they can be handled, then remove the paper and the weights.

3. Spread the jam in a thin layer on the bottom of each shell. Place the mazarin filling in a pastry bag with a no. 6 (12-mm) plain tip. Pipe the filling into the tarts in an even layer. Sprinkle sliced almonds evenly over the tops.

4. Roll out short dough ⅛ inch (3 mm) thick. Refrigerate the dough to make it firm and easier to handle. Cut into ¼-inch-wide (6-mm) strips using a fluted pastry wheel.

5. Arrange dough strips ¼ inch (6 mm) apart over the almonds; then arrange strips in the other direction so they form a diamond pattern (see example Figure 9–25, page 265). Press the strips lightly with your hand as you place them to make sure they stick together. Carefully brush the strips with egg wash.

6. Bake the tarts at 375°F (190°C) until golden brown, about 45 minutes. Let cool to room temperature.

7. Remove the tarts from the pans. Slice into the desired number of serving pieces, and sift powdered sugar lightly over the tops.

Tart Tatin

one 9-inch (22.5-cm) tart

6 ounces (170 g) Puff Paste (Classic, Quick, or scraps) (page 21)
12 medium-sized Red Delicious apples
3½ ounces (100 g) butter
7 ounces (200 g) granulated sugar
1½ cups (360 ml) Crème Fraîche, approximately (page 559)
Cinnamon Sugar (page 4)
strawberry halves

1. Roll out puff paste to a square approximately 10 × 10 inches (25 × 25 cm) and slightly thinner than ⅛ inch (3 mm) thick. Place on a sheet pan, prick well, and reserve in the refrigerator.

2. Peel, core, and cut the apples in half lengthwise.

3. Put the butter in a 10-inch (25-cm) skillet and melt over medium heat. Sprinkle the sugar evenly over the melted butter.

4. Place an 11-inch (27.5-cm) adjustable ring (or use the ring from a 10-inch [25-cm] springform, unclamped) in the skillet and quickly arrange the apples inside the ring, standing them on the stem end, and packing them tightly. (The ring will sit high on the side of the pan at first, but as the apples cook and become smaller, you can adjust it.)

5. Cook over medium heat, shaking the skillet gently to make sure the apples do not stick and pressing lightly on the top to compact them. As the apples shrink, tighten the ring around them. If you could not fit all of the apple pieces in the pan at the beginning, try to fit them in at this point. Continue cooking, still shaking the skillet and compacting the apples occasionally, until

the sugar turns a dark golden brown, about 30 minutes. Remove the skillet from the heat and let cool a few minutes.

6. Cut a 10-inch (25-cm) circle from the reserved puff paste square (save the scraps for another use). Cover the apples with the puff paste, tucking the dough between the apples and the ring.

7. Bake at 375°F (190°C) for about 30 minutes, or until the puff paste is baked through. Let cool for 10 minutes.

8. Invert a platter over the tart and flip them over together to unmold the tart onto the platter. Be careful of the hot caramel as you do this. Cut the tart into the desired number of slices.

9. Presentation: Place a tart slice on a dessert plate, spoon crème fraîche over the tip of the tart, and sprinkle cinnamon sugar lightly over the top. Fan a strawberry half and set it on the plate next to the crème fraîche.

NOTE: This tart is best served warm from the oven. If you must, serve it at room temperature, but never cold. Tart Tatin must be served the same day it is made.

Walnut-Caramel Tart

(see photograph in color insert)
two 11-inch (27.5-cm) tarts

2 pounds, 10 ounces (1 kg, 195 g)
 Short Dough (page 31)
Caramel Filling (recipe follows)
Egg Wash (page 5)
10 ounces (285 g) Ganache
 (page 567)
5 ounces (140 g) walnuts,
 finely chopped
Orange Sauce (page 561)
Chocolate Sauce for Piping
 (page 560)
raspberries
mint sprigs

1. Roll out 1 pound, 2 ounces (510 g) of the short dough ⅛ inch (3 mm) thick and use it to line two 11-inch (27.5-cm), 1-inch-deep (2.5-cm) tart pans (see Figure 2–11, page 33). These do not have to be false-bottom pans. Reserve the remaining dough. Place baking paper in the bottom of the pans and fill with dried beans or pie weights.

2. Bake at 375°F (190°C) until set, but not brown, about 12 minutes.

3. Remove papers and weights from the baked shells. Divide the caramel filling evenly between the shells.

4. Roll out the remaining short dough ⅛ inch (3 mm) thick.

5. Brush the edge of the baked shells with egg wash, then cover with the dough. Press the edges together to seal, and trim away any excess dough. Prick the top lightly to let air escape.

6. Bake the tarts at 350°F (175°C) until golden brown, about 30 minutes. If the pastry bubbles, press it down with the bottom of a cake pan or any other flat object while the tart is still hot from the oven. Let the tarts cool to room temperature.

7. Remove the tarts from the pans. Warm the ganache to a soft, but not runny, consistency; it should have a nice shine.

8. Spread a thin even layer of warm ganache on top of one tart. Place a 5- to 6-inch (12.5- to 15-cm) plain cookie cutter (or anything with a rim around it so it will not damage the ganache) in the center of the tart. Sprinkle the chopped walnuts around the

ring before the ganache hardens, taking care not to spill any in the middle. (Sprinkle the walnuts lightly; you should still be able to see as much uncovered ganache as you do nuts.) Remove the cookie cutter and refrigerate the tart to firm the ganache. Repeat with the remaining tart.

9. Cut the tarts into the desired number of slices using a sharp knife dipped in hot water.

10. Presentation: Place a slice of Walnut-Caramel Tart slightly off-center on a dessert plate. Pour a pool of Orange Sauce in the larger space, and decorate the sauce with Chocolate Sauce for Piping as shown on pages 518–519. Place three raspberries and a mint sprig on the opposite side of the plate.

NOTE: Walnut-Caramel Tart must be served at room temperature because the filling becomes too hard if refrigerated.

Caramel Filling

4 pounds, 3 ounces (1 kg, 905 g) filling

2 pounds (910 g) granulated sugar
juice of ½ lemon
1 cup (240 ml) heavy cream, at room temperature
10 ounces (285 g) butter
1 pound (455 g) walnuts, coarsely chopped

1. Caramelize the sugar with the lemon juice in a heavy-bottomed saucepan (see page 488).

2. Cook, stirring constantly with a wooden spoon, until the mixture reaches a light brown color, 335°F (168°C). Remove from heat.

3. Quickly add the cream and swirl it around to mix.

4. Stir in the butter, then the walnuts.

If made ahead, you may need to warm the filling before spreading it in the tart shells.

Sponge Cakes and Tea Cakes

Sponge Cakes and Other
Cake Batters
  Sponge Cake
  Almond Sponge
  Biscuit Viennoise
  Chocolate Biscuit
  Dobosh Sponge
  Hazelnut-Chocolate Biscuit
  Vanilla Butter Cake

Tea Cakes
  Apple Cinnamon Cake
  Banana Tea Cake
  Chocolate Crisp Cake
  Chocolate Gugelhupf
  Lingonberry Cake
  Raisin Cake
  Soft Gingerbread Cake
  Swedish Jam Roll
  Tiger Cake

*B*aking a sponge cake is a basic skill every baker or pastry chef must master: sponge cakes are the base for the majority of the cakes we create. Not having a properly made sponge to start with affects not only the taste of the cake, but also the final appearance, since it will be harder to decorate nicely.

Sponge cakes are made from the three ingredients no baker can do without—eggs, sugar, and flour—although some sponges also contain butter. Sponge cakes do not contain baking powder or baking soda—their volume and light texture come solely from the air whipped into the eggs.

There are two basic ways to make a classic sponge cake: the warm method and the cold method. In the warm method, eggs and sugar are mixed over simmering water to about 110°F (43°C), or until the sugar is melted, and are stirred constantly so that the eggs do not cook. The mixture is removed from the heat, placed in a mixing bowl, and whipped at high speed until creamy and light in color. It is then whipped at a lower speed for about 5 minutes longer to stabilize the batter. Sifted flour is folded in, followed by the melted butter, if used.

In the cold method, the eggs are first separated; the yolks are whipped with half of the sugar to a light and fluffy consistency, and the whites and the remaining sugar are whipped to soft peaks. The yolks are gradually folded

into the whites, then sifted flour is folded in, and last the melted butter, if used. The cold method produces a somewhat lighter sponge than the warm method. Due to the lightness of the cake, the cold-method sponge tends to shrink away from the sides of the pan more than is desirable. For this reason it is best not to grease the sides of the cake pan. Instead, cut the baked sponge free using a sharp, thin knife.

A third method, and probably the most common in the baking industry today, is the emulsifier method; it is quick, convenient, and almost foolproof. All ingredients, including the flour, are whipped together with an emulsifier for a specified time. The emulsifier method uses baking powder and does not rely on air as a leavening agent, so the sponge does not need to be baked immediately but can "wait its turn for the oven" just as any plain cookie—a big advantage in a busy bakery.

Another sponge variation is the classic ladyfinger sponge, which is used not only for cookies, but also for Othello shells and certain cake bottoms. In this method, more air is whipped into the batter so it can be piped into various shapes without running. Ladyfinger sponges are meant to be very dry after baking, but will easily absorb moisture from fillings or syrup.

Sponge batter must have a balanced gluten strength. Some gluten is required for a good baking structure, but too much will make the batter rubbery and hard to work with. You can balance the gluten structure in the flour by using part low-gluten flour, such as cake flour, or you can add cornstarch, potato starch, or cocoa powder, which do not contain any gluten at all.

Flours for sponge cake should always be sifted. If you use cocoa powder or any other dry ingredient, sift it in with the flour. You must be very careful when adding the flour to the batter not to break the air bubbles that you just whipped in; use a flat rubber spatula or your hand, and never stir.

Butter can be added to a sponge in an amount up to 75 percent of the weight of the sugar in the warm method, and up to 50 percent of the weight of the sugar in the cold method. The butter should be melted, but not hot. It is always added last, after the flour has been completely incorporated. Otherwise the butter will surround any small lumps of flour, and you won't be able to break them up without losing volume.

Almonds are sometimes added to a sponge batter in the form of either ground almonds or almond paste; they are best added to the cold method sponge. Almond paste can be added without adjusting the other ingredients, providing the weight of the almond paste does not exceed the weight of the sugar in the recipe. The almond paste is first softened (worked free of lumps) with some egg whites. The whipped egg yolks can then be folded in quickly and smoothly without causing lumps or losing volume. Ground almonds must be ground very fine and sifted with the flour. They can be added to a maximum half of the weight of the sugar. You must decrease the weight of the flour in equal proportion to the amount of ground almonds added.

To make a chocolate sponge, sift cocoa powder in with the flour. Use 3 ounces (85 g) of cocoa powder for each pound (455 g) of flour in your recipe. Decrease the weight of the lowest-gluten flour in the recipe by the same amount of cocoa powder used.

Divide the batter into pans and bake it immediately (unless you are using an emulsifier) or the air bubbles will start to break. Pans should be buttered and floured using a combination of four parts melted butter to one part flour, by volume. By brushing this mixture on the pans you only have to handle them once.

The oven should be around 400°F (205°C) for a typical 10- × 3-inch (25- × 7.5-cm) cake pan. The deeper and wider your cake pan, the lower you should have the heat. On the other end of the scale, if you are baking a ¼-inch (6-mm) roulade, the oven should be at 425°F (219°C) or the roulade will dry out as it bakes and be difficult (or impossible) to roll. To test a sponge for doneness, press down in the center with your finger. The sponge should spring right back and not leave any indentation.

Do not unmold any sponge before it has cooled completely. Store it covered or wrapped in plastic. If you do not need to reuse the pans, leave the cakes in the pans, turn them upside down to store, and unmold as needed. Sponge cake freezes exceptionally well, even for months if wrapped properly; both the professional baker and the home cook should always have some sponge in the freezer to create a last-minute dessert.

Sponge Cakes and Other Cake Batters

Sponge Cake
one 10-inch (25-cm) layer

6 eggs
8 ounces (225 g) granulated sugar
½ teaspoon (2.5 ml) vanilla extract
8 ounces (225 g) cake flour

1. Place the eggs, sugar, and vanilla in a mixing bowl and heat over a bain-marie, stirring constantly, to about 110°F (43°C). Remove from the heat, and whip at full speed until the mixture has cooled completely and is light and fluffy.

2. Sift the cake flour (and the cocoa powder, if used) and gradually fold (never stir) into the egg mixture by hand (Figures 7–1 and 7–2). Pour the batter into a greased and floured 10-inch (25-cm) cake pan.

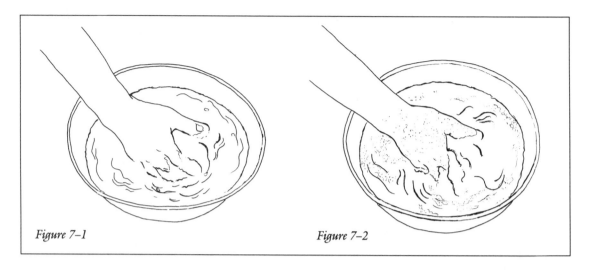

Figure 7–1   Figure 7–2

3. Bake immediately at 400°F (205°C) for about 20 minutes, or until the sponge springs back when pressed lightly in the center. Allow the cake to cool completely before unmolding. Store covered in the refrigerator.

Variation: Chocolate Sponge Cake

For Chocolate Sponge Cake, delete 1 ounce (30 g) of the flour and replace it with 1 ounce (30 g) of cocoa powder.

Almond Sponge

two ¼- × 14- × 24-inch (6-mm × 35- × 60-cm) sheets, or two 10-inch (25-cm) layers

3 egg whites
14 ounces (400 g) Almond Paste (page 4)
12 eggs, separated
10 ounces (285 g) granulated sugar
1 teaspoon (5 ml) vanilla extract
7 ounces (200 g) cake flour

1. Gradually mix the egg whites into the almond paste to soften it.
2. Whip the egg yolks with 3 ounces (85 g) of the sugar to the ribbon stage. Add the vanilla extract. Very gradually, add the yolk mixture to the almond paste; if you try to add it too fast, you are sure to get lumps.
3. Whip the egg whites to a foam. Gradually add the remaining 7 ounces (200 g) of sugar and whip to stiff peaks.
4. Sift the flour (and the cocoa powder, if used). Carefully fold the egg whites into the yolk mixture. Fold in dry ingredients.

To make sheets
Immediately spread the batter on paper-lined sheet pans to 14 × 24 inches (35 × 60 cm), taking care not to overwork the sponge. Bake at 425°F (219°C) for approximately 8 minutes or until just done.

To make layers
Line the bottoms of two 10-inch (25-cm) cake pans with baking paper (or grease and flour, but do not grease and flour the sides).

When the sponge is allowed to stick to the side of the pan, it does not shrink as it bakes. Divide the batter between the pans and bake at 400°F (205°C) for about 15 minutes or until the sponge springs back when pressed lightly in the middle. When cold, cut the sponge away from the side with a thin, sharp knife.

Variation: Cocoa Almond Sponge

To make Cocoa Almond Sponge, delete 3 ounces (85 g) of flour and substitute 3 ounces (85 g) of cocoa powder.

NOTE: If the oven is not hot enough or if the sheets are overcooked (and therefore dried out), the sponge will not bend without breaking. To remedy this, place a damp towel on a sheet pan and place the sponge on top, with the paper next to the towel. Invert a second sheet pan on top as a lid. Place in the oven (400°F/205°C) for 5 to 10 minutes to soften. If the sponge is to be used the next day, repeat the process as above, but soften in the refrigerator instead of in the oven.

Biscuit Viennoise

two 10-inch (25-cm) layers

12 eggs
2 egg whites
10 ounces (285 g) granulated sugar
1 teaspoon (5 g) salt
6 ounces (170 g) cake flour
6 ounces (170 g) bread flour
5 ounces (140 g) melted butter

1. Place whole eggs, egg whites, sugar, and salt in mixing bowl. Heat over simmering water to about 110°F (43°C), whipping continuously. Remove from heat and whip at high speed until mixture has cooled and is light and fluffy.

2. Sift the flours together and fold into the batter by hand. Fold in the melted butter. Divide the batter between two greased and floured 10-inch (25-cm) cake pans.

3. Bake immediately at 400°F (205°C) for approximately 15 minutes. Let the sponges cool before removing them from the pans.

Chocolate Biscuit

two 10-inch (25-cm) layers

12 eggs
2 egg whites
10 ounces (285 g) granulated sugar
1 teaspoon (5 g) salt
4 ounces (115 g) cake flour
6 ounces (170 g) bread flour
2 ounces (55 g) cocoa powder
5 ounces (140 g) melted butter

1. Place whole eggs, egg whites, sugar, and salt in mixing bowl. Heat over simmering water to about 110°F (43°C), whipping continuously. Remove from heat and whip at high speed until mixture has cooled and is light and fluffy.

2. Sift the flours and cocoa powder together and fold into the batter by hand. Fold in the melted butter. Divide the batter between two greased and floured 10-inch (25-cm) cake pans.

3. Bake immediately at 400°F (205°C) for approximately 15 minutes. Let the sponges cool before removing them from the pans.

Dobosh Sponge

one 16- × 24-inch (40- × 60-cm) sheet

10 ounces (285 g) softened butter
10 ounces (285 g) granulated
   sugar
10 egg yolks
1 teaspoon (5 ml) vanilla extract
1 teaspoon (5 g) salt
grated zest of ½ lemon
10 egg whites
7 ounces (200 g) sifted cake flour

1. Cream the butter with 5 ounces (140 g) of the sugar to a light and fluffy consistency. Beat in egg yolks a few at a time. Mix in vanilla, salt, and lemon zest.

2. Whip the egg whites until foamy. Gradually add the remaining 5 ounces (140 g) of sugar and whip to soft peaks. Carefully fold the whipped egg whites into the yolk mixture.

3. Gently fold in the flour (and cocoa powder, if used).

4. Spread the batter evenly over a 16- × 24-inch (40- × 60-cm) sheet of baking paper. Drag the paper onto a sheet pan (see Figure 15–3, page 422). Bake at 425°F (219°C) for about 10 minutes or until baked through.

Variation: Cocoa Dobosh Sponge

For Cocoa Dobosh Sponge, delete 1 ounce (30 g) of the cake flour and replace with 1 ounce (30 g) of cocoa powder sifted with the remaining flour.

Hazelnut-Chocolate Biscuit

two 10-inch (25-cm) layers

14 eggs
12 ounces (340 g) granulated
   sugar
1 teaspoon (5 ml) vanilla extract
1 teaspoon (5 g) salt
8 ounces (225 g) bread flour
6 ounces (170 g) hazelnuts,
   roasted and finely ground
3 ounces (85 g) dark
   chocolate, grated
4 ounces (115 g) melted butter

1. Combine eggs, sugar, vanilla, and salt in a mixing bowl. Heat over simmering water until mixture reaches about 110°F (43°C), whipping continuously. Remove from heat and whip at high speed until mixture has cooled and has a light and fluffy consistency.

2. Sift flour. Mix in hazelnuts and chocolate, then carefully fold into the batter by hand. Fold in melted butter. Divide the batter between two greased and floured 10-inch (25-cm) cake pans.

3. Bake immediately at 400°F (205°C) until the cake springs back when pressed lightly on top, approximately 15 minutes. Allow the sponges to cool completely before removing them from the pans.

Vanilla Butter Cake

two 10-inch (25-cm) layers

12 egg yolks
6 ounces (170 g) granulated sugar
8 egg whites
½ teaspoon (3 g) salt
1 teaspoon (5 ml) vanilla extract
6 ounces (170 g) bread flour
3 ounces (85 g) cake flour
3 ounces (85 g) melted butter

1. Whip egg yolks with 3 ounces (85 g) of the sugar until light and fluffy. Whip egg whites and salt to a foam. Gradually add the remaining 3 ounces (85 g) of sugar and whip to stiff peaks. Fold the yolk mixture carefully into the whites together with the vanilla.

2. Sift the flours together, then fold into the egg mixture. Slowly incorporate the melted butter.

3. Line the bottom of two 10-inch (25-cm) cake pans with baking paper (or grease and flour, but do not grease and flour the sides; the sponge will stick to the sides of the pans instead of shrinking). Divide the batter between the pans.

4. Bake at 400°F (205°C) for about 12 minutes or until done. Let cool completely, then cut the sponges away from the sides of the pans and unmold.

Tea Cakes

Several years ago I was asked to judge a decorated cake contest in San Francisco. My two fellow judges were Jeremiah Tower and another local celebrity chef who is also a well-known food show host. After seeing the large array of cakes we decided that we should each separately pick what we thought were the top five, and then together choose the winner and runners-up from this pool. When we told each other our choices my unnamed colleague had picked one tea cake among his five. Although the cake was iced and decorated, it had been baked in a tube pan and had not been split and filled. I agreed that it did taste good, but said I had disqualified this one as not being a legitimate decorated cake. We had a heated argument about this. My point was this: If I order a decorated cake at the local bakery this is not the type of cake I expect to receive. I ended up winning the argument but I realized later that in fact we were both right. There is certainly a gray area dividing tea cakes and decorated cakes.

Tea cakes are generally made from a richer and heavier batter than sponge cakes and therefore require a leavening agent such as baking powder or baking soda. Rather than adding the filling after the cake is baked, a flavoring or filling is added directly to the batter. For example, chopped nuts, sliced apples, chocolate chips, raisins, bananas, and spices are used to flavor the tea cakes in this chapter. Because the cakes are heavier, they are baked in a tube pan, loaf pan, or other narrow form so they will bake evenly. The decoration (if any) on a tea cake is usually kept very simple, often just a sprinkling of powdered sugar or a plain glaze. This makes tea cakes quick and easy to prepare. Tea cakes will remain fresh for several days in the refrigerator and actually become more moist after a few days. Sliced tea cakes are always included along with an assortment of petits fours or cookies at the traditional three o'clock coffee break in Sweden.

Apple Cinnamon Cake

four 1-pound, 5-ounce (595-g) cakes

melted butter
finely ground bread crumbs
4 small apples (Golden Delicious, pippin, or Granny Smith)
½ recipe Poaching Syrup II (page 6)
Cinnamon Sugar (page 4)
1 pound (455 g) granulated sugar
6 eggs
1 teaspoon (5 ml) vanilla extract
1 pound (455 g) bread flour
2 tablespoons (24 g) baking powder
1 teaspoon (1.5 g) ground cinnamon
1 teaspoon (2 g) ground cardamom
1 teaspoon (5 g) salt
12 ounces (340 g) melted butter
1¼ cups (300 ml) half-and-half, at room temperature

1. Brush melted butter on the inside of four 1-quart (960-ml) tube-style cake pans. Coat the pans with bread crumbs. Set aside.

2. Peel and core the apples. Poach them in syrup until soft. Remove the apples from the liquid. When cool enough to handle, slice them into ½-inch (1.2-cm) wedges. Toss the wedges in cinnamon sugar to coat, then arrange them evenly over the bottoms of the forms.

3. Whip the sugar, eggs, and vanilla together until light and foamy.

4. Sift together the flour, baking powder, cinnamon, cardamom, and salt. Fold into the egg mixture.

5. Combine the 12 ounces (340 g) of melted butter with the half-and-half. Add to the batter slowly. Divide the batter between the prepared cake pans, filling them no more than halfway.

6. Bake at 350°F (175°C) for about 45 minutes or until done. Unmold the cakes and let them cool on a cake rack. When completely cool, cover and refrigerate.

NOTE: To save time, cut the apples into ¼-inch (6-mm) chunks and fold them into the batter before pouring it into the forms.

Banana Tea Cake

three 1-pound, 5-ounce (595-g)
cakes

Butter and Flour Mixture
    (page 4)
10 ounces (285 g) butter
1 pound, 2 ounces (510 g)
    granulated sugar
3 eggs, at room temperature
1 teaspoon (5 ml) vanilla extract
1 pound, 5 ounces (595 g) puréed
    bananas, somewhat overripe
1 pound, 2 ounces (510 g)
    bread flour
2 teaspoons (10 g) salt
2 teaspoons (8 g) baking soda
9 ounces (255 g) coarsely
    chopped walnuts

1. Brush the butter and flour mixture over the inside of three gugelhupf forms or other desired molds with a 1-quart (960-ml) capacity.

2. Melt the butter and add the sugar. Beat together for a few minutes. Stir in the eggs, vanilla, and bananas.

3. Mix together the flour, salt, baking soda, and walnuts. Stir into the butter mixture.

4. Spoon the batter into the prepared forms. If you are using small forms, fill them only three-quarters full.

5. Bake at 350°F (175°C) for about 45 minutes or until baked through. You may need to use a second pan underneath to ensure that the cakes do not get too dark while baking. Unmold the cakes as soon as possible and let cool on a cake rack (they will get wet if left in the pans).

Chocolate Crisp Cake

four 1-pound, 5-ounce (595-g)
cakes

Butter and Flour Mixture
    (page 4)
12 ounces (340 g) softened butter
12 ounces (340 g) granulated
    sugar
8 eggs, at room temperature
1 teaspoon (5 ml) vanilla extract
1 pound, 5 ounces (595 g)
    bread flour
1 tablespoon (12 g) baking powder
7 ounces (200 g) dark chocolate,
    chopped
8 ounces (225 g) hazelnuts,
    roasted and crushed
grated zest of 1 orange
1¼ cups (300 ml) milk, at room
    temperature

1. Brush the butter and flour mixture on the insides of four rectangular, fluted forms with a 1-quart (960-ml) capacity.

2. Beat the softened butter with the sugar until fluffy. Add the eggs one at a time, then add the vanilla.

3. Sift the flour with the baking powder. Stir in the chopped chocolate, hazelnuts, and orange zest. Fold into the butter mixture in two additions, alternating with the milk. Divide the batter between the prepared pans.

4. Bake at 350°F (175°C) for about 50 minutes, or until baked through. Unmold as soon as possible and let the cakes cool on a cake rack. When cold, store in the refrigerator.

NOTE: You can serve these cakes plain or brushed with a thin layer of apricot glaze (see page 526) and covered with a thin layer of dark baker's chocolate. The cakes taste best one or two days after they are made.

Chocolate Gugelhupf

four 1-pound, 4-ounce (570-g) cakes

melted butter
finely crushed almonds
8 ounces (225 g) softened butter
1 pound, 2 ounces (510 g)
    granulated sugar
1½ teaspoons (7.5 ml) vanilla
    extract
6 eggs, at room temperature
11 ounces (310 g) boiled potatoes,
    mashed
15 ounces (430 g) cake flour
1½ ounces (40 g) cocoa powder
1½ tablespoons (18 g) baking
    powder
½ teaspoon (3 g) salt
8 ounces (225 g) blanched
    almonds, finely ground
1¼ cups (300 ml) heavy cream

1. Brush the melted butter on the inside of four gugelhupf forms or other 1-quart (960-ml) tube pans. Coat with crushed almonds.

2. Beat the softened butter and sugar together until light and fluffy. Add the vanilla to the eggs, and gradually add the eggs to the butter. Add the mashed potatoes.

3. Sift together the flour, cocoa powder, baking powder, and salt. Mix in ground almonds. Add to the butter mixture alternately with the cream. Divide the batter among the prepared forms. If you are using small forms, do not fill more than two-thirds full.

4. Bake at 350°F (175°C) for about 50 minutes. Immediately unmold and let the cakes cool on a cake rack. When completely cold, wrap in plastic and refrigerate.

Lingonberry Cake

four 1½-pound (680-g) cakes

melted butter
finely ground bread crumbs
12 ounces (340 g) black or English
    walnuts
1 pound, 2 ounces (510 g)
    granulated sugar
2 teaspoons (10 g) salt
8 ounces (225 g) soft butter
1 pound (455 g) cake flour
2 teaspoons (4 g) ground
    cardamom
1 teaspoon (2 g) ground nutmeg
1 teaspoon (4 g) baking soda
1 teaspoon (4 g) baking powder
1¼ cups (300 ml) heavy cream
1 cup (240 ml) buttermilk
5 eggs
1 pound (455 g) lingonberry jam

1. Brush four 1-quart (960-ml) rectangular, fluted cake pans with melted butter. Coat pans with bread crumbs and set aside.

2. Chop the walnuts into raisin-sized pieces. Toast them lightly, then set aside to cool.

3. Beat together the sugar, salt, and soft butter for a few minutes until well combined.

4. Sift together the flour, cardamom, nutmeg, baking soda, and baking powder.

5. Combine the heavy cream, buttermilk, and the eggs.

6. Incorporate the dry ingredients into the butter mixture in two additions, alternating with the liquid. Mix at medium speed for 4 to 5 minutes.

7. Stir the toasted walnuts into the batter. Stir in the jam.

8. Divide the batter between the prepared cake pans. If using smaller pans do not fill more than two-thirds full.

9. Bake at 375°F (190°C) for approximately 35 minutes, or until the top springs back when pressed lightly in the center.

10. Unmold immediately and let the cakes cool.

11. Store the cakes wrapped in plastic in the refrigerator. This cake will stay fresh for at least a week if stored properly, and actually becomes more moist after a few days in the refrigerator.

Raisin Cake

four 1-pound, 7-ounce (655 g)
cakes

melted butter
finely ground bread crumbs
1 pound, 8 ounces (680 g)
*   softened butter*
1 pound, 8 ounces (680 g)
*   granulated sugar*
1 teaspoon (5 ml) vanilla extract
10 eggs, at room temperature
13 ounces (370 g) bread flour
10 ounces (285 g) cornstarch
1½ tablespoons (18 g)
*   baking powder*
8 ounces (225 g) dark raisins

1. Brush melted butter inside four gugelhupf forms, or other tube pans with 1-quart (960-ml) capacity, and coat the forms thoroughly with the bread crumbs.

2. Beat the softened butter, sugar, and vanilla together until creamy. Mix in the eggs a few at a time.

3. Sift the flour with the cornstarch and baking powder. Add the raisins and mix to coat them with flour. Stir the flour into the butter mixture, taking care not to incorporate to much air by overmixing. Divide the batter equally between the prepared pans. If you use small pans, do not fill them more than two-thirds full.

4. Bake at 375°F (190°C) until the cake springs back when pressed lightly, about 30 minutes. Unmold and cool the cakes on a cake rack. When cool, wrap and store in the refrigerator.

NOTE: This batter can also be baked in muffin pans. Portion 4 ounces (115 g) batter for each small cake. Bake at 400°F (205°C) for about 25 minutes or until cakes spring back when pressed lightly.

Soft Gingerbread Cake

four 17-ounce (485-g) cakes

Butter and Flour Mixture
*   (page 4)*
1 pound (455 g) brown sugar
6 eggs
1 pound (455 g) bread flour
2 tablespoons (24 g) baking powder
1 teaspoon (4 g) baking soda
4 tablespoons (20 g) ground
*   cinnamon*
2 teaspoons (4 g) ground ginger
1 teaspoon (2 g) ground cloves
2 teaspoons (4 g) ground
*   cardamom*
1 teaspoon (5 g) salt
12 ounces (340 g) melted butter
1¼ cups (300 ml) half-and-half,
*   at room temperature*
powdered sugar

1. Brush the butter and flour mixture on the insides of four 1-quart (960-ml) rectangular fluted cake pans.

2. Whip the brown sugar and eggs together to a foamy consistency.

3. Sift together the flour, baking powder, baking soda, spices, and salt. Add to the egg mixture.

4. Combine the melted butter with the half-and-half. Add to the batter slowly. Divide the batter between the pans.

5. Bake at 350°F (175°C) for about 45 minutes or until the cakes spring back when pressed lightly in the center. Unmold the cakes and cool on a cake rack.

6. When the cakes have cooled completely, place a 1-inch-wide (2.5-cm) strip of baking paper on top of the cakes lengthwise. Sift powdered sugar over the cakes. Remove the paper template. Wrap the cakes in plastic and refrigerate.

NOTE: This recipe can also be made in muffin tins. Line every other space of muffin pans with paper cups, and grease the top of the pan around the cups with the butter and flour mixture. Pipe the batter into the cups using a no. 6 (12-mm) plain tip in your pastry bag. Bake at 375°F (190°C) for about 30 minutes or until baked through. Makes about twenty 3-ounce (85-g) muffins.

Swedish Jam Roll
(Rull Tårta)
two 11-inch (27.5-cm) rolls

1 recipe Roulade Batter
    (recipe follows)
granulated sugar
12 ounces (340 g) smooth
    strawberry or raspberry jam

This is a simple and delicious tea cake that can be made in a very short amount of time and does not even require a cake pan. It is actually a larger version of the roulade made to line the molds for Charlotte Royal.

1. Spread the sponge batter evenly over a sheet of baking paper that is 16 × 24 inches (40 × 60 cm), leaving approximately ½ inch (1.2 cm) of paper uncovered along all four sides. Drag the paper onto a sheet pan (see Figure 15–3, page 422).

2. Bake immediately at 425°F (219°C) for about 10 minutes, or until just done. Transfer the sponge to a second (cool) sheet pan after removing it from the oven so it will not dry out. Let the sponge sheet cool, then store it covered in the refrigerator if it is not to be rolled right away. If the sponge seems too dry to roll, follow the instructions given on page 163 to soften it.

3. Sprinkle granulated sugar lightly over a sheet of baking paper. Invert the sponge sheet on top. Peel the paper from the back. Trim the sheet to 15 × 22 inches (37.5 × 55 cm).

4. Spread the jam evenly over the entire surface of the sponge.

5. Pick up the two upper corners of the paper and roll the cake into a tight log, starting from the top long edge and rolling the cake toward you, using the paper underneath to help you form the roll. Leaving the paper in place around the cake, hold the bottom of the paper still with your left hand, and push a dowel or ruler against the roll with your free hand. The paper will wrap around the roll and tighten it (see Figure 15–4, page 426).

6. Place the pieces seam-side down on sheet pans lined with baking paper, cover and refrigerate until ready to serve.

7. Cut the roll into two 11-inch (27.5-cm) pieces, or into individual servings approximately ¾ inch (20 mm) wide.

Roulade Batter
one 16- × 24-inch (40- × 60-cm) sheet or one 10-inch (25-cm) layer

8 eggs
2 egg whites
6 ounces (170 g) granulated sugar
grated zest of ½ lemon
4 ounces (115 g) cake flour
4 ounces (115 g) bread flour
1 teaspoon (4 g) baking powder
3 ounces (85 g) melted butter

1. Place the whole eggs, egg whites, sugar, and lemon zest in a mixing bowl.

2. Heat over simmering water, whipping constantly, until the mixture reaches approximately 110°F (43°C). Remove from heat and whip at high speed until the mixture has cooled completely and is light and fluffy.

3. Sift the flours with the baking powder. Fold the flour into the batter by hand. Fold in the melted butter by hand.

Tiger Cake

four 17-ounce (485-g) cakes

melted butter
finely ground bread crumbs
8 eggs, at room temperature
1 pound, 2 ounces (510 g)
   granulated sugar
¾ cup (180 ml) milk,
   at room temperature
1 pound, 6 ounces (625 g)
   melted butter
14 ounces (400 g) cake flour
1 tablespoon (12 g) baking powder
1 ounce (30 g) cocoa powder
grated zest of 2 lemons
1 teaspoon (5 ml) vanilla extract

1. Brush the inside of four 1-quart (960-ml) capacity gugelhupf forms with melted butter and coat with the bread crumbs.

2. Separate the eggs. Whip the egg yolks with 9 ounces (255 g) of sugar until light and fluffy. Add the milk and melted butter (the butter should not be hot).

3. Sift the flour with the baking powder, then mix into the butter mixture.

4. Whip the egg whites until foamy. Gradually add the remaining sugar and whip to stiff peaks. Carefully fold the butter mixture into the whipped egg whites by hand.

5. Sift the cocoa powder into a bowl; gradually add one-third of the batter and mix to combine. Mix the lemon zest and the vanilla into the remaining two-thirds of the batter.

6. Starting and finishing with the white batter, spoon three or four alternating layers of white and chocolate batters into the prepared forms. If you are using small forms, fill each one only two-thirds full.

7. Bake immediately at 375°F (190°C) for about 40 minutes, or until the cake springs back when pressed lightly. Unmold onto a cake rack to cool. When the cakes have cooled completely, wrap them in plastic and store in the refrigerator.

Decorated Cakes

Apple Wine Cake
Apricot Cream Cake
Black Currant Cake
Black Forest Cake
Caramel Cake
Carrot Cake
Cheesecake
Chestnut Puzzle Cake
Chocolate and Frangelico
   Mousse Cake
Chocolate Decadence
Chocolate Hazelnut Cake
Chocolate Mousse Cake
   with Banana
Chocolate Truffle Cake
   with Raspberries
Coconut Cake Hawaii
Gâteau au Diplomate
Gâteau Istanbul

Gâteau Lugano
Gâteau Malakoff
Gâteau Moka Carrousel
Gâteau Saint-Honoré
Harlequin Cake
Lemon Chiffon Cake
Pariser Chocolate Cake
Poppy Seed Cake
Princess Cake
Queen of Sheba Cake
Raspberry Cake
Sacher Torte
Sicilian Macaroon Cake
Strawberry Kirsch Cake
Swedish Chocolate Cake
Tropical Mousse Cake
White Chocolate Pumpkin
   Cheesecake

*T*he *term decorated cake* is generally used to describe a cake that is filled, iced, and has some type of finishing touch on the icing. Whether or not the cake is decorated attractively can influence your sales to a great degree. The decoration should tempt the customer to try the product, and at the same time it should suggest the flavor and texture of the cake and filling. The decoration is the final wrapping, or packaging, designed to market your product.

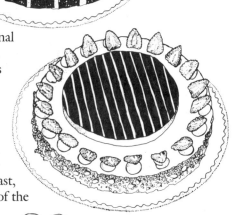

The degree of complexity of the cake decorations in this chapter ranges from Princess Cake, which traditionally has only a thin sheet of marzipan encasing the whole cake and a dusting of powdered sugar on top, to the more elaborately decorated Lemon Chiffon Cake. The latter is iced with whipped cream; the surface of the cake is covered with lemon glaze or chocolate shavings; the side of each serving is decorated with a thin handmade chocolate square; and last, rosettes of whipped cream are piped around the perimeter of the cake and topped with a small wedge of lemon.

Most of the cakes in this chapter are decorated after being marked or cut into serving pieces. This enables you to decorate each serving identically. If you are displaying the cakes in a pastry case, the servings will still look attractive even if only a few remain. Precut or marked slices can save time for the waitperson or retail clerk; it is also a good idea for the chef to designate the portion size from the standpoint of cost control. If you do choose to cut the pieces rather than mark them, you may want to cover the cut sides of each slice with small sheets of paper to prevent the cake from drying out. The slices should then be reassembled into the original shape for display. Any of the cakes in this chapter can also be decorated before cutting using the techniques and special-occasion designs described in the decorations chapter.

Before you can ice and decorate a cake, it is usually necessary to cut a baked sponge into two or three layers and stack these layers on top of the filling. Cutting and moving thin sponge layers is often a more challenging skill for students to master than some of the decorating procedures. Use a serrated knife to slice the layers and hold the blade of the knife parallel to the tabletop. Place your left hand flat on top of the cake (if you are right-handed) and turn the cake counterclockwise as you cut. Do not move the knife from side to side; hold it level and only move it away and toward you as you move the cake into the knife's path. Start by cutting the skin off the top of the cake and cutting the top flat at the same time if necessary. Then cut the desired number of layers, starting from the top and removing each layer before cutting the next. After making the cut for the first layer, leave the layer in place on the cake. Carefully slide a cardboard cake round into the cut, easing it in by wiggling it up and down a bit instead of just pushing it into the cut, which can break the cake. Then simply pick up the cardboard to move the layer to the side, and repeat to cut the remaining layers. It becomes more difficult to cut thin, even layers as the size of the sponge increases. Use the same technique for all sizes. With practice, and assuming the sponge has been baked correctly, it should be possible to move the layers of a standard 10-inch (25-cm) sponge using your hand, or by lifting the cake with the knife used for slicing, rather than using a cardboard.

When you are ready to stack the layers pick up the cardboard and hold the layer just above the cake where you want to place it. Slide the cake off the cardboard and onto the cake, guiding it into position with your free hand as you pull the cardboard away from the bottom (see Figure 8–12, page 213 as an example).

Note that many of the cakes in this chapter use gelatin to thicken the filling so the cakes can be sliced attractively. Gelatin is first softened by sprinkling it over a cold liquid (do not stir at this point or you will get lumps) and allowing it to stand two or three minutes. It is then heated to dissolve it completely. The degree to which the gelatin is heated depends on how it will be used. In Black Currant Cake, for example, the gelatin for the glaze is heated to a relatively low temperature: 110°F (43°C). It is added to only a small amount of liquid, and you want it to start setting up fairly quickly so you can spread it over the cakes. On the other hand, in the recipe for Chocolate Cognac Cream, you will see the instructions call for heating the gelatin to 150°F (65°C). Here the gelatin is added to a large amount of cold whipped cream, and you need time to mix it in thoroughly before it sets up. In this particular filling, melted chocolate, which is a thickening agent in itself, is also added at the same time; this causes the filling to set up more rapidly. In general, it is better to heat gelatin a bit too hot than to have the filling lump because the gelatin was too cold. However, never heat gelatin close to the boiling point, and discard any gelatin that boils accidentally as it will partially lose its ability to thicken.

Apple Wine Cake

two 10-inch (25-cm) cakes

*1 recipe Almond Sponge batter
    (page 162)*
*8 medium-sized apples (Golden
    Delicious, pippin, or Granny
    Smith)*
*3 cups (720 ml) muscat or
    riesling wine*
1 tablespoon (15 ml) lemon juice
1 cinnamon stick
⅔ cup (160 ml) calvados
4 ounces (115 g) dark raisins
*two 10-inch (25-cm) Short Dough
    Cake-Bottoms (page 32)*
4 ounces (115 g) soft apricot jam
*Calvados Wine Filling
    (recipe follows)*
*8 ounces (225 g) smooth
    raspberry jam*
1 cup (240 ml) heavy cream
*2 teaspoons (10 g) granulated
    sugar*
1 recipe Apricot Glaze (page 526)
*sliced almonds, toasted and
    lightly crushed*
*1 recipe Mousseline Sauce
    (page 561)*
¼ cup (60 ml) calvados
mint sprigs

1. Line the bottom of a 10-inch (25-cm) cake pan with baking paper (or grease and flour, but do not grease and flour the sides).
2. Pour a little more than half of the sponge batter into the pan and even the surface.
3. Pour the remainder of the batter onto a sheet of baking paper and spread into a 20- × 15-inch (50- × 37.5-cm) rectangle. Drag the paper onto a sheet pan (see Figure 15–3, page 422).
4. Bake both sponges at 400°F (205°C). The sheet will take approximately 8 minutes to bake and the round cake about 18 minutes, or until the top springs back when pressed lightly in the center.
5. Immediately transfer the thin sheet to a second (cool) sheet pan. Let both sponges cool completely.
6. Peel the apples, core, and cut into ½-inch (1.2-cm) thick wedges (not slices). To prevent oxidation, keep the apples in acidulated water as you are working.
7. Combine wine, lemon juice, cinnamon stick, and ⅔ cup (160 ml) calvados in a saucepan. Heat the liquid to boiling, then add the raisins and apple wedges. Simmer until the apples are soft, but not falling apart. Set the apples and raisins aside to cool in the liquid.
8. Cut the skin from the top of the round sponge cake. Slice the cake into four thin layers. Reserve two of the layers for another project or use them to make the variation of this recipe (instructions follow).
9. Place the short dough cake-bottoms ⊂ cardboard rounds for support. Divide the apricot jam between them and spread out evenly. Place one sponge layer on each.

10. Remove the cinnamon stick from the apples and raisins and discard it. Strain off the liquid. Reserve 1 cup (240 ml) of the poaching liquid to use in making the filling, and brush some of the remainder over the sponge cakes to soak them lightly. Discard the remainder of the liquid unless you are making the variation.

11. Remove about half of the raisins from the apple-raisin mixture and reserve them to use in the presentation. Divide the remaining apple-raisin mixture between the two cakes, arranging the apple wedges in concentric circles on top of the sponge.

12. Place 10-inch (25-cm) cake rings snugly around each sponge. (If the rings are not stainless steel, line them with strips of plastic or baking paper to prevent the metal from discoloring the filling.) Divide the Calvados Wine Filling between the two cakes. The filling should be just starting to thicken when you pour it into the rings. Refrigerate the cakes until the filling is set, approximately 2 hours.

13. Invert the thin sponge sheet onto a sheet of baking paper, then peel the paper off the back of the sponge. If the sponge has been made ahead and refrigerated carefully, scrape the skin off the top of the sponge first before inverting it. Cut the sponge in half lengthwise and transfer one half to a second sheet pan. Spread the raspberry jam over the entire surface of both sponge sheets. There should be just enough jam to make the surface sticky. Roll the sponge sheets lengthwise following the instructions in the recipe for Yule Logs (see Figure 15–4, page 426). Place the jelly rolls in the freezer to make them firm and easier to cut.

14. Remove the cake rings and the paper or plastic strips from the two round cakes. Trim away any excess short dough to even the sides of the cakes.

15. Whip the heavy cream and the sugar to stiff peaks. Ice the top and sides of the cakes with a thin layer of whipped cream.

16. Cut the jelly rolls into thin slices, approximately 1/8 inch (3 mm) wide. Starting at the edge of the cakes, arrange the slices in concentric circles covering the tops of the cakes. Place the rounds in each circle between those in the previous row to cover as much of the surface as possible.

17. Brush the jelly rolls with apricot glaze.

18. Cover the sides of the cakes with sliced almonds (see Figure 8–1, page 178).

19. Flavor the Mousseline Sauce with the calvados.

20. Cut the cakes into the desired number of servings.

21. Presentation: Place a slice of cake off-center on a dessert plate. Pour a pool of Mousseline Sauce in front of the dessert. Sprinkle some of the reserved raisins over the sauce and place a sprig of mint next to the sauce.

Variation

Omit the jelly rolls. Use all four sponge layers. Double the amounts of apples, raisins, and poaching liquid. Divide the mixture in half after cooking, reserving the most attractive apple wedges for decorating the cakes. Assemble the cakes as in the preceding recipe, placing the second sponges on top of the cream filling and brushing them lightly with some of the poaching liquid before refrigerating the cakes. Decorate the tops of the cakes with reserved apple wedges and raisins (instead of jelly roll slices) arranging the apples in concentric circles as in the layer inside.

Calvados Wine Filling

3 pounds, 8 ounces (1 kg, 590 g) filling

4 egg yolks
2 ounces (55 g) granulated sugar
5 cups (1 l, 200 ml) heavy cream
2 tablespoons (18 g) unflavored gelatin powder
1 cup (240 ml) strained liquid from poaching the apples, chilled
¼ cup (60 ml) calvados

1. Whip the egg yolks and sugar until light and fluffy.
2. Whip the cream to soft peaks. Combine the cream with the yolk mixture.
3. Soften the gelatin in the poaching liquid. Add the calvados, then heat the mixture to 125°F (52°C) to dissolve.
4. Rapidly mix the gelatin into a small part of the cream mixture; then, still working quickly, mix this into the remaining cream and yolks.

NOTE: Because you cannot reheat this filling to soften it, do not make it until you are ready to assemble the cakes.

Apricot Cream Cake

(see photograph in color insert)
two 10-inch (25-cm) cakes

two 10-inch (25-cm) Short Dough Cake-Bottoms (page 32)
4 ounces (115 g) smooth apricot jam
two 10-inch (25-cm) Vanilla Butter Cakes (page 165)
Apricot Whipped Cream (recipe follows)
1½ cups (360 ml) heavy cream
1 tablespoon (15 g) granulated sugar
almonds, roasted and lightly crushed
dark chocolate shavings
apricot wedges
Apricot Sauce (page 556)
mint sprigs

1. Place the short dough bottoms on cardboard cake rounds for support. Divide the jam between them and spread it out evenly.
2. Cut the butter cakes into two layers each. Place one layer on top of each short dough bottom. Place 10-inch (25-cm) cake rings around each sponge, setting them on top of the short dough. If the cake rings are not stainless steel, line them with strips of baking paper or plastic.
3. Divide the Apricot Whipped Cream between the two rings and spread it out evenly. Place the remaining cake layers on top of the filling. Refrigerate the cakes for at least 2 hours to set the filling.
4. Whip the heavy cream and granulated sugar to stiff peaks.
5. Remove the rings and paper or plastic strips from the cakes. Trim the short dough around the base of the cakes to make the sides even.
6. Ice the top and sides of the cakes with the whipped cream. Use just enough of the cream to cover the sponge. Place the remaining whipped cream in a pastry bag with a no. 6 (12-mm) plain tip and reserve. Cover the sides of the cakes with the crushed roasted almonds (Figure 8–1, page 178).

Figure 8–1

7. Cut a 6-inch (15-cm) circle out of the center of a 10-inch (25-cm) cardboard circle. Place the doughnut-shaped template on top of one of the cakes. Sprinkle the shaved chocolate over the top to cover the center of the cake. Carefully remove the template and repeat with the second cake.

8. Cut or mark the cakes into the desired number of pieces. Pipe a rosette of the reserved whipped cream at the edge of each slice; top each rosette with an apricot wedge.

9. Presentation: Place a slice of cake off-center on a dessert plate. Pour a small pool of Apricot Sauce in front of the slice. Place a mint sprig next to the sauce.

Apricot Whipped Cream
4 pounds (1 kg, 820 g)

6 egg yolks
5 ounces (140 g) granulated sugar
3 cups (720 ml) heavy cream
2 tablespoons (18 g) unflavored gelatin powder
½ cup (120 ml) cold water
½ cup (120 ml) Cointreau or other orange liqueur
¼ cup (60 ml) apricot juice
2 ounces (55 g) apricot purée
1 pound (455 g) apricot chunks

1. Whip egg yolks and sugar until light and fluffy.

2. Whip the cream to soft peaks; fold into yolk mixture.

3. Soften gelatin in the cold water. Heat to 125°F (52°C) to dissolve. Add Cointreau and apricot juice to gelatin.

4. Remove about one-fourth of the cream mixture and rapidly mix the gelatin into it. Working quickly, add this to the remaining cream. Fold in the apricot purée and chunks.

5. If the filling has not started to set up, wait a few minutes and mix again before using in the cakes to prevent the apricot chunks from sinking to the bottom of the filling.

Black Currant Cake

(see photograph in color insert)

two 10-inch (25-cm) cakes

*two 10-inch (25-cm) Short Dough
   Cake-Bottoms (page 32)*
*4 ounces (115 g) smooth
   apricot jam*
*one 10-inch (25-cm) Cocoa
   Almond Sponge (page 163)*
*¼ cup (60 ml) Black Currant
   Purée (recipe follows)*
¼ cup (60 ml) crème de cassis
*Black Currant Mousse
   (recipe follows)*
*Black Currant Glaze
   (recipe follows)*
*reserved black currants
   (see purée recipe)*
granulated sugar
Apricot Sauce (page 556)
*Chocolate Sauce for Piping
   (page 560)*
*fanned fresh apricot halves or
   other fruit in season*
mint sprigs

1. Place the short dough bottoms on cardboard cake rounds for support. Divide the jam between them and spread it out evenly.

2. Cut the skin off the top of the sponge cake, cutting the cake even at the same time. Slice into two layers and set them on the jam.

3. Combine the Black Currant Purée with the crème de cassis. Brush the mixture over the sponges, allowing all of the liquid to soak in.

4. Put 10-inch (25-cm) cake rings around the sponge layers, setting them on top of the short dough. If the cake rings are not stainless steel, line them with baking paper or plastic. Divide the Black Currant Mousse between the two cakes. Refrigerate for at least 2 hours to set the filling.

5. When the cakes are completely set, carefully run a thin knife dipped in hot water around the inside of the rings, then remove the rings. (If you have lined the rings with paper or plastic, just cut the mousse free from the paper, then remove the rings and peel away the paper.) Trim away any short dough that protrudes outside the sponge to make the sides even.

6. Pour half of the Black Currant Glaze on one cake and quickly spread it out with a metal spatula to cover the whole surface. Repeat with second cake. Be sure that the glaze is not too hot or it can melt the filling. Also, do not pour it straight down in one spot or it will make a hole.

7. Refrigerate the cakes for a few minutes to set the glaze. If any glaze has run down the sides, cut it away with a knife. Warm a metal spatula and use it to smooth the sides of the cakes.

8. Slice the cakes into the desired number of serving pieces using a thin knife dipped in hot water (let the warm knife melt through the glaze, then cut).

9. Roll the reserved black currants in granulated sugar to coat them. Place one at the edge of each slice. If necessary, attach them to the cake by touching a hot metal skewer or heated knife-tip to the glaze to melt it, then set the currant on top.

10. Presentation: Place a slice of cake off-center on a dessert plate. Pour a pool of Apricot Sauce in front of the slice and decorate it with the Chocolate Sauce for Piping (see pages 518–519). Place a fanned apricot half on the opposite side of the plate and place a mint sprig next to the apricot.

Black Currant Mousse

4 pounds (1 kg, 820 g)

3 cups (720 ml) heavy cream
6 egg whites
6 ounces (170 g) granulated sugar
8 ounces (225 g) white chocolate,
  melted
1½ cups (360 ml) Black Currant
  Purée (recipe follows)
2 tablespoons (18 g) unflavored
  gelatin powder
¾ cup (180 ml) cold water

1. Whip the cream to soft peaks. Reserve in the refrigerator.
2. Combine the egg whites and sugar. Heat the mixture over simmering water until it reaches 110°F (43°C), whipping constantly to prevent the egg whites from cooking on the bottom. Remove from the heat and continue whipping until the mixture is cold and has formed stiff peaks.
3. Stir the white chocolate into the Black Currant Purée.
4. Soften the gelatin in the water. Heat to 125°F (52°C) to dissolve.
5. Rapidly add the gelatin mixture to the currant purée (be sure that the purée is not any cooler than room temperature). Gradually fold this mixture into the reserved meringue. Fold into reserved whipped cream.
NOTE: Because gelatin sets fairly quickly, do not make this filling until you are ready to use it.

Black Currant Glaze

enough to cover tops of two 10-inch (25-cm) cakes

1 tablespoon (9 g) unflavored
  gelatin powder
3 ounces (90 ml) cold water
3 ounces (90 ml) Simple Syrup
  (page 7)
¼ cup (60 ml) Black Currant
  Purée (recipe follows)

1. Soften the gelatin in the water. Heat to 110°F (43°C) to dissolve.
2. Stir in the simple syrup and the currant purée and use as soon as the glaze shows signs of the thickening. Should the glaze thicken too much before it can be applied, reheat to insure a smooth glaze on the cakes.

Black Currant Purée

approximately 2 cups (480 ml)
purée

2 pounds (910 g) fresh or frozen
  black currants (see note)
1 cup (240 ml) water
4 ounces (115 g) granulated sugar

1. Reserve one whole black currant to decorate each serving of cake. Combine the remaining currants with the water and granulated sugar in a skillet.
2. Cook over low heat until the currants start to soften, about 5 minutes.
3. Purée the mixture, then pass the purée through a strainer. Divide as follows:

- ¼ cup (60 ml) to use in assembling the cakes
- ¼ cup (60 ml) to use in the glaze
- remainder, approximately 1½ cups (360 ml), to use in the mousse

NOTE: If using black currants in heavy syrup, strain and reserve the syrup before weighing the currants. Substitute 2 cups (480 ml) of syrup for the granulated sugar and the water.

Variation: Cranberry Mousse Cake

If black currants are not available, or if you want to make a dessert especially suitable for the holiday season, you can alter the recipe in the following ways:

- Substitute cranberry purée for the Black Currant Purée.
- Use whole cranberries instead of currants to decorate.
- Replace crème de cassis with cranberry juice.
- Serve cranberry sauce instead of chocolate sauce.
- Add an additional 8 ounces (225 g) of granulated sugar when you make the cranberry purée.

To make cranberry purée
Set aside the number of berries you need for decoration. Add the additional sugar to the remaining cranberries in a skillet or saucepan (add sugar and water in recipe). Cook over low heat for 2 or 3 minutes, or until the cranberries are soft and start to pop open. Purée.

Black Forest Cake

two 10-inch (25-cm) cakes

1 recipe Chocolate Sponge Cake batter (page 162)
¼ cup (60 ml) kirschwasser
2 tablespoons (30 ml) Simple Syrup (page 7)
2 cups (480 ml) heavy cream
two 10-inch (25-cm) Short Dough Cake-Bottoms (page 32)
4 ounces (115 g) smooth apricot jam
½ recipe Cherry Filling (page 565)
1½ cups (360 ml) heavy cream
1 tablespoon (15 g) granulated sugar
Dark Chocolate Squares (page 445)
dark chocolate shavings
powdered sugar
fresh cherries

1. Divide the Chocolate Sponge Cake batter between two 10-inch (25-cm) greased and floured cake pans. Bake at 400°F (205°C) for approximately 12 minutes. Set aside to cool.

2. Combine the kirschwasser and simple syrup. Reserve.

3. Whip 2 cups (480 ml) heavy cream with half of the kirschwasser mixture to stiff peaks. Reserve.

4. Place the short dough cake-bottoms on cardboards for support. Divide the apricot jam between them, and spread it evenly over the surface.

5. Unmold the cooled sponge cakes and cut them into two layers each. Place one layer on each jam-covered short dough round, saving the two better sponges for the top if there seems to be any difference.

6. Divide the cherry filling between the two cakes and spread it out carefully. Divide the whipped cream between the cakes and spread it out evenly on top of the filling.

7. Place the second sponge layers on top of the cream, making sure the cakes are level. Brush the remaining kirschwasser mixture over the sponges.

8. If you plan to precut the cakes into serving pieces you should cover them at this point and place them in the freezer until they are frozen solid. This will enable you to cut cleanly through the cream and the cherries without dragging one into the other.

Figure 8–2

9. On removing the cakes from the freezer, trim away any excess short dough that protrudes outside the sponge (Figure 8–2). Whip the remaining heavy cream with the granulated sugar to stiff peaks. Spread enough of the cream over the top and sides of the cakes to cover the sponge. Reserve the remainder.

10. When the cakes have thawed halfway, cut them into the desired number of pieces. Put the remaining whipped cream in a pastry bag with a no. 6 (12-mm) star tip and pipe a rosette at the edge of each slice. Place a chocolate square on the side of each slice. Sprinkle the shaved chocolate over the top of the cake, inside the piped rosettes. Sift powdered sugar lightly over the shavings. Place a cherry on each whipped cream rosette.

NOTE: If fresh cherries are not available, substitute a small wedge of fresh strawberry for decoration or leave the rosettes plain rather than using canned (or worse yet, the infamous maraschino) cherries.

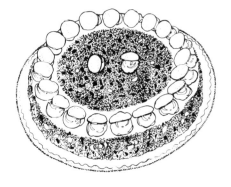

Caramel Cake

(see photograph in color insert)

two 10-inch (25-cm) cakes

one 10-inch (25-cm) Almond
  Sponge (page 162), see note
one 10-inch (25-cm) Cocoa
  Almond Sponge (page 163),
  see note
two 10-inch (25-cm) Short Dough
  Cake-Bottoms (page 32)
4 ounces (115 g) smooth
  apricot jam
Caramel Cream (recipe follows)
1½ cups (360 ml) heavy cream
1 tablespoon (15 g) granulated
  sugar
sliced almonds, roasted and
  lightly crushed
dark chocolate shavings
Caramel Sauce II (page 558)
Chocolate Sauce for Piping
  (page 560)
Sour Cream Mixture for Piping
  (page 564)

1. Cut the skin and ⅛ inch (3 mm) off the tops of the sponges, cutting them even at the same time. Cut each sponge into two layers.

2. Using a 5½-inch (13.7-cm) plain cookie cutter, cut a circle from the center of all four layers. Place the center circles from the light sponge inside the rings from the dark sponge and vice versa.

3. Place the short dough bottoms on cake cardboards for support. Spread the apricot jam evenly on top. Place one of the dark rings with a light center on top of the jam on each cake. Place adjustable cake rings around both cakes, fitting them snugly around the sponge layer, and set them on top of the short dough.

4. Divide the Caramel Cream between the two cakes and spread it out evenly. It should have a thick enough consistency that it will hold its shape as you spread it. If not, wait until the cream thickens a little more before using. Place the remaining sponge layers on top of the cream.

5. Refrigerate the cakes for about 2 hours to set the cream.

6. Whip the heavy cream and sugar to soft peaks. Trim away any excess short dough from the bottom of the cakes to make the sides even. Ice the top and sides of the cakes with the whipped cream.

7. Cover the sides of the cakes with the sliced almonds (see Figure 8–1, page 178). Place the 5½-inch (13.7-cm) cookie cutter in the center of one of the cakes and sprinkle the shaved chocolate around the outside of the cake. Repeat with the other cake. Cut the cakes into the desired number of slices.

8. Presentation: Place a slice of cake off-center on a dessert plate. Pour a pool of Caramel Sauce in front of the slice. Decorate the outer edge of the sauce using the Chocolate Sauce for Piping and the Sour Cream Mixture for Piping, as shown in the color insert.

NOTE: If you do not have sponges on hand, instead of making two separate sponges, make the Almond Sponge recipe, divide the batter in half, and add 1½ (40 g) of cocoa powder to one half.

Caramel Cream

3 pounds, 2 ounces (1 kg, 420 g)

12 ounces (340 g) granulated
  sugar
1 cup (240 ml) hot water
3½ cups (840 ml) heavy cream
4 teaspoons (12 g) unflavored
  gelatin powder
⅓ cup (80 ml) cold water

1. Caramelize the sugar to a light brown color (see note and page 448). Add the hot water. Cook out any lumps and cool completely. If you evaporate too much water while cooking the caramel, it will be too thick when it is cold to combine with the cream. Add just enough hot water to bring it to a syrupy consistency.

2. Whip the cream to soft peaks. Fold in the cooled caramel.

3. Soften the gelatin in the cold water, then heat to 125°F (52°C) to dissolve.

4. Rapidly mix the gelatin into a small portion of the cream, then quickly add that mixture to the remainder of the cream.

NOTE: It is important to caramelize the sugar dark enough; not only to color the filling, but also to give it a caramel flavor.

Carrot Cake

two 10-inch (25-cm) cakes

Carrot Sponges (recipe follows)
Cream Cheese Filling
  (recipe follows)
8 ounces (225 g) Vanilla
  Buttercream (page 501)
hazelnuts, toasted and
  finely crushed
10 ounces (285 g) white
  Marzipan (page 531)
powdered sugar
dark baker's chocolate, melted
Marzipan Carrots
  (procedure follows)

1. Cut the tops off the Carrot Sponges to make them level. Cut both sponges in half to make two layers each.

2. Divide the Cream Cheese Filling between the bottom layers; spread it out evenly. Place the top layers on the filling.

3. Ice the tops and sides of the cakes with a thin layer of buttercream. Cover the sides of the cakes with crushed hazelnuts.

4. Roll out the marzipan, using powered sugar to prevent it from sticking, to ⅛ inch (3 mm) thick. Cut out two circles the same size as the tops of the cakes. Place them on the cakes.

5. Place a cardboard circle on each cake and invert the cakes onto the cardboards. Place in the refrigerator (upside down) to flatten the tops and firm the filling (do not leave the cakes for more than two hours or the moist air will make the marzipan wet).

6. Turn the cakes right-side up and cut them into the desired number of serving pieces. Sift powdered sugar very lightly over the cakes. Pipe a dime-sized dot of melted baker's chocolate on each slice, ½ inch (1.2 cm) from the edge. Before the chocolate hardens, place a marzipan carrot on top.

Carrot Sponge

two 10-inch (25-cm) sponges

8 eggs
1½ cups (360 ml) vegetable oil
1 pound, 12 ounces (795 g)
  granulated sugar
1 teaspoon (5 g) salt
1 pound, 2 ounces (510 g)
  bread flour
3 tablespoons (15 g) ground
  cinnamon
1½ teaspoons (6 g) baking soda
½ teaspoon (2 g) baking powder
2 pounds (910 g) peeled carrots,
  shredded or grated finely
5 ounces (140 g) walnuts, chopped

1. Whip the eggs to a light and frothy consistency, then gradually add the oil. Turn mixer speed to low and mix in sugar and salt.

2. Sift together the flour, cinnamon, baking soda, and baking powder. Add to the egg mixture. Fold in the carrots and walnuts, evenly distributing them in the batter.

3. Divide the batter between two greased and floured 10-inch (25-cm) cake pans. Bake at 375°F (190°C) for about 50 minutes.

NOTE: The Carrot Sponge can be baked in a tube cake pan and served plain as a tea cake. The batter can also be baked in sheets, cut into bite-sized pieces, and topped with a small rosette of Cream Cheese Filling. When the sponges are made into decorated layer cakes it is necessary to level the tops before assembling. Baking powder and baking soda stop working at approximately 170°F (77°C); the batter next to the side of the pan reaches that temperature first (in part due to the hot metal), so a heavy sponge like this one always bakes higher in the middle.

Cream Cheese Filling

1 pound, 10 ounces (740 g)

14 ounces (400 g) cream cheese,
  at room temperature
4 ounces (115 g) softened butter
1 teaspoon (5 ml) vanilla extract
8 ounces (225 g) powdered sugar,
  sifted

1. Soften the cream cheese in a mixer without beating in any air.

2. Mix the butter in gradually. Add the vanilla and powdered sugar.

3. Mix until smooth and spreadable, but do not overmix.

Marzipan Carrots

24 carrot decorations

5 ounces (140 g) white Marzipan (page 531)
red, yellow, and green food coloring

1. Color 1 ounce (30 g) of the marzipan green. Reserve, covered. Use red and yellow food coloring to tint the remainder orange.

2. Roll the orange marzipan out to an 18-inch (45-cm) rope. Cut the rope into twenty-four ¾-inch (2-cm) pieces, one piece for each serving of cake. Keep the pieces covered with plastic to prevent them from drying out.

3. Roll the pieces one at a time (two at a time after some practice) into round balls between your palms. Roll the balls into cone shapes, about 1 inch (2.5 cm) long, by rolling them back and forth against the table.

4. Mark the cones crosswise with a small knife to make them look ringed like a carrot. Starting at the wide end, turn them slowly and make random vertical marks all around. Make a small round hole in the wide end of each carrot using a thin metal skewer.

5. Roll the green marzipan into a thin rope. Cut out 24 pea-sized pieces. Roll each one into a ½-inch (1.2-cm) string tapered on both ends.

6. Insert one end of the green stem into the hole in each carrot. Cut and fan the other end of each one to resemble a carrot top.

Cheesecake

two 10-inch (25-cm) cakes

8 ounces (225 g) graham cracker crumbs
4 ounces (115 g) melted butter
3 pounds, 7 ounces (1 kg, 565 g) cream cheese, at room temperature
7 eggs
1 pound (455 g) granulated sugar
3 pounds (1 kg, 365 g) sour cream
7 ounces (200 g) granulated sugar
flavoring (choices follow)

1. Mix the graham cracker crumbs with the melted butter. Divide the crumbs between two 10-inch (25-cm) springform pans, covering the bottoms of the pans, and pat the crumbs even with your hands. (If the springform pans are not stainless steel, line the inside of the rings with strips of baking paper to avoid staining the filling. Cut the paper to the exact height of the rings and fasten to the inside of the pan using melted butter.)

2. Soften the cream cheese in a mixer on low speed using the paddle attachment, or by stirring, until it has a smooth consistency. Take care not to incorporate too much air or you will end up with a dry and crumbly cheesecake.

3. Lightly mix the eggs and 1 pound (455 g) of sugar, stirring them together by hand. Gradually add the egg mixture to the cream cheese, scraping the bottom and sides of the mixing bowl frequently to avoid lumps. Divide the batter between the prepared pans and spread out evenly.

4. Bake at 375°F (190°C) until just done, about 30 minutes. The filling should move in one mass inside the forms when gently shaken. If it moves more in the center than on the sides, continue baking. The cakes become firmer once they have cooled, so do not

overbake them "just to play it safe;" the cakes will crack on the surface and taste dry and stale.

5. Mix the sour cream with the remaining 7 ounces (200 g) of sugar. Divide the mixture between the baked cakes. (You can do this as soon as they are baked, but be careful not to damage the tops of the cakes when you pour on the sour cream mixture.)

6. Place the flavoring in a pastry bag with the piping tip indicated in the flavoring instructions. Pipe the flavoring in a spiral pattern on top of each cake, starting in the center. Run the back of a paring knife through the spiral starting in the center and pulling toward the edge of the pan to make a spider-web pattern. See the example in Figure 18–26, page 519.

7. Bake the cakes at 375°F (190°C) for 5 minutes to set the sour cream. The sour cream will still look liquid, but will set as it cools.

Flavorings

Lingonberry

Lingonberries are an expensive Scandinavian delicacy that look like small cranberries but taste sweeter. They are available as a preserve in most grocery stores. Pipe lingonberry jam in a spiral pattern using a no. 4 (8-mm) plain tip (or larger if necessary for the berries to go through).

Chocolate

Reserve ¼ cup (60 ml) of the sour cream mixture per cake. Flavor the remainder with 2 tablespoons (16 g) cocoa powder per cake. Top the baked cheesecake with the cocoa-flavored sour cream and use the reserved plain sour cream mixture to pipe the spiral pattern on top, using a no. 2 (4-mm) plain tip.

Strawberry

Use good quality strawberry preserves. If the preserves have large chunks of purée or fruit, break up the chunks with a spoon. Pipe onto the cakes in a spiral pattern using a no. 2 (4-mm) plain tip. For a fresh strawberry topping, bake the sour cream mixture plain. Top the cooled cakes with strawberries cut into thin slices lengthwise. Brush the strawberries with Apricot Glaze (page 526).

Variation: New York Style Cheesecake
one 10-inch (25-cm) cake

Follow the procedure in the main recipe with these changes: Use 1 pound, 2 ounces (510 g) cream cheese; 4 eggs; 8 ounces (225 g) sugar; 1 pound, 8 ounces (680 g) sour cream; and the grated zest of one small lemon. Line the pan with graham cracker crumbs halfway up the side as well as on the bottom. Incorporate the sour cream and lemon zest after adding the egg and sugar mixture. Bake at 325°F (163°C) for approximately 1 hour, or until the filling is set. Serve with Blueberry Sauce (page 557).

Chestnut Puzzle Cake

(see photograph in color insert)
two 10-inch (25-cm) cakes

4 pounds, 8 ounces (2 kg, 45 g)
  Vanilla Buttercream (page 501)
12 ounces (340 g) unsweetened
  chestnut purée
12 ounces (340 g) dark chocolate,
  melted
two 10-inch (25-cm) Almond
  Sponges (page 162)
two 10-inch (25-cm) Cocoa
  Almond Sponges (page 163)
½ cup (120 ml) Frangelico liqueur
¼ cup (60 ml) water
dark chocolate shavings
Cold Chocolate Sauce (page 559)
Sour Cream Mixture for Piping
  (page 564)
strawberries

This is the showy kind of dessert that will have your customers and friends "oohing and aahing" even before they have discovered how delicious it is, trying to figure out how you managed to get the cake layers going in alternate directions! With this reward in mind, it is well worth the effort to make two different sponges, two flavors of buttercream, and go through all of the various steps.

1. Flavor 2 pounds (910 g) of the buttercream with the chestnut purée. Flavor the remaining buttercream with the melted dark chocolate. Set the buttercream aside.

2. Cut about one-third off the top of both Almond Sponges and reserve for another use (such as the refreshing Mandarin Tart with Armagnac, page 149). Slice the remaining two-thirds of each Almond Sponge in half.

3. Cut just enough off the top of the Cocoa Almond Sponges to make the tops even. Then cut the sponges into three layers each. (You need five ¼-inch (6-mm) layers of sponge cake, three cocoa and two almond, for each cake.) Cover two of the cocoa layers and reserve.

4. Place two of the remaining cocoa layers on cardboard cake rounds for support. Combine Frangelico and water; brush the layers with some of this mixture.

5. Spread 2 ounces (55 g) of the chestnut buttercream evenly over each layer.

6. Place an Almond Sponge on the buttercream on each cake, brush with the Frangelico mixture, and spread another 2 ounces (55 g) of the chestnut buttercream on top.

7. Continue layering, alternating one more cocoa and almond layer on each cake, brushing each sponge with the Frangelico mixture before spreading with 2 ounces (55 g) of buttercream. You should end with an almond sponge on top. Do not brush this one with the Frangelico mixture. Place the cakes in the refrigerator until the buttercream is completely set.

8. Using a serrated knife dipped in hot water, cut a cone-shaped piece from each cake, 8 inches (20 cm) in diameter at the top of the cake and approximately 2 inches (5 cm) in diameter at the bottom (Figure 8–3). Place one hand flat on the cake and, using the knife or a spatula to help you, remove the cone by inverting it onto your hand. Place the cone flat-side down on a cardboard. Repeat with the second cake.

9. Ice the inside of the "crater" and the remaining top edge of each cake with a ¼-inch (6-mm) layer of chocolate buttercream (Figure 8–4).

10. Place the reserved cocoa sponges flat on top of each cake. Place cardboard cake rounds on top and invert the cakes so the

Figure 8–3

Figure 8–4

Figure 8–5

Figure 8–6

uncut cocoa layers are on the bottom. (If possible, the cakes should be set aside at this point to allow the buttercream to soften, which makes it easier to form the top.)

11. Gently press the top around the hole in and down, so it touches the bottom of the cake, and you have a cone-shaped crater again (Figure 8–5). Repeat with the second cake.

12. Ice the new craters with a ¼-inch (6-mm) layer of chocolate buttercream. Replace the cones in the craters.

13. Trim the sides of the cakes to make them even. Ice the tops of the cakes with just enough chocolate buttercream to cover the sponge. Ice the sides with a ¼-inch (6-mm) layer of chocolate buttercream. Use a cake comb to make horizontal lines on the sides of the cakes (Figure 8–6). Even the top edges of the cakes.

14. Place the remaining chestnut buttercream in a pastry bag with a no. 3 (6-mm) plain tip. Pipe a spiral on top of each cake, piping the rings next to one another to cover the tops of the cakes completely (see example in Meringue Noisette, Figure 12–1, page 334).

15. Sprinkle shaved chocolate lightly on top. Refrigerate the cakes until the buttercream is firm. Cut the cakes into the desired number of serving pieces.

16. Presentation: Place a slice of cake off-center on a dessert plate. Pour a pool of Cold Chocolate Sauce in front of the slice and decorate the sauce with the Sour Cream Mixture for Piping (see pages 518–519). Place a strawberry half on the opposite side of the plate. Try to serve the cake at room temperature; buttercream tastes much better this way.

NOTE 1: If you are making only one cake, you can simplify things by making one recipe of Almond Sponge and baking one-third of the batter in a prepared 10-inch (25-cm) cake pan. Sift 1½ ounces (40 g) of cocoa powder over the remaining batter, carefully fold it in, and bake in a second prepared pan. Cut the plain sponge into two layers and the cocoa sponge into three layers, after cutting the tops even. Working the cocoa batter twice means you will get less volume and a slightly denser sponge, but you will save time.

NOTE 2: If you are having second thoughts about cutting the cone out of the cakes as described, try placing an instant-read meat thermometer or a metal skewer in the center of the cake, sticking it into the cardboard. Use it to guide the tip of your knife evenly around the bottom. You will not get the desired 2-inch (5-cm) hole in the bottom, but you will at least get an evenly cut cone.

Chocolate and Frangelico Mousse Cake

(see photograph in color insert)
two 10-inch (25-cm) cakes

one 10-inch (25-cm) Biscuit
*   Viennoise (page 163)*
two 10-inch (25-cm) Short Dough
*   Cake-Bottoms (page 32)*
4 ounces (115 g) currant jelly
Dark Chocolate Cream
*   (recipe follows)*
Frangelico Cream (recipe follows)
¾ cup (180 ml) heavy cream
1 teaspoon (5 g) granulated sugar
milk chocolate shavings
1-inch (2.5-cm) Chocolate Rounds
*   (page 445)*
½ recipe Mousseline Sauce
*   (page 561)*
1 ounce (30 ml) Frangelico liqueur
½ recipe Cold Chocolate Sauce
*   (page 559)*
seasonal fruit
mint sprigs

1. Slice the biscuit into three layers. Reserve the top layer for another use such as Rum Balls, page 254.

2. Place the short dough bottoms on cardboards for support. Divide the currant jelly between them and spread out evenly. Place the biscuit layers on top of the jelly.

3. Check the Chocolate Cream. If it seems too thin to hold its shape, stir until thickened. Divide the Chocolate Cream equally between the two cakes and spread it into a high dome shape.

4. Place adjustable cake rings snugly around the sponges. Unless the rings are made of stainless steel, line them with paper or plastic strips. Place the cakes in the refrigerator while you make the Frangelico Cream.

5. Divide the Frangelico Cream between the cakes and spread it out evenly on the top of the chocolate dome so the cakes are now level (Figure 8–7). Refrigerate the cakes until the fillings are set, about 2 hours. Also refrigerate the chocolate shavings to make them easier to put on the cakes.

6. Remove the rings and paper or plastic strips. Trim any short dough that protrudes outside the biscuit layer to make the sides even. Ice the sides of the cakes with a thin layer of whipped cream.

7. Place a 7-inch (17.5-cm) round template on the top of one of the cakes in the center. Use a spatula to pick up and gently pat the chilled chocolate shavings onto the side of the cake. Still using the spatula, sprinkle additional shavings over the top of the cake (if you were to use your hands, the shavings would melt as you touched them). Carefully remove the template and repeat with the second cake.

8. Whip the heavy cream with the sugar until stiff peaks form.

9. Mark or cut the cakes into the desired number of serving pieces. Place whipped cream in a pastry bag with a no. 6 (12-mm) plain tip. Pipe a mound of whipped cream on each slice, the size of a cherry, on the exposed cream just next to the shaved chocolate. Place a Chocolate Round on each mound.

10. Flavor the Mousseline Sauce with the Frangelico liqueur.

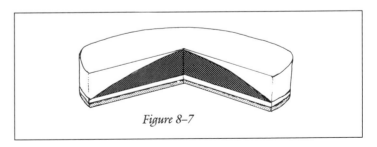

Figure 8–7

11. Presentation: Place a slice of cake in the center of a dessert plate. Pour pools of Cold Chocolate Sauce and Mousseline Sauce next to each other in front of the dessert. Swirl the sauces together where they meet (see photo in color insert). Place a small piece of fruit and a mint sprig behind the cake.

Dark Chocolate Cream

2 pounds, 6 ounces (1 kg, 80 g) cream

3 cups (720 ml) heavy cream
2 egg whites
2½ teaspoons (8 g) unflavored gelatin powder
¼ cup (60 ml) cold water
⅓ cup (80 ml) Simple Syrup (page 7)
¼ cup (60 ml) crème de cacao liqueur
4 ounces (115 g) dark chocolate, finely chopped

1. Whip the cream with the egg whites to a very soft consistency. The cream should fall in soft mounds, not peaks, when dropped from the whisk. If overwhipped, the mixture will break when you add the rest of the ingredients.
2. Soften the gelatin in cold water. Heat to 125°F (52°C) to dissolve.
3. Stir in the simple syrup, crème de cacao, and chocolate. Keep stirring until all the chocolate is melted.
4. Rapidly add this mixture to a small amount of the whipped cream. Then, still working quickly, add to the remaining cream. If the filling is not thick enough to hold its shape, just mix a little longer.

Frangelico Cream

2 pounds, 6 ounces (1 kg, 80 g) cream

3½ cups (840 ml) heavy cream
2 ounces (55 g) granulated sugar
4½ teaspoons (14 g) unflavored gelatin powder
½ cup (120 ml) cold water
½ cup (120 ml) Frangelico liqueur

1. Whip cream and sugar to soft peaks.
2. Soften the gelatin in cold water. Heat to 125°F (52°C) to dissolve. Add liqueur.
3. Rapidly stir the gelatin into a small part of the whipped cream. Then, still working quickly, add this mixture to the remaining cream.

Chocolate Decadence

(see photograph in color insert)
two 10-inch (25-cm) cakes

melted butter
12 ounces (340 g) dark chocolate
14 ounces (400 g) cocoa block
(bitter chocolate)
1¼ cups (300 ml) water
12 ounces (340 g) granulated
sugar
1 pound, 2 ounces (510 g)
softened butter
12 eggs
6 ounces (170 g) granulated sugar
3 cups (720 ml) heavy cream
2 tablespoons (30 g) granulated
sugar
toasted hazelnuts, crushed
dark chocolate shavings
Raspberry Sauce (page 563)
Sour Cream Mixture for Piping
(page 564)
raspberries or strawberries
for decoration
mint sprigs

1. Brush melted butter over the inside of two 10-inch (25-cm) cake pans. Place rounds of baking paper in the bottom and butter the papers. Set the pans aside.

2. Cut the dark chocolate and cocoa block into small pieces.

3. Bring the water and 12 ounces (340 g) of sugar to a boil. Remove from heat and add the chocolate; stir until the chocolate is melted and completely incorporated. Add the butter, in chunks, and stir until melted. Set aside at room temperature.

4. Whip the eggs with the 6 ounces (170 g) of sugar to the ribbon stage. Do not overwhip. Very gently, fold the mixture into the melted chocolate.

5. Divide the batter between the two prepared pans. Place the pans in a water bath.

6. Bake immediately at 350°F (175°C) for approximately 40 minutes, or until the top feels firm. Refrigerate the cakes at least 2 hours or, preferably, overnight. The chocolate must be completely set before you unmold or finish the cakes.

7. Unmold the cakes by briefly warming the outside of the pans (holding them over a gas flame is ideal), and invert them onto cardboard circles. If the cakes are where you want them to be when they are decorated, leave them as they are (upside down) since the tops of the cakes are drier and less likely to stick to the cardboard. If not, invert again onto serving platter or cardboard with doily.

8. Whip the cream with the 2 tablespoons (30 g) of sugar to stiff peaks. Ice the tops and sides of the cakes with a thin layer of cream. Cover the sides of the cakes with the hazelnuts.

9. Place the remaining whipped cream in a pastry bag with a no. 4 (8 mm) plain tip. Starting in the center of the cake (which can easily be located by marking the top into four pieces), pipe a spiral of whipped cream, with each circle touching the last one, over the entire top of the cake. Lightly sprinkle the chocolate shavings over the top. Cut the cakes into the required number of servings using a thin knife dipped in hot water. (See note.)

10. Presentation: Place the cake slice off-center on a dessert plate. Pour an oval pool of Raspberry Sauce in front. Decorate the sauce using the Sour Cream Mixture for Piping (see pages 518–519). Place three raspberries (or a fanned strawberry) and a mint sprig behind the cake slice.

NOTE: Chocolate Decadence must be cut when it is chilled, but should be served at room temperature. Due to the fragile consistency of this cake, it should be handled as little as possible. You cannot pick the cake up to move it; instead you must invert it onto a second platter if necessary.

Chocolate Hazelnut Cake

two 10-inch (25-cm) cakes

½ recipe Chocolate Sponge Cake batter (page 162)
2 pounds, 12 ounces (1 kg, 250 g) Vanilla Buttercream (page 501)
3 ounces (85 g) Hazelnut Paste (page 6)
4 ounces (115 g) dark chocolate, melted
two 10-inch (25-cm) Vanilla Butter Cakes (page 165)
hazelnuts, toasted and crushed
hazelnuts, toasted
Chocolate Rounds (page 445)
dark baker's chocolate, melted

1. Pour the Chocolate Sponge Cake batter into a greased and floured 10-inch (25-cm) cake pan and bake at 400°F (205°C) for about 12 minutes, or until done. Set aside to cool.

2. Flavor 1 pound, 8 ounces (680 g) of the buttercream with the hazelnut paste. Flavor the remaining buttercream with the dark chocolate.

3. Cut the chocolate cake into two layers. Cut the vanilla cakes into three layers each.

4. Place the chocolate cakes on cardboard cake rounds and spread a ⅛-inch (3-mm) thick layer of hazelnut buttercream on each. Place one of the vanilla layers on top of each and spread with hazelnut buttercream.

5. Add the remaining vanilla layers, two to each cake, layering with hazelnut buttercream between each layer the same way. Use all of the hazelnut buttercream.

6. Spread a thin layer of chocolate buttercream over the top and sides of the cakes. Reserve the remainder. Cover the sides of the cakes with crushed, toasted hazelnuts. Refrigerate the cakes until the buttercream is set.

7. Place one of the whole toasted hazelnuts in the middle of each chocolate round, securing it with the melted baker's chocolate. Make one decoration for each serving.

8. Cut or mark the cakes into the desired number of serving pieces. Place the remaining chocolate buttercream in a pastry bag with a no. 1 (3-mm) plain tip. Pipe two straight lines of buttercream, next to each other, down the length of each slice, starting about one-third from the center of the cake. Pipe a third line slightly longer, in between and on top of the first two. Place a chocolate round at a slight angle on top of the three lines at the end of each slice.

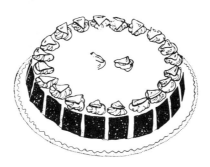

Chocolate Mousse Cake with Banana

two 10-inch (25-cm) cakes

one 10-inch (25-cm) Cocoa
*   Almond Sponge (page 163)*
4 ounces (115 g) currant jelly
two 10-inch (25-cm) Short Dough
*   Cake-Bottoms (page 32)*
5 medium-sized ripe bananas
Chocolate Cognac Cream
*   (recipe follows)*
1½ cups (360 ml) heavy cream
1 tablespoon (15 g) granulated
*   sugar*
sliced almonds, toasted and crushed
Dark Chocolate Figurines
*   (page 449)*

1. Cut the skin from the top of the Cocoa Almond Sponge and slice the cake into two layers.

2. Place the short dough bottoms on cardboards for support. Spread the jelly thinly and evenly on top.

3. Place the sponge layers on the jelly. Place 10-inch (25-cm) cake rings snugly around the sponge cakes. Unless the rings are stainless steel, line them with paper or plastic strips to prevent the metal from staining the filling.

4. Peel the bananas and slice in half lengthwise. Bend the halves carefully to accentuate the natural curve (they will break slightly but it will not show in the finished cakes) and make two circles of banana on each cake, placing them with the cut sides against the sponge. Make the first circle close to the edge and the second, smaller, circle about 2 inches (5 cm) toward the center.

5. Spread the Chocolate Cognac Cream smoothly and evenly on top of the cakes. Refrigerate the cakes until the cream is set, 1 to 2 hours.

6. Whip the heavy cream with the sugar until stiff peaks form.

7. Remove the rings and the paper or plastic strips. Spread a thin layer of whipped cream on the sides of the cakes. Cover the sides with the almonds (see Figure 8–1, page 178). Cut or mark the cakes into desired number of serving pieces.

8. Place the remaining whipped cream in a pastry bag with a no. 7 (14-mm) plain tip. Pipe a mound of whipped cream at the edge of each slice. Decorate each mound with a chocolate figure.

Variation

½ recipe Chocolate Cream
*   (page 566)*
1 cup (240 ml) heavy cream
2 teaspoons (10 g) granulated
*   sugar*
dark chocolate shavings

For a different presentation, substitute these ingredients for the whipped cream and chocolate figures.

1. Make the Chocolate Cream and place it in the refrigerator to set up.

2. Whip the heavy cream with the sugar to stiff peaks.

3. Divide the whipped cream between the two cakes and ice the tops and the sides. Cover the sides with toasted almonds. Cut or mark the cakes into the desired number of pieces.

4. When the Chocolate Cream has set, whip it smooth and place it in a pastry bag with a no. 7 (14-mm) star tip. Pipe a rosette of Chocolate Cream at the edge of each slice. Sprinkle the chocolate shavings on the center of the cakes within the rosettes.

Chocolate Cognac Cream

*3 pounds, 10 ounces (1 kg, 650 g)
   cream*

*2½ pints (1 l, 200 ml)
   heavy cream*
2 egg whites
*4½ teaspoons (14 g) unflavored
   gelatin powder*
½ cup (120 ml) cold water
*6 ounces (170 g) dark chocolate,
   melted*
*3½ ounces (100 ml) Simple Syrup
   (page 7)*
¼ cup (60 ml) cognac

1. Whip the cream and egg whites together until thickened to the consistency of ketchup. Do not overwhip or the cream may break when you add the chocolate.

2. Soften the gelatin in cold water. Heat to 150°F (65°C) to dissolve.

3. Combine the melted chocolate with the simple syrup and cognac. Stir in the gelatin.

4. Quickly add the chocolate mixture to a small amount of the cream. Then, still working rapidly, add this mixture to the remaining cream.

NOTE: Do not make this filling until you are ready to use it.

Chocolate Truffle Cake with Raspberries

two 10-inch (25-cm) cakes

*½ recipe Japonaise Batter
   (page 333)*
*1 recipe Chocolate Sponge Cake
   batter (page 162)*
*4 pounds (1 kg, 820 g) Ganache
   (page 567)*
¾ cup (180 ml) brandy
*¼ cup (60 ml) Simple Syrup
   (page 7)*
*two 10-inch (25-cm) Short Dough
   Cake-Bottoms (page 32)*
*5 pints (2 l, 400 ml) raspberries,
   approximately*
dark baker's chocolate, melted
Raspberry Sauce (page 563)
*Sour Cream Mixture for Piping
   (page 564)*
mint sprigs

1. Pipe the Japonaise Batter into two 10-inch (25-cm) circles, using the procedure for Meringue Noisette (Figure 12–1, page 334). Bake at 300°F (149°C) for approximately 30 minutes or until golden.

2. Divide the Chocolate Sponge Cake batter between two 10-inch (25-cm) greased and floured cake pans. Bake at 375°F (190°C) for about 15 minutes, or until cake springs back when pressed lightly in the middle. Set aside to cool.

3. Warm the ganache to soften it to a thick, sauce-like consistency.

4. Combine the brandy and simple syrup.

5. Spread a thin layer of ganache over the short dough bottoms and place the Japonaise circles on top. Spread another thin layer of ganache over the Japonaise.

6. Cut the sponges horizontally into two layers, about ¼-inch (6-mm) thick each. Place one sponge layer on each cake on top of the ganache. Brush with the syrup mixture. Arrange one-fourth of the raspberries on each sponge.

7. Make a collar of plastic strips or aluminum foil, or use an adjustable cake ring, and place snugly around the sponge. Don't worry if the short dough bottom and the Japonaise are larger; you will trim them later.

8. Reserve 1 pound (455 g) of the ganache and pour the remainder evenly over the raspberries (you may have to rewarm the ganache slightly to pour it).

9. Place the second sponge layers on top of the ganache and press down gently so they stick. Brush the cakes with the remaining syrup mixture. Refrigerate to set.

10. Remove the collars and trim the short dough and Japonaise as needed to make the sides even.

11. Rewarm the reserved ganache so it has a definite shine. Ice the top and sides with the ganache. Immediately, while the ganache is still sticky, arrange the remainder of the raspberries on top of the cakes, starting at the edge and making concentric circles next to each other.

12. Measure and cut out two strips of baking paper or plastic as wide as the cakes are high and the exact length of the circumference of the cakes. Place one of the strips on a flat surface and spread evenly with just enough of the dark baker's chocolate to cover the paper. Since this has to be done quickly, it is impossible to do this without spreading some of the chocolate outside the paper.

13. Before the chocolate has time to harden, pick up both ends of the chocolate-covered paper and position it around the cake so the chocolate sticks to the cake. Repeat with the second strip. Refrigerate for a few minutes.

14. Carefully pull the paper away from the chocolate. Cut the cakes into the desired number of pieces by first melting through the chocolate layer with a hot knife.

15. Presentation: Place a cake slice in the center of a dessert plate, pour a pool of Raspberry Sauce on the plate at the tip of the slice, and pipe the sour cream mixture into the sauce to decorate (see pages 518–519). Place a mint sprig next to the cake.

Coconut Cake Hawaii

two 10-inch (25-cm) cakes

1 recipe Sponge Cake batter
    (page 161)
4 ounces (115 g) smooth apricot
    marmalade
two 10-inch (25-cm) Hazelnut
    Short Dough Cake-Bottoms
    (page 32)
Coconut Cream Filling
    (recipe follows)

1. Make the sponge cake batter and divide it between two 10-inch (25-cm) cake pans. Bake at 400°F (205°C) for approximately 10 minutes. Set aside to cool.

2. Slice each sponge cake into two layers.

3. Spread the apricot marmalade on the short dough cake-bottoms. Place one sponge layer on each. Place 10-inch (25-cm) adjustable rings around the sponges, lining the rings with paper or plastic if they are not stainless steel.

4. Fill with the coconut cream, dividing it equally between the two cakes. Place a second sponge on top of the cream in each ring. Refrigerate the cakes for at least 2 hours to set.

5. Remove the rings and paper or plastic. Trim away any excess short dough to make the sides even. Brush the pineapple juice over the sponges to moisten them.

⅓ cup (80 ml) pineapple juice
1 quart (960 ml) heavy cream
2 tablespoons (30 g) granulated
    sugar
1 teaspoon (5 ml) vanilla extract
6 ounces (170 g) toasted
    macaroon coconut
3 ounces (85 g) dark chocolate
    shavings
Pineapple Sauce (page 562)
papaya or mango to decorate
mint sprigs

6. Whip the cream, sugar, and vanilla to stiff peaks. Spread over the top and sides of the cakes, using just enough to cover. Reserve the remaining cream.

7. Mark the center of the cakes using a 5-inch (12.5-cm) plain round cookie cutter. Place the remaining whipped cream in a pastry bag with a no. 4 (8-mm) plain tip. Pipe in a spiral pattern on top of the cakes, starting at the outside edge and stopping when you get to the mark in the center.

8. Lightly sprinkle the toasted coconut over the spiral, then press the remaining coconut onto the sides. Carefully place the shaved chocolate on top in the circle. Cut into the desired number of servings pieces.

9. Presentation: Place a slice of cake off-center on a dessert plate. Pour a pool of Pineapple Sauce next to the cake. Garnish with thin slices of papaya or mango and a mint sprig.

Coconut Cream Filling

4 pounds, 10 ounces (2 kg, 105 g)
filling

2 ounces (55 g) macaroon coconut,
    toasted
2 ounces (55 g) macadamia nuts,
    toasted
4 ounces (115 g) granulated sugar
2 cups (480 ml) milk
1 cup (240 ml) unsweetened
    coconut milk
1½ ounces (40 g) cornstarch
2 eggs
2 tablespoons (18 g) unflavored
    gelatin powder
¾ cup (180 ml) cold water
1 quart (960 ml) heavy cream

1. Finely grind the coconut and macadamia nuts with half of the sugar.

2. Scald the milk combined with the coconut milk.

3. Mix the remaining sugar, cornstarch, and the eggs in a bowl. While whipping rapidly, gradually add the scalded milk. Stir in the ground coconut mixture. Put the custard back in the saucepan and cook until it just begins to thicken.

4. Soften the gelatin in cold water. Heat to 110°F (43°C) to melt. Stir the gelatin into the custard while the custard is still hot. Set aside to cool, stirring occasionally.

5. Whip heavy cream to soft peaks. Fold into the cooled custard.

NOTE: Be sure the custard has cooled sufficiently before folding in the whipped cream or the cream will melt. The air whipped into the cream will be lost, resulting in a dense filling.

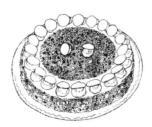

Gâteau au Diplomate

two 10-inch (25-cm) cakes

two 10-inch (25-cm) Biscuit
    Viennoise (page 163)
6 ounces (170 g) smooth
    strawberry jam
2 pounds, 7 ounces (1 kg, 110 g)
    Pastry Cream (page 569)
sliced almonds, lightly crushed
    (untoasted)
1 pound (455 g) Macaroon
    Decorating Paste (page 123)
fresh fruit
Apricot or Pectin Glaze
    (page 526)

1. Slice the biscuits into three layers each.

2. Divide the jam between the two bottom layers. Spread out evenly. Place the middle layers on the jam and cover each with a ¼-inch (6-mm) layer of pastry cream. Place the top layers on the pastry cream and spread another layer of pastry cream, ⅛ inch (3 mm) thick, on the top and sides of the cakes. Cover the sides of the cakes with crushed almonds (see Figure 8–1, page 178).

3. Place the cakes on a sheet pan lined with baking paper. Mark the cakes into the desired size serving pieces (not more than 16 pieces per cake).

4. Place the macaroon paste in a pastry bag with a no. 3 (6-mm) plain tip. Pipe a flower design on the top of each cake, just inside the marks for the individual pieces, forming one petal on each slice (Figure 8–8). The macaroon paste should be firm enough so that it will not run when it is baked. Add some additional almond paste if necessary. It will be somewhat difficult to pipe out.

5. Bake the cakes at 425°F (219°C), double-panned, for about 10 minutes or until the almond paste is light brown and the sliced almonds are toasted. Let the cakes cool completely.

6. Decorate the cakes with two or three different kinds of fruit on each slice, using the macaroon paste as a frame. Use small, soft fruits that can be cut into thin slices such as kiwi, strawberries, plums, or apricots (read the instructions for decorating Fruit Tartlets on page 234 for more information). Make the same design on each slice to create a uniform and elegant look. Cut the cakes following the marks between each flower petal.

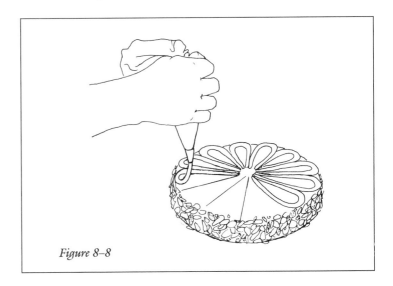

Figure 8–8

Gâteau Istanbul

two 10-inch (25-cm) cakes

two 10-inch (25-cm) Cocoa
  Almond Sponges (page 163)
two 10-inch (25-cm) Short Dough
  Cake-Bottoms (page 32)
Nougat Butter (recipe follows)
Hazelnut Cream (recipe follows)
1½ cups (360 ml) heavy cream
1 tablespoon (15 g) granulated
  sugar
almonds, toasted and crushed
cocoa powder
Chocolate Crescent Cookies
  (procedure follows)

1. Cut the skin from the tops of the sponge cakes and trim the tops to make them even, if necessary. Cut each sponge into two layers.

2. Place the short dough bottoms on cardboards. Divide the Nougat Butter between them and spread it out evenly. Place a sponge layer on top.

3. Spread the Hazelnut Cream evenly over the first sponge layers. Place the second sponge layers on the cream and press down lightly to even the tops.

4. Place the cakes in the freezer, covered, until completely frozen (this is not necessary if you plan to present the cakes whole rather than cut into serving pieces).

5. Trim off any short dough that protrudes outside the sponge to make the sides even.

6. Whip the cream with the sugar to stiff peaks and ice the tops and sides of the cakes with a thin layer of whipped cream. Reserve the remaining cream. Cover the sides of the cakes with crushed almonds (see Figure 8–1, page 178).

7. Place a 10-inch (25-cm) round template with a 6-inch (15-cm) hole cut out of the center on one of the cakes. Sift cocoa powder over the cake to cover the whipped cream. Remove the template carefully. Repeat with the second cake.

8. When the cakes are halfway thawed, cut into the desired number of serving pieces. Do not allow the cakes to thaw completely, or you will push the nuts into the cake rather than slicing through them.

9. Place the remaining whipped cream in a pastry bag with a no. 7 (14-mm) plain tip. Pipe a mound of whipped cream the size of a cherry at the edge of each slice. Place a Chocolate Crescent Cookie on each mound.

Nougat Butter

4 ounces (110 g)

2 ounces (55 g) softened butter
2 ounces (55 g) Hazelnut Paste
  (page 6)

Work the softened butter into the hazelnut paste gradually to make a smooth, lump-free mixture.

Hazelnut Cream

2 pounds, 14 ounces (1 kg, 310 g)

8 ounces (225 g) toasted hazelnuts
1 quart (960 ml) heavy cream
6 ounces (170 g) Hazelnut Paste
(page 6)

1. Rub the nuts between your palms to remove as much skin as possible. Do not attempt to remove all of it; it is just too time-consuming.

2. Very gradually mix enough of the cream into the hazelnut paste to make it soft and similar in consistency to lightly whipped cream. Whip the remaining cream to soft peaks.

3. Fold the cream into the hazelnut paste together with the roasted nuts. If the cream is overwhipped it can break when the rest of the ingredients are added. If it not whipped enough and the filling seems too runny, just mix a little longer.

Chocolate Crescent Cookies

24 cookies

1. Roll out 5 ounces (140 g) cocoa short dough (page 31; or flavor regular short dough with some cocoa powder) ⅛ inch (3 mm) thick.

2. Using a ¾-inch (2-cm) plain cookie cutter, cut out 24 crescents as described in making Fleurons (see Figure 2–8, page 24).

3. Bake the cookies at 375°F (190°C). Let them cool completely before placing on the whipped cream.

Gâteau Lugano

(see photograph in color insert)
two 10-inch (25-cm) cakes

two 10-inch (25-cm) Cocoa
Almond Sponges (page 163)
3 pounds (1 kg, 365 g) Vanilla
Buttercream (page 501)
¼ cup (60 ml) arrack or dark rum
almonds, toasted and
lightly crushed
cocoa powder
small strawberries

1. Cut the two sponge cakes into three layers each. Use a 6-inch (15-cm) round template or plain cookie cutter to cut both top layers into 6-inch (15-cm) circles. Cut them level and trim off the skins if necessary. Save the doughnut-shaped circles that are left for another use. (The bottom layers remain whole.)

2. Flavor the buttercream with the arrack or rum. Spread a ¼-inch (6-mm) layer of buttercream on each of the two bottom sponge layers. Place the middle layers on top.

3. Ice the top and sides of the cakes with additional buttercream. Cover the sides of the cakes with the crushed almonds (see Figure 8–1, page 178).

4. Ice the top and sides of the 6-inch (15-cm) layers with buttercream. Reserve the remaining buttercream for decoration. Refrigerate the four iced sponges until the buttercream is firm.

5. Place a cake cooler or aspic rack over the 6-inch (15-cm) layers. Sift cocoa powder through a fine sieve on top. Be very careful as you remove the cake cooler so that you do not disturb the pattern.

6. Set one of the 6-inch (15-cm) layers in the center of each of the 10-inch (25-cm) layers. Cut or mark the cakes into the desired number of pieces.

7. Place the remaining buttercream in a pastry bag with a no. 6 (12-mm) plain tip. Pipe a mound of buttercream, the size of a Bing cherry, at the edge of each piece.

8. Remove the stems from the strawberries and cut them in half lengthwise. Place one half, cut side up, on each buttercream mound. Although this cake looks best if cut while the buttercream is cold, it should be eaten when the buttercream is at room temperature.

Gâteau Malakoff

two 10-inch (25-cm) cakes

½ recipe Ladyfinger batter
(page 134)
two 10-inch (25-cm) Short Dough
Cake-Bottoms (page 32)
5 ounces (140 g) smooth
strawberry jam
two 10-inch (25-cm) Cocoa
Almond Sponges (page 163)
¾ cup (180 ml) Simple Syrup
(page 7)
½ cup (120 ml) light rum
Maraschino Cream (recipe follows)
8 ounces (225 g) Ganache
(page 567)
whipped cream

1. Place the Ladyfinger batter in a pastry bag with a no. 4 (8-mm) plain tip. Pipe out batter 1½ inches (3.7 cm) long on sheet pans lined with baking paper, making approximately 60 ladyfingers per cake. Bake as directed in recipe and reserve.

2. Place the short dough cake-bottoms on cardboard circles for support. Spread the jam evenly on top.

3. Cut the skin and about ¼ inch (6 mm) from the top of the sponge cakes. (Use the excess for Rum Balls, page 254). Slice each cake into two layers. Place one layer of sponge on each short dough cake base. Place an adjustable cake ring snugly around each sponge, lining the rings with paper or plastic strips if they are not stainless steel.

4. Combine the simple syrup and rum. Reserve 72 of the most attractive Ladyfingers to use in decorating. Place the remaining Ladyfingers in the syrup mixture and let them soak about 5 minutes to fully absorb the liquid.

5. Top each of the sponge cakes with one-fourth of the Maraschino Cream and spread it out evenly within the rings.

6. Arrange the soaked Ladyfingers flat-side down on the cream, with the long sides touching, making a circle 1 inch (2.5 cm) from the edge of the cake. Work quickly so that the filling does not set up.

7. Divide the remaining cream between the cakes and spread it out evenly on top. Place the remaining sponge layers on the cream and press down gently to even the tops. Refrigerate the cakes for at least 2 hours to set the cream.

8. Heat the ganache until liquid and very glossy. Spread ganache over the top of the cakes, using just enough to cover the sponge. As soon as the ganache starts to harden, score lines every ½ inch (1.2 cm) using the back of a chef's knife. Turn the cake 45° and score again to create a diamond pattern.

9. Cover the sides of the cakes with whipped cream.

10. Cut the cakes into the desired number of servings. Stand three Ladyfingers upright on the side of each slice. If the Ladyfingers are too tall, trim one end and place them with the cut end at the base of the cake.

Maraschino Cream

3 pounds, 6 ounces (1 kg, 535 g) cream

½ cup (120 ml) dry white wine
⅓ cup (80 ml) maraschino liqueur (or kirschwasser)
5 teaspoons (15 g) unflavored gelatin powder
4 egg yolks
3 ounces (85 g) granulated sugar
5 cups (1 l, 200 ml) heavy cream

1. Combine the wine and liqueur. Stir in the gelatin and let soften. Heat to 110°F (43°C) to dissolve the gelatin.

2. Whip the egg yolks and sugar until just combined, then quickly whip in the wine mixture. Place over simmering water and heat to about 125°F (52°C), whipping the mixture to a thick foam in the process. Remove from the heat.

3. Whip the cream to soft peaks. Working quickly, add the wine mixture to about a quarter of the whipped cream, and then rapidly mix the wine and cream combination into the remaining cream.

NOTE: Because you cannot reheat this filling to soften it, do not make it until you are ready to use it in the cakes.

Gâteau Moka Carrousel

(see photograph in color insert)
two 10-inch (25-cm) cakes

½ recipe Japonaise Batter (page 333)
1 recipe Cocoa Almond Sponge batter (page 163)
8 ounces (225 g) Ganache (page 567)
Mocha Whipped Cream (recipe follows)
1½ cups (360 ml) heavy cream
1 tablespoon (15 g) granulated sugar
sliced almonds, toasted and crushed
ground coffee
Marzipan Coffee Beans (procedure follows) or candy coffee beans
1 recipe Mousseline Sauce (page 561)
2 ounces (60 ml) Kahlua
cocoa powder
fanned apricot halves
mint sprigs

1. Draw two 10-inch (25-cm) circles on baking paper. Invert the paper on a sheet pan. Place the Japonaise Batter in a pastry bag with a no. 3 (6-mm) plain tip. Pipe the batter in a spiral within each of the circles as described in Meringue Noisette (see Figure 12–1, page 334). Bake at 275° to 300°F (135° to 149°C) until golden brown, about 35 minutes.

2. Line the bottom of a 10-inch (25-cm) cake pan with baking paper (or grease and flour, but do not grease and flour the sides). Pour about one-third of the cocoa sponge batter into the pan and spread it out evenly.

3. Pour the remaining batter onto a sheet of baking paper and spread it out to slightly less than 24 × 16 inches (60 × 40 cm), leaving a border approximately ¼ inch (6 mm) all around. Drag the paper onto a sheet pan (see Figure 15–3, page 422). Bake both sponges immediately at 400°F (205°C). The round cake will take about 15 minutes; the sheet will take about 10 minutes. Set the sponge cakes aside to cool.

4. Warm the ganache to soften. Place the Japonaise bottoms on cardboards for support, divide the ganache between them, and spread it out evenly. Place 10-inch (25-cm) cake rings on the ganache.

5. Cut the thin chocolate sheet lengthwise into strips 1 inch (2.5 cm) wide. Stand the strips up on the ganache in five evenly spaced concentric circles, starting at the outside against the ring on each cake.

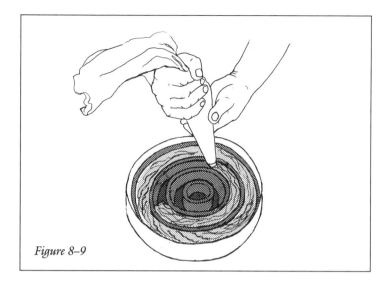

Figure 8–9

6. Place the Mocha Whipped Cream in a pastry bag with a no. 6 (12-mm) plain tip. Pipe the cream between the circles (Figure 8–9). Spread the excess evenly over the top with a spatula.

7. Cut the skin off the top of the 10-inch (25-cm) chocolate sponge and slice it into two layers. Place one on top of each cake. Press gently to be sure they are sticking to the mocha cream. Refrigerate the cakes until the cream is set (about 2 hours).

8. Remove the cake rings. Trim away any excess Japonaise that protrudes outside the sponge to make the sides even.

9. Whip heavy cream and sugar to stiff peaks. Cover the top and sides of the cakes with a thin layer of the cream. Cover the sides of the cakes with crushed almonds (Figure 8–1, page 178). Mark or cut the cakes into the desired number of pieces.

10. Place the remaining whipped cream in a pastry bag with a no. 6 (12-mm) star tip. Pipe a rosette at the edge of each slice. Sprinkle the ground coffee lightly on the whipped cream inside the piped rosettes. Place marzipan or candy coffee beans on the rosettes.

11. Add the Kahlua to the Mousseline Sauce.

12. Presentation: Place a slice of cake in the center of a dessert plate. Pour a half-moon of sauce in front of the dessert. Sprinkle cocoa powder very lightly on the sauce. Place a fanned apricot half and a mint sprig behind the cake.

Mocha Whipped Cream
3 pounds (1 kg, 365 g) cream

4 egg yolks
4 ounces (115 g) granulated sugar
1 quart (960 ml) heavy cream
4½ teaspoons (14 g) unflavored gelatin powder
½ cup (120 ml) dry white wine
⅓ cup (85 ml) Kahlua liqueur
¼ cup (60 ml) Coffee Reduction (page 5)
    or
1 teaspoon (4 g) mocha paste

1. Whip the egg yolks and sugar until light and fluffy.
2. Whip the cream to soft peaks and combine with the yolk mixture.
3. Soften the gelatin in the wine. Heat to 125°F (52°C) to dissolve the gelatin. Add the Kahlua and coffee reduction.
4. Rapidly combine the wine mixture with a small amount of the yolk and cream mixture. Still working quickly, combine with remaining cream.

NOTE: Do not make this filling until you are ready to use it.

Marzipan Coffee Beans
24 decorations

2 ounces (55 g) white Marzipan (page 531)
cocoa powder

1. Color the marzipan dark brown using a small amount of cocoa powder.
2. Roll the marzipan into a 12-inch (30-cm) rope. Cut the rope into 24 equal pieces.
3. Roll one piece at a time between your palms to make it smooth; then roll it into a ball. Roll the ball into an oval. Place the oval in the palm of your hand and use a marzipan tool or the back of a knife to make a mark lengthwise in the center. Push the tool halfway into the "bean." Make the remaining decorations in the same way.

Gâteau Saint-Honoré
two 11-inch (27.5-cm) cakes

1 pound (455 g) Classic Puff Paste (page 21)
½ recipe Pâte à Choux (page 15)
Bavarian Rum Cream (recipe follows)
1 pound (455 g) granulated sugar
strawberries
1 cup (240 ml) heavy cream
2 teaspoons (10 g) granulated sugar

1. Roll out puff paste ⅛ inch (3 mm) thick, 23 inches (57.5 cm) long, and 12 inches (30 cm) wide. Place on a sheet pan lined with baking paper. Refrigerate covered at least 20 minutes.
2. While the puff paste is resting, make the pâte à choux, and place it in a pastry bag with a no. 6 (12-mm) plain tip. Reserve.
3. Leaving the puff paste in place on the sheet pan, cut two 11-inch (27.5-cm) fluted circles from the dough and remove the scraps. (An easy way to cut them is to use an 11-inch/27.5-cm tart pan as a "cookie cutter.") Prick the circles lightly with a fork.
4. Pipe three concentric rings of pâte à choux, plus a small mound in the center, on each circle. Place a no. 3 (6-mm) tip over the no. 6 (12-mm) tip and, holding it in place (see Figures 12–2 and 12–3, page 340), pipe out 20 to 24 pâte à choux profiteroles the size of Bing cherries onto the paper around the cakes (Figure 8–10).
5. Bake the puff paste circles and the profiteroles at 400°F (205°C) until the pâte à choux has puffed, about 10 minutes. Reduce the heat to 375°F (190°C) and bake until everything is dry

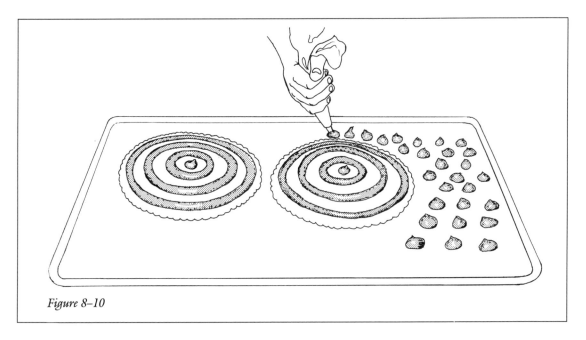

Figure 8–10

enough to hold its shape, about 35 minutes longer for the cake and about 8 minutes longer for the profiteroles. (Just pick the profiteroles up and take them out as they are done.)

6. Place approximately 6 ounces (170 g) of the Bavarian Rum Cream in a pastry bag with a no. 2 (4-mm) plain tip. Pipe the cream into the baked profiteroles by first pushing the tip into the bottom to make a hole, then piping in the cream. Do not make the hole any larger than necessary.

7. Divide the remaining Bavarian Rum Cream evenly between the two cakes, spreading it into a dome shape. Refrigerate the cakes for at least 2 hours to set the cream.

8. Caramelize the first measurement of sugar (see page 488). Dip the filled profiteroles into the hot caramel using two forks to avoid burning your fingers. Place them on a sheet pan. The caramel must be hot enough to go on in a thin layer. Reheat it if necessary as you work, but swirl, do not stir, the pan. Also avoid getting any Bavarian cream mixed in with the caramel, as mixing in air (stirring) or cream will cause the sugar to crystallize.

9. Whip the heavy cream and remaining sugar into stiff peaks. Place the whipped cream in a pastry bag with a no. 5 (10-mm) star tip. Slice the cakes into the desired number of servings. Pipe a whipped-cream rosette at the edge of each slice and set a profiterole on each rosette. Pipe two large shells of cream on each slice to fill in the wedge-shaped space. Place a small wedge of strawberry next to each profiterole.

Bavarian Rum Cream

Make 1½ recipes Vanilla Bavarian Cream (see page 570), substituting 4 ounces of rum for the 4 ounces of water in the recipe.

Harlequin Cake

two 10-inch (25-cm) cakes

*one 10-inch (25-cm) Chocolate
   Sponge Cake (page 162)*
½ cup (120 ml) Cognac or brandy
*White Chocolate Mousse Filling
   (recipe follows)*
*½ recipe Chocolate Cognac Cream
   (page 195)*
½ cup (120 ml) heavy cream
*10 ounces (285 g) White or
   Chocolate-Flavored Marzipan
   (page 531)*
dark baker's chocolate, melted
*dark Piping Chocolate, melted
   (page 449)*
candied violets
Raspberry Sauce (page 563)
fruit for decorating

1. Cut the Chocolate Sponge Cake into two layers; place them on cardboard cake rounds for support. Brush the Cognac onto the sponges. Use it all up and pay special attention to the edges. Fasten a cake ring, 3 inches (7.5 cm) high, around each sponge, lining them with paper or plastic strips if they are not stainless steel. If the plastic strips are heavy enough, you can use them alone, without the rings.

2. Divide the White Chocolate Mousse Filling between the cakes, smooth the tops level, and refrigerate to set.

3. Divide the Chocolate Cognac Cream between the cakes, on top of the mousse filling. Spread the top level, taking care not to smear any of the filling on the paper or plastic above the filling on the sides. Refrigerate to set, approximately 2 hours.

4. When the fillings are completely set, remove the rings from around the cakes. Whip the cream into stiff peaks, and ice the tops of the cakes with a thin layer, leaving the sides exposed.

5. Divide the marzipan into two pieces. Roll them out one at a time, using powdered sugar to prevent them from sticking, into round shapes about 12 inches (30 cm) in diameter and ¹⁄₁₆ inch (2 mm) thick. Place the marzipan rounds on cardboard circles and spread a thin layer of melted dark baker's chocolate on top. Use just enough to cover the circles evenly.

6. Use a guide, and trim each round into an even circle slightly smaller than the top of the cakes (save the trimmings for Rum Balls or chocolate-flavored marzipan).

7. Cut the marzipan circles into the same number of slices you will be cutting the cakes. Slide the cuts (chocolate side up) all at once onto the tops of the cakes (as shown for Raspberry Cake, Figure 8–12, page 213), or pick the pieces up one at a time and reassemble on the cakes.

8. Cut between the marzipan pieces to slice the cakes. Be sure to clean the knife after each cut. Pipe the melted piping chocolate decoratively on top of each slice. Place a small piece of candied violet at the wide end of each piece.

9. Presentation: Place a slice of cake in the center of a dessert plate. Pour a small pool of Raspberry Sauce on one side of the slice and decorate the opposite side with the fresh fruit.

NOTE: If the cakes are not to be precut, the chocolate marzipan tops should be cut the same size as the cakes and placed on the top whole.

White Chocolate Mousse Filling

Make one-half recipe of Raspberry White-Chocolate Mousse (see page 323), omitting the raspberry purée and the lemon juice.

Lemon Chiffon Cake

two 10-inch (25-cm) cakes

5 lemons
one 10-inch (25-cm) Sponge Cake (page 161)
6 egg yolks
1/3 cup (80 ml) water
4 ounces (115 g) granulated sugar
3 cups (720 ml) heavy cream
2 tablespoons (18 g) unflavored gelatin powder
1/2 cup (120 ml) water
Tartaric Acid Solution (page 596)
or
lemon juice
1 quart (960 ml) heavy cream
2 tablespoons (30 g) granulated sugar
Pectin Glaze (page 526)
or
Lemon Glaze (recipe follows)
Chocolate Squares (page 449)
lemon slices
Blackberry Sauce (see note on page 365)
Sour Cream Mixture for Piping (page 564)

1. Finely grate the zest of the lemons, juice them, and combine the juice with the zest. Set aside.

2. Cut the skin from the top of the sponge cake. Slice into two layers. Put the layers on cardboard cake rounds and place a 10-inch (25-cm) cake ring snugly around each one. Unless the rings are stainless steel, line them with paper or plastic strips to prevent the metal from reacting with the acidic filling.

3. Start whipping the egg yolks on medium speed in a mixer. Combine the first measure of water with the first measure of sugar and boil until the syrup reaches 230°F (110°C). Pour the hot syrup into the whipped egg yolks in a steady stream. Increase the mixing speed and continue whipping until the mixture is light and fluffy.

4. Whip the 3 cups (720 ml) of heavy cream to soft peaks.

5. Soften the gelatin in the 1/2 cup (120 ml) of water. Heat to 125°F (52°C) to dissolve. Combine egg yolk mixture, whipped cream, and lemon juice with zest. Place about one-fourth of this combination in a separate bowl and rapidly mix in the dissolved gelatin; quickly mix this into the remaining cream mixture. Add a few drops of tartaric acid or lemon juice to neutralize the gelatin flavor.

6. Divide the lemon filling between the two prepared sponge cake halves. Spread out evenly within the rings. Cover the cakes and refrigerate until the filling is set, about 2 hours.

7. Remove the rings and paper or plastic strips. Whip the remaining cream with the sugar to stiff peaks. Spread a 3/4-inch (2-cm) layer of cream on the top of the cakes, and just enough on the sides to cover the sponge. Reserve the remaining cream.

8. Cover the top of the cakes with a thin layer of pectin or lemon glaze, leaving a 1-inch (2.5-cm) border of cream uncovered around the outside edge. When the glaze has set up, cut or mark the cakes into the desired number of pieces. Place a chocolate square on the side of each slice; it should stick to the cream.

9. Place the remaining whipped cream in a pastry bag with a no. 6 (12-mm) star tip. Pipe a rosette of cream at the edge of each slice (on the plain cream border). (If you don't have time to make the glaze, cover the tops of the cakes with shaved dark chocolate instead, placing it within the piped rosettes.) Place a small wedge of sliced lemon on each rosette.

10. Presentation: Place a slice of cake in the center of a dessert plate. Pour a round pool of Blackberry Sauce in front of the dessert, and decorate the sauce with the sour cream mixture (see pages 518–519).

Lemon Glaze

1 cup (240 ml) glaze

1 tablespoon (9 g) gelatin powder
¼ cup (60 ml) cold water
½ cup (120 ml) strained lemon juice
¼ cup (60 ml) Simple Syrup (page 7)
¼ teaspoon (1.25 ml) Tartaric Acid Solution (page 596)

1. Soften gelatin in cold water; heat to 110°F (43°C) to dissolve. Stir in lemon juice, simple syrup, and tartaric acid solution. Use on the cakes as soon as the mixture shows signs of thickening. If the glaze should thicken too much before it can be applied, reheat before using to avoid ruining the appearance of the cakes.

NOTE: This glaze can be made in a larger quantity as a *mise en place* item; just melt the amount needed each time.

Pariser Chocolate Cake

two 10-inch (25-cm) cakes

¾ cup (180 ml) light rum
¼ cup (60 ml) Simple Syrup (page 7)
1 recipe Crème Parisienne (page 567)
two 10-inch (25-cm) Hazelnut-Chocolate Biscuits (page 164)
dark chocolate shavings
1 recipe Mousseline Sauce (page 561)
¼ cup (60 ml) Frangelico liqueur
Chocolate Sauce for Piping (page 560)
fresh fruit
mint sprigs

1. Combine rum and simple syrup. Reserve.
2. Whip Crème Parisienne to stiff peaks. Reserve.
3. Cut biscuits into three layers each. Brush the bottom layers with one-third of the syrup mixture. Spread a ¼-inch (6-mm) thick layer of Crème Parisienne on top. Place the second layers on the cream. Repeat the procedure adding more syrup, filling, and the remaining biscuit layers. Brush the remaining rum syrup on the top of the cakes. Ice the tops and sides of the cakes with a thin layer of Crème Parisienne.
4. Place about half of the remaining cream in a pastry bag with a no. 6 (12-mm) flat star tip (see Figure 18–2, page 182, instructions for basketweave pattern). Pipe vertical strips on the sides of the cakes, piping them next to each other, from the bottom to the top. Smooth the top edge all around the cakes with a spatula.
5. Place the remainder of the Crème Parisienne in another pastry bag with a no. 4 (8-mm) plain tip. Pipe lines ½ inch (1.2 cm) apart on the tops of the cakes, first in one direction, then at a 45° angle to create a diamond pattern.
6. Sprinkle chocolate shavings lightly over the cakes. Combine Frangelico liqueur with Mousseline Sauce. Reserve in the refrigerator. Cut the cakes into the desired number of servings.
7. Presentation: Place a slice of cake in the center of a dessert plate. Pour a pool of Mousseline Sauce at the tip of the slice so that the sauce runs out evenly on either side. Decorate the sauce with Chocolate Sauce for Piping (see pages 518–519). Place a piece of seasonal fruit and a mint sprig on the side.

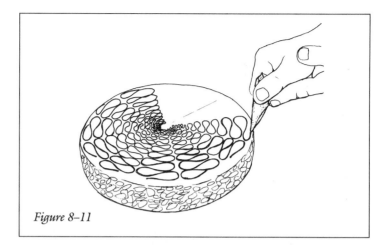

Figure 8–11

Poppy Seed Cake

two 10-inch (25-cm) cakes

Poppy Seed Cake Base
*   (recipe follows)*
1 quart (960 ml) heavy cream
2 tablespoons (30 g) granulated
*   sugar*
about 20 medium strawberries,
*   thinly sliced*
sliced almonds, toasted and
*   lightly crushed*
dark Piping Chocolate (page 449)
strawberry wedges

1. Cut the skin from the tops of the cakes and even the tops if necessary. Cut the cakes into three layers each.

2. Whip cream and sugar into stiff peaks. Spread a thin layer of cream, ⅛ inch (3 mm) thick, on both of the bottom cake layers. Cover the cream with a single layer of strawberry slices. Spread another thin layer of cream on top of the strawberries. Place the second cake layers on top of the cream and repeat the procedure. Add the top cake layers.

3. Ice the top and sides of the cakes with a thin layer of whipped cream. Use just enough to cover the sponge; you should have some left for decorating. Cover the sides of the cakes with the crushed almonds (see Figure 8–1, page 178).

4. Cut or mark the cakes into the desired number of serving pieces. Decorate the top of each slice with the piping chocolate (Figure 8–11). Place the reserved whipped cream in a pastry bag with a no. 4 (8-mm) star tip. Pipe a rosette at the edge of each slice. Place a small strawberry wedge on each rosette.

NOTE: If you do not have time to pipe the chocolate design, pipe the rosettes and then sprinkle dark chocolate shavings on top of the cakes within the rosettes.

Poppy Seed Cake Base
two 10-inch (25-cm) cakes

8 ounces (225 g) bread flour
8 ounces (225 g) cake flour
1½ teaspoons (6 g) baking soda
1 teaspoon (4 g) baking powder
5 ounces (140 g) poppy seeds
1 pound (455 g) softened butter
1 pound, 8 ounces (680 g)
  granulated sugar
10 egg yolks
1 tablespoon (15 ml) vanilla
  extract
1 pound (455 g) sour cream
12 egg whites
½ teaspoon (3 g) salt
½ teaspoon (1 g) cream of tartar

1. Grease and flour two 10-inch (25-cm) cake pans.

2. Sift the flours, baking soda, and baking powder together. Mix in the poppy seeds.

3. Cream the butter. Add 1 pound, 4 ounces (570 g) of the sugar and mix until light and fluffy. Add the egg yolks and vanilla. Mix two minutes.

4. Mix in half of the dry ingredients on low speed. Add the sour cream and mix until just combined. Mix in the remaining dry ingredients.

5. Whip the egg whites, salt, and cream of tartar to a foam. Gradually add the remaining 4 ounces (115 g) sugar and whip to soft peaks. Fold the whites into the batter one-quarter at a time. Divide the batter between the reserved cake pans.

6. Bake at 350°F (175°C) for approximately 35 minutes, or until the sponge springs back when pressed lightly in the center.

Princess Cake
(see photograph in color insert)
two 10-inch (25-cm) cakes

two 10-inch (25-cm) Biscuit
  Viennoise (page 163)
6 ounces (170 g) smooth
  strawberry jam
1 pound, 4 ounces (570 g) Vanilla
  Bavarian Cream (page 570)
5 cups (1 l, 200 ml) heavy cream
2 tablespoons (30 g) granulated
  sugar
1 pound, 4 ounces (570 g)
  Marzipan, light green
  (page 531)
powdered sugar
Strawberry Sauce (page 563)
Sour Cream Mixture for Piping
  (page 564)

1. Cut the skin from the top of the two cakes. Cut the cakes into three layers each.

2. Divide the jam between the two bottom layers and spread evenly. Place the middle layers on top of the jam. Spread half of the Bavarian cream on each of the middle layers. Place the top layers on the Bavarian cream.

3. Whip the cream and granulated sugar to stiff peaks. Divide the cream between the two cakes, spreading just enough on the sides to cover them. Spread the remaining cream into a dome shape on the tops, about ¾ inch (2 cm) thick in the center.

4. Divide the marzipan into two pieces. Roll them out one at a time into circles ⅛ inch (3 mm) thick and about 15 inches (37.5 cm) in diameter, using powdered sugar to prevent the marzipan from sticking.

5. Roll one circle onto a dowel and unroll over one of the cakes. Smooth the marzipan onto the cake with your hands, keeping the dome shape on top. Pay special attention to the sides to be sure the marzipan is not wrinkled. Trim the marzipan around the base of the cake to make it even. Repeat procedure to cover the second cake.

6. Cut or mark the cakes into the desired number of serving pieces. Cut from the edge of the cake toward the center to prevent the marzipan from being pushed into the whipped cream. If you have problems, cut through the marzipan layer first before cutting the cake. Sift powdered sugar lightly over the cakes.

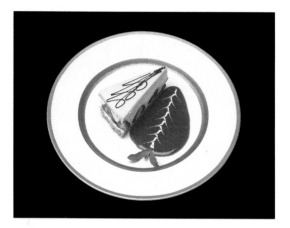

Strawberry Kirsch Cake

Fruit Barrels

Cobbler with Peaches and Cinnamon

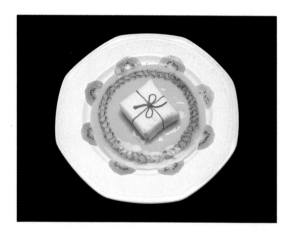

Tropical Surprise Packages

Puff Pastry with Fruit and Champagne Sabayon

Toasted Panettone with Mascarpone Sauce

Small Pear Tartlets with Caramel Sauce

*Petits Fours Sec
and Chocolate Candies*

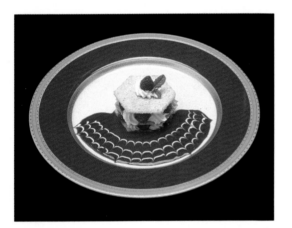

Raspberry Wafers

Swans (variation)

Apple Strudel, German Style

Strawberry Pyramids

Cookies

Gâteau Moka Carrousel

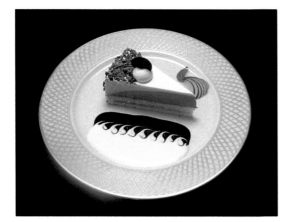

Chocolate and Frangelico Mousse Cake

Fig Tart

*Rhubarb Meringue and Swedish Hazelnut Tarts,
Clafoutis with Cherries, Walnut Caramel Tart*

Caramel Cake

Apricot Cream Cake

Chestnut Puzzle Cake

Princess Cake

Chocolate Decadence

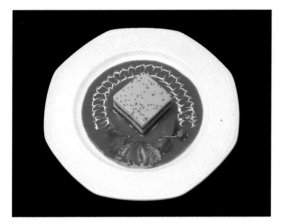

Tropical Mousse Cake

Black Currant Cake

Poached Pears with Ginger Ice Cream and Two Sauces

Peach Ice Cream in Florentina Baskets

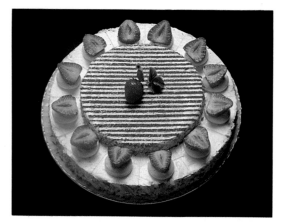

Gâteau Lugano

Bombe Monarch

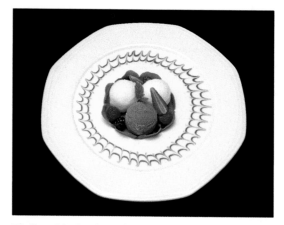

Medley of Sorbets in Tulips

Meringue Glacé Leda

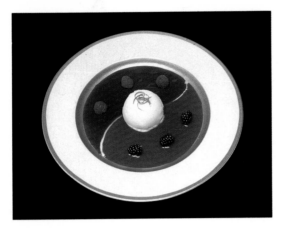

Champagne Sorbet

Pears California

Caramelized Pineapple Barbados

Lemon Chiffon Pouches

Blood Orange Sorbet in Magnolia Cookie Shells

Marzipan Bear Birthday Cake

Budapest Swirls

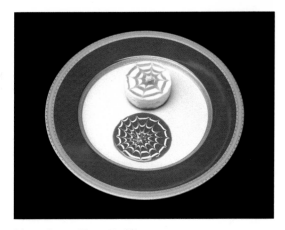

Lingonberry Cheese Pudding

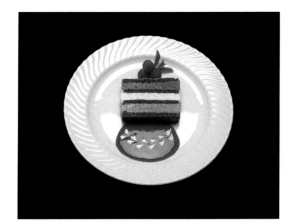

Triple Chocolate Terrine

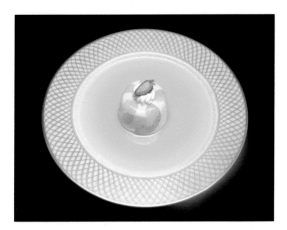

Pear Charlotte

Blueberry Soufflé

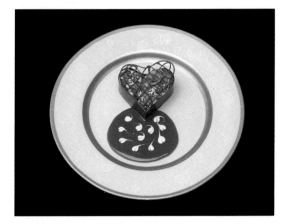

Cupid's Treasure Chest

Plum Fritters

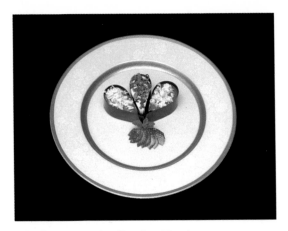

Chocolate Mousse in Chocolate Teardrops

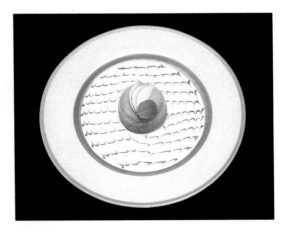

Apple Rum Charlotte

Vacherin with Plum Ice Cream

Blackberry Meringue Tartlets

Meringue Baskets with Raspberries

7. Presentation: Place a slice of cake off-center on a dessert plate. Pour a small pool of Strawberry Sauce in front of the dessert, and decorate the sauce with the sour cream mixture (see pages 518–519).

NOTE: Although it is traditional to use green marzipan, a very light pink color is also attractive. The marzipan can also be textured with a tread roller or waffle roller before it is placed on the cake. If you plan to decorate the cakes, sift the powdered sugar over the top after adding the decoration. Princess Cake is an excellent cake to make up ahead because the marzipan keeps the cake fresh for days if well-covered and refrigerated. To protect the marzipan from becoming wet from the whipped cream, brush or spread a thin layer of buttercream on the bottom side of the marzipan before placing it on the cake. You then have to invert the marzipan onto the cake and will not be able to avoid getting some buttercream on your hands, so be sure to clean them before smoothing the marzipan onto the cake.

Queen of Sheba Cake

two 10-inch (25-cm) cakes

*4 ounces (115 g) Short Dough
  (page 31)*
dark baker's chocolate, melted
*Queen of Sheba Cake Base
  (recipe follows)*
*2 pounds (910 g) Ganache
  (page 567)*
*14 ounces (400 g) Vanilla
  Buttercream (page 501)*
hazelnuts, toasted and crushed
*10 ounces (285 g) Marzipan,
  white (page 531)*

1. Roll out short dough to ⅛ inch (3 mm) thick. Cut out cookies using a 1-inch (2.5-cm) fluted cookie cutter. Cut three holes in each cookie using a no. 2 (4-mm) plain pastry tip. Bake the cookies at 375°F (190°C) until golden brown, about 10 minutes. Let the cookies cool, then place them next to each other and streak in one direction with melted baker's chocolate; (see example in Figure 6–1, page 150).

2. Cut the skins from the cake bases and, at the same time, cut the tops even. Slice each cake into two layers.

3. Reserve 10 ounces (285 g) of the ganache and mix the remainder with the buttercream. Spread the ganache mixture ¼ inch (6 mm) thick on the bottom cake layers. Invert the remaining cake layers and place on top. Ice the top and sides of the cakes with the ganache mixture, using just enough to cover the sponge. Reserve the remainder for decorating. Cover the sides of the cakes with crushed hazelnuts.

4. Roll out half of the marzipan into a ¹⁄₁₆ inch (2 mm) thick circle, slightly larger than 10 inches (25 cm) in diameter. Use powdered sugar to prevent it from sticking. Cut out a cardboard circle the same size as the cake you are going to put it on (use an adjustable cake ring as a guide if you have one). Carefully place the marzipan round on top of the cardboard circle and then slide the marzipan onto the top of the cake. Place the cardboard circle on top of the marzipan and invert the cake. Press down firmly to even the top of the cake. Repeat with the remaining cake.

5. Warm the reserved ganache until liquid. Turn the cakes right-side up again and spread ganache on top of the marzipan just thick enough to cover. Let the ganache sit for a few minutes to set up, then use the back of a chef's knife to mark a diamond pattern in the ganache. Make parallel marks every ½ inch (1.2 cm), then turn the cake a quarter-turn and repeat. Refrigerate the cakes until the ganache and buttercream are firm.

6. Mark or cut the cakes into the desired number of serving pieces. Place the remaining ganache and buttercream mixture in a pastry bag with a no. 6 (12-mm) plain tip. Pipe a small mound, the size of a cherry, at the edge of each slice. Place one of the cookies at an angle on each mound. This cake should be cut while chilled, but tastes better if served at room temperature.

Queen of Sheba Cake Base
two 10-inch (25-cm) cakes

1 pound (455 g) dark chocolate
½ cup (120 ml) dark rum
1 pound (455 g) softened butter
1 pound (455 g) granulated sugar
12 eggs, separated
8 ounces (225 g) Almond Paste
   (page 4)
10 ounces (285 g) bread flour
7 ounces (200 g) hazelnuts, toasted
   and finely ground

1. Melt the chocolate. Stir in the rum and set aside, but keep warm.

2. Beat the butter with 8 ounces (225 g) of the sugar until light and fluffy.

3. Gradually mix the egg yolks into the almond paste. You must mix them in a few at a time, or you will get lumps. Stir the yolk mixture into the butter mixture. Add the melted chocolate rapidly and mix until completely incorporated.

4. Whip the egg whites to a foam. Gradually add the remaining 8 ounces (225 g) of sugar and whip to stiff peaks. Carefully fold the chocolate mixture into the egg whites.

5. Sift the flour and mix with the nuts. Fold into the batter.

6. Line the bottom of two 10-inch (25-cm) cake pans with baking paper (or grease and flour, but do not grease and flour the sides). Divide the batter equally between the pans.

7. Bake at 350°F (175°C) for about 50 minutes, making sure the cakes are baked through. After the cakes have cooled completely, cut around the sides with a thin knife and unmold.

Raspberry Cake
two 10-inch (25-cm) cakes

two 10-inch (25-cm) Vanilla
   Butter Cakes (page 165)
two 10-inch (25-cm) Short Dough
   Cake-Bottoms (page 32)
4 ounces (115 g) raspberry jam
Raspberry Cream (recipe follows)

1. Cut the vanilla cakes into two layers each. Cut the tops even if necessary.

2. Place the short dough cake-bottoms on cardboards for support. Divide the jam between them and spread out evenly. Place one layer of vanilla cake on the jam on each. Place adjustable cake rings snugly around the cakes, setting them on top of the short dough. If the rings are not stainless steel, line them with strips of baking paper or plastic.

3. Pour one-fourth of the Raspberry Cream on each cake. Spread it out evenly within the rings.

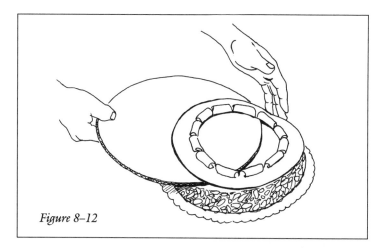

Figure 8–12

2 dry pints (960 ml) raspberries,
    approximately
8 ounces (225 g) Vanilla
    Buttercream (page 501)
sliced almonds, toasted and
    lightly crushed
10 ounces (285 g) Marzipan,
    white (page 531)
dark chocolate shavings

4. Arrange whole raspberries, stem-side down, in three concentric circles spaced evenly over the cream. Start the first circle about ½ inch (1.2 cm) from the cake ring. Use both hands to put the berries on the cakes quickly, before the remaining cream sets up.

5. Divide the remaining cream filling between the cakes, pouring it over the raspberries; spread it out evenly. Place the remaining two cake layers on top of the cream and press down lightly to make the tops level. Refrigerate the cakes until the filling is set, about 2 hours.

6. Remove the rings and paper or plastic strips. Spread a thin layer of buttercream over the top and sides of each cake. Cover the sides of the cakes with crushed almonds, gently pushing them into the buttercream (see Figure 8–1, page 178).

7. Roll out the marzipan to ¹⁄₁₆ inch (2 mm) thick, using just enough powdered sugar to prevent it from sticking. Make sure there is no powdered sugar underneath when you finish, as part of the bottom side will be visible in the final presentation. Mark the marzipan with a waffle roller.

8. Cut two circles of marzipan the same size as the tops of the cakes. These may be slightly smaller than 10 inches (25 cm). Place the marzipan circles on cardboard rounds and cut 3-inch (7.5-cm) circles out of the centers. Reserve the centers for another use.

9. Mark the marzipan rings into the desired number of slices for each cake. Then cut through the marks, cutting from the center of the rings and stopping 1 inch (2.5 cm) from the edge so that the pieces remain attached at the outside edge of the rings. Roll back the cut edge of each marzipan wedge toward the outside of the rings.

10. Carefully slide the rings onto the tops of the cakes (Figure 8–12). Cover the exposed center of the cakes with shaved choc-

olate. Cut the cakes into serving pieces cutting between the rolled marzipan pieces. Using a no. 6 (12-mm) plain tip on the pastry bag, pipe a small mound of buttercream on the flat part of the marzipan at the edge of each piece. Top each mound with a raspberry.

Raspberry Cream
3 pounds (1 kg, 365 g)

3 egg yolks
2 eggs
3 ounces (85 g) granulated sugar
½ cup (120 ml) dry white wine
5 teaspoons (15 g) unflavored
   gelatin powder
½ cup (120 ml) cold water
¼ cup (60 ml) raspberry liqueur
½ cup (120 ml) strained
   raspberry purée
3 cups (720 ml) heavy cream

1. Whip the egg yolks, whole eggs, sugar, and wine over simmering water until the mixture reaches 110°F (43°C). Remove from heat and continue whipping until the mixture is cold and has a light and fluffy consistency, about 10 minutes.

2. Soften the gelatin in cold water. Heat to 125°F (52°C) to dissolve. Add liqueur. Add gelatin mixture to egg yolk mixture. Stir in raspberry purée.

3. Whip the cream to soft peaks. Rapidly add the raspberry mixture to a small part of the whipped cream, then stir this mixture into the remaining whipped cream.

NOTE: Do not make the filling until you are ready to use it in the cakes.

Variation: Blackberry Cake

Substitute whole blackberries for the raspberries inside the cakes and in the decoration. In the cream filling, substitute ½ cup (120 ml) heavy cream for the raspberry purée and Chambord liqueur for the raspberry liqueur.

Sacher Torte
two 10-inch (25-cm) cakes

Sacher Biscuits (recipe follows)
3 cups (720 ml) Apricot Glaze
   (page 526)
1½ cups (360 ml) Chocolate Glaze
   (page 526)
dark or light Piping Chocolate
   (page 449)

1. Cut the skins from the tops of the biscuits (even the tops, if necessary) and cut each cake into two layers.

2. Heat the apricot glaze. Place one-fourth on each of the two bottom cake layers and spread it out quickly, forcing it into the cake before it has a chance to form a skin. Add the second cake layers and press them into the glaze. Use the remaining apricot glaze to ice the tops and sides of the cakes.

3. Move the cakes to a cake cooler or aspic rack with a sheet pan underneath. Be careful not to disturb the apricot glaze once it has started to form a skin. Spread a thin layer of chocolate glaze on the tops and sides of the cakes. It should be just thick enough to prevent you from seeing the apricot glaze underneath. Leave the cakes on the rack for a few minutes, then move them to cardboards before the glaze is completely set.

4. When the glaze is firm enough to be cut without running, mark or cut the cakes into the desired number of servings. Place light or dark piping chocolate in a piping bag and pipe a large S on each slice.

Sacher Biscuit

two 10-inch (25-cm) biscuits

14 eggs, separated
12 ounces (340 g) granulated
*   sugar*
6 ounces (170 g) bread flour
3 ounces (85 g) cake flour
3 ounces (85 g) cocoa powder
3 ounces (85 g) hazelnuts,
*   ground fine*
3 ounces (85 g) dark chocolate
7 ounces (200 g) butter

1. Whip the egg yolks with 5 ounces (140 g) of the sugar until light and fluffy.

2. Sift the flours and cocoa powder together. Mix in the ground nuts.

3. Melt the chocolate and butter together. Keep warm.

4. Whip the egg whites to a foam, gradually add the remaining 7 ounces (200 g) of sugar. Whip to stiff peaks. Fold the yolk mixture into the egg whites, then fold in the dry ingredients. Fold in the chocolate mixture last. Divide the batter equally between two greased and floured 10-inch (25-cm) cake pans.

5. Bake at 375°F (190°C) for about 20 minutes. Let the cakes cool completely before using them in the recipe.

Sicilian Macaroon Cake

two 10-inch (25-cm) cakes

½ recipe Japonaise Batter
*   (page 331)*
½ recipe Almond Sponge batter
*   (page 162)*
1 tablespoon (5 g) ground
*   cinnamon*
dark baker's chocolate, melted
two 10-inch (25-cm) Cocoa Short
*   Dough Cake-Bottoms (page 32)*
4 ounces (115 g) currant jelly
Macaroon-Maraschino Whipped
*   Cream (recipe follows)*
1-inch (2.5-cm) Almond Macaroon
*   Cookies (page 123)*
1 pint (480 ml) heavy cream
1 tablespoon (15 g) granulated
*   sugar*
almonds, toasted and lightly
*   crushed*
dark chocolate shavings

1. Draw two 10-inch (25-cm) circles on baking paper and invert the paper on a sheet pan. Place the Japonaise Batter in a pastry bag with a no. 4 (8-mm) plain tip. Pipe the batter in a spiral within each of the circles as described in Meringue Noisette (see Figure 12–1, page 334). Bake at 300°F (149°C) until dry, about 45 minutes.

2. Add the cinnamon to the sponge batter. Line the bottom of a 10-inch (25-cm) cake pan with baking paper (or grease and flour, but do not grease and flour the sides). Pour the cake batter into the pan. Bake at 400°F (205°C) for about 15 minutes or until done.

3. Brush melted baker's chocolate on one side of the Japonaise bottoms. Place the short dough bottoms on cardboards for support. Divide the currant jelly between the short dough bottoms and spread it evenly. Place the Japonaise bottoms on top, with the chocolate side up.

4. Put 10-inch (25-cm) cake rings on top of the Japonaise and press lightly to seal. If the rings are not stainless steel, line them with paper or plastic strips to prevent the metal from staining the filling. Divide the Macaroon-Maraschino Whipped Cream equally between the two cakes. The filling should be just starting to set up or it may run out.

5. Cut the top of the sponge even, then cut it into two layers. Place the layers on top of the cream on each cake. Refrigerate the cakes until the cream is set, about 2 hours.

6. While the cakes are chilling, dip the macaroon halfway in melted dark baker's chocolate.

7. Trim the sides of the cakes so that the short dough and Japonaise are even with the filling. Whip the heavy cream and sugar to stiff peaks. Ice the top and sides of the cakes with a thin layer of the cream, saving some for decoration.

8. Cover the sides of the cakes with toasted almonds (see Figure 8–1, page 178). Place a 6-inch (15-cm) plain cookie cutter in the center of the cakes. Sprinkle chocolate shavings inside the cutter, just thick enough to cover the cream. Mark or cut the cakes into the desired number of servings.

9. Place the remaining whipped cream in a pastry bag with a no. 5 (10-mm) plain tip. Pipe a small mound of cream at the edge of each slice. Place a macaroon on each whipped cream mound.

Macaroon-Maraschino Whipped Cream

3 pounds, 12 ounces (1 kg, 705 g)

10 ounces (285 g) Almond
   Macaroon Cookies (page 123)
½ cup (120 ml) maraschino
   liqueur
5 egg yolks
3 ounces (85 g) granulated sugar
1 quart (960 ml) heavy cream
½ cup (120 ml) cold water
⅓ cup (80 ml) milk
2½ tablespoons (23 g) unflavored
   gelatin powder

This is a good opportunity to use up some old and dry macaroon cookies. If they have to be made fresh, bake the macaroons slightly on the dry side so they do not fall apart when mixed with the cream.

1. Cut the macaroons into ½-inch (1.2-cm) pieces. Soak them in maraschino liqueur.

2. Whip the egg yolks and sugar until light and fluffy. Whip the cream to soft peaks and combine with the yolks.

3. Combine the cold water and milk. Add the gelatin to soften. Heat the mixture to 125°F (52°C) to dissolve the gelatin.

4. Rapidly add the gelatin mixture to a small portion of the cream. Still working quickly, add this mixture to the remaining cream. Fold in the soaked macaroon pieces.

Strawberry Kirsch Cake

(see photograph in color insert)
two 10-inch (25-cm) cakes

one 10-inch (25-cm) Sponge Cake
   (page 161)
two 10-inch (25-cm) Short Dough
   Cake-Bottoms (page 32)
4 ounces (115 g) strawberry jam
50 medium-sized strawberries,
   stemmed

1. Cut the skin from the top of the sponge cake and slice it into four thin layers.

2. Place the short dough cake-bottoms on cardboards for support. Divide the jam between them and spread it out evenly. Place one of the sponge layers on the jam on each cake. Place a 10-inch (25-cm) cake ring snugly around each cake. If the rings are not stainless steel, line them with strips of plastic or baking paper to prevent the metal from discoloring the filling.

3. Cut 32 strawberries in half lengthwise. Using 32 halves per cake, line the inside of each ring, placing them stem-end down with the cut side against the rings. Divide the remaining whole strawberries between the cakes, placing them evenly over the sponges, points up (Figure 8–13).

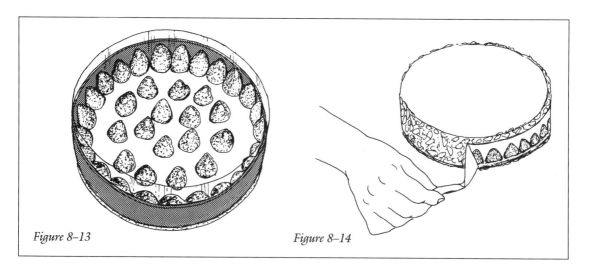

Figure 8–13   *Figure 8–14*

*Kirsch Whipped Cream
   (recipe follows)
Vanilla Buttercream (page 501)
12 ounces (340 g) sliced almonds,
   toasted and lightly crushed
10 ounces (285 g) Marzipan,
   white (page 00)
dark Piping Chocolate (page 449)
Strawberry Sauce (page 563)
Sour Cream Mixture for Piping
   (page 564)
small mint sprigs*

4. Divide the Kirsch Whipped Cream between the cakes. The cream should be just starting to set up or it will run between the strawberries and the ring, ruining the appearance of the cakes. Place the remaining two sponge cake layers on top of the cream filling. Refrigerate the cakes until the filling is set, at least 2 hours.

5. Remove the rings and the paper or plastic strips. Trim away any excess short dough to make the sides of the cakes even. Cut two new strips of baking paper, wide enough to cover the strawberries on the sides of the cakes, leaving the top and bottom sponges exposed. Wrap the paper strips around the strawberry layers, making sure you are not covering the sponge on the top or the bottom (make a mark on the cardboards where the ends of the paper meet so you will be able to find them easily later).

6. Ice the tops and the sides of the cakes, including the protective paper, with a thin layer of buttercream. Cover the sides of the cakes with crushed almonds, getting as few as possible on the paper strips. Carefully pull off the paper strips (Figure 8–14). Do not refrigerate the cakes before removing the paper.

7. Roll out half of the marzipan ⅛ inch (3 mm) thick, using powdered sugar to prevent it from sticking. Place the marzipan on a cardboard and cut out a circle the same size as the top of the cake. Repeat with the remaining marzipan. Carefully slide the circles onto the tops of the cakes.

8. Cut or mark the cakes into the desired number of serving pieces. Decorate the top of each slice with the piping chocolate (see Figure 16–16, page 452; the designs in the third row would be the most appropriate.

9. Presentation: Place a slice of cake off-center on a dessert plate. Pour a round pool of Strawberry Sauce next to the slice. Use a spoon to form the sauce into a strawberry shape (see photo in color insert). Decorate the sauce with the sour cream mixture (see pages 518–519). Place a mint sprig at the "stem end" of the sauce.

NOTE: This cake should not be frozen because the strawberries will lose their texture and look unpleasant when thawed.

Kirsch Whipped Cream

3 pounds, 10 ounces (1 kg, 650 g) cream

4 egg yolks
4 ounces (115 g) granulated sugar
5 cups (1 l, 200 ml) heavy cream
2 tablespoons (18 g) unflavored gelatin powder
1 cup (240 ml) dry white wine
¼ cup (60 ml) kirschwasser

1. Whip the egg yolks and sugar until light and fluffy. Whip the cream to soft peaks and combine with the yolk mixture.

2. Soften the gelatin in the wine, add the kirschwasser, and heat to 125°F (52°C) to dissolve.

3. Rapidly mix the gelatin into a small part of the cream and egg yolk mixture. Still working quickly, mix this into the remaining cream and yolks.

Swedish Chocolate Cake

two 10-inch (25-cm) cakes

two 10-inch (25-cm) Chocolate Biscuits (page 163)
1 pound, 12 ounces (795 g) Pastry Cream (page 569)
2 pounds, 10 ounces (1 kg, 195 g) Chocolate Buttercream (page 501)
chocolate sprinkles
4- × 1-inch (10- × 2.5-cm) Chocolate Rectangles (page 445)
Chocolate Squares (page 445)

1. Cut the skin off the Chocolate Biscuits. Cut each into three layers. Use the bottom layers as the base for each cake, but choose the better of the remaining layers for the tops.

2. Divide the pastry cream between the bottom cake layers and spread out evenly. Place the second cake layers on the cream, and spread a ¼-inch (6-mm) layer of chocolate buttercream on top.

3. Place the remaining cake layers on top and spread chocolate buttercream over the top and sides of the cakes. Spread just thick enough to cover the sponge, leaving some buttercream for decoration. Refrigerate the cakes until the buttercream is firm so that the cakes will slice cleanly.

4. Put the remaining buttercream in a pastry bag with a no. 4 (8-mm) plain tip. Making one decoration for each serving of cake, pipe a small mound of buttercream, about the size of a cherry half, onto a sheet pan lined with baking paper. Cover the mounds with chocolate sprinkles. Refrigerate the decorations until they are firm.

5. Cut the cakes into the desired number of slices. Pipe a straight line of buttercream next to one cut side of each piece. Place a chocolate rectangle standing at an angle on each slice, supported by the buttercream lines and angled slightly toward the center of the cake. Place a chocolate square on the side of each piece. Place one of the reserved decorations at the end of each slice.

Tropical Mousse Cake

(see photograph in color insert)
20 servings

Passion Fruit Jelly (recipe follows)
⅓ recipe Cocoa Almond Sponge batter (page 163)
Passion Fruit Mousse Filling (recipe follows)
¼ cup (60 ml) papaya or other tropical fruit juice
2 tablespoons (30 ml) light rum
Strawberry Sauce (page 563)
20 strawberry halves, fanned
Sour Cream Mixture for Piping (page 564)

1. Stretch a sheet of plastic wrap tightly over a sheet of cardboard or an inverted sheet pan (make sure the sheet pan has an even surface). Make a frame 12½ inches long, 10 inches wide, and 2½ inches high (31.2 × 25 × 6.2) from cardboard. Cut the pieces and tape them together at the corners. (Or use any form with approximately the same dimensions.) Place the frame on top of the plastic sheet. If the bottom of the frame does not sit tight against the plastic, the jelly will run out, so weigh it down by placing a heavy object on the corners. Or, better yet, roll some short dough or modeling clay into a rope and press it against the outside bottom edge of the frame to seal. Set the frame aside.

2. Make the Passion Fruit Jelly, let it start to thicken slightly, then pour it over the bottom of the frame. Chill in the refrigerator until set, about 30 minutes.

3. Make the Cocoa Almond Sponge batter. Immediately spread the batter into a 13- × 21-inch (32.5- × 52.5-cm) rectangle. Bake at 400°F (205°C) for about 10 minutes or until just done. Let the sponge sheet cool. Cut in half crosswise and trim the pieces to fit inside the frame.

4. Spread half of the mousse filling evenly on top of the jelly. Top with one of the sponge sheets. Combine the rum and fruit juice, and brush half of the mixture over the sponge. Spread the remaining mousse filling on top of the sponge, then set the second sponge sheet on the filling. Brush the remaining rum mixture over the sponge. Refrigerate for at least 3 hours to set the filling.

5. Invert the cake. Remove the sheet pan or cardboard and the plastic wrap. Cut around the inside of the frame and remove the frame. Trim the cake and cut it into twenty 2½-inch (6.2-cm) squares.

6. Presentation: Place a square in the center of a dessert plate. Pour Strawberry Sauce around the dessert to cover the surface of the plate. Place a fanned strawberry half in front of the cake. Decorate the Strawberry Sauce with the Sour Cream Mixture for Piping (pages 518–519), making a half-circle behind the cake.

Passion Fruit Jelly

11 ounces (330 ml)

2 teaspoons (6 g) unflavored gelatin powder
¾ cup (180 ml) papaya or other tropical fruit juice
½ cup (120 ml) passion fruit pulp
2 ounces (55 g) brown sugar

1. Soften the gelatin in ⅓ cup (80 ml) of the fruit juice.

2. Stir the passion fruit pulp into the remaining fruit juice. Add the sugar and bring to a boil in a saucepan.

3. Remove from heat, add the softened gelatin, and heat to 110°F (43°C) to dissolve. Skim any foam from the surface. Cool until the mixture just begins to thicken before using.

NOTE: If you do not want the seeds in the jelly, strain the mixture before adding the gelatin.

Passion Fruit Mousse Filling

4 pounds, 2 ounces (1 kg, 875 g)
filling

¼ recipe Italian or Swiss Meringue
(pages 333 and 334)
¾ cup (180 ml) passion fruit pulp
2 cups (480 ml) papaya or other
tropical fruit juice
2½ tablespoons (23 g) unflavored
gelatin powder
2½ cups (600 ml) heavy cream
1 cup (240 ml) unflavored yogurt

Variation: Kiwi Mousse Cake

1. Make the meringue and set aside.

2. Cut passion fruits in half and scoop out the pulp and seeds to make ¾ cup (180 ml). Stir in 1½ cups (360 ml) of the fruit juice. Heat to 150°F (65°C). Remove from heat. Strain to remove the seeds and reserve.

3. Soften the gelatin in the remaining fruit juice. Add to the hot liquid and stir until dissolved. Set aside.

4. Whip the cream to soft peaks. Fold into the yogurt. Fold the yogurt and cream into the reserved meringue. Quickly add the gelatin mixture to a small amount of the cream mixture; then add this back to the remainder, still mixing rapidly. If necessary, cool the mousse until it starts to thicken before using, but do not make the mousse until you are ready to use it in the cake.

Although passion fruit is certainly more tropical and unusual, its season is rather short. By substituting kiwi fruit when passion fruits are not in season, you can make this delicious cake any time of the year. Use 1 ounce (30 ml) less pulp in making both the jelly and the mousse filling. Use only fully ripe kiwis. Cut off the skin, remove the white vein in the center, and mash the fruit into a pulp. Proceed as directed for the Tropical Mousse Cake. Do not use a red-colored juice with the kiwi fruit jelly or it will turn a very unattractive color.

White Chocolate Pumpkin Cheesecake

two 10-inch (25-cm) cakes

Crust
7 ounces (200 g) graham cracker
crumbs
3 ounces (85 g) finely ground
almonds
1 teaspoon (2 g) ground ginger
1 teaspoon (1.5 g) ground
cinnamon
4 ounces (115 g) melted butter

Filling
2 pounds, 6 ounces (1 kg, 80 g)
cream cheese, at room
temperature

1. Combine all of the ingredients for the crust. Divide the mixture between two 10-inch (25-cm) springform pans. Use your hands to pat the crumbs in place covering the bottom of the pans. (If the springform pans are not made of stainless steel or aluminum, line the inside of the rings with strips of baking paper to avoid staining the filling. Cut the paper to the exact height of the rings and fasten to the inside of the pans using melted butter.) Set the pans aside.

2. Place the cream cheese in a mixer bowl and soften it by stirring on low speed with the paddle. Be careful not to overmix and incorporate too much air as this will result in a dry and crumbly cheesecake. Stir the white chocolate into the cream cheese, then add the eggs gradually. Scrape the sides and bottom of the mixing bowl frequently to avoid lumps. Combine the maple syrup, brandy, spices, and pumpkin purée. Add this mixture to the cream cheese mixture, stirring only long enough to combine. Divide the batter between the prepared pans and spread it evenly on top.

*1 pound (455 g) melted white
    chocolate*

6 eggs

¼ cup (60 ml) maple syrup

¼ cup (60 ml) brandy

2 teaspoons (4 g) ground ginger

2 teaspoons (3 g) ground cinnamon

1 teaspoon (2 g) ground nutmeg

*1½ cups (360 ml) canned or
    freshly cooked pumpkin purée
    (page 425)*

Topping

*2 pounds, 8 ounces (1 kg, 135 g)
    sour cream*

6 ounces (170 g) granulated sugar

2 tablespoons (30 ml) maple syrup

2 tablespoons (30 ml) brandy

decoration (choices follow)

Decoration

3. Bake the cheesecakes at 325°F (163°C) for approximately 40 minutes, or until the filling is set (see step 4, page 185).

4. Combine the topping ingredients. Divide the topping between the baked cakes. This can be done as soon as they come out of the oven if necessary, but pour the topping gently around the outside edges of the cakes to avoid denting the softer center.

5. Place the flavoring in a pastry bag with the size tip specified in the flavoring instructions. Pipe the flavoring in a spiral pattern on the top of each cake, starting in the center. Run the back of a paring knife through the spiral starting in the center and pulling toward the edge of the pan to make a spider-web pattern (see Figure 18–26, page 519).

6. Bake the cakes at 400°F (205°C) for 8 minutes to set the sour cream. The sour cream will still look liquid but will set as it cools.

Pumpkin

Reserve ¼ cup (60 ml) of the sour cream mixture per cake and flavor it with 2 tablespoons (30 ml) pumpkin purée. Pour the remaining sour cream mixture onto the cake (or cakes). Pipe the pumpkin-flavored sour cream on top using a no. 2 (4-mm) tip in the pastry bag.

Cranberry

Purée prepared cranberry sauce (use the thicker jellied type) or cranberry preserves. Pipe on top of the sour cream using a no. 3 (6-mm) plain tip in the pastry bag.

NOTE: For an elegant holiday presentation make individual White Chocolate Pumpkin Cheesecakes using the template and instructions for Lingonberry Cheese Pudding (page 315). Bake at 375°F (190°C) as specified in the recipe for Lingonberry Cheese Pudding; the pumpkin cheesecakes will take slightly less time. Be careful not to overbake. Follow the presentation instructions in step 11 of Lingonberry Cheese Pudding, substituting Cranberry Sauce (page 558) for the lingonberry sauce.

—NINE—

Individual Pastries

Almond Doubles
Almond Truffles
Apple Mazarins
Chocolate Eclairs
Chocolate Macaroons
Chocolate Triangles
Citrons
Cream Horns
Diplomats
Florentina Surprise
Fruit Tartlets
Fruit Waffles
Hazelnut Nougat Slices
Kirschwasser Rings
Lemon-Almond Tartlets
Linzer Tartlets
Macaroon Bananas
Mazarins
Noisette Rings
Orange Truffle Strips
Othellos
Petits Fours

Petits Fours Sec
  Brandy Pretzels
  Chocolate-filled Macadamia
    Morsels
  Hazelnut Cuts
  Hazelnut Flowers
  Macaroon Candies
  Miniature Palm Leaves
  Raspberry Cut-outs
  Strawberry Hearts
  Vienna Petits Fours
Polynées
Pretzels
Rum Balls
Small Princess Pastries
Streusel Kuchen
Swans
Swedish Napoleons
Tosca
Triangles
Trier Squares
Vanilla Macaroons
Walnut-Orange Tartlets

The term "pastries" includes small, decorated cuts of cakes or tarts, fancy individual pieces in numerous shapes, and the much larger classics such as napoleons and chocolate eclairs. These treats are perhaps best known in this country as "French pastries," which is actually a misnomer (they are called *les petits gateaux* or "small cakes" in France), as they are tremendously popular all over Europe.

Every country in Europe has pastry specialties that vary in flavor and style. The variations are influenced to some degree by the climate: It is much easier to work with chocolate and whipped cream (and more pleasant to eat them) in the cooler, northern part of Europe than in the heat of the Mediterranean. In southern France or Italy, you will find a tendency (too often in my opinion) to use fondant, candied fruits, and apricot glaze, which make the pastries very sweet. In the Scandinavian countries of northern Europe many pastries combine almond, chocolate, and fresh fruit. These pastries are typically covered with pectin glaze (a sugar syrup that develops a pleasant tart flavor when tartaric acid is added to it), which complements the fruit nicely. A similar style is popular in Germany, Switzerland, and Austria.

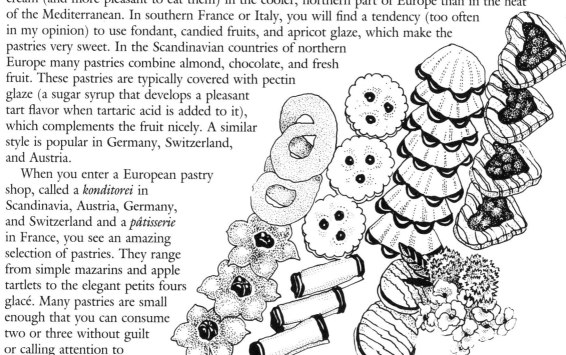

When you enter a European pastry shop, called a *konditorei* in Scandinavia, Austria, Germany, and Switzerland and a *pâtisserie* in France, you see an amazing selection of pastries. They range from simple mazarins and apple tartlets to the elegant petits fours glacé. Many pastries are small enough that you can consume two or three without guilt or calling attention to yourself. These desserts are appropriately eaten with the fingers and include filled cookies and petits fours sec.

Pastries based on pâte à choux or puff paste are made up fresh every day in the pastry shop. Other varieties, such as Orange Truffle Strips and Tosca, can be made once or twice a week because they are covered, wholly or partially, with chocolate, fondant, or marzipan and will keep fresh much longer.

Every week at the California Culinary Academy we serve a classic European buffet. The pastries are all miniatures, half or smaller than the typical size, and are presented on large mirrors for a spectacular display featuring the specialties of many countries, including America. When pastries are served on a buffet, they should be placed in small paper cups so the customers can help themselves. Known as petits fours cups, these containers are usually round but should be altered to fit individual shapes for the most finished appearance. This can be done by pressing a stack of cups with the appropriate size and shape of cookie cutter to enlarge the bottom (Figure 9–1) or by bending the sides to create a new bottom edge with your hands. If a dessert tray is to be presented to the table after a meal, it is not necessary to use paper cups as the waiter should place the selection on the plate using a cake spatula or tongs.

The pastries in this chapter are quite varied. Some must be started a day in advance of serving, while others can be made on the spur of the moment. Some have a plain finish and others require a bit of artistic ability. All of these recipes have proven to be very popular in this country, as I can attest from watching customers "load up" on the students' creations at the Academy.

Figure 9–1

Almond Truffles

88 pastries

1 pound, 5 ounces (595 g)
  Short Dough (page 31)
4 ounces (115 g) smooth
  apricot jam
4 pounds, 10 ounces (2 kg, 105 g)
  Mazarin Filling, soft
  (page 569)
1 pound, 8 ounces (680 g)
  Ganache (page 567)
melted dark baker's chocolate
melted light baker's chocolate
candied violets, optional
blanched pistachios, optional

1. Line the bottom of a half-sheet pan (16 × 12 inches/40 × 30 cm) with baking paper. Cover with the short dough, rolled to ⅛ inch (3 mm) thick.

2. Spread the jam evenly over the dough, then spread the mazarin filling evenly on top.

3. Bake the sheet at 375°F (190°C) for about 50 minutes.

4. When completely cold, preferably the next day, cut around the inside edge of the pan to loosen the skin, and unmold onto an inverted sheet pan or cardboard. If the sheet does not separate easily from the pan, do not force it. Instead place a hot sheet pan underneath and wait a few minutes. The heat will soften the butter, which is making it stick, without heating up the whole sheet.

5. Invert the sheet again so it is now right-side up. Cut off the skin and even the top at the same time, if necessary. Trim the two long sides. Cut the sheet into 11 strips lengthwise. Separate the pieces slightly.

6. Soften the ganache, if necessary, and place it in a pastry bag with a no. 8 (16-mm) plain tip. Pipe the ganache in a long rope down the center of each strip. The ganache should be soft enough to stick to the mazarin but still hold its shape. Refrigerate until the ganache is firm.

7. Cut each strip into eight equal slices using a thin, sharp knife. Dip each slice in melted dark baker's chocolate as described in the instructions for Tosca, page 266 (see Figures 9–26 through 9–30).

8. Streak thin lines of light chocolate over the tops for decoration. A small piece of candied violet or a half of a blanched pistachio is nice on top as further decoration. Attach these with a small dot of chocolate.

Apple Mazarins

35 pastries

1 pound, 14 ounces (855 g)
  Short Dough (page 31)
⅓ recipe Chunky Apple Filling
  (page 566)
1 pound (455 g) Mazarin Filling,
  soft (page 569)
1 pound, 8 ounces (680 g)
  Streusel Topping (page 8)
powdered sugar

1. Line mazarin forms with short dough rolled to ⅛ inch (3 mm) thick (see Figures 2–12 through 2–15, page 34).

2. Place the apple filling in a pastry bag with a no. 6 (12-mm) plain tip. Pipe the filling into the forms, filling them halfway.

3. Place the mazarin filling in the same pastry bag you used for the apple filling, and pipe over the apple filling to the rim of the forms.

4. Top the pastries with a small mound of streusel (it is a good idea to prepare the mazarins on one sheet pan and then transfer them to another because it is impossible not to spill the streusel around the forms).

5. Bake at 375°F (190°C) until golden brown, about 25 minutes, using steam during the first 10 minutes. Let cool to room temperature.

6. When they are cool, unmold each pastry carefully by cupping your hand over the streusel to hold it in place. Sift powdered sugar very lightly over the tops.

NOTE: If you do not have a steam oven, follow the directions given in the recipe for Baguettes on page 48, or simply spray a fine mist of water on top of the pastries after topping with streusel to hold the streusel in place.

Chocolate Eclairs

30 pastries

½ recipe Pâte à Choux (page 15)
Chocolate Glaze (page 526)
8 ounces (225 g) smooth
*   strawberry jam*
¼ recipe Crème Parisienne
*   (page 567)*
*   or*
½ recipe Chocolate Cream
*   (page 566)*

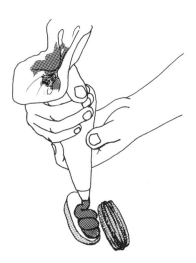

Figure 9–2

1. Place the pâte à choux in a pastry bag with a no. 8 (16-mm) star tip. Pipe out 4½-inch (11.2-cm) strips onto sheet pans lined with baking paper. Do not put more than 20 eclairs on a pan because there must be enough space around them to bake thoroughly (see note).

2. Bake the eclairs at 425°F (219°C) until puffed and starting to color, about 10 minutes. Reduce heat to 375°F (190°C) and bake until they are dry enough to keep their shape when you take them out, about 12 minutes longer. Let the eclairs cool.

3. Cut off the top third of each eclair. Brush the tops evenly with chocolate glaze. Set the tops next to the bottoms to speed up assembly.

4. Pipe a small ribbon of strawberry jam in the bottom of each eclair using a no. 5 (10-mm) plain tip. Pipe crème Parisienne or chocolate cream in a coil shape on top of the jam (Figure 9–2). The coil shape makes the cream more visible in the final presentation. It should be at least ½ inch (1.2 cm) higher than the base of the eclair.

5. Set the glazed tops on top of the cream at an angle so the filling shows nicely. Serve the eclairs as soon as possible—the pâte à choux will become soggy and rubbery if left to stand too long. Try not to fill any more eclairs than you will serve within the next few hours.

NOTE: If you are planning to freeze the eclairs before baking, pipe them as close together as possible to conserve freezer space. If well-covered, they can be frozen for weeks without losing quality. Bake as needed directly from the freezer.

Chocolate Macaroons

60 pastries

1 recipe Almond Macaroon Cookie
batter (page 123)
3 pounds, 8 ounces (1 kg, 590 g)
Chocolate Buttercream
(page 501)
melted dark baker's chocolate
60 whole hazelnuts, roasted and
skins removed

1. Place the macaroon batter (paste) in a pastry bag with a no. 8 (16-mm) plain tip. Line a sheet pan with baking paper and fasten the paper to the pan using a small dab of batter in the corners. Pipe the batter onto the paper, making cookies that are 2½ inches (6.2 cm) in length. As you pipe the cookies, hold the tip of the pastry bag close enough to the pan that the batter flattens slightly (becomes wider and lower than the size of the tip) rather than making ropes.

2. Bake immediately, following the instructions for Almond Macaroon Cookies, page 123.

3. Let the cookies cool, then invert the paper and peel it away from the cookies. Arrange the cookies in rows on a sheet pan flat side up. Press down lightly, if necessary, to flatten the tops (now the bottoms) so that the cookies do not wobble.

4. Place the chocolate buttercream in a pastry bag with a no. 7 (14-mm) plain tip. Pipe two small mounds on each cookie, wide enough to cover most of the surface and about ½ inch (1.2 cm) high (Figure 9–3). Refrigerate until the buttercream is firm.

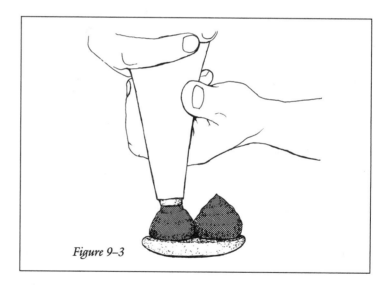

Figure 9–3

5. Holding a cookie upside down and touching only the edges of the macaroon, dip it into melted dark baker's chocolate to cover the buttercream mounds and the flat side of the macaroon. Move the cookie up and down a few times over the bowl to allow as much of the excess chocolate as possible to drip off, then place it (chocolate-side up) on a sheet pan. Set a hazelnut between the buttercream mounds before the chocolate hardens.

NOTE: Chocolate Macaroons can be kept at normal room temperature for up to one week. They should be well-covered if refrigerated.

Chocolate Triangles
about 40 pastries

two ¼- × 14- × 24-inch
  (6-mm × 35- × 60-cm)
  Cocoa Almond Sponges
  (page 163)
3 pounds, 8 ounces (1 kg, 590 g)
  Chocolate Buttercream
  (page 501)
1 pound (455 g) Marzipan,
  white (page 531)
melted dark baker's chocolate
melted light baker's chocolate

1. When the sponge sheets are cold, cut each in half lengthwise, leaving the baking paper attached. Invert one sponge strip and peel the paper from the back. Spread a ¼-inch (6-mm) layer of buttercream on the sponge.

2. Pick up a second sponge sheet, holding it by the paper, and invert it on top of the buttercream, lining up the edges evenly. Peel the paper from the back.

3. Add the remaining two sponge sheets in the same way, layering buttercream between them. Refrigerate until the buttercream is firm.

4. Trim the long sides of the layered sponge sheets. Cut in half lengthwise to create two strips, 24 inches (60 cm) long and approximately 3 inches (7.5 cm) wide.

5. Place one of the strips at the very edge of the table with the layers running horizontally. Using a long, serrated knife dipped in hot water, with the table edge as your guide, cut the strip in half diagonally, making two triangles (Figure 9–4).

6. Arrange the triangles so the two long uncut sides are back to back, with the layers running vertically (Figures 9–5, 9–6, and 9–7). Place a dowel about 2 inches (5 cm) behind the strips and tilt the back piece onto the dowel.

7. Spread a ¼-inch (6-mm) layer of buttercream on the back piece (Figure 9–8). Use the dowel to pick that piece up and put it back into place, with the buttercream in the middle (Figure 9–9). Lightly press the two pieces together with your hands (Figure 9–10). Transfer the cake to one side of an inverted sheet pan topped with baking paper.

8. Repeat steps 5 through 7 with the second cake, placing the finished triangle on the same sheet pan.

9. Ice the two exposed sides of the triangles with a thin film of buttercream.

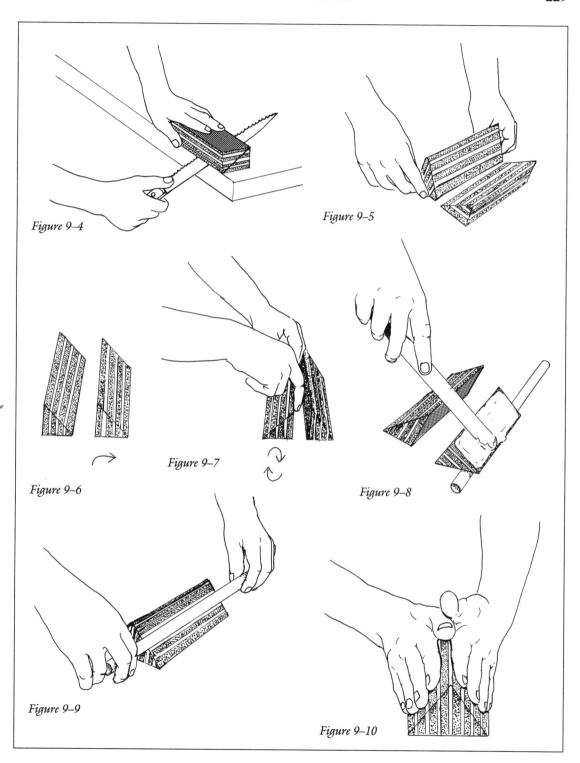

Figure 9–4

Figure 9–5

Figure 9–6

Figure 9–7

Figure 9–8

Figure 9–9

Figure 9–10

10. Roll out the marzipan (using powdered sugar to prevent it from sticking) to $1/16$ inch (2 mm) thick, approximately 7 inches (17.5 cm) wide, and twice as long as one strip. Cut it in half crosswise.

11. Roll one piece of marzipan up on a dowel and unroll it over one of the strips. Press it in place with your hands. Trim the excess marzipan even with the bottom of the cake on the long sides (do not worry about covering the ends or trimming the marzipan on the ends at this time). Cover the second cake with marzipan in the same way.

12. Working on one cake at a time, spread a layer of melted dark baker's chocolate over the marzipan just thick enough to prevent the marzipan from showing through. (If the chocolate layer is too thick it will be difficult to cut the cake.) Keep spreading the chocolate back and forth until it starts to set up. Repeat with second cake.

13. Decorate both cakes by streaking light baker's chocolate, crosswise, over the dark chocolate (see example in Figure 6–1, page 150).

14. Refrigerate the cakes just until the buttercream is firm (if you need to refrigerate them longer make sure they are well covered).

15. Trim the ends and cut the cakes into 1-inch (2.5-cm) slices using a thin, sharp (or serrated) knife dipped in hot water.

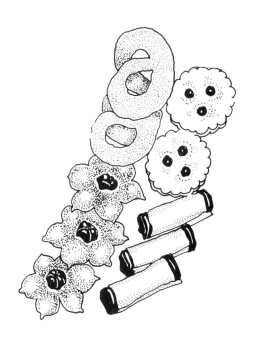

Citrons

forty-five 3-inch (7.5-cm) pastries

*1 pound, 2 ounces (510 g)
   Short Dough (page 31)*
*4 ounces (115 g) smooth
   strawberry jam*
*1 pound, 2 ounces (510 g)
   Mazarin Filling, soft
   (page 569)*
granulated sugar
*12 ounces (340 g) Vanilla
   Buttercream (page 501)*
*3 ounces (85 g) Lemon Curd
   (page 568)*
dark baker's chocolate, melted
*Marzipan (page 531),
   colored yellow*
Piping Chocolate (page 449)

1. Line 45 barquette forms, 3 inches long by ¾ inch high (7.5 cm × 2 cm), with short dough rolled to ⅛ inch (3 mm) thick.

2. Make a disposable pastry bag from baking paper (see page 505). Place the jam in the cone and pipe a ribbon of jam in each form.

3. Place the mazarin filling in a pastry bag with a no. 6 (12-mm) plain tip. Pipe into the forms on top of the jam, filling each two-thirds full.

4. Bake at 400°F (205°C) until golden brown, about 10 minutes.

5. As soon as you remove the tartlets from the oven, immediately sprinkle sugar over the tops, then turn the forms upside down on the pan so they will become flat on the top. Cool completely (upside down), then remove the forms.

6. Combine the buttercream and lemon curd. Place the mixture in a pastry bag with a no. 5 (10-mm) plain tip. Turn the barquettes right-side up and pipe a rope of buttercream straight down the center of each pastry. With a small spatula, spread both sides of the buttercream into a ridge in the center about ½ inch (1.2 cm) high (Figure 9–11). Refrigerate until the buttercream is firm.

7. Dip the tops of the pastries (the buttercream) into melted dark baker's chocolate.

8. Roll out the yellow marzipan to ¹⁄₁₆ inch (2 mm) thick. Cut out 45 strips, 1¾ × ⅜ inch (4.5 cm × 9 mm). Put the piping chocolate in a piping bag and use it to write "citron" on each strip.

9. Pipe a thin, diagonal line of chocolate on each pastry and place a marzipan strip on top.

NOTE: Citrons keep well for several days at normal room temperature. They should be well covered if refrigerated.

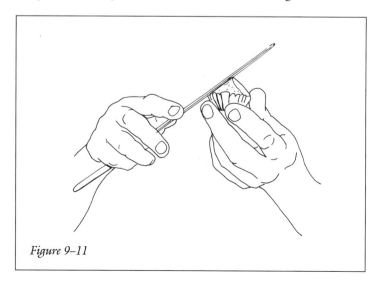

Figure 9–11

Cream Horns

18 pastries

1 pound, 8 ounces (680 g)
   Classic Puff Paste (page 21)
granulated sugar
5 ounces (140 g) strawberry jam
1½ cups (360 ml) heavy cream
1 tablespoon (15 g) granulated
   sugar
powdered sugar
strawberries

1. Roll out the puff paste to a ⅛-inch (3-mm) thick rectangle measuring 16 × 18 inches (40 × 45 cm). Cover the dough and place in the refrigerator to rest for a few minutes.

2. Cut the dough into eighteen ¾-inch-wide (2-cm) strips, crosswise. Brush the strips lightly with water.

3. Wind the dough around Cream Horn cones 5 inches (12.5 cm) long with a 1¼-inch (3.1-cm) opening. Place the wet side against the form, starting at the narrow end and overlapping each previous strip halfway as you go (Figure 9–12). Line them up next to each other on the table as you cover the remaining molds.

4. Brush the top and sides of the pastries with water. Invert onto granulated sugar to coat the top and sides. Roll them back and forth to get sugar on the sides, but do not get any on the bottom. Place sugar-side up on sheet pans lined with baking paper.

5. Bake at 400°F (205°C) for about 45 minutes. Just before the horns are done, pull out the forms and finish baking (see note). Allow to cool completely.

6. Place the strawberry jam in a disposable pastry bag made from baking paper. Pipe a thin string of jam along the inside of each horn.

7. Whip the cream and 1 tablespoon (15 g) sugar to stiff peaks. Place the cream in a pastry bag with a no. 5 (10-mm) star tip and pipe into the horns, filling them completely. Pipe a small rosette of whipped cream on each horn at the top edge.

8. Lightly sift powdered sugar over the pastries. Place a small wedge of strawberry on the whipped cream rosettes.

NOTE: The coiled puff paste strips have a tendency to slide off the forms during baking, curling into various interesting, but not very presentable, shapes. There are a number of tricks for keeping

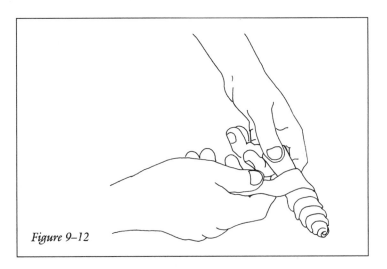

Figure 9–12

the paste on the molds, including freezing them before baking and standing them up during baking. Brushing the strips with water also works very well to secure them to the molds. However, you must remove the forms just before the pastries have finished baking and as soon as you can handle them after they come out of the oven. Stick a chef's knife (one you are not too fond of) into the opening of the metal cone and twist to remove the cone. Return the pastries to the oven to dry the inside as needed. If you let them cool completely before removing the cones, the pastries will break into little pieces.

Diplomats

45 pastries

1 recipe Biscuit Viennoise batter
  (page 163)
7 ounces (200 g) smooth
  strawberry jam
1 pound, 6 ounces (625 g)
  Pastry Cream (page 569)
sliced almonds, lightly crushed
¼ recipe or 14 ounces (400 g)
  Macaroon Decorating Paste
  (page 123)
strawberries
Pectin or Apricot Glaze
  (page 526)

1. Line the bottom of a half-sheet pan (16 × 12 inches/40 × 30 cm) with baking paper. Fill the pan with the Biscuit Viennoise batter, spreading it out evenly.

2. Bake immediately at 400°F (205°C) for about 15 minutes, or until the cake springs back when pressed lightly in the center. Let cool completely.

3. Cut around the side of the pan and invert it to remove the biscuit. Peel the paper from the back and turn right-side up. Cut away the skin from the top, then cut into two layers horizontally.

4. Spread strawberry jam on the bottom layer, then place the top layer on the jam.

5. Cut out forty-five 2-inch (5-cm) rounds using a plain cookie cutter. You will need to keep the cuts close together and stagger the rows to get 45 pieces. Reserve the leftover cake scraps for another use, such as Rum Balls (see page 254).

6. Spread a thin layer of pastry cream on the sides of each pastry (you will not use all of it). Roll the sides of the pastries in crushed almonds. Place the cakes on a sheet pan lined with baking paper.

7. Place the macaroon decorating paste in a pastry bag with a no. 3 (6-mm) plain tip. Pipe a ring of paste at the edge of each cake.

8. Place the remaining pastry cream in a pastry bag with a no. 4 (8-mm) plain tip. Pipe the pastry cream in a spiral, inside the macaroon paste border, to cover the sponge on the top of each cake.

9. Bake the cakes, double-panned, at 425°F (219°C) for about 8 minutes, or until the macaroon paste is light brown. Let the cakes cool completely.

10. Cut the strawberries across to get round slices; place one in the center of each cake. Glaze the tops of the cakes with apricot or pectin glaze.

NOTE: The macaroon paste should be just firm enough to be piped yet still stick to the surface it is piped on. If it is too soft it will run as it bakes and not be as attractive.

Florentina Surprise

60 pastries

1 pound, 8 ounces (680 g)
Short Dough (page 31)
½ recipe Florentina Batter
(page 131)
1 pound, 5 ounces (595 g) Vanilla
Buttercream (page 501)
5 ounces (140 g) Hazelnut Paste
(page 6)
or
2½ ounces (70 g) commercial
hazelnut paste
10 ounces (285 g) Ganache
(page 567)
⅓ cup (80 ml) light rum
melted dark baker's chocolate

1. Roll out the short dough to ⅛ inch (3 mm) thick. Cut out sixty 2-inch (5-cm) cookies using a plain cutter. Bake the cookies at 375°F (190°C) for about 10 minutes, or until light brown. Set aside to cool.

2. Draw sixty 2-inch (5-cm) circles on baking papers using a cookie cutter as a guide; invert the papers and place them on sheet pans. Divide the Florentina Batter between the circles, spread out, bake, and trim the cookies according to the instructions on page 130.

3. Flavor the buttercream with the hazelnut paste and place it in a pastry bag with a no. 5 (10-mm) plain tip. Pipe a ring of buttercream on each of the short dough cookies just inside the edge.

4. Flavor the ganache with the rum. Place it in a pastry bag with a no. 4 (8-mm) plain tip. Pipe a small mound of ganache inside the buttercream rings. Refrigerate until the buttercream is firm.

5. Holding a cookie upside down, dip the buttercream, ganache, and the top part of the short dough cookie into melted baker's chocolate. Gently shake off as much excess chocolate as possible by moving the cookie up and down a few times over the bowl so that the chocolate does not run out around the pastries before it hardens. Place the cookies on paper-lined sheet pans.

6. Before the chocolate hardens, place a Florentina on top of the buttercream and press gently to make it level. Do not refrigerate Florentina Surprise pastries.

Fruit Tartlets

thirty 2-inch (5-cm) pastries

14 ounces (400 g) Short Dough
(page 31)
melted dark baker's chocolate
14 ounces (400 g) Vanilla
Bavarian Cream (page 570)
fresh fruit
Apricot or Pectin Glaze
(page 526)

1. Line thirty 2-inch (5-cm) tartlet pans with short dough rolled to ⅛ inch (3 mm) thick (see Figures 2–12, 2–13, 2–14, and 2–15, page 34). Prick the dough lightly with a fork and bake the shells at 375°F (190°C) until light golden brown. Unmold while still warm, then cool the shells completely.

2. Brush melted dark baker's chocolate (or apricot glaze) on the inside of each shell so that the filling will not soften them.

3. Place the Bavarian cream in a pastry bag with a no. 6 (12-mm) plain tip. Pipe the cream into each shell, up to the rim, in a nice mound. Decorate the tartlets with the fresh fruit (see note).

4. Brush apricot or pectin glaze on the fruit. Place the finished tartlets in paper cups. Use these tarts the day they are made; they usually look a bit wilted the day after.

NOTE: Choose fruit that is in season. Use small fruits if possible, such as raspberries, blackberries, strawberries, kiwis, figs, plums, and blueberries. Leave the skin on when it is edible and adds to the appearance. Cut the fruit into thin slices to make it look more appealing: a whole or half strawberry may look good on a large tart, but on a small tartlet it looks clumsy. If you slice a half strawberry thinly and fan it out as you place it on the tartlet, it will look elegant. The entire top of the tartlet should be covered with fruit in a simple pattern; do not get too complicated.

Fruit Waffles
30 pastries

1 pound (455 g) Classic
  Puff Paste (page 21)
flour
granulated sugar
8 ounces (225 g) Pastry Cream
  (page 569)
frozen cooking apples, cut into
  small wedges
  or
fresh apples (see note 1)
Cinnamon Sugar (page 4)
Apricot or Pectin Glaze
  (page 526)

The name Fruit Waffles derives from the traditional method of making these pastries. The dough was rolled over a waffleboard, leaving a waffle-like impression.

1. Roll out the puff paste to ¼ inch (6 mm) thick and cut out circles using a fluted cookie cutter approximately 1¾ inches (4.5 cm) in diameter. Stagger the cuts to get 30 circles and minimize the scrap dough. Press the scrap pieces together, cover, and reserve in the refrigerator or freezer for another use. Place the cut circles in the refrigerator to firm up if necessary.

2. Set up your work station efficiently: If you are right-handed, place some flour in a pie tin on your left, granulated sugar directly on the table in front of you, and sheet pans lined with baking paper on your right.

3. Place half a dozen or so of the circles on top of the flour. One at a time, pick up a circle, invert it (flour-side up) onto the sugar in front of you, and use a dowel to roll it in the sugar making an oval about 4 inches (10 cm) long. If the dough sticks to the dowel, turn the puff paste back over in the flour again, but do not get any sugar on the flour side or it will burn when the pastries bake. Place each sugared pastry sugar-side up on the sheet pan.

4. Using a no. 3 (6-mm) plain tip, pipe a small oval of pastry cream in the center of each pastry oval, leaving a ¼-inch (6-mm) border of puff paste uncovered.

5. Arrange four to five small apple wedges at an angle in the pastry cream. Sprinkle with cinnamon sugar.

6. Bake at 400°F (205°C) just until the sugar caramelizes, about 20 minutes. Cool completely.

7. When the pastries have cooled, glaze with apricot or pectin glaze. The waffles should be served the same day they are made.

NOTE 1: If you use fresh apples, try to get Golden Delicious or Granny Smith. Peel, core, and cut the apples in half; poach them in Poaching Syrup II (see page 6) until soft. Cut in wedges.

NOTE 2: The waffles can also be baked without the apples (reduce the baking time to 15 minutes) and decorated with fresh fruit in season. Apricots and figs are especially nice with puff paste.

NOTE 3: Because these waffles, like all puff paste goods, should be baked fresh every day, make a large number to freeze and bake as needed. You can stack six layers of waffles (rolled in sugar), separated with baking paper, per sheet pan.

Variation: Pariser Waffles

15 pastries

1. Follow the directions for Fruit Waffles, but omit the apples and pastry cream. Instead, make three ¼-inch (6-mm) cuts at an angle on the top of each pastry. Let the pastries rest for at least 30 minutes.

2. Bake the ovals at 425°F (219°C) until they are golden and the sugar on top begins to caramelize, about 12 minutes. When they have cooled, turn half of them upside down reserving the best-looking ones to become the tops.

3. Flavor the buttercream with arrack or rum and pipe a border around each bottom waffle with a no. 4 (8-mm) plain tip. Pipe a small ribbon of strawberry jam down the middle.

4. Place the reserved waffles on top and press lightly into the buttercream so they adhere.

Hazelnut Nougat Slices

thirty 4- × 1½-inch (10- × 3.7-cm) pastries

1 recipe Sponge Cake batter (page 161)
½ recipe Pâte à Choux (page 15)
5 ounces (140 g) smooth apricot jam
Hazelnut Nougat Cream (recipe follows)
1½ cups (360 ml) heavy cream
1 tablespoon (15 g) granulated sugar
powdered sugar

1. Line the bottom of a half-sheet pan (16 × 12 inches/40 × 30 cm) with baking paper. Spread the sponge cake batter evenly on top. Bake at 400°F (205°C) for about 10 minutes, or until the cake springs back when pressed lightly in the center. Reserve.

2. Cut a piece of baking paper the same size as the sponge cake. Draw lines the length of the paper ½ inch (1.2 cm) apart. Turn the paper 45° and repeat to create a diamond pattern. Turn the paper upside down on a sheet pan.

3. Place the pâte à choux in a pastry bag with a no. 1 (2-mm) star tip. Pipe the pâte à choux onto the paper following the lines.

4. Bake the pâte à choux at 400°F (205°C) until golden brown and dry enough to hold its shape once removed from the oven, about 15 minutes.

5. Cut the reserved sponge free from the sides of the pan, invert onto a cardboard, remove baking paper, and turn right side up. Cut the sponge into two layers horizontally.

6. Spread the apricot jam on the bottom layer. Place the top layer on the jam.

7. Cover the top of the cake with the Hazelnut Nougat Cream. Refrigerate until the cream is set, about 2 hours.

8. Whip cream and sugar to stiff peaks. Spread the cream evenly on top of the hazelnut filling. Place the pâte à choux screen on top of the cream; lightly press it into place.

9. Trim the two long sides of the sheet to make them even. Use a thin, sharp knife to cut the sheet into three strips lengthwise. Cut each strip into pieces 1½ inches (3.7 cm) wide. Sift powdered sugar lightly over the slices.

Hazelnut Nougat Cream

3 pounds, 10 ounces (1 kg, 650 g) filling

5 cups (1 l, 200 ml) heavy cream
1 teaspoon (5 ml) vanilla extract
1 recipe Hazelnut Paste (page 6) or
4 ounces (115 g) commercial hazelnut paste
10 ounces (285 g) Pastry Cream (page 569)
4 teaspoons (12 g) unflavored gelatin powder
⅓ cup (80 ml) cold water

1. Whip heavy cream and vanilla to soft peaks.
2. Combine the hazelnut paste and pastry cream. Mix into the whipped cream.
3. Soften the gelatin in cold water. Heat to 125°F (52°C) to dissolve. Rapidly add the gelatin to a small part of the cream mixture. Then quickly mix this combination into the remaining cream mixture. Allow the filling to thicken slightly before using it.

Kirschwasser Rings

fifty 3½-inch (8.7-cm) pastries

melted butter
sliced almonds, lightly crushed
7 ounces (200 g) granulated sugar
1 pound, 6 ounces (625 g) Almond Paste (page 4)
12 ounces (340 g) softened butter
6 eggs
2 tablespoons (30 ml) kirschwasser
5 ounces (140 g) bread flour
½ teaspoon (2 g) baking powder
powdered sugar

1. Grease fifty 3½-inch (8.7-cm) savarin forms with melted butter, coat them with crushed almonds, and place the forms on a sheet pan.
2. Place the sugar and almond paste in a mixing bowl. Blend in the softened butter gradually, making sure there are no lumps. Add the eggs, two at a time, and the kirschwasser.
3. Sift the flour and baking powder together and stir it into the batter. Take care not to overwhip the mixture at this time, or you will incorporate too much air and the finished product will be dry and crumbly.
4. Place the batter in a pastry bag with a no. 6 (12-mm) plain tip. Pipe into the forms, filling each two-thirds full.
5. Bake at 400°F (205°C) for about 20 minutes, or until baked through and golden brown on the bottom as well as the top (unmold one to check). Let cool.
6. Unmold the pastries and sift powdered sugar over the tops. You may serve Kirschwasser Rings as is, or you can cut them in half and dip the cut ends into melted dark baker's chocolate (refrigerate before dipping). If you store the rings in the refrigerator, they will stay fresh for several days.

Lemon-Almond Tartlets

approximately 45 tartlets

1 pound, 2 ounces (510 g)
*   Short Dough (page 31)*
1 pound, 10 ounces (740 g)
*   Mazarin Filling, soft*
*   (page 569)*
granulated sugar
Apricot Glaze (page 526)
almonds, toasted and crushed
½ recipe Lemon Curd (page 568)

1. Line individual tartlet or mazarin pans (see page 241) with short dough rolled to ⅛ inch (3 mm) thick (see Figures 2–12, 2–13, 2–14, and 2–15, page 34).

2. Place the mazarin filling in a pastry bag with a no. 6 (12-mm) plain tip. Pipe the filling into the lined pans, filling each two-thirds full.

3. Bake at 400°F (205°C) until golden brown, approximately 12 minutes.

4. As soon as you remove the tartlets from the oven, dust the tops lightly with sugar and immediately turn them upside down on the pan to make the tops flat and even. Be careful: If the skin is damaged it will show in the finished product.

5. When the tartlets have cooled, brush the tops with apricot glaze and dip the tartlets into the almonds to coat.

6. Cut out the center of each tartlet using a plain 1-inch (2.5-cm) cookie cutter. Reserve the centers.

7. Fill the holes with lemon curd. Replace the cut-outs on top of the lemon curd. Store covered in the refrigerator.

Linzer Tartlets

forty-five 2-inch (5-cm) pastries

1 recipe Linzer Dough (page 14)
Butter and Flour Mixture
*   (page 4)*
1 pound (455 g) smooth
*   raspberry jam*
powdered sugar

Linzer Tartlets should be made with only the highest quality raspberry jam available. The forms must be lined one at a time due to the softness and composition of the dough; however, the tender and fragile crust is one of the things that makes this specialty from the town of Linz in Austria so delicious.

1. Roll out 10 ounces (285 g) of linzer dough ⅛ inch (3 mm) thick and as square as possible. Reserve in the refrigerator.

2. Brush the butter and flour mixture on the inside of 45 shallow tartlet forms about 2 inches (5 cm) in diameter and ½ inch (1.2 cm) high.

3. Roll out the remaining dough to ¼ inch (6 mm) thick. Cut out 2½-inch (6.2-cm) cookies. Gently press the cookies into the buttered forms, then cut away any excess on the tops to make them even.

4. Place the raspberry jam in a pastry bag with a no. 5 (10-mm) plain tip. Pipe the jam into the forms, filling them halfway.

5. Using a fluted pastry wheel, cut the reserved piece of dough into ¼-inch (6-mm) strips. Place two strips on top of each tartlet in an X, pressing the ends into the dough on the sides.

6. Bake at 350°F (175°C) for about 15 minutes, or until golden brown on top. Let cool completely before unmolding. Sift powdered sugar lightly over the tartlets. Linzer Tartlets taste best if they are served the same day they are baked; the jam begins to get dry and rubbery after that.

NOTE: To remove the forms, tap them gently against the table. If this does not work (or if you forgot to grease them), invert the forms, place a damp towel on top, and put them into a hot oven for a few minutes.

Macaroon Bananas

about 40 pastries

½ recipe Almond Macaroon Cookie batter (page 123)
8 ounces (225 g) Vanilla Buttercream (page 501)
5 ounces (140 g) smooth currant jelly
10 medium bananas
Piping Chocolate (page 449)
melted light baker's chocolate
Simple Syrup (page 7)

1. Place the macaroon batter in a pastry bag with a no. 8 (16-mm) plain tip. Use a small amount of batter to fasten a sheet of baking paper to a sheet pan so the paper will not move as you pipe. Pipe the batter into slightly curved cookies 3 inches (7.5 cm) in length, holding the pastry tip close to the paper so that the batter comes out flatter and wider than the opening of the tip.

2. Bake immediately following the instructions for Almond Macaroon Cookies. Let the cookies cool completely.

3. Invert the paper and peel it away from the cookies as shown in the Almond Macaroon Cookies recipe. Place them flat-side up on a sheet pan.

4. Place the buttercream in a pastry bag with a no. 2 (4-mm) plain tip. Pipe a border of buttercream, ⅛ inch (3 mm) from the edge, around the cookies.

5. Place the currant jelly in a piping bag. Pipe a small line of jelly inside the frame of buttercream.

6. Peel the bananas and cut them in half lengthwise (do not use overripe or bruised bananas). Cut each half in half again, crosswise, to make pieces about the same size and shape as the cookies.

7. Place a banana, flat-side down, on each of the cookies bending it slightly to fit the curve of the cookie if necessary (Figure 9–13). Press the banana down lightly to be sure it is firmly attached. There should not be any banana protruding outside of the macaroon. Refrigerate just until the buttercream is hard.

Figure 9–13

Figure 9–14

8. Place a cake-cooling rack over a sheet pan lined with baking paper. Arrange the pastries on the rack in straight rows, curved-side toward you.

9. Spoon melted dark baker's chocolate over the bananas, starting with the one in the upper right-hand corner, and working right to left, back to front, to avoid dripping chocolate on the bananas once they are coated (Figure 9–14). Be sure each pastry is completely covered in chocolate. When the chocolate has hardened, use a thin sharp knife to cut the pastries off the rack.

10. Melt the piping chocolate. Place it in a piping bag and cut a very small opening in the tip. Write the word "banana" on each pastry, or just decorate by streaking the light chocolate over the top.

NOTE: If the chocolate is applied correctly, the banana will be sealed from the air and the pastries will keep up to one week, well-covered, in a cool place (but not the refrigerator).

Mazarins

50 pastries

2 pounds, 10 ounces (1 kg, 195 g)
*   Short Dough (page 31)*
2 pounds (910 g) Mazarin Filling,
*   soft (page 569)*
granulated sugar
Apricot Glaze (page 526)
White Fondant or Simple Icing
*   (page 521 or 529)*

Mazarins are popular in most Scandinavian pastry shops, especially in Sweden. Traditional mazarin pans are small, round, plain (not fluted) forms, about 1¼ inches (3.1 cm) high and 2½ inches (6.2 cm) across the top, sloping down to about 1½ inches (3.7 cm) across the bottom.

1. Line mazarin forms with short dough rolled to ⅛ inch (3 mm) thick (see Figures 2–12, 2–13, 2–14, and 2–15, page 34).

2. Place the mazarin filling in a pastry bag with a no. 7 (14-mm) plain tip, and pipe the filling into the shells almost to the top of the forms.

3. Bake at 400°F (205°C) for about 20 minutes, or until filling springs back when pressed gently.

4. As soon as you remove the Mazarins from the oven, sprinkle sugar over the tops, then quickly invert them on the sheet pan to make the tops flat and even. A fast way to do this is to place an inverted sheet pan on top of the pastries and flip the whole thing at once. Allow them to cool upside down.

5. When cold, remove the forms and turn the pastries right-side up on a paper-lined sheet pan. Refrigerate briefly until firm.

6. Glaze the tops of the Mazarins with a thin layer of apricot glaze. Ice with a thin layer of fondant or simple icing by dipping the top surface of the pastries into the icing and removing the excess with a spatula.

NOTE: Before they are glazed, Mazarins will keep fresh for up to one week stored covered in the refrigerator. Glaze and ice as needed.

Noisette Rings

45 pastries

1 pound, 4 ounces (570 g)
Short Dough (page 31)
1 pound (455 g) Almond Paste
(page 4)
¼ cup (60 ml) dark rum
¼ cup (60 ml) water,
approximately
8 ounces (225 g) hazelnuts,
toasted, skins removed, and
coarsely crushed
melted dark baker's chocolate
soybean oil or a commercial
thinning agent

1. Roll out the short dough to ⅛ inch (3 mm) thick. Cut out forty-five 2¼-inch (5.6-cm) cookies using a fluted cutter. Place the cookies on paper-lined sheet pans. Cut a circle out of the center of each cookie using a 1-inch (2.5-cm) fluted cutter. Remove the small circles of dough and reserve for another use.

2. Bake at 375°F (190°C) for about 10 minutes or until light brown. Set aside to cool.

3. Add rum and enough water to the almond paste to make it just soft enough to pipe; the amount of water needed will vary depending on the consistency of the almond paste. Place the mixture in a pastry bag with a no. 5 (10-mm) plain tip. Pipe a ring of almond paste onto each cookie, holding the bag straight above the cookie to avoid moving the cookie sideways as you pipe. If you have trouble with the cookies sliding, the almond paste is probably too firm.

4. As soon as you finish the piping, invert the cookies into the crushed hazelnuts and press gently to make the nuts stick and to flatten the almond paste slightly (do not wait too long to do this or the almond paste will form a skin and the nuts will not stick). Reshape the almond paste circle so it is even.

5. Thin the baker's chocolate with soybean oil so that the hazelnuts will show through the coating: approximately 2 parts chocolate to 1 part oil by volume.

6. Hold the cookies upside down and dip into the chocolate to cover all of the almond paste as well as any short dough that is visible on the top. Move the cookies up and down a few times above the bowl to allow as much chocolate as possible to fall back in the bowl to prevent it from running out around the pastry before it hardens. Place the dipped pastries on paper-lined pans. Noisette Rings should not be refrigerated.

Orange Truffle Strips

60 pastries

½ recipe Japonaise Batter
(page 333)
1 recipe Chocolate Biscuit batter
(page 163)
⅓ cup (80 ml) Simple Syrup
(page 7)
½ cup (120 ml) Grand Marnier
liqueur

1. Spread the Japonaise Batter into a 16- × 12-inch (40- × 30-cm) rectangle on a sheet of baking paper. Slide the paper onto a sheet pan and bake at 300°F (149°C) until golden brown and dry, about 30 minutes. Set aside to cool.

2. Line the bottom of a half-sheet pan (16 × 12 inches/40 × 30 cm) with baking paper. Spread the Chocolate Biscuit batter evenly on top. Bake immediately at 400°F (205°C) for about 12 minutes, or until the cake springs back when pressed lightly in the center.

3. Flavor the simple syrup with about one-fourth of the Grand Marnier. Add the remaining Grand Marnier to the ganache.

3 pounds (1 kg, 365 g)
   softened Ganache (page 567)
cocoa powder
60 Marzipan Oranges
   (recipe follows)

4. Remove the Chocolate Biscuit from the pan by cutting around the edge and inverting. Peel the paper from the back and turn right-side up again. Slice into two layers horizontally. Place the bottom layer on a cardboard or inverted sheet pan. Brush some of the simple syrup mixture on top.

5. Reserve 1 pound, 8 ounces (680 g) of the ganache. Spread half of the remaining ganache on top of the sponge. Place the Japonaise layer upside down on the ganache; peel the paper from the back. Spread the other half of the ganache over the Japonaise.

6. Top with the second biscuit layer and press down to even the sheet. Brush the remaining simple syrup mixture over the biscuit. Refrigerate until the ganache is firm.

7. Trim the two long sides of the assembled sheet. Cut the sheet into four strips lengthwise. Ice the top and long sides of each strip with the reserved ganache (softened first to spread easily), dividing it equally between the strips.

8. Sift cocoa powder over the strips to cover the ganache. Using the back of a chef's knife, lightly press straight down to mark the cocoa powder with diagonal lines in both directions, creating a diamond pattern.

9. Cut each strip into fifteen 1-inch (2.5-cm) pieces, using a thin knife dipped in hot water. Drill a small hole in the center of each pastry with the tip of a paring knife. Place a marzipan orange on the hole.

NOTE: If 60 pastries are too many, rather than going through all the steps to make a half-recipe, cut the sheet in half lengthwise at the beginning of step 7, wrap one half and place it in the freezer. It will keep this way for up to four weeks.

Marzipan Oranges
60 pieces

5 ounces (140 g) Marzipan
   (page 531), colored orange
melted cocoa butter, optional

1. Divide the marzipan into two equal pieces and roll the pieces into ropes. Cut the ropes into 30 pieces each.

2. Roll the small pieces into balls, keeping them covered until you form them to prevent their drying out.

3. Roll the balls lightly on a fine grater to give them an orange peel texture. Use a toothpick to make a small indentation in one end where the stem would be.

4. The finished oranges can be stored for weeks. To keep them looking fresh, coat them with a thin film of cocoa butter.

Othellos

about fifty 2-inch (5-cm) pastries

Othello Batter (recipe follows)
1 pound, 10 ounces (740 g)
    Pastry Cream (page 569)
½ recipe Apricot Glaze
    (page 526)
2 pounds, 8 ounces (1 kg, 135 g)
    Fondant or Chocolate Glaze
    (page 521 or 526)
Dark or Light Piping Chocolate
    (page 449)

1. Place the batter in a pastry bag with a no. 7 (14-mm) plain tip. Pipe the batter onto sheet pans lined with baking paper in mounds slightly less than 2 inches (5 cm) in diameter and about ¾ inch (2 cm) high.

2. Bake immediately at 450°F (230°C) for approximately 10 minutes, or until golden brown. Let cool completely.

3. Use a melon baller to make a hole the size of a cherry in the bottom of each pastry. Place the pastries on a sheet pan with the holes facing up.

4. Put the pastry cream in a pastry bag with a no. 6 (12-mm) plain tip. Pipe it into the pastries. Sandwich the pastries together in twos, enclosing the cream. Brush apricot glaze over the tops of the pastries.

5. Place the Othellos on an aspic rack or cake cooler with a sheet pan underneath. Ice with fondant or chocolate glaze, following the instructions on page 524 for Glazing or Icing with Fondant (see Figures 18–31 and 18–32, page 525). (If you are using fondant, make sure it is thick enough to completely cover the apricot glaze.)

6. Place light piping chocolate, if you are using chocolate glaze, or dark piping chocolate, if you are using fondant, in a piping bag (see page 505) with a small opening. Pipe a spiral design on the top of each pastry, starting in the center.

Othello Batter

12 egg yolks
6 ounces (170 g) granulated sugar
6 ounces (170 g) cornstarch
14 egg whites
1 teaspoon (2 g) cream of tartar
5 ounces (140 g) bread flour

1. Whip the egg yolks with 2 ounces (55 g) of the sugar until light and fluffy. Reserve.

2. Combine the remaining 4 ounces (115 g) of sugar with about two-thirds of the cornstarch.

3. Whip the egg whites and cream of tartar together for a few minutes until they have quadrupled in volume, lower the mixer speed, and gradually add the sugar and cornstarch mixture. Whip to stiff but not dry peaks.

4. Sift the remaining cornstarch with the flour. Carefully fold half of the egg whites into the whipped egg yolks. Fold in the flour mixture, then fold in the remaining whites. Use immediately.

Petits Fours

about 80 pieces

one 16- × 24-inch (40- × 60-cm)
    Dobosh Sponge (page 164)
1 pound, 4 ounces (570 g)
    softened Ganache (page 567)

1. If the dobosh sheet has been stored for a day or more the skin on top will probably be loose. If this is the case, remove as much of it as will come away easily before using the sheet. Unmold and cut the sheet crosswise into three equal pieces, leaving the baking paper attached. Each sheet should be approximately 16 × 8 inches (40 × 20 cm).

1½ ounces (40 g) Vanilla
  Buttercream (page 501)
8 ounces (225 g) Marzipan,
  white (page 531)
4 pounds, 8 ounces (2 kg, 45 g)
  Fondant (page 521) (see note)
Simple Syrup (page 7)
dark Piping Chocolate (page 449)

2. Place one sheet (paper-side down) on an inverted sheet pan or a cake cardboard. Top with half of the ganache; spread out evenly. Invert a second sheet onto the ganache and peel the paper from the back. Spread the remaining ganache on the second sheet. Top with the third sheet, and press the top with a baking pan to make sure the ganache and sheets are firmly attached. Peel away the baking paper.

3. Spread a thin film of buttercream over the top sheet.

4. Roll out the marzipan (using powdered sugar to prevent it from sticking) to a rectangle just slightly larger than the stacked sponge sheets and ⅛ inch (3 mm) thick. Roll it up on a dowel and unroll it over the buttercream. Invert the cake, and peel the paper off the top. Trim away any marzipan protruding outside the cake. Refrigerate (upside down) until the ganache is firm, about 1 hour. (If you refrigerate the cake much longer, wrap it well to prevent the marzipan from getting wet.)

5. Leave the cake upside down and cut out desired shapes (Figure 9–15). Keep all of the shapes around 1¼ inches (3.1 cm) in size; in other words, make the rectangles longer than the squares but not quite as wide, and so on, so that all the pieces look uniform. Keep in mind that cutting squares, rectangles, and diamond shapes will give you more Petits Fours and less waste than cutting circles or hearts.

6. Place the Petits Fours, marzipan-side up, on an aspic or cooling rack set over a clean sheet pan. Space them at least 1 inch (2.5 cm) apart.

7. Warm the fondant, stirring constantly, over simmering water to around 100°F (38°C). Do not get it too hot or it will lose

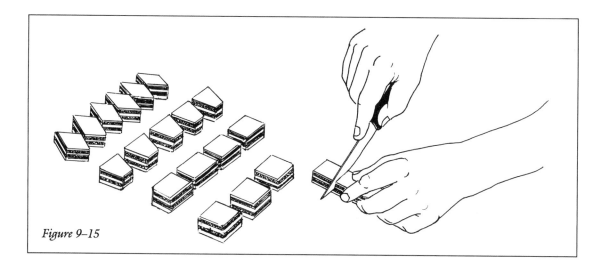

Figure 9–15

its shine when it dries. Thin to the proper consistency with simple syrup (adding some egg whites together with the simple syrup will give the fondant extra shine). Test the thickness by coating one or two pastries: You should be able to clearly see the layers on the sides through the fondant.

8. Coat the Petits Fours with fondant by either piping it on using a pastry bag with a no. 3 (6-mm) plain tip or by pouring it from a saucer (see Figures 18–31 and 18–32, page 525). Always start with the pastry farthest away from you so you will not drip over the pastries once you have coated them. Continue to warm the fondant as needed throughout the coating process so it is always at the correct temperature. If a skin forms on top of the fondant while you are working with it, cover it with hot water for a few seconds, then pour the water off, stir, and continue. The fondant that drips onto the sheet pan under the pastries can, of course, be warmed and used again. If you wish to tint the fondant see page 525. When all the Petits Fours are coated, let the fondant set completely before moving them.

9. Decorate the tops of the Petits Fours with piping chocolate, using the designs shown in Figures 16–15 and 16–16, pages 451 and 452. You can also enhance the decoration by adding a small piece of candied violet or a pistachio nut, or by filling in part of your design with piping gel.

NOTE: If you are making your own fondant, you can probably get away with making just three-fourths of the recipe (about 4 pounds/1 kg, 820 g of fondant), provided you keep it free of crumbs and mix the colors carefully so that you can use all the fondant. However, since fondant will keep for months if stored properly and has many other uses, I recommend that you make the full recipe.

Petits Fours Sec

The name "Petits Fours Sec" translates to "petits fours dry," which sounds rather unappealing and implies that these bite-sized pastries have no filling. In reality, a small amount of ganache, buttercream, or jam is used to either sandwich the pastries together or decorate the tops, and they are often dipped in chocolate. They are delicious, elegant, miniature creations, far from dry. They look beautiful lined up on silver trays for afternoon tea or as an accompaniment to after-dinner coffee. Petits Fours Sec can also garnish ice cream coupes, or any dessert where the serving dish is placed on a plate with a doily. Many of the cookies and pastries in this book can be used as Petits Fours Sec (just as many of the following recipes can be made into traditional pastries or cookies) by cutting or making them smaller, or by modifying the recipe.

Almond Doubles

eighty-five 2-inch (5-cm) cookies

2 pounds (910 g) Short Dough (page 31)
1 pound, 12 ounces (795 g)
  or
½ recipe Macaroon Decorating Paste (page 123)
10 ounces (285 g) smooth raspberry jam
10 ounces (285 g) smooth apricot jam
Simple Syrup (page 7)
melted dark baker's chocolate, optional

1. Roll the short dough to ⅛ inch (3 mm) thick. Cut out eighty-five 2-inch (5-cm) cookies using a fluted cookie cutter. Place them on a sheet pan lined with baking paper.

2. Place the macaroon paste in a pastry bag with a no. 3 (6-mm) plain tip. Pipe the paste onto the cookies by first going all the way around the edge, and then straight across the middle in one unbroken line.

3. Make two pastry bags from baking paper and fill one with raspberry and one with apricot jam. Pipe the jam within the macaroon frame, filling one side with each flavor.

4. Bake the cookies at 400°F (205°C) for about 12 minutes, or until golden brown.

5. As soon as the cookies come out of the oven, brush simple syrup on the macaroon border without disturbing the jam.

6. For a fancier look (and taste), dip the base of the cookie into melted baker's chocolate. Hold a dipping fork under the cookie and press lightly into the melted chocolate, coating the bottom and the sides up to the macaroon. Drag off the excess on the rim of the bowl and place cookies on sheet pans lined with baking paper (see Figures 9–26 to 9–30, page 267).

Brandy Pretzels

(see photograph in color insert)
72 cookies

6 ounces (170 g) granulated sugar
10 ounces (285 g) softened butter
¼ cup (60 ml) brandy
1 teaspoon (5 ml) vanilla extract
1 pound, 2 ounces (510 g) bread flour
Cinnamon Sugar (page 4)

1. Combine the sugar and butter. Add the brandy and vanilla extract. Incorporate the flour and mix to form a smooth dough. Refrigerate if the dough is too soft to work with.

2. Divide the dough into four 9-ounce (255-g) pieces. Roll into ropes and cut each of the four ropes into 18 small pieces. Roll each of the small pieces into a string 8 inches (20 cm) long and slightly tapered at the ends, using little or no flour. Form the strings into pretzels. Invert in cinnamon sugar. Place them sugar-side up on sheet pans lined with baking paper.

3. Bake at 375°F (190°C) for about 8 minutes or until light, golden brown and baked through.

Variation:
Chocolate-Covered Pretzels

Omit cinnamon sugar. Dip the baked pretzels (once they have cooled) into dark baker's chocolate thinned with soybean oil or a commercial thinning agent. (Use approximately 2 parts chocolate to 1 part oil by volume.)

Chocolate-filled Macadamia Morsels

(see photograph in color insert)
50 filled cookies

melted butter
bread flour
10 ounces (285 g) unsalted
  macadamia nuts
8 ounces (225 g) granulated sugar
6 ounces (170 g) softened butter
4 egg whites
6 ounces (170 g) bread flour
6 ounces (170 g) Ganache
  (page 567)
melted dark baker's chocolate

1. Lightly grease sheet pans with melted butter. Place a band of bread flour at the edge on one long side, and tilt the pan to spread the flour. Tap the pan against the table to remove any excess.

2. Grind the nuts and sugar together in a food processor to a very fine consistency. Reserve.

3. Beat the softened butter until light and creamy. Add the ground nut mixture. Add the egg whites one at a time, and beat until smooth. Mix in the flour.

4. Place the batter in a pastry bag with a no. 6 (12-mm) plain tip. Pipe out 100 mounds 1 inch (2.5 cm) wide and about ½ inch (1.2 cm) high onto the prepared pans.

5. Bake at 325°F (163°C) until deep golden brown around the edges, approximately 12 minutes. Let the cookies cool completely.

6. Turn half of the cookies upside down. Warm the ganache to a soft, paste-like consistency and place in a pastry bag with a no. 5 (10-mm) plain tip. Pipe a small amount of ganache on the inverted cookies. Place the remaining cookies on top, pressing lightly to sandwich the two flat sides together, and squeeze the ganache to the edge of the cookies.

7. Place the melted dark baker's chocolate in a piping bag and pipe straight lines close to each other (streak) across the cookies (see Figure 6-1, page 150), but pipe in one direction only. Store in airtight containers to keep the cookies crisp.

NOTE: These cookies are also delicious made with pine nuts.

Hazelnut Cuts

(see photograph in color insert)
about 80 cookies

1 cup (240 ml) egg whites
12 ounces (340 g) granulated
  sugar
14 ounces (400 g) hazelnuts,
  ground fine
2 ounces (55 g) cornstarch
melted dark baker's chocolate

1. Combine the egg whites and sugar in a mixing bowl, place over hot water, and heat to 110°F (43°C) while whipping constantly. Remove the bowl from the pan and continue whipping until mixture is cold and stiff peaks have formed.

2. Combine the hazelnuts with the cornstarch and fold into the meringue by hand.

3. Place the meringue in a pastry bag with a no. 5 (10-mm) plain tip. Pipe out ropes of meringue onto sheet pans lined with baking paper.

4. Bake at 300°F (149°C) for approximately 25 minutes, or until very light brown. Do not dry the meringue completely or it will break when you cut the cookies.

5. Before the meringue is completely cold (while still soft) cut the ropes into 2-inch (5-cm) pieces. Let cool completely.

6. Sandwich the flat sides of the pieces together with baker's chocolate by dipping only the surface into the chocolate and then placing a plain piece on top. After joining all the pieces, dip both ends of the pastries into chocolate to coat them about ¼ inch (6 mm) on each end.

Hazelnut Flowers

(see photograph in color insert)

about seventy-five 2-inch (5-cm) cookies

*1 pound, 8 ounces (680 g)
    Hazelnut Short Dough
    (page 32)
14 ounces (400 g)
    or
¼ recipe Macaroon Decorating
    Paste (page 123)
75 whole hazelnuts, lightly toasted,
    skins removed
Simple Syrup (page 7)*

1. Roll out a piece of the short dough ⅛ inch (3 mm) thick. Cut out star-shaped cookies using a cutter approximately 2 inches (5 cm) in diameter. Place the cookies on sheet pans lined with baking paper. Repeat with remaining dough and scraps until you have used all of the dough.

2. Place the macaroon decorating paste in a pastry bag with a no. 2 (4-mm) plain tip. Pipe the paste onto the cookies in a series of small teardrop shapes, starting at the end of each point of the star and ending in the center, to form a flower pattern. Place one hazelnut, pointed end up, in the center of each cookie.

3. Bake at 400°F (205°C) for about 12 minutes. Brush the cookies lightly with simple syrup as soon as they come out of the oven.

NOTE: If you do not wish to use hazelnuts for decoration, make an indentation in the center using your index finger (use some water to keep it from sticking) and fill the hollow with apricot jam.

Macaroon Candies

about 70 pastries

*3 pounds, 8 ounces (1 kg, 590 g)
    or
1 recipe Macaroon Decorating
    Paste (page 123) see note 1
food colorings
almonds, blanched and
    skins removed
pistachios
raisins or currants
Candied Orange Peel (page 520)
granulated sugar
Simple Syrup (page 7)
melted dark baker's chocolate*

This type of cookie is very popular in Europe, and even though it is not really a petit four sec, the color can really enliven a petits fours tray.

1. Warm the macaroon paste in a saucepan over low heat, stirring constantly, until it has a soft consistency and can be piped without effort. If you want to color the paste, use pale shades.

2. Pipe out the paste in various shapes onto sheet pans lined with baking paper, using a pastry bag with a plain or star tip, separately or in combination. Use your imagination and creativity, but keep the shapes 1½ to 2 inches (3.7 to 5 cm) in size.

3. Decorate with whole or slivered almonds, pistachios, raisins, and candied orange peels. Granulated sugar can be sprinkled over the tops, but this should be done immediately after the cookies are piped and decorated, before a skin forms on the top. Set the cookies aside at room temperature overnight to allow them to dry slightly before baking.

4. Bake the cookies, double-panned, at 425°F (219°C) for about 8 minutes or until they just start to show color. Brush with simple syrup as soon as they come out of the oven. Let cool completely before attempting to remove them from the paper. If they stick, follow the directions in Almond Macaroon Cookies on page 123. Dip some of the cookies partially into melted baker's chocolate for a nice contrast.

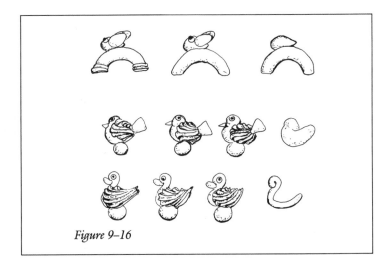

Figure 9–16

NOTE 1: Leave out two egg whites when you make the decorating paste. The paste will be too firm to pipe, but using the warming method to soften it, rather than adding egg whites, will keep the cookies from spreading while they bake.

NOTE 2: This paste can be used to make figures such as rabbits, chickens, and ducks as shown in Figure 9–16 (the rabbit's ears are made of sliced almonds, the chicken's tail is candied orange peel, and the duck's beak is a pine nut).

Miniature Palm Leaves

(see photograph in color insert)
about ninety 2-inch (5-cm) cookies

1 pound (455 g) Classic Puff Paste
*   (page 21)*
4 ounces (115 g) granulated
*   sugar, approximately*
melted dark baker's chocolate

1. Roll the puff paste in the granulated sugar to make a strip 20 × 8 inches (50 × 20 cm) and about ⅛ inch (3 mm) thick, following the directions for rolling out the sheet in Palm Leaves on page 136.

2. Fold the long sides in to meet in the center. Use a thin dowel to make a light indentation lengthwise down the center where the two edges meet. Fold in half on this mark to complete a double turn. Cut the strip in half crosswise to make it easier to move, and refrigerate the two strips until firm.

3. Slice and bake following the directions for Palm Leaves, but allow only 6 minutes before turning the cookies and be very careful not to burn them after they are turned over.

4. When cold, dip the wider end of each baked cookie into melted baker's chocolate.

NOTE: The cookies can also be served without chocolate, or sandwiched together as described in the recipe for the larger Palm Leaves, depending on what other selection of Petits Fours Sec you are serving.

Raspberry Cut-outs

(see photograph in color insert)
about ninety 1¾-inch (4.5-cm)
cookies

2 ounces (55 g) bread flour
1 recipe Spritz Rings dough
*   (page 140)*
12 ounces (340 g) raspberry jam
powdered sugar

1. Add the additional flour to the Spritz Rings when making the dough. Mix on low speed only until smooth. Refrigerate dough if needed.

2. Roll out a piece of dough to ⅛ inch (3 mm) thick. Cut out round cookies using a 1¾-inch (4.5-cm) fluted cutter. Place the cookies on sheet pans lined with baking paper. Repeat with remaining dough and scraps until all the dough is used. Cut three small holes in half of the cookies using a no. 4 (8-mm) plain piping tip.

3. Bake the cookies at 400°F (205°C) until they are golden, about 10 minutes. Let the cookies cool completely.

4. Place the jam in a disposable pastry bag made from baking paper (see page 505). Pipe a small dot of jam on top of the plain cookies. Place the cut cookies on the jam, and press down lightly. Sift powdered sugar lightly over the tops.

Strawberry Hearts

(see photograph in color insert)
about eighty-five 2-inch (5-cm)
cookies

2 pounds (910 g) Short Dough
*   (page 31)*
1 pound, 12 ounces (795 g)
*   or*
½ recipe Macaroon Decorating
*   Paste (page 123)*
12 ounces (340 g) smooth
*   strawberry jam*
Simple Syrup (page 7)
melted dark baker's chocolate

1. Roll out half of the short dough to ⅛ inch (3 mm) thick. Cut out heart-shaped cookies using a cutter approximately 2 inches (5 cm) in diameter. Place the cookies on sheet pans lined with baking paper. Repeat with remaining dough and scraps until all the dough is used.

2. Place the macaroon decorating paste in a pastry bag with a no. 3 (6-mm) plain tip. Pipe a border of paste around each heart. The paste should be just soft enough to stick to the dough; if it is too soft it will run when it bakes. If the cookies keep moving as you try to pipe the paste, place them in a warm oven for about 30 seconds, which will make them stick to the paper.

3. Place the jam in a disposable pastry bag made from baking paper (see page 505). Pipe just enough jam inside the macaroon border to cover the short dough.

4. Bake the cookies at 400°F (205°C) until golden brown, about 12 minutes. Brush the macaroon border with simple syrup as soon as the cookies come out of the oven, taking care not to smear the jam. Let the cookies cool completely.

5. Place the melted baker's chocolate in a piping bag and cut a very small opening. Streak the chocolate over the cookies as explained for Pecan Whiskey Tart (see Figure 6–1, page 150), but pipe the lines in only one direction, diagonally, across the cookies.

Vienna Petits Fours

about 85 pieces

*1 pound (455 g) Short Dough
    (page 31)
    or
1 pound (455 g) Hazelnut Short
    Dough (page 32)
    or
1 pound (455 g) Linzer Dough
    (page 14)
6 ounces (170 g) Almond Paste,
    approximately (page 4)
4 ounces (115 g) softened butter,
    approximately
2 tablespoons (30 ml) dark rum
8 ounces (225 g) Ganache
    (page 567)
2 tablespoons (30 ml) orange
    liqueur
6 ounces (170 g) Vanilla
    Buttercream (page 501)
½ teaspoon (2 g) mocha paste
    or
2 tablespoons (30 ml) Coffee
    Reduction (page 5)
melted dark or light baker's
    chocolate
Apricot Glaze (page 526)
    or
Red Currant Glaze (page 527)
slivered almonds
pistachios
hazelnuts
Candied Orange Peel (page 520)*

1. To produce the best look and variety in this type of petits four you need an assortment of individual small molds, 1½ inches (3.7 cm) in diameter and ½ inch (1.2 cm) high, or better yet, rows of molds fastened to a metal strip. Line the molds with short dough, hazelnut short dough, or linzer dough rolled ¹⁄₁₆ inch (2 mm) thick (see Figures 2–12, 2–13, 2–14, and 2–15, page 34). Prick the shells, then bake at 375°F (190°C) for about 8 minutes. Let the shells cool and remove from the molds.

2. Fill and decorate the shells. Here is a good chance to use your imagination as well as your good taste. You might, for example:

- soften the almond paste to a pipeable consistency with butter and flavor it with rum;
- add orange liqueur to the ganache; or
- flavor vanilla buttercream with mocha paste.

The amounts given in the ingredients list are based on using three separate fillings. If you wish to use just one or two fillings, adjust the quantities accordingly. Pipe these fillings into the shells in the shape of a mound or rosette.

3. Dip the tops of the pastries in melted baker's chocolate or brush them with apricot or currant glaze.

4. Decorate with slivered almonds, pistachios, hazelnuts, or candied orange peel.

Polynées

40 pastries

*1 pound, 8 ounces (680 g)
 Short Dough (page 31)*
*6 ounces (170 g) smooth
 strawberry jam*
*1 recipe Almond Macaroon Cookie
 batter (page 123)*
3 egg whites, approximately
powdered sugar

1. Roll out one-third of the short dough to ⅛ inch (3 mm) thick and reserve in the refrigerator. Roll out the remaining dough to ⅛ inch (3 mm) thick and use it to line 40 mazarin forms (see page 241) or other forms of similar size (see Figures 2–12, 2–13, 2–14, and 2–15).

2. Make a pastry bag from a half sheet of baking paper and fill it with the strawberry jam. Pipe the jam into the forms, dividing it evenly.

3. Add one to three egg whites to the cookie batter, beating it to a soft, creamy, yet still pipeable consistency. It should be liquid enough to flatten when piped. Place the batter in a pastry bag with a no. 4 (8-mm) plain tip. Pipe the batter into the forms on top of the jam, almost filling the forms.

4. Cut the reserved short dough into ¼-inch (6-mm) strips. Place two strips on top of each form, crossing them at a 90° angle and pinching the ends to the dough lining the sides.

5. Bake the pastries at 400°F (205°C) until golden brown, about 20 minutes. They should puff up and crack in the middle. Very lightly sift powdered sugar over the tops. Polynées will keep fresh for up to one week if stored, covered, in the refrigerator.

Pretzels

36 pastries

*1 pound (455 g) Classic Puff Paste
 (page 21)*
*1 pound (455 g) Short Dough
 (page 31)*
Egg Wash (page 5)
AA confectioners' sugar
sliced almonds, crushed
Simple Syrup (page 7)

Scrap dough from puff paste can be used in this recipe with excellent results.

1. Roll the puff paste into a rectangle 9 × 14 inches (22.5 × 35 cm). The dough should be about ⅛ inch (3 mm) thick. Place the dough on a cardboard or inverted sheet pan.

2. Roll the short dough to the same size as the puff paste. It will be slightly thicker.

3. Brush egg wash on the puff paste. Carefully, so you do not alter the shape, roll the short dough up on a dowel and unroll it on top of the puff paste. Press the two pieces together by rolling the dowel over them. Refrigerate until firm.

4. Mix equal amounts of confectioners' sugar and sliced almonds by volume. Place the mixture on a sheet pan and reserve.

5. With a dowel or ruler as a guide, use a sharp knife or pastry wheel to cut the sheet lengthwise into ¼-inch (6-mm) strips.

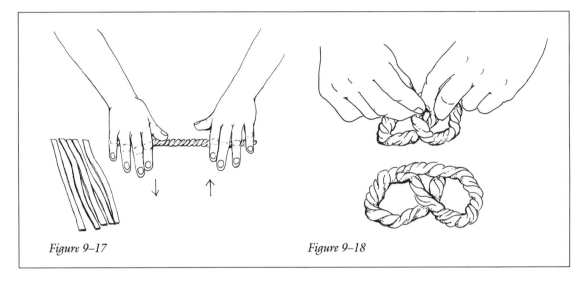

Figure 9–17   Figure 9–18

6. Twist each strip into a corkscrew by rolling the ends in opposite directions against the table (Figure 9–17), then form the corkscrew into a pretzel shape (Figure 9–18).

7. Set the Pretzel on the sugar and almond mixture and press gently to make sure the mixture adheres. Continue forming the remaining Pretzels in the same way.

8. When the pan of sugar mixture is full, transfer the Pretzels, sugar-side up, to a sheet pan lined with baking paper. Repeat with the remaining strips. If the strips get soft or sticky and hard to work with, refrigerate for a short time. Do not use any flour while forming the Pretzels.

9. Bake double-panned at 375°F (190°C) for about 15 minutes, or until golden brown. As soon as the pastries are removed from the oven, brush simple syrup lightly over the tops.

NOTE: Anything made with puff paste is best the day it is baked, so bake only as many Pretzels as you will use within a day or two. The formed Pretzels can be frozen and baked as needed.

Rum Balls

60 pastries

Rum Ball Filling (recipe follows)
melted dark or light baker's
*   chocolate*

Rum Balls are an excellent way of recycling good leftover pastries, end pieces, scraps, and other preparations. However, the Rum Ball bucket should not be mistaken for a garbage can: Only those scraps that will not spoil within a week or so should be added. No pastry cream or whipped cream should be used, and buttercream or buttercream-filled items should be used only if they are no more than one day old. The best kinds of scraps to use are slightly

2 pounds (910 g) dark or light baker's chocolate, melted and cooled, approximately (see note 1)

stale cookies, meringues or macaroons, Florentinas, Ladyfingers, pastries such as Tosca or Polynées that do not contain buttercream, light or dark sponge cake, and baked short dough cakebottoms. Danish or other yeast-dough pastries should not be used in a quality Rum Ball mixture.

The technique used for coating Rum Balls with chocolate is a little more complicated than the dipping technique used in many of the other recipes. However, because Rum Balls are so simple and inexpensive to make, there is no need to speed up the finishing process by simply dipping them or, worse yet, rolling them in chocolate sprinkles. I prefer to use light chocolate for coating Rum Balls because so many of the other pastries look better with dark chocolate, but of course they are interchangeable.

1. Divide the filling into five pieces approximately 1 pound, 2 ounces (510 g) each. Roll each piece into a 12-inch (30-cm) rope, using some powdered sugar to prevent the filling from sticking to the table. Cut each rope into 12 equal pieces. Roll the small pieces into round balls. Place the balls on sheet pans lined with baking paper. Refrigerate until firm.

2. Cover the Rum Balls with a thin layer of melted baker's chocolate by picking up some chocolate with your fingers and rolling a Rum Ball between your palms to coat. Place them back on the pans and reserve at room temperature.

3. Cool the other batch of melted baker's chocolate, stirring frequently so the consistency is even, until it is as thick as mayonnaise. Melt the chocolate early, so that it can cool to this point at room temperature. If you must speed up the process, place the chocolate over cold, not ice, water and stir constantly until it reaches the proper consistency.

4. Pick up some of the thickened chocolate with your fingers and roll the Rum Balls between your palms as before, but this time cover them with a thick layer of chocolate, with spikes and tails of chocolate standing up (Figure 9–19, next page). You must work quickly or the heat from your hands will melt the chocolate and you will not be able to achieve the rough texture: the finished pastry should be full of ridges and points like a properly rolled truffle.

5. Replace the Rum Balls on the pans and store in a dry box or covered in the refrigerator.

NOTE 1: I generally do not specify the amount of melted chocolate where the item is simply to be dipped in or decorated with chocolate. The baker usually has a supply of chocolate on hand, either melted or ready to melt, for this purpose. Also, the amount of chocolate the chef needs to work with is always quite

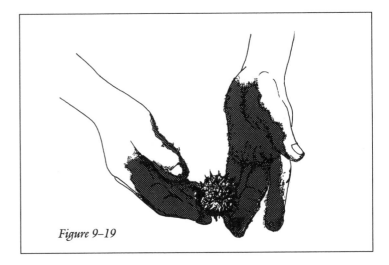

Figure 9–19

a bit more than is actually used on the finished pastries. I am specifying an amount in this recipe to emphasize that a fairly large amount is needed.

NOTE 2: The first coating is necessary to seal the surface of the Rum Balls before they are rolled in thick chocolate. This makes it possible to roll the Rum Balls in the thick chocolate at room temperature without having them fall apart. Simply firming them in the refrigerator will produce small cracks in the chocolate coating, as the filling expands when it reaches room temperature.

Rum Ball Filling

about 5 pounds, 8 ounces
(2 kg, 500 g) filling

⅓ cup (80 ml) light rum
4 ounces (115 g) dark raisins
4 pounds (1 kg, 820 g) scraps
¼ cup (60 ml) water,
*   approximately*
2 ounces (55 g) apricot jam
5 ounces (140 g) nuts, any variety,
*   crushed fine*
12 ounces (340 g) melted dark or
*   light chocolate*

1. Heat rum slightly, add raisins, and macerate for a few hours.

2. Place scraps and water in a mixing bowl, and mix with a paddle to a smooth consistency. You may have to adjust the amount of water depending on how many dry items you are using. Mix until you have a very firm, smooth dough, approximately 10 minutes. Add crushed nuts, apricot jam, and chocolate. Mix until combined. Incorporate the rum and raisin mixture.

3. Place on a sheet pan lined with baking paper. Refrigerate until the filling is firm before shaping. If the mixture is too soft to work with, add some additional scraps from dry items, finely ground, to absorb moisture. If the filling is dry and crumbly, mix in enough buttercream or ganache to bring it to a workable consistency.

Porcupines

60 pastries

5 pounds, 8 ounces (2 kg, 500 g)
    or
1 recipe Rum Ball Filling
    (page 256)
5 ounces (140 g) whole almonds,
    blanched and skins removed
    or
4 ounces (115 g) blanched, slivered
    (not sliced) almonds
melted dark baker's chocolate
Royal Icing (page 528)

1. Divide the filling into five pieces, approximately 1 pound, 2 ounces (510 g) each. Roll each piece into a 12-inch (30-cm) rope, using some powdered sugar to prevent the filling from sticking to the table. Cut each of the ropes into 12 equal pieces. Roll the small pieces into round balls.

2. Keeping the ball between your hands, taper one end to make a small cone, rounded at the wide end. To be sure the pastries will resemble porcupines (and not look like some strange rodent instead), make the cones only about 2 inches (5 cm) in length, with a definite point. Place the cones on sheet pans lined with baking paper and press lightly, just enough to prevent them from rolling. Refrigerate until firm.

3. If using whole blanched almonds, cut them into pointed strips (which is easiest to do while the almonds are still soft from blanching). Dry the almond strips in the oven until hard.

4. Push seven almond strips or slivers into the top of the wide end of each rum ball cone (Figure 9–20).

5. Set the Porcupines, one at a time, on a dipping fork, and dip into melted baker's chocolate, covering them completely. Be sure the Porcupines are near room temperature as you do this. As you remove each Porcupine, move it up and down over the bowl of chocolate a few times to remove as much excess chocolate as possible. Place the Porcupines on sheet pans lined with baking paper.

6. Make sure the royal icing is thick enough to keep its shape when piped. Put the royal icing in a piping bag and pipe two dots (the size of green peppercorns) on each Porcupine for eyes. Place melted dark baker's chocolate in a second piping bag and pipe a smaller dot of chocolate on the royal icing, making pupils in the eyes. Store Porcupines in a dry box or well covered in the refrigerator.

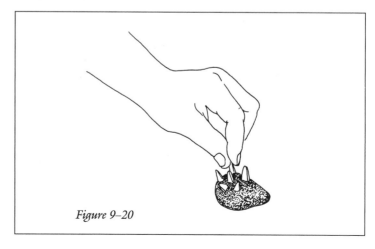

Figure 9–20

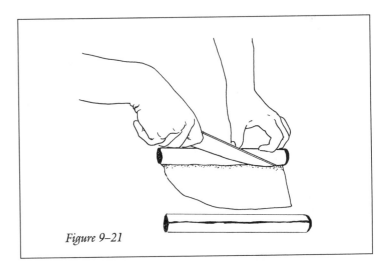

Figure 9–21

Rum-Chocolate Spools
40 pastries

2 pounds, 12 ounces (1 kg, 250 g)
   or
½ recipe Rum Ball Filling
   (page 256)
1 pound, 2 ounces (510 g)
   Marzipan, white (page 531)
2 ounces (55 g) Vanilla
   Buttercream (page 501)
melted dark baker's chocolate

1. Divide the Rum Ball Filling into four equal pieces, about 11 ounces (310 g) each. Roll each piece into a rope 20 inches (50 cm) long, using powdered sugar to prevent the filling from sticking to the table. Set the ropes aside on a sheet pan lined with baking paper.

2. Roll out a portion of the marzipan to ⅛ inch (3 mm) thick, the same length as the ropes (use powdered sugar to keep it from sticking also). Trim the sides to make them even and straight. Turn the marzipan upside down, and spread a thin film of buttercream over it.

3. Set one of the rum ball ropes at the edge of the marzipan sheet, and roll up one full turn to encase it completely; the edges should line up, not overlap. Cut the rope away from the marzipan sheet (Figure 9–21).

4. Roll the covered rope against the table until it is 24 inches (60 cm) long, making it even at the same time. Carefully transfer the rope back to the sheet pan. Repeat with the remaining ropes, rolling out more marzipan as needed. Refrigerate the ropes, covered, until they are firm.

5. Cut each rope into ten equal pieces, about 2½ inches (6.2 cm) long.

6. Dip ⅛ inch (3 mm) of both ends of each pastry into melted dark baker's chocolate. Place the Rum-Chocolate Spools back on sheet pans lined with baking paper, in straight rows.

7. Place a small amount of the melted chocolate in a piping bag (see page 505). Pipe a small dot of chocolate, the size of a pea, in the center of each pastry.

Small Princess Pastries

50 pastries

1 recipe Biscuit Viennoise batter
   (page 163)
8 ounces (225 g) smooth
   strawberry jam
2 pounds (910 g) Marzipan,
   light pink (page 531)
10 ounces (285 g) Vanilla
   Buttercream (page 501)
1 pound, 8 ounces (680 g)
   Pastry Cream (page 569)
1 quart (960 ml) heavy cream
2 tablespoons (30 g) granulated
   sugar
strawberries
dark chocolate shavings

1. Line the bottom of a half-sheet pan (16 × 12 inches/40 × 30 cm) with baking paper. Fill the pan with the Biscuit Viennoise batter, spreading it out evenly. Bake immediately at 400°F (205°C) for about 15 minutes, or until the cake springs back when pressed lightly in the center. Let cool completely.

2. Cut around the side of the pan and invert to remove the biscuit. Peel the paper from the back and turn right-side up. Cut away the skin from the top, then cut into two layers horizontally.

3. Spread strawberry jam on the bottom layer, then place the top layer on the jam.

4. Cut out 1¾-inch (4.5-cm) rounds using a plain cookie cutter. Place the cuts close together and stagger the rows to get the full fifty circles. Save the scraps for another use, such as Rum Ball Filling.

5. Roll the marzipan, using powdered sugar to prevent it from sticking, to ⅛ inch (3 mm) thick. Texture the top of the marzipan with a waffle roller. Turn upside down and cut out fifty strips, 6 × 1½ inches (15 × 3.7 cm). Keep the strips together.

6. Spread a thin film of buttercream over the strips. Fasten a marzipan strip around the side of each cake so that the buttercream sticks to the sponge. The strips should overlap just slightly so you can press them together.

7. Place the pastry cream in pastry bag with a no. 4 (8-mm) plain tip. Pipe on the top of the cakes in a spiral pattern, covering the sponge completely.

8. Whip the heavy cream and sugar to stiff peaks. Place in a pastry bag with a no. 3(6-mm) star tip. Pipe the whipped cream decoratively on top of the pastry cream, within the marzipan border, making loops left to right and right to left (Figure 9–22).

9. Cut the strawberries into small wedges and place one on top of each pastry. Place a small amount of chocolate shavings next to the strawberry wedges. Small Princess Pastries should be served the same day they are finished. They can be refrigerated for about 6 hours without any ill effects but will not hold up overnight.

Figure 9–22

Streusel Kuchen

twenty-four 2- × 4-inch
(5- × 10-cm) pieces

melted butter
⅔ ounce (20 g) fresh
*   compressed yeast*
1 cup (240 ml) warm milk
*   (105°–115°F, 40°–46°C)*
2½ ounces (70 g) granulated
*   sugar*
½ teaspoon (3 g) salt
3 egg yolks
1 teaspoon (5 ml) vanilla extract
1 pound (455 g) bread flour,
*   approximately*
2 ounces (55 g) softened butter
Egg Wash (page 5)
10½ ounces (300 g) or ¼ recipe
*   Streusel Topping (page 8)*
1 pound (455 g) or ½ recipe
*   Vanilla Bavarian Cream*
*   (page 570)*
powdered sugar

1. Brush melted butter over the bottom and sides of a half-sheet pan (16 × 12 inches/40 × 30 cm). Lay a piece of baking paper on the bottom and reserve.

2. Dissolve the yeast in the warm milk. Add the sugar, salt, egg yolks, and vanilla extract. Incorporate approximately half of the flour. Add the softened butter and the remaining flour, and mix until you have a very soft, smooth dough, approximately 5 minutes. Mix in additional flour if necessary for the proper consistency. Place the dough in an oiled bowl, cover, and let rise in a warm place until doubled in volume.

3. Roll and stretch the dough to fit, and place it in the buttered sheet pan. Let rise again until half-doubled in volume.

4. Brush the dough with egg wash. Sprinkle the streusel topping over the dough.

5. Bake at 400°F (205°C) for about 10 minutes. Let cool.

6. Cut around the edges of the pan if necessary to loosen the cake. Invert the cake onto a sheet pan and peel away the baking paper. Invert again to turn the cake right-side up on an inverted sheet pan or cardboard. Slice the cake into two equal layers horizontally. Spread Bavarian cream on the bottom layer, then replace the top. Refrigerate to set the cream, approximately 1 hour.

7. Trim the sides of the cake. Cut into three equal strips lengthwise. Cut each strip into eight equal pieces. Sift powdered sugar lightly over the cut pieces.

Swans

approximately 55 pastries

2 pounds, 10 ounces (1 kg, 195 g)
*   or 1 recipe Pâte à Choux*
*   (page 15)*
6 ounces (170 g) smooth
*   strawberry jam*
1 quart (960 ml) heavy cream
2 tablespoons (30 g) granulated
*   sugar*
melted dark baker's chocolate
strawberry wedges
powdered sugar

1. Reserve about 1 cup (240 ml) of the pâte à choux to make the Swan necks. Place the remaining paste in a pastry bag with a no. 7 (14-mm) star tip. Pipe the paste in cone shapes 3 inches (7.5 cm) long and 1¾ inches (4.5 cm) wide, on sheet pans lined with baking paper. Start by making the wide end of the cone, piping in an up-and-over motion (Figure 9–23), then gradually relax the pressure on the bag and end in a narrow point. It is important that the wide end be quite a bit higher than the narrow end for nice-looking Swans.

2. Bake at 425°F (219°C) until puffed and starting to color, about 10 minutes. Reduce heat to 375°F (190°C) and continue to bake until the pastries will hold their shape when removed from the oven, approximately 10 minutes longer.

3. Place the reserved pâte à choux in a pastry bag with a no. 1 (2-mm) plain tip. Pipe out the necks, moving the tip quickly so the flow of paste is actually thinner than the tip. Pipe a ¼ inch (6 mm) strip (the beak), pause for a second so you get a lump for the head, then continue in the shape of a question mark forming the

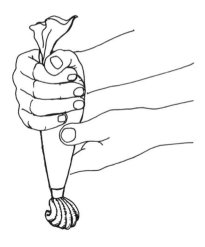

Figure 9–23

long, curved neck (Figure 9–24). Make 10 to 12 more necks than you have bodies to allow for breakage. Bake the necks at 375°F (190°C) for about 12 minutes. Let cool completely.

4. Cut the top third off the bodies; then cut this piece in half lengthwise to create two wings (scissors work best). Place the two wings on either side of the bodies, lining them up for assembly. Pipe a thin ribbon of strawberry jam in the bottom of each shell.

5. Whip the cream and sugar to stiff peaks and place in a pastry bag with a no. 7 (14-mm) star tip. Pipe the cream into the shells following the same up-and-over motion you used to pipe the shells, coming to a point at the narrow end (which will be the tail).

6. Arrange the wings in the whipped cream, pointing upward and meeting at the top.

7. Dip the bottom of each neck in baker's chocolate to prevent the whipped cream from softening it and causing it to fall. Push the necks into the whipped cream so they lean back slightly between the wings.

8. For some color, place a small wedge of strawberry at the back end as a tail. Sift a little powdered sugar over the top of the pastries. As with all pâte à choux products, Swans should be served the same day they are assembled.

Figure 9–24

Variation: Pâte à Choux Swans for Restaurant Service

(see photograph in color insert)
20 servings

1 pound, 5 ounces (595 g) or ½
recipe Pâte à Choux batter
(page 15)
½ recipe or 2 cups (480 ml) Cold
Chocolate Sauce (page 559)
1 quart (960 ml) heavy cream
2 tablespoons (30 g) granulated
sugar
4 ounces (115 g) raspberry jam
powdered sugar
strawberries
Sour Cream Mixture for Piping
(page 564)

This is an elegant and yet simple dessert that can be prepared hours ahead of serving and presented very quickly. It takes only a little knowledge of how to pipe out the shape of the swan body and neck.

1. When making the pâte à choux, be sure it has the proper consistency described in the recipe. Reserve about 1 cup (240 ml) of the batter for the necks (cover it tightly so it doesn't form a skin).

2. Place the remaining batter in a pastry bag with a number 6 (12-mm) star tip. Pipe the batter onto sheets lined with baking paper in small cone shapes (the wide end should be about the size of an unshelled walnut), following the instructions in the main recipe for Swans. You are making them the correct size if you have used about half of the batter after making 20 (there are two Swans per serving).

3. Pipe out the necks using a no. 0 (1-mm) plain tip (see preceding illustration and instructions). Bake the bodies and necks as instructed in the main recipe.

4. Adjust the chocolate sauce as needed. The sauce should be thin enough to cover the plate, yet stay in place without running.

5. Whip the heavy cream and the sugar to stiff peaks.

6. When the Swans have cooled, assemble and fill them as directed in the main recipe. Lightly sift powdered sugar over the tops.

7. Presentation: Pour the chocolate sauce to cover half of the plate and place two Swans at the edge of the sauce facing each other. Place a fanned strawberry spread out behind each Swan. Decorate the chocolate sauce by piping hearts using the sour cream mixture (pages 518–519). Serve immediately.

Swedish Napoleons

15 pastries

1 pound, 8 ounces (680 g) Quick,
Classic, or scrap Puff Paste
(page 21)

If you are making puff paste only for napoleons, make quick puff paste. Alternatively, if you have it on hand, this is a good recipe for using up scrap dough. Be sure you do not knead the scraps together; instead overlap the edges and press them together to preserve the layered structure. If you are using fresh classic puff paste, you will need to roll it a bit thinner than specified in the recipe.

1. Roll out the puff paste to ⅛ inch (3 mm) thick, the length of a full sheet pan (24 inches/60 cm) and 14 inches (35 cm) wide. Prick the dough well and let it rest in the refrigerator for at least 30 minutes. Bake at 375°F (190°C) about 25 minutes. Let cool.

5 ounces (140 g) smooth
   strawberry jam
3 ounces (85 g) Fondant or
   Simple Icing (page 521 or 529)
Simple Syrup (page 7)
1 pint (480 ml) heavy cream
1 tablespoon (15 g) granulated
   sugar

2. Cut three strips from the pastry sheet, the full length of the sheet and 4 inches (10 cm) wide for regular servings or 3 inches (7.5 cm) wide for buffet servings.

3. Select the nicest strip for the top and turn it upside down. Spread a very thin film of strawberry jam, just enough to color it, over the flat side of the top strip. Spread a slightly thicker layer of jam on one of the remaining strips, which will become the bottom.

4. Spread a thin layer of fondant or simple icing (thinned to a spreadable consistency with simple syrup, a little thinner than for Petits Fours), on the top strip, blending it gently with the jam. Set the top strip aside for about 30 minutes to set the glaze, or place it in a warm oven for 30 seconds.

5. Whip the heavy cream and sugar to stiff peaks. Place in a pastry bag with a large, plain tip. Place the middle strip on the bottom strip and pipe the whipped cream on top in a 1-inch (2.5-cm) layer.

6. Cut the glazed top layer crosswise into 1½-inch (3.7-cm) pieces. Reassemble the top strip on top of the whipped cream. Using the top pieces as a guide, cut through the other layers. Napoleons must be served the same day they are made.

Variation: Classic Napoleons

Follow the recipe above with the following changes:

1. Omit the strawberry jam.

2. Substitute 2 pounds (910 g) Pastry Cream (see page 569) flavored with 1 tablespoon (15 ml) kirschwasser for the whipped cream. Spread it equally on both layers.

3. For decoration spread the fondant directly on the top layer of puff paste. With melted dark chocolate or brown piping gel, pipe 8 to 10 narrow straight lines, lengthwise, on the fondant. Immediately draw a knife through the chocolate every ½ inch (1.2 cm) to create a fishbone pattern.

Triangles

55 pastries

*1 pound, 5 ounces (595 g)
    Short Dough (page 31)*
*4½ ounces (130 g) smooth
    strawberry jam*
*4 pounds, 10 ounces (2 kg, 105 g)
    Mazarin Filling (page 569)*
*2 ounces (55 g) Vanilla
    Buttercream (page 501)*
*1 pound (455 g) Marzipan, white
    (page 531)*
melted dark baker's chocolate

1. Line the bottom of a half-sheet pan (16 × 12 inches/40 × 30 cm) with baking paper. Roll out the short dough to ⅛ inch (3 mm) thick to fit the bottom of the pan and place in pan. Spread the jam over the short dough. Top with the mazarin filling and spread it out evenly. Bake at 375°F (190°C) until baked through, about 55 minutes. Cool to room temperature, then refrigerate.

2. When the mazarin sheet is cold (preferably the day after baking), cut off the skin and even the top of the sheet. To do this, leave the mazarin sheet in the pan and cut with a serrated knife held parallel to the top of the cake, using the edge of the pan as a guide for your knife. Cut around the edges and unmold. If the bottom of the sheet does not come away from the pan, place a hot sheet pan underneath for a few seconds to soften the butter in the short dough; then try again. Once unmolded, turn right-side up. Spread a thin film of buttercream on top of the mazarin filling.

3. Roll out the marzipan slightly larger than the mazarin sheet, ⅛ inch (3 mm) thick. Mark the marzipan with a waffle roller. Roll it up on a dowel, and unroll it on top of the buttercream. Place a clean cardboard on top and invert. With the pastry upside down, trim away the excess marzipan. Refrigerate until thoroughly chilled, but no longer than a few hours or the marzipan will get soggy.

4. Still working with the pastry upside down, cut it lengthwise into five strips, holding the knife at a 90° angle so the edges are straight. A serrated knife or the very tip of a sharp chef's knife works best. Cut each strip into eleven triangles (save the scraps for Rum Ball Filling).

5. Dip each triangle into melted dark baker's chocolate, coating the bottom and sides up to the marzipan (as shown for Tosca, Figures 9–26 through 9–30, page 267).

NOTE: If more than a half-sheet is needed, make one full sheet rather than two halves so that there will be fewer scraps when you cut. These pastries will stay fresh four to five days, covered, at room temperature, but should not be refrigerated or the marzipan will become wet.

Trier Squares

*forty-eight 1½-inch (3.7-cm)
square pastries*

*2 pounds, 3 ounces (1 kg)
    Short Dough (page 31)*

1. Roll out the short dough to ⅛ inch (3 mm) thick. Cut a piece 16 × 12 inches (40 × 30 cm), and use it to line a half-sheet pan. Refrigerate both pieces of dough for a few minutes until firm.

2. Spread the jam in a thin layer over the short dough in the pan. Spread the Trier Filling evenly over the jam.

*4½ ounces (130 g) smooth
    apricot jam*
Trier Filling (recipe follows)
Egg Wash (page 5)

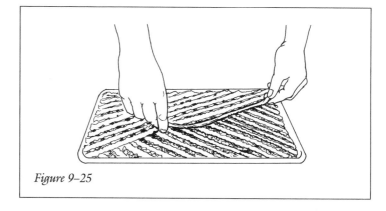

Figure 9–25

3. Place the remaining piece of short dough on a cardboard (or on an inverted pan so the sides will not be in your way when you cut) and cut into ¼-inch-wide (6-mm) strips with a fluted or plain pastry wheel.

4. Brush the top of the Trier Filling with egg wash. Arrange the dough strips diagonally, ¼ inch (6 mm) apart, over the filling. Then arrange strips in the other direction so they form a diamond pattern (Figure 9–25). Press the strips lightly with your hand as you place them to make sure they stick. Brush the strips with egg wash.

5. Bake at 375°F (190°C) until golden brown and baked through, about 40 minutes. Let the pastry cool completely. Unmold the sheet and trim the edges. Measure and cut into 2-inch (5-cm) squares, using a ruler as a guide. (Cut six strips the long way and cut each strip into eight pieces.)

Trier Filling

*2 pounds, 13 ounces (1 kg, 280 g)
filling*

15 ounces (430 g) sliced almonds
*14 ounces (400 g) granulated
    sugar*
½ cup (120 ml) milk
5 ounces (140 g) butter
6 ounces (170 g) golden raisins
¼ cup (60 ml) lemon juice
grated zest of 1 lemon
*1 tablespoon (5 g) ground
    cinnamon*

1. Combine the almonds, sugar, and milk.

2. Melt the butter and allow it to brown slightly; add to the almond mixture.

3. Mix in the raisins, lemon juice, lemon zest, and cinnamon.

Tosca

60 pastries

1 pound, 5 ounces (595 g)
  Short Dough (page 31)
4½ ounces (130 g) smooth
  strawberry jam
4 pounds, 10 ounces (2 kg, 105 g)
  Mazarin Filling (page 569)
½ recipe or 13 ounces (370 g)
  Florentina Batter (page 131)
melted dark baker's chocolate

1. Line the bottom of a half-sheet pan (16 × 12 inches/40 × 30 cm) with baking paper. Roll the short dough to ⅛ inch (3 mm) thick and place it in the pan. Spread the jam in a thin layer over the dough. Spread the mazarin filling evenly on top.

2. Bake at 375°F (190°C) until baked through, about 50 minutes (keep in mind the pastry will be baked an additional 5 minutes with the topping). Let cool to room temperature, then refrigerate.

3. When the mazarin sheet is cold (preferably the day after baking), cut off the skin and even the top. To do this, leave the mazarin sheet in the pan and cut with a serrated knife, using the edge of the pan as a guide for your knife.

4. Spread the Florentina Batter over the mazarin, using a spatula dipped into hot water to make it slide more easily. Place the mazarin sheet, still in its original pan, onto a second pan the same size (double-panning).

5. Bake at 425°F (219°C) until the Florentina topping begins to bubble and turn golden brown, about 5 minutes. Let cool to room temperature.

6. Cut the sheet loose from the sides of the pan. Place a cardboard on top, invert, and unmold onto the cardboard. Refrigerate until cool and hard.

7. While still upside down, cut the sheet lengthwise into four strips; then cut each strip into 15 pieces. Hold the knife at a 90° angle so that the edges are straight.

8. Dip the bottom and sides, but not the top, of each pastry into dark baker's chocolate using a dipping fork inserted part way into the pastry. Carefully move the pastry up and down over the bowl a few times to allow as much excess chocolate as possible to fall back into the bowl. Drag the bottom against the side of the bowl. Place the slices in straight rows on sheet pans lined with baking paper (Figures 9–26 through 9–30).

NOTE: Stored covered at room temperature, these pastries will stay fresh four to five days. Do not refrigerate Tosca or the topping will become wet and sticky. If 60 pastries are more than you can use, follow the procedure above through step 2. Then cut the sheet in half and use the other half to make Almond Truffles (page 225) or Triangles (page 264).

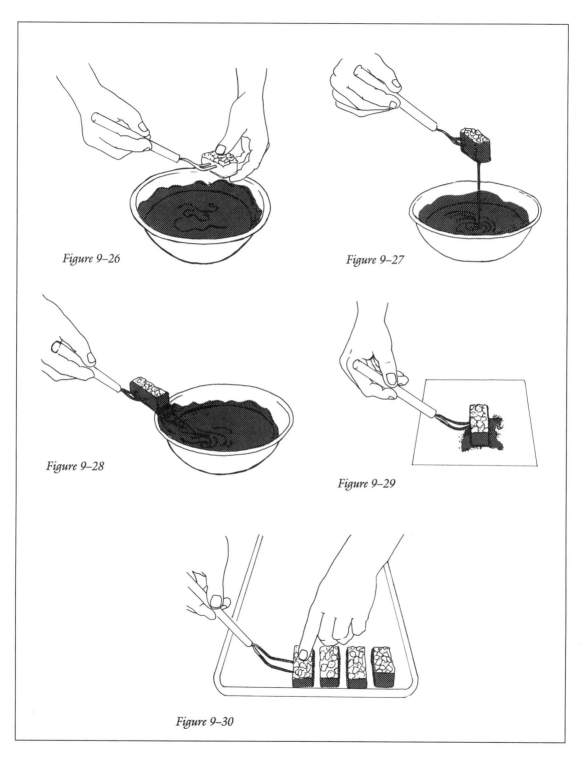

Figure 9–26

Figure 9–27

Figure 9–28

Figure 9–29

Figure 9–30

Vanilla Macaroons

60 pastries

60 Almond Macaroon Cookies
    (page 123)
2 pounds (910 g) Vanilla
    Buttercream, softened
    (page 501)
melted dark baker's chocolate
melted light baker's chocolate

Figure 9–31

1. Remove the cookies from the baking paper as instructed and shown in the recipe. Arrange them in rows, flat-side up. Press down lightly to flatten the cookies so they do not wobble.

2. Place the soft buttercream in a pastry bag with a no. 6 (12-mm) plain tip. Pipe a mound of buttercream, the size of a large egg yolk, onto each cookie. Use a soup spoon to smooth and shape the buttercream into an even mound about ½ inch (1.2 cm) thick in the center, tapering down to the sides of the cookie (Figure 9–31). Refrigerate until the buttercream is firm.

3. Holding the pastries upside down and touching only the macaroon, dip the buttercream mound into the melted dark baker's chocolate. Hold each dipped pastry over the bowl of chocolate for a few moments, moving the pastry up and down to allow as much of the excess chocolate as possible to fall back into the bowl. Place the cookies on a sheet pan in straight rows chocolate-side up.

4. Put a small amount of melted light baker's chocolate in a piping bag (see page 505). Cut a small opening in the tip. Moving the piping bag over the macaroons in an even motion, pipe (streak) straight thin lines on top of the dark chocolate. Then turn the pan 90° and pipe in the other direction to make a diamond pattern on the pastries (see Figure 6–1, page 150).

NOTE: Vanilla Macaroons will keep for up to one week at normal room temperature. They should not be kept in the refrigerator after they have been dipped in chocolate.

Walnut-Orange Tartlets

30 pastries

1 pound, 2 ounces (510 g)
    Short Dough (page 31)
6 ounces (170 g) Almond Paste
    (page 4)
2 ounces (55 g) granulated sugar
4 ounces (115 g) softened butter
3 eggs
1 ounce (30 g) bread flour
grated zest of one lemon
2 ounces (55 g) Candied Orange
    Peel, finely chopped (page 520)
4 ounces (115 g) walnuts, finely
    chopped

1. Roll the short dough ⅛ inch (3 mm) thick and use it to line 30 plain round tartlet pans 1¼ inches (3.1 cm) high and 2½ inches (6.2 cm) across the top (see Figures 2–12 to 2–15, pages 33 and 34). (Mazarin pans will also work fine.) Combine the short dough scraps and roll the dough again to ⅛ inch (3 mm) thick. Place the lined forms and the rolled sheet in the refrigerator.

2. Place the almond paste and the sugar in a mixing bowl. Add the butter gradually while mixing on low speed using the paddle. Mix only until the ingredients are combined and smooth. Add the eggs one at a time. Combine the flour, lemon zest, orange peel, and walnuts. Add the flour mixture to the almond paste mixture.

3. Place the filling in a pastry bag with a no. 7 (14-mm) plain tip. Pipe the filling into the reserved forms, filling them almost to the top. Use the rounded tip of a small metal spatula to spread the filling evenly to the edge all around the forms, making it slightly concave in the center. Place the filled shells back in the refrigerator long enough to firm the filling.

*1¼ cups (300 ml) or ¼ recipe
Royal Icing (page 528)
30 small walnut halves (or
large quarters) for decorating*

4. Spread a thin layer of royal icing on top of the filling. If the icing is too thick to spread easily, thin with a little egg white. Place a walnut half in the center of each pastry on top of the icing.

5. Cut the reserved short dough sheet into strips ¼ inch (6 mm) wide using a fluted pastry wheel. Center one small strip of short dough on either side of, and parallel to, the walnut. Use your thumbs to sever the ends of the strips against the sides of the forms to remove the excess dough and secure the strips to the sides. Set the forms aside until the royal icing has formed a crust on top, about 30 minutes.

6. Bake the tartlets at 400°F (205°C) for about 15 minutes, or until baked through. Let cool; unmold. Stored in a cool, dry place, Walnut-Orange Tartlets will stay fresh for up to three days. The tartlets may also be stored uncooked in the refrigerator or freezer for up to one week. Before baking, let them sit at room temperature until the icing has formed a crust.

Variation: Caramel Walnut Tartlets

30 pastries

*1 pound, 8 ounces (680 g)
Short Dough (page 31)
½ recipe Caramel Filling
(page 157), walnuts chopped
fine rather than coarse
powdered sugar
6 ounces (170 g) Ganache,
softened (page 567)
30 small walnut quarters
for decorating*

1. Line 30 tartlet forms with short dough as described in step 1 of the main recipe, rolling the short dough slightly thinner than ¹⁄₁₆ inch (2 mm) and reserving the remaining dough rather than rolling it out again. Prick the bottom of the shells with a fork.

2. Bake the shells at 375°F (190°C) for approximately 12 minutes, or until they start to brown lightly. Remove from the oven and let cool for a few minutes.

3. Place the caramel filling in a pastry bag with a no. 7 (14-mm) plain tip. Pipe the filling into the shells. Flatten the top of the filling if necessary. Push the tartlets as close together as possible.

4. Roll the reserved short dough ¹⁄₁₆ inch (2 mm) thick, roughly in the same shape as the forms on the sheet pan. Roll the dough up on a dowel and unroll over the top of the tartlets. Press down on the top of each one with the palm of your hand to trim the short dough around the sides of the forms. Spread the tartlets out over the pan. Use a fork to prick the top of the dough.

5. Bake the tartlets at 325°F (163°C) for approximately 12 minutes, or until the tops are baked (they should not brown; see note). Let the tartlets cool.

6. Unmold and sift powdered sugar lightly over the tops. Place the ganache in a pastry bag with a no. 5 (10-mm) star tip. Pipe a small rosette of ganache in the center of each pastry. Place a walnut quarter on the ganache. If you do not have ganache on hand, omit the powdered sugar and dip the top of the tartlets into melted dark baker's chocolate instead. Place a walnut half in the center before the chocolate hardens.

NOTE: Do not bake the tartlets in a hotter oven or longer than necessary or you risk having the filling boil over in the forms, making the tartlets impossible to remove from the pans.

Desserts for Restaurant Presentation

Apple Strudel, Austrian Style
Apple Strudel, German Style
Budapest Swirls
Cobbler with Apples and Ginger
Cobbler with Peaches and
    Cinnamon
Cobbler with Rhubarb and
    Honey
Crepes Suzette
Crisp Waffles
Florentina Cones with
    Seasonal Fruit
Florentina Noisettes
Fruit Barrels

Plum Fritters
Puff Pastry with Fruit and
    Champagne Sabayon
Raspberry Wafers
Rum Babas
Savarins
Small Pear Tartlets with
    Caramel Sauce
Small Swedish Pancakes
Strawberry Pyramids
Swedish Profiteroles
Toasted Panettone with
    Mascarpone Sauce
Tropical Surprise Packages

*F*or many hundreds of years, sweet and elegant desserts have been a favorite way to reward ourselves and those who are special to us. They are a small luxury that, even though not an essential part of one's everyday diet, has played an important role in cultural history. From the first sweets, which were probably nothing more than a plate of fruit topped with honey, cooking and baking have developed into a creative and sophisticated art. This is especially evident in dessert presentations, which are often a meaningful part of celebrations and special occasions.

Some of the more elaborate recipes in this chapter require time and patience, but they yield breathtaking results. However, any of these desserts, even the quickest and most humble, should be presented in its own elegant way, served on an attractive plate and accompanied by an appropriate sauce and/or garnish. Even the simple and homey-looking cobbler can be dressed up with a little effort, although this type of dessert is not meant to compete with the artistry and complexity of, for example, Tropical Surprise Packages.

The size of the serving plate alone can make a big difference in a dessert's appearance. The dessert should not touch the rim of the plate, so for most items, it is essential to use a 10- to 12-inch plate to display the pastry, sauce, and garnish without crowding. It is best to use plates that have no pattern on the surface and just a simple design on the rim so as not to detract from the dessert. This is especially important if decorating with two or more sauces or the result can look like a bad example of modern art. Keep in mind that the serving plate, garnish, and sauce are there to enhance the dessert, not compete with it. Strive for a well-balanced presentation.

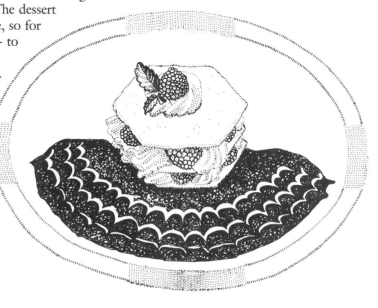

Many of the pastries in this chapter would be suitable for the showcase in a pastry shop or for a dessert buffet, instead of plate service, just by leaving out the sauce and garnish. The Budapest Swirls, babas, profiteroles, and both varieties of apple strudel, are examples. Conversely, some of the individual pastries found in the preceding chapter—eclairs, napoleons, and Orange Truffle Strips, for example—can easily be turned into elegant plated desserts by serving with a sauce and garnish.

In either case, whether you serve an elegant petits fours tray or an artistically decorated serving of Florentina Cones with Seasonal Fruit, when your customers are finished they should say, "It was worth every calorie."

Apple Strudel, Austrian Style

about 25 servings

2 pounds, 8 ounces (1 kg, 135 g) peeled, cored, and thinly sliced apples
4 ounces (115 g) granulated sugar
1 pound (455 g) bread flour
1 egg
2 ounces (55 g) softened butter
½ teaspoon (3 g) salt
1 cup (240 ml) cold water, approximately
6 ounces (170 g) small white-bread croutons
3 ounces (85 g) melted butter
8 ounces (225 g) dark raisins
8 ounces (225 g) coarsely crushed nuts
Cinnamon Sugar (page 4)
7 ounces (200 g) firm butter
powdered sugar
Vanilla Custard Sauce (page 564) or
sweetened whipped cream

1. Combine the sliced apples and granulated sugar and set aside.

2. Place the flour in a bowl or on the table. Make a well in the middle and add the egg, softened butter, salt, and enough of the cold water to make a soft dough. Knead the dough until it is smooth and elastic, about 5 minutes. Divide the dough into two pieces and roll out each one, on a cloth dusted with flour, into a small rectangle. Let the dough rest for 5 minutes, then stretch it out with your hands and let it rest 5 minutes longer.

3. Sauté the croutons in the melted butter until golden brown and crisp. Reserve any leftover melted butter to brush on the strudel during baking.

4. Finish stretching the dough into rectangles, making them about 28 × 14 inches (70 × 35 cm). Sprinkle the apples, including any juice that has developed, over the dough. Divide the raisins, nuts, cinnamon sugar to taste, croutons, and firm butter (cut into small chunks) between the two pastries, distributing all of the ingredients evenly over the dough.

5. Using the cloth to help, roll up each strudel starting from the long side (see Budapest Swirls, Figure 10–3, page 275), rolling it toward you and pressing down at the same time to form a tight roll that will not flatten out too much when baked. Place each strudel, seam-side down, in a horseshoe shape on a sheet pan.

6. Bake at 375°F (190°C) for about 35 minutes, brushing from time to time with the juices that run out. If there are no juices after 15 to 20 minutes of baking, melt some butter and brush it on.

7. When the strudels have cooled somewhat, slice and sift powdered sugar over the slices. Serve hot or cold with Vanilla Custard Sauce or with whipped cream flavored with sugar and vanilla.

Apple Strudel, German Style

(see photograph in color insert)

fifteen 1½-inch (3.7-cm) servings

12 ounces (340 g) Short Dough
    (page 31)
1 pound (455 g) Classic or
    Quick Puff Paste (page 21)
one ¼- × 14- × 24-inch
    (6-mm × 35- × 60-cm)
    Almond Sponge (page 162)
2 pounds (910 g) apples,
    peeled and cored
Poaching Syrup I (page 6)
6 ounces (170 g) walnuts,
    halves or pieces
8 ounces (225 g) dark raisins
1 ounce (30 g) Cinnamon Sugar
    (page 4)
3 ounces (85 g) Mazarin Filling
    (page 569) (see note)
apricot jam
Egg Wash (page 5)
Apricot Glaze (page 526)
Simple Icing (page 529)
water
2¾ cup (660 ml) or ½ recipe
    Vanilla Custard Sauce
    (page 564)
fresh fruit

1. Roll out a strip of short dough to ⅛ inch (3 mm) thick, the length of a full sheet pan (24 inches/60 cm) and 4 inches (10 cm) wide. Refrigerate.

2. Roll out the Puff Paste to ⅛ inch (3 mm) thick, 8 inches (20 cm) wide, and as long as the short dough. Refrigerate.

3. Cut the sponge sheet 3½ inches (8.7 cm) wide and as long as the short dough. Tear the remainder of the sponge sheet into small pieces and reserve.

4. Lightly poach the apples in the syrup (they should still be firm) and cut them into ½-inch (1.2-cm) slices.

5. Chop the walnuts to the size of the raisins. Mix thoroughly with apples, raisins, cinnamon sugar, and mazarin filling. Add the reserved sponge cake pieces.

6. Spread a thin layer of jam on the short dough, leaving ¼ inch (6 mm) of the dough exposed on the long sides. Place the sponge cake strip on top of the jam. Use your hands to place the filling on top of the sponge cake, shaping the apple mixture so that it is slightly rounded, and leaving a ¼-inch (6-mm) edge of short dough exposed on each long side.

7. Fold the puff paste lengthwise over a dowel, positioning the dowel 2 inches (5 cm) away from the fold. With the back of a chef's knife (using the dowel as a guide) lightly mark (do not cut) a line parallel to the fold and approximately 1½ inches (3.7 cm) away from it, toward the dowel. Cut through the fold, up to the mark, at ¼ inch (6 mm) intervals (Figure 10–1).

8. Brush the exposed short dough on the strudel with the egg wash. Move the dowel to the fold of the puff paste, and use the dowel to lift the puff paste and unfold it over the strudel (Figure 10–2), positioning it so that the slits are centered over the filling. Fasten the puff paste to the short dough with your thumbs. Trim

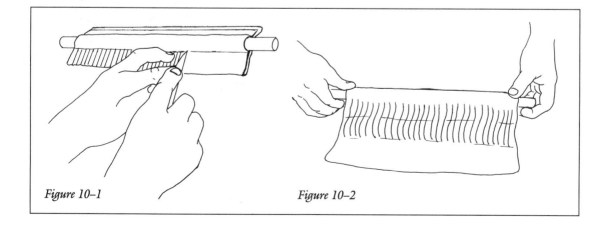

Figure 10–1   *Figure 10–2*

the excess from the sides (do not worry about sealing the short ends). Brush with egg wash.

9. Bake at 375°F (190°C) until golden brown, about 45 minutes. You may need to place a second pan underneath to prevent the bottom from becoming too dark. Let cool.

10. Glaze the strudel with apricot glaze, then brush with simple icing that has been thinned enough with simple syrup to look transparent. Do not just warm the icing to make it thin enough to use, or the glaze will be too thick when it sets.

11. Presentation: Pour 1½ ounces (45 ml) Vanilla Custard Sauce on a dessert plate, covering half of the plate, off-center. Cut the strudel into 1½-inch (3.7-cm) slices and place a slice in the middle of the plate next to the sauce. Place the fruit behind the strudel on the opposite side. The strudel can be served hot or cold.

NOTE: Frozen or canned apples are an excellent substitute, but they must not be too soft. Add them directly to the filling without poaching. If you do not have mazarin filling on hand, substitute Almond Paste (page 4).

Budapest Swirls

(see photograph in color insert)
24 servings

Butter and Flour Mixture
(page 4)
2 recipes Japonaise Batter
(page 333)
1 recipe Vanilla Bavarian Cream
(page 570)
Orange Segments from 2 oranges
(directions follow)
powdered sugar
Orange Sauce (page 561)
Sour Cream Mixture for Piping
(page 564)
orange segments for decoration
mint sprigs

1. Line two full-sized sheet pans (16 × 24 inches/40 × 60 cm) with baking paper. Lightly grease the papers with the butter and flour mixture. Place the Japonaise Batter in a pastry bag with a no. 5 (10-mm) plain tip. Pipe the batter into strings, side by side and touching, running the full length of the pans. You should get about 20 strings on each pan. Make the two sheets the same size.

2. Bake the sheets at 300°F (149°C) for about 15 to 20 minutes. They should show some color and have a crust on top, but should not be dry all the way through. (To put it another way, remove the sheets from the oven when they are only half baked as compared to regular Japonaise sheets.) Let cool completely (see note).

3. Invert the cold Japonaise sheets onto baking papers and peel the other paper off the back. Divide the Bavarian cream between them and spread it out over the sheets. Arrange the orange segments in a straight line, lengthwise, approximately 1 inch (2.5 cm) from the top long edge on each sheet. Refrigerate for about 15 minutes to partially set the cream.

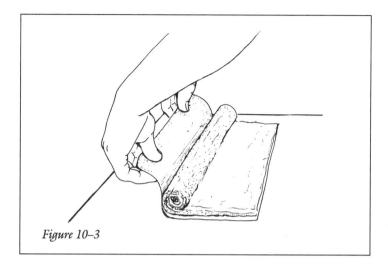

Figure 10–3

4. Roll up the sheet as for a roulade by lifting the back of the paper and letting the pastry roll toward you (Figure 10–3). Refrigerate again until the cream is completely set.

5. Cut the roll into 2-inch (5-cm) slices at an angle. Sift powdered sugar lightly over the top of the pastries.

6. Presentation: Place a Budapest Swirl in the center of a dessert plate. Pour a small pool of Orange Sauce in front of the pastry. Decorate the sauce with the Sour Cream Mixture for Piping (see pages 518–519). Arrange three thin orange segments and a mint sprig on the opposite side of the plate.

NOTE: Ideally, the Japonaise sheets should be baked the day before assembly and placed in the refrigerator overnight to ensure that they will be soft enough to roll. If necessary, follow the directions for softening the sponge sheet given on page 163. Although the sheets can be made one day ahead of time, the Budapest Swirls should be assembled the day they are to be served; if left too long the meringue will absorb moisture from the filling and become soggy.

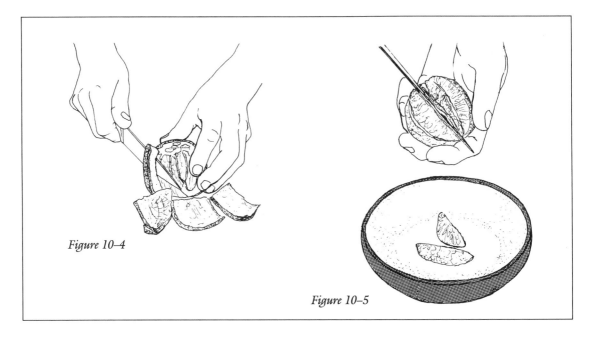

Figure 10–4

Figure 10–5

To cut orange segments

1. Cut the top and bottom off the orange and set the orange on a cutting board.

2. Cut away the skin on the sides, cutting from top to bottom, removing all of the white pith, and keeping the natural shape of the orange (Figure 10–4). Hold the orange in your hand over a bowl to catch the juice.

3. With a small sharp paring knife, cut between the inside membranes to remove the segments (Figure 10–5).

Cobbler with Apples and Ginger

two 10-inch (25-cm) cobblers

1½ ounces (40 g) candied or crystallized ginger
15 medium-sized tart cooking apples (pippin or Granny Smith are good choices)

Cobblers are a very simple and quick way of using fresh seasonal fruit to create a delicious ending to a meal. Peach cobbler is an American favorite and is probably the best-known version; topped with fresh vanilla ice cream it is almost synonymous with Fourth of July celebrations for some people. The only thing I do not like about cobblers made in the traditional form is that they really do not present very well and can often end up looking like a pie gone wrong! But then, a cobbler that does not look a little bit messy is not the genuine article. If the cobbler is not to be plated in the kitchen, use any presentable baking dish, such as an earthenware casserole, with a 2-quart (1 l, 920 ml) capacity.

¼ cup (60 ml) lemon juice
8 ounces (225 g) granulated sugar
4 ounces (115 g) butter
Cobbler Topping (recipe follows)
Cinnamon Sugar (page 4)
Bitter Orange Sauce (page 561)
mint sprigs

1. Finely chop ginger and reserve.

2. Peel apples, core, and cut into wedges. Place the wedges in a bowl with the lemon juice as you cut them, tossing them in the juice to coat.

3. Transfer to a skillet or saucepan and add sugar and butter. Cook over medium heat, stirring, until the apples are soft but not mushy. Mix in candied ginger.

4. Divide the apples, including all of the liquid, between two 10-inch (25-cm) cake pans with 2-inch (5-cm) sides. Press the pieces into the pans firmly.

5. Use your hands or two spoons to place the topping on the apples in random piles, leaving 1 inch (2.5 cm) of apples uncovered around the outside of the pans to allow the batter to bake out. Do not smooth the batter over the top; this is not an authentic cobbler if you do so. Sprinkle cinnamon sugar lightly over the top.

6. Bake at 425°F (219°C) for approximately 40 minutes, or until the crust is golden brown and baked through. Set the cobblers aside for at least 30 minutes before serving to allow the crust to absorb part of the liquid in the pan. Warm before serving if necessary; the cobbler should be served warm or hot, never chilled. Divide into the desired size pieces.

7. Presentation: Place a portion of cobbler on a dessert plate. Pour a pool of Bitter Orange Sauce on the side and decorate with a sprig of mint.

Variation: Cobbler with Whipped Cream

Try serving cobbler with a bourbon- or calvados-flavored whipped cream; it is much easier than making the Bitter Orange Sauce and it tastes great with the apples. Follow the directions for Brandied Whipped Cream (see page 424), substituting bourbon or calvados for brandy.

Cobbler Topping

3 pounds, 6 ounces (1 kg, 535 g)

1 pound, 6 ounces (625 g)
bread flour
1 teaspoon (5 g) salt
3 tablespoons (36 g) baking powder
4 ounces (115 g) cold butter
3¼ cups (780 ml) heavy cream

1. Sift together the flour, salt, and baking powder. Cut the butter into small chunks, add, and cut into the flour mixture to the size of peas.

2. Pour in the cream all at once and stir rapidly with your hand to form a soft dough.

3. Place on a floured work surface and pat out to a rectangle 1½ inches (3.7 cm) thick. Make two rough single turns (see page 96), shaping the dough with your hands and not a rolling pin.

NOTE: Do not make the topping until you are ready to use it.

Cobbler with Peaches and Cinnamon

(see photograph in color insert)
two 10-inch (25-cm) cobblers

12 medium-sized peaches
3 ounces (85 g) Cinnamon Sugar
  (page 4)
1 recipe Cobbler Topping
  (page 277)
1 recipe Mascarpone Sauce
  (page 561)
ground cinnamon

1. Wash the peaches, remove the pits, and cut each one into about eight wedges leaving the skin on. Place in a bowl and toss with cinnamon sugar to coat. Divide between two 10-inch (25-cm) cake pans, lightly pressing the fruit into the forms with your hands.

2. Add the Cobbler Topping and bake following instructions in Cobbler with Apples and Ginger, page 276.

3. Presentation: Place a portion of cobbler on a dessert plate. Spoon Mascarpone Sauce on one side, letting the sauce run onto the plate. Lightly sprinkle cinnamon on the sauce.

Cobbler with Rhubarb and Honey

two 10-inch (25-cm) cobblers

5 pounds (2 kg, 275 g) rhubarb
2 ounces (55 g) cornstarch
12 ounces (340 g) granulated
  sugar
¾ cup (180 ml) honey
2 ounces (55 g) candied or
  crystallized ginger
1 recipe Cobbler Topping
  (page 277); see step 3
1 recipe Romanoff Sauce
  (page 563)
mint sprigs

1. Wash and dry the rhubarb. Trim the top and bottom off the stalks and discard. Cut the stalks into ½-inch (1.2-cm) slices. If any stalks are wider than 1 inch (2.5 cm), cut in half.

2. Place a stainless steel bowl in the oven until it is hot. Stir the cornstarch and sugar together in the bowl, add the rhubarb pieces, and toss to coat them thoroughly. Mix in the honey and set aside for about 30 minutes.

3. Chop the ginger and add to the Cobbler Topping mixed with the dry ingredients.

4. Transfer the rhubarb, with all of the liquid, to a saucepan. Cook over low heat, stirring constantly until the rhubarb starts to turn a little soft. Do not overcook or the rhubarb will fall apart very quickly at this point.

5. Divide the rhubarb mixture between two 10-inch (25-cm) cake pans, lightly pressing the fruit into the pans with your hands. Use two spoons or your hands to drop the Cobbler Topping over the rhubarb in random piles, leaving 1 inch (2.5 cm) of rhubarb uncovered around the outside of the pans to allow the topping to bake out. Do not smooth the batter over the top.

6. Bake at 425°F (219°C) for about 30 minutes or until the topping is golden brown and baked through. Set the cobblers aside for at least 30 minutes before serving to allow the crust to absorb part of the liquid in the pan. Warm before serving if necessary. The cobbler should be served warm or hot, never chilled. Divide into the desired size pieces.

7. Presentation: Place a portion of cobbler on a dessert plate. Pour a pool of Romanoff Sauce on the side and decorate with a sprig of mint.

Variation

Rhubarb Cobbler is excellent served with Honey-Vanilla Frozen Yogurt (see page 386) rather than Romanoff Sauce.

Crepes Suzette
4 servings

12 Crepes (page 388)
2 oranges
1 lemon
6 ounces (170 g) granulated sugar
6 ounces (170 g) softened butter
¼ cup (60 ml) orange liqueur
   (Cointreau or Grand Marnier)
½ cup (120 ml) cognac or brandy

This is the most famous of all crepe recipes. It is usually prepped by the pastry shop and prepared tableside on a *gueridon* by the waiter. The crepe sauce can also be prepared in the kitchen and then flambéed at the table. The dessert is generally made for two to four people at a time. For larger servings the crepes should be prepped in the kitchen, or two *gueridons* should be used, as it is not practical to heat more than 12 crepes in one chafing dish or sauté pan. (You can stretch this a little by serving two crepes per serving rather than the usual three.)

Dining room method

1. Arrange your *mise en place* neatly and in sequence on the *gueridon*. Grate the zest of one orange and half the lemon; reserve. Juice the oranges, strain, and reserve the juice (do not mix with the zest).

2. Place the sugar in the chafing dish (or a copper sauté pan). Squeeze and strain the juice from the lemon into the sugar.

3. Adjust the flame to medium. Heat the sugar, stirring constantly, until all of the sugar is melted and it just starts to caramelize.

4. Add half of the orange juice and the grated zest and blend thoroughly. Add the butter and stir for a few seconds until the sauce is smooth. Stir in the orange liqueur.

5. Reduce the flame. Add the crepes one at a time with the best side facing up. After a few seconds use a fork and spoon to turn the crepe over to ensure that both sides are well coated with the sauce and the crepe is hot. Fold the crepe into quarters and move to the side of the chafing dish.

6. Add the remaining crepes in the same way, arranging them in an overlapping circle around the edge of the pan after coating them with the sauce. (If the chafing dish is too small to hold all of the sauced crepes while you are working, transfer part of them to a side dish while finishing the remainder, then heat them up in the sauce before flaming.) If necessary, thin the sauce with the remaining orange juice during this process.

7. Move the crepes to the center of the pan. Add the cognac, and allow it to warm up for a few seconds but do not stir to mix it with the sauce.

8. Turn up the flame and tilt the pan to ignite the cognac. Turn the crepes over in the flambéed sauce, then serve immediately

using the spoon and fork to arrange three crepes per serving on warm dessert plates. Top each with a portion of the sauce.

NOTE: Instead of heating the cognac in the pan with the crepes, you can pour the cognac into a ladle (move the pan of crepes to the side) and warm the cognac over the flame. Return the pan to the stand, ignite the cognac in the ladle, and pour it flaming over the crepes.

Kitchen method

1. Cream the butter and sugar until fluffy. Add the lemon juice, orange juice, and grated zest. Stir to combine. (If the butter or juice is cold, the mixture might separate; this will not make any difference except for the appearance, but it is a good idea to warm the mixture until it is homogenized.)

2. Give this mixture, together with the crepes, orange liqueur, and cognac, to the waiter. The waiter will heat the sauce mixture in the chafing dish until it starts to bubble, then allow it to simmer for a minute or two to ensure that the sugar is melted. The orange liqueur is then added, and the crepes and cognac are introduced in the same way as described in the preceding method.

Crisp Waffles
about 16 servings

1 pound, 8 ounces (680 g)
    bread flour
10 ounces (285 g) cornstarch
2 ounces (55 g) granulated sugar
1 teaspoon (5 g) salt
1 quart (960 ml) warm water
6 eggs
6 ounces (170 g) melted butter
finely grated zest of ½ lemon,
    optional
1 quart (960 ml) heavy cream
2 teaspoons (10 ml) vanilla extract
powdered sugar
Apple Jam with Calvados
    (instructions follow)
Calvados Whipped Cream
    (recipe follows)

To many people waffles are synonymous with breakfast, but I think you will find that this crisp light waffle makes a tempting dessert when paired with cream and apple jam. The waffles should be served as soon as they are made, while still warm, to taste their best. If it is necessary to make them ahead of time, reserve them in a single layer placed on a cake rack in a low oven (200°F/94°C). The waffles will stay crisp for about 15 minutes. Any leftover waffle batter can be kept covered in the refrigerator and used for two to three days with no loss in quality.

1. Sift the flour and cornstarch into a mixing bowl. Stir in the sugar and salt.

2. Gradually incorporate the water, mixing with a whisk. Whisk in the eggs and then the butter and lemon zest, if used. Mix until you have a smooth paste, about 3 minutes longer.

3. Cover the batter and let it rest for 30 minutes.

4. Whip the heavy cream and the vanilla extract to stiff peaks. Fold the cream into the waffle batter.

5. Heat a waffle iron (grease if not using a nonstick iron). Portion 1 to 2 cups (240 to 480 ml) of waffle batter onto the iron and quickly spread it out a little (see note). Close the lid and bake approximately 3 minutes per side if using a stove-top iron, or about 5 minutes total if using an electric iron.

6. Presentation: Place two or three waffles (depending on size) off-center on a dessert plate, placing one of the waffles leaning against the other(s). Sift powdered sugar lightly over the tops of the waffles and over the plate. Spoon a large dollop of warm apple jam on the plate next to the waffles. Pour a pool of Calvados Whipped Cream in front of the dessert and over a corner of the waffles. Serve immediately.

NOTE: The amount of batter needed for each waffle will vary depending on the type of iron used. Belgian waffle irons use more batter because of the deep grooves.

Apple Jam with Calvados

Make ½ recipe Apple Cinnamon Filling (page 307), substituting calvados for the rum and omitting the pectin powder.

Calvados Whipped Cream

2¼ cups (540 ml) cream

1 pint (480 ml) heavy cream
1 tablespoon (15 g) granulated sugar
¼ cup (60 ml) calvados
1 teaspoon (5 ml) vanilla extract

Whip the cream and sugar until the mixture is fairly thick, yet still pourable. Stir in the calvados and vanilla. Reserve covered in the refrigerator. If needed, adjust the consistency of the sauce at serving time by adding additional cream to thin it, or whip it a little longer to thicken. The sauce should be thick enough not to run on the plate.

Variation

Try serving these waffles for brunch with the following Strawberry-Lime Sauce and whipped cream flavored with vanilla. You will need 1 cup (240 ml) heavy cream and ½ teaspoon (3 ml) vanilla extract.

Strawberry-Lime Sauce

2½ cups (600 ml) sauce

2 pounds (910 g) fresh strawberries
6 ounces (170 g) granulated sugar
3 tablespoons (45 ml) honey
½ cup (120 ml) lime juice
2 tablespoons (16 g) cornstarch
2 tablespoons (30 ml) strained raspberry purée, optional

1. Remove stems from strawberries (a small melon baller works well for this). Wash, purée, and strain them.

2. Add the sugar, honey, and lime juice. Stir the cornstarch into a small part of the liquid, then mix into the remainder.

3. Bring to a boil and cook for about 2 minutes over low heat to eliminate any aftertaste from the cornstarch.

NOTE: If the sauce is pale from using strawberries that were not perfectly ripe, adding the raspberry purée will give the sauce a more attractive color.

Florentina Cones with Seasonal Fruit

25 servings

*1 pound, 10 ounces (740 g) or
    1 recipe Florentina Batter
    (page 131)*
*3 pounds (1 kg, 365 g) assorted
    fresh fruit, approximately*
*2 pounds (910 g) or 1 recipe
    Vanilla Bavarian Cream
    (page 570)*
6 ounces (170 g) whipped cream
Bitter Orange Sauce (page 561)
*Chocolate Sauce for Piping
    (page 560)*
*Sour Cream Mixture for Piping
    (page 564)*
strained strawberry jam

1. Draw twenty-five 4¾-inch (11.8-cm) circles on baking paper using a plain cookie cutter as a guide. Invert the papers on sheet pans. Divide the Florentina Batter between the circles. Spread out, bake, and trim the cookies as directed in the recipe for Florentinas.

2. Reheat the trimmed cookies until they are soft enough to bend. Immediately form them into cones by wrapping them, top-side out, around a cone-shaped object. Press the edges together where they meet so the cone will hold together (Figure 10–6). If you do not have an appropriate form, you can make one by cutting it out of styrofoam and covering it with aluminum foil. The cone should be about 4 inches (10 cm) long and 2½ inches (6.2 cm) across at the base. If the cookies become too firm to bend easily, just reheat them. Reserve the finished cones, covered, in a dry place.

3. Use four or five different kinds of fruit for a colorful presentation. Cut the fruit into raspberry-sized chunks. If using peaches or apricots, leave the skin on. Take care to make uniform cuts. Do not use apples or pears unless they have been poached. Apricots, peaches, blueberries, raspberries, and strawberries work well. Add either kiwi or honeydew melon for contrasting color. Blend the cut fruits carefully so you do not damage them, and take extra care if you use raspberries. If you do not plan to serve all of the mixed fruit within a few hours, leave the varieties separated, then combine them as needed to protect the fruits from "bleeding" and staining each other.

4. Presentation: Fill a cone halfway with Bavarian cream. Pipe a rosette of whipped cream off-center on a dessert plate using a no. 4 (8-mm) star tip. Pour an oval pool of Bitter Orange Sauce

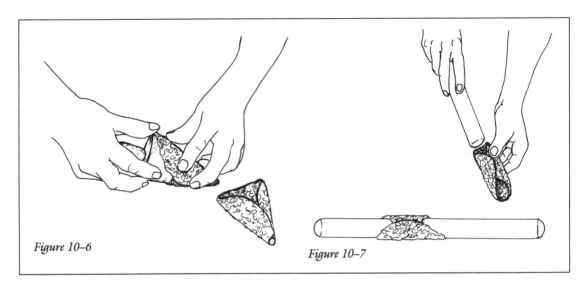

Figure 10–6

Figure 10–7

on the larger part of the plate. Hold the cone vertically and fill with about 2 ounces (55 g) of the fruit mixture on top of the Bavarian cream. Gently place the cone (on its side) on the whipped cream rosette with the wide end in the orange sauce. Part of the fruit should fall out onto the orange sauce naturally. Decorate the sauce using the chocolate sauce, sour cream mixture, and jam (see pages 518–519). Serve immediately.

Florentina Noisettes

25 servings

*1 pound, 10 ounces (740 g) or
    1 recipe Florentina Batter
    (page 131)*
*4 ounces (115 g) Short Dough
    (page 31)*
melted dark baker's chocolate
*25 hazelnuts, roasted and skins
    removed*
1 quart (960 ml) heavy cream
*2 tablespoons (30 g) granulated
    sugar*
1 teaspoon (5 ml) vanilla extract
*1 recipe Hazelnut Paste (page 6)
    or*
4 ounces commercial hazelnut paste
Vanilla Custard Sauce (page 564)
*mocha paste or Coffee Reduction
    (page 5)*
*Chocolate Sauce for Piping
    (page 560)*
strawberry halves, fanned

1. Draw twenty-five 4¾-inch (11.8-cm) circles on baking paper. Invert the papers and place on sheet pans. Divide the Florentina Batter between the circles, spread out, bake, and trim as instructed in the recipe for Florentinas.

2. Return the cookies to the oven for a few minutes until soft. Immediately roll each cookie, top-side out, around a dowel so that the ends of the cookie overlap slightly. Push the ends together between the dowel and the table to make sure they stick. Turn the cookie a half turn so it will not stick to the dowel as it cools. Let each Florentina roll cool completely before sliding it off the dowel (Figure 10–7).

3. Roll out the short dough to ⅛ inch (3 mm) thick. Cut out twenty-five 1¼-inch (3.1-cm) cookies using a fluted cutter. Bake at 375°F (190°C) until golden brown.

4. Place a small amount of melted baker's chocolate in a piping bag and pipe a pea-sized dot of chocolate in the center of each cookie. Fasten a hazelnut on top, point up, before the chocolate hardens. Set the cookies aside.

5. Whip the cream, sugar, and vanilla to soft peaks. Add a small amount of the cream to the hazelnut paste and mix until softened. Add the paste back to the remaining cream and whip to stiff peaks.

6. Place the cream in a pastry bag with a no. 6 (12-mm) star tip. Fill each of the Florentinas with the cream mixture by piping it into both ends. Do not fill any more cookies than you plan to serve within a few hours because they become soft quickly.

7. Flavor the Vanilla Custard Sauce with mocha paste or coffee reduction.

8. Presentation: Pipe a small rosette of cream off-center on a dessert plate and place a Florentina on top to prevent the pastry from sliding. Pipe a second, smaller dot of cream on top of the roll and set a short dough cookie on top. Pour a small pool of Vanilla Custard Sauce in front of the pastry and decorate the sauce with the Chocolate Sauce for Piping (see pages 518–519). Place a fanned strawberry half behind the roll.

Fruit Barrels

(see photograph in color insert)
25 servings

1 recipe Vanilla Tulips batter
    (page 546)
1 recipe Sponge Cake batter
    (page 161)
Butter and Flour Mixture
    (page 4)
½ teaspoon (1 g) cocoa powder
3 cups (720 ml) heavy cream
1½ tablespoons (23 g) granulated
    sugar
1 teaspoon (5 ml) vanilla extract
fresh blueberries
    and/or
fresh raspberries
Blueberry Sauce *(page 557)*

It is best to make the Vanilla Tulip batter first, then make the sponge cake batter while it is resting.

1. Spread the sponge cake batter evenly over a half-sheet pan lined with baking paper. Bake at 400°F (205°C) for about 15 minutes, or until the cake springs back when pressed lightly in the center.

2. Make the Fruit Barrel template (Figure 10–8). The template as shown is the correct size for the recipe. However, due to the size of this particular template, it is only possible to show half of it on the page. Trace as shown, invert your paper, match the dotted line in the center, and trace the other half of the template so it looks like the small sample shown. Cut the template out of ⅟₁₆-inch (2-mm) thick cardboard (cakeboxes work fine for this).

3. Brush the butter and flour mixture on the back of several clean, even sheet pans. Remove 3 tablespoons (45 ml) of the tulip batter and color it with the cocoa powder. Place it in a piping bag and set aside. Spread the remaining batter on the sheet pans following the outline within the template (as shown in Figures 18–47 and 18–48, page 548). Take care not to spread the batter too thick or it will be difficult to form the barrels. With the reserved cocoa-colored batter, pipe out two lines the length of each barrel and two dots in the "handles" (Figure 10–9).

4. Bake at 400°F (205°C) until the batter begins to brown in spots, about 8 minutes. Remove from the oven and immediately bend into oval barrels. Press firmly with a dowel or other suitable tool on the overlapping ends to seal them. You will need to work quickly once the barrels are out of the oven. If they become too brittle to bend, reheat to soften them.

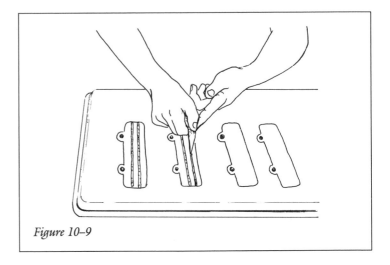

Figure 10–9

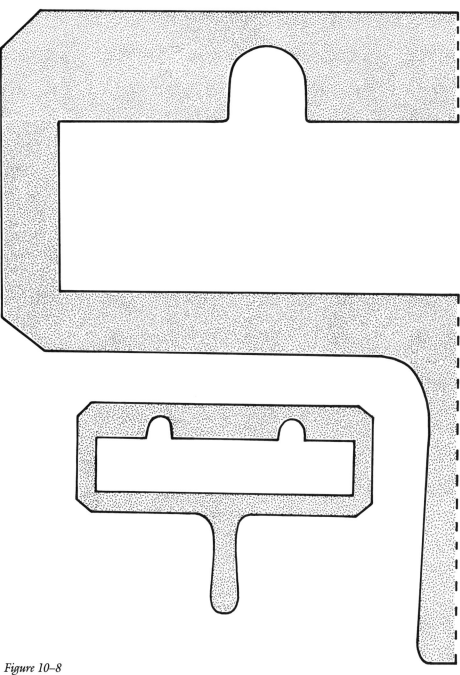

Figure 10–8

5. Cut out ½ inch (1.2 cm) thick pieces of sponge cake the same size as the inside of the barrels and place one in the bottom of each barrel.

6. Whip the cream, sugar, and vanilla to stiff peaks. Pipe the whipped cream into the barrels, filling them almost to the top. Top the cream with the blueberries and/or raspberries. The barrels should look as if they are full of fruit, almost overflowing.

7. Presentation: Place a barrel off-center on a dessert plate and pour a pool of Blueberry Sauce in front of it.

Variation

If you would like to make barrels with a bottom (to omit the sponge, or just for a more finished look) use the alternate template (Figure 10–10). The same instructions apply for cutting out the template as described above. When the barrels come out of the oven, bend the bottom up first, then bend the sides around until they are even with the bottom. Lay the barrels on their sides with the seam against a dowel or other object until they are firm to prevent them from unfolding.

Plum Fritters
(Beignets)
(see photograph in color insert)
15 servings

15 medium-sized whole plums
1 recipe Poaching Syrup I
*   (page 6)*
Apricot Glaze (page 526)
15 plum halves, fanned
oil for deep frying
bread flour
Fritter Batter (recipe follows)
Cinnamon Sugar (page 4)
Apricot Sauce (page 556)
powdered sugar

1. Cut the whole plums into quarters. Poach them gently in the poaching syrup for about 5 minutes. They should be soft but not mushy. Remove and set aside to drain on paper towels.

2. Lightly brush apricot glaze on the fanned plum halves. Reserve for garnish.

3. Heat the frying oil to 375°F (190°C). Coat the poached plums with bread flour to help the batter adhere. Dip them into the Fritter Batter and carefully drop them into the oil. Do not add too many pieces at one time or the fat will cool rapidly and the fritters will become greasy and heavy from absorbing the oil. Fry for about 5 minutes or until golden brown, turning the fritters in the oil so they will color evenly.

4. Remove the fritters with a slotted spoon or skimmer and place them on paper towels or napkins to drain. Sprinkle cinnamon sugar lightly over the fritters and keep them warm as you fry the remaining pieces.

5. Presentation: Place a reserved plum half in the center of a dessert plate. Pour Apricot Sauce in a large pool in front of the plum (be sure the sauce is at room temperature or it will cool the fritters). Sift powdered sugar over four warm fritters and arrange them on the opposite side of the plate. Serve immediately.

NOTE: Use only a quarter plum to make each garnish if the plums are large. Be sure to use a sharp knife that will cut through the skin cleanly, allowing you to make thin, elegant slices. Instead

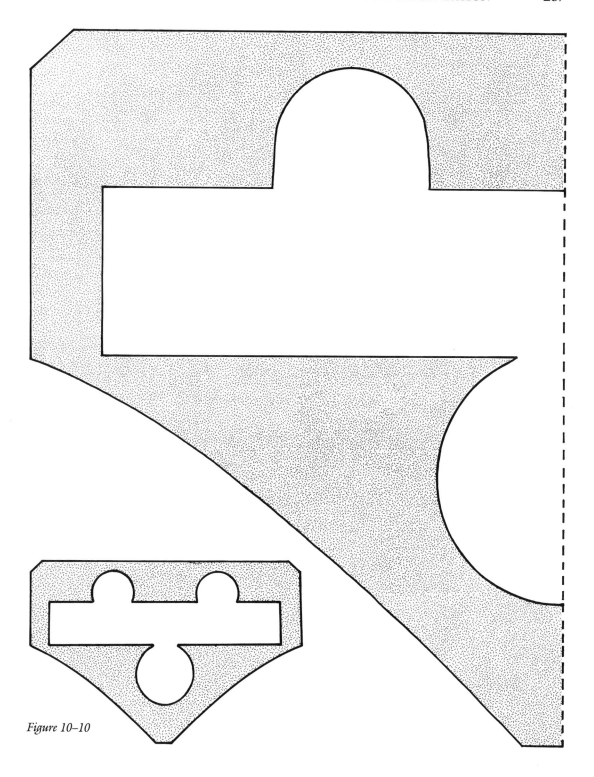

Figure 10–10

Fritter Batter

5 ounces (140 g) bread flour
1/2 teaspoon (3 g) salt
2 egg yolks
4 ounces (115 g) granulated sugar
finely grated peel of 1 lemon
1 cup (240 ml) sweet white wine
1 teaspoon (5 ml) vanilla extract
2 egg whites

Variation: Fritters with Fresh Berries

Puff Pastry with Fruit and Champagne Sabayon

(see photograph in color insert)
twenty 3½-inch (8.7-cm) squares

2 pounds, 8 ounces (1 kg, 135 g)
   Classic Puff Paste (page 21);
   see note
Egg Wash (page 5)

of using fanned plums as a decoration, it looks very nice to make a rose out of plum peel as shown in the color insert.

1. Sift flour and salt together. Beat egg yolks, 2 ounces (55 g) of the sugar, and lemon peel just to combine. Add wine and vanilla extract. Gradually stir this mixture into the dry ingredients and mix until completely smooth. Refrigerate about 30 minutes.

2. Just before batter is to be used, whip the egg whites with the remaining 2 ounces (55 g) of sugar to stiff peaks. Gradually fold the reserved batter into the egg whites. For the best result, the batter should be used within 30 minutes. If you know you will not be able to use the batter right away, whip just one egg white and add to half the batter at a time.

Try this delicious combination when fresh blackberries, or any of the hybrids such as boysenberries or loganberries, are available.

1. Follow the recipe and instructions for plum fritters using fresh peaches or nectarines instead of plums. Cut the fruit into ¾-inch (2-cm) wedges and allow five pieces per serving.

2. Serve with Blackberry Sauce, made by using the recipe for Raspberry Sauce on page 563, substituting blackberries for raspberries.

3. Presentation: Arrange five warm fritters in a half circle on one side of a dessert plate. Pour a small pool of Blackberry Sauce in front and decorate the sauce with Sour Cream Mixture for Piping (see page 564 for the recipe and pages 518–519 for decorating instructions). Serve immediately.

1. Roll out the puff paste to a rectangle, 14 × 17½ inches (35 × 43.7 cm) and ¼ inch (6 mm) thick. Trim the edges if necessary. Let the dough rest in the refrigerator for 30 minutes.

2. Cut the puff paste into 3½-inch (8.7-cm) squares. It is important that the dough is firm and that you use a sharp knife. As you cut, be sure to hold the knife at a 90° angle so that your cuts are straight.

3. Brush the squares with egg wash, being careful not to let any drip down the sides, which can keep the paste from puffing. Lightly score the tops with parallel lines, marking diagonally in both directions.

4. Place the squares on sheet pans lined with baking paper. Bake at 425°F (219°C) for approximately 12 minutes. Lower the heat to 375°F (190°C) and continue baking until dark golden brown and dried all the way through. Set aside to cool.

5. Cut the fresh fruit into pieces the size of raspberries (see step 3 in recipe for Florentina Cones with Seasonal Fruit, page 282).

fresh fruit
powdered sugar
1 recipe Cold Sabayon, made with
   champagne (page 398)
1 recipe Vanilla Bavarian Cream
   (page 570)
Chocolate Sauce for Piping
   (page 560)
mint sprigs

6. Cut off the top third of the baked pastry squares. Place the "lids" on a separate pan and lightly sift powdered sugar over them.

7. One half hour before serving, make the sabayon and reserve in the refrigerator.

8. Presentation: Pipe a small amount of Bavarian cream (about 1½ ounce/40 g) on top of a "bottom" puff paste square. At the same time pipe a small dot in the center of a dessert plate. Fill the pastry square with cut fruit, arranging it on top of the cream. Place the square on top of the dot of cream on the plate to prevent it from sliding. Pour a little less than 2 ounces (60 ml) of sabayon over the fruit and on to the plate in front of the pastry. Sprinkle a little additional fruit on top of the sauce in the center. Place a "lid" on top at an angle so you can see the fruit inside. Use the chocolate sauce to make a decoration in the sabayon (see pages 518–519). Place a mint sprig on the fruit inside the case and serve immediately.

NOTE: The puff paste dough should be made the day before it is used and left to rest overnight, covered, in the refrigerator.

Raspberry Wafers

(see photograph in color insert)
20 servings (approximately sixty
3-inch/7.5-cm wafers)

6 ounces (170 g) toasted hazelnuts
7 ounces (200 g) granulated sugar
4 ounces (115 g) softened butter
½ teaspoon (3 g) salt
¼ cup (60 ml) heavy cream
4 egg whites
2 tablespoons (30 ml) dark rum
4 ounces (115 g) bread flour
Butter and Flour Mixture
   (page 4)
2½ cups (600 ml) heavy cream
1 tablespoon (15 g) granulated
   sugar
3 dry pints (1 l, 440 ml)
   raspberries, approximately
powdered sugar
mint sprigs
Raspberry Sauce (page 563)
Sour Cream Mixture for Piping
   (page 564)

1. Grind the hazelnuts with half of the sugar to a fine consistency. Cream the butter with the remaining sugar and mix in the ground nuts, salt, and ¼ cup (60 ml) cream. Add the egg whites and rum. Sift the flour and incorporate it into the batter. Let the batter rest for 1 hour.

2. Meanwhile make the Raspberry Wafer template (Figure 10–11). The template as shown is the correct size required for this recipe. Trace the drawing, then cut the template out of ⅙-inch (2-mm) thick cardboard (cake boxes work fine for this). Brush the butter and flour mixture on the back of clean, even sheet pans.

3. Spread the batter onto the prepared sheet pans, spreading it flat and even within the template (see Figures 18–47 and 18–48, page 548). Adjust the consistency by adding more flour if needed (it should not be runny).

4. Bake at 410°F (210°C) until slightly brown at the edges, approximately 6 minutes. Allow the wafers to cool before removing them from the pans.

5. Assemble the wafers within 30 minutes before serving. Whip the 2½ cups (600 ml) of heavy cream with 1 tablespoon (15 g) sugar to stiff peaks. Place in a pastry bag with a no. 4 (8 mm) star tip. Use three wafers per serving: Pipe six small rosettes of cream around the edges of two wafers, piping them at

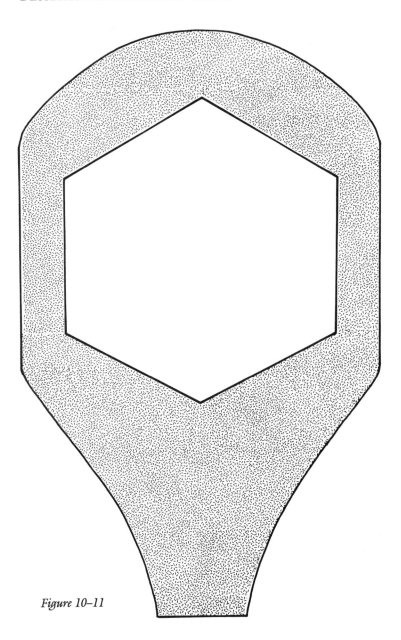

Figure 10–11

the points of the hexagons. Place six raspberries per wafer between the rosettes of cream. Stack one wafer on top of the other, then top with a plain wafer. Sift powdered sugar lightly over the top layer of the stacked wafers. Pipe a small rosette of cream in the center on top. Place one raspberry and a mint sprig on the cream.

6. Presentation: Pipe a dot of whipped cream in the center of a dessert plate and carefully set a wafer stack on top. Pour just enough Raspberry Sauce in front of the wafers to cover half of the plate, then decorate the sauce with the Sour Cream Mixture for Piping (see pages 518–519). For a more dramatic presentation, sift the powdered sugar over the wafer stack after you put it on the plate (before you add the sauce), sifting sugar over the entire plate at the same time. Pour the sauce around the dessert. The sugar will melt into the sauce but will remain on the rim of the plate as a border. Be careful not to get fingerprints on the rim when serving.

Rum Babas

30 servings

Rum Syrup (recipe follows)
2 ounces (55 g) dark raisins
Butter and Flour Mixture
*   (page 4)*
Baba Dough (recipe follows)
½ cup (120 ml) heavy cream
1 teaspoon (5 g) granulated sugar
strawberries

Babas are traditionally made in small, thimble-shaped forms about 3 inches (7.5 cm) deep and 1¾ inches (4.5 cm) wide. They are usually soaked in a delicious rum syrup so you can hardly eat one without a bib, glazed with apricot jam, and decorated with a cherry. In France babas are sold as a hand-held pastry in a paper cup. I have adapted a slightly different version that is more appropriate as a restaurant dessert.

1. Reserve a third of the rum syrup for the sauce. Add the raisins to the remainder of the syrup and set aside to plump.

2. Brush the butter and flour mixture on the inside of thirty 2-ounce (60-ml) brioche forms. Reserve.

3. Place the baba dough in a pastry bag with a no. 7 (14-mm) plain tip. Pipe the batter into the reserved forms, filling each half full. Let the babas rise until they fill the forms. Make sure they have proofed enough or the baked babas will not be able to absorb enough syrup.

4. Bake at 400°F (205°C) until golden brown and baked through, about 15 minutes. Remove from the forms as soon as possible and let cool.

5. Cut the crust from the top of the babas, making them flat at the same time.

6. Heat the rum syrup and raisin mixture to scalding. Remove the plumped raisins with a slotted spoon and reserve for decoration. Place a few babas at a time in the hot syrup. Push them down and let them soak long enough to absorb as much of the syrup as they can. Cut one in half to see whether it is soaked all the way through. Carefully remove the babas from the syrup and place them on a cooling rack set over a sheet pan to drain. Reheat the syrup, if necessary, while you soak the remaining babas.

7. Whip the cream and sugar to stiff peaks. Place in a pastry bag with a no. 6 (12-mm) star tip.

8. Presentation: Place a baba in the middle of a dessert plate. Pour enough of the reserved rum syrup on top of the baba so it runs down and covers the plate. Sprinkle a few of the reserved raisins in the sauce. Pipe a rosette of whipped cream on top of the baba and decorate the cream with a small wedge of strawberry.

Baba Dough

2 pounds, 12 ounces (1 kg, 250 g) dough

⅔ ounce (20 g) fresh compressed yeast
¾ cup (180 ml) warm milk (105°–115°F/40°–46°C)
7 ounces (200 g) bread flour
6 eggs
1 teaspoon (5 ml) vanilla extract
½ teaspoon (3 g) salt
8 ounces (225 g) softened butter
10 ounces (285 g) cake flour
3 ounces (85 g) dark raisins

1. Dissolve the yeast in the warm milk. Stir in 4 ounces (115 g) of the bread flour and mix until you have a smooth, soft sponge. Let rise, covered, in a warm place until the sponge starts to bubble and fall.
2. Mix the eggs, vanilla extract, salt, and butter into the sponge. Add the remaining bread flour and the cake flour. Mix until it becomes a soft, smooth paste. Mix in the raisins.

Rum Syrup

2 quarts (1 l, 920 ml)

5 cups (1 l, 200 ml) water
2 pounds (910 g) granulated sugar
1 orange (with skin), quartered
1 cup (240 ml) light rum

1. Place the water, sugar, and orange in a saucepan. Bring to a boil and cook for about two minutes, until all of the sugar has dissolved.
2. Remove from the heat, strain, and add the rum.

Savarins

18 individual pastries or two savarin rings serving 8 to 10 each

Butter and Flour Mixture (page 4)
1 recipe Baba Dough (this page), without raisins
12 seedless mandarins
Orange Syrup (recipe follows)
3 cups (720 ml) or ½ recipe Mandarin Sorbet (page 366)
mint sprigs

Savarins are simply babas in a different shape, without raisins. They are typically made in individual doughnut-shaped ring molds, but it is very practical to make a large ring to serve 8 to 10 people. Present the larger savarin whole on a silver tray decorated with scoops of sorbet before it is cut and plated. To make a large savarin, use a 3½-cup (840-ml) mold.

1. Brush the butter and flour mixture on the inside of eighteen 3½-ounce (105-ml) capacity ring molds or two 3½-cup (840-ml) molds.
2. Place the dough in a pastry bag with a no. 7 (14-mm) plain tip. Pipe the dough into the forms, filling each half full. Let the savarins rise until they have doubled in volume. Do not take any

short cut here: A savarin that has not been left to proof properly will not be able to absorb enough liquid and will be dry and unpleasant to eat.

3. Bake at 400°F (205°C) until golden brown and baked through, about 25 minutes (40 minutes for the larger size). Remove from the forms as soon as possible and let cool on a cooling rack.

4. Peel the mandarins by hand and remove any white pith clinging to the fruit. Separate the segments by pulling them apart with your hands. (Do not cut mandarin segments from the membrane with a knife, as you would oranges.) Reserve.

5. Cut the crust from the top of the savarins, making them flat at the same time.

6. Reserve one-third of the orange syrup to use for the sauce. Heat the remaining orange syrup to scalding. Place a few savarins at a time in the hot syrup, push them down into the syrup, and let them soak long enough to absorb as much of the syrup as possible before carefully removing them. Place on a cooling rack set over a sheet pan to drain. Reheat the syrup, if necessary, while you soak the remaining savarins. (If you are making the larger savarin, place it directly on the cooling rack after trimming the crust and spoon the hot syrup evenly over the top until you are sure it has penetrated all the way through. Let the savarin drain, then use two metal spatulas to carefully place it on a serving tray.)

7. Presentation: Place a savarin (flat-side down) in the center of a dessert plate. Pour enough of the reserved orange syrup over the pastry to cover the plate. Place a small scoop of Mandarin Sorbet in the center of the ring. Decorate the sorbet with a mint sprig. Place six mandarin segments in the sauce around the savarin. Or, omit the sorbet and fill the center of the ring with mandarin segments instead of using them in the sauce.

Orange Syrup
2 quarts (1 l, 920 ml)

5 cups (1 l, 200 ml) water
2 pounds (910 g) granulated sugar
1 orange (with skin), quartered
1 cup (240 ml) orange liqueur

1. Place the water, sugar, and orange in a saucepan. Bring to a boil and cook for about two minutes to ensure that all of the sugar has melted.

2. Remove from the heat, strain, and add the orange liqueur.

Small Pear Tartlets with Caramel Sauce

(see photograph in color insert)
24 servings

12 medium-sized pears
2½ quarts (2 l, 400 ml) or
    2 recipes Poaching Syrup I
    (page 6)
5 pounds (2 kg, 275 g) or ½ recipe
    Classic Puff Paste (page 21)
8 ounces (225 g) Pastry Cream
    (page 569)
8 ounces (225 g) Mazarin Filling
    (page 569)
Cinnamon Sugar (page 4)
Apricot Glaze (page 526)
2 recipes Caramel Sauce II
    (page 558)
Chocolate Sauce for Piping
    (page 560)
1½ cups (360 ml) Crème Fraîche
    (page 559)
strawberries or raspberries

1. Peel, core, and cut the pears in half, placing them in acidulated water as you work to prevent them from browning. Poach the pear halves in poaching syrup until soft. Take care not to overcook or they will become difficult to work with. Remove from the syrup and cool.

2. Roll out the puff paste slightly thicker than ⅛ inch (3 mm) and as square as possible. Refrigerate the dough until firm. Using a sharp knife, cut out rectangles 5 × 3 inches (12.5 × 7.5 cm) and place them on sheet pans lined with baking paper.

3. While the dough is still firm (you may need to refrigerate some of the rectangles while you are working), cut halfway through to make a smaller rectangle within each one, leaving a ¼-inch (6-mm) border (Figure 10–12). Do not cut all the way through the dough. Prick the inside rectangle.

4. Combine the pastry cream and mazarin filling. Place in a pastry bag with a no. 2 (4 mm) plain tip. Pipe a layer of the cream over the inside rectangle. [If you do not have mazarin filling on hand you can use 4 ounces (115 g) of almond paste instead, and increase the pastry cream by the same amount. Mix the pastry cream into the almond paste gradually to avoid lumps.]

5. If needed, trim the width of the pears to fit within the puff paste frame. Slice the pears crosswise into thin slices. Arrange four to five overlapping slices at each end of the rectangles, meeting in the center to form a butterfly. Sprinkle a small amount of cinnamon sugar over the top.

6. Bake at 375°F (190°C) about 35 minutes or until the puff paste is golden brown. Brush apricot glaze over the tartlets once they have cooled.

7. Presentation: Heat the caramel sauce and keep it warm over hot water. Place a tart on a warmed dessert plate. Pour caramel sauce around the tart, covering the plate. Spoon 1 tablespoon (15 ml) crème fraîche in the center, on top of the tart. Place a small wedge of strawberry or a raspberry next to the cream. Decorate the edge of the caramel sauce with the chocolate sauce (see pages 518–519). Serve immediately.

Variations

Rectangles are not only the fastest shape to make, they also give you the least amount of leftover dough. However, if you have a use for scrap dough or if you are only making a few tarts, make them in round or pear shapes. To make round tarts, cut the dough using the inside fluted circle left over from making the large Tulip template (see Figure 18–46, page 547); then cut halfway through on the inside using a fluted cookie cutter that is slightly smaller to make a frame. Prick the dough inside the frame, then pipe on the cream. Using half a pear for each tart, arrange the pear slices in overlapping circles, starting at the edge and building slightly higher in the center; continue as for rectangles.

For pear-shaped tarts, make the pear-shaped template (Figure 10–13). The template as shown is the correct size for this recipe. Trace the drawing, then cut the template out of ¹⁄₁₆-inch (2-mm) cardboard (cake boxes are ideal for this purpose). Cut the puff paste using the template as a guide (Figure 10–14, page 296). Cut again halfway through ½ inch (1.2 cm) from the edge to create a frame. Prick the dough inside the frame, then pipe on the cream as directed above. Slice the pear halves, fan the slices slightly, and place them on the cream (Figure 10–15). Continue as for rectangles. (It also looks nice to slice the pear halves lengthwise, starting just below the neck of the pear, so the slices are still attached at the top.)

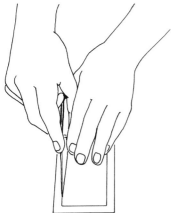

Figure 10–12

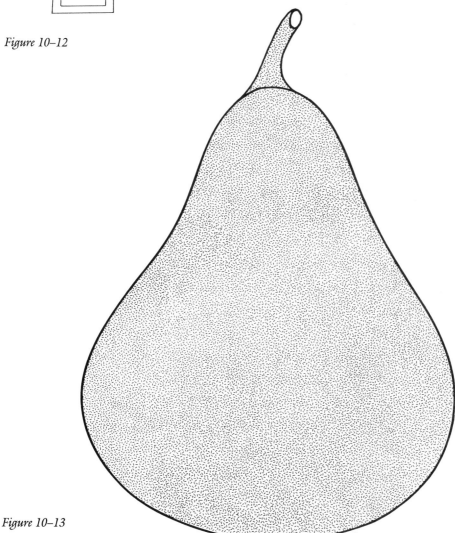

Figure 10–13

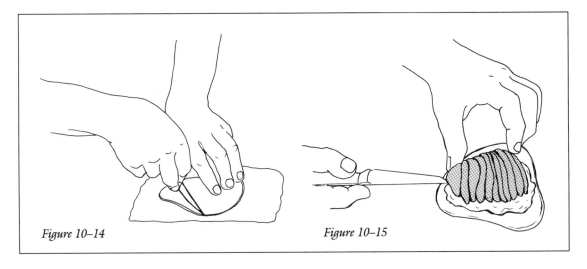

Figure 10–14   *Figure 10–15*

Small Swedish Pancakes
(Plättar)
14 servings

6 eggs
1 ounce (30 g) granulated sugar
1 cup (240 ml) heavy cream
7 ounces (200 g) cake flour
3½ cups (840 ml) milk
1 teaspoon (5 g) salt
1 teaspoon (5 ml) vanilla extract
6 ounces (170 g) melted
   clarified butter
½ cup (120 ml) heavy cream
1 teaspoon (5 g) granulated sugar
powdered sugar
8 ounces (225 g) lingonberry jam
mint sprigs

These delicious little pancakes are so tender that they seem to just dissolve on your tongue as you eat them. Being so delicate, they would be impossible to handle if they were made the same size as a standard pancake. *Plättar* are traditionally enjoyed in Sweden after the yellow pea soup on Thursdays. Served warm, dusted with powdered sugar and topped with lingonberries, they make an un-usual light dessert. Or, try them on your breakfast or brunch table.

I remember how the American passengers fell in love with Swedish pancakes when I was working on the Swedish American Lines cruise ships in the sixties. One woman in particular was so enamored that she asked the pastry kitchen to make her a special order so she could attach them to her dress and go to the masquerade ball as a small Swedish pancake!

Plättar should, if at all possible, be made to order. If you must make them ahead, you can keep them covered in a low oven (200°F/94°C) for a short time.

1. Beat the eggs with 1 ounce (30 g) sugar for about 2 minutes to blend well.

2. Mix in 1 cup (240 ml) heavy cream and the flour to make a smooth paste.

3. Warm the milk to body temperature, and gradually add to the egg mixture along with the salt, vanilla extract, and butter. The batter will be quite thin.

4. Whip the ½ cup (120 ml) of heavy cream with the 1 teaspoon (5 g) of sugar to stiff peaks. Place in a pastry bag with a no. 6 (12-mm) star tip. Reserve in the refrigerator.

5. Heat the *plättiron* (the traditional Swedish sectional pancake pan; see page 604) or a pancake griddle or cast-iron skillet large enough to accommodate at least five 3-inch (7.5-cm) pancakes until it is hot enough that a small drop of water evaporates instantly when it touches the surface.

6. Pour 1 ounce (30 ml) of the batter into each depression in the pan. The iron does not need to be greased due to the large amount of butter in the batter (if you are using a skillet, it may need to be greased for the first batch). Turn the pancakes using a narrow metal spatula as soon as they become light brown on the bottom, about 1 minute. Cook for approximately 1 minute longer to brown the other side. Turning the pancakes takes some practice: It has to be done very rapidly as the batter is not completely set at this point and the pancakes are very tender.

7. Quickly transfer the pancakes to a warm plate and keep them covered if it is necessary to make additional *Plättar*. Make sure that the iron does not get too hot or you will risk burning the last few pancakes. This recipe requires quick action even with the iron at the correct temperature. Try the technique of stacking two or three pancakes before removing them from the pan.

8. Presentation: Arrange five *Plättar* in a circle on a dessert plate, overlapping them just enough to leave a small opening in the center. Sift powdered sugar on top of the pancakes and over the exposed part of the plate. Spoon a small dot of lingonberry jam, the size of a hazelnut, in the center of each pancake. Pipe a rosette of whipped cream in the center of the plate. Decorate with a sprig of mint and serve immediately.

Strawberry Pyramids
(see photograph in color insert)
16 pastries

one 14- × 24-inch (35- × 60-cm)
   Almond Sponge (page 162)
granulated sugar
25 to 30 medium-sized strawberries
1 recipe Kirsch Whipped Cream
   (page 218)
Strawberry Sauce (page 563)
Sour Cream Mixture for Piping
   (page 564)
16 fanned strawberry halves
mint sprigs

To make the pyramids you will need a triangular form 24 inches (60 cm) long with an inside diameter of approximately 3½ × 3½ inches (8.7 × 8.7 cm). If you do not have one you can make a temporary form using cardboard (directions follow). If the sponge sheet has been refrigerated and seems a little sticky (wet) on top, leave it out at room temperature long enough to prevent it from adhering to the form.

1. Sprinkle the top of the sponge lightly with granulated sugar. Pick the sponge up by the paper and invert on top of another piece of baking paper. Carefully peel the paper from the back of the sponge and trim it to 12 inches (30 cm) wide. Again, picking up the sponge by the paper, place it inside the triangular mold with

the paper against the mold and one long edge even with one long edge of the form. Support the top one-third of the sponge that is outside of the form with a rolling pin or some cans. If necessary, add a piece of sponge at the end to line the full 24 inches (60 cm) of the form.

2. Clean the strawberries and cut off both the stem ends and approximately ¼ inch (6 mm) of the tips (save the tips for sauce). Line the strawberries up end-to-end on their sides next to the form, to determine how many you need and to make the assembly go quicker.

3. Pour the Kirsch Whipped Cream into the sponge-lined form to fill it halfway. Quickly place the strawberries on the cream (end-to-end with the cut sides touching). Top with the remaining cream. You may have a small amount of the cream left over depending on the thickness of the sponge and the size of the strawberries: Do not overfill the form. Fold the supported sponge over the top and trim off any excess. Refrigerate for at least 2 hours.

4. Cut the ends loose from the mold, unmold the pyramid onto a cardboard or inverted sheet pan and remove the paper. Slice into sixteen servings. Arrange the pastries standing up, seam-side down. Heat a metal skewer by holding it against an electric burner or in a gas flame. Quickly use the skewer to mark four horizontal lines on both sides of each pastry by caramelizing the sugar.

5. Presentation: Place a slice, off-center, on a dessert plate (standing on end). Pour a pool of Strawberry Sauce in front on the larger uncovered space. Decorate the sauce with the sour cream mixture (see pages 518–519). Place a mint sprig and a fanned strawberry half behind the dessert.

Making a triangular cardboard form

1. See Figure 10–16. Cut a sturdy piece of cardboard 24 × 7 inches (60 × 17.5 cm). Score (cut halfway through the thickness of the cardboard) a line lengthwise down the center to make it easier to bend the cardboard. Turn the cardboard sheet upside down so the score is on the bottom, then bend the cardboard along the line and tape the top so that the opening is 3½ inches (8.7 cm) wide.

2. Cut out two triangles of cardboard 3½ inches (8.7 cm) on all sides. Tape the triangles to the ends of the form, and remove the tape on the top.

3. Cut out two pieces of cardboard 12 inches (30 cm) long and 4 inches (10 cm) wide. Score a cut in the center (lengthwise) on each piece; turn upside down and fold. Tape the folded pieces to the sides of the form for support.

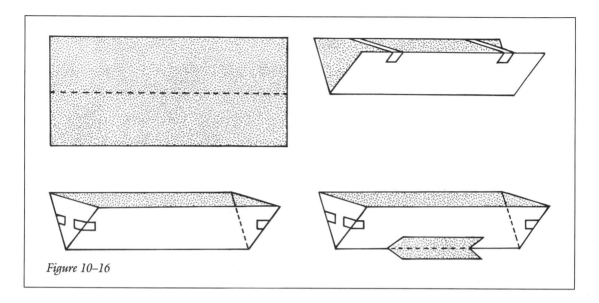

Figure 10–16

Swedish Profiteroles

28 servings (about 84 profiteroles)

*8 ounces (225 g) Short Dough
(page 31)*
3 ounces (85 g) granulated sugar
*1 pound, 5 ounces (595 g) or ½
recipe Pâte à Choux (page 6)*
*2 pounds (910 g) or 1 recipe
Vanilla Bavarian Cream
(page 570)*
powdered sugar
*6 cups (1 l, 440 ml) or 1½ recipes
Cold Chocolate Sauce
(page 559)*
*Sour Cream Mixture for Piping
(page 564)*
*thinly sliced strawberries, plums,
apricots, or kiwis*

1. Mix the granulated sugar into the short dough. Roll the dough to ¹⁄₁₆ inch (2 mm) thick and cut out circles using a 1¼-inch (3.1-cm) cookie cutter. Set aside.

2. Place the pâte à choux in a pastry bag with a no. 4 (8-mm) plain tip. Pipe out mounds 1 inch (2.5 cm) in diameter onto sheet pans lined with baking paper. The profiteroles should be about the size of golf balls when baked. Do not place more than 24 to 30 on a pan. Place a short dough circle on each mound and press lightly with your fingers to be sure they stick (see note). The short dough circles must be placed on the pâte à choux as soon as you have piped out one pan or the batter will form a skin and the short dough will not stick.

3. Bake the profiteroles at 400°F (205°C) until puffed, about 10 minutes. Reduce heat to 375°F (190°C) and bake until they will hold their shapes, about 10 minutes longer. Let the puffs cool completely.

4. Make a small slit in the bottom of each puff just large enough to insert the pastry tip. Put the Bavarian cream in a pastry bag with a no. 3 (6-mm) plain tip and pipe it into the profiteroles. Dust the tops lightly with powdered sugar.

5. Presentation: Sift powdered sugar lightly over a dessert plate. Pour just under ¼ cup (60 ml) of chocolate sauce on the plate. The sauce should be thin enough to spread over the bottom of the plate. Place three profiteroles together in the center of the sauce. Pipe the sour cream mixture in a thin ring around the

profiteroles and curl it (see Figure 18–23, page 518). Decorate with small, thin slices of fruit at the edge of the plate, on top of the powdered sugar but not in the sauce (take care not to get any fingerprints on the rim while serving).

NOTE: The profiteroles can be frozen after they have been piped out and topped with the cookies. Bake straight from the freezer without thawing. I try to place them in the freezer long enough to harden even when they are to be baked right away because they seem to puff up better if baked frozen.

Variation: Maria Puffs

The Swedish Profiteroles recipe was developed from a typical Swedish pastry known as *Maria Bollar* or Maria Puffs. To make the original version, omit the chocolate sauce and the sour cream mixture and follow the preceding recipe with these changes: Use a cookie cutter slightly larger than 2 inches (5 cm) for the short dough. Pipe out 30 mounds of pâte à choux 2 inches (5 cm) in diameter and ¾ inch (2 cm) high. Follow the same procedure for baking except for time; these will take a bit longer. When they are cold, fill the puffs, dust lightly with powdered sugar, and place in paper cups.

Toasted Panettone with Mascarpone Sauce

(see photograph in color insert)
16 servings

*½ recipe Italian Easter Bread
    (panettone) dough (page 62)*
16 small fresh figs
*5 cups (1 l, 200 ml) or 1 recipe
    Poaching Syrup II (page 6)*
*4 cups (960 ml) or 1 recipe
    Mascarpone Sauce (page 561)*
*2 ounces (55 g) Candied Orange
    Peel, chopped (page 520)*
mint sprigs

1. Follow steps 2, 3, and 4 for Italian Easter Bread.

2. Divide the dough into two pieces. Pound and roll each piece into an oval loaf 9 inches (22.5 cm) long. Leave the ends rounded so the loaves are shaped like sausages. Place the loaves on a sheet pan lined with baking paper. Follow the instructions for proofing, baking, and decorating, omitting the almonds in the decoration.

3. Poach the figs in poaching syrup until soft, approximately 5 minutes. Leave them to cool in the liquid. (If the figs are really ripe you may not need to poach them.)

4. When the panettone loaves have cooled, trim off the ends, then cut each into sixteen ⅜-inch (9-mm) slices. Place on a sheet pan and lightly toast the slices in a 450°F (230°C) oven. The toast should be crisp on the outside but still soft in the center.

5. Presentation: Place two slices of toast in the center of a dessert plate. Pour about ¼ cup (60 ml) of the Mascarpone Sauce over one-third of each slice, letting it run out into an even pool on the plate in front of the dessert. Sprinkle candied orange peel on top of the sauce. Cut a fig in half and place the pieces, with the cut sides up, next to each other beside the sauce. Decorate with a sprig of mint.

NOTE: When figs are not available, I substitute three orange segments, placed in a fan shape, on one side of the toast.

Tropical Surprise Packages

(see photograph in color insert)
20 servings

Tamarind Parfait (recipe follows)
1 recipe Pirouettes batter
*   (page 138)*
1 teaspoon (2.5 g) cocoa powder
about 8 medium-sized kiwi fruit
4 cups (960 ml) or 1 recipe
*   Mango Sauce (page 560)*
Chocolate Sauce for Piping
*   (page 560)*

1. Make a rectangular frame measuring 12 × 9 inches (30 × 22.5 cm) from cardboard cut into 1½-inch (3.7-cm) wide strips. Tape the strips together at the corners. Place the frame on a sheet pan, or on a sheet of cardboard, and line the bottom and sides with plastic wrap.

2. Pour the Tamarind Parfait into the frame, and place in the freezer to harden.

3. Make the template (Figure 10–17) using ¹⁄₁₆ inch (2 mm) thick cardboard (cake boxes are ideal for this). The template as shown is the correct size for use in this recipe. However, due to the size of this template it is possible to show only half of it on the page. Trace the template as shown, then turn your paper over, match the dotted lines in the center, and trace the other half to make the shape shown in the illustration. Lightly grease and flour the back of even sheet pans; reserve.

4. Color about 2 ounces (60 ml) of the Pirouettes batter with the cocoa powder. Set aside.

5. Spread the remaining batter on the reserved sheet pans using the template as a guide, spreading the batter thin, flat, and even within the template (see Figures 18–47 and 18–48, page 548). Place the cocoa-colored batter in a piping bag. Pipe a design (which will look like ribbons tying the package closed) on each one by first piping straight lines in the center, the full length of the cross in both directions, then piping a bow where the lines meet; reserve in the refrigerator. You can prepare the "wrappers" up to this point several hours ahead of time if desired.

6. Once the Tamarind Parfait has frozen firm, cut it into 2¼-inch (5.6-cm) squares using a knife dipped in hot water. Place the squares back in the freezer and remove them individually as you are ready to wrap the packages.

7. Bake the prepared Pirouette batter at 400°F (205°C) until the wrappers start to turn golden brown at the edges, approximately 5 minutes. Do not overbake (see note). Remove from the oven and quickly turn them, one at a time, upside down onto the table. Place a reserved parfait square in the center of a cookie. Quickly wrap the three short sides around the square, then fold the long side on top of these. Place the package back in the freezer and assemble the remainder in the same way. The wrapped packages will stay crisp in the freezer for days; keep them well covered.

8. Peel the kiwifruit using a vegetable peeler or small knife, removing only the skin and keeping the natural shape of the kiwi (or use the method described on page 583). Cut in half lengthwise. Place the halves cut-side down and cut into thin slices (you should get 7 or 8 slices from each half). It is preferable to use kiwis that are firm and slightly underripe than to use overripe fruit, as it is impossible to cut a soft kiwi into thin slices.

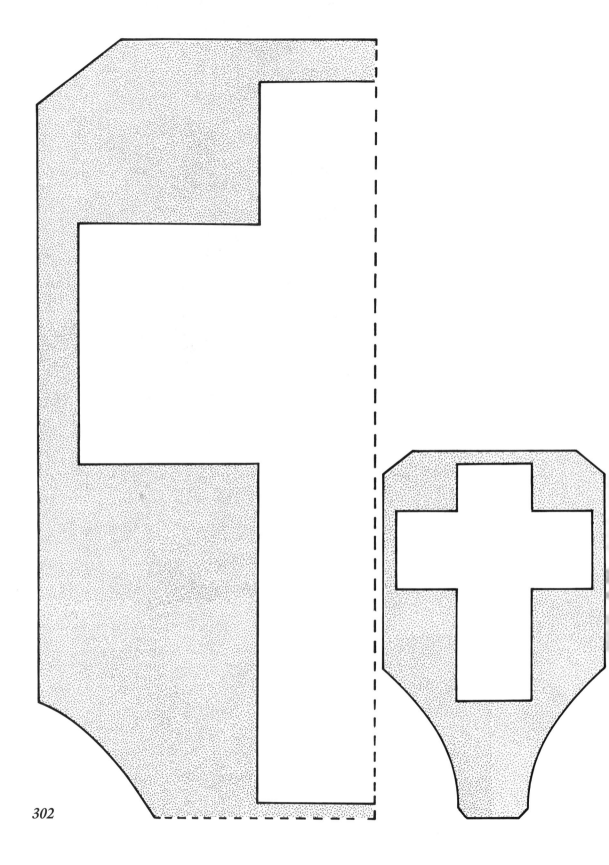

9. Presentation: Pour just enough Mango Sauce on a dessert plate to cover the surface. Place six kiwi slices around the rim of the plate next to the sauce. Decorate the edge of the Mango Sauce with the Chocolate Sauce for Piping (see pages 518–519). Place one of the Tropical Surprise Packages in the center of the sauce; serve immediately.

NOTE: If the wrappers are left in the oven too long, because you either overbaked them or baked them at too low a temperature, they will crumble and fall apart before you have had a chance to cover the parfait. The best method is to only bake two or three wrappers at a time so you can form them quickly while they are still warm. If properly baked, the wrappers may be returned to the oven to soften if they should cool off before you can form them.

Tamarind Parfait

12 ounces (340 g) tamarind pods,
approximately
or
6 ounces (170 g) tamarind paste
(see note)
1½ cups (360 ml) hot water
10 ounces (285 g) granulated
sugar
3 ounces (90 ml) water
10 egg yolks
2½ cups (600 ml) heavy cream

1. Peel the tamarind pods and remove the seeds and the stringy membranes from the flesh. Cut the flesh into chunks and place in a bowl. Cover with the hot water and leave to soak for a few hours or, if possible, overnight.

2. Transfer the mixture to a saucepan and cook over low heat until it reaches a fairly thick consistency, approximately 10 minutes. Press as much as possible through a fine sieve and set it aside to cool; discard the contents of the sieve.

3. In a heavy saucepan, dissolve two thirds of the sugar in the 3 ounces (90 ml) water. Bring to a boil and cook to 240°F (115°C) on a sugar thermometer. While the syrup is cooking, whip the egg yolks and the remaining sugar until light and fluffy. Lower the mixer speed and gradually pour the hot syrup into the yolk mixture. Whip at medium speed until cold. Whip heavy cream to soft peaks. Add the cooled tamarind purée to the yolk mixture; gradually fold this combination into the heavy cream.

NOTE: If you are using the more convenient tamarind paste, rather than the tamarind pods, you will need to reduce the sugar in the recipe by about half, as the paste is usually prepared with sugar. The amount varies depending on the brand used.

Charlottes and Bavarois, Custards, Mousses, and Soufflés

Charlottes and Bavarois
  Apple Rum Charlotte
  Apricot Bavarois
  Charlotte Charente
  Pear Charlotte
  White Chocolate Bavarois
    with Macadamia and
    Pistachio Nuts
Custards
  Brandy Bread Pudding
  Crème Caramel with Ginger
  Chocolate Rum Pudding
  Crème Brûlée
  Lingonberry Cheese Pudding
  Riz à la Malta

Trifle with Fresh Fruit
Vanilla Pots de Crème
Mousses
  Chocolate Mousse in
    Chocolate Teardrops
  Cupid's Treasure Chest
  Raspberry–White Chocolate
    Mousse
  Triple Chocolate Terrine
Soufflés
  Blueberry Soufflé
  Crepe Soufflé
  Grand Marnier Soufflé
  Pecan-Raisin Soufflé

The chief similarity of the desserts in this chapter is that they all contain eggs, but they are totally different in technique and presentation. Custards are simple to prepare, can be made one to two days in advance, and need little or no finishing touches. When the custard is to be unmolded, a ratio of two yolks per cup of liquid is required; an example of this is crème caramel. If a thinner, more fragile consistency is desired, one yolk per cup of liquid is the norm. These custards are then presented in their baking cups, as in pots de crème and crème brûlée. Custards are generally baked in individual earthenware cups, but can be made in larger ovenproof dishes to serve on a buffet. A custard should always be placed in a pan with at least 1 inch of hot water around it, and then baked at 350°F (175°C) to avoid overcooking, which would result in watery and curdled custard.

Mousses are made in a variety of flavors, with the old standby chocolate mousse being the most common. They do not require any cooking. Instead, air is whipped into eggs and cream to make them light and smooth, and then a thickening agent (chocolate in the case of chocolate mousse, gelatin for a fruit mousse) is added. A mousse is generally piped into a glass or other individual serving dish and left to set up in the refrigerator. A mousse should be just thick enough that a rosette of whipped cream can be piped on top for decoration without sinking into the mousse.

By comparison, just enough additional gelatin is added to the filling of a charlotte so the dessert can hold its shape when unmolded. The filling, called a bavarois, is then put into a lined mold. The molds are lined with sliced jelly rolls in charlotte royal, and with ladyfingers in charlotte russe, to name two of the most well-known varieties. The filled molds are left to set up in the refrigerator, then unmolded directly onto the serving plate.

The bavarois filling, which could be described as an unbaked custard, is an excellent dessert by itself, chilled and unmolded like the charlotte, but made in unlined forms. Both the charlotte and the bavarois can be kept several days in the refrigerator, provided they are well covered in their original molds.

Soufflés have a reputation for being complicated and difficult, and when compared to the desserts described above, this certainly is true. A soufflé requires quick and precise steps; if something goes wrong you usually do not have the opportunity to start over. Timing is essential and requires good cooperation with the dining room: The waiter must know when to "fire" the order and must be there to pick it up at the prescribed time. It is said that "a soufflé is just a sauce that takes a deep breath, and holds it," so you must be sure that the waiter takes the soufflé directly to the customer before it starts to fall. Made and presented correctly, a soufflé is the ultimate "ooh and aah" dessert, rivaled only by the fire shows of baked Alaska.

The most common soufflé variety, the liqueur soufflé, is basically a pastry cream with whipped egg whites and liqueur folded in before baking. The air whipped into the egg whites expands in the oven and makes the soufflé rise. In fruit soufflés, the fruit pulp is first reduced, then added to the pastry cream before the egg whites are folded in. The third soufflé variety, crepe soufflé, combines a thin pancake and a small amount of soufflé batter served on a dessert plate instead of in a ramekin. The sauce is served on the plate, unlike the liqueur and fruit soufflés, in which the sauce is served in a small dish on the side.

Charlottes and Bavarois

Apple Rum Charlotte

(see photograph in color insert)
approximately fifteen 3-ounce (90-ml) servings

4 ounces (115 g) dark raisins
¼ cup (60 ml) dark rum
1½ Brioche loaves (page 85)

1. Combine the raisins and ¼ cup (60 ml) rum. Set aside to macerate for at least 30 minutes.

2. Slice the brioche ⅟₁₆ inch (2 mm) thick (do not use the crust). Use 3-ounce (90-ml) oval forms such as those used for eggs-in-aspic or any other plain (not fluted) forms of the same size. Cut bread slices to fit, dip in melted butter, and line the bottoms and sides of the forms.

12 ounces (340 g) melted butter
Apple Cinnamon Filling
   (recipe follows)
2 tablespoons (30 ml) dark rum
Vanilla Custard Sauce (page 564)
Chocolate Sauce for Piping
   (page 560)
thin apple slices
mint leaves

3. Fill the forms with Apple Cinnamon Filling, mounding the filling slightly. Cut more bread to fit the tops of the filled molds, dip in melted butter, and put in place over the filling to enclose it completely.

4. Bake the charlottes at 400°F (205°C) for approximately 30 minutes, or until the brioche is golden brown (invert one to check). Let the charlottes cool slightly before attempting to unmold them. However, if you leave them until they are completely cold you will have to reheat them slightly or the butter will cause them to stick to the forms. (This dessert should be served warm, or at room temperature; never chilled.)

5. Add the remaining rum to the Vanilla Custard Sauce.

6. Presentation: Pour enough custard sauce on a dessert plate to cover the base of the plate. Decorate the sauce with the Chocolate Sauce for Piping (see pages 518–519). Place an inverted charlotte in the center of the plate, and place two or three apple slices and a mint leaf on top.

NOTE: You can make the full recipe for brioche loaves and reserve the leftover in the freezer to use in bread pudding, for example, or you can use any plain white bread, although a loaf made in a rectangular bread pan would be the most suitable.

Apple Cinnamon Filling
3 pounds (1 kg, 365 g)

3 ounces (85 g) dark raisins
¼ cup (60 ml) dark rum
4 pounds (1 kg, 820 g) cooking
   apples, Granny Smith or
   Golden Delicious
2½ quarts (2 l, 400 ml) or
   2 recipes Poaching Syrup II
   (page 6)
4 ounces (115 g) brown sugar
½ cup (120 ml) reserved
   poaching liquid
juice from 1 lemon
1 ounce (30 g) pectin powder
1 teaspoon (2 g) ground cinnamon

1. Combine the raisins and rum. Set aside to macerate for at least 30 minutes.

2. Peel, core, and cut the apples in half. Cook in the poaching syrup until soft. Drain; reserve ½ cup (120 ml) of the liquid and discard the remainder. Chop the apples into small pieces.

3. Combine the apples, half of the sugar, the reserved poaching liquid, and the lemon juice in a saucepan. Cook over medium heat until the apples start to fall apart. Mix the pectin powder and cinnamon with the remaining sugar and add it to the apple mixture. Continue cooking, adding additional water if necessary to prevent the filling from sticking, until the mixture is reduced to a paste-like consistency. Remove from the heat and stir in the raisin and rum mixture.

Apricot Bavarois

twenty 5-ounce (150-ml) servings

*1½ pounds (680 g) apricots, pitted
    fresh or strained canned*
*5 cups (1 l, 200 ml) or 1 recipe
    Poaching Syrup II (page 6)*
8 egg yolks
2 ounces (55 g) granulated sugar
2 tablespoons (18 g) gelatin powder
½ cup (120 ml) cold water
3 cups (720 ml) heavy cream
*¼ recipe Italian Meringue
    (page 333)*
Apricot Sauce (page 556)
*Chocolate Sauce for Piping
    (page 560)*
10 small apricots

1. Lightly poach the fresh apricots in poaching syrup (if you substitute canned apricots, do not poach them). Purée the apricots, strain the purée, and cook it over low heat, stirring from time to time, until reduced by one third. You should have about 1 cup (240 ml) purée.

2. Whip the egg yolks and sugar to the ribbon stage.

3. Soften the gelatin in cold water and then heat to 110°F (43°C) to dissolve completely. Working quickly, add the gelatin and the yolk mixture to the apricot purée. Cool to about 110°F (43°C).

4. Whip the heavy cream to soft peaks and fold into the meringue. Gradually fold the cooled apricot mixture into the cream mixture.

5. Fill 5-ounce (15-ml) capacity molds and refrigerate to set, about 2 hours.

6. Presentation: Unmold a bavarois to the center of a dessert plate by briefly dipping the mold in hot water. Pour an oval pool of Apricot Sauce in front and pipe the chocolate sauce into the Apricot Sauce to decorate (see pages 518–519). Cut a small apricot in half and slice thin. Place the slices in a half circle behind the bavarois.

Charlotte Charente

20 servings

*1½ recipes Chocolate Ladyfinger
    batter (page 135)*
Charente Bavarois (recipe follows)
1 quart (960 ml) heavy cream
*2 tablespoons (30 g) granulated
    sugar*
*6 cups (1 l, 440 ml) or 1 recipe
    Mousseline Sauce (page 561)*
*2 tablespoons (30 ml)
    cognac or brandy*
*Chocolate Sauce for Piping
    (page 560)*
dark chocolate shavings
small strawberry wedges

1. Place the Ladyfinger batter in a pastry bag with a no. 4 (8-mm) plain tip. Pipe the batter onto two full-sized sheet pans (16 × 24 inches/40 × 60 cm) lined with baking paper, making seven 1¾-inch (4.5-cm) wide strips, the full length of the pans. Each strip should be made up of Ladyfingers close enough together so that they just touch. Pipe left to right and right to left, continuing within the 1¾-inch (4.5-cm) width, so that once the Ladyfingers are baked, they form a solid, wavy strip as illustrated.

2. Bake at 425°F (219°C) for about 10 minutes. Immediately transfer the strips (attached to the paper) to cold sheet pans or the tabletop, to prevent them from drying out as they cool.

3. Line the sides of twenty 3-inch (7.5-cm) diameter soufflé ramekins with strips of waxed paper or plastic to prevent the Ladyfingers from sticking.

4. Trim enough from one long side of each Ladyfinger strip to make them even. Cut each strip into three 8-inch (20-cm) pieces. Fit one strip inside of each of the prepared ramekins, arranging the strip so the trimmed, even edge is in the bottom of the mold, and the flat (bottom) side faces the inside of the mold (Figure 11–1). (You can also use rings, set on a sheet pan lined with baking paper, rather than ramekins.) If you have trouble

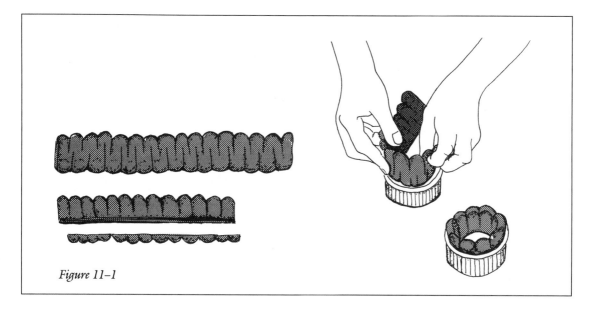

Figure 11–1

bending the strips, follow the directions for softening a roulade sheet on page 163.

5. Divide the bavarois between the lined forms. Refrigerate until set, at least 2 hours.

6. Whip the heavy cream with sugar to stiff peaks. Place in a pastry bag with a no. 4 (8-mm) plain tip. Reserve in the refrigerator.

7. Make the Mousseline Sauce and stir in cognac or brandy. Reserve.

8. Presentation: Unmold a charlotte from the soufflé ramekin by dipping the bottom very briefly into hot water. If you are using rings, simply remove them. Place the charlotte in the center of a dessert plate. Pour enough of the Mousseline Sauce around the dessert to cover the plate. Decorate the Mousseline Sauce with the Chocolate Sauce for Piping (see pages 518–519). Pipe dots of whipped cream, the size of hazelnuts, on top of the charlotte, covering the entire surface. Decorate the whipped cream with shaved chocolate and a small strawberry wedge.

Variation: Charlotte Russe

Follow the instructions for lining the forms with Ladyfingers, as described; then fill the molds with Classic Chocolate Bavarian Cream (see page 567). Follow the same presentation instructions given with Charlotte Charente.

Charente Bavarois

2 quarts (1 l, 920 ml) bavarois or
sixteen 4-ounce (120-ml) servings

3 ounces (85 g) currants
1 cup (240 ml) port wine
8 egg yolks
¼ cup (60 ml) Simple Syrup
  (page 7)
1 pint (480 ml) heavy cream
¼ cup (60 ml) cognac or brandy
1 tablespoon (9 g) unflavored
  gelatin powder
¼ recipe Italian Meringue
  (page 333)

Variation

1. Macerate the currants in one-quarter of the port wine, preferably the day before, but at least several hours before proceeding with the recipe.

2. Whip the egg yolks and simple syrup until light and fluffy.

3. Whip the cream to soft peaks.

4. Add the cognac or brandy to the remaining port. Soften the gelatin in the mixture. Heat to 130°F (54°C) to dissolve the gelatin. Quickly incorporate the gelatin and wine mixture into the egg yolk mixture. Fold this into the whipped cream, then fold in the Italian meringue and the macerated currants, including the port.

NOTE: Do not make the Charente Bavarois until you are ready to fill the molds.

Charente Bavarois can be served as a dessert by itself. Omit the ladyfingers and pipe the mixture into small individual molds. Unmold when set and decorate with a small rosette of whipped cream.

Pear Charlotte

(see photograph in color insert)
eighteen servings

5 medium-sized pears
5 cups (1 l, 200 ml) or 1 recipe
  Poaching Syrup II (page 6)
1 pound, 4 ounces (570 g)
  granulated sugar
1 pint (480 ml) water,
  approximately
Pear Bavarois (recipe follows)
¾ cup (180 ml) heavy cream
1 teaspoon (5 g) granulated sugar
strawberry wedges

1. Peel the pears. Poach in poaching syrup until they are soft. Set aside to cool.

2. Caramelize the first measure of sugar to a dark brown color (see page 488). Immediately add the water and cook out any lumps that form. Be careful of spattering when you add the water. Remove from the heat and let cool. Thin the caramel, if necessary, by adding some additional water. The caramel should be the consistency of simple syrup.

3. Remove the pears from the poaching liquid, core, and cut in half lengthwise. Slice the pear halves into thin slices crosswise, using just the wider part of the pears. Put the pear slices in the thinned caramel, cover, and set aside to macerate at room temperature. Start macerating the pears at least 4 hours before you assemble the desserts, or preferably the day before, to ensure that the pear slices absorb the color and flavor of the caramel.

4. Remove the pear slices from the liquid and pat dry with paper towels. Strain the liquid through a fine mesh strainer and reserve for the sauce.

5. Line the sides of eighteen 5-ounce (150-ml) pots de crème cups using four or five pear slices for each one, evenly spaced, in a tulip pattern (Figure 11–2). If pots de crème cups are not available, any form that has a similar shape and is smooth inside can be used.

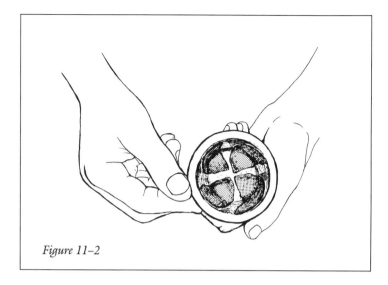

Figure 11–2

6. Divide the bavarois between the cups. Refrigerate for at least 2 hours.

7. Whip the heavy cream with the sugar to stiff peaks. Place in a pastry bag with a no. 7 (14-mm) star tip.

8. Presentation: Quickly dip the bottom of a pots de crème cup into hot water (not too long or you will melt the bavarois) and unmold the charlotte in the center of a dessert plate. Pour just enough of the reserved caramel around the sides to cover the plate. Pipe a rosette of whipped cream on top of the dessert, and decorate the cream with a wedge of strawberry.

Pear Bavarois

2½ quarts (2 l, 400 ml) bavarois or sixteen 5-ounce (150-ml) servings

8 egg yolks
2 ounces (55 g) granulated sugar
3 cups (720 ml) milk
1 vanilla bean, split
    or
1 teaspoon (5 ml) vanilla extract
3 tablespoons (27 g) unflavored gelatin powder
¾ cup (180 ml) cold water
½ cup (120 ml) pear brandy
3 cups (720 ml) heavy cream
¼ recipe Italian Meringue (page 333)

1. Beat the egg yolks and sugar just enough to combine. Heat the milk with vanilla bean (if used) to the scalding point (remove the bean and reserve for another use). Gradually pour the milk into the egg mixture, beating constantly.

2. Soften the gelatin in cold water and stir into the milk mixture. Add the vanilla extract (if used) and pear brandy. Set aside to cool, stirring occasionally. If you want to speed up the cooling process, place the mixture over ice water and stir until it is slightly warmer than body temperature. (Should you get it too firm, or lumpy, reheat the mixture and start again.)

3. Whip the cream to soft peaks. Gradually fold the milk mixture into the cream. Fold that combination into the Italian Meringue. Do not incorporate the bavarois with the Italian Meringue until the bavarois has started to thicken or the two will separate.

NOTE: Do not make the bavarois until you are ready to use it.

Variation

Pear Bavarois makes an excellent quick dessert by itself. Instead of lining forms with the macerated pear slices, just pour the bavarois directly into small, fluted forms. Unmold and serve with Caramel Sauce I (see page 557).

White Chocolate Bavarois with Macadamia and Pistachio Nuts

eighteen 4-ounce (120 ml) servings

4 ounces (115 g) macadamia nuts
1¼ cups (300 ml) milk
1 vanilla bean, split
    or
1 teaspoon (5 ml) vanilla extract
2 ounces (55 g) pistachio nuts
6 eggs
6 ounces (170 g) granulated sugar
10 ounces (285 g) white chocolate, finely chopped
2½ tablespoons (23 g) unflavored gelatin powder
½ cup (120 ml) cold water
2½ cups (600 ml) heavy cream
¼ cup (60 ml) macadamia nut liqueur
½ cup (120 ml) heavy cream
½ teaspoon (3 g) granulated sugar
4 cups (960 ml) or 1 recipe Kiwi Sauce (page 560)
mango or papaya slices

1. Roast the macadamia nuts. Grind to a paste with ¼ cup (60 ml) of the milk. Mix into the remaining milk and add the vanilla bean. Bring the mixture to a boil, then set aside to steep for 15 minutes.

2. Blanch the pistachio nuts and remove the skins (a pinch of salt added to the blanching water helps bring out the green color). Reserve 18 of the best-looking nuts for the garnish. Chop the remaining nuts coarsely: Large pieces make the dessert look more attractive and also prevent a grainy texture.

3. Separate the eggs. Mix the egg yolks with half of the sugar until well combined. Reheat the milk mixture to boiling, remove the vanilla bean, and gradually pour the milk into the egg yolk mixture, stirring rapidly. Strain through a fine mesh strainer. Stir in white chocolate, and continue to stir until all the chocolate has melted.

4. Soften the gelatin in cold water, then heat to 110°F (43°C) to dissolve. Add to the warm mixture (add the vanilla extract if using). Set aside to cool.

5. Whip the 2½ cups (600 ml) heavy cream to soft peaks. Whip the egg whites with the remaining 3 ounces (85 g) sugar to soft peaks. Gradually add the white chocolate/custard mixture to the whipped cream, then fold this into the whipped egg whites. Fold in the chopped pistachios and the liqueur. Pour into 4-ounce (120-ml) molds and refrigerate to set, at least two hours. Whip the ½ cup (120 ml) heavy cream with the sugar to stiff peaks. Place in a pastry bag with a no. 4 (8-mm) tip; reserve in the refrigerator.

6. Presentation: Unmold a bavarois and place it off-center on a dessert plate. Pour an oval pool of Kiwi Sauce in front of the dessert (the larger space). Place three small slices of mango or papaya in the space behind the bavarois. Pipe a rosette of whipped cream on top of the bavarois, and place one of the reserved pistachio nuts on the rosette.

Custards

Brandy Bread Pudding

one pan 12 × 20 inches (30 × 50 cm) or twenty-eight 3- × 2¾-inch (7.5- × 7-cm) servings

5 ounces (140 g) melted butter
three 1-pound (455-g) Brioche
    loaves (page 85)
10 ounces (285 g) softened butter
8 ounces (225 g) sugar
12 eggs
2 cups (480 ml) scalded milk
½ cup (120 ml) brandy
1 teaspoon (5 ml) vanilla extract
1 teaspoon (1.5 g) cinnamon
8 ounces (225 g) golden raisins
1 quart (960 ml) heavy cream
12 ounces (340 g) Streusel Topping
    (page 8)
½ recipe Brandied Whipped
    Cream (page 424), made
    without nutmeg

1. Use some of the melted butter to butter the baking pan. Set aside. Trim the crust from the bread, cut into ¼-inch (6-mm) slices, and place on a sheet pan. Brush with the remainder of the melted butter and toast in a 400°F (205°C) oven for approximately 10 minutes or until golden brown.

2. Beat the softened butter and sugar together. Beat in the eggs. Add the warm milk, brandy, vanilla, and cinnamon.

3. Make a level, single layer of bread in the baking pan. The sides of the bread should touch, completely covering the pan. Sprinkle the raisins evenly on top. Pour half the custard slowly and equally over the bread. Cover with a second bread layer and press with your hands to make the top level. Pour the remaining custard evenly over the second layer. Press down again.

4. Pour 3 cups (720 ml) of the cream over the top. Cover with baking paper and place another pan, just slightly smaller, over the paper and weight down the top with cans. Let sit at room temperature for 1 hour.

5. Remove the weights, top pan, and baking paper. Pour the remaining 1 cup (240 ml) of cream evenly over the pudding. Sprinkle with streusel.

6. Bake covered at 350°F (175°C) for 30 minutes. Uncover and bake approximately 10 minutes longer. Let cool slightly, then cut into the desired number of serving pieces. Serve warm or at room temperature with Brandied Whipped Cream.

Crème Caramel with Ginger

fourteen 5-ounce (150-ml) servings

1 tablespoon (15 ml) finely chopped
    fresh ginger root
5 cups (1 l, 200 ml) milk
2 pounds (910 g) granulated sugar
5 drops lemon juice
12 ounces (340 g) sugar
10 eggs
Caramel Sauce I (page 557)

1. Combine ginger root and milk in a saucepan and bring to the scalding point. Set aside to infuse.

2. Caramelize the first measurement of sugar with the lemon juice (see page 488). Pour a ⅛-inch (3-mm) layer of caramel on the bottom of soufflé ramekins or other appropriate forms.

3. Reheat the milk to the scalding point. Whisk together the remaining sugar and eggs. Gradually add the hot milk, whisking constantly. Strain and discard ginger.

4. Pour the custard into the forms. Place the forms in a larger pan and add hot water around them to reach halfway up the sides.

5. Bake at 350°F (175°C) for approximately 35 minutes or until the custard is set. Let cool completely; then refrigerate.

6. Unmold and pour Caramel Sauce around the dessert.

Chocolate Rum Pudding

sixteen 4-ounce (120-ml) portions

6 ounces (170 g) toasted white
*   bread crumbs*
3 cups (720 ml) heavy cream
2 teaspoons (10 ml) vanilla extract
melted butter
finely ground almonds
8 ounces (225 g) dark chocolate
8 ounces (225 g) softened butter
8 ounces (225 g) granulated sugar
8 eggs, separated
½ cup (120 ml) dark rum
6 ounces (170 g) finely ground
*   almonds*
6 cups (1 l, 440 ml) or 1 recipe
*   Mousseline Sauce (page 561)*
Chocolate Sauce for Piping
*   (page 560)*
powdered sugar
fanned strawberry halves

1. Combine the bread crumbs, cream, and vanilla. Set aside for 15 minutes.

2. Brush the inside of sixteen 4-ounce (120 ml) ramekins, or other ovenproof molds, with melted butter. Coat with finely ground almonds.

3. Melt the dark chocolate. Set aside but keep warm.

4. Beat the softened butter with half of the sugar to a light and creamy consistency. Add the egg yolks a few at a time. Quickly incorporate the melted chocolate. Add the 6 ounces (170 g) of ground almonds, ¼ cup (60 ml) of the rum, and the bread crumb mixture.

5. Whip the egg whites and remaining sugar to soft peaks. Gradually fold the chocolate mixture into the egg whites. Fill the prepared molds with the batter. Set the forms in a larger pan and add hot water around the forms to come halfway up the sides.

6. Bake at 350°F (175°C) for about 35 minutes. The puddings should spring back when pressed lightly.

7. Combine the Mousseline Sauce with the remaining ¼ cup (60 ml) rum. Reserve. Unmold the puddings and sift powdered sugar over the tops (crust-side down). Reserve at room temperature.

8. Presentation: Place a pudding in the center of a dessert plate. Pour Mousseline Sauce around the dessert to cover the plate (if the sauce seems too thick, thin with a little heavy cream). Pipe three concentric circles of chocolate sauce in the Mousseline Sauce. Drag a line through the circles every 1 inch (2.5 cm) (see Figure 18–26, page 519). Place a fanned strawberry half on top of the pudding.

Crème Brûlée

twenty-four 5-ounce (150-ml)
servings

16 egg yolks
8 eggs
12 ounces (340 g) brown sugar
2 quarts (1 l, 920 ml) heavy cream
1 teaspoon (5 g) salt
2 teaspoons (10 ml) vanilla extract
6 ounces (170 g) brown sugar
24 Pirouettes (page 138)

1. Mix, do not whip, the egg yolks, eggs, and 12 ounces (340 g) brown sugar until combined. Heat the cream to the scalding point and gradually pour it into the egg mixture, while stirring constantly. Add the salt and vanilla.

2. Divide the custard between twenty-four 5-ounce (150-ml) ovenproof forms, such as soufflé ramekins. Be sure to fill the forms to the top because Crème Brûlée, like any custard, will settle slightly once it is cooked. Place the forms in hotel pans, or other suitable containers, and add hot water around the forms to reach halfway up the sides.

3. Bake at 350°F (175°C) for about 30 minutes, or until the custards are set. Do not overcook or you will have a broken and unpleasant finished product (see note). Remove the custards from the water bath and let them cool slightly at room temperature, then refrigerate until thoroughly chilled.

4. Place the brown sugar on a sheet pan lined with baking paper, and dry in the oven for a few minutes. Let cool. Use a rolling pin or dowel to crush the sugar and separate the grains. Reserve.

5. Presentation: Sift or sprinkle just enough of the dry brown sugar on top of a custard to cover. Wipe away any sugar that is on the edge of the form. Caramelize the sugar in a salamander or under a broiler. Place the form on a dessert plate lined with a doily. Serve immediately with a Pirouette on the plate.

NOTE: If you are not certain your oven temperature is accurate, test it with an oven thermometer. If you do not have a removable thermometer, start cooking the custards at 325°F (163°C); if after 30 minutes the custard is still as liquid as when you started, your thermostat is incorrect and you should increase the temperature. Wasting a half hour is better than overcooking the custard in a poorly calibrated oven.

Lingonberry Cheese Pudding

(see photograph in color insert)
twenty-four 5-ounce (150-ml) servings

melted butter
12 ounces (340 g) graham
   cracker crumbs
4 ounces (115 g) melted butter
   approximately
3 pounds (1 kg, 365 g) cream
   cheese, at room temperature
6 eggs
1 pound, 4 ounces (570 g)
   granulated sugar
2 pounds, 12 ounces (1 kg, 250 g)
   sour cream
1¼ cups (300 ml) puréed and
   strained lingonberries (see note)
water
Sour Cream Mixture for Piping
   (page 564)

1. Grease the inside of twenty-four 5-ounce (150-ml) ramekins with melted butter. Reserve. Cut out strips of baking paper to line the forms (Figure 11–3). This drawing is the correct size for typical soufflé ramekins that are approximately 2½ inches (6.2 cm) in diameter across the bottom, measured on the inside. Trace the drawing, then cut 24 of the shapes out of baking paper. Line the buttered forms with the papers, pressing the flaps against the sides. The flaps should extend about ¾ inch (2 cm) above the form on either side so you can hold on to them to remove the dessert. Test before cutting all of the papers to be sure the flaps are long enough and adjust as needed.

2. Mix the graham cracker crumbs with the 4 ounces (115 g) of melted butter. Divide among the forms and press the crumbs evenly over the bottoms.

3. Soften the cream cheese in a mixer on low speed, taking care not to incorporate too much air. Lightly combine the eggs with 14 ounces (400 g) of the sugar by hand. Gradually add the mixture to the cream cheese, scraping the sides and bottom of the bowl frequently to avoid lumps.

4. Place the batter in a pastry bag with a no. 6 (12-mm) plain tip. Pipe the batter into the forms, dividing it equally between them. Be very careful not to get any batter on the sides at the top of the forms, as this will detract from the presentation.

5. Bake the puddings at 375°F (190°C) for approximately 20 minutes or until just done. Take into consideration that they will set further as they cool.

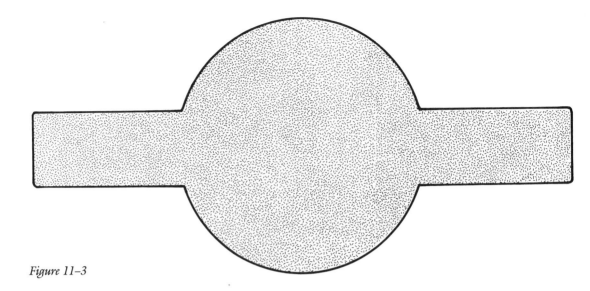

Figure 11–3

6. Mix the sour cream with the remaining 6 ounces (170 g) of sugar. Place the mixture in a pastry bag with a no. 6 (12-mm) plain tip and pipe it on top of the puddings. Flatten the top of the sour cream with the back of a spoon, moving it up and down a few times on top of the sour cream layer.

7. Place the lingonberry purée in a pastry bag with a no. 1 (2-mm) plain tip. Pipe a small amount of the purée in a spiral pattern on top of the sour cream layer in each of the forms, starting in the center. Reserve the remaining purée for the sauce. Pull a toothpick from the center of the spiral to the outside to create a spider-web pattern (see Figure 18–26, page 519).

8. Bake the puddings for 4 minutes at 375°F (190°C) to set the sour cream. Let cool completely.

9. Thin the remaining lingonberry purée with water to a sauce-like consistency. Reserve.

10. Unmold the puddings by cutting around the edge with a small, thin knife, then carefully lifting the pudding out by the paper flaps.

11. Presentation: Place a pudding off-center on a dessert plate. Pour a small, round pool of sauce in front of the pudding. Decorate the sauce with the Sour Cream Mixture for Piping, making the same spider-web design used on the pudding.

NOTE: It is assumed that you are using canned and sweetened lingonberries for the purée. You will need approximately 1 pound, 8 ounces (680 g) to make the amount called for in the recipe. If you are fortunate enough to find fresh lingonberries, cook and sweeten them before puréeing.

Riz à la Malta

fifteen 4-ounce (120-ml) servings

1 teaspoon (3 g) unflavored
gelatin powder
1 tablespoon (15 ml) cold water
2 cups (480 ml) or 1 recipe
Cherry Sauce (page 558)
2½ cups (600 ml) milk
1 vanilla bean, split
or
1 teaspoon (5 ml) vanilla extract
5 ounces (140 g) long-grain rice,
blanched (see note)
4 teaspoons (12 g) unflavored
gelatin powder
¼ cup (60 ml) cold water
2 cups (480 ml) heavy cream
6 ounces (170 g) granulated sugar
Sour Cream Mixture for Piping
(page 564)

1. Soften 1 teaspoon (3 g) gelatin in 1 tablespoon (15 ml) water. Stir into 5 ounces (150 ml) of the Cherry Sauce (reserve the remaining sauce). Heat to 110°F (43°C) to dissolve the gelatin. Pour on the bottom of fifteen 4-ounce (120-ml) brioche forms and place in the refrigerator to set.

2. Bring the milk to the scalding point with the vanilla bean, if used. Add the rice and cook over medium heat, stirring from time to time, until the rice is tender and the mixture has started to thicken (see note). Remove from the heat and add the vanilla extract, if used, or remove the vanilla bean.

3. Soften the 4 teaspoons (12 g) gelatin in ¼ cup (60 ml) of water. Heat to 110°F (43°C) to dissolve. Stir into the rice mixture. Set aside to cool to room temperature.

4. Whip the heavy cream and sugar to soft peaks. Gently fold the cream into the rice. Fill the prepared forms and return to the refrigerator until the pudding has set up, about 2 hours.

5. Presentation: Dip the bottom of a form into hot water very briefly and unmold in the center of the dessert plate. Pour Cherry Sauce around the dessert and decorate the sauce with the Sour Cream Mixture for Piping (see pages 518–519).

NOTE: Before adding the rice to the milk, wash it in cold water, drain, and cover with fresh water, approximately 3 times the amount of the rice. Bring to a boil and cook over low heat for 5 minutes. Drain the rice and proceed with the recipe. Blanching the rice before cooking it in milk will speed up the cooking process and reduce your chances of burning the rice. As an alternative to cooking the rice on the stove, you can cook it covered in a shallow pan in a 400°F (205°C) oven, stirring from time to time. With either method, avoid stirring the rice with a whip and be careful not to break or smash the grains as the rice begins to get tender. Remove from heat when the grains flatten easily when pressed gently between your fingers. Do not use converted rice.

Variation: Riz Impératrice

Replace the Cherry Sauce with Strawberry Sauce (see page 563). Follow the preceding recipe through step 3. In step 4 omit the ½ cup (120 ml) of the heavy cream and replace with 6 egg yolks. Whip the yolks with the granulated sugar until light and fluffy. Whip the remaining heavy cream to soft peaks separately. Add the whipped yolk mixture to the rice together with the cream. Stir in 6 ounces (170 g) chopped mixed candied fruit. Continue as directed.

Trifle with Fresh Fruit

10 to 12 servings

*4 cups (960 ml) prepared fresh
  fruit*
*one 10-inch (25-cm) Sponge Cake
  (page 161)*
  or
*about the same amount of leftover
  sponge pieces*
*1 cup (240 ml) orange liqueur,
  approximately*
*1 teaspoon (3 g) unflavored
  gelatin powder*
*3 pounds (1 kg, 365 g) or ½ recipe
  Pastry Cream, freshly made
  (page 569)*
1½ cups (360 ml) heavy cream
1 teaspoon (5 ml) vanilla extract
*2 teaspoons (10 g) granulated
  sugar*
dark chocolate shavings

English trifle, also popular in Italy where it is known as *Zuppa Inglese* (English Soup), should be assembled in, and served from, a large glass bowl so that all of the layers can be seen. It is therefore better suited to buffet service, or use on a pastry cart, than as a dessert served directly from the kitchen. Trifle is an excellent way of using leftover sponge pieces or dry sponges. Instead of the traditional raspberry jam, I prefer to use seasonal fresh fruit. However, the variations of this dessert are endless. Here are two of my favorites.

1. Prepare the fruit. A nice combination is peaches, cherries, oranges, and strawberries (the flavor of peaches and strawberries goes very nicely with the orange liqueur). Poach, peel, pit, and slice the peaches (if perfectly ripe, omit poaching). Peel and section the oranges. Pit cherries and cut in half. Remove stems from strawberries and cut in halves or quarters. If you use small berries, such as raspberries or blueberries, leave them whole.

2. Cut the skin from the top of the sponge cake. Slice into two layers. Use bite-sized chunks from half of the cake to cover the bottom of a glass serving bowl approximately 10 inches (25 cm) in diameter. Sprinkle approximately 6 tablespoons (90 ml) of the orange liqueur generously over the sponge pieces. You may need to use more liqueur than called for in the recipe, depending on how dry the sponge is. The pieces should be well saturated—after all, trifle is not known as "tipsy pudding" for nothing!

3. Soften the gelatin in 2 tablespoons (30 ml) of the orange liqueur, heat to dissolve, then whisk into the warm pastry cream. Spoon half of the custard over the sponge and spread it out to the edge of the bowl.

4. Reserve some of the fruit to use for decoration. Sprinkle half of the remaining fruit on top of the custard. Layer the reserved sponge, remaining orange liqueur, custard, and fruit (saving the fruit for decorating) in the same manner. Place the trifle in the refrigerator to chill.

5. Whip the heavy cream to stiff peaks with the sugar and vanilla. Spread enough cream on top of the trifle to cover the fruit. Place the remaining whipped cream in a pastry bag with a no. 6 (12-mm) star tip. Pipe a border around the edge. Sprinkle shaved chocolate in the center and decorate around the chocolate with the reserved fruit.

NOTE 1: If you would prefer not to use alcohol, substitute fruit juice for the liqueur.

NOTE 2: Although in a pinch you can use a chilled custard that is already made (providing it is smooth and soft), the trifle will look much nicer if warm custard is draped over the sponge, filling all the crevices and holding the sponge chunks together when set.

Variation: Amaretto-Chocolate Trifle

Replace the sponge cake with Cocoa Almond Sponge (see page 163). Use amaretto rather than orange liqueur. Try using cherries instead of mixed fresh fruit, if they are in season.

Vanilla Pots de Crème

eighteen 5-ounce (150-ml) servings

10 egg yolks
6 eggs
10 ounces (285 g) granulated
  sugar
2 quarts (1 l, 920 ml)
  half-and-half
1 vanilla bean, split
  or
1 teaspoon (5 ml) vanilla extract
whipped cream, optional
candied violets, optional

1. Whip the egg yolks, eggs, and sugar just until combined. Heat the half-and-half to the scalding point with the vanilla bean, if used. Remove the bean and reserve for another use. Gradually stir the half-and-half into the egg mixture. Add vanilla extract, if used.

2. Strain the mixture and pour it into pots de crème cups, filling them all the way to the top. Place the lids on the pots de crème cups. If these forms are not available, use 5-ounce (150-ml) soufflé ramekins. Skim off any foam that forms on the top of the custards. Place the forms in a larger pan and add hot water around the forms to come halfway up the sides.

3. Bake at 350°F (175°C) for about 30 minutes or until the custard is set. Be careful not to overcook (see note following Crème Brûlée, page 315). Transfer the custards to a sheet pan. Let cool slightly at room temperature, then refrigerate, covered, until needed.

4. Presentation: Traditionally, pots de crème are served just as they are. If you are not using pots de crème forms, however, you may want to dress them up a bit. Pipe a rosette of whipped cream on the top, using a no. 4 (8-mm) star tip in your pastry bag. Place a small piece of candied violet in the cream.

NOTE: Pots de crème should not have any skin on top, just a glossy surface. If you do not have pots de crème cups with individual covers, cover the whole pan with a lid or a sheet of foil, leaving a small opening to allow steam to escape.

Variation: Chocolate Pots de Crème

Cut 6 ounces (170 g) of cocoa block (bitter chocolate) and 6 ounces (170 g) of dark chocolate into very small pieces. Stir into the hot half-and-half (off the heat) and keep stirring until all of the chocolate is melted before stirring into the egg mixture.

Mousses

Chocolate Mousse in Chocolate Teardrops

(see photograph in color insert)

twenty 4-ounce (115-g) servings

3 cups (720 ml) heavy cream
5 ounces (140 g) cocoa powder
1 cup (240 ml) warm water
3 ounces (90 ml) dark rum
10 ounces (285 g) semisweet
    chocolate
8 egg yolks
2 ounces (55 g) granulated sugar
¼ recipe Swiss Meringue
    (page 334)
⅓ recipe White Chocolate Mousse
    Filling (page 207)
dark baker's chocolate, melted
cocoa powder
white chocolate shavings
dark chocolate shavings
fanned strawberry halves
mint sprigs

1. Whip the heavy cream to stiff peaks and set aside in the refrigerator.

2. Mix the cocoa powder into the warm water. Add the rum. Melt the semisweet chocolate and add it to the cocoa powder mixture. Set aside and keep warm.

3. Whip the egg yolks and sugar until thick and fluffy. Fold the warm chocolate mixture into the egg yolks. Fold into the reserved whipped cream, then gradually add this mixture to the Swiss Meringue (see note 1). Place covered in the refrigerator.

4. Make the White Chocolate Mousse Filling. Cover and refrigerate while making the Chocolate Teardrops.

5. Cut out ten 9- × 1½-inch (22.5- × 2.5- to 3.7-cm) plastic strips. Place the strips one at a time on a baking paper in front of you. Spread, or brush, a thin layer of melted dark baker's chocolate over one strip. To cover the strip completely you will need to spread a little chocolate onto the baking paper.

6. Use the tip of a paring knife to find the edge of the strip at two corners and lift it up from the paper. Holding onto the plastic at one short end, run your thumb and index finger down both long edges to smooth them. Stand the strip on its side vertically and bend (with the chocolate on the inside) to make the ends meet; attach a paper clip to hold the ends together while the chocolate is setting. Transfer the teardrop to a sheet pan lined with baking paper. Repeat with the other nine plastic strips.

7. Place the teardrops in the refrigerator for just a few minutes; this will ensure a glossy surface.

8. Remove the paper clips and gently pull the plastic strips away from the hardened chocolate.

9. Repeat, using the same plastic strips, until you have made 60 teardrops. Store the finished chocolate shells, covered, in the dry box.

10. Place the White Chocolate Mousse Filling and the reserved chocolate mousse in two pastry bags both with no. 6 (12-mm) plain tips. Reserve in the refrigerator.

11. Presentation: Sift cocoa powder lightly over a dessert plate. Wipe the rim of the plate clean. Place three chocolate teardrops, off-center, on the plate with the points angled toward each other. Pipe White Chocolate Mousse Filling into the center shell. Pipe dark chocolate mousse into the two other shells. Place dark chocolate shavings on the white mousse and white chocolate shavings on the dark mousse. Place a fanned strawberry where the tips of the teardrops meet. Place a mint sprig next to the strawberry.

NOTE 1: You should make the Swiss Meringue before you start to assemble the remainder of the recipe so that you can mix it in quickly when it is called for.

NOTE 2: This presentation, while quite elegant, is a bit more time-consuming than the traditional one. However, the shells will keep for weeks stored in a cool dry place and can be made up anytime there is a slow day, and the mousse can be made up to three days ahead if it is properly stored in the refrigerator. If there is little time, make just one type of mousse and pipe it into champagne glasses (not flutes) or other suitable serving containers; pipe whipped cream on top, and sprinkle the shaved chocolate on the cream.

Variations

This basic idea can, of course, be used to make many different shapes and be used with a variety of fillings. If desired, you can also make a bottom on the shells by following the instructions given in Molding Chocolate Strips (see page 459).

Cupid's Treasure Chest

(see photograph in color insert)
20 servings

8 ounces (225 g) melted dark baker's chocolate
melted Piping Chocolate (page 449)
one 10-inch (25-cm) Sponge Cake (page 161)
orange liqueur
½ recipe Raspberry–White Chocolate Mousse (page 323)
dark chocolate shavings
20 Marzipan Rose Buds (page 541)
20 Marzipan Leaves (page 541)
4 cups (960 ml) or 1 recipe Raspberry Sauce (page 563)
Sour Cream Mixture for Piping (page 564)

This is a dessert created especially for Valentine's Day, but it makes a beautiful presentation for other special occasions as well, such as a romantic anniversary dinner.

1. Cut 20 thin plastic strips 1¼ inches (3.1 cm) wide and exactly as long as the inside circumference of a heart-shaped cookie cutter that is 4 inches (10 cm) across at the widest point, approximately 12¾ inches (32 cm). (The strips will not follow the heart shape precisely, but don't worry; if anything, this just adds to the appearance.)

2. Spread a thin layer of melted baker's chocolate over one of the strips, covering it completely. Carefully lift up the plastic at one end by sliding the tip of a knife underneath. Hold the plastic at one short end and run your thumb and index finger along the edges on both sides for a cleaner look. Position the strip inside the heart cutter with the plastic side against the cutter and the two ends meeting at the point of the heart. Press lightly to make sure that the bottom edge lines up evenly. Refrigerate for a few minutes to set. (It will obviously go faster if you have more than one cutter, but if not, you can be working on the lids as you wait.)

3. When the chocolate has set, brush some additional chocolate at the tip where the ends join (this chocolate will set immediately since the heart is cold). Carefully remove the heart from the mold (run a thin knife around the inside perimeter if it is stuck), leaving the plastic strip attached. Place on a sheet pan. Repeat to make twenty hearts. Place the hearts in the refrigerator for 1 minute to ensure a glossy finish (do not leave them too long or they will become brittle and break). Remove from refrigerator and carefully peel off the plastic strips. Reserve.

4. To make the lids for the heart boxes, place one chocolate heart on top of a piece of thick paper such as a cake box. Trace around, and cut out the shape. Use this template to draw 25 hearts on a sheet of baking paper (you need to make a few extra lids to allow for breakage). Invert the baking paper.

5. Place melted piping chocolate in a piping bag (see pages 505–506). Pipe the chocolate, tracing the outline of the heart first, then filling in by piping back and forth at a diagonal, in both directions, spacing the lines about ½ inch (1.2 cm) apart. Make sure you connect with the outline on each side. Set aside to harden.

6. Cut the skin from the top of the sponge cake, cutting it even at the same time. Slice the sponge into three thin layers. Cut out 20 hearts using the template used to trace the lids, or use a smaller heart-shaped cutter if you have one (a template is best because cake cut with a cutter will not fix exactly and the filling may run out at the bottom). Brush the cake pieces with orange liqueur. Reserve covered in the refrigerator.

7. Place the Raspberry–White Chocolate Mousse in a pastry bag with a no. 7 (14-mm) plain tip. Reserve in the refrigerator.

8. Presentation: Place a heart-shaped sponge in the bottom of a chocolate heart. Place off-center on a dessert plate. Pipe raspberry mousse into the shell to fill to the top. Sprinkle chocolate shavings over the mousse. Place a marzipan rosebud and leaf in the upper right side of the heart, sticking the bud lightly into the filling. Run a thin knife under the piped lids to loosen them. Place one of the lids on top of the heart, sticking it partially into the filling on the left side to hold it in a half-open position. Pour a small pool of Raspberry Sauce in front of the dessert, and decorate the sauce with the sour cream mixture, making a series of hearts (see Figure 18–27, page 519). Serve immediately.

NOTE: If you wish to make a chocolate bottom for the treasure chests instead of, or in addition to, the sponge cake, place a sheet of baking paper on a cardboard or inverted sheet pan and spread a thin layer of melted dark baker's chocolate over the paper. Set the chocolate hearts on top, moving them back and forth just a little to make sure they adhere. Pipe a border of dark chocolate all around the inside of the base. Let the chocolate set at room temperature, then cut around the outside of each heart and carefully break off the excess chocolate. (At this stage the hearts can be reserved, covered, in a cool, dry place for up to two weeks.)

Raspberry–White Chocolate Mousse

twenty-two 4-ounce (120-ml) servings

3 cups (720 ml) heavy cream
1 ounce (30 g) powdered pectin
8 ounces (225 g) granulated sugar
1 cup (240 ml) egg whites
10 ounces (285 g) melted
    white chocolate
3 cups (720 ml) strained raspberry
    purée (see note)
1/2 cup (120 ml) lemon juice
4 teaspoons (12 g) unflavored
    gelatin powder
1/2 cup (120 ml) cold water
3/4 cup (180 ml) heavy cream
1 teaspoon (5 g) granulated sugar
dark chocolate shavings
fresh raspberries
22 Almond Macaroon Cookies
    (page 123)

1. Whip 3 cups (720 ml) of heavy cream to soft peaks. Reserve in the refrigerator.

2. Combine the pectin powder with 8 ounces (225 g) granulated sugar. Add the egg whites. Heat the mixture over a bain-marie until it reaches 120°F (49°C), whipping constantly to make sure that the egg whites on the bottom do not get too hot and cook. Remove from the heat and whip until the mixture is cold and has formed stiff peaks. Reserve the meringue.

3. Stir the melted white chocolate into the raspberry purée. Add the lemon juice (make sure that the raspberry purée is not colder than room temperature).

4. Soften the gelatin in cold water; heat to 125°F (52°C) to dissolve. Quickly add the gelatin to the raspberry mixture. Gradually (to avoid lumps) fold this mixture into the reserved meringue. Fold into the reserved whipped cream. Pipe into dessert cups or glasses. Refrigerate for about 2 hours to set.

5. Whip 3/4 cup (180 ml) heavy cream with 1 teaspoon (5 g) granulated sugar to stiff peaks. Place in a pastry bag with a no. 7 (14-mm) star tip. Reserve in the refrigerator.

6. Presentation: Pipe a rosette of whipped cream in the center of a mousse. Decorate the cream with a small amount of the shaved dark chocolate. Arrange a ring of raspberries circling the rosette. Place the glass on a dessert plate lined with a doily. Serve with an Almond Macaroon Cookie on the plate.

NOTE: You will need approximately 2 1/2 pounds (1 kg, 135 g) fresh or frozen raspberries to make the purée. If fresh raspberries are out of season or too expensive, substitute frozen berries and omit them from the decoration. If the berries are frozen in sugar or sugar syrup, use only half the amount of sugar called for in the recipe.

Triple Chocolate Terrine

(see photograph in color insert)
two 10- × 3-inch (25- × 7.5-cm)
molds, about 30 servings

Baked Chocolate Sheet
   (recipe follows)
Triple Chocolate Fillings
   (recipes follow)
Raspberry Sauce *(page 563)*
Sour Cream Mixture for Piping
   (page 564)
raspberries

This dessert is fairly complicated to make, but the presentation is very appealing and the taste is every chocoholic's dream. Any leftover terrine can be kept, well covered, in the freezer for several weeks with no loss in quality.

1. Line the bottom and the two long sides of two terrine molds (see note) with baking paper. Cut the chocolate sheet into eight pieces the size of the bottom of the molds. Place one piece in the bottom of each mold.

2. Add the Milk Chocolate Filling. Place a second sheet of cake on top. Add the White Chocolate Filling, place another cake layer on top. Add the Dark Chocolate Filling. Top with the remaining cake sheets. Place in the freezer for at least 3 hours to harden.

3. Presentation: Unmold the terrines and remove the baking paper. Position them so that the layers are running vertically. Cut into ¾-inch (2-cm) slices using a thin knife dipped in hot water. Place the slices onto dessert plates as you cut them (make sure the slice has thawed before serving). Pour a pool of Raspberry Sauce in front of the slices and decorate the sauce with the sour cream mixture (see pages 518–519). Place three or four raspberries behind the dessert.

NOTE: If the baker is using all of his bread forms, and the *garde manger* will not part with his pâté molds, you can make a form by cutting strips of heavy cardboard to the appropriate size and taping them together at the corners. Place the sides on another sheet of cardboard or on a sheet pan which will serve as the bottom.

Baked Chocolate Sheet

12 eggs, separated
8 ounces (225 g) granulated sugar
12 ounces (340 g) semisweet dark
   chocolate, melted

1. Beat the egg yolks with 3 ounces (85 g) of the sugar until light and fluffy. Set aside.

2. Whip the egg whites to a foam. Gradually add the remaining 5 ounces (140 g) sugar and whip to soft peaks.

3. Combine the melted chocolate and egg yolk mixture. Carefully fold in the egg whites. Spread the batter out to a 16- by 20-inch (40- × 50-cm) rectangle on a sheet of baking paper. Drag the paper onto a sheet pan (see Figure 15–3, page 422).

4. Bake immediately at 375°F (190°C) for about 15 minutes.

Triple Chocolate Filling Base

6 ounces (170 g) granulated sugar
10 egg yolks
2 eggs
2½ cups (600 ml) heavy cream
individual filling ingredients
   (recipes follow)

Prep the base and the other ingredients for all three fillings simultaneously, but assemble and add them to the terrine one at a time as you are ready to use them.

1. Combine sugar, egg yolks, and whole eggs in a mixing bowl. Set the bowl over simmering water and heat the mixture, stirring constantly, to 110°F (43°C). Remove from heat and whip at high speed until the mixture is cold.

2. Whip the heavy cream to soft peaks, then carefully fold the egg mixture into the cream. Divide into three 1-pound (455-g) parts and proceed as follows.

Milk Chocolate Filling

10 ounces (285 g) melted
   milk chocolate
⅓ Triple Chocolate Filling Base
1 teaspoon (3 g) unflavored
   gelatin powder
2 tablespoons (30 ml) cold water

1. Gradually stir the chocolate into the base.

2. Soften the gelatin in the water. Heat to 110°F (43°C) to dissolve. Quickly mix the gelatin into a small part of the chocolate mixture, then stir into the remaining mixture.

White Chocolate Filling

10 ounces (285 g) melted
   white chocolate
⅓ Triple Chocolate Filling Base
1 teaspoon (3 g) unflavored
   gelatin powder
2 tablespoons (30 ml) cold water

Follow the directions for Milk Chocolate Filling. Take care not to overheat the white chocolate or it will become grainy.

Dark Chocolate Filling

10 ounces (285 g) melted
   dark chocolate
⅓ Triple Chocolate Filling Base
1 teaspoon (3 g) unflavored
   gelatin powder
2 tablespoons (30 ml) cold water

Follow the directions for Milk Chocolate Filling.

Soufflés

Blueberry Soufflé

(see photograph in color insert)
15 servings

½ recipe Grand Marnier Soufflé
batter (page 327)
1 pound, 6 ounces (625 g) fresh or
thawed frozen blueberries
3 ounces (85 g) granulated sugar
powdered sugar
4 cups (960 ml) or 1 recipe
Raspberry Sauce (page 563)

1. Prepare one-half of the full recipe of soufflé batter through step 4, omitting the Grand Marnier liqueur and using only 8 egg whites rather than 10.

2. Purée the blueberries with the sugar. Place in a heavy saucepan and reduce by half over low heat, forming a thick pulp. Stir from time to time, especially when the blueberries start to thicken, to prevent the mixture from burning. Remove from the heat and reserve.

3. Prepare fifteen 5-ounce (150-ml) soufflé ramekins as directed in the recipe for Grand Marnier Soufflé.

4. Add the blueberry pulp to the soufflé batter base.

5. About 30 minutes before the soufflés are to be served, whip the egg whites and sugar to stiff peaks and fold the soufflé base into the egg whites. Pipe the batter into the prepared ramekins, filling them to the top.

6. Bake immediately at 400°F (205°C) for approximately 20 minutes, or until done. The sides should have a light brown color.

7. Sift powdered sugar lightly over the tops. Serve immediately with Raspberry Sauce. For à la carte service, follow the directions in Grand Marnier Soufflé but use 1½ parts base to 2 parts egg white.

Variations

The recipe for Blueberry Soufflé can be used with other fruits and berries as well. Depending on the natural sweetness of the fruit you choose, you may need to adjust the amount of sugar added when you purée it. Fruits such as apricots or plums are excellent choices when in season. Use the same amount of fruit as in the Blueberry Soufflé (weigh the fruit after you have removed the stones). Leave the skin on if using plums, it will add a nice color to the pulp. Purée and reduce as directed in Blueberry Soufflé. Another variation that looks and tastes very distinctive uses black currants. Follow the directions for Blueberry Soufflé substituting black currants for the blueberries. Serve with Apricot Sauce. If using canned black currants in heavy syrup, drain and discard the syrup before weighing the fruit (or use it for sorbet after adjusting the Baumé), and omit the sugar in the purée.

Crepe Soufflé
16 servings

16 Crepes (page 388)
½ recipe Grand Marnier Soufflé
    batter (this page)
2 tablespoons (16 g) cornstarch
4 cups (960 ml) or 1 recipe
    Strawberry Sauce (page 563)
Sour Cream Mixture for Piping
    (page 564)
powdered sugar

1. Place the crepes, browned-side down, on top of sixteen 5-ounce (150-ml) soufflé ramekins, 3 inches (7.5 cm) wide. Push the crepes halfway into the forms, and reserve.

2. Thirty minutes before the Crepe Soufflés are to be served, whip the egg whites for the soufflé batter as directed in the recipe. Add the additional cornstarch to the sugar and cornstarch mixture before folding it in.

3. Pipe the soufflé batter into the ramekins on top of the crepes so that the crepes are pushed to the bottom and line the sides and bottoms of the ramekins. Fill the forms to about ½ inch (1.2 cm) above the rims.

4. Bake immediately at 400°F (205°C) for approximately 25 minutes. These do not puff up as high as a regular soufflé but will stick to the crepe and crack on the top.

5. Presentation: A few minutes before the soufflés come out of the oven, cover the bottom of the dessert plates with the Strawberry Sauce. Decorate the outer edge with the Sour Cream Mixture for Piping (see pages 518–519). Remove the soufflés from the oven and sift powdered sugar lightly over the tops. Unmold each soufflé gently by inverting it into your hand, then place it right-side up in the center of the prepared plate. Serve immediately.

Grand Marnier Soufflé
25 servings

melted butter
granulated sugar to coat forms
10 ounces (285 g) granulated
    sugar
3 ounces (85 g) cornstarch
3½ ounces (100 g) bread flour
3½ ounces (100 g) softened butter
1 quart (960 ml) milk
15 egg yolks
20 egg whites, at room temperature
1 teaspoon (5 ml) vanilla extract
¾ cup (180 ml) Grand Marnier
    liqueur
5½ cups (1 l, 440 ml) or 1 recipe
    Vanilla Custard Sauce
    (page 564)
powdered sugar

1. Use the melted butter to thoroughly grease the insides of 25 (or 5 for the small recipe) 3-inch (7.5-cm) wide, 5-ounce (150-ml) soufflé ramekins. Fill one of the forms halfway with granulated sugar. Twist the form so that the sugar coats the entire inside, then pour the sugar into the next form. Repeat until all the forms are coated, adding more sugar as necessary. Set the forms aside.

2. Combine about one-third of the second measurement of sugar with the cornstarch. Reserve.

3. Mix the flour and butter to form a paste. Heat the milk to the scalding point in a heavy saucepan. Add the butter and flour mixture to the milk and whisk to combine it with the milk. Quickly mix in one-third of the egg yolks. Bring to a boil over low heat, stirring constantly. Cook the mixture until it thickens, about 1 minute. Remove from the heat but continue to stir for 10 to 15 seconds to ensure a smooth cream.

4. Add the remaining egg yolks, vanilla, ½ cup (120 ml) of Grand Marnier liqueur (2 tablespoons/30 ml for the small recipe), and the sugar and cornstarch mixture. Cover the mixture and reserve. It will keep one day if refrigerated.

5 servings

melted butter
granulated sugar to coat forms
2 ounces (55 g) granulated sugar
1½ tablespoons (12 g) cornstarch
¾ ounce (20 g) bread flour
¾ ounce (20 g) softened butter
¾ cup (180 ml) milk
3 egg yolks
4 egg whites, at room temperature
¼ teaspoon (1.25 ml) vanilla
   extract
¼ cup (60 ml) Grand Marnier
   liqueur
1½ cups (300 ml) or ¼ recipe
   Vanilla Custard Sauce
   (page 564)
powdered sugar

5. Flavor the custard sauce with the remaining Grand Marnier liqueur. Reserve until time of service. If refrigerated, bring to room temperature before serving.

6. About 40 minutes before serving, whip the egg whites until they have quadrupled in volume and have a thick and foamy consistency. Gradually whip in the reserved two-thirds of the sugar, then whip a few seconds longer until the egg whites are stiff but not dry. Gradually fold the reserved custard mixture into the egg whites.

7. Immediately place the soufflé batter in a pastry bag with a no. 8 (16-mm) plain tip. Pipe into the prepared soufflé ramekins, making a smooth mound slightly above the rim of the ramekin. Be sure the batter does not actually stick to the rim itself.

8. Bake at once at 400°F (205°C) for about 25 to 30 minutes, or until done. The sides and top should be light brown.

9. Presentation: Quickly remove soufflés from the oven and sift powdered sugar lightly over the tops. Place the ramekins on dessert plates lined with doilies. Serve immediately with the accompanying sauce.

NOTE 1: For à la carte service, whip your egg whites and sugar as needed for each order as it comes in. Until you have enough experience to divide those ingredients into single portions by eye, whip extra whites and use more sugar than is called for rather than less. Combine approximately 2 parts whipped egg whites with 1 part custard base and spoon into the form. Unless you have another order immediately, do not use the leftover whipped egg whites, just adjust the amount you use for the next order. If you know you will need all of the soufflés, but not all at the same time, you can assemble the soufflés all together and hold them (unbaked) in a hot bain-marie (about 160°F/71°C). You can keep them for up to 30 minutes before baking without compromising the quality. When you are ready to proceed, remove them from the bain-marie and bake as directed, reducing the baking time by a few minutes. This method is also helpful when you have a misunderstanding with the dining room about when the order was fired.

NOTE 2: Traditionally, a liqueur soufflé is always served with sabayon sauce. However, Vanilla Custard Sauce is much more convenient, as it can be made ahead of time and therefore allows the chef to concentrate on the soufflé at the last moment.

Variation: Liqueur Soufflés

This recipe can be used to make any type of liqueur soufflé. Just substitute the desired flavor for the Grand Marnier in the soufflé base, then use the same liqueur to flavor the sauce. If the amount of liqueur called for in the recipe does not give the soufflé enough flavor, intensify it by soaking Ladyfingers (see page 134) in liqueur and placing two in the middle of the soufflé batter as you fill the forms.

Chocolate Soufflé

Prepare the recipe as directed with the following changes:

1. Omit the liqueur from the batter and the sauce.
2. Mix 3 ounces (85 g) cocoa powder with the cornstarch.
3. Add 2 ounces (55 g) melted dark chocolate to the warm custard.
4. Add 2 additional egg whites.

For the small recipe, add 3 tablespoons (24 g) cocoa powder, 1 tablespoon (15 ml) dark chocolate, and 1 extra egg white.

Harlequin Soufflé

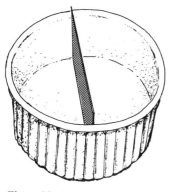

Figure 11–4

After coating the soufflé cups with butter and sugar, stand a piece of cardboard in the center of each form (Figure 11–4). Reserve. Prepare the full recipe as directed, making the following changes:

1. Divide the custard, reserved sugar, and egg whites in half, separately.
2. Add 1½ ounces (40 g) of cocoa powder and 1 ounce (30 ml) melted dark chocolate to one portion of the custard.
3. Add 1 additional egg white to one portion of the egg whites. Set next to the chocolate-flavored custard to distinguish.
4. Combine the custard with the sugar and egg whites as directed, making two separate batters and using the larger group of egg whites in the chocolate batter to compensate for the addition of the chocolate.
5. Fill one side of each of the prepared forms with the plain and chocolate batters. Pull the cardboard *straight* up and out. Bake and serve as directed.

Pecan–Raisin Soufflé

25 servings

1 recipe Grand Marnier Soufflé batter (page 327)
¾ cup (180 ml) whiskey
5½ cups (1 l, 320 ml) or 1 recipe Vanilla Custard Sauce (page 564)
½ recipe Caramelized Pecans (page 488)
2 tablespoons (24 g) Hazelnut Paste (page 6)
4 ounces (115 g) dark raisins
powdered sugar

1. Prepare the full recipe of Grand Marnier Soufflé batter through step 4, substituting ½ cup (120 ml) whiskey for the Grand Marnier liqueur.
2. Add ¼ cup (60 ml) whiskey to the sauce and reserve. If refrigerated, bring the sauce to room temperature before serving.
3. Coarsely crush the caramelized pecans. Mix the pecans, hazelnut paste, and raisins into the soufflé batter before combining with the whipped egg whites. Fill the prepared soufflé forms and bake as directed in Grand Marnier Soufflé.
4. Sift powdered sugar lightly over the tops, and serve immediately with the whiskey-flavored sauce.

Meringues

Basic Meringues
  French Meringue
  Italian Meringue
  Japonaise Batter
  Meringue Noisette
  Swiss Meringue
Meringue Desserts
  Baked Alaska
  Blackberry Meringue Tartlets
  Frozen Raspberry Mousse
    with Meringue
  Gâteau Arabe

Ice Cream Cake Jamaica
Japonaise
Marjolaine
Meringue Baskets
  with Raspberries
Meringue Black Forest Cake
Meringue Glacé Leda
Meringue Landeck
Mocha Meringues
Vacherin with Plum
  Ice Cream

$\mathcal{M}$*eringue is a key ingredient* in the pastry kitchen. It is used to make vacherin and glacées; baked layers of meringue are used in cakes and pastries such as the famous marjolaine; it is made into cookies, added to buttercream, and used to top desserts such as baked Alaska and lemon meringue pie. In Europe today, many pastry shops do not make their own meringue, but to save time and money buy it from companies that specialize in baked meringue products.

Meringue is made of egg whites and sugar whipped together to incorporate air and form soft or stiff peaks. The usual ratio of sugar to egg whites is 2 to 1, measured by weight. Egg whites whipped without sugar are not meringue, they are simply egg whites whipped to a dry consistency.

Meringue whipped to a soft peak will not hold its shape; it will slowly settle, or fall, instead. Meringue properly whipped to a stiff peak will not change shape as you pipe it from a pastry bag or work with it; you should actually be able to turn the bowl of meringue upside down with no problem (or mess). Be observant: There is a fine line between stiff peaks and overwhipped, dry peaks. Meringue that is overwhipped and dry is hard to pipe out into precise shapes, and is impossible to fold into a batter without getting small lumps. Meringue whipped to stiff peaks should still appear shiny, not dry or broken.

For perfect meringue, follow these guidelines.

(1) Use egg whites at room temperature.

(2) Be sure the egg whites are not so old that they have started to deteriorate and get cloudy.

(3) Because fat prevents egg whites from expanding, make sure they are clean and free of any egg yolk particles. The mixing bowl and whip or whisk must also be clean.

(4) Using a copper bowl and/or a balloon whisk can be helpful when making meringue, but they are not absolutely necessary. Copper bowls are preferable because of their acidity, but a

small amount of cream of tartar or lemon juice added to the egg whites will have the same effect.

There are three basic types of meringue: French, Swiss, and Italian. The ingredients for each of the three types is essentially the same, but the methods of preparation and the end results are different.

French Meringue is best for baking *au naturel*, mixing with nuts, and using as a cake base. If made and baked correctly, French Meringue is very tender, light, and fragile. It should not be held for more than 10 minutes before baking or the egg whites may start to separate from the sugar.

Italian Meringue is a better choice if the meringue must stand for some time. It is denser because the egg whites are partially cooked and therefore it holds up longer before baking. If made properly it will keep for several hours. Italian Meringue is also preferable to use in a dessert when the meringue is eaten raw or with only partial further cooking as, for example, when it is added to a filling or when only the outside is browned as in baked Alaska. When Italian Meringue is baked all the way through it is harder than French Meringue, and not as tender.

Swiss Meringue could be described as a mixture between the French and Italian Meringues. It is usually used in buttercreams and fillings, but it can be piped out in different shapes, then baked or dried.

In the recipes that follow, egg whites are measured by volume rather than by number. This measurement is not only more precise, it is also easier in professional kitchens, where a supply of egg whites is usually on hand. There are approximately seven egg whites in 1 cup (240 ml).

Meringue should be baked at a low temperature. For most types of meringue this is around 200°F (94°C). The most notable exception is a meringue containing ground nuts, such as a japonaise. Here, the nuts will absorb some of the moisture in the egg whites and allow the meringue to dry more quickly. You do not bake meringue so much as you dry it out. Meringue should not color as it is baked, but should remain white. However, a slight hint of color (off-white) is acceptable. Always store baked meringue in a warm, dry place. Baked meringue will keep for weeks unless nuts have been added, as the nuts can become rancid.

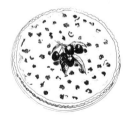

Basic Meringues

French Meringue

approximately 3 quarts (2 l, 880 ml) meringue

1 pint (480 ml) egg whites, at room temperature
3 drops lemon juice or Tartaric Acid Solution (page 596)
2 pounds (910 g) granulated sugar

1. If you are using a copper bowl to whip the meringue, omit the lemon juice or tartaric acid solution. Whip the egg whites, a handful of the sugar, and the lemon juice or tartaric acid for about 2 minutes or until the mixture has tripled in volume and has the consistency of a thick foam.

2. Still whipping at high speed, gradually add the remaining sugar; this should take about 3 minutes. Continue to whip the meringue at high speed until stiff peaks form. Do not overwhip (see chapter introduction).

3. Pipe or spread the meringue into the desired shape as soon as possible.

4. Bake at 200°F (94°C) until dry, following the instructions given in the individual recipes.

Italian Meringue

approximately 5 quarts (4 l, 800 ml) meringue

1 pint (480 ml) egg whites
1 pound, 8 ounces (680 g) granulated sugar
12 ounces (340 g) (or 1 cup/ 240 ml) light corn syrup
1 cup (240 ml) water

1. Place the egg whites in a mixing bowl so you will be ready to start whipping them when the sugar syrup is ready.

2. Boil the sugar, corn syrup, and water. When the syrup reaches 230°F (110°C), begin whipping the egg whites on high speed. Continue boiling the syrup until it reaches 247°F (120°C).

3. Remove the syrup from the heat and lower the mixer speed to medium. Pour the syrup into the egg whites in a thin, steady stream. Turn the mixer back up to high and continue to whip the meringue until it forms stiff peaks, approximately 5 minutes longer.

NOTE: If you do not have a sugar thermometer, boil the syrup for about 8 minutes on medium heat before you start whipping the egg whites. Then let the syrup boil about 6 minutes longer before you add it to the whipped whites.

Japonaise Batter

four 10-inch (25-cm) or ninety 2¼-inch (5.6-cm) shells

8 ounces (225 g) blanched almonds
½ ounce (15 g) cornstarch
11 ounces (310 g) granulated sugar
1 cup (240 ml) egg whites

1. Prepare your sheet pans, a pastry bag, and a template, if you are using one.

2. Grind the almonds, cornstarch, and half of the sugar to a fine consistency.

3. Whip the egg whites to a foam. They should quadruple in volume. Gradually add the remaining half of the sugar and whip to stiff peaks. Gently fold the ground nut mixture into the egg whites by hand. Pipe or spread into the desired shape immediately.

4. Bake as directed in individual recipes.

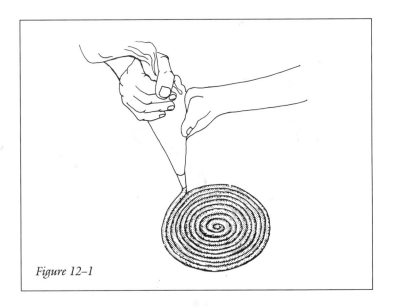

Figure 12–1

Meringue Noisette

*four 10-inch (25-cm) or fifty
3-inch (7.5-cm) shells*

*4 ounces (115 g) toasted hazelnuts
1 ounce (30 g) cornstarch
1 cup (480 ml) egg whites
1 pound (455 g) granulated sugar
1 teaspoon (5 ml) vanilla extract*

1. Draw four 10-inch (25-cm) circles on two sheets of baking paper. Place them upside down on sheet pans and set aside.

2. Remove as much of the skins from the toasted hazelnuts as comes off easily and grind them to a fine consistency. Combine with the cornstarch.

3. Whip the egg whites to a thick foam, until quadrupled in volume. Still whipping, gradually add the sugar, taking 3 to 4 minutes to add all of it. Continue to whip the meringue until it forms stiff peaks. Add the vanilla extract. Carefully fold the nut and cornstarch mixture into the meringue by hand.

4. Place the noisette batter in a pastry bag with a no. 4 (8-mm) plain tip. (Use a no. 3 (6-mm) tip if making the smaller size.) Pipe the batter in a spiral within the four circles drawn on the papers, starting in the center and working to the outside (Figure 12–1).

5. Bake immediately at 250°F (122°C) for approximately 1 hour, or until dry.

Swiss Meringue

2 quarts (1 l, 920 ml) meringue

*1 pint (480 ml) egg whites
2 pounds (910 g) granulated sugar*

1. Combine the egg whites and sugar in a mixing bowl. Place the bowl over simmering water and heat to 120°F (49°C), whipping constantly to avoid cooking the egg whites. Make sure all of the sugar is dissolved.

2. Remove from the heat and whip the mixture at high speed until it is completely cool and has formed stiff peaks.

Meringue Desserts

Baked Alaska

10 to 12 servings

*2½ cups (600 ml) Vanilla
    Ice Cream (page 364)*
*2½ cups (600 ml) Strawberry
    Ice Cream (page 364)*
*2½ cups (600 ml) Chocolate
    Ice Cream (page 358)*
*one 14- × 24-inch (35- × 60-cm)
    Almond Sponge (page 162)*
orange liqueur
*¼ recipe Italian Meringue
    (page 333)*
powdered sugar
glacéed red cherries
Strawberry Sauce (page 563)
151 proof rum

Baked Alaska is a popular "show dessert," equalled by few when presented to the table flambéed, yet it is a very simple creation. I call it "the cruise-ship dessert" because it is a standard item on these ships and is usually served at the traditional captain's farewell dinner.

1. Layer the three ice creams in a chilled bread pan or other rectangular pan approximately 11 inches long, 4 inches wide, and 4 inches deep (27.5 × 10 × 10 cm). You will need to soften the ice cream a bit first to create smooth, even layers. Let each layer harden in the freezer before adding the next.

2. Cut a strip from the sponge sheet that is as wide as the pan is long, and long enough to wrap all the way around the ice cream block.

3. Unmold the ice cream by dipping the mold briefly into hot water. Then place the ice cream on the sponge sheet and roll it up to completely cover all four long sides. Use some scrap pieces of sponge to cover the ends. Place on a chilled silver tray.

4. Lightly sprinkle orange liqueur over the top of the sponge. Spread a ½-inch (1.2-cm) thick layer of meringue over the top and all four sides, using a metal spatula to achieve a smooth and even finish.

5. Place the remaining meringue in a pastry bag with a no. 4 (8-mm) star tip. Pipe the meringue onto the iced rectangle, decorating after your own taste and incorporating a place for three eggshell halves in your design.

6. Lightly sift powdered sugar over the meringue. Decorate with cherries and place three eggshell halves in the meringue to hold the rum. Push the eggshells into the meringue far enough so they are as inconspicuous as possible.

7. Place the tray in a hot oven or salamander to brown the meringue.

8. Pour Strawberry Sauce on the base of the tray around the dessert.

9. Turn down the lights in the dining room, pour a little rum into the eggshells, ignite, and present immediately.

NOTE: Any liqueur or spirit with an alcohol level of 80 percent can be used to flambé, although 151 proof rum is convenient and foolproof since it will ignite cold. If you use alcohol with a lower proof, you must warm it before igniting. Before using 151 proof rum for flambé work, take into consideration that the flavor of the rum may interfere with the flavor of the dessert if it is spooned over the top or used as part of the sauce (as in Persimmon Pudding, for example).

Individual Baked Alaskas
24 servings

one 14- × 24-inch (35- × 60-cm)
    Almond Sponge (page 162)
2½ quarts (2 l, 400 ml) or
    2 recipes Vanilla Ice Cream
    (page 364)
½ recipe Italian Meringue
    (page 333)
powdered sugar
glacéed cherries
Strawberry Sauce (page 563)

1. Cut twenty-four 3-inch (7.5-cm) circles from the sponge sheet and place them on a sheet pan lined with baking paper. Place a small scoop of ice cream on top of each circle. Reserve in the freezer.

2. Presentation: Place the meringue in a pastry bag with a no. 4 (8-mm) plain tip. Place a frozen sponge circle with ice cream in the center of an ovenproof dessert plate. Quickly, completely cover the sponge and ice cream with meringue by piping circles of meringue on top of each other starting at the base (see Figure 12–4, page 344).

3. Sift powdered sugar over the meringue and the dessert plate, including the border. Place a cherry on top of the meringue in the center.

4. Brown the dessert in a very hot oven or salamander. Take care not to get any fingerprints on the powdered sugar border as you work. Cover the base of the plate with Strawberry Sauce and serve immediately.

NOTE: If you are expecting to serve a lot of these, or know you have a large order coming up, you can place them 3 inches (7.5 cm) apart on sheet pans lined with baking paper. Make sure that the ice cream scoops are small enough to allow you to pipe the first row of meringue on the sponge and not on the sheet pan. Pipe the meringue as directed above. Reserve in the freezer until needed. (They can be left this way for up to 24 hours.) Sift powdered sugar on top just before browning. For a dramatic presentation, pour some hot brandy on the dessert after browning the meringue, ignite, and quickly present to the guest. This technique is more practical for the larger version.

Blackberry Meringue Tartlets
(see photograph in color insert)
15 pastries

¼ recipe French Meringue
    (page 333)
1 pound (455 g) Lemon Curd
    (page 568)
blackberries

1. Draw fifteen 4-inch (10-cm) circles, properly spaced, on sheets of baking paper. Invert the papers and place on sheet pans.

2. Place the meringue in a pastry bag with a no. 4 (8-mm) plain tip. Pipe a ring of pointed dots ("kisses") next to each other all around the insides of the circles. For a perfectly clean look, use your finger or a small spoon to straighten up the points. To make the bottom of the cases, pipe rings of meringue inside the dots using the same technique as for Meringue Noisette (see Figure 12–1, page 334), but holding the tip closer to the sheet pan to make the bottom thinner and allow enough space for the filling later.

Blackberry Sauce (see note,
    page 365)
Sour Cream Mixture for Piping
    (page 564)

3. Bake immediately at 200°F (94°C) for approximately 2 hours, or until the meringue has dried all the way through.

4. Presentation: Fill a meringue shell with 1 ounce (30 g) of lemon curd. Place the shell off-center on a dessert plate (put a dab of curd underneath to prevent it from sliding). Arrange whole fresh blackberries on top of the filling. Pour an oval pool of Blackberry Sauce on the plate in front of the dessert, and decorate the sauce with the Sour Cream Mixture for Piping (see pages 518–519).

NOTE: Any of the blackberry hybrids such as boysenberries, loganberries, or olallieberries will work well, but I prefer blackberries as they are smaller and make a more attractive arrangement on top of the meringue shell.

Frozen Raspberry Mousse with Meringues

eighteen 5-ounce (150-ml) servings

Raspberry Mousse Filling
    (recipe follows)
1 recipe Meringue Noisette batter
    (page 334)
1½ cups (360 ml) heavy cream
1 tablespoon (15 g) granulated
    sugar
6 cups (1 l, 440 ml) or 1 recipe
    Mousseline Sauce (page 561),
    made with 2 ounces (60 ml)
    Riesling wine
fresh raspberries
Chocolate Sauce for Piping
    (page 560)

1. Fill soufflé ramekins 3 inches (7.5 cm) in diameter (or any other forms of about the same size with a 5-ounce (150-ml) capacity) with Raspberry Mousse Filling. Even the tops with a spatula. Cover and place in the freezer for approximately 3 hours or until the mousse is firm.

2. Place the Meringue Noisette batter in a pastry bag with a no. 3 (6-mm) plain tip. Pipe out 3-inch (7.5-cm) circles, following the instructions for Meringue Noisette (see Figure 12–1, page 334). You need 36 circles for this recipe, but the batter will make about 50. Bake at 250°F (122°C) for about 40 minutes or until dry. Set aside the best-looking shells to use for the tops.

3. Unmold each frozen mousse by dipping the forms briefly into hot water, just long enough to loosen them from the molds. Take care not to get any water on the mousse itself. Hold the forms upside down over the meringue circles and unmold one mousse onto each meringue. Use a fork to gently help you remove them. Place back in the freezer.

4. Whip the cream and sugar to stiff peaks. Place in a pastry bag with a no. 3 (6-mm) star tip. Reserve in the refrigerator until ready to serve.

5. Presentation: Pour just enough Mousseline Sauce on a dessert plate to cover the surface of the plate. Put a frozen raspberry mousse in the center of the plate. Place one of the reserved meringue shells on the top. Pipe a border of small dots, or "kisses," on the top meringue. Place five raspberries, standing on end, within the cream border. Decorate the Mousseline Sauce with the Chocolate Sauce for Piping (see pages 518–519). Serve immediately.

Raspberry Mousse Filling

about 2¾ quarts (2 l, 640 ml)
filling

3 cups (720 ml) heavy cream
2 tablespoons (18 g) powdered
    pectin
14 ounces (400 g) granulated
    sugar
6 egg whites
3 ounces (90 ml) Chambord
    liqueur
12 ounces (340 g) fresh raspberries,
    puréed and strained

1. Whip the cream to stiff peaks and reserve in the refrigerator.

2. Combine the pectin powder with the sugar. Add the egg whites. Heat mixture over simmering water, whipping constantly, until it reaches 110°F (43°C). Be careful not to let the egg whites get too hot and cook. Remove from the heat and whip the mixture until it is cold and has formed stiff peaks.

3. Add the liqueur to the raspberry purée. Gradually (to prevent lumps) fold the purée into the reserved whipped cream. Fold this mixture into the whipped egg whites.

NOTE: If you substitute frozen or canned raspberries packed with sugar syrup, decrease the amount of sugar in the recipe by half.

Gâteau Arabe

two 10-inch (25-cm) cakes

Butter and Flour Mixture
    (page 4)
½ recipe Chocolate Biscuit batter
    (page 163)
2 pounds, 8 ounces (1 kg, 135 g)
    Vanilla Buttercream (page 501)
1 teaspoon (4 g) mocha paste
    or
¼ cup (60 ml) Coffee Reduction
    (page 5)
4 ounces (115 g) smooth
    currant jelly
four 10-inch (25-cm) Meringue
    Noisette (page 334)
sliced almonds, toasted and
    lightly crushed
light Piping Chocolate (page 449)
Chocolate Rounds (page 445)

1. Brush the butter and flour mixture over two 10-inch (25-cm) cake pans. Divide the biscuit batter evenly between them. Bake at 400°F (205°C) for approximately 15 minutes, or until the sponge springs back when pressed lightly in the middle (these sponges will only be about an inch high). Let the sponges cool completely.

2. Flavor the buttercream with the mocha paste or coffee reduction and work it smooth at the same time. Reserve.

3. Cut the skin from the top of the sponges and even the tops, if necessary. Cut each sponge into two layers. Divide the jelly between two of the sponge layers and spread it out evenly. Place a Meringue Noisette on top of each one.

4. Set aside 6 ounces (170 g) of the buttercream for decoration. Spread some of the remaining buttercream in a ⅛-inch (3-mm) layer on the Meringue Noisettes that are on the sponges. Place the remaining two Meringue Noisettes on top of the buttercream layer. Spread a ⅛-inch (3-mm) layer of buttercream over the meringues. Top with the remaining sponge layers. Spread a thin layer of buttercream over the tops and sides of the cakes, using just enough to cover the sponge.

5. Place 6-inch (15-cm) round cookie cutters on top of the cakes in the centers; cover the sides of the cakes, and the outside top around the cutters, with the crushed almonds (see Figure 8–1, page 178). Refrigerate the cakes until the buttercream is firm.

6. Place the piping chocolate in a piping bag and cut a very small opening. Pipe a letter *A* on each chocolate round. Cut or mark the cakes into the desired number of serving pieces. Place the reserved 6 ounces (170 g) of buttercream in a pastry bag with a

no. 2 (4-mm) plain tip. Pipe two straight lines of buttercream in the center of each slice, covering the length of the slice. Place a chocolate round on top of the buttercream lines at the wide end of each piece.

Ice Cream Cake Jamaica

two 10-inch (25-cm) cakes

*½ recipe Swiss Meringue
    (page 334; see step 2)
1 ounce (30 g) cocoa powder
2 ounces (55 g) granulated sugar
melted dark baker's chocolate
Rum Parfait (recipe follows)
2½ cups (600 ml) or ½ recipe
    Vanilla Ice Cream (page 364)
1 quart (960 ml) heavy cream
2 tablespoons (30 g) granulated
    sugar
dark chocolate shavings
strawberry wedges
2½ cups (600 ml) or ½ recipe
    Mousseline Sauce (page 561),
    made with 2 tablespoons
    (30 ml) rum
Chocolate Sauce for Piping
    (page 560)*

1. Draw four 10-inch (25-cm) circles on baking papers. Invert the papers, place them on sheet pans, and set aside.

2. Combine the cocoa powder and 2 ounces (55 g) of granulated sugar and add to the meringue on low speed when it is finished whipping.

3. Place the meringue in a pastry bag with a no. 4 (8-mm) plain tip. Pipe the meringue inside the circles on the reserved papers, starting in the center and making a spiral to the outside (see Figure 12–1 on page 334).

4. Bake at 200°F (94°C) for approximately 1 hour or until dry. Let the meringues cool completely, then brush a thin layer of melted baker's chocolate on the top side of all four meringues.

5. Place two of the meringues, chocolate-side up, on cake cardboards for support. Place 10-inch (25-cm) cake rings on top of the meringues and press down gently to seal. If the rings are not made of stainless steel, line the insides with paper or plastic strips to prevent the metal from staining the filling. Set aside.

6. Gradually add the Rum Parfait to the Vanilla Ice Cream (the ice cream needs to be reasonably soft). Divide the mixture between the two prepared forms. Place the remaining meringue shells, chocolate-side down, on top of the filling. Trim the meringues if necessary to fit them inside the rings. Cover and place in the freezer for at least 3 hours, or until firm.

7. Whip the cream with the remaining sugar to stiff peaks. Remove the cake rings and paper or plastic strips from the cakes. Trim away any excess meringue to make the sides even. Return one cake to the freezer. Spread just enough whipped cream on the top and sides of the other cake to cover.

8. Cut into serving pieces. Sprinkle dark chocolate shavings over the center 6 inches (15 cm) of the cake. Return the cake to the freezer. Repeat with second cake.

9. Place the remaining whipped cream in a pastry bag with a no. 7 (14-mm) star tip. Reserve in the refrigerator until ready to serve.

10. Presentation: Pipe a small dot of whipped cream, slightly off-center, on a chilled dessert plate. Put a slice of cake on top. Place a no. 4 (8-mm) plain tip on the outside of the pastry bag and hold

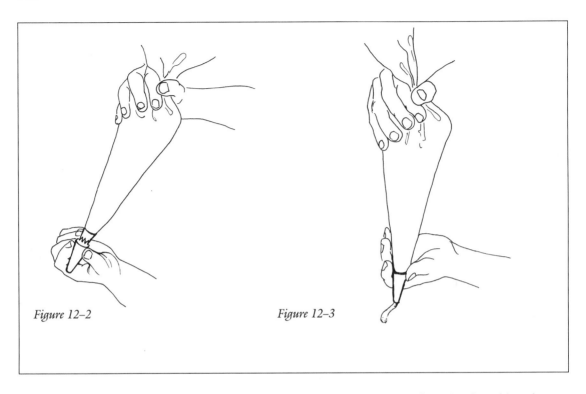

Figure 12–2   Figure 12–3

it in place as you pipe (Figures 12–2 and 12–3). Pipe whipped cream onto the iced side of the slice in a vertical zigzag pattern. Remove the plain tip and pipe a rosette on top of the slice near the end. Place a strawberry wedge on the rosette. Pour a small pool of Mousseline Sauce on the plate in front of the cake and decorate the sauce with the Chocolate Sauce for Piping (see pages 518–519).

Rum Parfait

5 ounces (140 g) golden raisins
¾ cup (180 ml) dark rum
8 egg yolks
5 ounces (140 g) granulated sugar
4½ cups (1 l, 80 ml) heavy cream
1 tablespoon (9 g) unflavored
   gelatin powder
¼ cup (60 ml) cold water

1. Combine the raisins and rum in a saucepan and heat to about 175°F (80°C). Remove from the heat and let the raisins macerate in the rum overnight.

2. Whip the egg yolks and sugar together over simmering water to approximately 110°F (43°C). Make sure that the sugar is completely dissolved. Remove from the heat and whip until cold and fluffy. Reserve.

3. Whip the cream to soft peaks. Reserve.

4. Soften the gelatin in cold water and heat to 120°F (49°C) to dissolve. Rapidly mix the gelatin into a small part of the whipped cream, then stir into the remaining cream. Gradually fold the rum, raisins, and the egg mixture into the cream.

NOTE: If you do not have time to macerate the raisins overnight it is better to omit them. If the raisins have not absorbed enough rum, they will be hard and unpleasant when frozen.

Japonaise

40 pastries

1 recipe Japonaise Batter
  (page 333)
2 pounds (910 g) Vanilla
  Buttercream (page 501)
6 ounces (170 g) Hazelnut Paste
  (page 6)
  or
3 ounces (85 g) commercial
  hazelnut paste
dark baker's chocolate, melted

1. The fastest and most efficient way of making Japonaise shells is to spread the batter over rubber templates made expressly for this purpose. If these are not available, you can make a pattern by drawing 2¼-inch (5.6-cm) circles, spaced 1 inch (2.5 cm) apart, on baking paper using a heavy pen. (Draw the circles before you make the batter.) Fasten the pattern to the table with a dab of batter in each corner. Place a second sheet of parchment on top.

2. Place the batter in a pastry bag with a no. 2 (4-mm) plain tip. Pipe the batter following the pattern under the paper, starting in the center of the circles and working to the outside, to fill in the circles completely as in the Meringue Noisette (see Figure 12–1, page 334). Drag the filled paper onto a sheet pan (see Figure 15–3, page 422) and repeat to make the remaining shells. If you are just making a few shells, invert the paper with the pattern and pipe the shells directly on the back of the paper. After you have had some practice you can eliminate this step completely and just pipe the batter into circles, keeping the shells the same size by piping an equal number of rings for each one.

3. Bake immediately at 300°F (149°C) until the meringues are completely dry, about 30 minutes. Make sure that the oven is not too hot; too high a temperature will cause the shells to puff up, become brittle, and be very hard to work with.

4. Set aside about 10 of the least attractive shells. Trim any of the remaining shells as needed so that they are round and all about the same size.

5. Flavor the buttercream with the hazelnut paste. Place it in a pastry bag with a no. 4 (8-mm) plain tip. Pipe a ¼-inch (6-mm) layer of buttercream on half of the shells, using the same piping technique that you used to make the shells. Invert the remaining shells on top and press down lightly making sure the sides are lined up evenly. Refrigerate until the buttercream is firm.

6. Crush the 10 reserved shells, as well as any shavings from the others, to very fine crumbs.

7. Spread a very thin layer of buttercream on the sides and top of the chilled pastries. (You can do this faster by holding two together while you ice the sides.) Roll the sides in the reserved crumbs and sprinkle crumbs over the tops to completely cover the buttercream. Pipe a small dot of melted baker's chocolate, about ½ inch (1.2 cm) in diameter, in the center of each Japonaise.

Variation

Classic Japonaise are filled with hazelnut-flavored buttercream. For a delightful variation, try filling them with coffee-flavored buttercream instead. Replace the chocolate dot with a candy coffee bean or one made out of marzipan (page 204).

Marjolaine

*thirty-five 2¼-inch (5.6-cm)
square pastries*

1 recipe Cocoa Almond Sponge
   batter (page 163)
Nut Meringue (recipe follows)
Praline Buttercream
   (recipe follows)
½ recipe Chocolate Cream
   (page 566)
1 pound, 6 ounces (625 g)
   Ganache (page 567)
Cream Chantilly (recipe follows)
cocoa powder
Raspberry Sauce (page 563)
raspberries
mint sprigs
Sour Cream Mixture for Piping
   (page 564)

This fabulous dessert is worth all of the trouble it takes to make. It is the best-known recipe of the late French chef, Fernand Point, owner of the three-star restaurant La Pyramide. Exactly why he picked the name Marjolaine I do not know, but it could have something to do with a special lady who liked chocolate. (Marjolaine is a girl's name in France.) The original recipe has been changed (possibly improved) over the years to suit each chef's taste. Here is my version.

1. Line the bottom of a half-sheet pan (16 × 12 inches/40 × 30 cm) with baking paper. Spread the sponge batter evenly over the pan. Bake immediately at 400°F (205°C) for about 15 minutes, or until the sponge springs back when pressed lightly in the middle. Set aside to cool.

2. Make the Nut Meringue, Praline Buttercream, and Chocolate Cream. Do not make the Cream Chantilly until you are ready to use it.

3. Cut the meringue sheets in half to make four layers, 16 × 12 inches/40 × 30 cm each. Do not separate the meringue from the baking paper at this time.

4. Cut the sponge sheet free from the sides of the pan. Unmold the sponge onto an inverted sheet pan or a cardboard. Remove the baking paper.

5. Soften 14 ounces (400 g) of the ganache and spread it evenly on top of the sponge sheet. Pick up one of the meringue layers, holding it by the baking paper, invert it on top of the ganache, and peel off the paper. Spread the Chocolate Cream on top of the meringue. Add a second meringue sheet, using the same method as before. Top this one with the Praline Buttercream. Add the third meringue sheet. Refrigerate while you make the Cream Chantilly.

6. Make the Cream Chantilly and spread it evenly on top of the third meringue sheet. Place the last meringue sheet on top of the cream. If necessary, press the top of the pastry lightly with the bottom of a sheet pan to level the top.

7. Warm the remaining ganache until it is liquid. Spread a thin layer over the top of the Marjolaine. Before the ganache sets up completely, use the back of a chef's knife to mark diagonal lines, ½ inch (1.2 cm) apart in both directions, making a diamond pattern in the ganache. Refrigerate until firm.

8. Dust cocoa powder lightly over the top. Using a thin, sharp knife dipped in hot water, trim about ¼ inch (6 mm) from one of the long sides of the rectangle to make a clean edge. Starting from that edge, mark or cut the Marjolaine into 2¼-inch (5.6-cm) pieces. Hold the knife at a 90° angle so that the sides of the pastries will be straight. This cake will keep for several days in the

refrigerator if left whole, so it is best to cut the servings as you need them.

9. Presentation: Place the Marjolaine slightly off-center on a dessert plate. Pour a small pool of Raspberry Sauce in front of the dessert and form it into a heart shape using a spoon. Place three raspberries and a mint sprig next to the sauce. Decorate the Raspberry Sauce with the sour cream mixture (see pages 518–519).

Nut Meringue

12 ounces (340 g) toasted almonds
8 ounces (225 g) toasted hazelnuts
1 ounce (30 g) bread flour
16 egg whites
1 pound (455 g) granulated sugar

1. Grind the almonds and hazelnuts to a fine consistency. Mix in the flour.

2. Whip the egg whites until they are foamy and have doubled in volume. Add the sugar gradually and whip to stiff peaks. Carefully fold in the ground nut mixture by hand.

3. Divide the batter equally between two sheets of baking paper, 24 × 16 inches (60 × 40 cm). Using a spatula, spread the batter in an even layer over the papers to cover them completely. Drag the papers onto sheet pans (see Figure 15–3, page 422).

4. Bake immediately at 350°F (175°C) for about 15 minutes or until golden brown and dry.

Praline Buttercream

1 pound, 4 ounces (570 g) Vanilla
Buttercream (page 501)
4 ounces (115 g) Hazelnut Paste
(page 6)
or
2 ounces (55 g) commercial
hazelnut paste
¼ teaspoon (1 g) mocha paste
or
1 tablespoon (15 ml) Coffee
Reduction (page 5)

1. Mix a small amount of buttercream into the hazelnut paste to soften it. Mix back into the remaining buttercream together with the coffee flavoring. Continue to mix until smooth.

NOTE: Buttercream tends to break when liquid is added, especially if the buttercream is cold. Should this happen, stir the mixture over simmering water until it is smooth.

Cream Chantilly

1 quart (960 ml) heavy cream
2 tablespoons (30 g) granulated
sugar
1 teaspoon (5 ml) vanilla extract
1 tablespoon (9 g) unflavored
gelatin powder
⅓ cup (80 ml) cold water

1. Whip the cream, sugar, and vanilla to soft peaks.

2. Soften the gelatin in cold water. Heat the mixture to 125°F (52°C) to dissolve. Rapidly mix the gelatin into a small portion of the cream. Then, still working quickly, add this combination to the remaining cream.

Meringue Baskets with Raspberries

(see photograph in color insert)
20 servings

Butter and Flour Mixture
(page 4)
½ recipe French Meringue
(page 333)
6 ounces (170 g) Short Dough
(page 31)
melted dark baker's chocolate
1 cup (240 ml) heavy cream
½ teaspoon (2.5 ml)
vanilla extract
Raspberry Sauce (page 563)
fresh raspberries
Sour Cream Mixture for Piping
(page 564)

1. Cut ½ inch (1.2 cm) from the tips of 20 paper cones (like those made of heavy waxed paper and used for shaved ice). Cut enough from the opposite end so that you have 2-inch (5-cm) tall (somewhat mutilated) cones. Thoroughly coat the outside of the cones with the butter and flour mixture. Place them on a sheet pan lined with baking paper.

2. Place the French Meringue in a pastry bag with a no. 4 (8-mm) plain tip. Pipe the meringue around the cones in concentric circles, one on top of the other, starting the first circle on the baking paper at the base of the cone (Figure 12–4).

3. Place a no. 3 (6-mm) plain tip, outside of the pastry bag, over the tip inside and hold it in place as you pipe (see Figures 12–2 and 12–3, page 340). Pipe out 20 (or a few extra to allow for breakage) 2-inch (5-cm) tall handles in the shape of an upside down *U*, onto a sheet pan lined with baking paper. Make sure the bottoms of the handles are not wider than the insides (tops) of the baskets.

4. Bake the cones and the handles at 200°F (94°C) for about 3 hours for the cones and slightly less for the handles, or until they are completely dry.

5. Roll out the short dough to ⅛ inch (3 mm) thick. Cut out 20 cookies using a 2-inch (5-cm) fluted cookie cutter. Bake the cookies at 375°F (190°C) until golden brown.

6. Carefully remove the meringue baskets from the paper cones using a small, thin knife. Trim the narrow end of the cones so they are flat and will stand straight.

7. Brush melted baker's chocolate on the inside of the cones to cover the bottom 1 inch (2.5 cm) of the narrow ends. This will

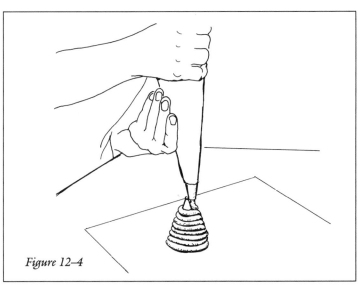

Figure 12–4

reinforce the bottom so the cones will be sturdier when filled. Dip the top rim of the cones into melted baker's chocolate, moving them up and down a few times over the bowl to remove all the excess so the chocolate will not drip on the sides as they are placed right side up. Stand the cones on their narrow ends, and let the chocolate set up. Dip the top edge of the handles in chocolate and set aside.

8. Dip the short dough cookies into melted baker's chocolate, coating them completely. Use the same up-and-down motion to remove excess chocolate and scrape the bottom of the cookies against the side of the bowl before placing them on paper. Set on baking paper and stand a cone on top of each one before the chocolate sets up.

9. Whip the heavy cream, vanilla, and a few tablespoons of the Raspberry Sauce to stiff peaks. Place in a pastry bag with a no. 6 (12-mm) plain tip.

10. Presentation: Pipe the whipped cream into a basket, filling it to ¼ inch (6 mm) from the rim. Place a handle on top of the basket, securing it in the cream. Arrange fresh raspberries on top of the cream. Pipe a small dot of cream off-center on a dessert plate. Set the basket on top to prevent it from sliding. Pour a pool of Raspberry Sauce in front of the basket. Decorate the Raspberry Sauce with the sour cream mixture (see pages 518–519).

Meringue Black Forest Cake

two 10-inch (25-cm) cakes

3 pounds (1 kg, 365 g) Crème Parisienne (page 567)
⅓ cup (80 ml) kirschwasser
four 10-inch (25-cm) Meringue Noisette (page 334)
melted dark baker's chocolate
one 10-inch (25-cm) Chocolate Biscuit (page 163)
Dark Chocolate Triangles (page 445)
1½ cups (360 ml) heavy cream
2 teaspoons (10 g) granulated sugar
Dark Chocolate Squares (page 445)
cocoa powder

1. Combine the Crème Parisienne and kirschwasser and whip to stiff peaks. Reserve.

2. Brush a thin layer of melted baker's chocolate on the top sides of the Meringue Noisettes.

3. Cut the skin from the top of the Chocolate Biscuit. Cut it into two layers and place them on cardboard cake circles for support. Place one-quarter of the Crème Parisienne on each of the sponge layers; spread it out evenly. Place a meringue, chocolate-side down, on top of the cream on each cake and press down firmly. Divide the remaining cream on top of the meringues and spread it out evenly. Place the remaining two meringues, chocolate-side down, on top of the cream and press down firmly. Do not worry if the meringues stick out beyond the sponge; you will trim them later. If you plan to present the cakes in serving pieces rather than whole, place the cakes in the freezer at this point until they are hard before finishing them. This will make them easier to cut.

4. Make the chocolate triangles 1½ inches (3.7 cm) tall and ¾ inch (2 cm) wide at the bottom. Reserve.

5. Trim any meringue that protrudes outside the sponge so that the sides are even. Whip the heavy cream and sugar to stiff peaks. Divide the cream between the cakes and ice the tops and sides, spreading just a thin layer of cream on the sides and the remainder on the tops.

6. Cut or mark the cakes into the desired number of serving pieces, making sure the cakes are still half-frozen when you cut them to avoid smashing the layers.

7. Decorate the length of each slice with the dark chocolate triangles. Start by placing one triangle at the tip of the slice, then two behind it, and three behind those, continuing as the piece becomes wider. Stick the pointed ends into the cream so that the triangles stand up at a very slight angle. Fasten a chocolate square to the side of each slice. Sift cocoa powder lightly over the top.

Meringue Glacé Leda

(see photograph in color insert)
25 servings

1/2 recipe French Meringue
  (page 333)
1 recipe Hippen Decorating Paste
  (page 527)
1 teaspoon (2.5 g) cocoa powder
1 recipe Spun Sugar, colored light
  pink (page 495); see note
1 1/2 cups (360 ml) heavy cream
1 tablespoon (15 g) granulated
  sugar
5 cups (1 l, 200 ml) or 1 recipe
  Vanilla Ice Cream (page 364)

This dessert is made in the shape of a swan and is named for Leda of Greek mythology. Leda was loved by Zeus, who appeared to her in the form of a swan and carried her away on his back.

1. Place the meringue in a pastry bag with a no. 8 (16-mm) star tip. Pipe into twenty-five 3-inch (7.5-cm), cone-shaped shells on sheet pans lined with baking paper (see Figure 9–24, page 261). Bake at 200°F (94°C) for approximately 3 hours or until dry.

2. Color about 1 ounce (30 g) of the hippen paste with the cocoa powder. Reserve.

3. Make the templates for the wings and neck (Figure 12–5). The template as shown is the correct size for this recipe. Trace the drawings and then cut them from 1/16-inch (2-mm) cardboard (cake boxes work fine for this).

4. Lightly grease the back of even sheet pans, coat with flour, and shake off as much flour as possible. Adjust the hippen paste, if necessary, until it is easily spreadable but not runny (see recipe). Spread the paste flat and even within the templates on the prepared pans (see Figures 18–47 and 18–48, page 548). Make a few extra necks to allow for breakage. Make 25 wings, then turn the template over and make 25 more so you will have a left and right wing for each swan.

5. Place the reserved cocoa-colored paste in a piping bag. Pipe one small dot on each head for an eye.

6. Bake at 375°F (190°C) until they start to color slightly, about 10 minutes. Let cool completely before removing from the sheet pans. Reserve in an airtight container. The necks and wings can be stored for up to one week at this point.

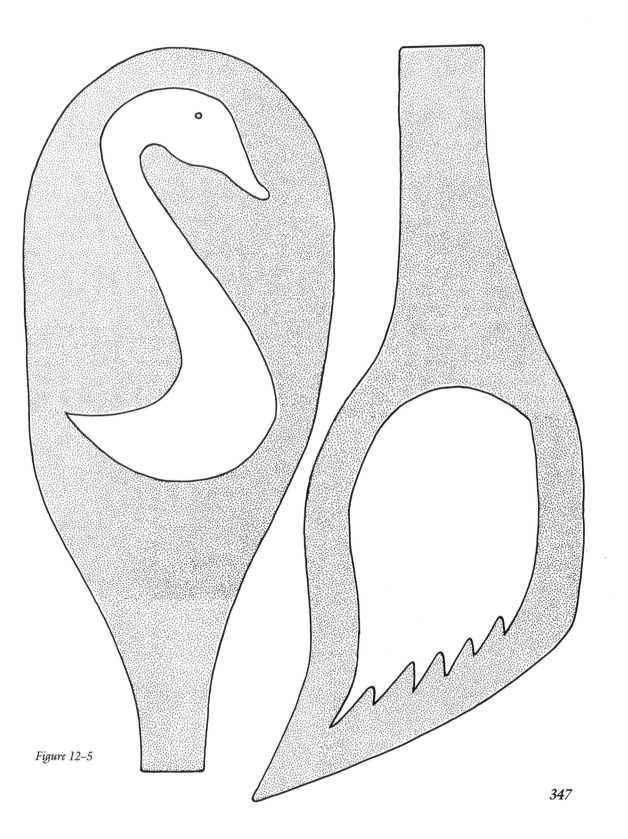

Figure 12–5

347

7. Make the spun sugar as close to serving time as possible. Reserve in an airtight container.

8. Trim just enough off the thicker part of the sides of the meringue shells to make them flat.

9. Whip the heavy cream and sugar to stiff peaks. Place in a pastry bag with a no. 8 (16-mm) star tip. Reserve in the refrigerator.

10. Presentation: Pipe a small dot of whipped cream in the center of a chilled dessert plate. Place a meringue shell on the cream. Place a scoop of ice cream, large enough to slightly protrude beyond the cut sides, on top of the meringue. Fasten one left and one right wing, top side facing out and flat side against the ice cream, on the sides. Place a neck between the meringue and ice cream, angled back over the body. Pipe a small amount of whipped cream at the back for a tail. Arrange spun sugar on the plate around the swan. Serve immediately.

NOTE: If the weather is humid or rainy, it will be very difficult to produce attractive spun sugar. You may want to substitute Chocolate Sauce (page 559) with a decoration made using the Sour Cream Mixture for Piping (page 564). The decoration shown in Figure 18–28, page 519, would be appropriate to suggest waves.

Meringue Landeck

15 servings or one 24- × 4-inch (60- × 10-cm) strip

½ recipe French Meringue (page 333)
½ recipe Ladyfinger batter (page 134)
4 ounces (115 g) smooth apricot jam
Mocha Cream (recipe follows)
melted dark baker's chocolate
powdered sugar

1. Place the French Meringue in a pastry bag with a no. 8 (16-mm) plain tip. Pipe out ropes of meringue on a full sheet pan (16 × 24 inches/40 × 60 cm) lined with baking paper, piping the ropes the full length of the pan. The ropes should not touch each other. Bake the meringue at 212°F (100°C) for about 4 hours or until completely dry.

2. Line a second full sheet pan with baking paper. Use enough of the Ladyfinger batter to spread a strip the full length of the pan, about 5 inches (12.5 cm) wide and ¼ inch (6 mm) thick. Place the remaining batter in a pastry bag with a no. 8 (16-mm) tip. Pipe out four ropes of batter the full length of the sheet pan. Bake at 425°F (219°C) until golden brown, about 12 minutes (slightly less time for the strip).

3. Trim the ladyfinger strip to make it 4 inches (10 cm) wide. Spread the apricot jam on top. Place two meringue ropes and one ladyfinger rope on top of the jam, with the ladyfinger rope in the center.

4. Spread half of the Mocha Cream over the top. Place two ladyfinger ropes and one meringue rope on the cream layer, this time with the meringue in the center.

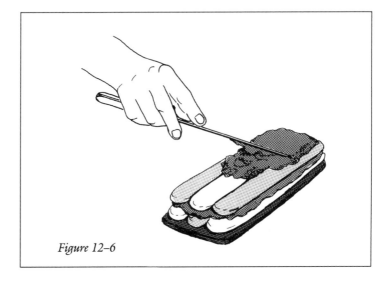

Figure 12–6

5. Ice the top and the long sides of the strip using all of the remaining Mocha Cream (Figure 12–6). Make a final layer using two meringue ropes and one ladyfinger rope, placing the lady-finger rope in the center.

6. Brush a thin layer of melted baker's chocolate over the two top meringue ropes. Refrigerate the strip for at least 2 hours to set the cream.

7. Cut the strip into 1½-inch (3.7-cm) slices using a serrated knife. Sift powdered sugar lightly over the pastries.

Variation: Chocolate Meringue Landeck

Follow the instructions as given, replacing the Mocha Cream with 2 pounds, 8 ounces (1 kg, 135 g) Crème Parisienne (see page 567).

Mocha Cream

7 cups (1 l, 680 ml) cream

5 eggs
3 ounces (85 g) granulated sugar
1 teaspoon (4 g) mocha paste
  or
¼ cup (60 ml) Coffee Reduction (page 5)
3 cups (720 ml) heavy cream
4 teaspoons (12 g) unflavored gelatin powder
⅓ cup (80 ml) cold water

1. Whip the eggs and sugar over simmering water for a few minutes until the mixture reaches 110°F (43°C). Remove from the heat and continue whipping until cold. Mix in the mocha paste or coffee reduction.

2. Whip the cream to soft peaks and fold into the egg mixture.

3. Soften the gelatin in cold water and heat to 125°F (52°C) to dissolve. Rapidly stir the gelatin into a small part of the cream mixture. Still working quickly, add this to the remaining cream.

NOTE: Do not make Mocha Cream until you are ready to use it.

Mocha Meringues

about 50 pastries

½ recipe French Meringue
  (page 333)
1 pound, 8 ounces (680 g) Vanilla
  Buttercream (page 501)
½ teaspoon (2 g) mocha paste
  or
2 tablespoons (30 ml) Coffee
  Reduction (page 5)
sliced almonds, toasted and
  lightly crushed
one hundred 1½-inch (3.7-cm)
  Chocolate Curls (page 444)
powdered sugar

1. Place the meringue in a pastry bag with a no. 8 (16-mm) plain tip. Pipe it onto sheet pans lined with baking paper in 1½-inch (3.7-cm) domes. Leave the tops as flat as possible as you pipe, without "tails" sticking up.

2. Bake at 250°F (122°C) until slightly puffed, about 5 minutes. Lower the heat immediately to 200°F (94°C) and leave the oven door open for a few minutes to help reduce the temperature quickly. Continue to bake the meringues at this temperature until completely dry, 3 to 4 hours. The meringues can be made to this point weeks in advance if they are kept covered in a warm place.

3. Flavor the buttercream with the mocha paste or coffee reduction, mixing until soft and smooth. Place in a pastry bag with a no. 2 (4-mm) plain tip. Pipe a mound of buttercream the size of a cherry on top of half of the meringues. Invert the remaining meringues on top of the buttercream, and press down lightly to level the tops.

4. Spread enough buttercream on the sides of the stacked meringues to completely fill in the gap between them and make the sides straight. Then roll the sides in the crushed almonds to coat. Using the same tip as before, cover the tops of the meringues with parallel lines of buttercream.

5. Set two chocolate curls on top of each pastry, arranging them diagonally across the buttercream lines.

6. Place six to eight pastries next to each other. Place a ¾-inch-wide (20-mm) strip of cardboard on top, perpendicular to the curls. Sift powdered sugar over the pastries. Remove the cardboard and repeat with the remaining pastries.

NOTE: If you do not have time to make the chocolate curls, substitute small Chocolate Rectangles (see page 445).

Vacherin with Plum Ice Cream

(see photograph in color insert)
16 servings

½ recipe French Meringue
  (page 333)
melted dark baker's chocolate
3 cups (720 ml) or ½ recipe
  Plum Ice Cream (page 363)
1 cup (240 ml) heavy cream
1½ teaspoons (8 g) granulated
  sugar

1. Draw thirty-two 3-inch (7.5-cm) circles on baking paper. Invert the papers on sheet pans. Place the meringue in a pastry bag with a no. 4 (8-mm) plain tip. Pipe the meringue onto the prepared baking papers using the circles as a guide (see Figure 12–1, page 334). As you come to the outside of each circle, pipe two additional rows of meringue on top of the outside ring to form the sides of the case. Make 16 cases. The remaining 16 circles are used as a guide to pipe out lids: Using a no. 2 (4-mm) plain tip held in place on the outside of the bag as you pipe (see Figures 12–2 and 12–3, page 340), pipe five equally spaced, parallel lines of meringue across one circle, then pipe five additional lines at a 45° angle to the first set to make a diamond pattern.

4 small plums
4 cups (960 ml) or 1 recipe
   Plum Sauce (page 562)

2. Bake immediately at 200°F (94°C) until dry. The cases will take approximately 4 hours and the lids about 2 hours. Made up to this point, the meringue shells will keep for several weeks if kept in a warm, dry place. Therefore, finish only the amount you expect to serve right away.

3. Holding the cases upside down, dip the rims of the cases into melted dark baker's chocolate. Carefully shake off excess chocolate before setting them right-side up to prevent any chocolate from dripping on the sides. Allow the chocolate to harden.

4. Fill each vacherin with plum ice cream. Place the filled meringue shells in the freezer.

5. Whip the cream and sugar to stiff peaks. Place in a pastry bag with a no. 3 (6-mm) plain tip; reserve in the refrigerator. Cut the plums into quarters. Fan the pieces and reserve in the refrigerator. Chill dessert plates in the refrigerator.

6. Presentation: Pipe the whipped cream in a spiral on top of a vacherin, starting in the center and continuing to the chocolate-covered rim, in the same way that you piped the base of the shells. Place a lid on top. Top with a fanned plum garnish. Pipe a small dot of whipped cream off-center on a dessert plate and place the finished vacherin on top to prevent it from sliding. Pour a small pool of Plum Sauce in front of the vacherin. Serve immediately.

NOTE: The vacherin or variation can, of course, be made with another ice cream of your choice. Change the name, sauce, and decoration accordingly.

Variation:
Meringue Glacé Chantilly

Vacherin Glacé is actually Meringue Glacé Chantilly in a fancy shape. You can make this classic by using the same ingredients but you will need a full recipe (6 cups/1 l, 440 ml) of ice cream as well as dark chocolate shavings. Use the following procedure.

1. Place the meringue in a pastry bag with a no. 6 (12-mm) star tip. Pipe it out into twenty-five 2½-inch (6.2-cm) corkscrews (like a telephone cord) or other pretty shapes.

2. Bake, cool, and dip the pieces halfway into melted dark baker's chocolate.

3. Place the whipped cream in a pastry bag with a no. 9 (18-mm) star tip. Pipe a large rosette of cream on the serving plate; sprinkle some chocolate shavings on top.

4. Arrange the ice cream, meringue, Plum Sauce, and a fanned plum in a nice presentation around the rosette. Do not forget to put a little whipped cream under the ice cream to prevent it from sliding. The variation makes 25 servings.

THIRTEEN

Ice Cream and Frozen Desserts

Ice Cream
  Banana Poppy Seed
    Ice Cream
  Caramel Ice Cream
  Chocolate Ice Cream
  Fresh-Coconut Ice Cream
  Macadamia Nut Ice Cream
  Papaya Ice Cream
  Peach Ice Cream
  Pistachio Ice Cream
  Plum Ice Cream
  Strawberry Ice Cream
  Vanilla Ice Cream
  White-Chocolate Ice Cream
    with Ginger
Sorbet
  Champagne Sorbet
  Honeydew Melon Sorbet
  Mandarin Sorbet
  Raspberry Sorbet
Bombes
  Basic Bombe Mixture

Bombe Aboukir
Bombe Bourdaloue
Bombe Ceylon
Bombe Monarch
Coupes
  Coupe Bavaria
  Coupe Belle Hélène
  Coupe Hawaii
  Coupe Niçoise
  Coupe Sweden
Frozen Desserts
  Baked Figs with
    Honey-Vanilla Frozen
    Yogurt
  Cherries Jubilee
  Frozen Hazelnut Coffee
    Mousse
  Ginger Soufflé Glacé
  Lingonberry Parfait
  Medley of Sorbets in Tulips
  Poached Pears with Ginger
    Ice Cream and Two Sauces

*I*ce creams and other frozen desserts in different shapes and combinations have always been favorites of guests and chefs alike. Ice cream seems to bring out the child in us, making it almost impossible to resist. The taste is refreshing, which is especially appreciated in the summer, and the light consistency makes it easy to digest. Ice cream is also an ideal dessert for chefs because it can be made days in advance. Today, the home cook can make wonderful ice creams as effortlessly as the professionals with the small electric ice cream freezers available at a reasonable cost. Churning ice cream by hand has become almost obsolete.

For a finished product of the highest quality, absolute cleanliness is a must. Because the ice cream mixture is a perfect breeding ground for bacteria, the equipment and utensils that come in contact with the ice cream must be stainless steel or another noncorrosive material and must be cleaned thoroughly after each use. Never pour the warm ice cream mixture directly into the ice cream freezer, but let it cool slowly and then refrigerate it for a few hours or overnight. The extra cooling time will result in a smoother finished product and a larger yield. When the ice cream has churned to the desired consistency, turn off the freezer unit of the ice cream maker but keep the churner on for a few minutes longer, if your machine has this option; then remove the finished ice cream.

This way less ice cream will stick to the sides of the container.

The amount of air churned into the ice cream determines the volume and lightness of the finished product. As a rule, higher-quality ice cream has less volume, when compared by weight. Because an ice cream made with heavy cream is more compact in its composition, it yields less than an ice cream made with milk or half-and-half, and is richer and smoother.

Custard-based ice creams are the most common type and are usually what we mean when referring to ice cream. A custard ice cream is really nothing more than a frozen vanilla sauce in which the egg yolks and sugar have been adjusted to suit a particular flavor. Gelato ice cream is richer and creamier, made with heavy cream, and almost no air is incorporated while churning.

Sorbets, also known as fruit and water ices, are made of fruit purée and/or juice combined with a simple syrup at a density of 16° to 18° Baumé. Sorbets are also made from liqueurs and wines. Some chefs add a small amount of Italian Meringue to give the sorbet a smoother texture, but in my opinion the meringue takes away some of the flavor. When a large amount of Italian Meringue is added to a sorbet it is called a "spoom." A granité is like a sorbet except that it is not churned during freezing; instead it is frozen in a hotel pan or other shallow container. The sugar density of a granité is only 12° to 14° Baumé, which produces a somewhat grainy texture as the name suggests. Granités are typically served as palate cleansers between courses of formal dinners. Unlike ice creams, sorbets and granités can be thawed, adjusted, and refrozen without adverse effect.

A parfait is a delicate frozen dessert made from a mixture of egg yolks and sugar syrup whipped to the ribbon stage, with whipped cream and flavoring added. To achieve the distinctive, light texture of this dessert you must combine the ingredients very carefully, preserving the air that has been whipped in. The parfait mixture is then poured into tall slender molds and frozen without churning.

There does seem to be a difference of opinion as to what constitutes a parfait. The name is used in many American cookbooks to mean alternating layers of ice cream, fruit, and liqueur in tall glasses, topped with whipped cream. This is actually a coupe, by classic definition. The "new world" parfait version probably got its name because the tall glasses resemble classic parfait molds.

Parfaits can also be combined with ice cream to create elegant ice bombes, or they can be used for, or as part of, the filling in frozen cakes. Another light and delicious variation is soufflé glacé, made by mixing Italian Meringue, ice cream, and the parfait mixture and freezing it in soufflé cups lined with collars.

Ice bombes are elaborately decorated creations formed in the spherical molds that gave them their name. They are usually made to serve 8 to 10 people and are traditionally presented whole on a silver platter before being sliced.

Coupes, or sundaes, are a very quick and practical ice cream dessert. They are a combination of ice cream or sorbet, liqueur, sauces, fruit, and often whipped cream. They are served in champagne glasses, goblets, or silver ice cream bowls. The most classic combinations, such as coupe melba, belle hélène, or coupe jacques, were created years ago by various master chefs and are still popular today. Coupes can be decorated very simply or in a way that makes the dish extraordinary.

Sorbets taste best when freshly made and still soft. Sorbets and parfaits should not be kept longer than one or two weeks at the most. It is possible to store ice cream for three to four weeks without any loss of volume or quality, provided it is stored in airtight containers. Ice cream should be frozen at 6°F (−15°C) so it will harden quickly. It should then be stored between 6°F and 14°F (−15°C and −9°C). However, the ice cream should be served at a higher temperature so that it is pleasant to eat, and easy to scoop and work with. The ideal temperature for serving varies with different flavors and types. Ice cream and other frozen desserts can be unmolded or scooped into serving glasses one to two hours in advance and held in the freezer, but final touches and garnishes must be applied at the last moment.

Many of the frozen desserts that were created years ago are now classics, such as soufflé glacé, vacherin, and peach melba, but there is still plenty of room for your particular taste and imagination.

Ice Cream

Banana Poppy Seed Ice Cream

6 cups (1 l, 440 ml)

8 ounces (225 g) granulated sugar
10 egg yolks
3 cups (720 ml) milk
2 cups (480 ml) heavy cream
4 medium-sized ripe bananas,
    puréed
2 ounces (55 g) poppy seeds
⅓ cup (80 ml) Frangelico liqueur
Strawberry Sauce (page 563)
Vanilla Tulips (page 546)
*Sour Cream Mixture for Piping
    (page 564)*

1. Beat the sugar and egg yolks together lightly to combine. Heat the milk and cream to the scalding point. Stirring constantly, gradually pour the hot liquid into the egg mixture. Place over simmering water and, continuing to stir, heat until the custard thickens enough to coat a spoon. (Be careful not to overcook and break the custard.)

2. Cool, then stir in the banana purée, liqueur, and poppy seeds. (As with any custard-based ice cream, Banana Poppy Seed Ice Cream will have a smoother texture if you rest the custard in the refrigerator for about 8 hours before freezing. Do not prepare, or stir in, the banana purée until you are ready to freeze.)

3. Process immediately in an ice cream freezer. Place a bowl in the freezer at the same time so it will be chilled to hold the finished product. Chill dessert plates in the refrigerator.

4. Presentation: Pour just enough Strawberry Sauce on a dessert plate to cover the surface. Place a tulip in the center, and fill with a scoop of ice cream. Decorate the Strawberry Sauce with the Sour Cream Mixture for Piping (see pages 518–519). Serve immediately.

Caramel Ice Cream

9 cups (2 l, 160 ml)

1¼ cups (300 ml) or ½ recipe
    Caramel Sauce I (page 567)
1 quart (960 ml) half-and-half
10 egg yolks
3 ounces (85 g) granulated sugar
2 cups (480 ml) heavy cream
7 ounces (200 g) or ¼ recipe
    Nougatine Crunch (page 493)

1. Place the caramel sauce and half-and-half in a saucepan and heat to the scalding point.

2. Whip the egg yolks and sugar until fluffy. Gradually add the scalded half-and-half mixture to the egg yolks while whipping rapidly. Heat the mixture over simmering water, stirring constantly, until it coats a spoon. Remove from the heat and stir in the heavy cream. Let the custard cool slightly at room temperature, then refrigerate until thoroughly chilled.

3. Process in an ice cream freezer. Stir in the Nougatine Crunch and store the finished ice cream, covered, in the freezer.

Caramel Ice Cream in a Cage

20 servings

2 pounds (910 g) granulated sugar
¼ teaspoon (1 ml) lemon juice
*Butter and Flour Mixture
    (page 4)*

1. Chill dessert plates in the refrigerator.

2. Caramelize the sugar with the lemon juice using the dry method (see page 488) to just a light golden color, so you can reheat it several times without getting it too dark. Let the caramel cool slightly while you grease the ladles or forms.

3. Use a ladle (or any other dome-shaped object, such as a small bowl) large enough for the finished cage to fit over the ice cream

2 cups (480 ml) heavy cream
9 cups (2 l, 160 ml) or 1 recipe
   Caramel Ice Cream
light chocolate shavings
Cold Chocolate Sauce (page 559)
Sour Cream Mixture for Piping
   (page 564)

and chocolate shavings, without touching them. Hold the ladle upside down and grease the back with the butter and flour mixture, using the palm of your hand to apply it rather than a brush. You want only a thin film because too much will cause the caramel to slide off as you streak it on.

4. Dip a paring knife into the cooled caramel and, letting it run off in a thin stream, streak it across the ladle in thin lines about ½ inch (1.2 cm) apart. Turn the ladle 90° and repeat to form lines going in the opposite direction (Figure 13–1). Finish the bottom of the cage with a thin line of caramel all around. Place the handle of the ladle in a tub of sugar to hold it as the caramel hardens slightly. Repeat the process with a second ladle.

5. The cages should be cool enough to be removed from the ladle without changing shape, but do not let them cool completely or they will stick and break. To remove, cup your hand around the cage and twist gently to loosen it. As you continue to make cages, the caramel will become too thick, the lines will become unattractive, and the cages will tend to slide off the ladle. At this point

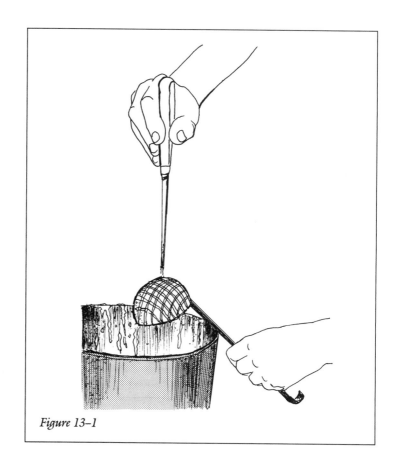

Figure 13–1

you need to reheat the caramel. Swirl, do not stir, the caramel while it reheats.

6. Store the cages in an airtight container. They will keep for several days.

7. Presentation: Whip the cream to stiff peaks and place it in a pastry bag with a no. 4 (8-mm) plain tip. Pipe a small dot of whipped cream in the center of a chilled plate and top with a scoop of ice cream. Pipe additional whipped cream in a pearl-shaped band around the base of the scoop. Place chocolate shavings on top of the ice cream. Set a caramel cage over the ice cream, on top of the whipped cream band. Quickly pour a small amount of chocolate sauce on the plate around the dessert, and decorate the sauce with the sour cream mixture (see pages 518–519). Serve immediately.

NOTE: Don't be discouraged if your first attempts at making cages are not successful. This recipe will make enough caramel that you can afford to break a few cages, and with a little practice, you will find it is not difficult to make thin, elegant cages. Timing is important when letting the caramel cool, and most likely it will require trial and error on your part to learn the correct consistency. If you attempt to apply the caramel when it is too hot, it will penetrate the coating and be impossible to remove in one piece. Even if you do get lucky with a few very thin cages, they will probably be too fragile to be practical. On the other hand, if the caramel becomes too thick it will not stick at all and will simply slide off. It is a good idea to have a bowl of ice water nearby as you are working, in case you get any hot caramel on your hands. Plunge the burn into the cold water immediately to be able to remove the caramel. Take care not to use any more lemon juice than specified. Although it prevents the sugar from darkening prematurely, it also softens the finished cages and they will not harden.

Chocolate Ice Cream
6 cups (1 l, 440 ml) ice cream

1 quart (960 ml) half-and-half
1 vanilla bean, split
 or
1 teaspoon (5 ml) vanilla extract
8 egg yolks
6 ounces (170 g) granulated sugar
6 ounces (170 g) cocoa block (bitter chocolate)
4 ounces (115 g) semisweet chocolate

1. Scald the half-and-half with the vanilla bean, if used.

2. Whip the egg yolks with the sugar until light and fluffy. Remove the vanilla bean from the half-and-half and reserve for another use, or add the vanilla extract, if used. Gradually pour the hot cream into the yolk mixture while stirring rapidly. Place over simmering water and heat, stirring constantly, until the mixture is thick enough to coat a spoon. Set aside.

3. Chop both chocolates into small pieces and melt over the simmering water. Stir the chocolate mixture into the reserved cream mixture. Cool completely.

4. Process in an ice cream freezer. Store covered in the freezer.

Fresh-Coconut Ice Cream

6 cups (1 l, 440 ml)

2 fresh coconuts, about 6 pounds
    (2 kg, 730 g)
3 cups (720 ml) coconut milk from
    fresh coconuts
milk, optional
1 vanilla bean, split
    or
1 teaspoon (5 ml) vanilla extract
2 cups (480 ml) heavy cream,
    approximately
10 egg yolks
3 ounces (85 g) granulated sugar

1. When selecting the coconuts, test for freshness by shaking them. There should be plenty of milk inside. Puncture the three eyes and drain the coconut milk, reserving 3 cups (720 ml). If the coconuts do not contain that much liquid, add regular milk to the liquid to make the amount needed.

2. Tap the coconuts all around with a hammer or heavy cleaver to help loosen the meat from the shell. Crack the coconuts open using the same tool. Remove the meat from the shell, then use a vegetable peeler to remove the brown skin from the meat. (If some pieces did not separate from the shell, place them on a sheet pan and bake at 350°F (175°C) for about 30 minutes.) Chop the coconut meat finely in a food processor.

3. Combine the coconut meat, coconut milk, and vanilla bean (if used) in a saucepan. Heat to scalding, remove from the heat, cover, and let infuse for at least 30 minutes.

4. Strain the mixture, pressing with a spoon to remove as much liquid as possible from the coconut meat. Remove the vanilla bean and save for another use. Discard the coconut meat. Add enough heavy cream to the strained coconut milk to measure 5 cups (1 l, 200 ml). Return to the saucepan and heat to scalding.

5. Beat the egg yolks and sugar together for a few minutes. Gradually pour the hot liquid into the yolk mixture, whisking continuously. Heat the mixture over simmering water, stirring constantly, until it thickens enough to coat the back of a spoon. Remove from the heat and continue to stir for a minute to prevent overcooking on the bottom or sides. Add the vanilla extract, if used. Cool completely.

6. Process in an ice cream freezer. Store covered in the freezer.

Quick Coconut Ice Cream

If you just cannot live with yourself if you use anything but fresh coconut to make your coconut ice cream (and I agree there is a difference), use the preceding recipe. However, if you are short on time, this is a very good quick compromise: Use the recipe for Vanilla Ice Cream (see page 364), replacing 2 cups (480 ml) of the half-and-half with unsweetened, canned coconut milk, and use only 4 ounces (115 g) of sugar. This makes 5 cups (1 l, 200 ml).

Macadamia Nut Ice Cream

2 quarts (1 l, 920 ml), 25 servings

1 pounds (455 g) unsalted
   macadamia nuts
1 quart (960 ml) milk
1 vanilla bean, split
   or
1 teaspoon (5 ml) vanilla extract
12 egg yolks
14 ounces (400 g) granulated
   sugar
2 cups (480 ml) heavy cream
whipped cream
25 Chocolate Tulips (page 546)
Mango Sauce (page 560)
Chocolate Sauce for Piping
   (page 560)
thinly sliced kiwis
raspberries
dark chocolate shavings

1. Roast the macadamia nuts, cool, and reserve 25 nice-looking whole nuts for garnish. Grind or crush the remaining nuts coarsely, combine with ½ cup (120 ml) of the milk, and grind to a paste in a food processor.

2. Add the vanilla bean to the remaining milk (3½ cups/840 ml) and bring it to a boil. Mix in the nut paste. Remove the pan from the heat (if using the vanilla extract, add now), cover, and set aside in the saucepan.

3. Whip the egg yolks and sugar until light and fluffy (ribbon stage). Reheat the milk mixture to boiling, strain, and gradually add it to the beaten yolks, stirring constantly. Cook the custard over hot water until it thickens enough to coat a spoon. Add the heavy cream. Chill the mixture until it is completely cold.

4. Process in an ice cream freezer. Be sure to have a container pre-chilled in the freezer to hold the finished ice cream. Chill dessert plates in the refrigerator.

5. Presentation: Pipe a small dot of whipped cream, off-center, on a dessert plate. Place a Chocolate Tulip on top. Pour an oval pool of Mango Sauce in front of the tulip (in the larger open space). Decorate the Mango Sauce with Chocolate Sauce for Piping (see pages 518–519). Arrange the kiwis and raspberries behind the tulip. Place a scoop of ice cream in the tulip and garnish the ice cream with shaved dark chocolate and a whole macadamia nut. Serve immediately.

Papaya Ice Cream

7 cups (1 l, 680 ml), 25 servings

1 recipe Vanilla Ice Cream,
   unfrozen (page 364)
3 cups (720 ml) papaya purée
5 limes
whipped cream
25 Chocolate Tulips (page 546)
Candied Lime Peels (page 520)
Kiwi Sauce (page 560)

1. Make Vanilla Ice Cream through step 3. Combine the ice cream and papaya purée. Place in the refrigerator to cool.

2. Zest the limes. Reserve the zest to make the candied lime peels. Juice the limes and add the juice to the cooled custard.

3. Process in an ice cream freezer. While the ice cream is freezing, chill a container to hold the finished product. When the ice cream is ready, place it in the container, cover, and store in the freezer until time of service. Chill dessert plates in the refrigerator.

4. Presentation: Pipe a small dot of whipped cream, off-center, on a dessert plate (it is just there to keep the tulip from sliding). Place a Chocolate Tulip on the cream and fill with a scoop of ice cream. Sprinkle a few candied lime peels on top. Pour a small pool of Kiwi Sauce in front of the dessert. Serve immediately.

Variation: Mango Ice Cream

This recipe can be used to make an excellent mango ice cream with only one change: The mango purée must be strained before it is combined with the custard. Use a *chinois* rather than an *étamé* to strain the purée.

Peach Ice Cream

6 cups (1 l, 440 ml)

2 pounds (910 g) peaches,
*   ripe but firm*
⅓ cup (80 ml) amaretto liqueur
2½ cups (600 ml) or ½ recipe
*   Poaching Syrup II (page 6)*
5 ounces (140 g) granulated sugar
10 egg yolks
2 cups (480 ml) heavy cream
2 cups (480 ml) milk

1. Wash the peaches, cut in half, and discard the pits. Pick out one-third of the firmest peaches and cut into pea-sized chunks. Macerate the peach chunks in the amaretto for 4 to 5 hours, or preferably overnight (see note).

2. Remove the skin from the remaining peaches. If you are losing too much pulp as you do this, add an additional peach. Place the peaches in a saucepan with the poaching syrup. Simmer until the fruit starts to fall apart. Remove the fruit from the syrup. Purée the fruit and set the mixture aside to cool. Discard the poaching syrup.

3. Whip sugar and egg yolks to the ribbon stage. Scald the cream and milk and gradually combine with the egg mixture, stirring rapidly. Set over simmering water, stirring constantly, and thicken the custard until it coats a spoon. The custard is ready when you pull a wooden spoon out of the mixture and cannot see the wood. Be careful not to overheat or you will coagulate the yolks. Remove the custard from the heat and cool completely before freezing.

4. Add the peach chunks and peach purée to the custard, and process the mixture in an ice cream freezer. Place in a chilled container and store, covered, in the freezer.

NOTE: For the best results with this ice cream, prepare the macerated peaches and the custard (separately) one day before freezing the ice cream. The custard will have a smoother texture if allowed to mature, and the fruit should absorb as much sugar as possible or it will freeze rock-hard in the ice cream. Rather than use canned peaches in this recipe, I suggest you substitute a different ice cream made with fruit in season.

Peach Ice Cream in Florentina Baskets

(see photograph in color insert)
25 servings

1 recipe Florentina Batter
*   (page 131)*
2½ cups (600 ml) or 1 recipe
*   Caramel Sauce II (page 558)*
2 tablespoons (30 ml)
*   amaretto liqueur*
whipped cream
6 cups (1 l, 440 ml) or
*   1 recipe Peach Ice Cream*
strawberries
thinly sliced peaches with skin

1. Draw twenty-five 4¾-inch (11.8-cm) circles on baking paper. Invert the papers onto sheet pans. Divide the Florentina Batter between the circles and spread out. Bake and trim the cookies following the instructions for Florentinas.

2. Reheat the cookies until they are soft enough to bend. Immediately bend ½ inch (1.2 cm) of the edge of each cookie up 45° to form a shallow basket with six sides (crust side facing out). Alternatively, fold the cookies over the back of a small bowl

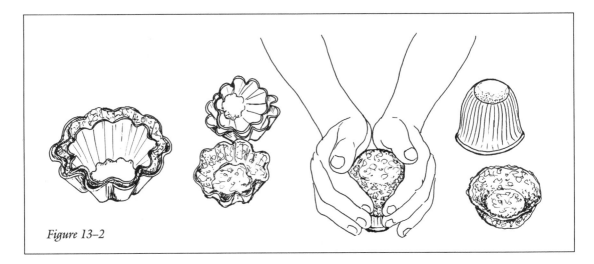

Figure 13–2

or jar, or use two brioche molds to make the baskets by placing a smaller mold inside a larger mold, with the cookie pressed between them (Figure 13–2).

3. Flavor the Caramel Sauce with the amaretto. Chill dessert plates in the refrigerator.

4. Presentation: Pipe a dot of whipped cream in the center of a dessert plate, set a Florentina basket on top, and fill with a scoop of ice cream. Arrange the peach slices fanned on top of the ice cream. Pour a pool of Caramel Sauce in front of the basket. Place a fanned strawberry on the sauce. Serve immediately.

Pistachio Ice Cream

2 quarts (1 l, 920 ml)

10 ounces (285 g) pistachio nuts
3 cups (720 ml) milk
1 recipe Vanilla Ice Cream, unfrozen (page 364)

Contrary to the impression you might get from some of the commercial pistachio ice cream on the market, pistachio nuts have a very mild flavor and are not nearly green enough to color the ice cream to the bright shade often found. This recipe makes an ice cream with a delicious, subtle taste and just a hint of green color, which comes naturally from the nuts.

1. Boil the pistachios in water for 1 minute. Drain, cool, and remove the skin with your fingers. Toast the nuts at 325°F (163°C) until they start to color lightly. Reserve 2 ounces (55 g) of the nuts and grind the remainder finely.

2. Combine the ground pistachios with the milk in a saucepan. Heat to scalding, then remove from the heat, cover, and allow to steep for 30 minutes. Strain through a fine mesh strainer, forcing all of the liquid from the nuts by pressing with a spoon. Discard the nuts.

3. Make the Vanilla Ice Cream through step 3. Stir the strained pistachio liquid into the ice cream custard. Crush the reserved pistachios coarsely and add. Cool the custard, then process in an ice cream freezer.

Plum Ice Cream

6 cups (1 l, 440 ml)

*2 pounds (910 g) tart plums
    (see note)*
*2 ounces (60 ml) Simple Syrup
    (page 7)*
*2 ounces (60 ml) plum brandy
    or liqueur*
*5 cups (1 l, 200 ml) or 1 recipe
    Poaching Syrup II (page 6)*
5 ounces (140 g) granulated sugar
10 egg yolks
2 cups (480 ml) milk
2 cups (480 ml) heavy cream

While I generally try to get the Laroda or Casselman variety of plum for cooking, the tart skin of the Santa Rosa plums gives this ice cream a wonderful taste. Keep in mind that Santa Rosa plums do produce a large amount of juice as they are cooked, which could be a problem in a dessert such as a tart.

1. Wash the plums, cut in half, and discard the pits. Cut one-third of the fruit into pea-sized chunks. Combine the chunks with the simple syrup and brandy. Set aside to macerate for a few hours or preferably overnight.

2. Place remaining plums in a saucepan with the poaching syrup and cook until the plums are soft and begin to fall apart. Remove from the heat and strain off the poaching liquid, reserving 1 quart (960 ml) to use as sauce for the ice cream if desired, or discard. (To use the poaching liquid as a sauce, reduce it by half.) Set the strained fruit aside to cool.

3. Whip sugar and egg yolks to ribbon stage. Heat the milk and cream in a saucepan to scalding. Gradually pour the hot milk into the egg yolk mixture while whisking rapidly. Place the mixture over simmering water and heat, stirring constantly, until the custard is thick enough to coat a spoon. Remove from the heat and stir in the reserved poached plums and the macerated plum chunks.

4. Let cool completely, then process the cold mixture in an ice cream freezer. Place the finished ice cream in a chilled container and store covered in the freezer.

NOTE: Should the short season for fresh plums be over, canned tart plums may be substituted. Drain and use the liquid as part of the poaching syrup, adjusting the sweetness and amount as needed.

Strawberry Ice Cream

7 cups (1 l, 680 ml)

Vanilla Ice Cream (this page);
*   see step 1*
1 pound (455 g) fresh,
*   ripe strawberries*
4 ounces (115 g) granulated
*   sugar, approximately*
½ cup (120 ml) strained
*   raspberry purée, approximately*

1. Make Vanilla Ice Cream through step 3, cutting the amount of sugar in half.

2. Clean and stem the strawberries. Chop into small pieces. Place in a saucepan with the sugar and cook over medium heat, stirring from time to time, until the mixture starts to thicken, about 10 minutes.

3. Add to the ice cream custard, together with the raspberry puree. Cool completely, then freeze in an ice cream freezer.

NOTE: Because this recipe does not use any artificial ingredients, the color may not be as bright as you are used to seeing. The raspberry juice is used to add some color. Adjust the amount of juice according to how ripe (and red) the strawberries are.

Vanilla Ice Cream

5 cups (1 l, 200 ml)

1 quart (960 ml) half-and-half
1 vanilla bean, split
*   or*
1 teaspoon (5 ml) vanilla extract
10 egg yolks
10 ounces (285 g) granulated
*   sugar*

1. Heat the half-and-half with the vanilla bean (if used) to scalding.

2. Beat the egg yolks and sugar until light and fluffy. Remove the vanilla bean from the half-and-half and save for another use. Gradually pour the half-and-half into the whipped egg yolk mixture while whisking rapidly (place a towel under the bowl to keep it from turning with your whisk). Add the vanilla extract, if used.

3. Heat the mixture over simmering water, stirring constantly, until it thickens enough to coat a spoon. Take care not to overheat and break (coagulate) the custard. Remove from the heat and continue to stir for a few seconds to keep the mixture from overcooking where it touches the hot bowl. Cool the custard completely.

4. Process the mixture in an ice cream freezer. Place an empty bowl in the freezer to chill while the ice cream is churning and use it to hold the finished ice cream.

NOTE: Vanilla Ice Cream will improve in texture if the custard is made the day before churning and left to rest in the refrigerator.

White-Chocolate Ice Cream with Ginger

5 cups (1 l, 200 ml)

1 ounce (30 g) fresh ginger
*   root, sliced*
3 cups (720 ml) half-and-half
2 cups (480 ml) heavy cream

1. Combine the fresh ginger root, half-and-half, and cream in a saucepan. Heat to scalding. Set aside to steep for 30 minutes.

2. Beat the egg yolks with the sugar until light and fluffy. Strain the ginger root from the cream mixture, and reheat to the scalding point. Gradually whisk the hot cream into the egg yolk mixture.

3. Place over simmering water and heat, stirring constantly (do not whip), until the custard is thick enough to coat the spoon.

8 egg yolks
3 ounces (85 g) granulated sugar
8 ounces (225 g) white chocolate,
   cut in small chunks
½ ounce (15 g) candied ginger,
   chopped fine

4. Remove from the heat and add the white chocolate, stirring until all the chunks are melted. Stir in the candied ginger. Cool the custard completely.

5. Process in an ice cream freezer. Transfer the finished ice cream to a chilled container and store, covered, in the freezer.

NOTE: You will get a richer tasting ice cream if you make the custard the day before, or at least several hours before, freezing (you must keep the custard base in the refrigerator).

White-Chocolate Ice Cream

Omit the ginger root and candied ginger, and increase the white chocolate by 2 ounces (55 g).

Sorbet

Champagne Sorbet

2 quarts (1 l, 920 ml), or
20 servings

3½ cups (840 ml) dry champagne
2½ cups (600 ml) Simple Syrup,
   at room temperature (page 7)
1½ cups (360 ml) water (see note)
juice of 2 lemons
Raspberry Sauce (page 563)
Sour Cream Mixture for Piping
   (page 564)
20 Chocolate Tulips (page 546)
mint sprigs

Variation

(see photograph in color insert)

1. Combine the champagne, simple syrup, water, and lemon juice.

2. Process in an ice cream freezer. Place in a chilled container and store, covered, in the freezer.

3. Presentation: Pour enough Raspberry Sauce on a dessert plate to cover the surface. Pipe straight lines, ½ inch (1.2 cm) apart, across the plate using the sour cream mixture. With a toothpick, draw a spiral through the sauces, working from the center to the outer edge. Place a tulip in the center of the plate. Fill with a scoop of Champagne Sorbet. Garnish with a mint sprig and serve immediately.

NOTE: If the tap water has a noticeable chlorine taste, use mineral water.

When blackberries are available, try this colorful presentation. Force a small amount of strawberry jam through a fine sieve and place in a pastry bag with a no. 1 (2-mm) plain tip. Divide the dessert plate in half by piping a slightly curved line across the center. Cover one half with Raspberry Sauce and the other with Blackberry Sauce. Omit the sour cream piping and the tulip. Instead, place a small, thin, round of sponge cake (smaller than the sorbet scoop so it does not show) in the center of the plate. Place a scoop of sorbet on the cake. Place three blackberries in the Raspberry Sauce, and three raspberries in the Blackberry Sauce. Garnish the sorbet with a mint sprig and serve immediately.

NOTE: To make Blackberry Sauce, follow the instructions for Raspberry Sauce, substituting blackberries for raspberries.

Honeydew Melon Sorbet

approximately 7 cups (1 l, 680 ml)

2 medium-sized honeydew melons
3 cups (720 ml) Simple Syrup,
    at room temperature (page 7)
1½ cups (360 ml) water,
    approximately
*few drops Tartaric Acid Solution
    (page 596) or lemon juice*

1. It is important that the melons be fully ripe, not just for the flavor, but so you will get enough juice out of the pulp when you purée them. Cut the melons into sections, scoop out the seeds, and cut the meat away from the rind. Purée to a pulp and force through a medium strainer. Measure 3 cups (720 ml). Discard remainder or save for another use.

2. Combine the strained melon juice and simple syrup. Add enough water to bring the mixture to between 16° and 18° Baumé (see page 615). (If you do not have a Baumé thermometer, use trial-and-error to determine the desired sweetness.) Add the tartaric acid or lemon juice.

3. Process in an ice cream freezer. When finished, transfer to a chilled bowl and store in the freezer.

NOTE: Use a chilled container for storage or the sorbet will start to liquify immediately. The amount of water needed in the recipe can vary quite a bit depending on the time of year or the sweetness of the melon.

Mandarin Sorbet

approximately 6 cups (1 l, 440 ml)

10 medium-sized mandarins,
    approximately
2 cups (480 ml) Simple Syrup,
    at room temperature (page 7)
2½ cups (600 ml) water,
    approximately
*few drops Tartaric Acid Solution
    (page 596) or lemon juice*

1. Juice the mandarins. Strain the juice and measure 2 cups (480 ml).

2. Combine the mandarin juice and simple syrup. Add enough water to bring the mixture to between 16° and 18° Baumé (see page 615). (If you do not have a Baumé thermometer, use trial-and-error to determine the proper sweetness.) Add the tartaric acid or lemon juice.

3. Process in an ice cream freezer. When finished, transfer to a chilled bowl and store in the freezer.

NOTE: Use a chilled container for storage or the sorbet will start to liquify immediately.

Orange Sorbet

Substitute orange juice for the mandarin juice.

Raspberry Sorbet

approximately 9 cups (2 l, 160 ml)

5 cups (1 l, 200 ml) loosely packed
    fresh raspberries, approximately
3 cups (720 ml) Simple Syrup,
    at room temperature (page 7)

1. Purée raspberries in a food processor. Strain and measure 3 cups (720 ml) of juice. Discard remainder or save for another use.

2. Combine the raspberry juice and simple syrup. Add enough water to bring the mixture to between 16° and 18° Baumé (see page 615). (If you do not have a Baumé thermometer, use trial-and-error to determine the proper sweetness.) Add the tartaric acid or lemon juice.

3½ *cups (840 ml) water,*
   approximately
few drops Tartaric Acid Solution
   (page 596) or lemon juice

3. Process in an ice cream freezer. When finished, transfer to a chilled bowl and store in the freezer.

NOTE: Use a chilled container for storage or the sorbet will start to liquify immediately. The amount of water needed in the recipe can vary quite a bit depending on the time of year or the sweetness of the particular variety of raspberry.

Bombes

Bombes lend themselves to opulent decorations, so the pastry chef can really express his or her style and fantasy. If bombes are presented to guests before being sliced and served, the accompanying sauce should be served separately in a sauce boat. The most common size bombe mold serves 8 to 10 people, so bombes are a great time-saver for the chef, especially since they can be prepared well in advance, then unmolded and decorated just before they are needed.

In creating the different variations, follow these basic steps in each bombe recipe:

1. Lightly oil the inside of the molds and place in the freezer until thoroughly frozen.

2. Line the chilled molds with a ¾-inch (2-cm) layer of softened ice cream using a spoon dipped in hot water. Should the ice cream become too soft, refreeze until you can work with it again. Freeze the ice cream layer in the molds.

3. Pour the bombe mixture into the ice cream shell, cover, and freeze until hard, at least 4 hours.

4. To unmold the bombe, place a thin sheet of sponge cake (the same size as the base of the mold) on the surface of the filling to prevent the bombe from sliding on the serving platter. Dip the mold quickly into hot water and invert onto a chilled silver tray or other serving platter. Decorate and present immediately.

Basic Bombe Mixture

enough for two 5-cup (1-l, 200-ml) bombes

8 ounces (225 g) granulated sugar
½ cup (120 ml) water
10 egg yolks
3 cups (720 ml) heavy cream

1. Dissolve two-thirds of the sugar in the water in a heavy saucepan and heat to 240°F (115°C) (see page 469 for information on how to boil sugar).

2. While the syrup is cooking, whip the egg yolks with the remaining sugar until light and fluffy. With the mixer running at slow speed, gradually add the hot syrup to the egg yolks, then whip at medium speed until cool.

3. Cover the mixture and place in the refrigerator until needed. It can be kept for up to one week at this point.

4. When you are ready to fill a bombe, whip the heavy cream to soft peaks, then carefully fold the yolk mixture and the desired flavoring into the cream. Pour the filling into the prepared bombe mold, cover, and place in the freezer.

Bombe Aboukir

two 5-cup (1-l, 200-ml) bombes

1 quart (960 ml) or ½ recipe
    Pistachio Ice Cream (page 362)
1 recipe Basic Bombe Mixture
    (this page)
½ recipe Hazelnut Paste (page 6)
    or
1½ ounces (40 g) commercial
    hazelnut paste
1 ounce (30 g) pistachios, blanched
    and skins removed
thin sheets of Sponge Cake
    (page 161)
whipped cream
Chocolate Figurines (page 449)
hazelnuts, roasted, skins removed
fresh fruit
Cold Chocolate Sauce (page 559)

1. Line the bombe molds with the ice cream. Reserve in the freezer.

2. Add a little of the bombe mixture to the hazelnut paste to soften it, then mix into the remaining mixture.

3. Chop the pistachio nuts and add to the filling. Pour the filling into the reserved shells. Freeze and unmold as described on page 367.

4. Decorate the bombes with whipped cream rosettes, chocolate figurines, hazelnuts, and fruit. Serve with Cold Chocolate Sauce.

Bombe Bourdaloue

two 5-cup (1-l, 200-ml) bombes

*5 cups (1 l, 200 ml) or 1 recipe
    Vanilla Ice Cream (page 364)
1 recipe Basic Bombe Mixture
    (page 368)
3 tablespoons (45 ml)
    anisette liqueur
thin sheets of Sponge Cake
    (page 161)
whipped cream
candied violets
Strawberry Sauce (page 563)*

1. Line the bombe molds with ice cream. Reserve in the freezer.

2. Flavor the bombe mixture with anisette. Pour into the reserved shells. Freeze and unmold as described on page 367.

3. Decorate the bombes with whipped cream rosettes and candied violets. Serve with Strawberry Sauce.

Bombe Ceylon

two 5-cup (1-l, 200-ml) bombes

*1 recipe Vanilla Ice Cream,
    unfrozen (page 364)
4 teaspoons (16 g) mocha paste
    or
¼ cup (60 ml) Coffee Reduction
    (page 5)
1 recipe Basic Bombe Mixture
    (page 368)
¼ cup (60 ml) dark rum
thin sheets of Chocolate Sponge
    Cake (page 162)
whipped cream
roasted coffee beans
Chocolate Figurines (page 449)
Cold Chocolate Sauce (page 559)*

1. Make Vanilla Ice Cream through step 3. Flavor the custard with the mocha paste or coffee reduction. Process in an ice cream freezer. If you are using mocha paste, mix a little of the custard into the paste to thin it before mixing the paste into the remaining custard, to avoid lumps.

2. Line the bombe molds with the coffee-flavored ice cream. Reserve in the freezer.

3. Flavor the bombe mixture with rum. Pour into the reserved shells. Freeze and unmold as described on page 367.

4. Decorate the bombes with whipped cream rosettes, coffee beans, and chocolate figurines. Serve with Cold Chocolate Sauce.

Bombe Monarch

(see photograph in color insert)
two 5-cup (1-l, 200-ml) bombes

3½ cups (840 ml) or ½ recipe
    Strawberry Ice Cream
    (page 364)
1 recipe Basic Bombe Mixture
    (page 368)
3 tablespoons (45 ml)
    Benedictine liqueur
thin sheets of Sponge Cake
    (page 161)
whipped cream
Chocolate Butterfly Ornaments
    (page 455)
fresh fruit
Cherry Sauce (page 558)

1. Line the bombe molds with the ice cream. Reserve in the freezer.

2. Flavor the bombe mixture with Benedictine liqueur. Pour into the reserved shells. Freeze and unmold as described on page 367.

3. Decorate the bombes with whipped cream rosettes, chocolate butterflies, and fresh fruit. Serve with Cherry Sauce.

Coupes

These popular individual ice cream servings can look very elegant if served in suitable dishes and attractively decorated. In every *konditorei* or pastry shop all over Europe, you will find a separate menu (usually illustrated) describing the coupes served. They are usually named for different countries according to their composition, and some are elaborately decorated with cookies and marzipan or chocolate figures. Coupes must always be assembled and decorated to order. The following are some of the most popular and classic variations, along with a few of my own creations.

Coupe Bavaria

Chocolate Ice Cream (page 358)
sweet dark cherries
maraschino liqueur
whipped cream
strawberry wedges
Chocolate Curls (page 444)
Raspberry Cut-outs (page 251)

Place a scoop of Chocolate Ice Cream in a coupe glass or dessert bowl. Top with cherries. Lightly sprinkle maraschino liqueur over the cherries and ice cream. Decorate with whipped cream rosettes, strawberry wedges, and two chocolate curls. Place the glass on a plate lined with a doily and serve immediately with a Raspberry Cut-out on the plate.

Coupe Belle Hélène

poached pear halves (page 6)
Vanilla Ice Cream (page 364)
Hot Fudge Sauce (page 559)
pistachios, blanched, skins removed,
    and coarsely chopped
Pirouettes (page 138)

Fan one pear half per serving and reserve. Place a scoop of Vanilla Ice Cream in a coupe glass or dessert bowl. Place one of the reserved pear halves on top of the ice cream. Pour Hot Fudge Sauce over the bottom part of the pear. Sprinkle pistachio nuts on the sauce. Set the glass on a dessert plate lined with a doily and serve immediately with a Pirouette on the plate.

Coupe Hawaii

Hippen Decorating Paste
    (page 527)
melted dark chocolate
Fresh or Quick Coconut Ice Cream
    (page 359)
whipped cream
fresh pineapple
Chocolate-filled Macadamia
    Morsels (page 248)

1. Make the templates for the palm trees. The templates in Figure 13–3 are the correct size for this recipe. Trace the drawings (allow enough cardboard around the trunk for a frame, as is shown with the crown), then cut the templates from ¹⁄₁₆-inch (2-mm) cardboard (cake boxes work fine).

2. Lightly grease the back of even sheet pans, coat with flour, and shake off as much flour as possible. Adjust the hippen paste, if necessary, until it is easily spreadable but not runny (see recipe). Spread the paste flat and even within the templates on the prepared pans (see Figures 18–47 and 18–48, page 548).

3. Bake at 375°F (190°C) until the paste starts to color slightly, about 10 minutes. Let cool completely before removing from the sheet pans. Fasten the palm crowns to the trunks with a small dot of dark chocolate. Reserve. (Assemble only as many as you plan to use. The remaining pieces can be stored for up to a week in an airtight container and heated to recrisp if necessary.)

4. Presentation: Place a scoop of coconut ice cream in a coupe glass or dessert bowl. Decorate the ice cream with whipped cream rosettes and fresh pineapple. Stand one of the reserved palm trees in the center. Push the tree down far enough into the ice cream so that it stands up straight. Place the glass on a plate lined with a doily and serve immediately with a macadamia morsel on the plate.

Coupe Niçoise

mixed fresh fruit salad
Mandarin or Orange Sorbet
    (page 366)
curaçao liqueur
whipped cream
raspberries or strawberries
Orange Macaroons (page 136)

Place a portion of fruit salad in the bottom of a coupe glass or dessert bowl. Place a scoop of Mandarin or Orange Sorbet on top. Sprinkle curaçao liqueur on the sorbet. Decorate with whipped cream rosettes and raspberries (use strawberry wedges if raspberries are not available). Place the glass on a plate lined with a doily and serve immediately with an Orange Macaroon on the plate.

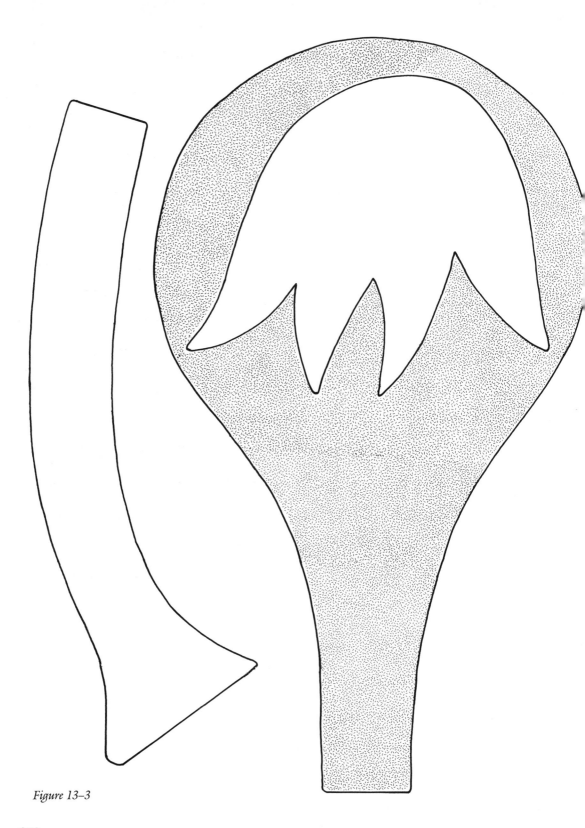

Figure 13–3

Coupe Sweden

Chunky Apple Filling (page 566)
White-Chocolate Ice Cream
  (page 365)
calvados
whipped cream
chocolate shavings
Florentinas (page 130)
Almond Macaroon Cookies
  (page 123)

Cover the bottom of a coupe glass or dessert bowl with the apple filling. Place a scoop of White-Chocolate Ice Cream on top. Sprinkle calvados on the ice cream. Decorate with whipped cream rosettes, chocolate shavings, and a Florentina. Place the glass on a dessert plate lined with a doily and serve immediately with a macaroon cookie on the plate.

Frozen Desserts

Baked Figs with Honey-Vanilla Frozen Yogurt

16 servings

32 medium-sized fresh figs
¼ cup (60 ml) water
8 ounces (225 g) granulated sugar
8 ounces (225 g) toasted pine nuts
2 tablespoons (30 ml) honey
⅓ cup (80 ml) Armagnac
2½ cups (600 ml) or ½ recipe
  Honey-Vanilla Frozen Yogurt
  (page 386)
melted dark chocolate
whipped cream
mint sprigs

1. Place the whole figs, standing on end, in a buttered oven-proof dish just large enough to hold them in one layer.

2. Heat the water and sugar in a saucepan until the mixture is simmering and the sugar dissolves. Pour the syrup over the figs. Bake at 375°F (190°C) for 15 minutes, basting the figs with the cooking liquid from time to time. Add the pine nuts and continue cooking for approximately 10 minutes longer, or until the figs are soft.

3. Transfer the figs to another dish (leaving the pine nuts in the liquid) and let them cool at room temperature.

4. Pour the cooking liquid and the nuts into a skillet. Add the honey and Armagnac. Cook the sauce, stirring constantly, until the ingredients are completely incorporated. Let the sauce cool to room temperature.

5. Scoop out 16 small scoops of frozen yogurt, taking care to keep them neat and uniform. Place them on a chilled sheet pan lined with baking paper.

6. Place the chocolate in a piping bag. Streak the chocolate across the frozen yogurt scoops, in two directions, as shown in Figure 6–1, page 150. Reserve in the freezer.

7. Presentation: Place two figs close together, off-center, on a dessert plate. Put a small drop of whipped cream in front (in the larger space) and place one of the prepared yogurt scoops on top. Spoon a portion of the sauce over the figs, making sure you include some of the pine nuts. Decorate with a sprig of mint; serve immediately.

Cherries Jubilee

8 servings

*1 pound, 6 ounces (625 g) pitted
   cherries (preferably black)
   or
1 pound, 8 ounces (680 g)
   canned cherries
1½ cups (360 ml) or ½ recipe
   Poaching Syrup II (page 6) or
   ¾ cup (180 ml) liquid from
   canned cherries
1 cup (240 ml) kirschwasser
2½ cups (600 ml) or ½ recipe
   White-Chocolate Ice Cream
   (page 365)
1 tablespoon (8 g) cornstarch*

There was a time when Cherries Jubilee was considered *the* dessert to end an elegant dinner. There is not too much you can do to change or improve this classic flambéed dessert, except possibly when it comes to the flamboyance of the presentation. Although it is traditional to serve vanilla ice cream with Cherries Jubilee in America, I suggest White-Chocolate Ice Cream instead because its rich texture is a perfect complement to the cherries. It is always a good idea to keep macerated cherries on hand in the refrigerator should you want to pamper an unexpected guest or friend. This dessert is very simple to prepare and people always seem to enjoy the theatrics of any flambéed dish.

1. Poach fresh cherries as directed for Cherry Sauce (page 558). Reserve ¾ cup (180 ml) of the poaching syrup or the same measurement of juice from canned cherries. Discard the remaining syrup or juice. Add the cherries and ¾ cup (180 ml) of the kirschwasser to the poaching syrup or juice. Macerate the cherries in the liquid for about an hour.

2. Scoop ice cream into individual servings, place on a serving platter, and reserve in freezer.

3. Fifteen minutes before serving, dissolve the cornstarch in a small portion of the macerating liquid, then stir back into the remaining liquid and cherries. Transfer to a chafing dish or copper sauté pan. Bring to a boil over medium heat, stirring constantly. Reduce heat and let simmer about 1 minute to eliminate the cornstarch flavor.

4. Presentation: Transfer the chafing dish or sauté pan filled with cherries to the stand of the *guéridon* in the dining room. Put the prepared ice cream and appropriate serving dishes or dessert plates nearby. Spoon the ice cream onto the serving dishes. Continue simmering the cherries, stirring from time to time, for a few minutes. Pour the remaining kirschwasser over the cherries in the pan, turn up the flame, and let the liqueur heat up a few seconds. Do not stir the liqueur into the sauce. Tilt the pan to ignite the liqueur (this looks a little more "showy" than using a match) and spoon the flaming cherries over the ice cream. Serve immediately.

NOTE: Because the cherry season is so short, you will probably prepare this recipe with canned cherries most of the time. Using canned cherries also makes more sense economically since poaching and pitting fresh cherries takes a lot of time.

Frozen Hazelnut Coffee Mousse

twenty 5-ounce (150-ml) servings

3 ounces (85 g) toasted hazelnuts
8 ounces (225 g) granulated sugar
2 eggs
6 egg yolks
1 teaspoon (4 g) mocha paste
  or
1 tablespoon (15 ml) Coffee
  Reduction (page 5)
1 quart (960 ml) heavy cream
¼ recipe Italian Meringue
  (page 333)
whipped cream
Strawberry Sauce (page 563)
Sour Cream Mixture for Piping
  (page 564)
strawberry wedges

1. Remove as much skin as possible from the roasted hazelnuts by rubbing them between your palms. Grind the nuts with half of the sugar in a food processor to a very fine consistency.

2. Combine the eggs, egg yolks, and remaining sugar. Whip the mixture over simmering water until it reaches 110°F (43°C). Remove from heat and whip until completely cooled, light, and fluffy. Mix in the hazelnuts and the mocha paste or coffee reduction. If you are using mocha paste, mix a little of the egg mixture into the paste to thin it first.

3. Whip the heavy cream to soft peaks and fold it into the egg mixture. Fold this mixture into the Italian Meringue.

4. Fill twenty 5-ounce (150-ml) soufflé ramekins (or any molds with the same capacity) with the mousse and freeze for at least 4 hours to harden.

5. Presentation: Pipe a small dot of whipped cream in the center of a dessert plate, unmold a mousse by dipping the mold briefly into hot water, and invert the mousse onto the cream to keep it from sliding. Pour Strawberry Sauce around the mousse, using just enough to cover the plate. Decorate the sauce with the sour cream mixture (see pages 518–519). Pipe a small rosette of whipped cream on top of the mousse and place a strawberry wedge in the cream. Serve immediately.

Ginger Soufflé Glacé

fifteen 8-ounce (240 ml) servings

1 ounce (30 g) candied ginger
2 tablespoons (30 ml)
  orange liqueur
1 teaspoon (5 ml) vanilla extract
6 egg yolks
8 ounces (225 g) granulated sugar
1 tablespoon (15 ml) honey
3 cups (720 ml) heavy cream
2½ cups (600 ml) or ½ recipe
  Vanilla Ice Cream (page 364)
12 egg whites
cocoa powder
julienne of candied ginger
Pirouettes (page 138)

1. Finely chop the candied ginger. Combine with the orange liqueur and set aside.

2. Prepare fifteen 3-ounce (90-ml) soufflé molds by fastening a collar around the outside with a rubber band (see note). The collars can be made of a plastic strip or a folded piece of aluminum foil. Cut the strips 2 to 2½ inches (5 to 6.2 cm) wide and a bit longer than the circumference of the molds. Reserve the molds in the freezer.

3. Whip the egg yolks, 3 ounces (85 g) of the sugar, and honey over simmering water until the mixture reaches about 110°F (43°C) and the sugar is dissolved. Remove from the heat and continue whipping until the mixture has cooled and is light and fluffy.

4. Whip the heavy cream to soft peaks. Fold into the egg yolk mixture together with the candied ginger and orange liqueur. Carefully stir in the ice cream (softened first, if necessary). Reserve the mixture in the freezer.

5. Whip the egg whites with the remaining sugar to stiff peaks. Fold the ice cream mixture into the egg whites.

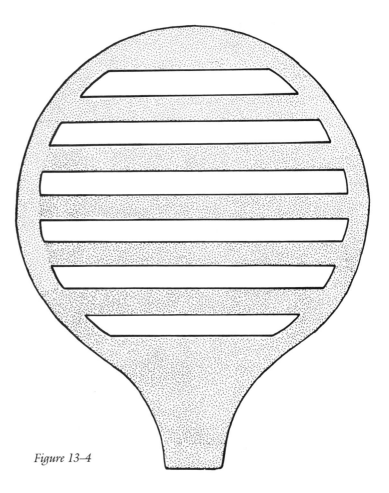

Figure 13–4

6. Working quickly, place the filling in a pastry bag with a no. 7 (14-mm) plain tip and pipe into the prepared molds. It should extend about 2 inches (5 cm) above the rim of the molds for an authentic soufflé look. Place the souffles in the freezer for at least 4 hours or, preferably, overnight.

7. Trace the drawing in Figure 13–4, then cut the template out of thin cardboard. Cake boxes 1/16 inch (2 mm) thick work fine.

8. Presentation: Remove the collar from a soufflé. Place the template on top and sift cocoa powder lightly over the template. Remove the template carefully without disturbing the pattern, then place a few pieces of julienned candied ginger in the center of the soufflé. Place the mold on a plate lined with a doily and serve immediately with a Pirouette on the plate.

NOTE: Using a smaller soufflé mold, rather than the typical 5-ounce (150-ml) capacity, will make the soufflé glacé higher and more attractive.

Variation

To make any type of liqueur soufflé glacé, omit the candied ginger and orange liqueur and replace with 6 tablespoons (90 ml) of the liqueur of your choice. Omit the candied ginger in presentation and substitute an appropriate garnish for the liqueur you have chosen.

Lingonberry Parfait
fourteen 5-ounce (150-ml) servings

10 ounces (300 ml) lingonberries
juice of 1 lime
3 eggs
2 egg yolks
2 ounces (55 g) granulated sugar
2½ cups (600 ml) heavy cream
whipped cream
Cranberry Sauce (page 558)
Sour Cream Mixture for Piping
    (page 564)

1. Purée the lingonberries. (Do not over-purée or you will add too much air and the mixture will lose color.) Add the lime juice and set aside.

2. Whip the eggs, egg yolks, and sugar over simmering water until the mixture reaches 110°F (43°C) and all of the sugar is dissolved. Remove from heat and continue whipping until completely cooled. The mixture should be light and fluffy.

3. Whip the heavy cream to soft peaks. Gently fold it into the whipped egg mixture, being very careful not to deflate. Fold in the lingonberry purée.

4. Fill fourteen 5-ounce (150-ml) parfait forms (or other suitable molds) with the mixture and place them in the freezer for about 4 hours to harden.

5. Unmold the parfaits by dipping the forms briefly into hot water. Place the parfaits on a sheet pan and return the pan to the freezer. Only unmold as many of the parfaits as you will be serving within a few hours. The parfaits left in the forms can be stored for several days in the freezer.

6. Presentation: To prevent the parfait from sliding on the plate as it is served, pipe a small dot of whipped cream in the center of a chilled dessert plate and set the parfait on top. Pour enough Cranberry Sauce around the parfait to cover the plate. Decorate the sauce with the sour cream mixture (see pages 518–519). Serve immediately.

NOTE: The recipe assumes that you are using lingonberries from a can or jar, which have added sugar. Depending on the sweetness of a particular brand, you may want to adjust the amount of sugar in the recipe. In the event that you are lucky enough to find fresh or frozen berries to work with, you must first cook them to a jam-like consistency, adding sugar to taste.

Medley of Sorbets in Tulips

(see photograph in color insert)

25 servings

25 Chocolate Tulips (page 546);
    see step 1
whipped cream
1 quart (960 ml) or ½ recipe
    Champagne Sorbet (page 365)
3½ cups (840 ml) or ½ recipe
    Raspberry Sorbet (page 366)
3½ cups (840 ml) or ½ recipe
    Honeydew Melon Sorbet
    (page 366)
Sabayon (page 398) made with
    champagne
Chocolate Sauce for Piping
    (page 560)
raspberries, strawberries,
    blueberries, and/or blackberries
    for garnish
mint sprigs

1. Make the Chocolate Tulips using the regular size of template, but form them over a larger cup or bowl than specified in the recipe, one that will give you a 3½-inch (8.7-cm) opening in the finished tulip. This larger size will allow you to place the scoops of sorbet side by side instead of on top of each other.

2. Pipe a small amount of whipped cream (about the size of a hazelnut) onto a serving plate, slightly off-center. Place a tulip on top of the cream so it will not slide. Place one scoop of each of the three sorbets in the tulip, using a 1-ounce (30-ml) ice cream scoop. Pour sabayon around the tulip to cover the plate. Decorate the sabayon with the Chocolate Sauce for Piping (see pages 518–519). Garnish with the mint sprigs and the berries.

Poached Pears with Ginger Ice Cream and Two Sauces

(see photograph in color insert)

16 servings

8 pears
7½ cups (1 l, 800 ml) or 1½
    recipes Poaching Syrup I
    (page 6)
4 small pieces of fresh ginger root,
    about the size of a quarter
½ recipe Sponge Cake batter
    (page 161)

1. Peel the pears and cut in half lengthwise. Place them directly into the poaching syrup as you are working, to prevent oxidation. Add the fresh ginger and poach the pears until they are tender. Remove from heat and let cool in the syrup.

2. Pour the sponge cake batter into a 10-inch (25-cm) greased and floured cake pan. Bake at 425°F (219°C) for about 8 minutes or until done. Set aside to cool.

3. Blanch the pistachios using a pinch of salt in the blanching water to amplify the green color of the nuts. Remove the skins and dry the nuts. Crush to a fine consistency. (If you dry the nuts in an oven, do not toast them or you will lose the color.)

4. Slice the sponge cake into two thin layers. Reserve one layer for another use. Cut 16 rounds out of the remaining layer using a 2-inch (5-cm) plain cookie cutter. Cover the cake circles and reserve.

2 ounces (55 g) pistachio nuts
5 cups (1 l, 200 ml) or 1 recipe
*   White-Chocolate Ice Cream*
*   with Ginger (page 364)*
Raspberry Sauce (page 563)
Romanoff Sauce (page 563)
16 Marzipan Leaves (page 541)
melted dark baker's chocolate

5. Remove the pear halves from the poaching liquid, core, and pat dry with towels. Chill dessert plates in the refrigerator.

6. Presentation: Place a sponge round in the center of a dessert plate. Put a small scoop of ice cream on top and lightly flatten the ice cream with the back of the scoop. Arrange a pear half on top of the ice cream (flat-side down), pressing it down to secure. Cover the stem half of the pear with Romanoff Sauce, spooning or pouring straight across the center and letting it run out to cover the plate next to the pear. Spoon Raspberry Sauce over the bottom half of the pear in the same manner. Make sure that the sauces are thick enough to cover the pear, but at the same time run out onto the plate. Sprinkle a thin line of pistachios across the center where the two sauces meet. Pipe a small, slightly curved line of chocolate in the sauce for the stem. Place a marzipan leaf next to the stem of the pear and serve immediately.

FOURTEEN

Light Desserts

Baked Bananas with
    Banana-Tofu Ice Cream
Blood Orange Sorbet in
    Magnolia Cookie Shells
Caramelized Pineapple
    Barbados
Crepes Vienna
Fresh Strawberries with
    Champagne Sabayon
Fruit Valentines

Lemon Chiffon Pouches
Lychee Charlotte Royal
Orange Gratin
Pears California
Sabayon
Salzburger Soufflé
Strawberry-Peach Yogurt
    Creams
Winter Fruit Compote
Zinfandel Poached Pears

We live in an era of heightened health awareness as well as food consciousness. People all over the world are realizing they cannot eat whatever and whenever they want and still remain healthy. More and more people exercise regularly and watch what they eat, whether to lower cholesterol, lose weight, reduce blood pressure, or just to feel more fit. I have always been fortunate because my love of exercise has offset any weight gain from my love of food. (Of course, there are always those who say you should never trust a skinny chef!)

The desserts in this chapter should not be confused with dietetic desserts, which in my experience usually taste as if something is missing. Instead, these lower-calorie desserts taste terrific and can be enjoyed by non-dieters as well as those who want to keep track of their calories. In fact, many are recipes I have been preparing for years, long before there was so much emphasis on lighter food.

Many restaurants today offer reduced-calorie alternatives to their regular menu selections. But a tasty and attractive finale is not as easy to produce as, for example, grilling fish instead of frying it, or sautéing chicken breasts in reduced stock instead of butter. The principal ingredients in

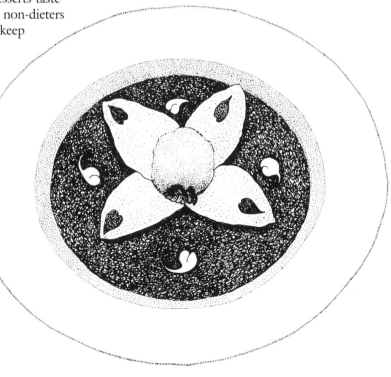

many desserts are virtually bursting with calories. Butter has an amazing 1,600 calories per cup, sugar 875 calories, eggs 320 calories, flour 800 calories, and heavy cream 840 calories. This limits the classic dessert possibilities quite a bit.

It is feasible, in some cases, to achieve fairly good results by replacing a calorie-rich ingredient in a recipe with a low-calorie one, such as substituting meringue for whipped cream, or using yogurt or tofu as a base for ice cream instead of egg yolks and heavy cream, but often this makes for a less satisfying dessert. It is more reliable to use a recipe that is light in calories by itself, or has been created as a light dessert and tested (like these).

Pastry chefs are often blamed for tempting the hapless consumer to consume excess calories. You can certainly gain weight, and plenty of it, by overindulging in some of the recipes in this book if you do not have the willpower to limit yourself to occasional, or small, portions. However, I do feel dessert—in moderation—can be part of a balanced diet. I like good, flavorful food and believe in the old saying, "If I cannot have what I want, I am not going to settle for what I can get." I would rather have an apple or an orange than a watered-down dessert that has no taste or uses artificial sweeteners and flavorings, as do many of the so-called diet desserts. The recipes in this chapter are all sweet and satisfying, yet none contains more than 300 calories per serving and none uses artificial ingredients. These recipes simply use ingredients naturally low in calories; many also recommend serving smaller portions. These desserts can be enjoyed not only for what they are not, but also for what they are: delicious!

Baked Bananas with Banana-Tofu Ice Cream

16 servings, approximately 240 calories each

3 oranges
¼ cup (60 ml) honey
1 tablespoon (15 ml) vanilla extract
8 medium-sized ripe bananas
lemon juice

1. Remove the zest from the oranges in long threads using a zester. Extract the juice from the oranges and combine with the zest, honey, and vanilla extract. Set aside.

2. Peel the bananas and cut in half lengthwise. Rub a little lemon juice on them to keep them from getting brown. Place cut-side up in a hotel pan or other ovenproof dish (see note). Place a piece of butter on top of each one. Cover the dish with aluminum foil, crimping the foil against the edge of the dish to seal it tightly.

3. Bake the bananas at 375°F (190°C) for approximately 6 minutes, or until they are soft (the time will vary depending on the ripeness of the fruit).

2 ounces (55 g) softened butter
Banana-Tofu Ice Cream
   (recipe follows)
mint sprigs

4. Presentation: Cut one of the banana halves in five or six places along one edge, cutting at a 45° angle and going almost to the opposite side. Place it flat-side up on a dessert plate and bend into a half-circle to fan out the cut pieces. Spoon some of the orange juice mixture over the banana without using any of the zest. Place a small scoop of the ice cream inside the circle and sprinkle some of the orange zest on the ice cream. Garnish with a mint sprig and serve immediately.

NOTE: If you wish to cook the bananas à la carte, or if you are only making a few servings, cut pieces of aluminum foil to the appropriate size, place a banana half on one side of each piece of foil, and top with butter as above. Fold the foil over and crimp the edge to seal. Place the individual packets on a sheet pan to bake.

Banana-Tofu Ice Cream
6 cups (1 l, 440 ml)

12 ounces (340 g) tofu
4 medium-sized ripe bananas
1/2 cup (120 ml) vegetable oil
1 1/2 cups (360 ml) milk
1/2 cup (120 ml) honey
2 teaspoons (10 ml) vanilla extract

1. Blend the tofu and peeled bananas in a food processor until smooth. Transfer to a bowl and stir in oil, milk, honey, and vanilla.
2. Process in an ice cream freezer. Transfer to a chilled bowl and store, covered, in the freezer.

Blood Orange Sorbet in Magnolia Cookie Shells
(see photograph in color insert)
20 servings, approximately
270 calories each

melted butter
bread flour
1 recipe Vanilla Tulip batter
   (page 546)
1/2 teaspoon (1 g) cocoa powder
Blood Orange Sauce (recipe follows)
Blood Orange Sorbet
   (recipe follows)
Sour Cream Mixture for Piping
   (page 564)
mint sprigs

1. Make the tulip batter and, while it is resting, prepare the sheet pans and the template. Brush a thin film of melted butter on the back of even sheet pans. Coat with flour and tap sharply to remove the excess. Make the magnolia template (Figure 14–1). The template as shown is the correct size for use in the recipe. Trace the drawing, then cut the template out of 1/16-inch (2-mm) thick cardboard. Cake boxes work fine for this.
2. Reserve about 2 ounces (55 g) of the tulip batter. Spread the remaining batter, flat and even within the template, on the prepared sheet pans (see Figures 18–47 and 18–48, page 548), making 20 flowers.
3. Mix the cocoa powder into the reserved tulip batter to turn it light brown (you may need to add a few drops of additional egg white if the batter seems too firm). Place the cocoa-colored batter in a piping bag and cut a small opening. Pipe a pea-sized dot of batter on each of the flower petals near the tip. Drag a toothpick through the dots to form hearts pointing toward the tips (see Figure 18–27, page 519).

Figure 14–1

4. Bake one pan at a time at 425°F (219°C) for approximately 8 minutes, or until there are a few light brown spots on the cookies. Leave the sheet pan in the oven and remove the cookie shells one at a time.

5. Working quickly, form them (with the hearts facing up) by pressing each cookie gently between two small forms, as shown in Figure 13–2, page 362 (example on left). The form on the bottom should be 2½ inches (6.2 cm) in diameter. Center the cookie over the form, center a small form (approximately 2 inches (5 cm) in diameter) on top, and press the center of the cookie into the form so the petals point straight up. Gently bend the top half of the petals over and down immediately, while they are still soft. It is easiest to work with two sets of forms at a time. As you finish forming the second flower, the first should be firm enough to remove and set aside. Repeat to form the remaining flowers. The cookie shells can be kept for several days at this point if stored in an airtight container at room temperature.

6. Presentation: Cover the base of a dessert plate with a thin layer of Blood Orange Sauce. Place a cookie shell in the center and fill with a scoop of Blood Orange Sorbet. Decorate the sauce with the sour cream mixture (see pages 518–519). Put a mint sprig on the sorbet. Serve immediately.

NOTE: If blood oranges are not available, replace with Raspberry Sorbet (see pages 366–367), and Raspberry Sauce (see page 563).

Blood Orange Sorbet

approximately 6 cups (1 l, 440 ml)

2 cups (480 ml) blood orange juice, strained
2 cups (480 ml) Simple Syrup, at room temperature (page 7)
1 cup (240 ml) water, approximately
few drops Tartaric Acid Solution (page 596) or lemon juice

1. Since most blood oranges are smaller than regular oranges, you will need approximately 15 to make the juice. Combine the orange juice and simple syrup. Adjust the mixture between 16° and 18° Baumé (see page 615) by adding water. If you do not have a Baumé thermometer, use trial-and-error to determine the proper sweetness. Add tartaric acid or lemon juice.

2. Process in an ice cream freezer. When finished, transfer to a chilled container and store, covered, in the freezer.

Blood Orange Sauce

Follow the directions for Orange Sauce (see page 561), substituting blood oranges.

Caramelized Pineapple Barbados

(see photograph in color insert)
12 servings, approximately
230 calories each

fresh pineapple
4 ounces (115 g) granulated sugar
2 cups (480 ml) or ½ recipe
　　Orange Sauce (page 561)
¼ cup (60 ml) honey
½ cup (120 ml) dark rum
2 tablespoons (30 ml) green
　　peppercorns, finely chopped
2½ cups (600 ml) or ½ recipe
　　Honey-Vanilla Frozen Yogurt
　　(recipe follows)
fresh pineapple leaves for decoration

1. Cut the top and bottom off the pineapple. Trim off the skin, cutting deep enough to remove all of the "eyes." Cut the pineapple into slices that are slightly heavier than 4 ounces (115 g) each. Cut the core out of each slice using a plain cookie cutter, then trim the sides to make the slices octagonal. Make 12 slices.

2. Place the pineapple on sheet pans lined with baking paper. Sprinkle half of the granulated sugar evenly over the top. Turn over and sprinkle sugar on the other side. Reserve.

3. Combine the Orange Sauce, honey, and rum in a saucepan. Bring to a boil over high heat and reduce to a sauce-like consistency. Pour into a container and reserve at room temperature.

4. Place the pineapple slices under a hot salamander and cook until the sugar is caramelized. Quickly turn the slices and caramelize the other side (see note).

5. Presentation: Pour a round pool of sauce in the center of a dessert plate. Place a slice of pineapple on top. Sprinkle some of the chopped peppercorns on the pineapple. Place a small scoop of frozen yogurt in the center of the slice and decorate the plate with a few pineapple leaves. Serve immediately.

NOTE: While it would be ideal to cook the pineapple slices to order, this is often not practical. However, they should not be cooked more than one hour in advance, and they should be held at room temperature. If you do not have a salamander, cook the pineapple in a very hot skillet to caramelize the topping.

Caramelized Pineapple with Coconut Ice Cream

Caramelized pineapple is wonderful served with Coconut Ice Cream (see page 359) if you do not need to watch calories. Spoon Caramel Sauce II (see page 558) on the base of the plate and set the pineapple on top. Decorate the caramel sauce with Chocolate Sauce for Piping (see page 560) around the edge of the plate. Sprinkle a few candied lime peels (see page 520) or toasted macadamia nuts on the ice cream. Garnish with fresh pineapple leaves.

Honey-Vanilla Frozen Yogurt

5 cups (1 l, 200 ml)

6 ounces (170 g) granulated sugar
⅓ cup (80 ml) honey
1 tablespoon (15 ml) lemon juice
1 tablespoon (15 ml)
　　vanilla extract
2 eggs, separated
4 cups (960 ml) plain yogurt

1. Place half of the sugar, the honey, and the lemon juice in a saucepan. Bring to a boil over low heat. Boil for 1 minute, then remove from the heat. Add the vanilla.

2. Beat the egg yolks, stir in some of the sugar syrup to temper, then add the remaining syrup. Cool to room temperature.

3. Beat the egg whites until they are foamy. Gradually add the remaining sugar and beat to stiff peaks.

4. Place the yogurt in a bowl and stir smooth with a whisk. Fold in the syrup and egg yolk mixture, then the whipped egg whites. Process in an ice cream freezer.

Fruit-flavored Frozen Yogurt

The honey-vanilla recipe can be used to make delicious fruit-flavored frozen yogurt as well. To make strawberry frozen yogurt, replace the honey with 3½ cups (840 ml) of Strawberry Ice Cream (see page 364), omitting the vanilla custard. Follow the procedure for preparing the strawberries in step 2 of the ice cream recipe, and add to the frozen yogurt instead of the honey. Continue as directed. To make other flavors, add approximately the same amount of fruit pulp (8 ounces/225 g) and approximately 8 ounces (225 g) additional sugar. Strain the fruit pulp as necessary, depending on the variety used. You may also need to adjust the amount of extra sugar, depending on the sweetness of the fruit.

Crepes Vienna

20 servings, approximately
200 calories each

2 tablespoons (30 ml)
   orange liqueur
1 ounce (30 g) dark raisins
1 ounce (30 g) golden raisins
½ recipe Crepe batter
   (recipe follows)
5 oranges
1 dry pint (480 ml) raspberries
⅓ cup (80 ml) heavy cream
½ teaspoon (3 g) granulated sugar
4 cups (960 ml) or 1 recipe
   Orange Sauce (page 561)
fresh raspberries
mint sprigs

1. Warm the liqueur just a little and add the raisins. Set them aside to plump.

2. Make the crepes following the directions with the recipe, but do not cook any more than you expect to use right away. (The crepe batter can be stored for up to three days in the refrigerator, but cooked crepes will become tough and rubbery the day after cooking and should not be used in this recipe.)

3. Cut the peel from the oranges and cut out the segments (see Figures 10–4 and 10–5, page 276). Hold the oranges over a bowl as you cut them to catch the juice for the orange sauce. Cut the orange segments in half crosswise.

4. Place the crepes in front of you with the golden brown side down. Place four or five pieces of orange, and an equal amount of raspberries in a line down the center of each crepe. Roll the crepes up tightly around the fruit and place them, seam-side down, next to each other on paper-lined sheet pans.

5. Whip the heavy cream and sugar to stiff peaks. Place in a pastry bag with a no. 7 (14-mm) star tip. Reserve in the refrigerator.

6. Gently stir the plumped raisins and the orange liqueur into the Orange Sauce.

7. Presentation: Place a crepe, seam-side down, in the center of a dessert plate. Spoon Orange Sauce across the crepe in the center so that there is a small pool of sauce on either side. Pipe a rosette of whipped cream on top of the crepe in the center. Place a raspberry on the cream, and set a mint sprig next to it.

NOTE 1: If raspberries are out of season, or are too expensive, substitute small wedges of strawberries.

NOTE 2: If you are serving this as part of your regular menu and the calorie count is not crucial, use two crepes per serving.

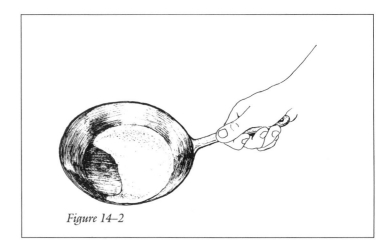

Figure 14–2

Crepes
about forty 6-inch (15-cm) crepes

6 ounces (170 g) cake flour
6 ounces (170 g) bread flour
3 ounces (85 g) granulated sugar
2 teaspoons (10 g) salt
6 eggs
6 egg yolks
6 ounces (170 g) melted butter
3 cups (720 ml) warm milk
⅓ cup (80 ml) brandy
clarified butter

1. Sift the flours together and combine with the sugar and salt in a mixing bowl.

2. Lightly beat the eggs with the egg yolks, just to mix. Gradually stir into the dry ingredients. Add the melted butter, milk, and brandy. Mix until smooth. If the batter appears broken, the milk was probably too cool. To remedy this, warm the batter over simmering water, stirring constantly, until smooth. Let the batter rest at room temperature for 1 hour.

3. Heat two 6-inch (15-cm) crepe pans and brush with clarified butter (see note). Do not use a nylon brush. Cover the bottom of the pans with a thin film of batter by quickly tilting and rotating the pan (Figure 14–2). Try to avoid making the batter run up on the sides of the pans. Pour any excess batter back into the bowl. With practice you should be able to add just the right amount of batter each time.

4. Flip the crepes when the bottoms have a nice golden brown color, using a spatula and the fingers of one hand, or flip them in the air, if you have the knack. The second side need only cook for a few seconds, until it is no longer sticky; overcooking the crepes will make them dry.

5. Slide the crepes out of the pans and stack them on top of each other on a plate to prevent their drying out as you make the remaining crepes. After you have made a few crepes, adjust the batter, if necessary. If large bubbles form as the crepe cooks, the batter is probably too thin (or the pan may be too hot). Thicken the batter by whipping in some additional flour. If the batter is too thick (does not pour in a thin film) add milk to thin it. Once you have the batter and the heat adjusted correctly, making a few dozen crepes is easy. Store the crepes, covered with an inverted

plate, at room temperature. Wipe the crepe pans clean with a towel; do not use water under any circumstance.

NOTE: If you are using properly seasoned crepe pans you probably will have to grease the pans only for the first few crepes. In any case, avoid using too much butter as this saturates the crepes as well as adds additional calories.

Fresh Strawberries with Champagne Sabayon

15 servings, approximately
230 calories each

3 pounds, 8 ounces (1 kg, 590 g)
strawberries, perfectly ripe
2 tablespoons (30 ml)
curaçao liqueur
2 recipes Sabayon, made with
champagne (page 398)
Candied Lime Peels (page 520)

This refreshing dessert is very simple to prepare; it should be made only when you can get strawberries that are fully ripe, red, and sweet.

1. Clean the strawberries and reserve 15 of the largest and most attractive berries. Cut the remaining strawberries into ½-inch (1.2-cm) chunks. Macerate the cut strawberries in the curaçao liqueur for at least one hour, tossing gently from time to time. Cut the reserved berries into thin slices lengthwise.

2. Presentation: Line the sides of fifteen 6-ounce (180-ml) saucer-type champagne glasses with the sliced strawberries, placing the cut sides against the glass. Divide the macerated berries evenly between the glasses. Pour hot sabayon on top. Decorate with the candied lime peels and serve immediately.

Fruit Valentines

sixteen 3½-inch (8.7-cm) servings,
approximately 225 calories each

½ recipe French Meringue
(page 333)
melted dark baker's chocolate
Fresh Fruit Filling
(instructions follow)
1 tablespoon (15 ml)
orange liqueur
2 tablespoons (30 ml)
Simple Syrup (page 7)
Raspberry Sauce (page 563)
Sour Cream Mixture for Piping
(page 564)

This is a light and tempting dessert, not just for a special occasion such as Mother's Day or Valentine's Day, but anytime you need a nice presentation for low-calorie fresh fruit.

1. The template shown in Figure 14–3 is the correct size for use in this recipe. Trace the drawing, then cut the template out of ¼-inch (6-mm) cardboard, such as corrugated cardboard used for cake rounds. Draw 16 hearts on baking paper, tracing around the inside of the template. Reserve.

2. Invert sheet pans and cover with baking paper (not the paper with the tracing). Fasten the papers to the pans with a little meringue to keep them from slipping. Make 16 hearts, spreading the meringue flat and even within the template, on the sheet pans (see Figures 18–47 and 18–48, page 548).

3. Place the remaining meringue in a pastry bag with a no. 3 (6-mm) plain tip. Pipe two ropes of meringue, one on top of the other, around the edge of the hearts.

4. Invert more sheet pans and attach the reserved baking papers as before, inverting the papers so the tracing is on the bottom.

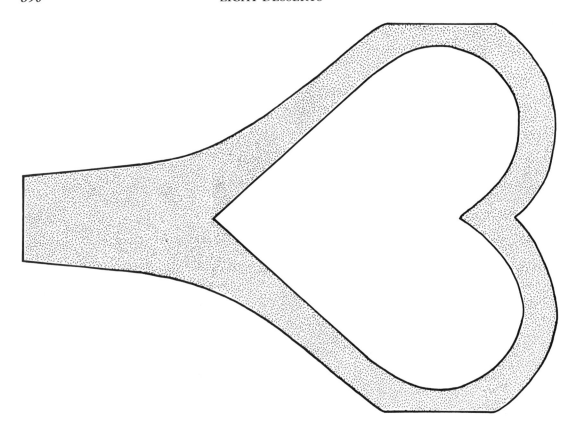

Figure 14–3

Place a no. 2 (4-mm) plain tip on the outside of the pastry bag and hold it in place as you pipe (see Figures 12–2 and 12–3, page 340). Pipe a border of meringue around the hearts, then pipe four diagonal lines across the inside, attaching the lines on either end.

5. Bake all of the meringue at 200°F (94°C) for approximately 2 hours, or until dried through. Remove the thinner hearts sooner if they begin to show color. Let the meringues cool completely.

6. Place a small amount of melted baker's chocolate in a piping bag and cut a small opening. Streak the chocolate in diagonal lines at right angles to the lines of meringue, on the thinner hearts.

7. Just before serving, gently fold the orange liqueur and simple syrup into the well-chilled fruit filling.

8. Presentation: Pipe a small dot of sour cream mixture off-center on a dessert plate. Place a meringue case on top. Fill the case with mounded fruit filling, letting it spill out onto the plate on one side. Place the lid leaning against the other side of the filled heart. Pour a small pool of Raspberry Sauce in front of the dessert, and decorate the sauce with the Sour Cream Mixture for Piping (see pages 518–519). Serve immediately.

NOTE: These desserts should be assembled to order to prevent the fruit from making the meringue soggy.

Fresh Fruit Filling

You will need approximately ¾ cup (180 ml) of filling per serving. Use small varieties such as blueberries, raspberries, strawberries, kiwis cut into small pieces, or small melon balls. Try to use at least four types of fruit, and choose colors that look good together.

Variation

This is a very attractive alternative should you not have time to make the meringue shells.

1. Prepare the appropriate amount of fresh fruit filling using orange segments, peaches, apricots, and several types of melon balls. Reserve.

2. Make enough Orange Sauce (see page 561) to allow ¼ cup (60 ml) per serving. Add the fruit to the sauce while the sauce is hot, together with 2 tablespoons (30 ml) of orange liqueur for every 16 servings. Set the fruit aside to cool in the sauce.

3. Force a small amount of strawberry jam through a fine sieve, and place in a pastry bag with a no. 1 (2-mm) plain tip.

4. Make the template shown in Figure 14–4. This template is the correct size for this recipe, but can be altered to better fit a particular plate. Trace the drawing, then cut the template from ¹⁄₁₆-inch (2-mm) cardboard (cake boxes work fine).

5. Presentation: Place the template in the center of a dessert plate. Lightly sift powdered sugar over the exposed part of the plate, including the rim. Carefully remove the template. Pipe a thin string of jam next to the powdered sugar following the outline left by the template. Arrange approximately ¾ cup (180 ml) of the well-chilled fruit and sauce mixture attractively within the border of jam, letting the sauce flow out to the edge of the jam, but not over it. Sprinkle a few fresh raspberries, blueberries, or cut strawberries on top. Be careful not to get any fingerprints on the powdered sugar border when serving.

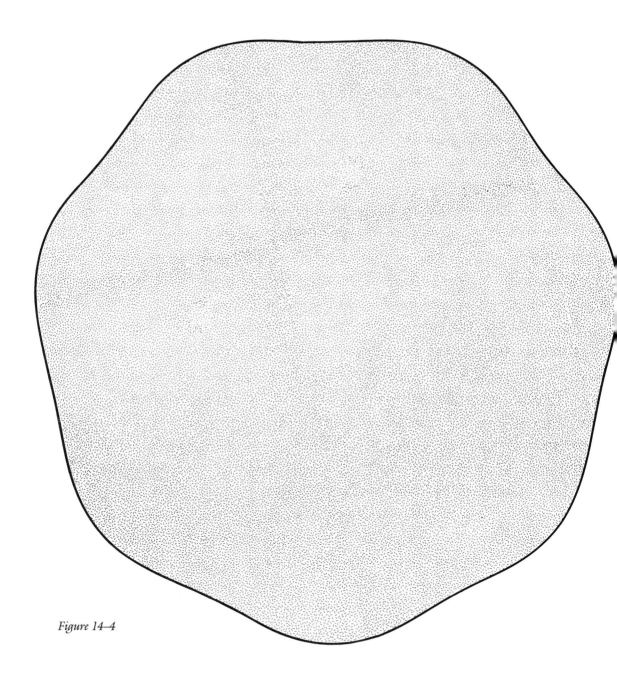

Figure 14-4

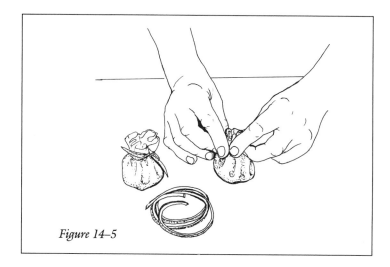

Figure 14–5

Lemon Chiffon Pouches

(see photograph in color insert)
16 servings, approximately
275 calories each

½ recipe Lemon Chiffon Cake
  filling (page 207); see step 1
½ recipe Crepe Batter (page 388)
oranges
1 recipe Raspberry Sauce or
  Strawberry Sauce (page 563)

1. To make the lemon filling, follow the recipe for Lemon Chiffon Cake, completing steps 1, 3, 4, and 5.

2. Make sixteen 7-inch (17.5-cm) crepes. Make sure they are thin, as well as uniform in size and shape. If they are not round, place a plate or other round object of the correct size on top and trim. Cover and reserve.

3. Using a citrus stripper, cut sixteen 8-inch (20-cm) strips of orange rind to use as strings to tie the pouches closed. Reserve.

4. Center the crepes on top of 3-inch (7.5-cm) diameter soufflé ramekins (or other forms of approximately equal size) with the nicest side on the bottom. Push the center of each crepe into the forms.

5. When the lemon filling has started to set slightly, place it in a pastry bag with a no. 6 (12-mm) plain tip. Divide the filling equally between the forms. Working with one at a time, bring up the sides of the crepes, lift them out of the forms, and tie them closed with the orange rind (Figure 14–5). Place on a sheet pan lined with baking paper and refrigerate just long enough to set the filling. Serve at room temperature.

6. Presentation: Cover the center of a dessert plate (but not the whole base) with a thin layer of Raspberry or Strawberry Sauce. Place one pouch on top of the sauce. Serve immediately.

NOTE: Should the calorie count not be an issue, use two pouches per serving.

Lychee Charlotte Royal

16 servings, approximately
290 calories each

½ recipe Almond Sponge batter
(page 162)
8 ounces (225 g) smooth
raspberry jam
Lychee Bavarois (recipe follows)
Red Currant Glaze (page 527)
Raspberry Sauce (page 563)

1. Spread the sponge batter out evenly to ¼ inch (6 mm) of the edge on all sides on a 16- × 24-inch (40- × 60-cm) sheet of baking paper. Drag the paper onto a sheet pan (see Figure 15–3, page 422). Bake immediately at 425°F (219°C) for about 8 minutes, or until just done. To prevent the thin sponge from drying out, slide it onto a second (cool) sheet pan or onto the table. Let cool.

2. Invert the sponge sheet onto a second sheet of baking paper, then peel the paper off the back. (If the sponge has been made ahead and refrigerated, the skin must be removed from the top before the sponge is inverted.) Spread the raspberry jam over the sponge (you want just enough to make the sponge sticky). Roll the sheet lengthwise as directed for Yule Logs (see step 7, page 426). Place the sponge roll in the freezer to firm up while you are making the Lychee Bavarois.

3. Cut the sponge roll into slices ⅛ inch (3 mm) thick. Use the slices to line the bottom and sides of deep, round bavarois molds, or other suitable molds with an approximate capacity of ½ cup (120 ml). Fill the molds with Lychee Bavarois as soon as it shows signs of thickening. Refrigerate for at least 2 hours to set.

4. Gently unmold the charlottes with the help of a spoon (you may need to dip them in hot water briefly). Place on a sheet pan lined with baking paper. Brush currant glaze over the jellyroll slices.

5. Presentation: Place a Lychee Charlotte Royal in the center of a dessert plate. Pour Raspberry Sauce around the dessert.

NOTE: If you are not serving this as a light dessert, add a rosette of whipped cream on top and decorate the Raspberry Sauce with Sour Cream Mixture for Piping (see page 564 for recipe, pages 518–519 for decorating instructions).

Variation I

1. Make a full recipe of Almond Sponge batter and make a second sponge sheet the same size as the first. Prepare one of the sheets as directed above. Weigh out an additional 8 ounces (225 g) of jam. Use soufflé ramekins that are 3 inches (7.5 cm) in diameter and have a 5-ounce (150-ml) capacity instead of the bavarois molds.

2. Invert and remove the paper from the second sponge sheet. Cut a rectangle approximately 8½ inches (21.2 cm) wide the length of the sheet. Adjust the width, if necessary, so that it matches the circumference of the inside of the ramekins you are using. Reserve the remaining piece of sponge.

3. Cut the rectangle across into four equal pieces, each approximately 8½ × 5¾ inches (21.2 × 14.3 cm). Cut two more pieces the same size from the reserved piece of sponge. Save the remainder for another use.

4. Stack the pieces, layering raspberry jam between them. Place in the freezer to firm the sponge and make it easier to slice.

5. Use ⅛-inch (3-mm) slices of the roulade (the rolled sponge sheet) to line the bottoms of the ramekins. (You will have some roulade left; wrap and reserve it in the freezer for another use.) Cut ⅛-inch (3-mm) slices lengthwise from the layered sponge strip, and use these pieces to line the sides of the ramekins. (A serrated knife dipped in hot water works best for slicing.)

6. Fill the lined ramekins and follow instructions for main recipe.

Variation II: Classic Charlotte Royal

Follow the instructions for lining the forms as described in Lychee Charlotte Royal. Fill with Classic Bavarian Cream (see page 566). Present garnished with whipped cream, Raspberry Sauce, and Sour Cream Mixture for Piping (see recipe, page 564; decorating instructions, pages 518–519).

Lychee Bavarois

2 quarts (1 l, 920 ml)

8 egg yolks
2 ounces (55 g) granulated sugar
2 tablespoons (18 g) unflavored gelatin powder
½ cup (120 ml) cold water
2 cups (480 ml) strained lychee purée
1 vanilla bean, split
  or
1 teaspoon (5 ml) vanilla extract
¼ recipe Swiss Meringue (page 334)
1 cup (240 ml) heavy cream

1. Whip the egg yolks and sugar until light and fluffy. Reserve.

2. Soften the gelatin in cold water. Reserve.

3. Bring the lychee purée to the scalding point with the vanilla bean, if used. Gradually pour the hot liquid into the yolk mixture while whipping rapidly. Return the mixture to the heat and bring back to the scalding point, stirring constantly. Do not boil. Remove from the heat, stir in the reserved gelatin, and set aside to cool, stirring from time to time.

4. Whip the cream to soft peaks. Remove the vanilla bean from the custard and save for another use, or add the vanilla extract, if used. Gradually stir the cream into the Swiss Meringue. When the custard has cooled, slowly stir it into the cream and meringue mixture.

NOTE: Your chances of finding fresh lychees are small, and the canned variety works just fine. You will need approximately 1 pound, 4 ounces (570 g) strained lychees to get 2 cups (480 ml) of strained purée. Strain the canned lychees and reserve the liquid. Purée the fruit, and pass it through a fine sieve. Add some of the reserved liquid as needed to make 2 cups (480 ml). The recipe presumes you are using lychees canned in sugar syrup.

Orange Gratin

16 servings, approximately
300 calories each

¼ recipe Vanilla Tulips batter
(page 546)
melted butter
bread flour
16 blood (or navel) oranges
1 ounce (30 g) fresh ginger root
3 fresh pomegranates
*   or*
1 tablespoon (15 ml) grenadine
⅓ cup (80 ml) honey
¾ cup (180 ml) water
2 tablespoons (30 ml) orange
*   liqueur*
½ teaspoon (1 g) ground allspice
5 egg yolks
¾ cup (180 ml) yogurt
1¼ cups (300 ml) heavy cream
2½ cups (600 ml) or ½ recipe
*   Honey-Vanilla Frozen Yogurt*
*   (page 386)*
melted dark chocolate

1. Make the Vanilla Tulips batter and set aside to rest. Lightly grease the back of even, inverted sheet pans with melted butter, coat them with flour, and tap sharply to remove the excess. Reserve.

2. Make the smaller size (the inside fluted circle) of the tulips template (Figure 18–46, page 547), following the directions in the tulip recipe.

3. Peel the oranges and cut out the segments (see Figures 10–4 and 10–5, page 276), holding the oranges over a bowl to catch the juice. Reserve the segments and juice. Peel the ginger root and cut into two or three slices. Reserve. Cut the pomegranates in half and extract the seeds and juice. Reserve.

4. Place the honey and water in a saucepan. Heat to simmering, then add the ginger root. Reduce the syrup by half. Add the reserved orange juice and the orange liqueur. Mix in the pomegranate seeds and juice (or grenadine), and the allspice.

5. Cool the mixture slightly, then strain over the reserved orange segments. Avoid mixing, to prevent breaking the segments. Cover and refrigerate for at least 4 hours (preferably longer) to develop the flavors.

6. Spread the tulip batter on the reserved sheet pans, spreading it flat and even within the template (see Figures 18–47 and 18–48, page 548). Make 16 tulips. Bake one pan at a time at 425°F (219°C) for approximately 5 minutes, or until there are a few light brown spots on the cookies.

7. Leave the sheet pan in the oven and remove the cookie shells one at a time. Working quickly, form them by pressing each cookie gently between two small forms as shown in Figure 13–2, page 362, example on left. Center the cookie over the form, center a smaller form on top, and press the center of the cookie into the form to make a tiny cup. It is easiest to work with two sets of forms at a time. When you finish forming the second cup, the first should be firm enough to remove and set aside. Repeat to form the remaining tulips. Reserve until time of service. (The cookie shells can be kept for up to a week at this point if stored in an airtight container at room temperature.)

8. Beat the egg yolks for a few seconds just to combine, then mix in the yogurt. Whip the cream to soft peaks, and fold the yogurt mixture into the cream.

9. Strain the liquid from the orange segments, measure off ¾ cup (180 ml), and stir into the cream mixture. Discard the remainder or save for another use.

10. Line the orange segments up on paper towels and pat somewhat dry to ensure that the sauce will adhere properly. Reserve.

11. Scoop out 16 small scoops of frozen yogurt, taking care to keep them neat and uniform. Place them on a chilled sheet pan lined

with baking paper. Place the chocolate in a piping bag. Streak the chocolate across the frozen yogurt scoops, in two directions, as shown in Figure 6–1, page 150). Reserve in the freezer.

12. Presentation: Place 10 orange segments per serving on oven-proof serving plates, arranging the segments in a spoke pattern. Pour just enough of the yogurt and cream mixture on top of the oranges to coat them and the surface of the plates. Try to avoid pouring any more than necessary on the plate surface (if the cream is too thin and runs off the segments without coating them, whip it until you have the proper thickness). Place under a hot broiler or salamander until light brown. Place a tulip cup in the center of the dessert. Place one of the reserved yogurt scoops in the tulip. Serve immediately or the yogurt will melt on the warm plate.

Pears California

(see photograph in color insert)
20 servings, approximately
300 calories each

20 medium-sized pears, with stems
Poaching Syrup I (page 6)
14 ounces (400 g) Almond Paste
*   (page 4)*
2 tablespoons (30 ml) honey
¼ cup (60 ml) water,
*   approximately*
6 cups (1 l, 440 ml) or 1½ recipes
*   Apricot Sauce (page 556)*
Chocolate Sauce for Piping
*   (page 560)*
Sour Cream Mixture for Piping
*   (page 564)*
Chocolate Leaves (page 447)

Try to find nicely shaped, small to medium pears for this dessert. A large pear looks clumsy on the dessert plate. If necessary, trim larger pears to a smaller size, retaining their natural shape.

1. Peel the pears, leaving the stems attached. Place them in acidulated water as you work to prevent browning. Poach the pears in poaching syrup until soft and tender. This can take anywhere from 5 to 45 minutes, depending on the type of pear and the stage of ripeness (see page 6). Let the pears cool in the syrup to fully absorb the flavor of the spices.

2. Combine the almond paste and honey. Add just enough water to make the mixture pipeable. Place in a pastry bag with a no. 6 (12-mm) plain tip and reserve.

3. Remove the pears from the poaching syrup and pat them dry with a napkin. Make a horizontal cut ½ inch (1.2 cm) below the stem, going three-quarters of the way through the pear to keep the stem attached. Push a corer up through the bottom of the pears and remove the cores. Pipe the almond paste mixture into the cavity. Reserve the pears in the refrigerator until ready to serve.

4. Presentation: Pour just enough Apricot Sauce on a dessert plate to cover the surface. Decorate a 2-inch-wide (5-cm) band at the outer edge of the sauce with Sour Cream Mixture for Piping and Chocolate Sauce for Piping (see pages 518–519). On a separate plate, pour Apricot Sauce over one of the filled pears so it is completely covered. Carefully, without disturbing the sauce coating, transfer the pear to the center of the decorated sauce. Cut a small slit ¼ inch (6 mm) below the stem and fasten a chocolate leaf inside. Serve immediately.

Sabayon

*about 4 cups (960 ml) or eight
4-ounce (120-ml) servings,
approximately 155 calories each*

*6 egg yolks
6 ounces (140 g) granulated sugar
1½ cups (360 ml) dry white wine
    or dry champagne*

Sabayon can be served as a dessert by itself, sprinkled lightly with nutmeg, or poured over fresh strawberries. As a sauce it is the classic companion to a liqueur soufflé. Try to make the Sabayon as close to serving time as possible; it can lose some of its fluffiness or separate if it stands too long.

1. Beat the egg yolks and sugar in a stainless steel bowl until light and fluffy. Add wine or champagne.

2. Place over simmering water and continue to whip constantly until the mixture is hot and thick enough to coat a spoon. Serve hot as soon as possible.

Cold Sabayon

Soften ½ teaspoon (1 g) unflavored gelatin powder in 1 tablespoon (15 ml) of the wine or champagne. Stir into the remaining liquid. Continue as for hot Sabayon. When the mixture is thickened, place over ice water and whip slowly until cold. Stir in additional wine or champagne as needed, depending on how you are serving the Sabayon.

NOTE: To make the original Sabayon, the Italian zabaglione, substitute sweet marsala for the wine and use only 4 ounces (115 g) of sugar.

Salzburger Soufflé
(Nockerln)

*4 servings, approximately
250 calories each*

*6 egg whites
4 ounces (115 g) powdered
    sugar, sifted
3 egg yolks
1 tablespoon (15 g) Vanilla Sugar
    (page 8)
grated zest from ¼ lemon
⅔ ounce (20 g) bread flour
⅔ ounce (20 g) butter
2 tablespoons (30 ml) half-and-half
1 teaspoon (5 ml) vanilla extract
powdered sugar*

Anyone who has traveled in Europe and dined in Salzburg has certainly been exposed to this wonderful dessert specialty in one form or another. Salzburger Soufflé is basically a meringue, lightly baked and browned in the oven. It requires a delicate touch when folding in the egg yolks, and the dish must be presented immediately after baking, before the meringue begins to collapse. Just as with a hot soufflé, the Nockerln is always made to order for two or more persons.

1. Take the usual precautions for whipping meringue (see page 331), and whip the egg whites at full speed to about three times their original volume. Lower the speed and gradually add the 4 ounces (115 g) of powdered sugar. Continue whipping at high speed to stiff peaks but do not overwhip.

2. Beat the egg yolks with the vanilla sugar for a few seconds, just to combine. Stir in the lemon zest and flour. Carefully fold the egg yolk mixture into the egg whites, mixing them only halfway: You should still be able to see swirls of yolk in the whites.

3. Place the butter in a shallow, ovenproof, oval dish. Warm the dish in the oven until the butter is melted. Add the half-and-half and vanilla to the melted butter. Using a rubber spatula,

Figure 14–6

add the egg mixture to the baking dish, placing it in three large, triangular ridges (Nockerln) (Figure 14–6).

4. Bake at 450°F (230°C) for about 8 minutes, or until the top is dark brown. The inside should remain creamy. Sift powdered sugar lightly over the top and serve immediately.

NOTE 1: You will need an oval dish approximately 12 inches (30 cm) long if, as is traditional, you are baking and presenting the dessert in the same dish.

NOTE 2: Nockerln also tastes good served with Chocolate Sauce (see page 559) or with Vanilla Custard Sauce (see page 564) and fresh raspberries or strawberries.

Strawberry-Peach Yogurt Creams

twenty-four 4-ounce (120-ml) servings, approximately 180 calories each

Aspic

1½ teaspoons (5 g) unflavored
   gelatin powder
3 ounces (90 ml) cold water
½ teaspoon (2.5 ml) lime juice

Cream

4½ cups (1 l, 80 ml) peach pulp
   (about 8 peaches peeled and
   pitted)
2 pounds (910 g) plain yogurt
4 ounces (115 g) granulated sugar
3 tablespoons (27 g) unflavored
   gelatin powder
⅓ cup (80 ml) lime juice
⅓ cup (80 ml) orange juice
strawberries
2½ cups (600 ml) heavy cream
Strawberry Sauce (page 563)
Sour Cream Mixture for Piping
   (page 564)

1. Make the aspic by softening the gelatin in the water and juice, then heating to 110°F (43°C) to dissolve. Pour a 1/16-inch (2-mm) film of aspic in the bottom of twenty-four 4-ounce (120-ml) molds, just enough to cover. Place the molds in the refrigerator to set.

2. For the cream, purée the peach pulp with the yogurt and sugar in a food processor until completely smooth.

3. Soften the gelatin in the lime and orange juices. Heat to dissolve. Stir the warm gelatin into the peach mixture. Set aside to cool slightly.

4. Cut the strawberries into thin slices crosswise. Place one slice on top of the hardened aspic in each mold.

5. Whip the cream to stiff peaks and fold it into the peach mixture. Fill the molds with the peach cream and chill to set, about 2 hours.

6. Presentation: Unmold by dipping the molds briefly into hot water. Place one yogurt cream off-center on a dessert plate. Pour Strawberry Sauce around the cream and decorate the sauce with Sour Cream Mixture for Piping (see pages 518–519). Serve immediately.

NOTE: The strawberries will bleed slightly if this dessert is made a day ahead. However, you can almost eliminate this problem by using firm strawberries that are not overripe.

Winter Fruit ~~ote

~~roximately

1. Soak the prunes, apricots, and peaches in hot water for 10 minutes.

2. Slice the orange into quarters and put in a saucepan along with the wine, cinnamon, vanilla bean, bay leaf, and sugar. Tie the cloves and peppercorns in a piece of cheesecloth and add to the wine mixture. Bring to a boil and let simmer for 10 minutes.

3. Peel, core, and cut the pears into quarters. Add to the wine mixture. Drain the dried fruits, pat them dry, and add to the wine ~~xture. Simmer until the pears are lightly poached but not falling ~~t (see page 6). Remove from the heat and let the fruit cool in ~~e liquid.

4. Remove the vanilla bean and save for another use. Remove and discard the cinnamon stick, bay leaf, orange pieces, and the spices in the cheesecloth bag. Reserve the poached fruit, in the poaching liquid, at room temperature until ready to serve.

4 whole black peppercorns
3 pears
6 tablespoons (90 ml) Crème
    Fraîche (page 559)
12 Caramelized Walnut Halves
    (page 488)
mint sprigs

5. Presentation: Spoon one prune, two apricot halves, two peach halves, and one pear quarter into a glass serving bowl or onto a dessert plate. Top with some of the poaching liquid. Spoon approximately ½ tablespoon (8 ml) crème fraîche on top of the fruit. Place a caramelized walnut on the crème fraîche, and garnish with a sprig of mint.

Zinfandel Poached Pears

*16 servings, approximately
180 calories each*

12 medium-sized pears
1 recipe Poaching Syrup I
    (page 6)
1 pint (480 ml) zinfandel
8 ounces (225 g) granulated sugar
Cointreau Pear Sauce
    (recipe follows)
Candied Orange Peels (page 520)

1. Peel the pears, keeping the stems intact. Place the pears in acidulated water to prevent them from becoming brown. Place the four least-attractive pears in the poaching syrup and poach until soft. Remove the pears and set aside to use for the sauce.

2. Add the zinfandel and sugar to the poaching syrup. Add the remaining pears and poach until soft. (To check if the pears are done, press lightly with your fingers.) Remove the pan from the heat and set the pears aside in the liquid to macerate for at least 8 hours. Keep the pears submerged in the liquid and do not crowd them or they will have light spots.

3. Remove the pears from the syrup. Carefully cut them in half lengthwise, including the stems. Gently remove the core (but not the stem) from both halves using a melon baller. Starting ½ inch (1.2 cm) from the stem end, cut the pears vertically into thin slices, leaving the top intact. Reserve.

4. Presentation: Place a pear half, flat side down, on the top half of a serving plate with the stem facing away from you. Fan the pear slices out decoratively. Pour a pool of Cointreau Pear Sauce below the pear. Sprinkle a few candied orange peels over the sauce.

NOTE: Leaving the pears in the liquid for 8 hours will make the zinfandel color penetrate about ½ inch (1.2 cm). Leave them in longer if you would like the color to go deeper. If you want the color to go all the way through, replace the water in the poaching syrup with additional zinfandel. Poach the pears for the sauce separately.

Cointreau Pear Sauce

2 cups (480 ml)

4 poached pears (from
    preceding recipe)
1 cup (240 ml) water,
    approximately
2 teaspoons (10 ml) lemon juice
2 ounces (55 g) granulated sugar,
    approximately
2 tablespoons (30 ml) Cointreau
2 tablespoons (16 g) cornstarch

1. Cut the pears in half, core, and purée. Add the water, lemon juice, sugar, and cointreau.

2. Combine the cornstarch with a small amount of the liquid, then stir back into the remaining purée mixture.

3. Heat to simmering, and simmer for about 1 minute. Sweeten with additional sugar, if necessary, and thin with water if too thick.

FIFTEEN

Holiday Breads and Desserts

Breads
   Braided Stollen
   Christmas Stollen
   Lucia Buns
   Sweet Pig's Head
   Swedish Spice Bread
   Triestine Bread
Desserts
   Chestnut Rum Torte
   Chocolate Snow Hearts
   Christmas Cookie Ornaments

Cinnamon Stars
Florentine Torte
Fruit Cake
Gingerbread Cookies
Persimmon Charlotte
Persimmon Cream Slices
Persimmon Pudding
Pumpkin or Sweet Potato Pie
Yule Logs
Gingerbread Houses

Having grown up on a farm in Sweden, with all of the traditional customs, it saddens me to see Christmas so commercialized today. At home the holiday season started four weeks before Christmas, with Advent and the lighting of the first of four candles; one more would be lit each week until Christmas, when all four would be burning. We children had our Advent calendar with a window to open on each day of December, each showing a different picture and ending with a picture of *Jultomten* (Santa Claus) on Christmas Eve. My dad saved a few wheat husks from the harvest which we would attach to a broomstick and put out for the birds as soon as the first snow covered the ground.

Every year my dad and a neighbor slaughtered the pig in early December. The two families shared it, and my mom made delicious dishes from the pig for the Christmas table. There was also baking to be done, from the *vörtbröd* to the gingerbread figures that my sister and I helped decorate for the Christmas tree. And there could not be a Christmas

without marzipan candies, one of which was always a pig with a red apple in its mouth. In addition we would arrange an abundance of nuts, bunches of large, dried raisins on the stem, dates, and citrus fruits from California. In the midst of all of these preparations, Lucia Day, the darkest day of the year, was celebrated with a special ceremony and traditional breakfast pastries, including Lucia Buns.

The week before Christmas my dad and I walked out into the snow-covered forest to cut down the pre-selected tree. We put it in a special stand with water to keep it from getting dry. This was especially important since we used real candles to decorate the branches. After the other ornaments were placed on the tree, it remained in place until the thirteenth of January, twenty days after Christmas.

On Christmas Eve, the culmination of all of this preparation and anticipation, we shared the most lavish meal of the year with our friends and relatives. It was customary to save the broth from cooking the ham, and the feast officially started with the *doppa i grytan* or "dip in the pot," where everyone would dip a piece of *vörtbröd* into the broth. The traditional porridge was served for dessert, with one bitter almond hidden inside; the story was that whoever found the almond would marry the next year.

The Christmas Eve buffet was always eaten early so there would be time for my dad to "go to the neighbors' house to give a helping hand," and every year, by coincidence, this was when *Jultomten*, or Santa, would arrive dressed in his red suit and carrying our presents! After Santa left, we moved the furniture (Dad was always back by then to help) and brought the Christmas tree to the center of the room. Everyone then joined hands around the tree and sang Christmas songs.

On Christmas Day we ate *lutfisk* (sun-dried and lime-cured ling cod) for dinner, accompanied by a white sauce and homemade mustard. And for dessert the custom called for *Riz à la Malta*, a light, fluffy pudding usually made from the leftover porridge, whipped cream, and chopped almonds, and served with cherry sauce.

In the pastry shops preparations started in late November for all of the candies, chocolates, and marzipan items. The first Sunday of Advent was also the big "window display Sunday" all over Sweden. The shops would try to outdo each other as well as their own display from the previous year, and people would crowd outside the windows to view the fantasy worlds inside.

Today, a large part of all of these food preparations and work is just a memory. Only the most dedicated continue to slaughter their own pigs and make all of the sweets at home. Instead, most Christmas food is purchased ready-made.

Although many items are made only at Christmas time, many of the recipes in this chapter can be made anytime, for different holidays: Snow Hearts for Valentine's Day, Cinnamon Stars for the Fourth of July, and Pumpkin Pie for Halloween or Thanksgiving. Gingerbread cookies and cakes, or stollen, can be adapted to serve year-round. For the recipes using persimmon, you can substitute another fruit of approximately the same texture (apricots and peaches, for example).

Conversely, you can dress up many standard pastries and desserts for holidays by substituting an appropriate decoration on top for the one called for in the recipe. For example, Rum Balls can be made in a log shape, lightly dusted with powdered sugar, and topped with a tiny gingerbread heart with a red dot piped in the center. The Princess Cake, with its green marzipan cover, lends itself very well to a Christmas presentation: Pipe a Christmas tree outline on each slice, dot it with red piping gel for ornaments, and sift powdered sugar lightly over the top for snow.

Breads

Braided Stollen

four 1-pound, 2-ounce (510-g) loaves

2 ounces (55 g) fresh compressed yeast
1½ cups (360 ml) warm water (105°–115°F, 40°–46°C)
1 ounce (30 g) malt sugar
3 ounces (85 g) granulated sugar
½ ounce (15 g) salt
grated zest of 1 orange
½ teaspoon (2.5 ml) orange flower water
½ teaspoon (2.5 ml) vanilla extract
2 eggs
3 ounces (85 g) blanched almonds, finely ground
4 ounces (115 g) softened butter
7 ounces (200 g) golden raisins
2 pounds (910 g) bread flour, approximately
Egg Wash (page 5)
Cinnamon Sugar (page 4)

1. Dissolve the yeast in warm water. Add the malt sugar, granulated sugar, and salt. Combine the orange zest, orange flower water, vanilla extract, and eggs, and add to the yeast mixture, together with the almonds, butter, and raisins.

2. Reserve a handful of the bread flour, incorporate the remaining flour into the mixture, and knead for a few minutes. Adjust the consistency of the dough by adding the reserved flour, if necessary, to make a soft and elastic dough. Cover the dough and let rise in a warm place until doubled in volume.

3. Punch the dough down and divide it into four equal pieces, about 1 pound, 2 ounces (510 g) each. Divide each of these into four pieces again. Pound and roll each of the 16 small pieces into a rope 12 inches (30 cm) long, following the same method given for braided bread (see page 50). Braid each group of four ropes following the instructions for a four-string braid on page 52.

4. Place the braided loaves in greased bread pans 8 × 4 inches (20 × 10 cm) in size. Brush them with egg wash, then sprinkle cinnamon sugar over the tops. Let the loaves rise until half-doubled in volume.

5. Bake at 400°F (205°C) for approximately 30 minutes, or until baked through. Remove from the pans immediately and transfer to racks to cool.

NOTE: The bread can also be baked on sheet pans if desired. Try using Braided Stollen to make toast; it is delicious with melted butter.

Christmas Stollen

three 1-pound, 5-ounce (595-g) loaves

2 ounces (55 g) glacéed cherries
4 ounces (115 g) candied
    orange peel
4 ounces (115 g) pecans
4 ounces (115 g) golden raisins
4 ounces (115 g) dark raisins
3 tablespoons (45 ml) dark rum
1½ ounces (40 g) fresh
    compressed yeast
¾ cup (180 ml) warm milk
    (105°–115°F, 40°–46°C)
1½ teaspoons (8 g) salt
1½ teaspoons (5 g) malt sugar
1½ ounces (40 g) granulated
    sugar
2 eggs
¼ teaspoon (.5 g) ground cloves
1½ teaspoons (3 g) ground
    cardamom
1 teaspoon (1.5 g) ground
    cinnamon
½ teaspoon (1 g) ground allspice
1 pound, 6 ounces (625 g)
    bread flour, approximately
10 ounces (285 g) softened butter
melted butter
Quick Vanilla Sugar
    (recipe follows)

1. Chop the cherries, orange peel, and pecans into raisin-sized pieces. Add the golden and dark raisins, and the rum. Let macerate for at least 24 hours, stirring from time to time if possible.

2. Dissolve the yeast in the warm milk. Add the salt, malt sugar, granulated sugar, eggs, and spices. Mix in about half of the flour. Add the softened butter and remaining flour.

3. Knead until an elastic (glutenous) dough has formed, about 10 minutes. Cover the dough and let proof in a warm place until doubled in volume.

4. Knead in the fruit mixture by hand. Cover and let the dough rise until doubled a second time.

5. Punch the dough down and divide it into three 1-pound, 5-ounce (595-g) pieces. Knead the pieces into round loaves (pick up any nuts or fruit that falls off and push them back into the dough). Shape the pieces into oval loaves with the palms of your hands (see Figures 3–1 and 3–2, page 49). Roll the loaves slightly tapered at the ends and place them seam-side down on the table.

6. Using a dowel, roll the loaves flat, keeping the same general shape. Fold the flattened pieces almost in half lengthwise to make the bottom part about ½ inch (1.2 cm) wider than the top half. Bend the loaves into a slightly curved shape, with the fold on the inside of the curve. Place on sheet pans lined with baking paper. Let rise until half-doubled in volume.

7. Bake double-panned at 375°F (190°C) for about 1 hour or until baked through. Brush the loaves with melted butter as soon as they come out of the oven. When they are cool enough to handle (as soon as possible), invert the loaves into the vanilla sugar.

Quick Vanilla Sugar

12 ounces (340 g)

1½ teaspoons (7.5 ml) vanilla
    extract
8 ounces (225 g) granulated sugar
4 ounces (115 g) powdered sugar

Rub the vanilla extract into the granulated sugar, using your hands. Mix in the powdered sugar.

Lucia Buns

thirty 2-ounce (55-g) rolls

1 recipe Cinnamon Swirls dough
   (page 92)
saffron
dark raisins
Egg Wash (page 5)
AA confectioners' sugar, optional
sliced almonds, optional

Lucia Buns (also called Lucia Cats because some of the shapes resemble a cat) are traditionally made in Sweden for Lucia Day, the thirteenth of December. This is the darkest, shortest day of the year, and we celebrate the fact that the days start to get lighter, and longer, from that point.

Every city or village crowns a Lucia or *Ljusets Drottning*, which means the "Queen of Light." Wearing a wreath on her head made of pine boughs studded with candles, and a long, plain white dress, she would bring light to the darkest day. Lucia appears in the morning, singing the song "Saint Lucia" and offering coffee, Lucia Buns, and gingerbread hearts.

The Lucia Buns are made from cardamom dough flavored with saffron, although it is a good idea to make some plain, as not everyone likes saffron. Saffron wreaths and breads are also traditionally made for the Christmas holidays in Sweden. They are always left undecorated except for the raisins, either in the dough or on top, and the sugar and almonds sprinkled over them.

1. Reserve whatever portion of the Cinnamon Swirls dough (if any) you do not want to flavor with saffron. Add a few grams of saffron to the remainder of the dough; the amount will vary depending on how much dough you are flavoring, your taste, and your pocketbook, since saffron is very expensive: about $2 per gram. Dissolve the saffron in water before adding it to the dough, using 1 tablespoon (15 ml) water for 1 to 5 grams of saffron. Cover the dough and let rest 10 minutes. At this stage, the dough can be placed in the freezer, well covered, for later use.

2. Divide the dough into thirty 2-ounce (55-g) pieces. A simple way to do this is to divide the dough into three 20-ounce (570-g) pieces, roll each piece into a rope, and cut it into 10 equal pieces (mark the middle first and then cut five from each side). Keep the pieces well covered.

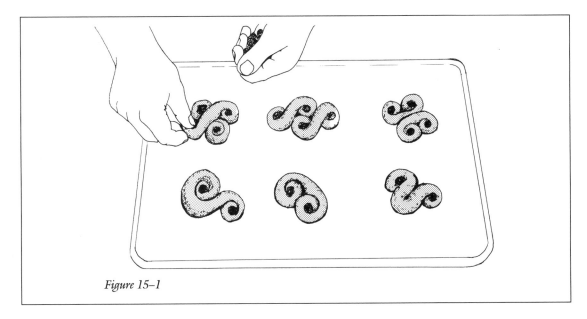

Figure 15–1

3. Divide each 2-ounce (55-g) piece in half when you are ready to roll them out. Roll the 1-ounce (30-g) pieces into ropes about 5 inches (12.5 cm) long and taper the ends. Use two ropes per roll, and form the desired shape or shapes (Figure 15–1).

4. Place the formed buns on sheet pans and decorate with raisins, as shown. Be sure to press the raisins in firmly, all the way to the bottom of the dough, or they will fall off. Let the buns rise until half-doubled in volume.

5. Brush the buns with egg wash and bake at 400°F (205°C) for about 15 minutes, or until golden in color and baked through.

NOTE: You can also form the dough into braided loaves and wreaths (see page 5 and Mayor's Wreath, page 112). Sprinkle these with a combination of equal parts AA confectioners' sugar and sliced almonds, then bake them at a slightly lower temperature for a little longer time.

Sweet Pig's Head
9 breakfast pastries

*1 recipe Cinnamon Swirls dough
    (page 92)*
Egg Wash (page 5)
*¼ recipe or 1½ pounds (680 g)
    Pastry Cream (page 569)*
whole wheat flour
Royal Icing (page 528)
dark baker's chocolate

Sweet Pig's Head is another traditional Swedish Christmas pastry. The pig is very celebrated in Sweden at that time because so many items on the Christmas smörgåsbord are made from it.

1. Roll the dough to ⅛ inch (3 mm) thick. Place in the refrigerator until firm. (You should start with a chilled dough.)

2. Cut out eighteen 6-inch (15-cm) circles and nine 2½-inch (6.2-cm) circles. You may have to press the scrap pieces together and roll them out again to do this. With a no. 4 (8-mm) plain pastry tip, cut two holes across the middle of the small circles. Brush egg wash over nine of the larger circles.

3. Put the same pastry tip used to cut the holes in a pastry bag, and add the pastry cream. Pipe the cream, dividing it evenly, over the nine egg-washed rounds, starting at the center and making concentric circles toward the outside. Stop to leave a ½-inch (1.2-cm) border at the edge.

4. Place the nine remaining large circles on top of the filling and press down hard all around to make sure the edges stick or the filling will ooze out as it bakes. Brush the tops of the filled circles, and the small circles with the holes (the snout), with egg wash. Invert the small circles onto whole wheat flour, then place them, flour-side up, on the lower half of the filled circles (the head).

5. Roll the remaining dough scraps to ¹⁄₁₆ inch (2 mm) thick. Using a plain 3½-inch (8.7-cm) cookie cutter, cut out nine circles. Cut two ears out of each circle using the same cutter, and making two cuts meeting in the center, giving you two pointed ovals. Brush egg wash on the ears and invert them in whole wheat flour. Attach the ears to the top half of the head (flour-side up), sticking them to the egg wash and folding the tips over.

6. Bake at 375°F (190°C) until golden brown and baked through, about 25 minutes. Let cool.

7. When the pastries have cooled, pipe two pea-sized dots of royal icing, fairly close together, between the ears and the snout to look like eyes. Pipe a small dot of baker's chocolate on the royal icing to mark the pupils (you can have some fun here by making the pig look left, right, or cross-eyed).

Variation: Dinner Rolls
18 rolls

*½ recipe Braided White Bread
    dough (page 49)*

The pig's head can also be made into a whimsical dinner roll, any time you want to show someone what you think of their appetite!

1. Roll the dough ¼ inch (6 mm) thick. Cut out eighteen 4-inch (10-cm) circles and eighteen 1½-inch (3.7-cm) circles. Use a no. 2 (4-mm) plain tip to cut the snouts from the smaller circles.

2. Brush with egg wash, invert in flour, and attach as in main recipe. Cut and attach the ears as in step 5, rolling the dough 1/8 inch (3 mm) thick and using a 2-inch (5-cm) cutter. Let rise until half-doubled in volume.

3. Bake at 400°F (205°C) for about 15 minutes. Decorate as directed in main recipe.

Swedish Spice Bread (Vörtbröd)

four 1-pound, 2-ounce (510-g) loaves

1 cup (240 ml) molasses
2 cups (480 ml) water, heated to 130°F (54°C); see note
1½ ounces (40 g) fresh compressed yeast
1 pound, 2 ounces (510 g) bread flour
9 ounces (255 g) medium rye flour
2 teaspoons (4 g) ground cloves
2 tablespoons (12 g) ground ginger
2 tablespoons (12 g) ground anise seed
2 tablespoons (12 g) ground fennel seed
1 tablespoon (15 g) salt
8 ounces (225 g) Candied Orange Peel, finely chopped (page 520)
2 ounces (55 g) softened butter
4 ounces (115 g) bread flour, approximately
4 ounces (115 g) dark raisins
medium rye flour
olive oil

It is important not to let the dough temperature fall below 75°F (25°C). The large amount of sugar in the recipe means that the yeast needs a warm dough. Be sure to start with the higher-than-normal temperature for the liquid.

1. Combine molasses and water. Add the yeast and mix to dissolve. Incorporate the first measure of bread flour and mix to form a smooth sponge. Place the dough in an oiled bowl and let rise, covered, in a warm place until doubled in volume.

2. Combine rye flour, spices, and salt. Mix into the sponge, together with the orange peel and butter. Add the remaining bread flour, adjusting the amount to form a very soft dough. Knead with the dough hook until smooth and elastic (about 5 minutes). Add the raisins and mix just until incorporated. Place the dough in an oiled bowl and let rise in a warm place until doubled in volume.

3. Punch the dough down and divide it into four 1-pound, 2-ounce (510-g) pieces. Shape the pieces into oval loaves, slightly tapered at the ends (see Figures 3–1 and 3–2, page 49). Place the loaves on sheet pans dusted with rye flour. Let rise until half-doubled in volume.

4. Bake at 375°F (190°C) for approximately 40 minutes, using a second pan underneath to protect the bottom of the loaves from becoming too brown. Brush the baked loaves with olive oil and transfer to a rack to cool.

Triestine Bread

four 13-ounce (370-g) loaves

Sponge

²/₃ cup (160 ml) warm milk
  (105°–115°F, 40°–46°C)
¹/₃ ounce (10 g) fresh
  compressed yeast
6 ounces (170 g) bread flour

Dough

²/₃ cup (160 ml) warm milk
  (105°–115°F, 40°–46°C)
1¹/₂ ounces (40 g) fresh
  compressed yeast
5 teaspoons (15 g) malt sugar
3 ounces (85 g) granulated sugar
2 teaspoons (10 g) salt
2 eggs
grated zest of ¹/₂ lemon
¹/₄ teaspoon (1.25 ml) orange
  flower water
2¹/₂ ounces (70 g) softened butter
1 pound (455 g) bread flour,
  approximately
4 ounces (115 g) Candied Orange
  Peel, finely chopped (page 520)
4 ounces (115 g) glacéed or
  candied cherries, finely chopped
4 ounces (115 g) sliced almonds

Topping

1¹/₂ ounces (40 g) finely
  ground almonds
¹/₂ ounce (15 g) granulated sugar
1 egg white, approximately
1¹/₂ ounces (40 g) sliced almonds
powdered sugar

1. Make the sponge by dissolving the yeast in the warm milk. Mix in the flour. Let rise, covered, until doubled in volume.

2. Using the ingredients listed for the dough, dissolve the yeast in the warm milk. Stir this into the sponge, then add the remaining dough ingredients in the order listed, but hold back a little of the flour in case you do not need it all. The dough should be fairly firm. Let rest, covered, 10 minutes.

3. Divide the dough into 13-ounce (370-g) pieces and knead into round loaves (see Figures 3–1 and 3–2, page 49). The loaf has been kneaded enough if the dough springs back when pressed lightly. Flatten the loaves slightly with your hands to make a surface for the topping.

4. Make the topping by combining the ground almonds and sugar; then add enough of the egg white to make the mixture spreadable but not runny. Spread over the tops and halfway down the sides of the loaves. Top with sliced almonds, pressing them on with your hands so they stick. Let the loaves rise until doubled in volume.

5. Sift enough powdered sugar over the tops to cover the almonds. Bake the loaves at 375°F (190°C) until golden brown, about 35 minutes. Cool on racks. You may need to protect the loaves from overbrowning by placing a second pan underneath or by covering the tops with baking paper.

Desserts

Chestnut Rum Torte

one 10-inch (25-cm) torte

Butter and Flour Mixture
    (page 4)
8 ounces (225 g) softened butter
9 ounces (255 g) granulated sugar
5 eggs, separated
3 tablespoons (45 ml) dark rum
2½ cups (600 ml) Chestnut Purée
    (recipe follows)
2 cups (480 ml) heavy cream
2 teaspoons (10 g) granulated
    sugar
½ teaspoon (5 ml) vanilla extract
finely chopped pecans
dark chocolate shavings

Chestnuts, like persimmons, are available fresh only for the few months from late fall to Christmas time, which makes the seasonal treats prepared with them so much more special.

1. Brush the butter and flour mixture over the inside of two 10-inch (25-cm) cake pans. Set aside.

2. Cream the butter with half of the first measurement of sugar (4½ ounces/130 g) until the mixture is light and fluffy. Beat the egg yolks lightly, then stir into the butter mixture, together with the rum and chestnut purée, mixing the ingredients together thoroughly.

3. Whip the egg whites to stiff peaks, gradually adding the remainder of the sugar (4½ ounces/130 g). Carefully fold about one-third of the egg whites into the batter, then fold in the remainder. Take care not to overmix and deflate the egg whites. Divide the batter between the reserved cake pans.

4. Bake immediately at 350°F (175°C) for approximately 45 minutes, or until baked through. Let the tortes cool for at least several hours, or preferably, refrigerate them until the next day.

5. Whip the heavy cream, 2 teaspoons (10 g) of sugar, and vanilla to stiff peaks.

6. Carefully cut the skin from the top of the sponges, cutting them level at the same time, if necessary. Place one layer on a cardboard cake round. Spread a ¼-inch (6-mm) layer of cream on top. Place the second layer on the cream. Ice the torte with the remaining cream.

7. Cover the side of the torte with the chopped pecans and sprinkle shaved chocolate on the top. Cut into the desired number of servings.

Chestnut Purée

2½ cups (600 ml)

You will need approximately 2½ pounds (1 kg, 135 g) of chestnuts to make the purée.

1. Cut a small *X* in the flat side of each nut, using the point of a paring knife.

2. Place the chestnuts in a saucepan with enough water to cover. Bring to a boil, reduce the heat, and simmer for 15 to 30 minutes. Be careful not to overcook the chestnuts. Peel one and check the inside: It should be dry and have a mealy texture something like a baked potato.

3. Drain the chestnuts and let them cool until they can be handled comfortably, but don't let them cool completely or they will be much more difficult to peel. Remove the shells and skin, and purée in a food processor just until smooth. Do not allow the chestnuts to become gummy.

Variation: Chestnut Cake

two 10-inch (25-cm) cakes

1 pound (455 g) softened butter
1 pound, 2 ounces (510 g) granulated sugar
10 eggs, separated
1/3 cup (80 ml) dark rum
4 ounces (115 g) bread flour
2 teaspoons (8 g) baking powder
2 1/2 cups (600 ml) unsweetened canned chestnut purée
Chestnut Rum Filling (recipe follows)
1 quart (960 ml) heavy cream
2 tablespoons (30 g) granulated sugar
2 teaspoons (10 ml) vanilla extract
dark chocolate shavings

Making the Chestnut Rum Torte in a large quantity is, unfortunately, too time-consuming in most professional kitchens. This variation using canned chestnut purée is a very nice substitute.

1. Cream the butter with half of the first measurement of sugar (9 ounces/255 g) until the mixture is light and fluffy. Beat the egg yolks lightly, then stir into the butter mixture, together with the rum. Sift the flour and baking powder together and add to the batter with the chestnut purée, mixing the ingredients together thoroughly.

2. Whip the egg whites to stiff peaks, gradually adding the remainder of the sugar (9 ounces/255 g). Carefully fold about one-third of the egg whites into the batter, then fold in the remainder. Take care not to overmix and deflate the egg whites. Divide the sponge batter between two full sheet pans (16 × 24 inches/40 × 60 cm) lined with baking paper. Spread the batter out to the full length of the pans but only 14 inches (35 cm) wide.

3. Bake at 375°F (190°C) for about 20 minutes or until done. Let cool and cut two 10-inch (25-cm) circles from each sheet. Tear the scrap pieces into small chunks and reserve for the filling.

4. Place two of the layers on cardboard cake rounds for support. Place adjustable cake rings snugly around each cake. If the rings are not made of stainless steel, line them with paper or plastic strips. Divide the filling evenly between the cakes. Place the remaining sponge layers on top. Refrigerate, covered, until set.

5. Whip the heavy cream, sugar, and vanilla to stiff peaks. Remove the rings from the cakes and ice the tops and sides with just enough whipped cream to cover the sponge.

6. Place the remaining cream in a pastry bag with a no. 4 (8-mm) plain tip. Decorate the sides of the cakes by piping the cream up and down in one continuous line (see Figure 11–1, page 309). Smooth the top of the cakes with a spatula, removing any whipped cream from above the edge.

7. Pipe a pearl-pattern border (see Figure 18–7, page 504) around the top edges of the cakes. Sprinkle the shaved chocolate over the entire surface, within the border.

Chestnut Rum Filling

6½ pints (3 l, 120 ml) filling

*1½ cups (360 ml) dark rum
reserved cake chunks from
    chestnut sponge
1½ quarts (1 l, 440 ml)
    heavy cream
2 ounces (55 g) granulated sugar
2 tablespoons (18 g) unflavored
    powdered gelatin*

1. Sprinkle ½ cup (120 ml) of the rum over the cake scraps.
2. Whip the heavy cream and sugar to soft peaks.
3. Soften the gelatin in the remaining rum and heat to about 110°F (43°C) to dissolve. Rapidly mix the gelatin into a small part of the cream, then add to the rest.
4. Carefully fold in the sponge chunks without breaking them apart.

NOTE: Do not make the filling until you are ready to use it.

Chocolate Snow Hearts

120 cookies

*1 pound, 6 ounces (625 g)
    blanched almonds, finely ground
1 pound (455 g) powdered sugar
4 egg whites
14 ounces (400 g) melted dark
    chocolate
granulated sugar*

1. Process the ground almonds, half of the powdered sugar, and the egg whites in a food processor to make a fine paste. Transfer to a mixing bowl and stir in remaining powdered sugar and the chocolate. Cover and refrigerate until firm.
2. Roll out the dough, using granulated sugar to keep it from sticking, to ¼ inch (6 mm) thick. Cut out cookies using a 2-inch (5-cm) heart cutter. Try to plan the cuts for a minimum of scrap dough. Place the cookies on sheet pans lined with baking paper. Knead the scrap dough together and roll out and cut cookies in the same manner.
3. Bake the cookies at 425°F (219°C) for about 8 minutes, or until slightly puffed. Be careful: They are very easy to overbake because of their color. Do not try to remove the cookies from the paper before they are completely cold. Follow the instructions for removing the cookies from the paper in Almond Macaroon Cookies, Figure 5–1, page 123. Store in airtight containers.

Christmas Cookie Ornaments

65 cookies

*8 ounces (225 g) Gingerbread
    Cookie dough (page 419)
Lemon-Butter Cookie Dough
    (recipe follows)
Egg Yolk Wash (page 5)
whole blanched almonds
Piping Chocolate (page 449)*

It is traditional in Sweden to decorate the Christmas tree in part with edible ornaments, such as chocolate figures, marzipan Santas, and a variety of decorated gingerbread cookies. The cookies were not to be touched by any eager little children's hands, only looked at with big eyes. We each picked out our favorites long before Christmas day, when we were finally allowed to taste them.

1. Make the gingerbread dough the day before you plan to use it and reserve in the refrigerator.
2. Roll out the Lemon-Butter Cookie Dough to ⅜ inch (9 mm) thick. Mark the top with a tread-type rolling pin (see page 605) or, if you do not have that tool, drag a fork across the dough

Royal Icing (page 528)
powdered sugar
dark baker's chocolate

to mark it. Transfer the dough to a sheet pan or cardboard. Brush egg yolk wash over the dough and place in the refrigerator or freezer for a few minutes to dry the egg wash a little.

3. While the lemon dough is in the refrigerator, roll out the gingerbread dough to ¹⁄₁₆ inch (2 mm) thick. Transfer to a sheet pan or cardboard and reserve in the refrigerator.

4. Remove the lemon dough from the refrigerator and cut out stars, hearts, and round shapes about 2 inches (5 cm) in diameter. Place on sheet pans lined with baking paper. Knead the scrap dough together well, roll it out, and cut more cookies. Repeat until all of the dough has been used. Set the cookies aside.

5. Remove the gingerbread dough from the refrigerator. Cut out small shapes that will fit on top of the lemon cookies, using your imagination to contrast with the lighter cookie dough. Smaller heart and star shapes look good placed in the center of a lemon cookie of the same shape, as does a small gingerbread heart in the center of a round lemon cookie, surrounded by four or five blanched almonds. If you have holiday cutters that are small enough, use these.

6. Decorate the lemon cookies with the gingerbread shapes and blanched almonds. Use a no. 3 (6-mm) plain piping tip to cut a hole in each cookie for the string if you plan to hang them on the tree.

7. Bake at 375°F (190°C) for about 15 minutes or until golden brown. When the cookies have cooled, decorate with piping chocolate, royal icing, or sifted powdered sugar. Or, dip whole cookies in thinned dark baker's chocolate (see Noisette Rings, page 242) and decorate with royal icing or piping chocolate, writing "Merry Christmas" or a person's name. When the icing is dry, tie gold threads through the holes.

NOTE: You can also reverse the decorations and place the lemon dough on top of the gingerbread. In that case, of course, you will need more gingerbread dough. Roll both doughs to ⅛ inch (3 mm) thick. Mark the lemon dough with the tread roller in the same way, but do not try to mark the gingerbread dough.

Lemon-Butter Cookie Dough

14 ounces (400 g) powdered sugar
14 ounces (400 g) softened butter
3 eggs
grated zest of 1 lemon
1 teaspoon (5 ml) vanilla extract
1 pound, 12 ounces (795 g)
    bread flour

1. Mix the powdered sugar and butter well, but do not cream. Add the eggs, lemon rind, and vanilla.

2. Incorporate the flour and mix just until combined. It is important not to overmix this dough, because the additional air will make the cookies "bake out" and change shape.

3. Refrigerate the dough, if necessary, to make it easier to handle.

Cinnamon Stars

90 cookies

1 pound, 5 ounces (595 g)
   blanched almonds, finely ground
1 pound (455 g) granulated sugar
2 tablespoons (30 ml) light corn
   syrup
4 egg whites
3 tablespoons (15 g) ground
   cinnamon
1 cup (240 ml) Royal Icing
   (page 528)

1. Combine the almonds, sugar, corn syrup, egg whites, and cinnamon. Mix to form a smooth paste. Roll out to ¼ inch (6 mm) thick, using flour to prevent the dough from sticking. Place on a cardboard or inverted sheet pan.

2. Adjust the royal icing to a spreadable but not runny consistency by adding additional powdered sugar or egg whites as needed. Spread just enough on top of the dough to cover the surface. Refrigerate for a few minutes to firm the dough and icing.

3. Cut out the cookies using a 2¼-inch (5.6-cm) star cutter (try to cut so you have a minimum of scrap dough). Place the cookies on sheet pans lined with baking paper. Work the scrap dough to completely incorporate the royal icing, then roll out and spread with more icing as you did the first time. Continue to cut the cookies and re-roll the dough until all the dough has been used.

4. Bake at 425°F (219°C) for about 6 minutes, or until the icing just starts to turn light brown at the edges. Let the cookies cool completely before removing them from the paper. Store in airtight containers.

Florentine Torte

two 10-inch (25-cm) cakes

melted butter
finely ground hazelnuts
1 pound, 4 ounces (570 g)
   mixed nuts (see note 1)
14 ounces (400 g) granulated
   sugar
14 ounces (400 g) grated
   dark chocolate
3 ounces (85 g) finely chopped
   Candied Citron or Orange Peel
   (page 520)
16 eggs, separated
2 teaspoons (10 ml) vanilla extract
powdered sugar
rum
Ganache, softened (page 567)
pecan halves

1. Line the bottoms of two 10-inch (25-cm) cake pans with circles of baking paper. Brush melted butter over the papers and the sides of the pans. Coat with ground hazelnuts.

2. Grind the mixed nuts with 7 ounces (200 g) of the sugar to the consistency of whole wheat flour (the sugar will absorb some of the fat in the nuts and prevent them from turning into a paste). Mix the chocolate, citron or orange peel, egg yolks, and vanilla with the ground nuts.

3. Whip the egg whites to a foam. Gradually add the remaining 7 ounces (200 g) sugar and whip to stiff peaks. Add a small amount of the whipped egg whites to the nut mixture to loosen it, then carefully fold the nut mixture into the remaining whites. Pour the batter into the prepared cake pans.

4. Bake at 350°F (175°C) for about 30 minutes. Let the tortes cool completely.

5. Make the star template (Figure 15–2). (See note 2.) The template as shown is the correct size for a 10-inch (25-cm) cake. Trace the drawing, then cut the template from ¹⁄₁₆-inch (2-mm) cardboard. A cake box works fine.

6. Unmold the tortes and immediately turn right-side up again to prevent damage to the skin.

7. Center the template on top of one torte. Sift powdered sugar lightly over the top. Carefully remove the template and repeat with the second torte.

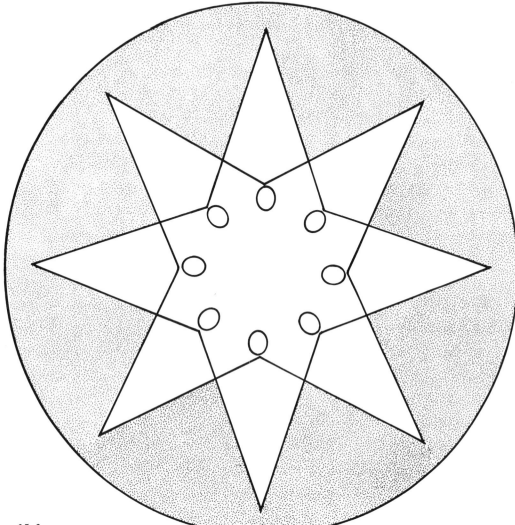

Figure 15–2

8. Using a small brush, "paint" rum in a ½-inch (1.2-cm) band next to the edge of the tortes to melt the powdered sugar and make the ganache stick to the cakes.

9. Place ganache in a pastry bag with a no. 4 (8-mm) plain tip. Pipe a pearl-pattern border of ganache (see page 504) at the edge of the cakes. Place pecan halves around the edge, sticking them into the ganache, spacing them evenly to give one per serving.

NOTE 1: You can use any combination of hazelnuts, walnuts, almonds, or pecans. Try to make this torte a few days in advance and store in the refrigerator. The nuts will absorb moisture during this time improving the flavor and texture of the torte.

NOTE 2: The star template can be used to give a holiday theme to desserts other than the Florentine Torte. The template can also be used in several different ways. You may cut out the star (leaving the circular frame), place the template on a dessert, and sift powdered sugar over the top to create a star pattern with the sugar. Or, you can do the opposite and place the cut-out star on top of the cake, then sift powdered sugar over the exposed part to create a star silhouette. The second method looks especially nice on a cake or tart iced with chocolate such as Gâteau Malakoff or Caramel Walnut Tart. You can also mark the places where the ovals are shown in the template, then pipe small teardrops of ganache, pointed in toward the center of the dessert, on the ovals. Place a pecan half on each. Lastly, the template can be traced using either of the two methods described for tracing a design on marzipan (see page 531). Start at the outline and pipe following every other oval as a loop in one unbroken line. Then pipe over the remainder of the outline and loops in the same way.

Fruit Cake

two 2-pound (910-g) loaves

Fruit Mixture

½ cup (120 ml) brandy
8 ounces (225 g) golden raisins
8 ounces (225 g) currants
8 ounces (225 g) pecan quarters
6 ounces (170 g) candied citron peel, chopped to raisin-size pieces
6 ounces (170 g) dried apricots, coarsely chopped
6 ounces (170 g) glacéed cherries, coarsely chopped

Batter

melted butter
10 ounces (285 g) softened butter
10 ounces (285 g) granulated sugar
5 eggs
1 ounce (30 ml) golden syrup

1. Combine all of the ingredients in the fruit mixture and let macerate for 24 hours.

2. Brush the melted butter on the inside of two 8- × 4-inch (20- × 10-cm) loaf pans. Line with strips of baking paper and brush the paper with melted butter. Reserve.

3. Cream the softened butter with the sugar until light and fluffy. Incorporate the eggs one at a time. Combine the syrup, 2 tablespoons (30 ml) of brandy, and citrus zest. Add to the sugar mixture.

4. Sift the flours together. Remove a handful of flour and toss with the fruit mixture. Mix the remaining flour into the batter. Fold in the fruit mixture. Divide the batter between the reserved pans.

5. Bake at 300°F (149°C) for 1 hour. Lower the heat to 275°F (135°C) and continue to bake approximately 1 hour longer (a wooden skewer inserted in the middle of the cake should come out dry). Unmold onto a cake-cooling rack and allow to cool.

2 tablespoons (30 ml) brandy
grated zest of 1 orange
grated zest of 1 lemon
6 ounces (170 g) bread flour
6 ounces (170 g) cake flour
½ cup (120 ml) brandy
additional brandy for brushing

6. Pierce the bottom of the cakes all over with a skewer; brush the bottom and sides of the cakes with the ½ cup (120 ml) of brandy. Wrap the cakes tightly. Uncover and brush with additional brandy every day for seven days, keeping the cakes tightly covered in between. Don't be a miser here: you should be using ⅓ to ½ cup (80 to 120 ml) every time you brush the cakes!

Gingerbread Cookies

about ninety 3-inch (7.5-cm)
cookies

15 ounces (430 g) butter
15 ounces (430 g) granulated
* sugar*
1 pound, 2 ounces (510 g)
* corn syrup*
¾ cup (180 ml) milk
2 pounds, 10 ounces (1 kg, 195 g)
* bread flour*
3 teaspoons (12 g) baking soda
4 tablespoons (20 g) ground
* cinnamon*
2 tablespoons (12 g) ground cloves
2 tablespoons (12 g) ground ginger

1. Place the butter, sugar, corn syrup, and milk in a saucepan. Heat to about 110°F (43°C), stirring the mixture into a smooth paste.

2. Sift the flour, baking soda, and spices together. Incorporate into the butter mixture.

3. Line the bottom of a sheet pan with baking paper. Dust the paper with flour and place the dough on top. Flatten the dough, then refrigerate, covered, overnight.

4. Roll out the dough, a small portion at a time, to ¹⁄₁₆ inch (2 mm) thick. Keep the dough you are not working with in the refrigerator. The dough will feel sticky, but do not be tempted to mix in additional flour. The flour used in rolling the dough will be enough, and too much flour will make the baked cookies too hard and not as pleasant tasting.

5. Cut out cookies with a 2½-inch (6.2-cm) plain cookie cutter. Place the cookies, staggered, on sheet pans lined with baking paper. Add the dough scraps to the fresh dough as you roll out the next batch.

6. Bake the cookies at 400°F (205°C) for about 10 minutes or until they have a rich brown color.

NOTE 1: This dough can be used to make cookies of any size or shape, as well as the traditional gingerbread figures made for Christmas. The dough should be rolled a bit thicker (⅛ inch/ 3 mm) for figures. Gingerbread Cookies can be kept for many weeks if stored — perhaps I should say hidden — in airtight containers or in a dry place.

NOTE 2: When using this dough to make gingerbread houses, replace the butter with margarine and increase the flour by 6 ounces (170 g) to make a firmer dough. You do not necessarily need the butter flavor in a gingerbread house and it may cause shrinkage with the additional flour.

Persimmon Charlotte
twenty 5-ounce (150-ml) servings

5 medium-sized Fuyu persimmons
Persimmon Bavarois (recipe follows)
Chocolate Decorations
*   (procedure follows)*
1 cup (240 ml) heavy cream
2 teaspoons (10 g) granulated
*   sugar*
1 cup (240 ml) or ½ recipe Red
*   Currant Glaze (page 527)*
3 cups (720 ml) or 1 recipe
*   Cranberry Sauce (page 558)*
Sour Cream Mixture for Piping
*   (page 564)*

1. The Fuyu persimmons should be firm to the touch. Cut off the stem end and peel them with a vegetable peeler to keep the natural shape. Place the persimmons on their sides, and slice as thin as possible using a sharp knife (ignore the tiny core in the center). Use a plain cookie cutter that has the same circumference as the bottom of the soufflé ramekins, and cut the slices round. Repeat until you have enough to line the bottoms of twenty 5-ounce (150-ml) soufflée ramekins, or other forms of approximately the same size with smooth sides. Place the slices in the bottom of the forms. Since it is impossible to cut the whole persimmon into large enough slices to line the forms, save the leftover pieces to use in the bavarois.

2. Fill the forms with Persimmon Bavarois. Refrigerate until set, about 2 hours.

3. Whip the heavy cream and sugar to stiff peaks. Place in a pastry bag with a no. 4 (8-mm) plain tip. Reserve in the refrigerator until ready to serve.

4. Presentation: Unmold a charlotte by dipping the bottom of the mold very briefly into hot water, invert, and unmold to the center of a dessert plate. Glaze the persimmon slice with a thin layer of red currant glaze. Pipe a border of whipped cream in a pearl pattern around the top edge of the charlotte. Place a chocolate decoration on top of the whipped cream. Pour just enough of the Cranberry Sauce around the charlotte to cover the plate. Decorate the Cranberry Sauce with the Sour Cream Mixture for Piping (see pages 518–519). Serve immediately.

Persimmon Bavarois
3 quarts (2 l, 880 ml)

Follow the recipe for Apricot Bavarois (see page 308) through step 4, substituting 1½ cups (360 ml) of persimmon purée and 1 tablespoon (15 ml) of lime juice for the apricots. Do not reduce the mixture. Use Hachiya persimmons for the bavarois if they are perfectly ripe as the jelly-like pulp is easier to remove (see Persimmon Pudding, pages 423–424). If you are using Fuyu persimmons, soften them by quickly freezing and thawing the fruit. To remove the flesh, cut the persimmons in half and use a spoon to scoop out the inside. Discard skin, seeds, and stem. Purée in a blender, then pass through a sieve to strain.

Chocolate Decorations
25 decorations

1. Find a cookie cutter that will just fit inside the forms you are using for the charlotte. Using the cutter as a guide, draw 25 circles on baking paper. Invert the paper.

2. Melt dark piping chocolate (see page 449) and place in a piping bag with a small opening. Pipe the chocolate onto the paper, first tracing around the circles, then piping within the

circles, going back and forth in a zigzag pattern. Space the lines ¼ inch (6 mm) apart and touch the circle on each end.

3. Let the chocolate harden, then slide a knife underneath and lift the decorations off the paper and onto the dessert.

Persimmon Cream Slices

30 servings

Gingerbread Sponge (recipe follows)
Persimmon Filling (recipe follows)
½ recipe Cream Chantilly
    (page 343)
5 Fuyu persimmons
Apricot Glaze (page 526)
powdered sugar
Cranberry Sauce (page 558)
Sour Cream Mixture for Piping
    (page 564)
fresh cranberries
granulated sugar
mint sprigs

1. Cut heavy cardboard into strips 2 inches (5 cm) wide and make a 16- × 12-inch (40- × 30-cm) rectangular frame, taping the pieces together at the corners (or use an existing pan of the same size). Line the bottom and sides with plastic wrap.

2. Cut the sponge sheet in half crosswise to make two sponges 16 × 12 inches (40 × 30 cm) each. Peel the paper from the back of the sponge sheets. Place one sponge in the prepared frame. Spread the Persimmon Filling on top of the sponge. Reserve in the refrigerator while you make the Cream Chantilly.

3. Spread the Cream Chantilly on top of the Persimmon Filling. Invert the remaining sponge sheet on top of the cream, placing it sugar-side up. Press the sponge lightly so it adheres. Place in the refrigerator for at least 2 hours to set completely.

4. Peel the persimmons using a vegetable peeler. Place them on their sides and slice thirty ¹⁄₁₆-inch (2-mm) slices (since it is hard to hold onto the persimmons to do this, use a slicer if you have one). Use a 2¼-inch (5.6-cm) plain cookie cutter to cut a round out of each slice (use a smaller cutter if needed to stay within the persimmon slice).

5. Place the rounds on a sheet pan lined with baking paper and brush them with apricot glaze. Reserve the garnishes at room temperature.

6. Remove the assembled cake from the refrigerator and invert onto a cardboard or upside-down sheet pan. Remove the plastic wrap, then invert the cake again so that the sugared side of the sponge is on top again. Using a thin sharp knife dipped in hot water, trim about ½ inch (1.2 cm) from one long side to make a clean edge. Starting from that edge, cut the cake lengthwise into five 2¼-inch (5.6-cm) strips. Trim the ends, then cut each of the strips into six 2¼-inch (5.6-cm) pieces. Be sure to hold the knife at a 90° angle so that the sides of the cake will be straight.

7. Presentation: Lightly sift powdered sugar over the slices. Place one of the reserved glazed persimmon garnishes on top of the powdered sugar, in the center of each slice. Place a slice, off-center, on a dessert plate. Pour a small pool of Cranberry Sauce in front of the dessert and decorate the sauce with the sour cream mixture (see pages 518–519). Quickly dip your clean

fingers in your container of Cranberry Sauce and roll two cranberries between them to make the berries sticky. Roll the cranberries in granulated sugar to coat them, then place them at the edge of the sauce on the plate. Place a mint sprig next to the berries and serve immediately.

Gingerbread Sponge

one 16- × 24-inch
(40- × 60-cm) sheet

5 ounces (140 g) softened butter
2 ounces (55 g) brown sugar
10 ounces (285 g) bread flour
3 teaspoons (6 g) ground ginger
½ teaspoon (1 g) ground nutmeg
1 teaspoon (4 g) baking soda
½ teaspoon (3 g) salt
4 eggs, separated
⅔ cup (160 ml) warm water
⅓ cup (80 ml) molasses
2 ounces (55 g) granulated sugar
granulated sugar

1. Beat the butter and brown sugar together until light and fluffy.

2. Sift together the flour, ginger, nutmeg, baking soda, and salt.

3. Beat the egg yolks a few seconds to combine. Slowly add the water and molasses.

4. Add the dry ingredients to the butter and sugar mixture in two portions, alternating with the egg yolk liquid.

5. Whip the egg whites to a thick foam. Gradually add the 2 ounces (55 g) of granulated sugar and continue to whip to stiff peaks. Gradually (to avoid lumps of egg white) add the reserved batter to the whipped egg whites.

6. Spread the batter out evenly to 16 × 24 inches (40 × 60 cm) on a sheet of baking paper. Slide the paper onto a sheet pan (Figure 15–3) and bake immediately at 375°F (190°C) for about 12 minutes, or until just baked through.

7. Sprinkle granulated sugar lightly on top of a baking paper. As soon as possible after the sponge has come out of the oven, cut it free from the pan, pick it up by the two corners on one long side of the paper, and invert it onto the sugar. Let cool completely. If the sponge is not to be used within a short time, cover and refrigerate.

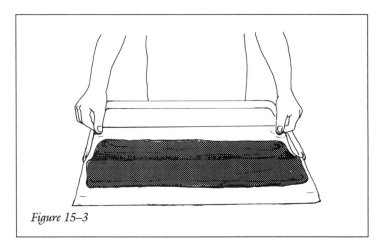

Figure 15–3

Persimmon Filling

2½ cups (600 ml) persimmon pulp
1 tablespoon (15 ml) lemon juice
½ cup (120 ml) Simple Syrup
    (page 7)
¼ cup (60 ml) orange liqueur
2½ cups (600 ml) heavy cream
2 tablespoons (18 g) gelatin powder
⅓ cup (80 ml) cold water

You must use perfectly ripe persimmons for the pulp. See the following recipe for Persimmon Pudding for information on how to extract the pulp. Do not make the filling until you are ready to assemble the dessert; it cannot be softened once it has set.

1. Strain the persimmon pulp through a very fine sieve. Stir in the simple syrup, lemon juice, and orange liqueur. Set aside.
2. Whip the cream to soft peaks. Reserve.
3. Soften the gelatin in cold water, heat to 110°F (43°C) to dissolve.
4. Gradually fold the persimmon mixture into the whipped cream. Quickly mix the dissolved gelatin into a small portion of the mixture, then quickly mix this back into the remainder of the filling.

Persimmon Pudding

two 2-quart (1 l, 920 ml)
puddings, 12 servings each

1 pound (455 g) dark and
    golden raisins
1½ cups (360 ml) brandy
Butter and Flour Mixture
    (page 4)
3 cups (720 ml) persimmon purée
    (see note)
1 pound, 12 ounces (795 g)
    granulated sugar
2 tablespoons (30 ml) vegetable oil
1 tablespoon (15 ml) vanilla
    extract
12 ounces (340 g) bread flour
1 tablespoon (12 g) baking soda
2 teaspoons (10 g) salt
1 teaspoon (2 g) ground cloves
1 teaspoon (2 g) ground nutmeg
10 ounces (285 g) coarsely
    chopped walnuts
1½ cups (360 ml) milk
Brandied Whipped Cream
    (recipe follows)
ground nutmeg
cranberries
mint sprigs

1. Combine the raisins and brandy and set aside to macerate.
2. Cut two rings of baking paper to fit the bottom of two 2-quart (1 l, 920 ml) angel food cake pans, or any other tube pan of the same size with a flat bottom. Place the paper in the pans, then brush the entire inside of the pans, including the paper, with the butter and flour mixture.
3. Mix the persimmon purée, sugar, oil, and vanilla. Sift together the flour, baking soda, salt, cloves, and 1 teaspoon (2 g) ground nutmeg. Mix the dry ingredients into the purée mixture. Stir in the walnuts, milk, and raisin mixture. Divide the batter equally between the reserved pans.
4. Bake at 325°F (163°C) for about 1 hour and 15 minutes, or until baked through. Let the puddings cool in the pans completely before unmolding. Cut the puddings into 12 slices each.
5. Presentation: Place a slice of Persimmon Pudding, cut-side up, in the center of a dessert plate. Spoon Brandied Whipped Cream over the narrow end of the slice, letting some fall onto the plate in front of the dessert. Sprinkle nutmeg lightly over the cream. Place three cranberries (in a triangle to look like holly berries) in the cream on the plate. Set a mint sprig next to the berries.
6. Holiday Presentation: Place a whole pudding on a serving platter. Heat ⅓ cup (80 ml) of brandy to the scalding point, but do not boil. Pour the brandy into a small, flameproof cup and place the cup in the middle of the cake ring. Turn down the room lights, ignite the hot brandy, and spoon it, flaming, on top of the pudding. Serve Brandied Whipped Cream on the side.
NOTE: To make the persimmon purée you will need approximately seven Hachiya persimmons or eight or nine Fuyu persimmons. Hachiya, the persimmon most commonly found in stores,

has a slightly oblong shape and is pointed at the bottom. The Hachiya are very high in tannin and can be eaten only when fully ripe (the fruit should be almost jelly-like throughout). Otherwise the fruits have an unpleasant, dry, almost rough taste. Instead of trying to peel the skin off the Hachiya, cut them in half and use a spoon to scoop out the flesh. Discard the stem, seeds, and skin. The smaller Fuyu persimmon is shaped like a tomato. It has very little tannin and can therefore be eaten before it is completely ripe and soft. This persimmon is easy to peel using a vegetable peeler.

With either variety the dry taste will disappear when the fruit is cooked, so it is acceptable to use unripe fruit in the Persimmon Pudding. Place unripe fruit in the freezer overnight so it will be soft when thawed, which makes it easier to purée. Or, if you are planning far enough in advance, place the fruit in a plastic bag with a ripe apple for a few days. This will speed up the ripening process and eliminate the dry taste.

If the fruit is very ripe and soft, just remove the stems, purée with the skin on, and then force the purée through a fine strainer. Prepared persimmon purée freezes well. Add 1 tablespoon lemon juice for every 2 cups of purée.

Brandied Whipped Cream

3 cups (720 ml) heavy cream
2 tablespoons (30 g) granulated
  sugar
1/3 cup (80 ml) brandy
1 teaspoon (2 g) grated nutmeg
1 teaspoon (5 ml) vanilla extract

1. Whip the cream and sugar until the mixture is thick but pourable. Stir in the brandy, nutmeg, and vanilla.

2. Reserve covered in the refrigerator. Adjust the consistency of the sauce at serving time. It should be just thick enough so it will not run on the plate.

Pumpkin or Sweet Potato Pie

two 10-inch (25-cm) pies

1/2 recipe Pie Dough (page 17)
5 eggs
3 cups (720 ml) cooked sweet
  potato or sugar pumpkin purée
  (see note)
12 ounces (340 g) granulated
  sugar

1. Roll out the pie dough 1/8 inch (3 mm) thick and line two 10-inch (25-cm) pie pans. Flute the edges (see Figures 2–1 and 2–2, page 18). Cover the dough with pieces of baking paper and fill the shells with dried beans or pie weights. Bake the shells at 375°F (190°C) until the dough is set, but has not yet started to color, about 12 minutes. Let the shells cool completely, then remove the paper and beans or pie weights. Reserve.

2. Beat the eggs lightly to mix. Stir in the sweet potato or pumpkin purée. Mix together 12 ounces (340 g) of granulated sugar, salt, cinnamon, ginger, and cloves. Add to the egg mixture.

1 teaspoon (5 g) salt
2 teaspoons (3 g) ground cinnamon
1 teaspoon (2 g) ground ginger
½ teaspoon (1 g) ground cloves
3½ cups (840 ml) half-and-half
1 pint (480 ml) heavy cream
1 tablespoon (15 g) granulated
    sugar

Stir in the half-and-half. Divide the filling evenly between the two pie shells.

3. Bake at 375°F (190°C) for approximately 50 minutes, or until the filling has puffed slightly and is firm around the edges. Let the pies cool.

4. Whip the heavy cream with 1 tablespoon (15 g) of granulated sugar to stiff peaks. Place the cream in a pastry bag with a no. 7 (14-mm) star tip. Pipe a shell border of cream around the edges of the pies (see Figure 18–7, page 504). Slice the pies into the desired size pieces. Serve at room temperature.

NOTE: If you use sweet potatoes you will need about 2 pounds (910 g) of raw potatoes, with skin. Boil them gently until soft, peel, and purée or force through a fine sieve. For the pumpkin purée you will need a 3-pound (1-kg, 365-g) sugar pumpkin. Bake the pumpkin at 400°F (205°C) until it feels soft when you press it with your thumb, about 1½ hours. Cool, peel or cut away the skin, cut in half, and remove the seeds (save the seeds and toast them for snacks). Purée or mash the pumpkin flesh and pass it through a sieve.

Yule Logs
(Bûche de Nöel)

two 11-inch (27.5-cm) logs
or 18 servings

1 recipe Cocoa Almond Sponge
    batter (page 163)
3 ounces (85 g) Marzipan,
    colored green (page 531)
½ ounce (15 g) Marzipan,
    colored red (page 531)
1 pound, 12 ounces (795 g)
    Chocolate Buttercream
    (page 501)
12 ounces (340 g) Marzipan,
    white (page 531)
4 ounces (115 g) melted
    dark baker's chocolate
8 ounces (225 g) Rum Ball Filling
    (page 256)
Piping Chocolate (page 449)
powdered sugar

1. Spread the sponge batter evenly over a sheet of baking paper 24 × 16 inches (60 × 40 cm). Drag the paper onto a sheet pan (see Figure 15–3, page 422). Bake at 425°F (219°C) for about 10 minutes, or until just done and let cool.

2. If the sponge is needed immediately but seems too dry to roll into a log, follow the procedure on page 163 to soften it. If made for later use, store the sponge sheet, covered, in the refrigerator.

3. Roll out the green marzipan (using powdered sugar to prevent it from sticking) to 1/16 inch (2 mm) thick. Cut out circles using a 2½-inch (6.2-cm) plain cookie cutter. Using the same cutter, make two cuts that meet in the center, giving you two pointed ovals. Make about 12 leaves for the two logs. Mark veins on the leaves using the back of a small knife. Use a no. 3 (6-mm) plain piping tip to cut out scalloped edges all around the leaves. Set the leaves on a dowel and leave them to dry in a curved shape. Roll the scraps to the same thickness and cut out two strips 5 inches (10 cm) long and 1 inch (2.5 cm) wide. Reserve.

4. Roll the red marzipan into pea-sized balls (berries). Make three balls for every two leaves. Reserve.

5. Peel the paper off the back of the inverted sponge sheet (leave the other paper underneath) and trim the sponge to 22 × 15 inches (55 × 37.5 cm). Reserve the scraps.

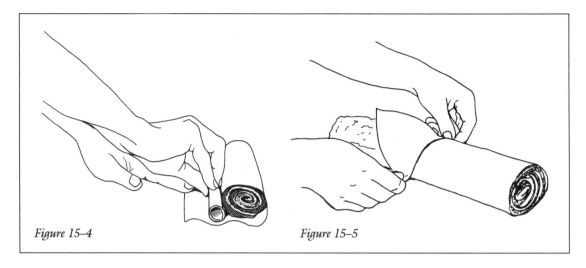

Figure 15–4

Figure 15–5

6. Spread approximately four-fifths of the chocolate butter-cream evenly over the sponge sheet (use less buttercream on the bottom 1 inch (2.5 cm) of the long edge or it will ooze out as the log is rolled).

7. Roll up the cake starting from the top long edge and rolling toward you. Pull the paper toward you as you roll to help make a tight log. Leaving the paper around the log, hold the bottom of the paper in place with your left hand, and push a dowel or ruler against the log on top of the paper; the paper will wrap around the log and make it tight (Figure 15–4). Refrigerate, covered, seam-side down, until the buttercream is firm.

8. Place the chilled log on an inverted sheet pan covered with baking paper. Spread a thin layer of the reserved buttercream over the log, spreading it to where the log meets the sheet pan. Do not try to spread it underneath. Even the buttercream by pulling a paper lengthwise around the log (Figure 15–5).

9. Roll out the white marzipan (using powdered sugar to prevent it from sticking) to 1/16 inch (2 mm) thick. Roll it wide and long enough to cover the log to where it meets the pan, but, like the buttercream, the marzipan does not go underneath or on the ends. Cover the log with the marzipan, smoothing it to fit with your hands. Cover and reserve the remaining marzipan.

10. Spread the dark baker's chocolate over the marzipan, spreading it back and forth rapidly until the chocolate starts to set up. It should not look completely smooth but rather show long marks from the spatula.

11. Cut the log into two 11-inch (27.5-cm) logs (or into 18 servings) using a hot knife. Cover the exposed ends of each log with part of the remaining chocolate buttercream.

12. Roll the Rum Ball Filling into ropes 1½ inches (3.7 cm) in diameter. (If you do not have Rum Ball Filling, use the reserved sponge scraps mixed with enough buttercream to make a dough-like consistency.) Cover the ropes with white marzipan rolled to ¹⁄₁₆ inch (2 mm) thick (see Figure 9–21, page 258). Refrigerate until cold.

13. Cut the ropes into 2-inch (5-cm) pieces, straight on one end and slanted on the other. Make two for each log. Dip these "branch stumps" into melted dark baker's chocolate to cover and let cool. Dip the slanted ends into chocolate again and fasten them to the top of the logs, one on each side, close to the ends. Do not make branch stumps if preparing the log as individual servings.

14. Decorate the logs with the marzipan holly leaves and berries, placing two leaves and three berries next to the branch stumps (or single decorations on each slice). Attach them with piping chocolate. Sift powdered sugar over the logs for a snow effect.

15. Write "Merry Christmas" on the reserved strips of green marzipan using piping chocolate. Make one for each log. Fasten them to the center of the logs using more piping chocolate.

Chocolate Roulade

1. Follow recipe above through step 10.

2. Cut the roulade into 1-inch-wide (25-mm) pieces with a serrated knife.

3. Place the slices in paper cups, pressing the bottom of the cups flat on both sides to create a stable base.

4. Decorate each slice by piping an *S* shape in chocolate buttercream, using a no. 1 (2-mm) plain tip in your pastry bag. Place a small candied violet in the center of the *S*.

Gingerbread Houses

Building and displaying a small gingerbread house is a traditional part of Christmas for many families in Sweden. It can be a project for the whole family; the children not only love to help assemble the house, but also to tear it apart after Christmas. A gingerbread house is also a typical part of the seasonal decor in the pastry shop. These are usually large, very elaborate creations that light up at night and are displayed in the shop windows. Smaller, simpler houses are made for sale. If the houses are made in an assembly-line fashion, they can be very profitable for your business, and they give the shop a feeling of old-fashioned Christmas spirit.

A good size for a small production house is 7 inches wide, 10 inches long, and 10 inches high (17.5 × 25 × 25 cm). The roof pieces for a small house should be cut large enough to allow for a ½-inch (1.2-cm) overhang on the sides and bottom; it is not necessary to make a center supporting wall. Smaller houses limit the decorating possibilities, which makes them suitable for decorating in an identical layout. For a small house, make the platform out of double layers of thick cardboard. The size will depend on how extensively you plan to decorate around the house. For the previously suggested size, make the platform 12 × 16 inches (30 × 40 cm).

These decorating instructions are for making a fairly large and ornate house measuring approximately 10½ inches wide, 15 inches long, and 15 inches high (26.2 × 37.5 × 37.5 cm). You can enlarge the templates accordingly to give you these dimensions, or enlarge or reduce them to any size you like to create smaller or larger houses. Of course, you must enlarge or reduce all of the templates equally to make them fit together.

One Large House

2 recipes Gingerbread Cookie
　dough (page 419); see step 1
½-inch (1.2-cm) plywood
2 recipes Royal Icing (page 528)
paper glue
red cellophane
½ recipe Boiled Sugar Basic Recipe
　(page 469)
powdered sugar
marzipan (optional)

1. Make the gingerbread dough, replacing the butter with margarine and increasing the flour by 6 ounces (170 g) per recipe. Place in the refrigerator overnight.

2. Enlarge, then trace the gingerbread house templates in Figures 15–6 through 15–10 or 15–11 and copy onto sturdy cardboard (the type used to mat framed artwork is an excellent choice). Cut the templates out using a carpet knife.

3. To prepare the platform, cut a rectangle measuring 16 × 24 inches (40 × 60 cm) out of ½-inch (1.2-cm) plywood. Cut out a square opening approximately 3 × 3 inches (7.5 × 7.5 cm), large enough to insert a light bulb (and your fingers), should you need to replace the light. To use the space on the platform in the most efficient way, I recommend that you place the house in one corner, with the long sides of the platform and the long sides of the house parallel, and of course with the front door facing the open, garden area. For the best effect with the light, the opening should be cut so that the bulb is just about in the center of the house once it is assembled. Keep the location of the house in mind when cutting the opening.

4. Cut out four small pieces of plywood from your scraps, and glue or nail one of these under each corner to raise the platform and allow space for the electrical cord.

5. Screw a light bulb holder to the plywood next to the opening and attach a cord that will reach just to one side of the platform. Attach a male plug to the end of the cord. (It is more

practical to use a short cord like this attached to the house itself and then combine it with whatever length extension cord is necessary so you will not have the long cord in your way, and you can use the same platform many times in different locations by changing only the extension cord.)

6. Work the gingerbread dough smooth with your hands. Roll out a portion at a time to ¼ inch (6 mm) thick (or slightly thinner for a small house), using as little flour as possible. Place the pieces on sheet pans lined with baking paper and reserve in the refrigerator.

7. When the dough is firm, place the templates on top and cut out the pieces with the point of a thin paring knife:

- Cut two identical pieces for the front and back except cut one with two windows and the other with one window and a door (Figure 15–6). When you cut out the piece for the door, save it to attach later.
- Cut two identical long pieces for the sides (Figure 15–7).
- Cut one piece for the center supporting wall (Figure 15–8).
- Make a balcony (Figure 15–9) to attach later to the front of the house. Cut two of each piece; the two long pieces will be the front side panel and the floor, and the short pieces will be the sides. Decorate the balcony pieces by cutting small hearts out of the sides. (You may want to make little marzipan children inside peeking out of the window; you only have to make their heads and support them on a piece of marzipan as that is all that will be visible).
- Choose one of the chimney designs. The one attached to the point of the roof (Figure 15–10) makes a small house look bigger. The other design (Figure 15–11) goes on the slope of the roof. Cut out two sets of either design (four pieces total). If you would like to make a brick design in the dough for the chimney, do it before you cut the pieces. Roll out scrap (not fresh) dough large enough for all four pieces and ⅛ inch (3 mm) thick. Use a straight piece of the cardboard used to make the templates or a ruler with an edge 1/16 inch (2 mm) thick, and press parallel lines into the dough every ¼ inch (6 mm). Cut a strip of cardboard ¼ inch (6 mm) wide and use the end to press lines, at a 90° angle to the parallel lines, staggering the rows to simulate bricks. Place the dough in the refrigerator if it has become soft while you were "laying the bricks," then cut out your chimney pieces.
- Cut out two rectangular pieces for the roof, allowing for a ¾-inch (2-cm) overhang at the sides and on the bottom. For the large house dimensions, this is 11½ × 16½ inches (28.7 × 41.2 cm).

- Cut out some backdrop material from your scrap dough: fence posts and planks (the planks should be bent uneven for a rough, natural look), several small pieces to use for a stack of firewood piled up outside, and whatever else you like, using your imagination to create your own personalized house.
- To decorate the roof, roll out a piece of gingerbread dough to ⅛ inch (3 mm) thick and cut out fifteen strips ½ inch (1.2 cm) wide and the length of the roof; you actually only need ten (five for each side) but it is always a good idea to make a few extra. Like the fence posts, the strips for the roof should be bent to be slightly uneven and resemble pieces cut from a tree that was not perfectly straight.
- Roll out more dough to 1/16 inch (2 mm) thick, and cut out approximately 120 hearts (you need about 100) using a 1¾-inch (4.5-cm) heart cutter (these will also be used to decorate the roof).
- You can either create a tree by tying small pieces of pine to a dowel, and then drilling a hole in the plywood to secure the tree trunk, or you can cut out large and small trees from scrap gingerbread dough.

8. Bake the pieces at 375°F (190°C) until they are dark brown and done. Make sure that the larger pieces are baked all the way through, and avoid placing large and small pieces on the same pan so you will not have to move them before they are cool. Set the pieces aside to cool completely.

9. When the gingerbread has cooled, trim the edges of the house pieces, if necessary, using a serrated knife or a coarse file, and turn them upside down.

10. Attach transparent red cellophane over the windows. Use any plain paper glue if the house is for a showpiece only (pipe a thin line of glue around the windows and press a small square of cellophane on top). If you suspect part of the house will be consumed, or if you are making houses for sale, use royal icing but pipe an additional line of icing on top of the cellophane and onto the gingerbread above and below the windows, then attach a narrow piece of gingerbread on top, securing the narrow piece to the main side piece.

11. Soften some additional icing by adding extra egg whites. Spread the icing in a thin film on the back side of the roof pieces, covering them completely. Set aside.

12. Pick out the pieces to be used for the fence posts and planks, the four chimney pieces, and the four balcony pieces.

Cover the backs of these with icing in the same way, being careful not to get any on the front. Set aside.

13. Turn the front, side, and back pieces right-side up. Pipe royal icing on the pieces in any decoration you wish around the outline of the door and windows, and around the edges. Set aside with the roof pieces.

14. Assemble the chimney once the icing on the back has dried enough to handle. Cut or file the edges of the four chimney pieces so they fit together. Pipe a thin line of royal icing on the edges of the long sides of the two wider pieces and fasten the other two pieces in between. Adjust so the edges line up correctly. Set aside.

15. Assemble the balcony once the icing on the back has dried enough to handle, trimming and gluing the pieces together as you did for the chimney. Set the balcony aside with the glazed roof pieces, the decorated front, back, and side pieces, and the chimney. Allow all of them to dry overnight before continuing.

16. Draw lines on the platform exactly where you want to attach the house (remember that, ideally, the light attachment should be in the center). Screw a 15- to 25-watt light bulb into the holder; plug it in, and test it to make sure it works before you build the house. Place a piece of foil over the bulb while you are working.

17. Spread a ¼-inch (6-mm) layer of royal icing in a 2-inch (5-cm) band around the perimeter of the platform where you plan to build the fence. Immediately measure and mark the spots where the fence posts will be fastened at intervals spaced correctly for the length of your fence planks (which should be approximately 4 inches/10 cm), placing the marks 1 inch (2.5 cm) away from the edge. Scrape the icing away at these marks so that the fence posts can be glued directly to the platform.

18. Boil the sugar to the hard crack stage, 310°F (155°C).

19. Use a knife and spread a little of the sugar on the edges of one side piece and the front piece. Quickly attach these to the platform and to each other (you can use the help of two extra hands at this point). Attach the remaining side and the back of the house in the same way. Spread a little sugar at the corners inside for extra support. Trim and attach the center supporting wall. Be careful as you complete these steps not to get any melted sugar on the windows or on the front side of the pieces.

20. Test the roof pieces to make certain they fit. If not, trim the edges of the frame on the platform as needed. Carefully, but quickly, spread sugar on the underside of the roof pieces in a 1-inch (2.5-cm) band where the roof will connect with the sides of the house. Attach the pieces one at a time, holding each one until secure.

21. A few minutes later, when the sugar has hardened, attach the chimney either in the center of the roof or over to one side. Before attaching, check to make sure that the angle of the chimney will fit with the angle of the roof. Trim the chimney if necessary. Attach to the roof with melted sugar. Take a good look at the chimney from all sides to be sure it is straight.

22. Trim and attach the balcony with melted sugar.

23. Dip the bottom of the fence posts in sugar (warm the sugar if necessary) and attach them to the platform at the marks in the royal icing you made earlier. Again, make sure these are standing straight up (see note 1).

24. Adjust the consistency of the royal icing, if necessary, until it is spreadable but not runny.

25. Spread enough icing on the roof to completely cover the gingerbread, including the sides of the chimney if you have not made "bricks." Smooth over and fill in any cracks where the chimney is attached to the roof, but do not make the icing completely smooth; it should look a little rustic. (Or you can leave the plain chimney without icing on the sides, and then decorate it with some piped icing later, as you would with the brick-style chimney.) Try to make the icing "hang over" the bottom edge of the roof, then make icicles by immediately pulling the icing down randomly across the sides. If the icing falls off in chunks instead, it is too soft.

26. Attach five roof planks on each side of the roof, pressing them lightly into the icing.

27. Place royal icing in a pastry bag with a no. 3 (6-mm) plain tip. Fasten rows of the gingerbread hearts between the roof planks with small dots of icing.

28. Glue the fence planks to the posts with royal icing, attaching one at the top of the posts and another halfway down (if they don't fit, trim them with a serrated knife).

29. Using all or part of your scraps, make one or two small hills on the platform by gluing the pieces together with icing. Spread a covering of icing over the hills and all of the remaining platform surface, being careful not to break the fence. Stack your firewood pieces in a pile.

30. Use your imagination to finish the landscaping, placing trees here and there and maybe a few deer (gingerbread) among the trees.

31. Attach the door in an open position. You might want to have a little face peering out and a Santa Claus walking up to the house, both made of marzipan, or you can place marzipan angels (see page 432) in front of the house or a few marzipan pigs (see page 439) near the fence.

32. Apply the trim by piping icing from top to bottom at each corner of the house. Pipe additional icing on the short sides of the roof, covering the exposed gingerbread. Use the piping tip to pull down icicles, as you did on the long sides. Pipe around the fence posts to cover the exposed sugar. Apply snow by piping icing around the top edge of the chimney, on top of the fence posts and planks (be sure they are dry or the weight of the snow will make them fall off) and any other exposed part of the landscape. Spot the branches of the trees and the firewood pile with icing.

33. Fasten some cotton inside the chimney to simulate smoke.

34. Dust the whole house and garden with powdered sugar, blowing at the same time to make some "snow" adhere to the sides of the house.

35. Plug in the cord, stand back and enjoy your masterpiece! A time-consuming and elaborate house like this one does not have to be thrown away after the holidays, but can be covered with a plastic bag, stored in a dry area, and used again next year (perhaps with some renovation or repair).

NOTE 1: The gingerbread house can be fully assembled using royal icing rather than sugar to attach the pieces, but you must do it in stages, letting the sides set for a few hours before adding the roof, chimney, and balcony, then allowing this to dry overnight before decorating. It is much more practical to use sugar, which makes it possible for you to decorate and finish the house immediately after assembling it.

NOTE 2: A house of this size should always be made with a light inside. The light bulb is not only decorative, it also keeps the house warm and prevents the gingerbread from getting soft and eventually collapsing as it absorbs moisture from the air. The light should therefore be turned on at least once every day during the evening and night. To prevent a small house without a light from softening, ice the back of all of the walls, as well as the roof, with a thin film of softened royal icing. Any gingerbread figures or trees standing out in the "garden" should be given the same treatment to prevent them from collapsing.

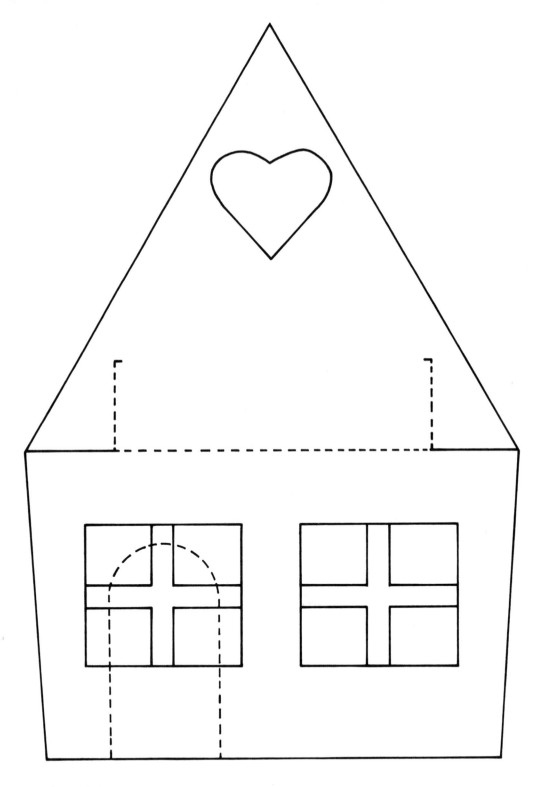

Figure 15–6

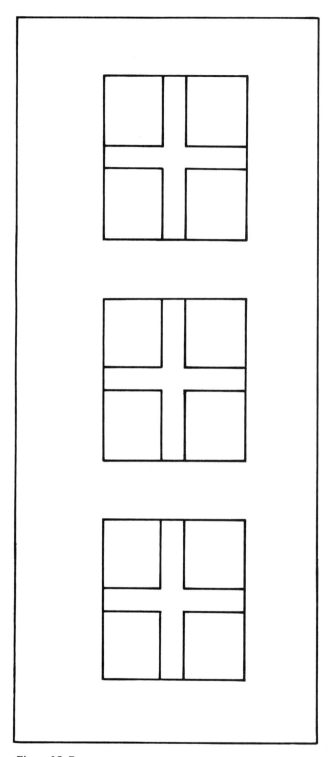

Figure 15–7

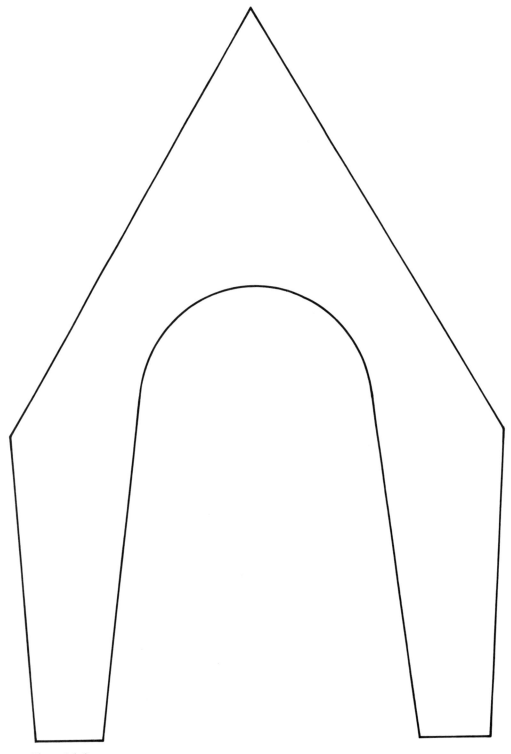

Figure 15–8

436

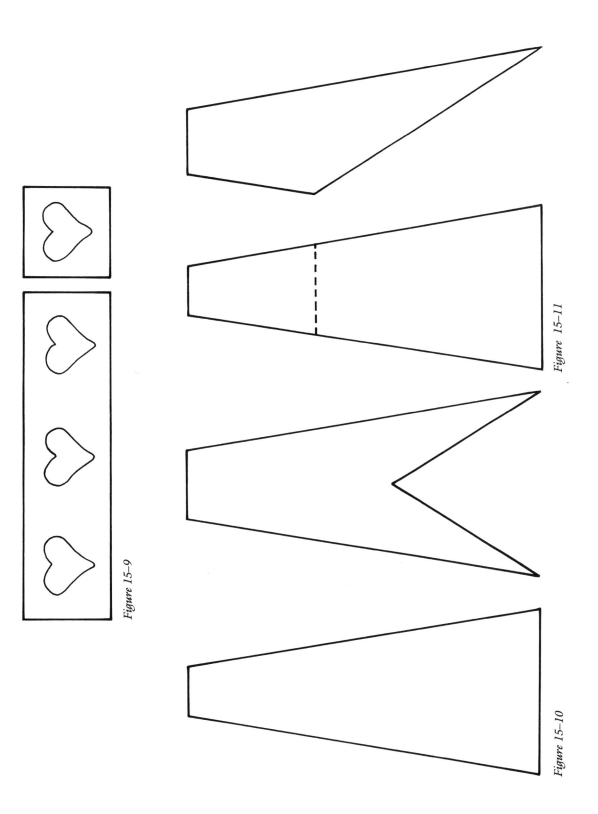

Figure 15-9

Figure 15-10

Figure 15-11

SIXTEEN

Chocolate and Chocolate Candies

Tempering Chocolate
Chocolate Decorations
  Chocolate Curls
  Chocolate Cut-outs
  Chocolate Leaves
  Chocolate Shavings
  Modeling Chocolate
  Piping with Chocolate
Chocolate Casting or Painting
Cocoa Painting
Hollow Chocolate Figures
  Using Molds

Molding Chocolate Strips
Chocolate Candies
  Fig Logs
  Gianduja
  Gianduja Bites
  Mimosa
  Nougat Montélimar
  Orange Moons
  Pistachio Slices
  Dark Truffles
  Light Truffles
  White Truffles

Chocolate is derived from the fruit of the cocoa tree, which the Swedish naturalist Carl von Linné (1707–1778) named *Theobromma* or "food of the gods." Besides being a heavenly pleasure for the palate, chocolate is a favorite source of quick energy. Athletes use chocolate to prevent fatigue and gain stamina during sporting events. Scientist Alexander von Humbolt (1769–1859) said, "Nature has nowhere else concentrated such an abundance of the most valuable foods in such a limited space as in the cocoa bean." Although nutritionists today probably would not endorse this assessment, the popularity of chocolate is more widespread than ever. There are books and monthly magazines devoted to the subject, as well as a growing number of people who refer to themselves as "chocoholics."

The cocoa tree can be found all through the equatorial belt where the average temperature is 80°F (26°C) and humidity is high. Like the citrus family, cocoa trees bear buds, blossoms, and fruit all at the same time. Each tree produces about 30 oblong fruits, or pods, which, unlike other types of fruit, grow directly on the trunk and branches. Each pod contains approximately 50 beans imbedded in the fleshy interior.

The cocoa fruits are generally harvested twice a year. The seeds, along with the white flesh, are scraped out and covered with banana leaves or placed in heaps. The beans are then left to ferment, a process that takes from one to three weeks, depending on the climate. The fermented beans are spread out on mats and dried in the sun to remove most of the water content. After drying, some of the bitter taste is gone, and the beans have developed a more pronounced cocoa aroma. At this stage the beans are ready to be packed into jute sacks and shipped.

When the beans arrive at the chocolate factories they are cleaned and roasted to develop the proper flavor and aroma. The beans are then crushed and the husks are removed. The roasted, crushed kernels of cocoa bean are milled very fine to produce cocoa paste. Also known as cocoa mass, this is the main ingredient for a variety of chocolate products (see Figure 16–1). Part of the cocoa mass is placed under high hydraulic pressure to extract the cocoa butter, a valuable aromatic fat that is an essential part of every chocolate recipe and gives chocolate a fine texture and attractive glaze. The cocoa cakes that are left after the fat has been removed are crushed, ground into a fine powder, and sifted to produce pure unsweetened cocoa powder.

Cocoa butter, sugar, and a flavoring such as vanilla (as well as milk powder, in the case of milk chocolate) are added to the cocoa mass to make chocolate. The combination is kneaded together in a mixer until a smooth, homogeneous mixture has developed. This can now be called chocolate, but it is not yet the smooth confection we think of when we use that name. To remove the gritty taste still present at this stage, the chocolate must go through an additional refining process, called conching. The chocolate is placed in machines that knead and roll the mixture on rotary bases continuously for up to three days. During this process, the mixture is warmed as high as 200°F (94°C) for some dark chocolate varieties. For the highest quality chocolate, additional cocoa butter is added, together with lecithin, to further reduce the viscosity. Lecithin (derived from soybeans), besides being less expensive than cocoa butter, brings out the cocoa flavor which might otherwise be overpowered by excess cocoa butter. The end result is a velvety-smooth chocolate product. The chocolate is poured and formed into blocks, wrapped, and stored in a cool, well-ventilated room. Dark chocolate will keep this way (if unopened) for up to one year, milk and white chocolates for slightly less time.

It can be a bit confusing seeing the term chocolate or chocolate coating on one manufacturer's label, and the word couverture on another. The French word couverture, roughly translated, means "to cover" or "to coat." (However, couverture is not the same as coating chocolate, which is another name for baker's chocolate.) To further the confusion, chocolate (or couverture, as the case may be) is available in several different grades. Generally, the

CHOCOLATE PRODUCTION

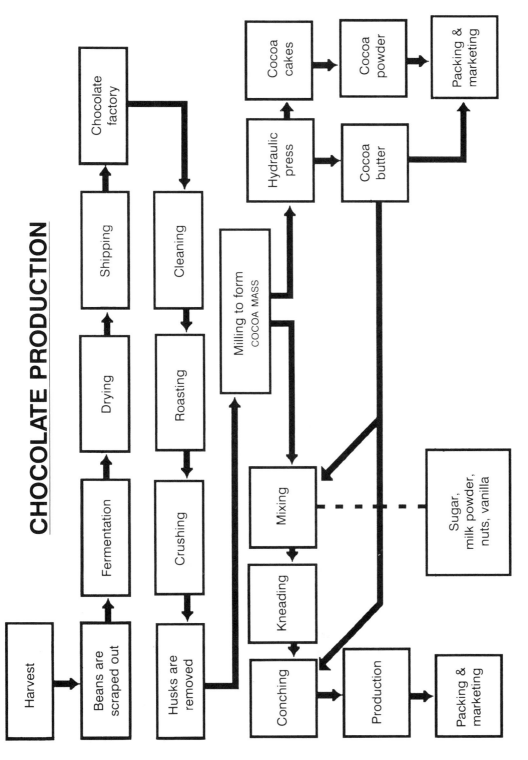

Figure 16–1

better-quality (more expensive) grades of chocolate are used for candy fillings and for dipping candies, or for any other application where superior taste and texture are crucial. Premium grades of chocolate are determined by a higher ratio of cocoa butter and a longer conching time.

True chocolate should not be confused with baker's chocolate, a much-used chocolate-flavored coating also known as non-temp or chocolate icing. This product does not need to be tempered because the cocoa butter has been replaced with other fats (such as hydrogenated palm kernel oil and lecithin). Baker's chocolate is easier to use than the real thing, and, although it falls short of genuine chocolate in both taste and texture, a high-quality baker's chocolate can be substituted for most of the recipes and techniques in this chapter with a good result. Candies or other products made with baker's chocolate must not be sold labeled as chocolate.

White chocolate contains no cocoa paste. Instead, it is a mixture that must contain a minimum of 20 percent cocoa butter and a maximum of 55 percent sugar. The remaining ingredients are milk solids and milk fats.

Tempering Chocolate

To achieve the desired high gloss and hard, brittle texture, and to make the chocolate more resistant to warm temperatures, it is necessary to temper it. The cocoa butter in chocolate consists of many different fat groups with melting points that vary between 60° and 115°F (16° and 46°C). The fats that melt at the higher temperature are also the first ones to solidify as the melted chocolate cools. These fats, when distributed throughout, are what gives the chocolate its gloss and solidity (a properly tempered chocolate should break with a crisp snap). One might say that these high-melting-point fats act as a starting point around which the remaining chocolate solidifies.

Two methods are used to temper chocolate by hand. Both consist of three basic steps: melting, cooling, and rewarming. The most commonly used method is called *tabliering*.

1. Cut the chocolate into small pieces and place it in a bowl over simmering water to melt. Stir it constantly to avoid overheating or burning, especially if you are working with milk chocolate, which tends to get lumpy if overheated. Stirring is essential when melting white chocolate, which can become grainy and useless very quickly. To completely melt all of the fats, heat the chocolate to approximately 115° to 120°F (46° to 49°C). The

chocolate must then be held at this temperature for at least 30 minutes. The temperature varies depending on the manufacturer, so it is a good idea to check the label.

2. Cool (temper) the melted chocolate by pouring about one-third of it onto a marble slab. Using a metal spatula in combination with a metal scraper, spread the chocolate out and scrape it back together until it cools and shows signs of thickening (the high-melting-point fats are starting to crystallize). Before the chocolate sets completely, stir it back into the remaining two-thirds of the chocolate and mix until it forms a homogeneous mass.

3. The chocolate is now too thick to use and must be warmed slowly over hot water back to 85° to 90°F (29° to 32°C), which is the correct working temperature. If the chocolate is still too thick at this temperature, thin it by adding a small amount of cocoa butter. Great care must be taken in this final (third) step. If you should let the chocolate get just a few degrees above the recommended temperature too much fat will melt and the chocolate will require a longer time to set. It also will not be as attractive since part of the fat will separate and show on the surface in the whitish pattern known as "bloom."

The second tempering method is called *seeding*.

1. Melt the chocolate over a water bath as above, remove it from the heat source, and stir grated chocolate in at a ratio of 1 part grated chocolate to 3 parts melted. Stir the grated chocolate in gradually, and wait for each addition to completely melt and incorporate before adding the next one.

2. When the chocolate is perfectly smooth and the temperature has dropped to about 82°F (28°C). Hold the chocolate at this temperature while stirring for at least 2 minutes, then slowly warm it back up to 85° to 90°F (29° to 32°C). In this method it is important that the grated chocolate was itself tempered before setting.

If you have a thermostatically controlled bain-marie, and you have no need to use the chocolate in a hurry (this process can take 12 to 24 hours), it is also possible to warm pre-tempered chocolate very slowly and omit the cooling process, provided that the temperature never exceeds 85° to 90°F (29° to 32°C) at any time.

Before starting to work with the product it is always a good idea to check if the chocolate has been tempered correctly, regardless of the method used. Do this by spreading a small amount of chocolate on a piece of baking paper and letting it cool at a room temperature of 64° to 69°F (18° to 20°C). Within 5 minutes the chocolate should have thickened enough so that it can be rolled into a chocolate curl.

Chocolate Decorations

Chocolate Curls
(Cigars)

1. Spread tempered chocolate on a marble slab using a metal spatula. Spread it as close to the edge as possible, in a thin strip about ¹/₁₆ inch (2 mm) thick, or as thin as possible without being able to see the marble through the chocolate. Make the strip a bit wider than the length you want the finished curls (Figure 16–2). Let the chocolate set up or, if using baker's chocolate, continue spreading back and forth until it has almost set up.

2. Cut the strip the long way to even the sides and make it as wide as the desired length of the finished curls (Figure 16–3).

3. Hold a chef's knife (or spatula) at a 45° angle to the slab and push the knife away from you to cut off and curl about 1 inch (2.5 cm) of the strip (Figures 16–4 and 16–5).

Getting the chocolate just the right consistency to curl is a bit tricky. If it is too soft it will just smear and stick to the knife

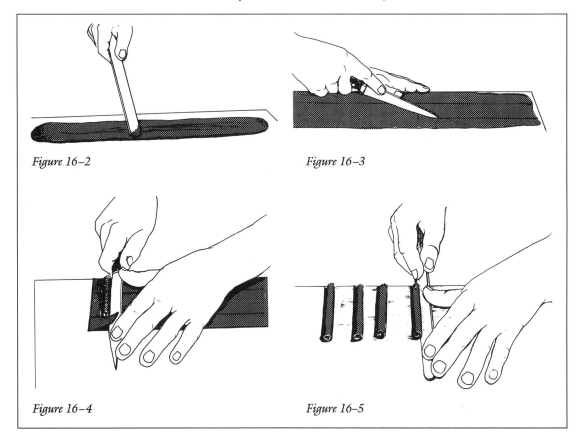

Figure 16–2

Figure 16–3

Figure 16–4

Figure 16–5

instead of curling. If this happens, wait a few seconds until it has set further. If that does not help (if the room or the marble slab is too warm), try placing a cold sheet pan on top. If it has set too hard, the chocolate will break when you try to curl it. Providing you have spread the chocolate thin enough, you can warm it by rubbing your hand over the top as you work your way down the strip.

Do not be discouraged if you are not successful at your first attempts at making chocolate curls. They take a bit of practice to master. One thing that is helpful to remember is that the ideal room temperature for chocolate work is approximately 68°F (20°C). The more the temperature varies from this figure, in either direction, the harder it will be to work with the chocolate.

Chocolate Cut-outs
(Squares, Rectangles, Circles, and Triangles)

This is a quick method for creating decorations that can be made up in advance. The assorted chocolate shapes can be used to decorate the sides of a cake or placed at an angle on top. They are used this way in Swedish Chocolate Cake, Meringue Black Forest Cake, and Gâteau Arabe, to name a few. Chocolate Cut-outs can be enhanced with the streaking technique described on page 455, applying the same or a different color chocolate for contrast. Chocolate Cut-outs are good to have on hand to use as a finishing touch; they can be placed on top of virtually any dessert to give it a special finesse.

1. Place a sheet of baking paper on the table and pour tempered chocolate on top. Spread it out very thin (1/16 inch/2 mm) and evenly using a metal spatula (Figure 16–6). Make sure the table around the paper is clean so you do not have to worry about spreading the chocolate onto the table if you have too much.

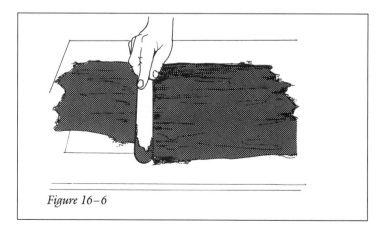

Figure 16–6

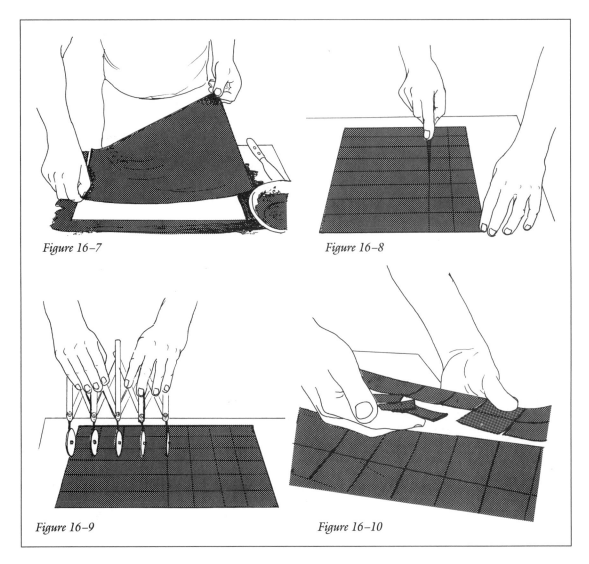

Figure 16–7

Figure 16–8

Figure 16–9

Figure 16–10

2. Immediately pick up the paper by two diagonal corners (Figure 16–7) and place it on a cardboard or inverted sheet pan. Allow the chocolate to set partially. Do not refrigerate.

3. Cut squares or rectangles using a sharp knife (Figure 16–8) or a multiple pastry wheel (Figure 16–9). Avoid cutting through the paper. Cut out circles, or other shapes such as hearts, using an appropriate size and shape cookie cutter. If necessary, heat the cutter by dipping it in hot water. Quickly shake off the water and dry the cutter on a towel before using. You can probably cut four or five pieces before reheating the cutter. Chocolate triangles can

be cut using the same pattern described in cutting croissants (see Figure 4–12, page 95) if you are making a full sheet of them, or just cut them out using a knife.

4. Store the chocolate cut-outs (still attached to the paper) in a dark cool place. Do not store them in the refrigerator. To remove them, place one hand underneath and push up gently to separate the decorations from the paper as you lift them off with your other hand (Figure 16–10). This technique is especially helpful when working with large, extra thin, or unusual shapes.

Chocolate Leaves

Method I

1. Spread tempered chocolate over a sheet of baking paper as described in the directions for chocolate cut-outs.

2. When the chocolate has set partially, use the tip of a small knife to cut out leaves of the appropriate size and shape (short and wide for rose leaves, longer and narrower for a pear leaf).

3. Carefully, without cutting all the way through, score the top to show the veins of the leaf (see Figure 18–44, page 543). Let set, store, and remove as directed in chocolate cut-outs.

Method II

1. A more eye-catching (but also more time-consuming) way to make chocolate leaves is to paint a thin layer of tempered chocolate on the back of a real leaf (typically a rose leaf) (Figure 16–11).

2. Let the chocolate set, then carefully peel the real leaf away from the chocolate one (Figure 16–12). You should be able to use the same leaf three or four times before the chocolate begins to stick.

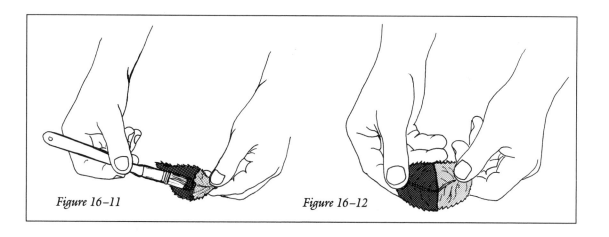

Figure 16–11   *Figure 16–12*

3. Any type of leaf can be produced in this manner as long as it is thin enough to be bent and peeled from the chocolate leaf without the chocolate breaking. (Naturally you want to make sure any leaves you use are nontoxic; citrus trees are safe and small citrus leaves produce a good result.)

Chocolate Shavings

Chocolate shavings are made by holding a small knife at a 90° angle to a piece of chocolate and scraping away from you, letting the shavings fall onto a paper-lined sheet pan (Figure 16–13). Again, the chocolate must have the correct consistency or you will experience the same problems described in the chocolate curls. Store the shavings, covered, in a cool, dry place to use as needed. Do not store them in the refrigerator. You can refrigerate the shavings for just a few minutes right before using them if it is necessary to keep them from melting and sticking to your hand (if you are placing them on the side of a cake for example). In most instances where the shavings are to be sprinkled on top of the dessert it is best to use a spoon and avoid contact with the heat of your hands. You can also use a melon baller with a sharp edge to create small, elegant 180° curled shavings, providing the chocolate is soft enough. Move the melon baller in short strokes, letting the curls fall onto a paper-lined sheet pan.

Figure 16–13

Modeling Chocolate

To prepare chocolate for modeling, add glucose or light corn syrup to chocolate (it does not have to be tempered) or baker's chocolate to make a thick paste. It can then be sculpted, much like marzipan, to make flowers and figures, or rolled into thin sheets, using a pasta machine, to cover cakes or pastries.

Chocolate Roses

8 to 10 medium-sized roses

6 ounces (170 g) milk, dark, or white chocolate or baker's chocolate, melted
5 teaspoons (25 ml) glucose or light corn syrup (see note)

1. Combine the chocolate and corn syrup and work into a dough. Cover and let rest for 6 hours or overnight.
2. Work the hardened mixture smooth (it will crumble at first) by forcing it against the table with the blade of a knife, then work it to the proper consistency with the warmth of your hands.
3. Form into roses using the directions and illustrations for marzipan roses (see Figures 18–38 to 18–44, pages 541–542).

NOTE: You may have to increase or decrease the amount of chocolate, depending on the brand you are using. With milk or white chocolate or baker's chocolate, you may need slightly less glucose or corn syrup.

Piping with Chocolate

Piping Chocolate

¼ cup (60 ml) piping chocolate

3 ounces (85 g) dark baker's chocolate
10 drops of Simple Syrup (page 7) or water, approximately

1. Chop the chocolate into small pieces. Place the chocolate in a small bowl or cup, preferably one with a handle.
2. Place the chocolate over simmering water and stir until melted. Do not overheat.
3. Using a drop bottle, add the simple syrup or water gradually. The number of drops needed will vary depending on the brand of chocolate. Stir in drops of syrup or water until the chocolate forms stiff peaks.
4. Place in a piping bag and use immediately or keep warm over hot water. Store leftover chocolate covered. Melt to reuse.

Chocolate Figurines

In addition to being used to coat and dip pastries, cookies, or cakes, baker's chocolate (dark, milk, or white) can be used to pipe out various decorative ornaments, either directly onto a cake or petit four freehand, or onto baking paper (sometimes with the help of a template) to place on the item after the decoration has hardened (tempered chocolate may also be used). The second method is a practical way of making fancy decorations when you are not too busy, because they can be made up far in advance and stored in a dark cool place (but not in the refrigerator). If you want the chocolate to float out slightly, use it as is. But if it is important to the design that the chocolate stay in precise lines, use piping chocolate.

Trace any of the small individual designs you would like to make from the examples shown in Figures 16–14 through 16–18) onto a sheet of paper, drawing as many as you need of each design.

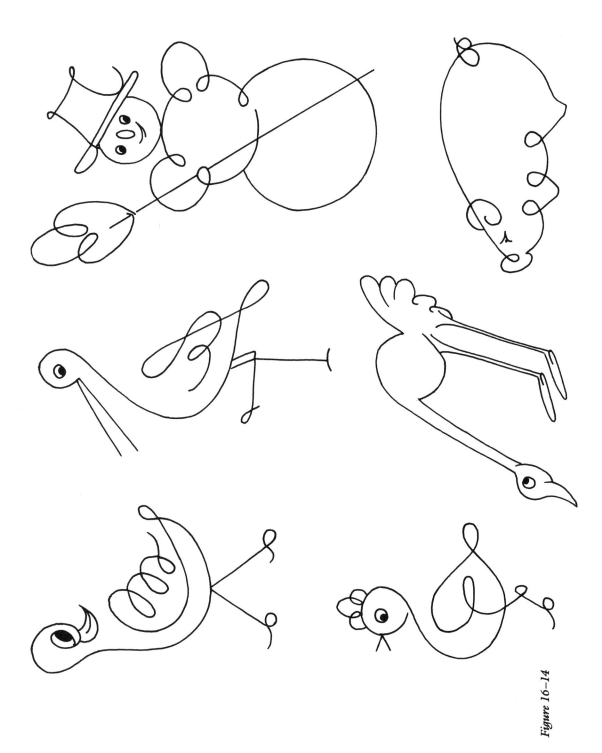

Figure 16-14

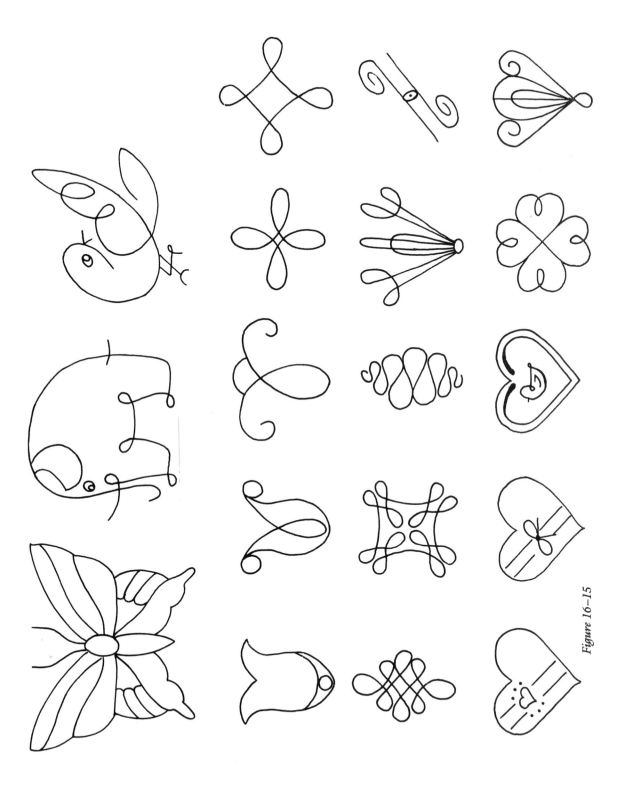

Figure 16–15

Figure 16–16

Figure 16–17

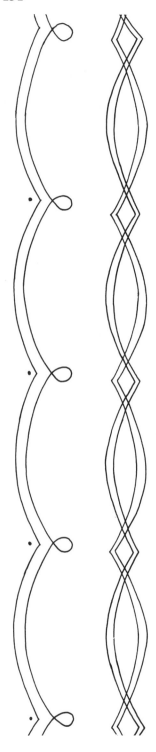

1. Attach the paper securely to a sheet of cardboard. Place a piece of baking or waxed paper on top, and attach it securely so it will not shift as you are piping the designs.

2. Make a piping bag (see page 505) and fill it with a small amount of baker's chocolate or piping chocolate. Cut a small opening in the bag. Pipe out, tracing the designs in one unbroken line as much as possible.

3. Let the chocolate harden, then store the figures attached to the paper. To remove them, place one hand under the paper and push up very gently to separate the chocolate from the paper, then lift the design off with the other hand. If they are very fragile, slide the blade of a thin knife under them instead.

Since the tip and the opening of the piping bag are so small, the chocolate will set up very quickly in that spot. When you pause while piping out the designs, hold the tip between your pinched fingers to keep it warm. If you forget, and only the chocolate at the very tip of the bag has set up, hold the tip of the piping bag against the side of a pot on the stove, or on the oven door, to melt it quickly.

You will never be able to get all of the chocolate out of the piping bag, but don't throw it out with the chocolate inside. Put the used bag in the refrigerator to harden, then open it up, and the chocolate will fall right out and can be put back into the bowl.

Some of the figurines look especially nice with a combination of dark, milk, and light chocolate in the same design. To create these, make the frame, using piping chocolate, and let it harden. Fill in the design with regular tempered chocolate in the desired shade or shades. When the chocolate has set, place these two-tone designs on the cake or pastry flat-side up. Different shades and colors can also be obtained by blending the dark, milk, and white chocolates (see Chocolate Casting, pages 456–457).

Figure 16–18

Chocolate Butterfly Ornaments

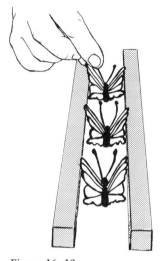

Figure 16–19

1. Trace the appropriate number of butterfly templates from Figure 16–15 onto a sheet of paper (you need only trace the wings; the antenna and the body are piped freehand).

2. Fasten the paper to a cardboard. Place a piece of baking or waxed paper on top, secure the paper with paper clips or tape so it will not move as you pipe.

3. Make dark piping chocolate and place a small amount in a piping bag (see page 505). Cut a small opening, and pipe the chocolate out following the outline and patterns of the wings.

4. Let these frames harden, then fill in the interior sections of the wings with milk and white baker's chocolate or tempered chocolate. (To make the monarch butterfly, color the white chocolate orange.) Let the chocolate set and reserve the wings.

5. Using dark piping chocolate, pipe out two antennae for each butterfly on a sheet of baking paper. This is done by piping a small dot about the size of the head of a pin, then attaching a slightly curved line approximately 1 inch (2.5 cm) long. Set the antennas aside.

6. Place two metal bars (or use dowels secured with a piece of dough) about 1½ inches (3.7 cm) apart on a sheet pan covered with baking paper. Place dark chocolate in a piping bag and cut a ⅛-inch (3-mm) opening. Pipe a small dot with a 1-inch (2.5-cm) tapered body (try to approximate the one in the drawing) behind it, between the bars.

7. Place two wings, flat-side up, into the chocolate, leaning them against the bars to get the proper angle. Repeat until all of the wings are attached. Once you can gauge how fast the chocolate is setting up you can pipe out several bodies at once.

8. Place the antennas in the refrigerator for a few minutes. Dip the straight ends in dark chocolate and fasten to the front of the butterfly in a *V* shape (Figure 16–19) (they will stick immediately since they have been chilled). Once the chocolate is firmly set you can remove the bars and store the butterflies in a cool, dark place; do not store them in the refrigerator.

Streaking

A very simple and elegant way to decorate petits fours, pastries, and candies, is to pipe a series of very thin lines across the item. The lines can be piped in just one direction, as in Strawberry Hearts, or in opposite directions as shown in Pecan Whiskey Tart (see Figure 6–1, page 150). Always use a small opening in the piping bag to keep the lines thin. Fill the bag with a small amount of tempered chocolate or baker's chocolate. Pipe the chocolate, moving the bag very quickly over the item alternating left to right and right to left. You need to extend the lines out just beyond the edge of the item and let them fall on a paper to get the desired effect.

Chocolate Casting or Painting

In addition to making individual decorations such as butterfly ornaments, you can apply the same basic technique to create stunning showpieces with chocolate. Again, the only prerequisites are a steady hand and a good eye for composing the various shades of chocolate in the design.

1. Draw or trace your picture on a sheet of paper. Try to use uncomplicated designs with clean lines. Attach the paper to a solid base, an inverted even sheet pan, or a sheet of cardboard. Remember that the design will be reversed (mirror image) in the finished piece. If that matters (for example, with lettering), follow the directions on page 523 to reverse the image.

2. Fasten a piece of plexiglas on top of the drawing or stretch a sheet of plastic wrap around it tightly. There must be no wrinkles because any imperfection here will show and be very disappointing when you turn over the finished piece.

3. Trace the drawing using piping chocolate (see page 449) in a piping bag with a small opening (see note). There is no reason to use pure chocolate here, since the finished piece is not meant to be eaten. Fill in the interior areas with different shades made by blending dark, milk, and white baker's chocolate, as necessary. If desired, you can color white baker's chocolate using fat-soluble coloring to make soft pastel shades. Think of the plastic or plexiglas as your canvas, the chocolate as your paint, the piping bag as your brush, and yourself as the artist.

4. When you have finished painting and the chocolate has set, move the painting to a corner or other safe place with the proper temperature, where it can set undisturbed. Do not attempt to move it once the background chocolate is poured.

5. Place metal bars around the edges, or use any other straight object that will prevent the poured chocolate from leaking out. Thick cardboard cut into strips will work if oiled on the side that will be next to the chocolate. Seal the outside with clay or even short dough. Apply the background by pouring baker's chocolate of the desired shade over the design within the frame. Make absolutely sure the temperature of the baker's chocolate is not above 105°F (41°C) or it can partially melt and destroy your piping underneath. On the other hand, if it is too cold (and therefore too thick), it will not flow out and cover properly, leaving an uneven and rough finish. The chocolate for the background should be poured very close to the painting, to avoid bubbles. Gauge the thickness of the background in proportion to the size of the painting. For example, if the painting is 12 ×

16 inches (30 × 40 cm), the background should be ½ inch (1.2 cm) thick for the proper strength. Leave your artwork to set for at least several hours.

6. In the meantime make a base and a stand. For the size painting above, pour baker's chocolate into a circle about 10 inches (25 cm) in diameter and ½ inch (1.2 cm) thick. For the rear support, pour a piece in the shape of a triangle with one long side at right angles to the short side, about 8 inches (20 cm) across the bottom, 14 inches tall (35 cm), and the same thickness as the base.

7. Place the painting in the refrigerator for 10 minutes to ensure a glossy finish. Carefully remove the metal bars from around the painting (cut them free with a thin knife if they do not separate easily). Place an inverted sheet pan or sheet of heavy cardboard on top, hold on securely with both hands, and turn the painting right-side up. Remove the other sheet pan or cardboard, as well as the plastic or plexiglas to reveal the painting. You may wish to add a border of piped chocolate or molded marzipan before placing it on the stand.

8. Chill the base of the stand and the rear support. Dip the bottom of the support in baker's chocolate and quickly fasten to the base. Hold it straight until it is set. Pipe some chocolate down the front of the support and carefully attach the painting. Hold until set. Pipe additional chocolate at the bottom behind the painting.

NOTE: If the piping chocolate sets up too hard, the thin lines will pull away from the surface (this will also happen if the room you are working in is too cold) and can cause the background chocolate to seep under later, when the background is poured. You can remedy this by thinning the piping chocolate slightly with soybean oil (or a commercial thinning agent).

Cocoa Painting

Although cocoa painting is quite an advanced decorating technique, with some practice and "help from a friend" (a stencil in this case), even a beginner can create simple designs with attractive results. Naturally it is helpful if you have some prior experience in drawing or in painting with watercolors.

The canvas for a cocoa painting is usually made of white marzipan rolled out in cornstarch, although pastillage can also be used. (I prefer the off-white color of marzipan, which blends in a more subtle way with the various cocoa tones, rather than the stark white of pastillage.) Powdered sugar is not used to roll out the marzipan in this case, as it leaves small grains of sugar on the surface that absorb the cocoa paint and leave unsightly dots on the finished piece. The sheet of marzipan must also be completely smooth for the same reason, and should be left to dry slightly after it is rolled out.

If you do not have a natural talent for drawing freehand, the stenciling technique described on page 531 can help frame an outline for your design. The stenciling should be done before the marzipan is left to dry.

The cocoa paint is made from cocoa powder diluted in water to produce an extensive number of varying shades. A few drops of clear liquor, such as vodka, can be added to create some of the lightest tones. Food color should be used sparingly (or your finished work will look like something you can buy at a garage sale).

Using artist brushes, start by applying the lighter shades first, then finish with the darker tones. Practice blending the shades together so that no clear line is visible where the lighter tone ends and the darker one starts. When completed, the painting can be used to decorate the top of a cake, or it can be framed in marzipan and used as a showpiece.

Hollow Chocolate Figures Using Molds

Only metal or plastic chocolate molds in perfect condition should be used to make hollow figures, because the smallest scratch can cause the chocolate to stick.

1. To prepare the molds, clean them using soap and hot water, rinse, and dry thoroughly. Polish the inside of the molds with cotton balls (if using metal molds, dip the cotton balls in a little powdered chalk, then remove any trace of the chalk with a clean cotton ball). For good results the molds as well as the work area must be at the proper temperature (around 68°F/20°C).

2. Before filling, coat the inside of the molds with a thin layer of tempered chocolate using a good brush to eliminate any small bubbles on the surface.

3. Immediately clip the two halves of the molds together and fill with chocolate. If the thin layer of chocolate is left to set up completely before filling, it can separate from the rest of the mold later.

4. Lightly tap the side of the mold with a dowel to break any bubbles that might have formed.

5. Wait a few minutes until a thick enough layer of chocolate has formed to be sure the mold will not break when handled (a larger mold will need a thicker layer), then invert the mold over the bowl of chocolate and allow the chocolate to run back out. Tap the mold lightly with a dowel to help remove the chocolate.

6. Place the molds on a sheet pan lined with baking paper. When they start to set, remove the clips and refrigerate for a few minutes until the chocolate has started to shrink away from the molds (this is easy to see with a plastic mold; you will just have to take an educated guess with a metal mold). Remove the molds.

7. To make the bottom, spread a thin layer of chocolate on a baking paper, place the hollow chocolate figure on top, and let it set. Cut away any excess chocolate around the figure. If a seam shows where the two halves were joined together, remove it after a few hours with a sharp, thin knife.

When making molds with two or more different chocolates (a white beard on a Santa, for example, or milk chocolate in spots on dark chocolate for a rabbit), brush or pipe on the contrasting color first, and allow it to set slightly before continuing. Milk, white, and dark chocolates can be mixed or tinted to create different shades for molding, as discussed in Chocolate Casting.

Molding Chocolate Strips

With this method it is possible to make containers of almost any shape to hold mousses, bavarois, or other dessert items (see pages 320 and 321).

1. Spread tempered chocolate (or baker's chocolate) in a thin layer on a strip of thin plastic that is cut as wide as you would like the height of the container, and to the precise length of the circumference of the finished container.

2. Pick up the sheet carefully before the chocolate has set and bend it into the desired shape.

3. Once the chocolate has hardened, peel away the plastic.

4. If you would like to put a base on the container, spread tempered chocolate out thinly on a sheet of baking paper and set the container on top. Pipe a string of chocolate around the inside bottom perimeter. Let the chocolate set partially. Cut around the outside with a thin knife and let it set completely.

A chocolate strip can also be wrapped around the side of the cake, as described in Chocolate Truffle Cake with Raspberries on page 195.

Chocolate Candies

Chocolate candies, known in Europe as pralines, have a liquid or solid filling (referred to as the interior) and are coated with a thin layer of chocolate using dipping tools. They are decorated in a simple, elegant manner after coating. As when working with any tempered chocolate, make sure the room temperature is approximately 68°F (20°C) when you dip the candies. The candy interiors should be the same, or a slightly higher temperature, for a satisfactory result. If the interiors are too cold, the chocolate will harden too quickly from the inside, resulting in a thicker coating than is desirable. Also, rather than a proper glossy finish, the surface can become dull and whitish-grey (you will see the same thing happen to a box of candies left in the sun, once the chocolate hardens again). Once the candies have been covered, they can be left to harden at a slightly lower temperature to speed up the process. A slow-moving fan can also be used. Candies should be stored in the same way as any chocolate: covered in a well-ventilated room with a temperature of 60° to 65°F (16° to 19°C).

Fig Logs

80 candies

4 ounces (115 g) dried figs
8 ounces (225 g) blanched almonds, lightly toasted
12 ounces (340 g) powdered sugar
1 tablespoon (15 ml) light rum
1 teaspoon (5 ml) vanilla extract
dark chocolate, tempered

1. Remove the stems from the figs. Place the figs in a saucepan with enough water to cover. Bring to a boil and cook for 10 minutes. Drain the water and purée the figs in a food processor. Set aside.

2. Process the almonds with half of the sugar in a food processor until very finely ground. Transfer to a bowl and stir in the remaining sugar, rum, vanilla, and fig purée. Adjust with additional rum as needed to make a firm paste.

3. Divide the filling into four equal pieces. Roll each piece into a 30-inch (75-cm) rope using powdered sugar to prevent it from sticking. Place the ropes next to each other and cut across, slicing each one into twenty 1½-inch (3.7-cm) pieces. Place them slightly separated on a paper-lined sheet pan, and allow them to dry overnight (place the sheet pan on a covered rack).

4. Dip the candies into tempered dark chocolate using a two-pronged dipping fork. Slide off onto sheet pans lined with baking paper. Before the chocolate sets, mark the top of the candies with the dipping fork, making two lines in the center of the logs, perpendicular to the long sides.

Gianduja

*3 pounds, 12 ounces (1 kg, 705 g)
Gianduja*

10 ounces (285 g) hazelnuts
*10 ounces (285 g) blanched
    almonds, lightly toasted*
1 pound (455 g) powdered sugar
*4 ounces (115 g) cocoa butter,
    melted*
*1 pound, 4 ounces (570 g)
    dark chocolate, melted*

Gianduja is a creamy chocolate confection flavored with roasted nut paste. While actually a candy, Gianduja is also used a great deal in the pastry shop as a flavoring, in fillings, and for decorations. It is quite easy to make but most professionals today purchase it from a supplier.

1. Lightly toast the hazelnuts and rub them between your hands or against a large-mesh drum sieve to remove the skins. Process the hazelnuts, almonds, and sugar in a high-speed food processor, continuing to grind the mixture until the oil begins to separate from the nuts and a thick paste is formed. If the mixture turns into a powder instead of a paste, just proceed with the recipe; the Gianduja will not be as smooth, but it will still be quite usable.

2. Combine the cocoa butter and chocolate. Add the nut mixture and stir until you have obtained a smooth mass. Place in a covered container. Store and reheat as you would chocolate. Gianduja will keep fresh for up to two months.

Gianduja Bites

100 candies

*1 pound (455 g) Gianduja,
    melted (this page)*
*12 ounces (340 g) milk
    chocolate, melted*
*6 ounces (170 g) sliced almonds,
    lightly toasted*
*100 blanched whole almonds,
    lightly toasted*
milk chocolate, tempered

1. Combine the Gianduja, melted milk chocolate, and sliced almonds. Pour into a 9-inch (22.5-cm) ring placed on a sheet pan or cardboard lined with baking paper. Allow to set.

2. Cut out rounds using a 1-inch (2.5-cm) plain candy or cookie cutter. Knead the scraps together, form, cut, and repeat until you have cut all of the filling. Fasten a whole almond to the top of each candy using a small drop of chocolate.

3. Dip the candies in the tempered chocolate using a three-pronged dipping fork.

Mimosa

60 candies

6 ounces (170 g) granulated sugar
¾ cup (180 ml) heavy cream, hot
1 pound, 4 ounces (570 g) milk
   chocolate, melted
milk chocolate, tempered
dark chocolate, tempered
candied violets

1. Caramelize the sugar in a heavy saucepan to a light golden color (see page 488). Quickly add the ¾ cup (180 ml) hot cream, reduce the heat, and cook, stirring out any lumps that have formed.

2. When smooth, remove from the heat and stir in the melted milk chocolate. If you overcaramelize the sugar, the mixture will separate. To bring it back together, add 1 tablespoon (15 ml) heavy cream. Return to the heat and stir until cream is mixed in and the mixture is smooth.

3. Pour the mixture into a 9-inch (22.5-cm) ring placed on a sheet pan lined with baking paper. Let set. Cut out ovals using a 1¼-inch (3.1-cm) oval cookie cutter. Knead the scraps of filling together, form, cut, and repeat until all of the filling is used.

4. Brush the top of the candies with a thin layer of tempered milk chocolate (to prevent them from sticking to the dipping fork).

5. Place the candies, chocolate-side down, on a two-pronged dipping fork and dip into tempered dark chocolate. Place them on sheet pans lined with baking paper, turning them over as you remove them from the fork to mark the tops (see note). Place a small piece of candied violet (about the size of a grain of rice) in the center before the chocolate hardens.

NOTE: Tempered chocolate is thick enough that the marks left by the dipping fork when the candy is inverted onto the baking paper will remain. If baker's chocolate is used, slide the candy off the fork instead, and wait until the chocolate starts to thicken (about 30 seconds if the chocolate is at the proper temperature). Then make two lines crosswise in the center of the candy by placing the dipping fork into the chocolate and pulling straight up.

Nougat Montélimar

80 candies

powdered sugar
5 ounces (140 g) blanched whole
   almonds, lightly toasted
5 ounces (140 g) whole toasted
   hazelnuts, skins removed
3 ounces (85 g) pistachios, skins
   removed, lightly dried
5 ounces (140 g) candied red
   cherries, coarsely chopped

1. Dust a small area of a marble slab or table with powdered sugar.

2. Combine the nuts and cherries. Reserve in a warm place, such as covered in a very low oven.

3. Warm the egg whites and honey in a large bowl placed over hot water to 120°F (49°C). Remove from heat and whip to soft peaks. Reserve.

4. Take the usual precautions for sugar boiling (see page 00) and boil the sugar, glucose or corn syrup, and water to 295°F (146°C). Immediately pour the hot syrup into the egg white mixture in a slow steady stream, while stirring constantly with a whisk. Return the mixture to the saucepan and continue to cook for about 10 minutes longer, stirring rapidly, over medium heat.

4 egg whites
¾ cup (180 ml) honey
12 ounces (340 g) granulated sugar
12 ounces (340 g) glucose or light corn syrup
½ cup (120 ml) water
melted cocoa butter
dark chocolate, tempered

Test to see if it is done by dropping a small piece in cold water: It should be quite firm.

5. Stir in the reserved (warm) nuts and cherries. Pour the nougat mixture on top of the prepared marble surface. Roll and form into a ¾-inch (2-cm) thick rectangle using a rolling pin dusted lightly with powdered sugar. Let cool partially.

6. Brush away the excess powdered sugar from the top and bottom of the nougat. Cut into strips 1¼ inches (3.1 cm) wide, then cut each strip into slices ⅜ inch (9 mm) thick (use a serrated knife with a sawing motion if the nougat sticks to the chef's knife).

7. Brush one cut side of each piece with a thin film of hot cocoa butter. Use a three-pronged dipping fork to dip the bottom and sides into melted dark chocolate, leaving the cocoa butter side exposed.

Orange Moons
65 candies

grated zest of 2 small oranges
6 ounces (170 g) softened butter
6 ounces (170 g) smooth Fondant (page 521)
2 tablespoons (30 ml) orange liqueur
1 pound (455 g) dark chocolate, tempered
milk chocolate, tempered
dark chocolate, tempered

1. Mix the orange zest into the butter and fondant and cream together well. Stir in the orange liqueur. Gradually mix in 1 pound (455 g) tempered dark chocolate (see note). Wait until the filling starts to thicken, then pour into a 9-inch (22.5-cm) ring set on a sheet pan or cardboard lined with baking paper. Allow the filling to set up.

2. Cut out 1½-inch (3.7-cm) rounds using a plain cookie cutter. Roll the scraps between sheets of baking paper, and continue to cut rounds until all the filling is used. Cut the rounds in half.

3. Dip each candy into tempered milk chocolate using a three-pronged dipping fork. Place on sheet pans lined with baking paper, turning the candies over as you remove them from the fork to mark the tops. When the coating is set, decorate the rounded edge by piping a design with dark chocolate.

NOTE: Generally chocolate does not need to be tempered when it is added to a filling. In this recipe, it helps harden the interior, but it is not absolutely necessary.

Pistachio Slices

80 candies

10 ounces (285 g) Praline Paste
  (page 7)
4 ounces (115 g) melted
  cocoa butter
4 ounces (115 g) melted
  milk chocolate
4 ounces (115 g) melted
  dark chocolate
4 ounces (115 g) blanched
  pistachios, skins removed
  and chopped fine
milk chocolate, tempered
dark chocolate, tempered

1. Combine the praline paste, cocoa butter, melted chocolate, and pistachios.

2. Adjust ½-inch (1.2-cm) thick metal bars to form an 8- × 7½-inch (20- × 18.7-cm) rectangle, or cut and tape heavy cardboard to size. Place the form on a paper-lined sheet pan or cardboard. Pour in the chocolate mixture and allow to set. You may want to help it along by placing it in the refrigerator briefly. Cut crosswise into five 1½- × 8-inch (3.7- × 20-cm) strips.

3. Brush a thin layer of tempered milk chocolate over the strips, and allow it to set. Place the strips, chocolate-side down, on a wire rack, positioning them so that the wires run at a 90° angle to the strips so that it will be easier to remove them later. Spread a thin layer of tempered milk chocolate on the top and sides with a spatula. Immediately transfer the strips to a sheet pan or cardboard lined with baking paper. Streak thin lines of tempered dark chocolate (the short way) across the strips. Let the chocolate set, then cut each strip crosswise into sixteen ½-inch (1.2-cm) wide slices.

Dark Truffles

65 candies

1 cup (240 ml) heavy cream
½ teaspoon (2.5 ml) vanilla
  extract
1 pound, 2 ounces (510 g)
  dark chocolate, chopped
3 ounces (85 g) softened butter
powdered sugar
dark chocolate, tempered

1. Heat the cream and vanilla to the boiling point. Remove from the heat and add the chopped chocolate, stirring until it is completely melted. Cool the mixture to approximately 86°F (30°C), then stir in the butter.

2. Wait until the filling starts to thicken, then transfer it to a pastry bag with a no. 6 (12-mm) plain tip. Pipe out in small mounds the size of cherries, or a little less than ½ ounce (15 g) each, on sheet pans lined with baking paper. Refrigerate for a few minutes to set.

3. Roll the centers into round balls between your hands, using powdered sugar to keep them from sticking. Let them firm up again, then precoat by rolling on a coat of melted chocolate with your hands. When the coating has hardened and the interiors have reached the proper temperature, dip them into melted dark chocolate using a round dipping fork. As they are dipped, transfer to a fine wire rack and roll to produce the typical uneven (spiked) surface.

Light Truffles

68 candies

1 cup (240 ml) heavy cream
½ teaspoon (2.5 ml) vanilla
   extract
1 pound, 5 ounces (595 g)
   milk chocolate, chopped
3 ounces (85 g) softened butter
powdered sugar
milk chocolate, tempered

Follow the instructions for Dark Truffles (preceding recipe).

White Truffles

75 candies

7 ounces (210 ml) heavy cream
1 pound, 2 ounces (510 g)
   white chocolate, chopped
3 ounces (85 g) Praline Paste
   (page 7)
3 ounces (85 g) softened butter
3 ounces (85 g) melted cocoa butter
powdered sugar
white chocolate, tempered

1. Heat the cream to the boiling point. Remove from the heat and stir in the chopped chocolate. Keep stirring until it has completely melted. Set aside to cool.

2. Combine the praline paste and butter, and beat to a creamy consistency. Stir into the chocolate mixture. Mix in the cocoa butter. Continue with steps 2 and 3 as directed for Dark Truffles (see page 464), precoating and covering the candies with white chocolate.

NOTE: If time does not permit making all three fillings for the truffles, make one kind and divide the filling into three parts. Roll and coat each with the various types of chocolate, and you will still have a nice assortment of truffles, in only half the time.

SEVENTEEN

Sugar Work

Boiled Sugar
  Boiled Sugar Basic Recipe
  Boiled Sugar Method I
  Boiled Sugar Method II
  Using Colors in Sugar Work
  Pulled and Blown Sugar
  Casting with Sugar
Caramelized Sugar
  Caramelized Sugar,
    Dry Method
  Caramelized Sugar
    with Water

Caramelized Almonds,
  Hazelnuts, Walnuts,
  and Pecans
Glazed Fruit
Gum Paste with Gum
  Tragacanth
Nougat
Pastillage
Rock Sugar
Spun Sugar

*S*ugar is a truly amazing commodity, and one that is indispensable to the baker. Part of the carbohydrate food group, sugar is the
product of an extensive refining process that begins with sugar
cane or sugar beets. Although these two plants are totally different
in their botanical composition and are cultivated on opposite
sides of the globe, you cannot identify by taste alone whether
the sugar you use to sweeten your coffee came from sugar cane
or sugar beets.

The word *sugar* is most commonly used to
refer to granulated table sugar. However,
many other types of sugar, with different
chemical structures, are used in the pastry
shop (see pages 593–595). Sugar is divided
into two basic groups: double-sugars, called
disaccharides, which include sucrose (granulated
sugar), maltose (known as malt sugar), and lactose
(the sugar found in milk); and single-sugars, called
monosaccharides, which include glucose and
fructose (both are forms of sugar found in
fruits, flowers, and honey). These different
types of sugar vary a great deal in their
sweetness. Lactose is less sweet than sucrose,
and fructose is sweeter than both lactose and
sucrose.

Sugar production has a long and interesting
history. Europeans first tasted sugar at the time
of the Crusades, but it had already existed in
tropical parts of the world for many thousands
of years. Presumably, sugar cane originated in
the islands of the South Pacific, spread west to

India and Persia (Iran), then eastward to what would later be known as America. Over time the taste of "red honey," as sugar was once called, improved with better refining techniques. However, this partially purified sugar still had a bitter aftertaste, and it was very expensive compared to honey, which had a better flavor. Sugar, therefore, was common more as a status symbol than as a sweetener. Nevertheless, by the time Columbus came to America (1492), sugar had become a major trade commodity. Europe was importing several tons annually, and a person with a large chunk of sugar (a sugarloaf) in their kitchen was considered very well-to-do. It was not until long after the Thirty Years' War (1618–1648) that sugar became generally available (at a lower price) because of improved cultivation techniques. This was when the confectioners', or "sugarbaker" (as it was appropriately called at that time), craft came into being. Since the majority of the sugar cane was still grown far away and had to be transported, availability and price continued to be dependent on world conditions. Unsuccessful attempts were made to cultivate sugar cane on the European continent until, in the mid-1700s, a German pharmacist discovered a way to boil the sap from a particular variety of beet that rendered a coarse grain with the look and taste of cane sugar. With this, the sugar beet industry was born, which, today, is responsible for almost half of the world's sugar production.

By looking at the ingredients listed in most pastry recipes, it becomes clear that a pastry chef would find it almost impossible to produce the majority of the traditional bakery products (keeping the desired flavor and appearance), without using some type of sugar. In addition to providing a sweet flavor, sugar acts as an emulsifying (creaming) agent when mixed with fat; becomes a foaming agent when mixed with eggs; weakens gluten structure of flour, contributing to a tender and fine-textured product; provides food for the developing yeast; caramelizes when heated to give an appetizing color and crust; and last, by retaining moisture, increases the shelf life of baked goods.

This chapter explains the artistic side of using sugar. Sugar can be boiled into a thick syrup and turned into a variety of shapes by casting, blowing, or pulling. Or, with the addition of gum tragacanth or gelatin, sugar can be made into a paste to be rolled, formed, or molded in almost any way imaginable. Royal icing is made by mixing powdered sugar and egg whites and is used to garnish pastries and cakes; it too can be made into a showpiece. Sugar is also spun into delicate threads and used as a decoration.

To master all or even a few of the many techniques for using sugar decoratively takes many years of experience. But the good news is that time is really the only investment you will need to make as very little equipment is used in most sugar work, and sugar itself is very inexpensive.

Boiled Sugar

Boiled Sugar Basic Recipe

3 cups (720 ml) or 1½ pounds (680 g)

1 cup (240 ml) water
2 pounds, 8 ounces (1 kg, 135 g) AA confectioners' or granulated sugar
8 ounces (225 g) glucose or light corn syrup
food color, optional for some uses
8 drops Tartaric Acid Solution (page 596), optional for some uses
or
½ teaspoon (1 g) cream of tartar dissolved in 1 teaspoon (5 ml) water (see note 2)

This recipe is used for spun sugar, cast sugar, and pulled or blown sugar. Make sure that your sugar and tools are absolutely clean. Scoop the top layer of sugar to one side in the bin before taking out what you need. Try to use AA confectioners' sugar if possible. And never use the flour scoop when measuring the sugar!

1. Place the water and sugar in a sugar pan (see page 605) or a heavy saucepan. Stir the mixture gently over low heat until all of the sugar has dissolved and the syrup has started to boil. If any scum has accumulated on top from impurities in the sugar, remove them with a skimmer or small sieve so that they do not cause the sugar to crystallize later. Add the glucose or corn syrup, stirring until it is thoroughly mixed in. Do not stir any further.

2. Turn the heat to medium, place a lid on the pan, and let the sugar boil hard for a few minutes. The steam trapped inside the pan will wash down the sugar crystals that form on the sides of the pan at this stage. (Or you can wash down the sides using a clean brush dipped in water instead.) (See note 3.)

3. Place a sugar thermometer in the pan. When the temperature reaches 265°F (130°C), add color if used. Stop brushing and boil the sugar to 280°F (138°C), then add the tartaric acid solution or cream of tartar solution, if used. Continue to boil, watching the temperature constantly, until the desired temperature is reached according to the specific recipe.

4. Remove the pan from the heat and dip the bottom in cold water to stop the temperature from going any higher.

NOTE 1: It is a good idea, especially if you are boiling a large amount of sugar, to remove the pan from the heat a few degrees before the specified temperature, watch the mercury rise off the heat, then plunge the pan into cold water.

NOTE 2: Be precise when measuring the acid. Using too much will make the finished sugar soft and difficult to work with.

NOTE 3: If you use this recipe frequently, you can make a larger batch. Cook the sugar through step 2, then store and finish cooking in smaller portions as needed.

Boiled Sugar Method I

These instructions are used for pulled and blown sugar.

1. Following the recipe and directions in the Boiled Sugar Basic Recipe, boil the syrup to 297°F (148°C). Quickly plunge the bottom of the pan into cold water to stop the cooking process. Let stand for about 10 seconds, then remove the pan from the water and wipe off the bottom with a damp cloth. Set the sugar aside a few seconds longer to allow most of the bubbles to subside. Remove the sugar thermometer and pour the syrup in a steady stream onto an oiled marble slab or table, pouring it into a round puddle (if you do not plan to use all of the sugar right away, see note).

2. As soon as the sugar has formed a skin, slide an oiled metal spatula under the edge of the sugar puddle and fold it in toward the center. Repeat, moving evenly around the circle until the sugar no longer runs and has cooled to the point that it can be pulled in your hands. Start to aerate the sugar as described in the recipe for Pulled and Blown Sugar, pages 473–474.

NOTE: Pour the extra sugar into a rectangular shape on the oiled marble. When a skin has formed on the top, use a metal scraper to mark the sugar into appropriate sized pieces. Let it solidify and cool completely. Break it into sections at the markings, then store the pieces in an airtight container with a small amount of Humisorb or silica gel to absorb any moisture. (Humisorb is a clay dessicant—a moisture-absorbing agent. Humisorb has no odor or taste, is nontoxic, and is less expensive than silica gel dessicants.) The sugar can be stored this way for up to 4 weeks.

To reheat the stored sugar, place it on the working frame under heat lamps. Depending on the amount of sugar and the number of heat lamps, it can take 5 to 25 minutes for the sugar to become soft enough to work with. Keep turning the sugar every few minutes to assure even heat distribution and prevent crystallization from overheating.

Boiled Sugar Method II

6 cups (1 1, 440 ml) or 3 pounds (1kg, 365 g) boiled sugar

2 pounds (910 g) AA confectioners' or granulated sugar

This recipe is also used for pulled and blown sugar. With this recipe the cooked sugar can be warmed and softened in a microwave.

1. Combine the sugar, corn syrup, and glucose in a sugar pan (see page 605) or heavy saucepan. Stir constantly over low heat until the mixture comes to a boil. Add the tartaric acid solution and continue boiling over medium heat. When the temperature reaches 265°F (130°C) add color, if used. Boil to 305°F (152°C). Immediately plunge the bottom of the pan into cold water for

3½ cups (840 ml) light corn syrup
10 ounces (285 g) glucose
> *or*

¾ cup (180 ml) corn syrup
12 drops Tartaric Acid Solution
> *(page 596)*
> *or*

½ teaspoon (1 g) cream of tartar
> *dissolved in 1 teaspoon (5 ml)*
> *water (see note 2)*

about 10 seconds to stop the cooking process. Remove the pan from the water and wipe off the bottom with a damp towel, wait a few seconds longer, then pour the sugar in a puddle on an oiled marble slab or table.

2. As soon as the sugar has formed a skin, slide an oiled metal spatula under the edge of the sugar puddle and fold it in toward the center. Repeat, moving evenly around the circle until the sugar no longer runs and has cooled to the point that it can be pulled in your hands. Start to aerate the sugar as described in the recipe for Pulled and Blown Sugar, pages 473–474.

If the sugar is to be stored, pour it directly into three or four microwavable plastic containers at the end of step 1 (if you are not sure they can stand up to the heat, test the containers first). When the sugar is completely cold, cover and store until needed. To use the sugar, reheat it in a microwave just long enough so the sugar can be removed from the container. It does not have to be totally liquid; do not boil it. Pour the sugar out onto the oiled marble slab or table. To ensure that the sugar cools evenly, use a lightly oiled metal scraper and fold the outside of the puddle in toward the middle continuously until the sugar has cooled to the point where it no longer runs. Start to aerate the sugar as described in the recipe for Pulled and Blown Sugar (pages 473–474) as soon as you can pick it up.

NOTE 1: If any sugar crystals form on the sides of the pan during the boiling period, they must be washed down as described in the preceding recipe.

NOTE 2: Be precise when measuring the acid. Using too much will make the finished sugar soft and difficult to work with.

Using Colors in Sugar Work

If the entire batch of sugar is to be colored (this applies to spun, cast, pulled, or blown sugar), add regular water-soluble food coloring when the sugar reaches 265°F (130°C), blending the three primary colors of red, yellow, and blue as desired to make various shades. It is not possible to make black; the best you can do is a heavily concentrated chocolate-brown. Milk-white is obtained by adding liquid whitener (a food coloring containing glycerin and titanium dioxide) at the rate of ½ teaspoon (2.5 ml) for the basic sugar recipe, or 1 teaspoon (5 ml) for Boiled Sugar Method II. The whitener is added at the same temperature as any other color (265°F/130°C), but for the best milk-white effect, stop boiling the sugar at 295°F (146°C). If you are unable to find liquid whitener, you can make your own by mixing calcium carbonate (precipitated chalk; this can be ordered from a laboratory) with water. Stir 8 ounces (225 g) of chalk into ⅔ cup (160 ml) of water and mix into a smooth paste. Store in a sealed glass jar and use as needed. This paste is only about one-third as strong as the commercial whitener; you will need to add three times as much solution to obtain a proper milk-white color. The liquid whitener or precipitated chalk can also be added to any other color to turn it opaque; this is especially desirable with cast sugar. Keep in mind when designing your project that adding a whitener will make the shade lighter. When making pulled sugar it is not necessary to color the sugar white. As the sugar is pulled the air that is worked into it produces a pleasant, opaque white color.

Spraying Colors

A different method is used when casting small figures because it is not practical to split the sugar into different boils and color them separately. Besides being time-consuming, it is hard to boil a very small amount to a precise temperature. You have to remove the sugar thermometer from its protective casing and tilt the pan to make the solution deep enough to get a reading. It is easy to overheat the sugar, which can caramelize in an instant at temperatures above 310°F (155°C). Therefore, it makes sense to cast the whole figure in one base color (preferably white), then spray on the desired shades. The color is sprayed (blown) on using a clever little tool called a fixative syringe. You submerge one end in the color and put the other in your mouth, then spray by blowing air into the syringe. You can obtain different shades by spraying at an angle to the flat surface because more color will adhere to the area closest to the sprayer. You can also mask part of the surface with paper to achieve a contrasting effect.

Make your own colors for spraying by mixing a small amount of water-soluble food coloring with marzipan lacquer (see note) in a small stainless steel cup. Try to make up only the amount you need at that time. Spray the color onto a paper first to check the effect and strength of the color before applying it to the cast sugar. Naturally, the closer you hold the sprayer to the sugar and the more forcefully you blow, the more concentrated the color will be. When you are finished, clean the container and the syringe with denatured alcohol. You can also apply colors in this manner to blown sugar pieces.

NOTE: The marzipan lacquer provides a protective coating along with the color. If that is not necessary, or you do not want to use the expensive lacquer, mix the colors with any clear spirit, such as vodka.

Pulled and Blown Sugar

This type of sugar work requires you to have an artist's hand and many years of practice before you can produce anything close to what you see in some of the specialty sugar books. Unfortunately, pulling and blowing sugar are becoming more and more obsolete today for these reasons. The problem is, of course, that learning to blow and pull sugar takes a large amount of time away from other chores and regular production work. You therefore must be interested enough in these types of sugar work to make it a hobby. The weather also plays an important role: If you live in a damp climate you will find it very difficult to work with sugar because the humidity accelerates crystallization. If you are a beginner, making a rose from pulled sugar, or blowing a small piece of fruit or even a vase, would be a realistic starting point once you have a basic knowledge of sugar work.

Both pulled and blown sugar can be made using the instructions for Boiled Sugar Method I (see page 470) or Boiled Sugar Method II (see pages 470–471). The procedure for cooking, aerating, and forming (pulling and blowing) the sugar is the same for both. Using Method II sugar may give you an edge because the sugar is less likely to crystallize, plus you can use the microwave to soften the sugar as often as needed while you are working.

After the sugar is cooked, aerate it by drawing it out evenly using your hands, folding it up, and pulling it out again as many times as necessary until enough air has been mixed in to give the sugar a silky sheen (Figures 17–1 and 17–2). To protect your hands from the heat if they are not calloused enough yet, use surgical gloves (if you have sweaty hands, you should also wear gloves at all times to protect the sugar). The sugar is now ready

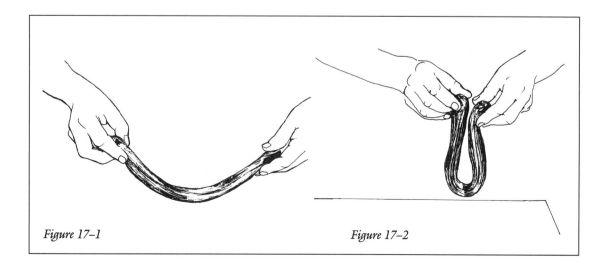

Figure 17–1

Figure 17–2

to use for either pulling or blowing, or it can also be stored in an airtight container at this stage for later use. Place a piece of Humisorb or silica gel in the bottom of the container to absorb moisture. Be careful not to work the sugar too long; if over-pulled it will crystallize and take on a dull, matte finish. This will also happen if the sugar is allowed to become too hard or cold while it is being pulled.

Pulling a Rose

Before you begin you will need a heat lamp or lamps, a workbox with a screen (see page 478), a pair of scissors, a Bunsen burner, a leaf mold, a hand-sprayer (called a fixative syringe), and pink and green pulled sugar.

1. Once the sugar has the proper consistency and shine, form it into a tight ball. Draw out a thin strip from the ball about 1 inch (2.5 cm) wide and 4 inches (10 cm) long. Cut this piece off with scissors.

2. Coil the strip into a small conical shape about 1 inch (2.5 cm) long to make the center of the rose. If the strip sets and becomes too firm to bend, warm it under the heat lamp until it is pliable. (You can also form the rose center using the technique for marzipan roses, page 542, Figure 18–41.)

3. Using the thumbs and forefingers of both hands, pull the top part of the sugar ball up into a thin ridge (Figure 17–3). Grasp the center of the ridge and draw the edge away to make a slightly elongated petal (Figure 17–4). Separate the petal from the sugar ball by pinching it off with your other hand. Quickly curl the top of the petal back as you would for marzipan roses (see Figure

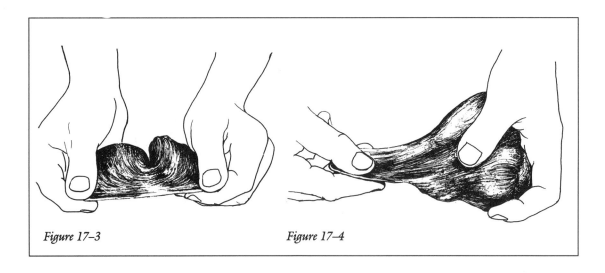

Figure 17–3   Figure 17–4

18–43, page 543), then attach it to the center of the rose immediately. Pull and shape two additional elongated petals of the same
size and attach them evenly around the center.

4. Make the remaining petals slightly larger and rounded,
folding the tops back a little more and forming them into a hollow
shape like a cupped hand. Attach them as you form them. Keep
the sugar warm under the heat lamp as you are working. If a thin
part of the surface of the sugar should harden, do not attempt to
mix it back into the remaining sugar without softening it first; the
hardened part will not melt, but break into small pieces, ruining
the appearance.

5. Make a rosebud using just the three elongated petals and the
center. Fasten the petals together in a close triangular shape
around the base, one inside the other. (See note.)

6. Pull small, pointed green leaves to the desired length using
the same technique as for the elongated petals. Bend the points
back, and attach the ends to the roses or buds. Make slightly larger
and wider leaves to go on the stem of the roses. Quickly and firmly
press them into the leaf mold to transfer the leaf pattern to the
sugar. Bend into a nicely curved shape (warm the sugar if necessary) and reserve to place around your rose display.

7. To make a stem for the rose, use a ridged wire (a coat hanger
works fine) cut to the desired size. Push the wire through the soft,
green sugar ball. The faster you push it through, the thinner the
coating of sugar will be. If you move too fast the sugar will simply
break, but after a few tries you will get just the right speed. Heat
the tip of the wire over the Bunsen burner, and push it into the
base of the rose. If you prefer not to have the wire inside (if you
are laying the rose on a cake or using it to garnish an individual
dessert serving) just pull out a thin rope of green sugar for the
stem. If you want to display the rose standing up, in a basket for
example, you must use the wire.

8. Curls or tendrils are easy to make, and are a very nice
complement to your rose display. To make them, lightly oil the
handle of a small wooden spoon or a ballpoint pen. Pull a thin
rope out of the green sugar ball and quickly wind it around the
spoon or pen like a telephone cord. Slide it off once it has
hardened.

9. Display your rose, or roses, with a few buds, leaves, and
tendrils on a small base cast in sugar, or within a frame made by
curling a thick rope of green sugar into a round disk.

10. To prevent the finished sugar pieces from deteriorating due
to moisture, keep them in an airtight container with some silica
gel or Humisorb, which absorbs the moisture in the air. The
pieces can also be sprayed with marzipan lacquer or, if they are to

be used for display purposes only, with a thin film of a fast-drying, clear shellac.

NOTE: Instead of attaching each petal to the center as you make it, you can make up all of the petals individually, then assemble the rose by heating the base of each hardened petal as you attach it. The drawback to this method is that you can no longer mold or shape the rose, as you can when the petals are attached while still soft.

Sugar Bow with Ribbons

one bow about 4 inches (10 cm) across with 6-inch (15-cm) long ribbons

Making a beautiful sugar bow to decorate a petits fours or candy tray, for example, or to use as part of a showpiece, can be done fairly quickly—especially if you already have some pieces of colored sugar left from previous sugar work. If so, follow the instructions for softening the sugar on page 470. If the sugar has already been aerated you will only need to pull it back and forth a few times to bring back its sheen. To make one bow with ribbons you need three or four pieces of colored sugar (one should be white) weighing about 12 ounces (340 g) each.

If you do not have any scrap sugar, make one recipe Boiled Sugar Method II (pages 470–471). After you add the tartaric acid continue boiling the sugar approximately 1 minute longer. Divide the syrup into three or four batches depending on the number of colors you want to use. Then, boil, color, and aerate each batch individually following the instructions. You should make at least three colors, one of them white.

1. Keep the colored sugar soft under a heat lamp. Pull out a rope of sugar about 4 inches (10 cm) long from each different color. The ropes should be approximately ¼ to ½ inch (6–12 mm) thick depending on how much of that particular color you want to use in your bow and ribbons. You can, of course, use the same color twice. Place the ropes next to one another (not stacked) in the desired pattern. The ropes should be warm enough to stick together. If necessary, leave them this way under the heat lamp until they are soft enough to stick, turning the ropes from time to time. Do not get any oil on the sugar ropes as this can prevent them from sticking together.

2. Once the ropes are attached side-by-side, take the whole strip out from under the lamp and let it cool for approximately 30 seconds, turning it over a few times; do not place it directly on a marble slab or marble table or it will cool too much.

3. Slowly and evenly pull the whole strip of sugar out lengthwise until it is about doubled in length.

4. Using an oiled pair of scissors cut the strip in half crosswise. Lay the two halves side-by-side under the heat lamp and leave

them until they stick together. Pull the strip out lengthwise a second time until doubled in length. You could stop at this point or you may repeat the cutting and pulling procedure one more time for a very elaborate ribbon, depending on how thin the sugar is at this point. If the strip is thinner and narrower than you would like, you are probably pulling too fast or working with sugar that is too soft (warm), or both.

5. To make the ribbons, start by pulling one end of the sugar out to make a thin strip approximately 1 inch (2.5 cm) wide and 12 inches (30 cm) long. (Don't just hold onto the end and pull it out to the final length all at once. To make the strip uniform in width and thickness you need to pull a few inches, then move your fingers back to where you started, pull a few inches further, start at the base again, and so on.)

6. Using oiled scissors trim away the very end of the strip, which is usually too thick and looks unattractive. Then cut off two 6-inch (15-cm) pieces, cutting them at an angle crosswise. Pleat the pieces slightly. Attach two narrow ends together to make an upside-down *V*. Set this piece aside.

7. To make the loops of the sugar bow you need thirteen pieces 4 inches (10 cm) long (it is a good idea to make a few extra to allow for breakage). Pull out one piece at a time from the thick piece of sugar, the same width and thickness as the ribbons. Continue to warm the sugar under the heat lamp as needed to keep the correct consistency. Cut off each piece as you pull it out and quickly form it into a smooth, curved loop by bending it in half over an oiled wooden dowel or other round object approximately ¾ inch (20 mm) thick; then pinch the flat ends together. Immediately pinch the attached flat edges in the opposite direction so that the bottom of the loop comes to a point and the sides of the loop pleat slightly. This will make it easier to fit the loops together when assembling the bow later. Warm the loop under the heat lamp while you are working so that it is soft enough to shape easily, but be sure that the sugar has cooled sufficiently to hold its shape before removing the loops from the dowel.

8. To assemble the bow, start by flattening a small disk of sugar approximately to the size of a nickel. Attach seven evenly spaced loops around the edge of the disk with the tips pointing in, first softening the tip of each loop until sticky by holding it over a Bunsen burner. You can also make the tip sticky by holding it right next to the heat lamp, but you risk deforming the thin loops. Attach a second layer of five loops in the same way, placing these overlapping the first set slightly, and attaching them closer to the center of the disk. Finish by attaching a single loop covering the center of the disk.

9. Attach the finished bow to the reserved ribbons by softening the sugar at the tip where the ribbons meet, then carefully setting the bow on top.

10. Spray the bow and ribbons with marzipan lacquer using a fixative syringe (do not forget to spray the bottom). Store in an airtight container with a piece of silica gel if desired for extra protection against moisture. If the sugar is completely sealed you should be able to use this mini-showpiece many times.

Sugar Workbox

1. Make a rectangle with the outside dimensions of 11½ × 16½ inches (28.7 × 41.2 cm) using 2½- to 3-inch × ½-inch (6.2- to 7.5-cm × 1.2-cm) strips of plywood or cut wood trim. (This size box will fit on a half sheet pan.)

2. Glue and screw the sides together, then sand the edges smooth. (It is bad enough you are going to get blisters on your fingers from the hot sugar; you don't need splinters too!)

3. Stretch a piece of nylon window screen tight across the top and staple it in place. The sugar should not actually be worked on the frame: The frame just supports the sugar while it is being softened or kept warm under the heat lamps.

NOTE: Use an old picture frame or a drawer of the appropriate size if you do not have time to build a frame.

Sugar Blowing

In addition to the tools needed for sugar pulling, you need a cooling fan, a small brush, and a one-way, hand-operated air pump with a wooden mouthpiece. If you do not have an air pump, you can blow the sugar by mouth, in much the same way that glass blowers produce their magic, using blow pipes with various openings. Sugar blowing was always done this way before the hand pump was developed some 60 years ago. Since sugar takes longer to cool than glass, and the blow pipes do not have a one-way valve to prevent the air from escaping, it is much easier to use the hand pump. The cooling time becomes a real issue when you blow larger pieces; using a more powerful fan can help.

1. Prepare the sugar as directed on page 473. Once it has been aerated and has developed the proper shine and temperature, cut off the amount you need with scissors (place the remainder under the lamps on the workbox).

2. Make an indentation in the cut surface with your finger, then securely attach the sugar around the wooden mouthpiece or blow pipe, leaving a small, natural air chamber from the indentation.

3. Pump the air in with one hand to expand the air chamber, while shaping the sugar with the other hand. If the ball of sugar has an uneven thickness, or is warmer on one side than the other,

the thinner and/or warmer side will expand faster. To control this, cool the warmer areas by covering them with your hand while you warm the cooler areas under the lamp.

4. Begin by making a sphere of the appropriate size. Gradually work the sphere away from the wooden tube to produce a small neck, which you will use later to separate the finished piece from the tube. For example, to make a pear, elongate the shape of the sphere, then warm the area close to the mouthpiece while stretching and bending it slightly to produce the curved neck of the pear. Start a vase the same way, but keep the elongated sphere straight, then warm the opposite end while pumping in air until it has expanded to the size you want. Flatten the bottom so the vase will stand straight.

5. Once the pieces are formed, cool them with a fan so they do not change shape. Preheat the neck later over a Bunsen burner and cut the mouthpiece away with scissors while the sugar is warm (smooth the cut so it will show as little as possible). Even the top off the vase by cutting it with a red-hot knife or wire.

6. Follow the directions for Using Colors in Sugar Work (see pages 471–472) to decorate the pieces. (To get the tiny spots that are typical on a pear, dip the top of the bristles of a fairly stiff brush in color, then bend them back to make the color fly off.)

7. Protect the finished pieces using the same methods described for pulled sugar. Blown pieces that are not too fragile can simply be painted rather than sprayed.

Casting with Sugar

For the average person casting is probably the easiest way of making spectacular showpieces with sugar, since it does not demand the years of practice and experience that pulled and blown sugar do. Casting sugar can be a relatively inexpensive occasional recreation, but you do need to have the basics down on how to boil and handle sugar. As in most artwork you need a good eye for color and proportions, you should be neat and precise, and yes, it does take a steady hand to pour the sugar, especially for the small and narrow shapes.

If you do not have much experience, start by casting small, simple figures such as the rooster, baker, or peasant girl (Figures 17–5, 17–6, and 17–7). Enlarge the templates to make the figures any size you like. The baker is designed to hold a tray in his hand as part of the display. You might want to make him 12 inches (30 cm) tall to hold a small tray with a few candies on it as a buffet showpiece, or as large as 3 feet (90 cm) tall to place in the shop window holding a large serving platter. When you cast the baker,

Figure 17–5

Figure 17–6

481

Figure 17–7

cast a small oval or circle of sugar in proportion to the size you make the figure, then attach it later as directed, placing it flat on his hand. This can be the actual tray for the small figure, or a real serving tray can be placed on top if you make the circle large enough to support it.

Since you will need so much sugar and must boil it in so many different batches (especially for large, complicated castings), it is a good idea to make a large quantity of basic sugar solution once you have made a reasonable calculation of how much you will need. It is better to make too much than not enough; leftover syrup can be stored in a sealed jar for many weeks.

1. Follow the recipe and instructions for Boiled Sugar Basic Recipe (see page 469), but omit the tartaric acid solution (see note 1, page 486). Let the sugar boil gently (brushing down the sides of the pan) for 1 minute after the glucose or corn syrup has been added to ensure that all of the sugar crystals have dissolved. Remove from the heat.

2. As you are ready to cast each section, in their various colors, measure off the amount of sugar needed, and continue boiling the smaller amount to the proper temperature. (When casting a small figure it is best to pour the various parts or sections in one color only, plain or white, and then apply the color with a brush or sprayer, since it is difficult to boil a small amount of sugar accurately).

You can make your own forms for casting using either metal strips (the kind that are used to secure crates and boxes) or plastilina, which is a sort of modeling clay. Or you can use both in combination. Metal strips are difficult and time-consuming to bend into small or intricate shapes, while plastilina can be rolled out to the required thickness and cut into any shape with a thin sharp knife or cookie cutter. Another way is to make a copy of your drawing, glue it to a piece of sturdy paper (a cake box works great) and cut out the shape with a razor blade or carpet knife. Transfer the rolled plastilina sheet to a cardboard, place the drawing on top, and cut it out, tracing around the shape. Then slide the cut piece back onto the oiled marble. The one drawback with this method is that you need a lot of plastilina, and you can only use the mold once. Just like the marble surface, any side of the plastilina that comes in contact with the sugar must be lightly greased with vegetable oil.

When making the mold using metal strips, place a piece of baking paper or other transparent paper on top of the drawing to keep it clean. Fasten the drawing to a sheet of cardboard. Form and solder the metal strips according to the directions on page 487. In making forms from either plastilina or metal strips, be sure you make them deep enough.

3. Lightly grease a marble slab or table with vegetable oil. Treat the inside of your individual forms or molds in the same way, and wipe off any excess with a cloth. Arrange the forms on the oiled marble. If any of them do not lay flush against the slab, weigh them down or the sugar will leak out. You can also place aluminum foil on top of any flat surface and arrange the forms, metal or plastilina, on this. Tape the corners down to secure the foil. The obvious advantage here is that you do not need a marble surface, and the cast piece can be easily moved when finished. The back of the cast sugar will also be free from oil since the foil does not need to be oiled, but will have an uneven surface. The foil is easily peeled off once the sugar has hardened.

4. Boil the measured amount of sugar to 256°F (130°C) and add color or whitening if using. Continue boiling until the sugar reaches 305°F (152°C). Immediately remove from the heat and plunge the bottom of the pan into cold water for a few seconds. Wipe the bottom of the pan dry.

5. As soon as bubbles stop appearing on the top, pour the sugar into the molds in a thin, steady stream (Figure 17–8). Vary the thickness of the sugar in proportion to the size of the piece. For a 12-inch (30-cm) figure pour the sugar ¼ inch (6 mm) thick; for a 3-foot (90-cm) figure cast the sugar ¾ inch (2 cm) thick.

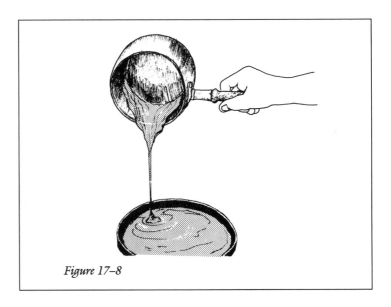

Figure 17–8

6. If you are making a mirror image (such as the chicken in Figure 17–5), wait a few seconds after the sugar is poured to allow the sugar closest to the form to harden a little. Tap the metal strip lightly with the back of a knife and remove the form. Invert the form and place it in another area on the marble. Then cast the chicken again (this time facing in the opposite direction). If the sugar in the pan starts to cool and thicken before you are finished, place it on the burner and swirl the pan to heat the sugar evenly, but do not stir. If any of the pieces are to be marked or outlined, for example lines in the baker's hat in Figure 17–6, do it as soon as a skin has formed on the top.

7. Loosen the cast pieces from the marble by carefully sliding the blade of a metal spatula underneath before they harden completely. Remember that disturbing them too soon will leave unsightly wrinkles.

8. When joining pieces by casting one next to the other, as in the neck and tail of the rooster, first burn off the connecting edges with a red-hot knife to remove any oil that would prevent the pieces from adhering. Heat an old knife over a Bunsen burner until it gets red-hot. Quickly wipe the knife on a wet towel to cool it slightly, then move the knife back and forth over the adhesion points. The larger that you make the figures, the more important this procedure is. (Make sure the knife is hot enough to melt the sugar, but not so hot that the sugar caramelizes, or it will leave ugly stains.)

9. When casting a small shape inside a large piece, cast the larger piece first so the heat will not soften and disturb the shape of the smaller one.

10. Before assembling the figures, first spray any pieces that are to be colored (see Using Colors in Sugar Work, pages 471–472). If individual pieces are to be assembled on top of each other, burn off the edges that are "glued." This can give the baker, for example, a more three-dimensional look: The baker's head, sleeve, and shoes (but not his hand) can be cast separately and pasted on top of the existing figure (you would still cast the entire figure first), to make it look as though his hand is coming out of his jacket.

11. To paste pieces together, reheat some of the sugar left over from casting. Let it start to thicken slightly before using, do not use too much, and do not use the sugar too hot or you can soften the pieces you are gluing. Always assemble the pieces lying flat on the table to ensure that the parts stay in the position you want until the sugar is cold.

12. Cast a wedge-shaped back support, as well as a base, for any figure that is to be displayed vertically. Make these pieces in proportion to the size of the figure and in the same thickness.

Shape the back support so that one long side of the wedge (the one attached to the figure) and the bottom are at right angles so that the figure stands straight. Once the base and back support have been cast and allowed to harden, carefully move the figure to the edge of the table and burn the bottom edge, where the base will go.

13. Carefully raise the figure (you now need an assistant to finish the assembly) and burn the back where the back support will attach. Attach the base with the "sugar glue," be sure the figure is standing straight, then glue on the back support using slightly thicker sugar; hold the figure until the back support is set. Coat the figure with marzipan lacquer or spray it with a fast-drying, clear lacquer as a protection against moisture and fingerprints.

Depending on the shape of the figure, you may need to attach a second support horizontally or vertically. The baker's outstretched hand and arm, for example, would slowly collapse if not supported. The second support should angle down to the main vertical support. This is especially necessary since the arm and torso are usually cast in white (the color of a chef's jacket), and white sugar is softer.

If you are not using white or another opaque color and you are not spraying on the colors after casting, the colored sugar will be transparent. This does not look good, especially if you are supporting the figure from the back, or if the figure can be seen from all sides. To remedy this, first cast a thin layer of the whole figure in milk white. Then, using that as the base, section off and cast the various colors on top of the white. The back of the figure will be clean, look good, and be well-supported (although it will look a little too thick from the side).

NOTE 1: Since a cast sugar figure must be solid enough to be able to support itself to some degree, and since tartaric acid (in addition to acting to inhibit crystallization) gives the sugar flexibility, leave it out when cooking sugar for casting to ensure maximum rigidity of the cast pieces.

NOTE 2: It is inevitable that you will break a piece of cast sugar, assembled or unassembled, now and then. The most precarious time is, of course, when you are attaching the base or raising the figure, but it also happens when you leave the piece too long on the table before loosening it. You can repair it quite easily by heating the two edges together over a Bunsen burner until the sugar is liquid and pressing them together again. Hold the pieces until set or, if you can, lay them flat. Put a little vegetable oil on your finger and smooth the cut while the sugar is still slightly soft. If it will not show from the front, fasten a piece of cast sugar on the back to act as a splint for the fracture and to give it added support.

Soldering the Metal Forms

Working with metal strips, also known as band iron, takes a little extra effort because they have to be soldered after they are shaped. But they can be used indefinitely, and one form can be used in either direction to make a mirror image. If you are making a butterfly, for example, you would only have to make one wing form. Metal strips may be a little hard to find because plastic strips are used more often today to secure boxes for shipping. If the local hardware store does not have any, you may find used strips at the lumberyard. If you have a choice, ½-inch-wide (1.2-cm) strips are the easiest to work with. You also need soldering wire, flux, some cold water, a blow torch (or Bunsen burner), flat- and round-nosed pliers, a metal cutter, and a metal file.

1. Form the strip, using your hands and the pliers, until it matches the drawing. Overlap the ends by ½ inch (1.2 cm).

2. Smear flux at the solder points or dip them into solder fluid.

3. Cut off a small piece of soldering wire, fold it in half, and place it between the two ends to be joined, holding them in place with the pliers. Make certain that the pieces line up exactly, or the form will not lay flat later on.

4. Heat the ends from both sides with the blowtorch until the solder melts. Dip into cold water and file off any excess solder to even the joint.

Caramelized Sugar

Sugar turns from golden to light brown in color and starts to caramelize when the temperature reaches 320°F (160°C). There are two ways of bringing the sugar to this temperature: the dry method or with water. Caramelizing sugar dry takes a little less time, but requires more attention because the sugar must be stirred constantly to prevent it from burning. If you use the dry method, do not use a skillet or pan that is any larger than necessary or you will have a larger area to cover when stirring and you may not be able to keep the sugar from getting too dark. In the second method, adding a small amount of water to the sugar means that the caramel does not need to be stirred during the entire cooking process, but it takes longer to caramelize because you must wait for the water to evaporate. Either way is much faster and easier if you use a sugar pan: an unlined copper pan made especially for cooking sugar. The acidity of the copper reacts with the sugar in such a way that some of the sugar breaks down into invert sugar, which is more resistant to crystallization. Invert sugar is a mixture of equal parts dextrose and levulose.

Caramelized Sugar, Dry Method

2¼ cups (540 ml) syrup

2 pounds (910 g) granulated sugar
1 teaspoon (5 ml) lemon juice

1. Place the sugar and lemon juice in a copper pan. Heat, stirring constantly, until the sugar starts to melt, lower the temperature, and stir until the sugar is completely melted.

2. Cook until the sugar has caramelized to the desired color.

3. Remove from the heat and immediately place the bottom of the pan in cold water to stop the cooking process. Use the caramel immediately. If you need to reheat the caramel, swirl, do not stir the saucepan to move the sugar around and prevent burning.

NOTE: If you are caramelizing more than 2 pounds (910 g) of sugar at one time, do not add all of it at the beginning. Instead, start with about one-quarter of the total amount. Once it has melted, but not changed color, add one-quarter more and repeat, adding the remaining sugar in the same way. This way you do not have to stir the entire amount from the start. If you still have lumps of unmelted sugar when the rest of the sugar is caramelized, the temperature was too high and/or the sugar was not stirred properly after it started to melt.

Caramelized Sugar with Water

2¼ cups (540 ml) syrup

2 pounds (910 g) granulated sugar
1 teaspoon (5 ml) lemon juice
1 cup (240 ml) water

1. Place the sugar, lemon juice, and water in a copper pan. Stir to combine.

2. Bring to a boil, then lower the heat to medium to assure that the liquid will not boil too hard. Do not stir once the sugar starts boiling. Instead, brush down the sides of the pan with water every 3 or 4 minutes until the sugar reaches 280°F (138°C), the crack stage. Keep boiling until the sugar has caramelized to the desired color.

3. Quickly remove the pan from the heat and place the bottom of the pan in cold water to stop the cooking process. Use immediately.

Caramelized Almonds, Hazelnuts, Walnuts, and Pecans

14 ounces (400 g) nuts

7 ounces (200 g) nuts
vegetable oil
6 ounces (170 g) granulated sugar
½ teaspoon (2.5 ml) lemon juice
2 tablespoons (30 ml) water
½ ounce (15 g) butter

1. Remove the skin from the nuts (see note). If using almonds, roast them to a golden brown color at 350°F (175°C) before caramelizing.

2. Lightly oil a marble slab or a sheet pan.

3. Place the sugar, lemon juice, and water in a copper or heavy-bottomed saucepan. Cook over medium heat until the temperature reaches 240°F (115°C) on a sugar thermometer. Brush down the sides of the pan with water a few times during the cooking process.

4. Remove the pan from the heat and immediately add the nuts. Stir gently with a wooden spoon or spatula.

5. Return the mixture to medium heat and reheat, continuing to stir gently. The mixture will appear crystallized at this point but will start to melt as it is heated. Keep stirring until the sugar starts to caramelize and turn golden brown, 320°F (160°C).

6. Remove the pan from the heat, add the butter, and stir until the butter is completely incorporated.

7. Pour the mixture onto the oiled marble or sheet pan. Use two forks to turn the nuts over, making sure the sugar coats all of the nuts and separating the nuts so that none of the sides touch. As the caramel starts to cool down you can do this more effectively with your fingertips. Store caramelized nuts in airtight containers.

If the nuts are to be crushed after they have been caramelized, there is no need to separate them individually. Instead let the mixture cool completely on the marble, then crush it to the desired coarseness. For a denser caramelization, crush the nuts first, caramelize, cool, and crush to desired size.

NOTE: To remove the skin from almonds, pour boiling water over them, cover, and let them soak for 5 minutes. Drain the water and immediately pinch the nuts between your fingers to remove the skin. Remove the skin on hazelnuts by placing the nuts in a 400°F (205°C) oven for about 10 minutes, or until they start to turn golden. Let cool, then rub them between your hands or a towel to remove the skin. Do not try to remove all of the skin on all of the hazelnuts; it simply will not come off. Instead, pick out the nice-looking ones for decorating and use the others where it does not matter as much. Walnuts and pecans are always caramelized (and otherwise used) with the skin on.

Glazed Fruit

vegetable oil
fresh or dried fruit or nuts
Boiled Sugar Basic Recipe
  (page 469)
Marzipan (page 531)
Simple Syrup (page 7)

Small, fresh, stemmed strawberries, glazed with sugar boiled to the hard crack stage, can be used as a garnish for a strawberry soufflé, as part of a petits fours tray after the meal, or on top of a Valentine dessert. They are elegant and look magnificent. Orange, apple, and pear wedges can be glazed and used to enhance the presentation of desserts made with those fruits, such as a pear or apple charlotte, or a Grand Marnier soufflé.

Because the juices of fresh fruits will eventually penetrate and melt the sugar shell, glazed fruits should be prepared as close as possible to serving time. Glazed dried fruits, on the other hand, hold up much better and can be kept in an airtight container for a few days. They are generally used as a colorful addition to a candy or petits fours tray, rather than to garnish a dessert.

1. Lightly oil a baking sheet to hold the glazed fruits.

2. Prepare the fruits or candies to be dipped in the following ways:

- Small strawberries: Leave whole, stem on if possible.
- Oranges: Pull the skin off the oranges by hand; do not peel with a knife. Pull the segments apart. Remove as much white pith as possible.
- Apples or pears: Leave the skin on for color, cut into thin wedges, and coat with lemon juice to prevent oxidation.
- Filled walnuts: Flavor a small amount of white marzipan with rum; roll into olive-shaped pieces; fasten a walnut half on each side using simple syrup.
- Filled dates, dried figs, or prunes: Cut open and remove the pits from medium-sized dates or prunes. Cut a small slit in dried figs. Color a small amount of marzipan light pink, and fill the fruit so that some of the marzipan can be seen along the cut. Form the fruit so the pieces are uniform in shape.
- Filled apricots: Flavor a small amount of white marzipan with pistachio extract. If desired, add a touch of green food coloring to tint the marzipan pale green. Sandwich the marzipan between two apricot halves. Shape them like the dates.

3. Insert a toothpick into each of the fruit pieces or candies (dip stemmed strawberries by holding onto the stem).

4. To glaze 25 pieces, make one recipe of Boiled Sugar Basic Recipe (you will have some sugar left over) and boil the syrup to 310°F (155°C). Immediately place the bottom of the saucepan in cold water for about 10 seconds to stop the cooking process. Remove the pan from the water and wait until most of the bubbles have disappeared before dipping the fruit.

5. Quickly dip each fruit or candy into the syrup, holding it by the toothpick, then gently move it up and down over the syrup to remove excess sugar. Lightly scrape the bottom against the side of the pan to remove the last drips. Place onto the oiled sheet pan. Reheat the syrup as it starts to cool and thicken. It is essential that the fruits have only a very thin shell of caramel or they will be unattractive and impossible to eat. Let cool completely, then remove the toothpicks by holding the candy in place with a fork as you pull them out. Avoid touching the glazed candies with your fingers.

Gum Paste with Gum Tragacanth

3 pounds (1 kg, 365 g) gum paste

*2 pounds, 10 ounces (1 kg, 195 g)
    powdered sugar, approximately*
*2 tablespoons (18 g) gum
    tragacanth powder*
4 ounces (120 ml) water
*2 tablespoons (30 ml) or
    light corn syrup*
1 tablespoon (15 ml) lemon juice
*1 ounce (30 g) white vegetable
    shortening*

Using gum tragacanth in gum paste, rather than gelatin, produces a paste that is more pliable and more convenient to work with since it does not dry out as quickly. This is also due in part to the addition of shortening, which acts as a moistening agent. Gum paste with gum tragacanth is ideal for small, time-consuming projects—for example, sculpting the head or arms of a figure, or when rolling the paste and marking an intricate design such as bricks in a castle wall—as the paste allows you more working time. The working time can be extended even further, up to 2 hours, by rubbing a thin film of white vegetable shortening over the surface as soon as the paste has been rolled, cut, or formed into the desired shape. This will delay the formation of a crust while you finish your design, and the shortening will slowly be absorbed by the paste and will not be visible in the finished piece. The drawback with using shortening in the paste and/or rubbed on the surface is that not only does the paste dry out more slowly while you are working, your finished showpiece will take up to a week longer to dry completely than if you use a gelatin-based paste. Gum paste with gum tragacanth is not practical for use when a large quantity of paste is called for as gum tragacanth is not readily available, and it costs about ten times more than powdered gelatin.

1. Sift the powdered sugar and reserve a few handfuls.

2. Thoroughly mix the gum tragacanth into the remaining sugar. Set aside in a mixing bowl.

3. Combine the water, glucose or corn syrup, and lemon juice, and warm the mixture slightly, stirring until well blended.

4. Using a dough hook, gradually incorporate the liquid into the powdered sugar mixture, adding some of the reserved powdered sugar if needed to make a fairly stiff paste. The consistency of the paste should be firm enough that it could easily be rolled out.

5. Mix in the shortening and continue kneading with the hook until you have an easily moldable paste. It takes some experience to get the consistency just right. You may need to add some additional shortening depending on the amount of powdered sugar used. If so, or if you are adding additional shortening to extend the working time, just rub it on top of the paste and knead it in by hand.

6. If any portion of the paste is to be tinted, use water-soluble food coloring and mix it in at this point. Cover with plastic wrap and store in an airtight container. Gum paste with gum tragacanth can be kept at normal room temperature for several weeks. It will harden a little, but it can be reworked with a small amount of additional shortening.

Nougat

about 1 pound, 10 ounces (740 g)
nougat

10 ounces (285 g) thinly
*   sliced almonds*
1 pound (455 g) granulated sugar
1 teaspoon (5 ml) lemon juice
2 ounces (55 g) butter, optional
Royal Icing (page 528)

Nougat is made of caramelized sugar and sliced almonds. It can be served as a candy, crushed and added to ice creams or fillings, made into shells for individual dessert presentations, or molded and cut into various shapes to create spectacular showpieces. Unlike other decorative materials, such as pastillage, nougat not only looks great, it is also very tasty. Although the recipe itself is quite simple, making nougat takes a lot of practice, proper planning, and fast precise steps to make a showpiece or even a dessert mold.

Before you begin, assemble the tools and equipment you will need to form the nougat. Cut out your pattern from heavy paper, such as a cake box. Lightly oil the mold or object you are planning to form the nougat in (or over) with vegetable oil or another flavorless oil. Clean and oil a heavy rolling pin, a metal spatula, and a chef's knife. Clean, dry, and lightly oil a marble slab. If marble is not available, use an inverted sheet pan.

1. Toast the almonds until golden brown. Set aside and keep warm.

2. Place the sugar and lemon juice in a heavy saucepan, preferably copper. Cook over low heat, stirring constantly, until all of the sugar has melted and it is light golden.

3. Stir in the almonds and continue stirring until the mixture turns a little darker golden, about 1 or 2 minutes. Stir in the butter, if used, and continue to stir until all of the butter is incorporated.

4. Quickly pour the nougat onto the prepared marble slab or sheet pan. Let it cool for a few seconds, then flip it over with the spatula so it will cool evenly. As soon as you can, roll the nougat to about ⅛ inch (3 mm) thick, never be more than ¼ inch (6 mm) thick.

5. Place your pattern on top and quickly cut out shapes with the oiled chef's knife. Form the pieces, if required. Let cool, then glue the pieces together with royal icing or sugar cooked to hard crack, 310°F (155°C).

If the nougat becomes too hard to work with at any time during rolling, cutting, or shaping, place it on a lightly oiled sheet pan and warm it in a 250°F (122°C) oven until soft. Be careful that you do not overheat the nougat and darken it or you might get several different shades in your finished showpiece, which does not look good.

To reuse scrap pieces, place them on top of each other, soften in the oven, then roll them out again. Or store scraps in airtight containers to use for candy or Nougatine Crunch.

NOTE: Nougat can be made without butter, but the butter will give the finished product an extra shine.

Nougatine Crunch

Crush cooled nougat into currant-sized pieces, using a heavy dowel or rolling pin. Store in airtight containers. Should the stored Nougatine Crunch become wet and sticky, dry it in the oven for a few minutes, then recrush it to separate the pieces.

Pastillage

5 pounds, 8 ounces (2 kg, 500 g) paste

1 ounce (30 g) unflavored gelatin powder
1¼ cup (300 ml) cold water
4 pounds, 3 ounces (1 kg, 905 g) powdered sugar
10 ounces (285 g) cornstarch
1 teaspoon (2 g) cream of tartar

Pastillage is also known as gum paste, from the time when a vegetable gum such as gum tragacanth was used in place of gelatin. It is a sugar paste perfectly suited for making show and display pieces or other decorative items. Pastillage is also preferred over marzipan as a canvas for cocoa paintings by some artists. It can be molded around almost any object and cut or pressed into many different shapes.

Theoretically pastillage is edible, but it is rarely intended to be (nor should it be) eaten when it is dry. It is as hard and brittle as glass, and I really do not recommend that you try it even if you have a ravenous appetite, strong teeth, and good insurance!

Pastillage is most typically left pure white, but it can be colored before it is rolled out and formed or painted or sprayed when dry. As always when using color on or in food, take care to keep the colors in soft pastel shades. The same precautions that must be taken when making marzipan apply to working with pastillage as well, to preserve its white color. Use a stainless steel bowl for mixing, never a corrosive bowl such as aluminum, which will turn the paste gray. Always wash and dry the work surface and rolling pin thoroughly (try to use marble, if possible, to give the rolled paste a smooth and even surface, which is essential for cocoa painting).

Pastillage dries and forms a crust almost immediately if left exposed, so assemble everything you will require ahead of time and keep the unused portion of the paste covered with a wet towel while you work. Have your templates cut out and ready, and be sure to use paper thick enough so you can quickly and precisely cut around the patterns with a thin, pointed, sharp knife. If the pastillage is to be molded, dust the forms (or object you are shaping it around) with cornstarch to keep it from sticking. Plan how you will cut the sheet of pastillage before you roll it out: Remember, you will not have time to stop and think once it is rolled. Try to use as much of each rolled sheet as possible since the scrap pieces cannot be softened and reused.

Use a very small amount of cornstarch to keep the pastillage from sticking. Too much will cause the surface to dry rapidly and form a crust, which will cause the paste to crack when it is shaped. Roll it out to ⅛ inch (3 mm) thick for the most attractive and elegant pieces. If rolled too thick, the pastillage looks clumsy and amateurish. Cut out the desired shapes, then carefully transfer the cut-outs to an even surface or to the mold, if you are using one. As soon as the pieces are partially dry and can be handled, turn them over or remove them from the molds to allow the bottom to dry. Continue to turn them from time to time so that they dry evenly (the moisture tends to sink to the bottom). This is especially important in large, flat pieces, which have a tendency to curl if not turned properly. Once dry, the pieces can be filed and sanded to help them fit together better and to smooth any sharp edges.

Pastillage is assembled using royal icing as cement. Take care not to use too much because none will be absorbed and the excess will squeeze out when the pieces are pressed together, spoiling the final appearance. Because royal icing does not set up quickly after it is applied (as chocolate and boiled sugar do), the pieces must be supported for several hours. Use any object that fits to hold a particular shape or angle. It can take several days to assemble a larger design. Once completely dry, the finished showpiece will keep forever if it is stored, covered, in a dry place.

This is intentionally a fairly small recipe, but since the paste is so quick and easy to make, and it does not stay workable very long, you might even consider measuring several half-batches and making each up as you use the previous one.

1. Soften the gelatin in the cold water. Heat to 110°F (43°C) to dissolve.

2. Sift together the sugar, cornstarch, and cream of tartar. Place in a stainless steel mixing bowl. Gradually add the gelatin mixture while mixing on low speed with a dough hook.

3. Continue mixing, scraping down the sides occasionally, until you have a smooth, elastic paste (it will still stick to the bottom of the bowl). Cover the paste with a wet towel immediately.

NOTE: Do not make any more pastillage than you will be able to use within an hour, and do not make it until you are ready to begin working with the paste. If the pastillage should become too firm, you can soften it to some degree by kneading it a little longer in the mixer.

Rock Sugar

1 cup (240 ml) water
2 pounds (910 g) granulated sugar
2 tablespoons (30 g) Royal Icing
    (page 528)
food coloring

Rock sugar, unlike other types of sugar, holds up very well to moisture. It is quite easy to make once you get the timing down.

1. Preheat an oven to 250°F (122°C). Line the inside of a medium bowl about 8 inches (20 cm) in diameter with aluminum foil. Have an absolutely clean wooden spoon available.

2. Combine the water and sugar in a large copper pan or heavy saucepan (the sugar mixture will swell to double in size, so the pan must be large enough to accommodate it). Stir over low heat until all of the sugar has dissolved and the mixture starts to boil. Take the usual precautions for boiling sugar: Remove any scum that accumulates on the surface, brush the sides of the pan clean from any sugar crystals, and partially cover the pan. Then turn the heat to medium and boil for a few minutes.

3. Uncover and place a sugar thermometer in the syrup. Add the coloring when the sugar reaches 255°F (124°C).

4. Continue boiling to 285°F (141°C). Remove the pan from the heat and quickly stir in the royal icing, mixing it in well. Do not overwork the mixture. You may have to try a few times to get the right feel here so don't be discouraged if it does not work the first time.

5. Stop stirring. The sugar will rise to almost double its original volume, fall slowly, and then start to rise again. If it fails to rise again you can help it along by stirring rapidly for a second or two.

6. After the second rising, quickly pour the sugar into the prepared bowl. The sugar will continue to increase in size. Immediately place the bowl in the oven for 10 minutes to harden the sugar and prevent it from falling again.

7. Set the sugar aside in a dry place, still in the bowl, for about 8 hours.

8. Remove the rock sugar from the bowl. Break or cut it with a serrated knife into pieces suitable for your decoration.

NOTE 1: Instead of adding the coloring to the rock sugar as it is cooking, you can spray colors on with a syringe to achieve special effects. This is best done once the pieces are placed on the showpiece.

NOTE 2: For a lighter and slightly more crumbly rock sugar, add a touch more royal icing.

Spun Sugar

Spun sugar is traditionally used to decorate ice cream desserts, but can be used to dress up many others as well. It looks very showy but is actually easy to make. The mass of thin, hair-like, sugar threads are also used to decorate *pièces montées*, such as croquembouche. Gâteau Saint-Honoré is also decorated with spun sugar on some occasions.

Unless the weather is dry, make the spun sugar immediately before serving. Moisture is gradually absorbed by the thin threads, which become sticky and eventually dissolve.

As with any sugar work, you should prepare everything you

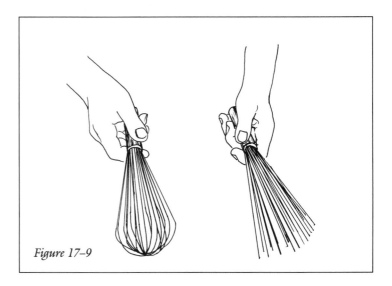

Figure 17–9

will need before you begin to boil the sugar. Clean, dry, and lightly oil two wooden or metal dowels. Place them, parallel, about 18 inches (45 cm) apart, extending over the edge of the table. Place a heavy cutting board on top at the back to hold them in place. Place a couple of sheet pans on the floor beneath the dowels to catch any drips. Cut the end off a metal whisk and spread the wires apart slightly (Figure 17–9). Have an airtight container handy to put the sugar in when it is ready.

1. Following the recipe and directions in the Boiled Sugar Basic Recipe, but omitting the tartaric acid or cream of tartar (see page 469), boil the syrup to 310°F (155°C) (hard crack stage). Immediately remove from the heat and plunge the bottom of the pan into cold water for a few seconds to stop the cooking process and cool the sugar a little. Let the syrup stand until slightly thickened before you start to spin it to prevent too many drops falling off the whisk during the spinning process. Do not stir the sugar.

2. Dip the cut whisk about ½ inch (1.2 cm) into the sugar. Gently shake off excess by moving the whisk in an up and down motion just above the surface of the sugar syrup. Do not hold the whisk up too high when you do this or the sugar drops will cool too much as they fall back into the pan and can cause the sugar to crystallize.

3. Spin the sugar by flicking the whisk back and forth in a rapid motion between the two dowels (Figure 17–10). Continue dipping and spinning the sugar until a reasonable amount has accumulated on the dowels.

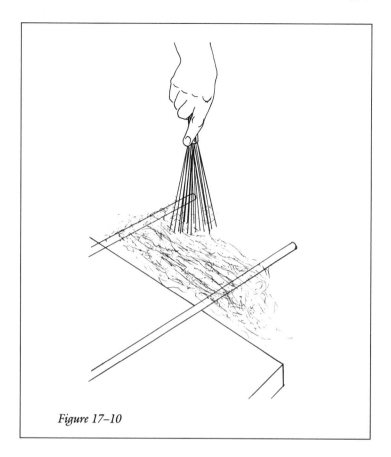

Figure 17–10

4. Gather the sugar off the dowels and place in the airtight container. Continue spinning the remaining sugar. Sugar will start to accumulate on the whisk and glue the wires together. Remove it by striking the whisk sharply against the edge of the sink. If the syrup cools down too much, warm it over low heat, swirling the pan to evenly distribute the heat. Avoid stirring, which can cause the sugar to crystallize.

NOTE 1: It is impossible to predict a precise yield when spinning sugar. On a rainy or humid day, you will get a much smaller volume. Also, depending on how many times you have to reheat the sugar, you may not be able to use all of the syrup.

NOTE 2: If you spin the sugar in a dry place you can store it for up to two days by lining the bottom of an airtight container with silica gel or Humisorb covered with foil.

—EIGHTEEN—

Decorations

Buttercream

Decorating with a Pastry Bag

Decorating with a Piping Bag

Decorating with Sauces

Candied Citrus Peels

Fondant

Glazes

Hippen Decorating Paste

Icings

Marzipan

Pâte à Choux for Decoration

Vanilla Tulips

Wedding Cake Assembly and
   Decorations

*H*andmade decorative ornaments and elaborate design work are labor-intensive skills that are becoming lost arts due to today's high labor costs. Unfortunately, more and more shops now use decorations made in factories. While in some instances it makes good sense to use prefabricated designs (marzipan and chocolate ornaments, for example), I believe that everything placed on a cake or pastry should be edible. Plastic cars and animals on a child's birthday cake, especially when combined with too many bright, artificial colors, can be frightful. One exception to using only edible ornaments is the use of fresh flowers. When artistically arranged on a wedding cake, flowers are an easy, refreshing alternative to traditional white buttercream alone.

The key to decorating (besides a steady hand and an awareness of neatness and symmetry) is to make the finished product look tasteful and elegant, rather than busy or cluttered. This chapter offers you methods and techniques, as well as a few tricks of the trade, for using very basic materials to create decorations quickly and economically.

Buttercream

Buttercream is indispensable in the pastry kitchen. It is mostly used to fill, ice, and decorate cakes and pastries, but it is also used to make buttercream roses and leaves. Buttercream should be light and smooth, and should always be made from a high-quality sweet butter. Icings made with margarine or shortening can be very unpleasant to eat (because of their higher melting point they tend to leave a film of fat in your mouth), but a small amount of margarine or shortening added to the buttercream stabilizes it without detracting from the taste. On very hot days, or in hot climates, you can increase the ratio of butter to margarine to equal amounts, but only if absolutely necessary to prevent the buttercream from melting.

Buttercream can be stored at normal room temperature for three to four days and in the refrigerator for up to two weeks. It can also be frozen for longer storage. Buttercream that is kept in the refrigerator should be taken out in plenty of time to soften before using. If you need to soften it quickly, warm it slightly over simmering water, stirring vigorously, until smooth. Be careful not to overheat and melt the buttercream; you should continue to stir after you take it off of the heat because the bowl will stay hot and can melt the buttercream on the sides. Use the same warming technique to repair buttercream that has broken (this usually happens when you add flavorings). I have had excellent results with softening buttercream on a low setting in the microwave. This is a technique you might want to try if it is more convenient for you.

Meringue-based buttercream (soft butter beaten into whipped egg whites and sugar) is probably the most widely used. It is quick and easy to make, and has a very light and fluffy texture. French or Italian buttercream is made from whole eggs or egg yolks whipped to a thick foam with hot sugar syrup added and butter whipped in. This is a very rich, yet light buttercream.

In an emergency, you can make a quick buttercream by creaming together equal amounts of soft butter and pastry cream. Adjust the sweetness with powdered sugar. If you do not have pastry cream, cream together two parts soft butter and one part fondant. Both these methods will result in a rather heavy product, not nearly as palatable as real buttercream, and should only be used as a last resort.

The following buttercream recipes can easily be multiplied, or scaled down, with no loss of flavor or texture.

Chocolate Buttercream

4 pounds, 6 ounces (1 kg, 990 g)

2 pounds (910 g) softened butter
14 ounces (400 g) granulated
*   sugar*
⅓ cup (80 ml) water
1 tablespoon (15 ml) light
*   corn syrup*
4 eggs
2 egg whites
1 teaspoon (5 g) salt
1 teaspoon (5 ml) vanilla extract
1 pound, 8 ounces (680 g) melted
*   dark chocolate at 130°F (54°C)*

1. Cream butter until light and fluffy. (Warm first if necessary.)
2. Combine sugar, water, and corn syrup in a saucepan. Boil to 245°F (118°C), brushing down the sides of the pan. Do not stir.
3. While the syrup is boiling, whip the eggs, egg whites, salt, and vanilla just to combine. Remove syrup from the heat, wait about 10 seconds, then gradually pour the syrup into the egg mixture while mixing on medium speed. Increase to high speed and whip until cold.
4. Reduce to low speed and slowly mix in the reserved butter. Remove the mixing bowl from the machine. Place one third of the butter mixture in a separate bowl and quickly mix in the melted chocolate. Still working quickly, add this to the remaining buttercream.

Vanilla Buttercream

5 pounds, 4 ounces (2 kg, 390 g)

2 pounds (910 g) softened butter
10 ounces (285 g) softened
*   margarine or shortening*
1 recipe Swiss Meringue (page 334)
2 teaspoons (10 ml) vanilla extract

1. Thoroughly combine the butter with the margarine.
2. When the meringue has been whipped to stiff peaks and is almost cold, lower the speed, add the vanilla extract, then gradually whip in the butter mixture on low speed.

NOTE: If you replace the margarine with sweet butter, add 2 teaspoons (10 g) salt.

Decorating with a Pastry Bag

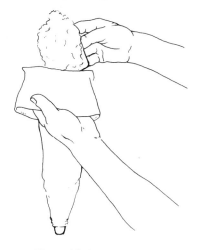

Use a large pastry bag that will allow you to fill the bag only half to two-thirds full. This will prevent the contents from being forced out through both ends.

1. Cut the opening of the bag so that the point of your largest piping tip just barely shows through, to make sure that the opening will not be too large for the smaller tips.
2. Fold the top half or one-third of the empty bag open.
3. Place the tip in the bag. It is a good idea, even though it is not always necessary, to force a small part of the bag, closest to the tip, inside the tip to lock the bag and stop the filling from running out.
4. Place the filling in the bag (Figure 18–1). Straighten out the fold and slide the top of the bag between your thumb and forefinger from the top to where the filling is, on both sides of the bag, to move the filling away from the top and remove any air pockets. Twist the bag closed.
5. Hold the bag by resting the twisted top between your thumb and fingers and apply pressure to the top of the bag only

Figure 18–1

with the palm of your hand. Use your other hand to guide the tip, or to hold onto the item being filled or decorated; do not apply pressure with this hand.

6. Squeeze out some of the filling back into the bowl to make sure there are no air pockets before piping on the item you are decorating.

Basketweave

This design can be done with any type of tip, but it looks best made with a flat tip (plain or star). If you do not have one, you can flatten a regular tip yourself.

1. Start by piping a vertical line close to one edge of the item you are decorating. (In the case of a round cake you can start anywhere on the sides.)

2. Pipe horizontal lines on top of the vertical line, leaving a space between them the same size as the width of the lines. The length of the horizontal lines should be three times the width, and the ends must line up evenly.

3. Pipe a second vertical line, one line-width from the first one, just slightly overlapping the ends of the horizontal lines.

4. Pipe more horizontal lines between the first rows, going over the second vertical line. Repeat, alternating vertical and horizontal lines, until finished (Figure 18–2).

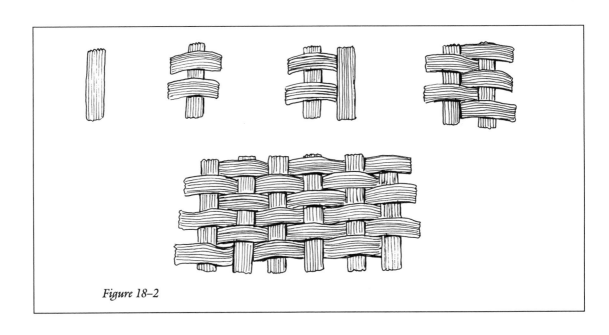

Figure 18–2

Buttercream Roses

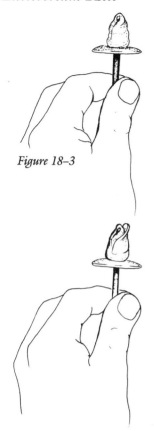

Figure 18–3

Figure 18–4

It is easier than it looks to make a buttercream rose, but it does require practice. You also need a very smooth buttercream that is not too soft, a decorating nail (it looks like a nail with a very large head) about 1½ inches (3.7 cm) in diameter, and a special rose-petal tip for the pastry bag (no. 124 for a medium-size rose).

1. Place the buttercream in the pastry bag with the rose-petal tip. Hold the stem of the decorating nail between the thumb and forefinger of your left hand. Hold the pastry bag so that the opening in the tip is perpendicular to the nail, with the wider end of the opening at the bottom.

2. Start by making the base of the rose. Place the bottom of the tip directly on the nail just outside the center. Angle the top of the tip just a little toward the center and pipe while turning the nail one complete turn. You should now have a small cone in the center of the nail. Make a second cone on top of the first one, slightly smaller and coming to a point at the top (Figure 18–3).

3. To form the petals, pipe the buttercream in a clockwise direction while turning the nail counterclockwise. Hold the bag the way you did to make the cone: wide end at the bottom. For the first row of petals, place the bottom of the tip slightly above the base of the cone, and the top of the tip angled out just a little (Figure 18–4). The first row should look fairly closed. Pipe three petals, evenly spaced, around the cone, lifting the tip up and then down in an arc, to make the rounded shape (Figure 18–5).

4. Make a second row of three petals in the same way, starting the bottom of these petals just below the first row, angling the top out a little further so the second row of petals has opened a bit more than the first, and placing the second row so the petals are staggered, not directly on top of the other three (Figure 18–6).

Figure 18–5

Figure 18–6

5. The third row should contain four or five petals. Using the same turning and piping method, start this row a little below the row before, angle the top out a bit more, and again stagger the petals so they fall between those in the second row. You can stop at this point, with three rows, or continue to add more rows.

6. To remove the rose from the nail, cut it off with a thin knife and set it on the cake. The roses are easier to cut off if you chill them first.

7. If you are making up buttercream roses in advance, cut squares of baking paper just slightly larger than the head of the decorating nail, attach the paper to the nail with a little buttercream, and form the roses on the paper squares. Lift the paper off the nail and set the roses on sheet pans in the refrigerator. To use, peel the roses off the paper with the tip of a knife.

8. Pipe buttercream leaves directly on the cake after you have set the rose in place. Use a leaf tip in the pastry bag. Hold the bag at a 45° angle with the base of the tip against the cake. Squeeze the bag with the palm of your hand while holding the tip in place for a split second to make the base of the leaf flow out. Gradually decrease the pressure as you pull the tip along, making the leaf narrower and bringing it to the length you want. Stop pressing on the bag and pull the tip away to bring the end of the leaf to a point. If you have difficulty forming a point at the end, the buttercream is not soft enough.

Rosettes

1. Place a star tip in the pastry bag. Add the filling. Hold the bag almost straight up and down above the place you want the rosette.

2. As you apply pressure, simultaneously move the bag in a tight 360° circle.

3. Stop the pressure, then lift the bag to finish the rosette.

Pearl and Shell Patterns

The technique used to make these two patterns is the same. You simply use a plain tip to make the pearls (also known as a bead pattern), and a star tip for the shells.

1. Hold the bag at an approximately 45° angle. The tip should just barely touch the surface you plan to pipe on.

2. Squeeze the bag with the palm of your hand, applying enough pressure to make the filling flow out to a wide base for the shell or bead, then gradually relax the pressure as you slowly move the tip toward you, to form the narrow point of the shell or bead.

3. Stop squeezing and pull the bag away to finish the design. This design is used individually or as part of a border design. For a border, start the next shell or bead just slightly overlapping the narrow tip of the last one (Figure 18–7).

Figure 18–7

Decorating with a Piping Bag

Making a Piping Bag

1. Cut a standard full-size sheet (24 × 16 inches/60 × 40 cm) of baking paper into six 8-inch (20-cm) squares. Fold each square diagonally and cut into two triangles.

2. Start by holding the triangle horizontally in such a way that the longest side is in front of you. Fold into a cone shape so that the long side becomes the tip, and the point of the original triangle (the opposite side) becomes the opening of the cone (Figures 18–8 through 18–11).

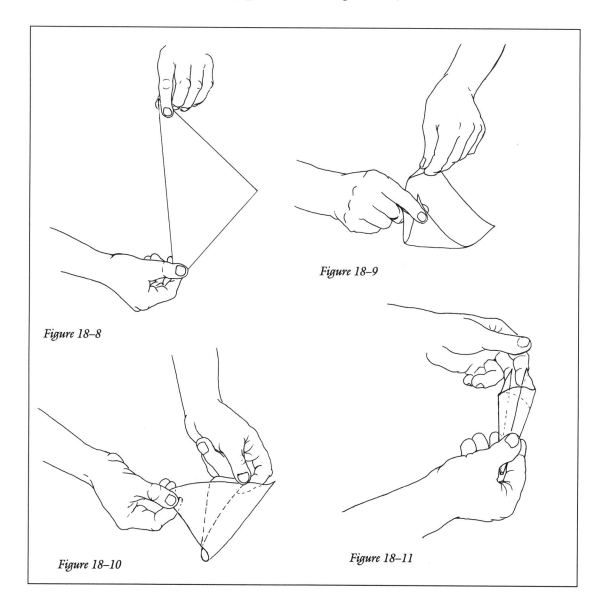

Figure 18–8

Figure 18–9

Figure 18–10

Figure 18–11

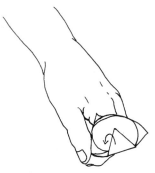

Figure 18–12

3. Fold the top into the cone to secure the shape (Figure 18–12).

4. Fill the cone only halfway. Close the top securely and cut the tip into the desired size opening.

Piping Designs for Special-Occasion Cakes

The templates or illustrations in Figures 18–13 through 18–22 suggest particular motifs such as Christmas, Valentine's Day, Easter, a child's birthday, and so on. They can serve as inspiration, or they can be used as a pattern to press into marzipan, as described in Decorating with Fondant—Method II (page 523). Once made in this fashion, the "stamps" can be kept virtually forever. You may also want to use these templates to create designs on marzipan by following the instructions for tracing onto marzipan, on pages 529–531.

The templates are approximately 70 percent of the size you need to decorate a standard 10-inch (25-cm) cake.

Piping Gel

Piping gel is purchased ready to use. It is made from sugar, corn syrup solids, and vegetable gum, such as gum arabic. It is very sweet and not very pleasant to eat by itself (as you can probably imagine from the ingredient list), but it is one of the most practical decorating materials in today's pastry shop. Although it looks artificial next to a chocolate decoration (for special petits fours or showpieces you should use piping chocolate), nevertheless the fact that piping gel is so inexpensive and easy to work with makes it useful for everyday decorating or adding just a small touch of color. For example, you can use it to fill in some of the small loops in a piped decoration. Piping gel is available in a clear, colorless form as well as in various colors. Because many of the colors are a bit bright, I recommend buying the clear gel and coloring it yourself to pastel shades.

Figure 18–13

Figure 18–14

Figure 18–15

Figure 18–16

Figure 18–17

Figure 18–18

Figure 18–19

Figure 18–20

Figure 18–21

Figure 18–22

Decorating with Sauces

Decorating desserts, and even savory dishes, with sauces has become very fashionable in restaurants. It is an excellent and easy way to dress up the presentation, personalize the dessert, and make it stand out as something memorable. Although to "paint" you need to use enough sauce to cover the base of the plate, or to cover one portion of it, be careful not to overdo it. Too much sauce can be overwhelming, as well as messy, and take away from the flavor of the dessert.

The instructions for making the various designs described here assume that the serving plates are large enough to give you space around the dessert to use as a "canvas." Ideally the base of the dessert plate should be about 8 inches (20 cm) across, with a simple border around the edge of the china so as not to distract from the presentation. These instructions also assume you have prepared the dessert item the same size as called for in the recipe or, in the case of a slice of cake, that a 10-inch (25-cm) cake has been cut into 12 to 14 pieces.

These are general decorating ideas for sauce. They can, of course, be combined or changed to suit a particular taste or occasion. The designs shown in a small pool of sauce can be done on the entire surface of the plate as well, and vice versa. Keep in mind that the more complicated the design, the less suitable it is for serving a large number. Even though the sauce can be poured on the plates in advance, piping on the decoration must be done just before the desserts are served or it will start to deteriorate.

As specified in the recipes for Sour Cream Mixture for Piping (see page 564) and Chocolate Sauce for Piping (see page 560), it is essential that the piping mixture or contrasting sauce, and the sauce on the plate, be the same consistency. You will not get a good result if they are not. The contrasting sauce should be applied with a piping bottle with a small opening. I use small plastic, squeeze bottles purchased at the drugstore that are designed for applying hair dye. In a pinch you can use a piping bag (see page 505), but it is much less convenient.

Corkscrew Pattern

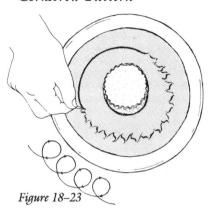

Figure 18–23

This decoration is quick and looks especially good with a round dessert, such as a charlotte or bavarois, or whenever the sauce is served encircling the dessert.

1. Place the dessert in the center of the plate and pour sauce all around to cover the base of the plate in a thin layer.
2. Pipe a circle of the contrasting sauce between the dessert and the edge of the plate.
3. Use a toothpick or small wooden skewer to draw a "corkscrew" pattern through the two sauces (Figure 18–23).

String of Hearts Pattern

Figure 18–24

This design takes a little longer to complete. It is especially elegant when you do not have too much space between the dessert and the edge of the plate.

1. Place the dessert in the center of the plate and pour sauce all around to cover the base of the plate in a thin layer.
2. Pipe a series of small dots, about 1 inch (2.5 cm) apart, between the dessert and the edge of the plate.
3. Drag a toothpick or small wooden skewer through the center of the circles in one continuous motion to create a string of hearts (Figure 18–24). You can also pick the skewer up and wipe it off between each heart to get a different effect.

Weave Patterns

Figure 18–25

1. Place the dessert on the plate, slightly off center. Pour a small oval pool of sauce in front (the side that will be facing the customer).
2. Pipe three or four horizontal lines of the contrasting sauce across the pool.
3. Drag a toothpick or small wooden skewer through the lines toward the edge of the plate. You can also alternate directions to make a herringbone pattern (Figure 18–25), or drag the lines through on the diagonal.

Spiderweb Pattern

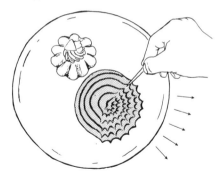

Figure 18–26

1. Place the dessert on the plate, slightly off center. Pour a small oval or round pool of sauce in front (the side that will be facing the customer).

2. Pipe a thin spiral of the contrasting sauce on top, making it oval or round to correspond with the pool.

3. Drag a toothpick or small wooden skewer from the center to the outside in evenly spaced lines (Figure 18–26) or from the outside toward the center, or alternate directions.

Curved String of Hearts Pattern

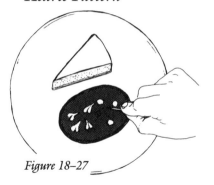

Figure 18–27

This is a variation of the string of hearts pattern.

1. Place a slice of cake on the dessert plate, slightly off center. Pour a small oval or round pool of sauce in front (the side that will be facing the customer).

2. Pipe the contrasting sauce on top in a random series of dots.

3. Drag a toothpick or small wooden skewer through the dots, making a succession of smooth turns, to create a curved string of hearts (Figure 18–27).

Ripple Pattern

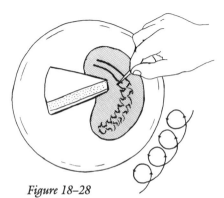

Figure 18–28

This design is very fast to make, and is especially useful when there is a limited amount of space on the plate.

1. Place a slice of cake in the center of the dessert plate. Pour a small oval pool of sauce at the tip of the slice (letting the sauce float out on both sides of the slice).

2. Pipe two lines of the contrasting sauce, close to each other, at the edge of the pool.

3. Drag a toothpick or a small wooden skewer through the two lines, making connected circles as for the corkscrew pattern (Figure 18–28).

Candied Citrus Peels
(Orange, Lemon, or Grapefruit)

2 pounds (910 g) candied peels, approximately

1 pound, 10 ounces (740 g) citrus fruit shells, prepared as described in step 1
1 tablespoon (15 g) salt
20° Baumé Sugar Syrup (recipe follows)
3 ounces (90 ml) glucose or light corn syrup

This recipe should really be referred to as sugar preservation of citrus peels rather than candied, as, accurately speaking, the peel must be preserved before it can be candied. The true procedure for making candied fruit involves covering the exterior surface of sugar-preserved fruit with a thin, crystallized layer of sugar, which prevents it from drying out too rapidly. These days most people do not have the time to go through this rather lengthy process and instead either purchase candied fruit already prepared or use the quick-method variation that follows this recipe.

1. Cut the oranges, lemons, or grapefruits in half, juice them (reserve the juice for another use), and scrape out the remaining flesh from the shells. Cut the shells in half again to make quarters.

2. Blanch the shells in boiling water for a few minutes. Pour off the water, add fresh water, and blanch for a few minutes longer. Repeat this step once more to remove the bitter taste from the peels.

3. Add fresh water again (just enough to cover), together with the salt, and simmer until the peels are soft (about 30 minutes). Plunge into cold water to cool.

4. The white part of the peel, the pith, is usually left on but can be removed at this point with a small spoon or a melon baller.

5. Stack the peels inside each other in a flat, noncorrosive pan such as a hotel pan. Weigh them down with a lid or plates to prevent them from floating to the surface when you add the syrup.

6. Pour the hot sugar syrup over the peels to cover. Let sit for 24 hours.

7. Pour the syrup off into a saucepan. Boil it until it is 4° higher on the Baumé thermometer (this can be accelerated by adding more sugar to the syrup). Pour the syrup back over the peels and let stand another 24 hours.

8. Repeat step 7 until the syrup reaches 34° Baumé. This will usually take four or five days. Heat the peels in the syrup to scalding every other day. When the syrup is heated for the last time, add the glucose or corn syrup to prevent crystallization. During the entire process the peels should be kept covered at room temperature. Store the peels in the syrup (it will be very thick at this point), covered, at room temperature. The candied peels will keep for months.

20° Baumé Sugar Syrup

5 pints (2 l, 400 ml) syrup

1½ quarts (1 l, 440 ml) water
1 pound, 8 ounces (680 g)
  granulated sugar
1½ cups (360 ml) glucose or
  light corn syrup

Quick Method for Candied Citrus Peels

4 ounces (115 g) candied peels

8 ounces (225 g) orange, lemon, or
  grapefruit peel, removed with a
  vegetable peeler, without any
  white pith
2 ounces (55 g) powdered sugar

Fondant

2 quarts (1 l, 920 ml)

vegetable oil
2 cups (480 ml) water
4 pounds (1 kg, 820 g) granulated
  sugar
⅔ cup (160 ml) glucose or
  light corn syrup, warmed
½ teaspoon (1 g) cream of tartar
1 cup (240 ml) cold water

1. Combine water, sugar, and glucose or corn syrup in a saucepan. Heat to boiling and boil for 1 minute.

2. Remove the pan from the heat and skim off any scum that has developed in the surface of the syrup. Use hot.

NOTE: This quantity of syrup will probably appear to be a great deal more than you need for the amount of citrus peel you are preparing. It is necessary to begin with a large amount as the peels absorb part of the syrup, and the syrup is reduced several times, during the process.

1. Cut the peels into very thin julienne.

2. Blanch the strips in water for a few minutes to remove the bitter taste. Strain and pat dry with a towel. Spread the peels in a single layer (but not too far apart) on a sheet pan lined with baking paper. Sift powdered sugar over the top.

3. Dry the peels at 100°F (38°C) for approximately 30 minutes, or until they begin to dry out. Move the peels around to make sure all sides are coated with the sugar and they are not sticking together.

4. Continue drying the peels about 30 minutes longer. Be careful not to overcook them. When cold, store candied peels in an airtight container to use as needed.

Fondant is widely used in the pastry shop for glazing and decorating. If properly applied, it dries to a silky-smooth icing that not only enhances the appearance of the pastry but preserves it as well, by sealing it from the air. Fondant is a sugar syrup that is crystallized to a creamy white paste. Glucose and cream of tartar are used to invert part of the sugar to achieve the proper amount of crystallization. Without these ingredients the cooked sugar would harden and be impossible to work with. Conversely, if too much glucose or cream of tartar is used, there will not be enough crystallization, and the fondant will be soft and runny.

Although fondant is inexpensive and relatively easy to make (once you get the hang of it), it is almost always purchased in a professional kitchen either in a ready-to-use paste or as a powder to which you add water. To make your own fondant you will need a precise sugar thermometer (test in boiling water to determine accuracy), a sugar pan (see page 605) or a heavy saucepan, a wide spatula or bench scraper, a marble slab (2 × 2 feet/60 × 60 cm for this recipe), four steel or aluminum bars, and, as in all sugar work, quick reaction time when the sugar has reached the proper temperature.

1. Clean, dry, and lightly oil the marble slab and metal bars with vegetable oil. Place the bars at the edge of the marble to make a frame to hold the hot syrup when it is poured on the slab. Oil a stainless steel scraper and place the cold water close by.

2. Combine the 2 cups (480 ml) water and the granulated sugar in a saucepan. Bring to a boil, stirring to dissolve the sugar. Reduce the heat to medium, stop stirring, and brush the sides of the pan with water. Be sure to brush down all of the crystals. It takes only a few particles of sugar left on the sides to make the mixture crystallize when the sugar becomes hotter.

3. When the temperature reaches 225°F (108°C), add the warm glucose or corn syrup and the cream of tartar dissolved in as little hot water. Continue boiling until the syrup reaches 238° to 240°F (114° to 115°C). Pay close attention, the syrup will reach this temperature quicker than you might think.

4. Immediately pour the syrup onto the prepared surface and sprinkle a little cold water on top to prevent it from crystallizing. It is critical that the temperature not exceed 240°F (115°C), so if your marble is not right next to the stove, place the saucepan in a bowl of cold water for a few seconds first to prevent overcooking. Insert the sugar thermometer into the thickest part of the puddle and let the sugar cool to 110°F (43°C).

5. Remove the bars and start to incorporate air. Using the oiled, stainless steel scraper, work the sugar by sliding the scraper under the edge, lifting it, and folding in toward the center. After awhile the sugar will start to turn white and become firmer. Continue to work the fondant slowly, either by hand or in a mixing bowl (see note), until it has a smooth and creamy consistency.

6. Pack the fondant against the bottom of a plastic container and pour the cold water on top to prevent a crust from forming. Store at room temperature.

7. The fondant must rest about 24 hours before it will be soft enough to use. Fondant will keep for weeks if covered properly. Pour off the water before using and keep the bowl covered with plastic wrap while you are working. Add a new layer of water and then cover to store until the next use.

NOTE: If you are making a large batch of fondant you can work the sugar in a mixer instead of by hand. Place the cooled syrup in the mixing bowl carefully. Do not get any on the sides of the bowl (hold the bowl next to the table and scrape the mixture in with the bench scraper). Use the paddle and mix on low speed until the fondant starts to turn off-white and is smooth and creamy. You may need to scrape down the sides of the bowl to ensure that all of the fondant is mixed evenly. Scoop the fondant into a container and cover with the cold water as above.

Decorating with Fondant

Fondant is an excellent decorating material for making designs using a piping bag. It needs to be fairly cold for piping the outline (85° to 95°F, 29° to 34°C) and quite firm. Add only enough simple syrup so you can pipe it—it should still hold its shape once it is piped out. To fill in the piped designs, warm the fondant just a little (not over 100°F, 38°C), then thin it, as needed, with simple syrup so it will flow out slightly within the outline. Be sure to keep the fondant covered at all times to prevent a skin from forming.

Method I

1. To make small, individual ornaments, place a perfectly flat transparent plastic sheet about 1/16 inch (2 mm) thick on top of your drawing (you may want to use designs shown in Figures 16–15 and 16–16, pages 451–452, or your own creations) and secure the plastic so it will not shift as you pipe.

2. Put a small amount of fondant in a piping bag and pipe a thin frame of fondant around the figures. (Unlike chocolate ornaments made using a similar method, these are placed on the cake or pastry right-side up. Small detail lines within the figure are piped on the top after filling in with warm fondant. They are not piped out at the same time as the outline.) Fill in with the warmer fondant, moving the piping bag back and forth to get a smooth surface and to build up your design and create height. Be careful not to disturb the frame. The fondant can be tinted with water-soluble food coloring or chocolate if desired. See Glazing and Icing with Fondant, pages 524–525, steps 4 and 5, for information on mixing colors.

3. Let the design dry overnight, then loosen it by moving the plastic over a sharp edge, bending it down lightly. Place the finished decoration on top of your cake or pastry. If you are not using the decoration right away, leave it attached to the plastic until you need it.

Method II

Fondant can also be piped directly on top of a cake or pastry in the same way as Method I if you have the skill to pipe the design freehand. Even if you are not a great artist you can use the following tracing method to make almost any design you like.

1. Draw or copy the design onto a paper. If necessary, rub vegetable oil onto the paper to make it transparent and invert the paper. If it does not matter that the design will be reversed on the cake, then you do not need to do this step.

2. Tape the drawing to a sheet of cardboard. Place a small piece of plexiglas (thick enough that it will not bend) on top of the drawing.

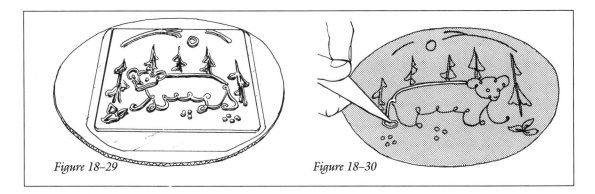

Figure 18–29   *Figure 18–30*

3. Make a small amount of royal icing. Put the icing in a piping bag, cut a small opening, and trace over your design (Figure 18–29). Let the icing harden overnight.

4. Roll out marzipan to ⅛ inch (3 mm) thick. Cut out rounds the same size as the design. Hold the glass upside down and press the design into the marzipan. Remove the glass and trace over the design with fondant (or royal icing or chocolate), using a piping bag with an opening just large enough to cover the lines (Figure 18–30). The design can be left as is with just the outline, or filled in with additional fondant, as in Method I.

This is a good way to make up a supply of cake decorations on a slow day to have ready at a busy time like Easter, Mother's Day or Christmas. You can keep the marzipan from looking old and dry by coating it with a thin layer of cocoa butter before you press out the pattern. To use this method on a cake that is entirely covered with marzipan (Princess Cake, for example), press the design into the marzipan just before you place it on the cake, then pipe over it.

NOTE: Instead of plexiglas, you can have a glass shop make rectangles 8 × 9 inches (20 × 22.5 cm) from regular window glass. Make sure they round the corners and sand the edges smooth. It is important that the glass or plexiglas is clean and free of fingerprints.

Glazing or Icing with Fondant

1. Warm the fondant over simmering water, stirring constantly, until it reaches approximately body temperature, 98°F (37°C). Do not heat over 100°F (38°C), or the fondant will become hard and unpleasant to eat as well as less shiny when dry. Should you overheat the fondant, wait until it has cooled to the correct temperature before you apply it. On the other hand, if the fondant is not hot enough, it will take too long to form a skin and will not have a nice satin shine; further, the pastries will be sticky and hard to work with and can collect dust while drying.

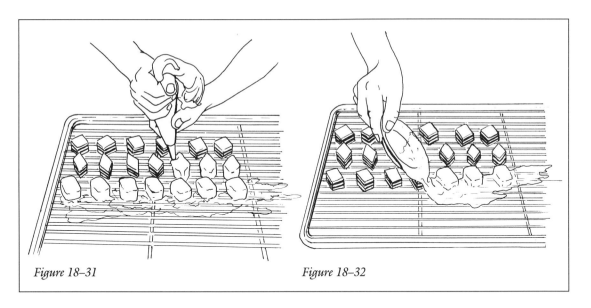

Figure 18–31　　　　　　　　　　*Figure 18–32*

2. Thin the warm fondant to the proper consistency with simple syrup (adding egg white along with the simple syrup will add an extra shine to the fondant). Test the thickness by coating a few pastries. The contours and separate layers of a petit four should be clearly visible through the icing.

3. Either pipe or pour fondant on top of petits fours or Othellos. Never coat them by dipping the pastry into the fondant or you will get crumbs in the fondant. If you are only coating a few dozen pastries, pipe it on (Figure 18–31). When covering a large number, pour the fondant from a saucer. Line up your pastries or petits fours to be covered on an aspic or cooling rack as you would if you were piping the fondant. Hold the bowl of fondant in one hand and the saucer in the other. Scoop up fondant in the saucer and pour it slowly and evenly over the pastries, holding it just above them (Figure 18–32). Always start with the pastry farthest away from you so you will not drip on the pastries once they are coated. You should be able to cover two or three rows in one stroke. The drawback with this method is that you need to work with a large amount of fondant.

4. If you wish to tint the fondant, start by coating as many petits fours as desired in white, then tint the white fondant yellow. Use leftover yellow when making green fondant, and reserve any leftover green. Next make and apply pink fondant. If any of that is left, combine it with the green to make a mocha color.

5. To make chocolate fondant, quickly add melted unsweetened chocolate to the warm fondant. The chocolate will thicken the fondant, so you will need to add more simple syrup.

Glazes

Apricot Glaze

2 cups (480 ml) glaze

1 pound (455 g) smooth apricot jam
3 ounces (85 g) granulated sugar
⅓ cup (80 ml) water

1. Place the jam, sugar, and water in a heavy-bottomed saucepan. Bring to a boil over medium heat, stirring constantly.

2. Lower the heat and continue cooking until the mixture can be pulled into a ¼-inch (6-mm) thread between your thumb and index finger, about 10 minutes.

3. Quickly remove the pan from the heat, strain, and use immediately. Store leftover glaze at room temperature. Reheat leftover glaze and, if too thick, add a small amount of water.

NOTE: If you cook the glaze too long it will become too thick to use properly. Unless it has started to caramelize, just add a small amount of water and cook to thread test again.

Chocolate Glaze

4½ cups (1 l, 80 ml) glaze

1 pound (455 g) dark chocolate
1 cup (240 ml) water
10 ounces (285 g) granulated sugar
½ cup (120 ml) glucose or light corn syrup
1 tablespoon (9 g) unflavored gelatin powder
¼ cup (60 ml) cold water
4 ounces (115 g) cocoa powder

1. Cut the chocolate into small chunks and reserve.

2. Combine 1 cup (240 ml) water, sugar, and glucose or corn syrup in a saucepan. Heat to boiling.

3. Soften the gelatin in the cold water, then stir into the sugar mixture. Whisk in cocoa powder and remove from heat.

4. Add the reserved chocolate chunks and stir until all of the chocolate is melted. Use immediately. Store leftover glaze in a covered container. To use, heat the glaze to about 175°F (80°C) but do not boil. If (after reheating) the glaze seems too thick to spread easily, thin with additional water.

NOTE: If a skin forms on the glaze, pour enough hot water on top to cover, wait a few seconds, then pour the water off. For a firmer glaze, you can increase the amount of chocolate, but you will lose some of the shine.

Pectin Glaze

8 cups (1 l, 920 ml)

5 cups (1 l, 200 ml) water
2 tablespoons, 1½ teaspoons (22 g) pectin powder
3 pounds (1 kg, 365 g) granulated sugar
Tartaric Acid Solution (page 596)

Unfortunately, pectin powder of the proper strength for making pectin glaze is not readily available in this country. Before trying this recipe make sure the pectin you are using is 150 percent strength, or the finished product simply will not gel. Put pectin powder on your shopping list the next time you go to Europe. It is inexpensive, has years of shelf life as long as it is kept dry, and a little goes a long way. Pectin glaze is used in combination with tartaric acid, which acts as a catalyst to make the glaze gel and gives it a slightly tart flavor that is especially complementary to fruit. The ability to gel quickly prevents the glaze from soaking into the fruit. Instead it leaves a thin, shiny coat on the top.

1. Heat the water to the scalding point in a saucepan. In the meantime, mix the pectin powder with 6 ounces (170 g) of the sugar. Whisk into the water when the water is ready, making sure it is thoroughly combined.

2. Bring the mixture to a boil, then stir in the remaining sugar. Bring back to a boil again, but this time check to see exactly when the mixture begins to boil, then reduce the heat and boil for 5 minutes.

3. Remove from the heat and let cool. Skim off any foam or scum that appears on the surface. The pectin glaze will keep for months at this stage if stored covered in the refrigerator.

4. To use the glaze, add two or three drops of tartaric acid solution for every 1 ounce (30 ml) of pectin glaze. The flavor should definitely be tart but not to the point where it is unpleasant (also adding too much liquid can prevent the glaze from setting). Stir in the tartaric acid quickly and use the glaze immediately. Add tartaric acid only to the amount of glaze you are ready to use at the moment because the glaze cannot be softened once it has set. You can keep the glaze from setting up while you are working by stirring it every few seconds.

NOTE: If the glaze gels too fast, thin it with additional water. If it does not set, or it is slow to set, boil it for another minute or so to reduce it.

Red Currant Glaze

2 cups (480 ml) glaze

1 pound (455 g) red currant jelly
4 ounces (115 g) granulated sugar

1. Place the jelly and sugar in a saucepan. Stirring constantly, bring to a boil over low heat. Keep stirring until all of the lumps have dissolved.

2. Lower the heat, and simmer for a few minutes until the mixture has a glossy shine. Strain, then use immediately. Store leftover glaze covered. Reheat to a liquid consistency to use again.

Hippen Decorating Paste

3 cups (720 ml) or 1½ pounds (680 g) paste

1 cup (240 ml) or approximately 7 egg whites
1 pound (455 g) Almond Paste (page 4)
1 ounce (30 g) bread flour
½ teaspoon (3 g) salt
pinch of ground cinnamon
2 to 3 drops lemon juice
milk

This paste is used in making decorations and containers to hold assorted desserts. It is always spread directly onto greased and floured sheet pans, following the shape of a template. Hippen paste is quite versatile because it can be tinted in various colors and bent 360°.

1. Add five of the egg whites to the almond paste one at a time to avoid lumps. Mix in the flour, salt, cinnamon, and lemon juice. Mix in the remaining egg whites. Let the mixture rest covered for 30 minutes.

2. Adjust the consistency with milk if necessary. The paste should be thin enough to spread out easily, but should hold the shape made by your template without floating out.

Icings

Royal Icing

*6 cups (1 l, 440 ml) or 3 pounds,
7 ounces (1 kg, 565 g) icing*

*2 pounds, 8 ounces (1 kg, 135 g)
    powdered sugar, sifted*
½ teaspoon (1 g) cream of tartar
*1 cup (240 ml) egg whites,
    approximately*

This type of icing is also called decorating icing, because that is its principal use. Royal icing is one of the best materials with which to practice piping. It is inexpensive and easy to make, and can be piped and formed into almost any shape. Royal icing is used a great deal around Christmas time to decorate gingerbread and Christmas cookies, and it is essential for making gingerbread houses. Because royal icing contains egg whites, it is hard and brittle when dry, so it is used mostly for decorations rather than for eating. However, it is traditional in some countries to use it on special-occasion cakes, such as wedding cakes. Personally, I limit its use to showpieces or for piping small amounts on cakes or pastries. Fancy royal icing ornaments or showpieces are easy to make.

1. Place a thin sheet of plastic or wax paper on top of your "blueprint." Fasten them together with paper clips so that they will not move as you pipe. (For small ornaments you may want to use some of the designs shown in Figures 16–15 and 16–16, pages 451–452.)

2. Trace over your design by piping with royal icing in a piping bag. Before the icing hardens you can bend the sheet into any shape you like.

3. Let the design dry overnight, then carefully peel away the paper or plastic. Join the shapes together with additional royal icing as needed. Frequently a combination of pastillage and royal icing is used to make the showpiece more durable.

Royal icing can also be used to pipe on plexiglas or glass templates for decorations on marzipan, as described in Decorating with Fondant, Method II (see pages 523–524).

This recipe gives you a large amount of royal icing. If you only need a small amount, simply add powdered sugar to one or two egg whites until you reach the proper consistency, stir rapidly until the mixture is light and fluffy, then add a small pinch of cream of tartar to prevent the icing from yellowing.

Make sure you keep royal icing covered at all times and clean off any icing on the side of your cup or bowl. The icing dries very quickly and the small lumps will interfere with your piping. A wet towel on top of the bowl works well while you are working, but use plastic wrap or some water on the icing for longer storage.

1. Place the powdered sugar and cream of tartar in a mixing bowl. With the machine set at low speed, gradually add enough egg whites to make a smooth paste.

2. Beat at high speed for just a few seconds if you are using the royal icing for piping. If you will be spreading the icing—on the

top of a gingerbread house, for example—beat the icing a bit longer to make it light and fluffy.

3. Immediately transfer to a clean, covered container to prevent a skin from forming. Or if you are going to use the icing within a few minutes, place a damp towel on top. Stored in the refrigerator, royal icing will keep for up to 1 week.

Simple Icing

3 cups (720 ml) icing

2 pounds (910 g) powdered sugar
3 tablespoons (45 ml) light corn syrup
¾ cup (180 ml) hot water, approximately

This icing is also known as flat icing or water icing.

1. Place the powdered sugar in a mixing bowl. Pour the corn syrup into the hot water and stir until melted. Add the liquid to the powdered sugar and mix until smooth.

2. Adjust the thickness with additional water as needed. The icing should be the consistency of sour cream.

3. Cover the surface with a thin layer of water to prevent a crust from forming (pour off before using). Store covered at room temperature.

NOTE: The corn syrup prevents the icing from crystallizing when stored for several weeks. If you use this icing as part of your daily routine, here is a simple way to make it: Fill your storage container with powdered sugar and add as much hot water as the sugar will absorb. Do not stir, but let it settle for a few minutes. Pour enough additional water on top to cover the surface in a 1-inch (2.5-cm) layer. Let the icing sit overnight. The next day not only do you have pefectly fine simple icing, but the water on the top of the icing can be poured off and used instead of simple syrup on Danish pastries or puff pastry items. Store covered at room temperature.

Marzipan

Marzipan is used extensively in European pastry shops, particularly in Germany, Austria, Switzerland, and Scandinavia. It is made of almond paste and powdered sugar with the addition of a moistening agent such as glucose or corn syrup. Some recipes substitute egg whites or even fondant, but the purpose is the same.

There was a time when every pastry chef had to make his own almond paste by grinding the blanched almonds with an equal weight of sugar until it became a fine paste. Today almond paste is readily available, making it much more convenient to make your own marzipan in large quantities. Of course, marzipan can be purchased from bakery supply houses as well, but it is much more economical to make it. Marzipan must be made in a stainless steel bowl to prevent discoloration.

Due to its large sugar content (60 to 70 percent), marzipan

dries very quickly when exposed to air and should be kept covered at all times. If the marzipan becomes dry (but has not dried all the way through), you can reconstitute by kneading in a small amount of water; this will shorten its shelf life considerably. Keep your tools and work place scrupulously clean, and always wash your hands immediately prior to rolling or molding marzipan with your hands. The almond oil, which is brought to the surface as you work the marzipan, will pick up and absorb even a small trace of dirt on your hands, which not only ruins the off-white color of the marzipan but can lead to spoilage.

Marzipan is rolled out in the same manner as short dough (but powdered sugar is used instead of flour to prevent the paste from sticking) and can be left smooth, or textured in various patterns before being used to cover cakes, petits fours, and pastries. It is an ideal surface to decorate and pipe on, either freehand or using the tracing method that follows. It is also used on petits fours and pastries that are to be coated with fondant or chocolate to keep the coating from soaking into the sponge and to achieve an even surface. A thin layer of marzipan on a yule log or chocolate cake prevents the thin layer of chocolate coating from mixing with the buttercream on top of the cake. Not only does the marzipan make a smooth finish possible, but the combination of chocolate and marzipan also gives the pastry a very special and distinctive flavor. With very few exceptions, marzipan should never be rolled out thicker than 1/8 of an inch (3 mm), or it can look clumsy and unattractive.

You can use water-soluble food coloring to tint the marzipan, but keep the colors to soft pastel shades as much as possible. A green color (such as for the Princess Cake) should usually be toned down with the addition of a few drops of yellow. When adding color to a small amount of marzipan, or when you need only a hint of color, put a drop of color on a piece of baking paper and add some of it to the marzipan using the tip of a knife. Knead the marzipan until the color is completely worked in. Use cocoa powder to produce brown in various shades unless you do not want, or need, the chocolate flavor (it is obviously a lot less expensive to use food color). Work the desired amount of cocoa powder into the marzipan and keep kneading it until all of the marbled effect is gone and you have a smooth, evenly colored marzipan. If you add a large amount of cocoa powder you may have to compensate by working in some simple syrup or water to prevent the marzipan from getting too dry.

Marzipan will keep almost indefinitely if you take proper care in the mixing and handling. It should be placed in airtight containers and stored in a very cool place or the refrigerator. It can also be stored in the freezer should you need to keep it for a long time. If the oil separates from the marzipan after it has thawed, making it crumbly and hard to work with, add a small amount of water and some powdered sugar. Continue to knead the marzipan until it is smooth and elastic.

Marzipan

approximately 4 pounds, 6 ounces
(1 kg, 990 g)

2 pounds (910 g) Almond Paste
(page 4)
½ cup (120 ml) glucose or
light corn syrup
2 pounds (910 g) powdered sugar,
sifted, approximately

1. In a stainless steel mixing bowl, use the hook to mix the almond paste with the glucose or corn syrup, at low speed, until combined.

2. Start adding the sugar, scraping the sides of the bowl down as necessary. Add enough of the powdered sugar to make a fairly firm, yet workable, dough.

3. Store the marzipan, wrapped in plastic, inside an airtight container in a cold place.

NOTE: The amount of powdered sugar needed will depend on the consistency of the almond paste. Always mix at low speed and take care not to overmix. The friction will make the marzipan warm, thereby softening it, and you will end up adding too much powdered sugar.

Tracing onto Marzipan

The templates and illustrations in this book (or any other drawings) can be traced quite easily on top of a sheet of marzipan using one of the following methods.

Method I

1. Roll out high-quality marzipan a little thinner than ¹⁄₁₆ of an inch (2 mm), using the smallest possible amount of powdered sugar. This will make the marzipan transparent.

2. Place the marzipan on top of the drawing and cut the edges to the proper size and shape.

3. Trace the design using either piping chocolate or piping gel. Transfer the finished piece to the top of a cake or save it to use later.

Method II

If you use tinted marzipan it may not be transparent when rolled thin.

1. Trace the drawing on top of a sheet of baking paper using a soft pencil.

2. Roll out the marzipan to ⅛ inch (3 mm) thick, using no powdered sugar at all on the top so that this side will stay fairly sticky.

3. Invert your drawing on top of the marzipan and roll a rolling pin gently over the drawing, pressing the image onto the marzipan. (Remember, this will be a mirror image. Follow the procedure given on page 523 to avoid this. You will have to draw the picture twice.

Marzipan Angel

one 3½-ounce (100-g) figure

4½ ounces (130 g) Marzipan,
*   white (pages 529–531)*
yellow food coloring
powdered sugar
red food coloring
egg white
Royal Icing (pages 528–529)
melted dark baker's chocolate
1 small candle (such as a
*   birthday cake candle)*

4. Remove the drawing and pipe over the pencil marks as directed above. Since you will be pressing the lead from the pencil onto the marzipan, this method is not recommended for anything other than show or display cakes.

1. See Figure 18–33 as a guide in constructing the angel. As always when working with marzipan, be sure your hands and working area are spotlessly clean. Divide the marzipan into four pieces: two ⅓ ounce (10 g) pieces and one 2½ ounce (70 g) piece, with a bit more than 1 ounce (40 g) left.

2. Color this remaining piece pale yellow. Roll it out a little thinner than ⅛ inch (3 mm), using powdered sugar to prevent it from sticking.

3. Cut out a heart, using a heart-shaped cutter 2½ inches (6.2 cm) wide. Place the heart on a sheet of cardboard. Make a cut in the wings (heart), starting at the pointed tip and going three-quarters of the way toward the top. Spread the cut apart at the tip so it is open ½ inch (1.2 cm). Set the wings aside.

4. To make the hair you can color a piece of the scraps left from the wings with cocoa powder to a dark brown, or leave it yellow. Roll it out even thinner and cut out a fluted circle using a ½-inch (1.2-cm) cutter. Reserve this piece (which will be the hair), covered. (You will have some yellow marzipan left over since it would be impossible to roll out the exact amount needed.)

5. Use a very small amount of red food coloring to color one of the small (⅓-ounce/10-g) pieces pale pink. Or color it brown, with cocoa powder. Pinch off a tiny piece the size of a pin head, and color this piece red to use for the mouth. Reserve. Roll the rest of the piece (the head) into a perfectly round ball. Holding it carefully in one of your palms (so that it will remain perfectly round), mark two small indentations for the eyes using a marzipan tool or other small blunt object.

6. Roll the small red piece for the mouth round between your thumb and index finger of your free hand, and then fasten to the head using egg white to make it stick. Using a pointed marzipan tool or an instant-read meat thermometer, press in the center of the mouth to make a small round hole; the mouth should look as if the angel is singing.

7. Fasten the reserved round, fluted piece (the hair) to the top of the head using egg white. Reserve this piece.

8. Take out the large, reserved piece and roll it between your hands until it is soft and pliable. Then roll it into a ball. Place the ball on the table and roll into a 3-inch (7.5-cm) long cone with a

Figure 18–33

blunt tip at the narrow end. Pick up the cone and firmly tap the wide end against the table a few times to flatten it so the angel will stand upright.

9. Brush some egg white down the center of the reserved wings above the cut. Lay the cone on top of the wings, placing the narrow end level with the top in the center.

10. Roll the final reserved piece of marzipan into a 4-inch (10-cm) rope tapered at both ends. Fasten the rope (arms) to the body with egg white, draping them from the shoulders to the waist. Leave the body laying flat for 24 hours to allow the wings to dry sufficiently.

11. Stand the angel up (cut the bottom flat if necessary) and attach the head to the body with egg white. Pipe two dots of royal icing in the indentations for the eyes, using a piping bag with a small opening. Place melted chocolate in a second piping bag and pipe two very small dots on the royal icing for pupils. Pipe a very fine line above each eye for eyebrows. Gently place the candle in the arms.

NOTE: If you wish to decorate the body with royal icing (buttons above the arms or a pattern to mark the skirt), do this while the figure is lying down. If you plan to keep the figure for any length of time, brush a thin film of hot cocoa butter over the figure before piping.

Figure 18–34

Marzipan Bear

(see photograph in color insert)
one 3½-ounce (100-g) figure

3½ ounces (100 g) white
   Marzipan (pages 529–531)
egg white
Royal Icing (pages 528–529)
melted dark baker's chocolate

1. See Figure 18–34 as a guide in constructing the bear. Be certain that your hands and your work area are absolutely clean. Divide the marzipan as follows: One ⅔-ounce (20-g) piece for the rear legs; one ½-ounce (15-g) piece for the front legs; one ½-ounce (15-g) piece for the head; one ⅙-ounce (5-g) piece for the tail. Cover these pieces with plastic to prevent them from drying out.

2. Use the remaining marzipan for the body. Roll this large piece between the palms of your hands for a few seconds to make it soft and pliable. Roll it into a smooth, round ball. Position the ball between the lower part of your palms and taper one-half of the ball almost to a point. Form the opposite side to narrow it slightly, leaving the center of the ball in a rounded shape which will be the stomach of the bear. Roll and shape the body to make it 2 inches (5 cm) long. Slightly flatten the narrow end on top (the neck). Set the body aside.

3. Divide the piece of marzipan reserved for the rear legs (⅔ ounce/20 g) into two equal pieces. Roll the pieces (separately) to make them soft, then roll them into smooth, round balls. Place them, one at a time, between the lower part of your palms and roll to 2 inches (5 cm) long, tapering one end slightly. Bend the front

part of the narrow end on each leg to form the bear's paws. Apply a small amount of egg white to the inside of the legs where they will touch the body. Attach the legs to the wide end of the body (placing the bear so it is seated), pressing to flatten and widen the rear part of the legs at the same time. Position the body in the way that you want the bear to be posing: leaning forward or sitting back.

4. Repeat step 3 using the piece reserved for the front legs (½ ounce/15 g), but roll the front leg pieces to only 1¾ inches (4.5 cm) long. Fasten them to the upper part of the body. Depending on how you arrange the front legs you may need to use some type of support until the pieces are firm.

5. Pinch off a raisin-sized piece of marzipan from the piece reserved for the head (½ ounce/15 g); this small piece will be used to make the ears. Roll the remainder of the marzipan for the head to make it soft, then roll into a smooth, round ball. Place the ball between the lower part of your palms and taper one side to a small delicate point; leave the opposite side of the head round, not oblong. Hold the head in the palm of one hand. Use the tip of a small knife to make a ¼-inch (6-mm) cut for the mouth just below the tip of the nose. Twist the knife to open up the mouth slightly. Use a marzipan tool or other object with a small rounded end to make 2 shallow indentations for the eyes. Carefully (so you do not deform the head in the process) fasten the head to the body using egg white. To be able to attach the head in the exact position desired, apply a thin film of egg white to both the neck and the bottom of the head. Wait until the egg white is almost dry, but is still sticky. Very carefully place the head on the neck giving it a slight twist at the same time to seal the pieces together. Part of a toothpick, pressed into the body first so that just the tip is sticking out from the neck, can be very helpful to support the head. However, a toothpick should be used only if the figure is exclusively for display.

6. Roll the small piece for the ears between your thumbs to make it soft. Divide in half and roll the pieces one at a time into smooth, round balls. You may need to adjust the size of the pieces if they look too large; remember, bears have very small ears. Use the same rounded tool that you used to make the indentations for the eyes, and press the ears into the top of the head, using egg white as glue.

7. Roll the remaining piece of marzipan soft and round. Roll it into an oblong shape and fasten it to the back of the bear as the tail.

8. Make 3 small grooves in the end of each paw to make the bear's claws, using a marzipan tool or a blunt pointed object such as an instant-read meat thermometer.

9. Set the figure aside for a few hours or until the next day to allow the surface to dry slightly.

10. Place a little royal icing in a piping bag with a small opening. Pipe icing in the indentations made for the eyes.

11. Place melted baker's chocolate in a second piping bag with a small opening. Pipe a small dot of chocolate in each of the marks made for the claws. Pipe a larger dot of chocolate on the tip of the bear's nose. Wake the bear up by piping a small dot of chocolate on top of the icing in the eyes to mark the pupils. Last, pipe a thin eyebrow above each eye.

NOTE: If the figure is to be kept for some time, brush a thin film of hot cocoa butter over the marzipan before piping on the royal icing or the chocolate.

Marzipan Easter Bunny
one 3-ounce (85-g) figure

3 ounces (85 g) Marzipan, white (pages 529–531)
egg white
Royal Icing (pages 528–529)
melted dark baker's chocolate

1. See Figure 18–35 as a guide in constructing the bunny. Weigh out 2⅓ ounces (65 g) of marzipan to use for the body. Cover and reserve the remaining ⅔ ounce (20 g) to use for the head. Be sure that the work area and your hands are impeccably clean.

2. Roll the larger piece of marzipan between your hands for a few seconds until soft, then form into a completely smooth, round ball.

3. Place the marzipan on the table in front of you and roll the ball into a 4-inch (10-cm) long cone-shaped body with a blunt tip at the tapered end.

4. Use a thin, sharp knife to cut a very small slice off the thick end to flatten it enough that it will not roll. Reserve the piece you cut off to use later for the tail.

5. Stand the wide end so it is flat on the table and carefully bend the marzipan so that the front one-third is also on the table, and the middle is up about 1½ inches (3.7 cm) high (like the silhouette of a pouncing cat).

6. Make a cut in the front end, lengthwise, and twist the pieces toward the center so that the cut edges are against the table. Spread the two pieces apart slightly to form the front legs of the bunny. (Keep in mind that these steps must be completed rather quickly to prevent the softened marzipan from hardening again, and cracking or wrinkling as you mold it.)

7. Set the body aside, placing it over a dowel of suitable thickness to hold the curved shape, if necessary.

8. Roll the piece of marzipan reserved for the head to make it soft, then roll it into a round ball. Form the ball between the lower part of your palms to make it into a shape resembling a bowling pin, but tapered at the wide end. The piece should be 2¼ inches (5.6 cm) in length.

9. Place the head on the table and make a 1-inch (2.5-cm) cut lengthwise, starting at the narrow end. Spread the two pieces

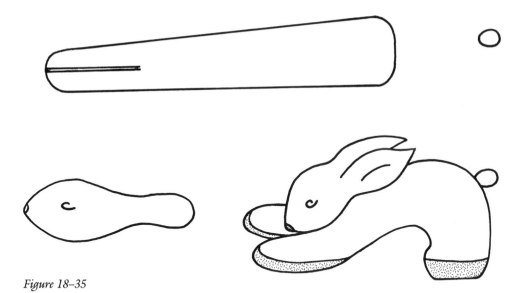

Figure 18–35

apart and flatten with your fingers a little to form the ears. Make two small indentations for the eyes.

10. Using egg white as glue, attach the head to the body, placing the nose between the front legs. Roll the small remaining piece into a ball, and glue in place as the tail. Set the figure aside for a few hours or overnight to allow the surface to dry somewhat.

11. Dip the bottom ¼ inch (6 mm) of the bunny in melted chocolate. Pipe a small dot of royal icing in the indentations made for the eyes. Last, make the bunny come alive by piping a smaller dot of melted chocolate on the tip of the nose and on top of the royal icing to make pupils in the eyes.

NOTE 1: If you wish to keep the figure fresh for some time, brush a thin film of hot cocoa butter on the marzipan before dipping it in chocolate and applying the royal icing.

NOTE 2: For a different look to the bunny, cut the thick end of the cone instead of the narrow end. Bend the cut halves so that the flat ends face the table, and spread them out and forward alongside the body on both ends like a rabbit about to jump. Flatten the uncut narrow end slightly and place the head on top. Or taper both ends of the body when rolling it out, cut both ends, position one front leg over the other, and arrange the rear legs to resemble a resting rabbit.

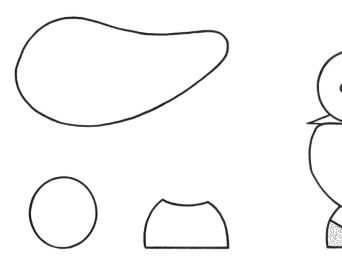

Figure 18–36

Marzipan Easter Chicken

one 2-ounce (55-g) figure

*⅓ ounce (10 g) Marzipan, white
(pages 529–531)*
egg white
*slightly more than 1½ ounces
(43 g) Marzipan, pale yellow
(pages 529–531)*
*1 blanched almond or
sliver of almond*
Royal Icing (pages 528–529)
melted dark baker's chocolate

1. See Figure 18–36 as a guide in constructing the chick. Make sure that your work area and hands are very clean. Roll the white marzipan in your hands until soft, then roll into a ball. Place on the table and make a shallow depression on the top with your thumb, pressing hard enough to make the ball slightly flat on the bottom so that it will not roll (it should be the size of a quarter). Set this piece, the nest, aside.

2. Cover and reserve a little less than ⅓ ounce (8 g) of the yellow marzipan. Roll the remainder between your palms to soften, then roll into a smooth, round ball. Roll the ball between the lower part of your palms to form a 2½-inch (6.2-cm) long cone, rounded on both ends.

3. Bend the narrow end up slightly, and press to flatten it a bit. Mark two lines on top of the flattened part using a modeling pin, or the back of a paring knife, to form a tail.

4. With a small pair of scissors make a thin cut from the rear about midway on either side of the wide end to form the wings. Bend the cut parts down slightly, and mark each wing in two places, as for the tail. Use a little egg white as glue and attach the chicken to the reserved nest.

5. Cut a pointed piece out of the almond to use for the chicken's beak.

6. Roll the reserved piece of yellow marzipan soft, then into a perfectly round ball. Make a small depression in the chicken's body where the head should go and attach the head, using egg white.

7. Place the beak between the head and the body. Mark two

small points with a marzipan tool (or other small pointed object) on either side of the head (not in the front) where the eyes will be. Allow the figure to dry for a few hours or overnight.

8. Dip the bottom ¼ inch (6 mm) of the nest in melted dark chocolate. Place the royal icing in a piping bag and pipe a small dot of icing in the impressions made for the eyes. Pipe an even smaller dot of chocolate on top of the icing for pupils. If you plan to keep the figure for some time, follow the preceding instructions in note 1 for the Easter bunny.

Marzipan Pig
one 3½-ounce (100-g) figure

3⅓ ounces (95 g) Marzipan, light pink
red food coloring
egg white
Royal Icing (pages 528–529)
melted baker's chocolate

1. See Figure 18–37 as a guide in constructing the pig. Starting with clean hands and a clean working surface, work a small piece of the marzipan soft in your hands, then roll it out, or flatten it, to ¹⁄₁₆ inch (2 mm) thick. Cut out two triangles (these will be the pig's ears) with 1-inch (2.5-cm) sides. Cover and reserve.

2. Color a small piece of the scraps, the size of a pea, with red food coloring. Roll it round and reserve.

3. Combine the scraps with the remaining marzipan. Pinch off a piece about the same size used to make both ears, cover it, and reserve for the tail.

4. Roll the remaining marzipan soft in your hands and roll it into a round ball. Place the ball on the table and roll it out to a 4-inch (10-cm) cone, keeping the wide end nicely rounded.

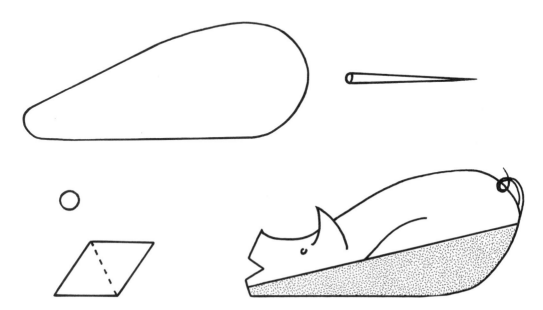

Figure 18–37

5. Place your thumb and index finger on either side of the narrow end, press lightly and, at the same time, use a small knife to flatten the narrow end of the cone, moving the knife from the bottom to the top to form the snout of the pig. Make a small cut for the mouth about two-thirds of the way from the top. Open the cut and place the reserved red ball (the apple) in the mouth.

6. Use the cone-shaped marzipan tool (or an instant-read meat thermometer) to make two deep holes for the ears to sit in, placing them about 1 inch (2.5 cm) from the snout. One at a time, form the reserved triangles around the tip of the cone tool, put a little egg white on them first, then push them into the holes. Arrange the ears so that they point slightly forward.

7. Make two small indentations close together between and below the ears for the pig's eyes, using the same tool. Make two identical marks in the upper part of the snout.

8. Place both index fingers on the sides of the pig about ¼ inch (6 mm) behind the head. Angle them 45° toward the back, and press hard, making two deep indentations to form the pig's body. Use a marzipan tool or a paring knife to make a vertical line in the center of the back end of the pig.

9. Roll the small piece of marzipan reserved for the tail smooth, then roll it into a 2-inch (5-cm) long thin rope, tapered to a point at one end. Use a little egg white to fasten the tail to the body, curling the pointed end. Let the pig dry for a few hours or, preferably, overnight.

10. Using a piping bag, pipe two small dots of royal icing in the indentations made for the eyes: Remember, pigs have small eyes set very close together. Pipe two smaller dots of chocolate on the royal icing to indicate the pupils. Dip the bottom of the pig into the melted chocolate, holding it at an angle to coat the pig about ¼ inch (6 mm) in the front and halfway up the sides in the back.

NOTE: Brush a thin film of cocoa butter on the figure before piping the eyes or dipping it in chocolate to keep it from drying if you plan to keep it more than a week or so.

Marzipan Roses and Leaves

A marzipan rose may not be as elegant as the famed pulled-sugar rose, but it certainly is more practical, because it can be made in minutes and can be eaten. Although a marzipan rose made for a special occasion should have twelve or more petals (depending on the shape and size of the rose), a nice-looking "production rose" can be made using only three petals attached to the center. The three-petal rose is naturally quicker and easier to make, and actually looks very much like a rose that is just about to bloom out.

Try to use either a marble slab or a wooden cutting board or table to work on. The surface must be clean and dry. Make sure the marzipan has a firm, smooth, consistency. If it is too dry or hard the marzipan will crack when you shape the petals. If it is too soft it cannot be worked thin enough without it sticking to the knife and falling apart. Adjust with a small amount of water or powdered sugar as needed.

To make eight medium-sized ⅔-ounce (20-g) roses you need to start with 10 ounces (285 g) of marzipan (you will have quite a bit left when you finish and cut off the bottoms).

1. Start by working one-fourth of the marzipan smooth and pliable (keep the remainder covered with plastic). Roll it out to a 16-inch (40-cm) rope.

2. Place the rope approximately 1 inch (2.5 cm) away from the edge of the table in front of you. Use your palm to flatten the rope into a wedge shape, with the narrow side toward the edge of the table (Figure 18–38). Keep the rope in a straight line and make sure it sticks to the table (use powdered sugar to prevent the marzipan from sticking to your hand).

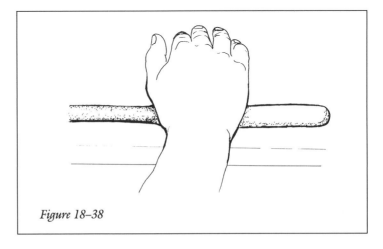

Figure 18–38

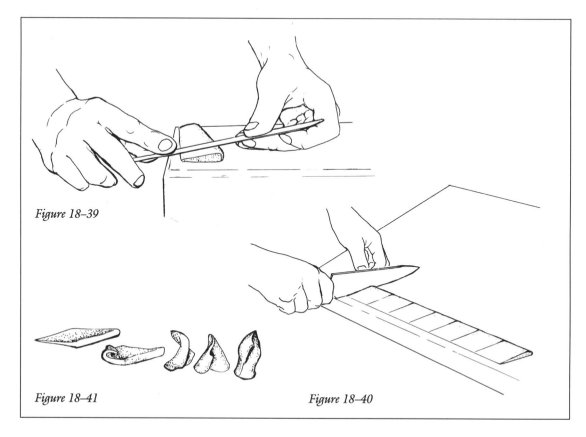

Figure 18–39

Figure 18–41

Figure 18–40

3. Lightly oil a spatula or knife with vegetable oil. Holding the spatula at an angle to keep the wedge shape, work the spatula over the rope, making long even strokes and using enough pressure to flatten the rope to a 1-inch (2.5-cm) wide strip (Figure 18–39). The strip should be paper-thin in the front.

4. Cut the flattened strip away from the table by quickly sliding a thin knife underneath, moving under the length of the strip in one smooth motion. Cut the strip diagonally into eight 2-inch (5-cm) pieces (Figure 18–40).

5. Roll each piece around itself so that it forms a cone, with the narrow part of the piece at the top. Then fold one end back slightly so that it looks like a bud about to open.

6. Squeeze the bottom of the bud to secure the shape, and set the bud on the table in front of you (Figure 18–41). Repeat with the remaining seven pieces. When you have finished making the centers, clean the work surface by scraping off any marzipan left from making them.

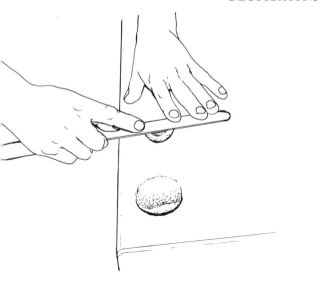

Figure 18–42

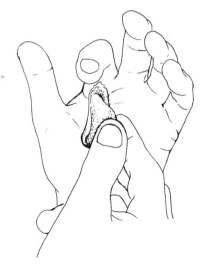

Figure 18–44

7. Work the remaining marzipan soft. Roll it out to a 16-inch (40-cm) rope. Cut the rope into 24 equal pieces. Roll the pieces into round balls. Place three to six balls (depending on how much work space you have) 8 inches (20 cm) apart, in a row in front of you at the edge of the table or marble slab. (Keep the remaining pieces covered with plastic.)

8. Flatten one side of each ball, as you did with the rope, to make them wedge-shaped. The flattened part should be on the sides, rather than the back or front. Make sure the pieces are stuck to the table.

9. Use an oiled knife or spatula held parallel to the table to enlarge the pieces, keeping the round shape, and working them out paper-thin on the flat side (Figure 18–42). This can also be done with the top of a light bulb or a plastic scraper.

10. Cut the petals free from the table by sliding a knife underneath, but leave them in place. Use the tip of your index finger to make an indentation on the thicker side of the petal (Figure 18–43). This will make it easier to bend the petal into the proper shape.

11. Pick up the petals, one at a time, and curl the thin edge back slightly to form a petal (Figure 18–44).

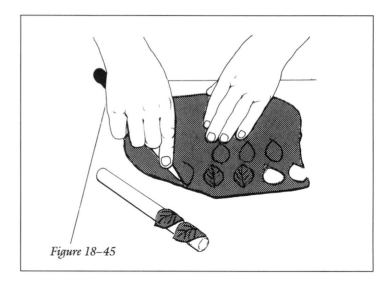

Figure 18–45

12. Fasten three petals around the center of the rose made earlier. Squeeze the base of the rose to secure the petals and make them open out slightly.

13. Cut away the excess marzipan from the bottom (save and use again). Repeat to make the remaining roses. Take care not to flatten too many petals at one time, or they will dry quickly and become difficult to form. The completed roses, however, can be made up days in advance without looking wilted. The thin edges will dry and become lighter in color, but that makes them look more authentic.

14. For a rose stem, roll light green marzipan to a thin string. Make the thorns by cutting the stems here and there with scissors. As on a real rose stem, the thorns should point upward.

15. Make rose leaves (Figure 18–45) by rolling out light green marzipan to $\frac{1}{16}$ inch (2 mm) thick. Using a sharp paring knife, cut out leaves of the appropriate size. Keep the tip of the knife clean and free from any pieces of marzipan, or the cuts will have a ragged and unattractive appearance. Mark veins on the leaves using the back side of the knife. Place a dowel on a sheet pan and prevent it from rolling (and throwing all the leaves off) by fastening a small piece of marzipan under each end. Put the leaves on the dowel so they will dry with a slightly bent, elegant curve. Let the leaves dry in a warm place for a few hours or, preferably, overnight.

Pâte à Choux for Decoration

4 ounces (115 g) paste

¼ cup (60 ml) milk
½ ounce (15 g) butter
3 tablespoons (36 g) bread flour
small pinch of salt
2 egg yolks

Piping out small, individual decorations with pâte à choux is done in much the same way as with chocolate, the main difference being that pâte à choux must then be baked before it is transferred to the pastry or cake, and is therefore never piped directly on top of the item, as chocolate is in many cases. The fact that this method is so easy to use (the pâte à choux will not set up if you work slowly) and is not very well known makes the finished pastries it is used on unusual and personalized. If possible, reserve a small amount of pâte à choux in the freezer when you make eclairs or cream puffs, for use later in making decorations. If none is available, you probably will only need to use the following proportions, since a little goes a long way. Follow the directions for making the paste on pages 15–16. Pass the pâte à choux through a fine sieve before piping it out. If the pâte à choux seems too stiff to pipe, stir in a small amount of milk.

1. Make a piping bag and cut a small opening. Pipe the figures onto baking papers following the same designs and techniques used for chocolate decorations (see Figures 16–14 to 16–16, pages 450–452). If the figures are complicated, or you want them to be identical, draw or trace the patterns onto the baking paper with a heavy pencil, invert the papers, and pipe on the other side so that the pâte à choux does not come in contact with the lead. If it matters that the figures will be reversed, or if you are making several of the same shape, place a second paper on top of the one with the tracings and secure the corners so that the papers will not slide as you pipe (a little pâte à choux makes an excellent glue).

2. Leave just the outline or fill in the designs, partially or fully, using a slightly modified version of hippen decorating paste (instructions follow). The paste can be left plain or tinted to light pastel colors to contrast with the golden pâte à choux: for example, a New Year's bell filled with light brown hippen paste, or an oak leaf with a pale green tint. Use a thicker grade of baking paper if you are filling in with the hippen paste because the thinner paper tends to curl from the moisture.

3. Bake the decorations at 375°F (190°C) until they start to turn light brown in a few spots (watch them like a hawk, it does not take very long and this is not something you want to burn). After they are cool place them on the cake or pastries.

Modified Hippen Decorating Paste

½ cup (120 ml) or 4½ ounces (130 g) paste

1 egg white
2½ ounces (70 g) almond paste
3 tablespoons (30 g) powdered
   sugar, sifted
2 teaspoons (8 g) bread flour
milk

1. Add the egg white to the almond paste and mix until smooth.
2. Incorporate the powdered sugar, flour, and, if necessary, enough milk so that the paste will just barely run out to the edges when piped inside the patterns.
3. For brown color add cocoa powder to the shade you want. If necessary add a few extra drops of milk.

Vanilla Tulips

25 to 30 cookie shells

7 ounces (200 g) granulated sugar
8 egg whites
1 teaspoon (5 ml) vanilla extract
5 ounces (140 g) bread flour
2 tablespoons (16 g) cornstarch
7 ounces (210 ml) clarified butter

1. Mix (do not whip) the sugar, egg whites, and vanilla together for about 1 minute. Sift the flour with the cornstarch and fold into egg white mixture. Add the clarified butter. Set the batter aside to rest for 30 minutes.
2. Make the larger version of the tulip template (Figure 18–46). The template as shown is the correct size for use in this recipe (the small template shown in the center is used in other recipes). Trace the drawing, then cut the template out of ¹⁄₁₆-inch (2-mm) cardboard (cake boxes are ideal).
3. Grease the back of even sheet pans very lightly. Coat with flour, then shake off as much flour as possible.
4. Spread the tulip batter onto the prepared pans spreading it flat and even within the template (Figure 18–47). Be careful when you pick up the template from the pan after spreading each one. Hold down the opposite end with your spatula as you lift off the template to avoid disturbing the batter (Figure 18–48).
5. Bake at 425°F (219°C) for approximately 8 minutes, or until there are a few light brown spots on the cookies. Leave the sheet pan in the oven and remove the tulips one at a time.
6. Working quickly, form the tulips (with the brown-side out) by pressing each cookie gently over an inverted bowl or cup. Use something that will give you a 3-inch (7.5-cm) opening at the top of your finished tulip. If you are making quite a few at once, form them by pressing a second bowl or cup on top of the tulip instead of using your hands; this way you can go on to forming the next one without waiting for each tulip to become firm. (See Figure 13–2, page 362.)

Variation: Chocolate Tulips

Delete the cornstarch and replace it with an equal amount of cocoa powder.

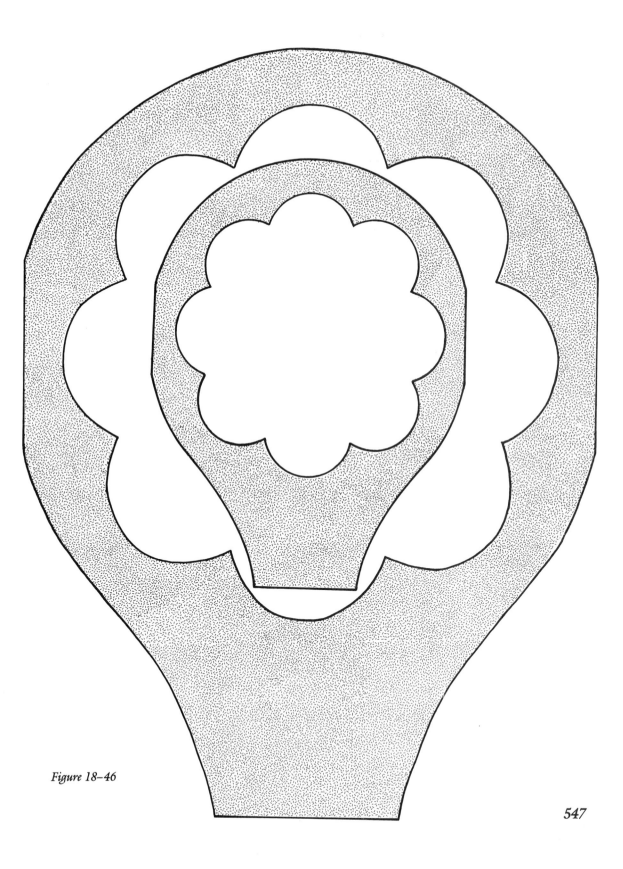

Figure 18–46

547

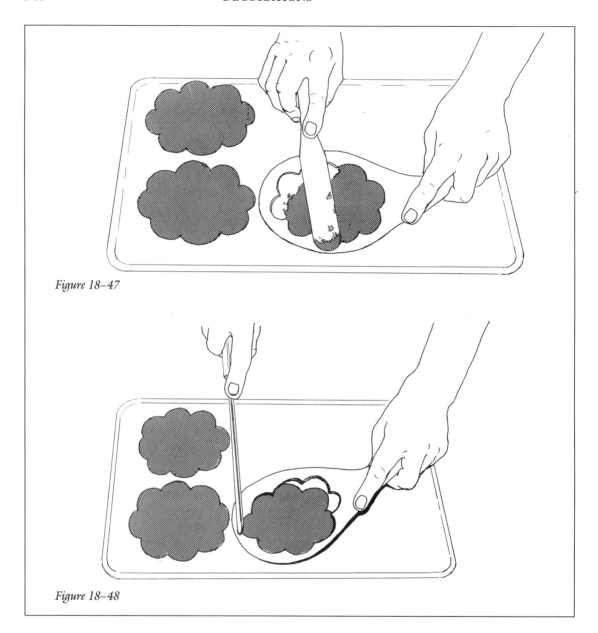

Figure 18–47

Figure 18–48

Wedding Cake Assembly and Decorations

There are so many different types and variations of wedding cakes that the topic can easily fill a book all by itself. The following is a very basic guide for assembling a simple, traditional cake, a starting point from which you may create your own interpretation.

Some of the cakes I've seen recently are a bit overdone in my opinion, including one with a waterfall cascading down through the tiers and another where the top tier was turning and blinking like a Christmas tree! This is not my idea of a wedding cake, but I must admit I have made some strange ones myself. After seeing some of my marzipan figures, one customer insisted on having nearly two dozen marzipan lions, tigers, elephants, and monkeys decorating all five tiers of the cake instead of flowers; the bride and groom were going on an African safari for their honeymoon. Another wanted marzipan sailboats all over the cake (they had the ceremony at a yacht club). But the strangest of all had to be the couple who requested two large, pink marzipan pigs (wearing running shoes!) on the top tier, one marzipan cat hidden in some fresh flowers on the middle tier, and sixteen marzipan crocodiles, nose-to-tail, encircling the bottom tier! Even after inquiring discreetly about this particular combination I never did fully understand its significance.

The classic wedding cake, of course, has none of this. The layers are typically separated and placed on a stand, usually with five tiers. The base is generally 18 inches (45 cm) in diameter, the top around 8 inches (20 cm), and each layer is between 4 and 5 inches (10 to 12.5 cm) in thickness. The cake is usually iced and decorated in white buttercream, with buttercream or marzipan roses tinted in a shade to coordinate with the color scheme of the wedding.

If the bottom tier is made of a regular chocolate or light sponge cake, even the largest sizes can be baked whole, although to ensure that they are fully cooked in the center you sometimes have to overbake the edges a little (this is usually not a problem because the cake must be trimmed to fit the cake stand anyway). With heavier cakes such as carrot, or a chocolate cake such as the Queen of Sheba, the larger sizes should always be baked in two or even three layers.

Cake Stand Assembly

1. Place the cake plates from the stand on top of cake cardboards (use the heavy, double-lined variety) and trace around them with a pen. If the stand you are using has supporting pillars going through the center, mark this spot on the cardboards also.

2. Draw a second line ⅛ inch (3 mm) inside the circles, using the cake plates as a guide (draw part of the way, move the plate, draw a bit more, etc., until you end up where you started).

3. Using a sharp carpet knife, cut out the smaller circles. Cut a space for the center support, if applicable.

4. Cut the skin from the top of the sponges, cutting them even at the same time. Check the bottoms and cut off the crust if this is too dark (usually on the larger sizes).

5. Place your cut cardboards on top of the appropriate sponges, and cut straight down, trimming the sides of the sponge to fit the cardboard exactly.

6. Cut the cakes into two or three layers. Place one layer on the cardboard, then fill and stack the layers. It is a good idea to brush the sponge with a mixture of simple syrup and a liqueur that is complementary to the flavor of the filling as you layer the sponges and filling, to be sure that the cake will be moist. This is especially important if you cut each sponge into only two layers.

7. To make sure that the buttercream is smooth and free from any air bubbles, soften it (over hot water if necessary) and place it in the mixer about 10 minutes before it is needed. Stir it, using the paddle attachment, on low speed.

8. Unless the buttercream is applied to the cakes in a very thick layer it is impossible to do so without getting some cake crumbs in it. For this reason you must first apply a crumb layer or crumb coat of buttercream. Ice the top and sides of the cakes with a thin layer of buttercream just as carefully as if you were icing the final layer. Place the cakes in the refrigerator long enough to harden the buttercream and glue the crumbs in place.

9. Remove one layer at a time from the refrigerator and place it on the corresponding cake-stand plate, attaching the cardboard to the plate with a piece of tape rolled into a loop, sticky-side out.

10. Place on a cake-decorating turntable, and ice the top and sides with buttercream in a perfectly even layer. This would have been quite hard, as well as time-consuming, if the cake had been the same size as the cake plate. However, since the stand is slightly wider than the cake, it is easy to fill the space and make the sides even by holding the spatula against the cake stand, straight up and down, while rotating the turntable. Ice all of the layers in the same manner.

11. If the layers are to be decorated with the typical drop-loop pattern (which can be done very quickly and simply or made as complicated as you wish) it is essential that the pattern come together evenly. You do not want the last loop to be one-quarter of the size of the others, since you usually decorate the top following the pattern on the sides (also, you will not always be able to display the cake in a corner to hide any imperfections from prying eyes!). Check the pattern and the remaining space to be decorated when you are three-quarters of the way around, to either increase or decrease the size of the loops gradually and make

them come out even. Or, evenly mark the top edge of the cake very lightly before piping to show where the loops begin and end. These marks can be covered when you decorate the top.

12. The top of the cakes are usually decorated with a simple pearl pattern piped around the edge (see Figure 18–7, page 504) and a rosette piped where the ends of each loop meet. The cakes can then be decorated with flowers, either buttercream (see page 500), marzipan (see pages 529–531), or fresh.

13. If the cakes have to be transported to another location for the reception, which is usually the case, take great care because a wedding cake, as opposed to a regular cake, has the same circumference as the base it is placed on, and it is therefore very easy to ruin the piping on the sides, and all of your careful work, with one careless move. (In fact, I have heard it said that there are only two people trustworthy enough to deliver a wedding cake: the person who made it and the person who is paying the bill!) I place each layer in an oversized box, with a double layer of heavy cardboard in the bottom, and attach the cake-stand plate to the cardboard with loops of masking tape (in addition to sternly cautioning the driver to drive carefully). While it is unlikely that you will be able to close the lids of the cake boxes, it is a good idea to try and cover the cakes to some degree because any fine dust or ash blowing in the air will stick immediately to the soft buttercream and be impossible to remove without leaving a mark.

Stacked Wedding Cakes

This is a much easier and quicker method of making wedding cakes, plus there is no cake stand to take a deposit on, or to check to see if all of the pieces were returned. And if the cake is decorated with fresh flowers, as is so popular now, making this type of wedding cake is not any more difficult than making any large cake.

1. Cut out cardboards slightly smaller than your sponge layers, using a sharp carpet knife so you can cut precisely and evenly. It is essential that you use the thick grade of cardboard, not just to ensure proper support for the cake, but to avoid having the cardboard warp. Cut out two extra cardboards, one about 1 inch (2.5 cm) smaller and one 3 inches (7.5 cm) larger, than the piece cut for the base of the stacked cake.

2. Glue small 5-inch (12.5-cm) round lace doilies all around the perimeter of the largest cardboard. They should protrude out beyond the cardboard just a little bit. Do not use staples to attach the doilies; they can very easily come loose and get into the cake. Glue the smaller extra cardboard in the center of the one covered with doilies. Set aside. You can of course place the cake on top of

one of the cake plates from the traditional cake stand and avoid having to make this base, but that takes away the convenience of not having to worry about getting the stand back.

3. Cut hollow, clear plastic pipes, ½ to ¾ inches (1.2 to 2 cm) in diameter, into lengths slightly longer than the height of the cake layers. You need four to support each of the larger layers, and three to support each of the smaller sizes, using the dimensions given for the tiers earlier. Make sure that all of the pillars used for each layer are exactly the same height, or the cake will lean.

4. Fill, layer, and ice the cakes with the crumb layer as described in the preceding directions.

5. When the crumb layer is chilled, place the layers one at a time on the turntable, and ice the tops.

6. A nice way to decorate the sides of a stacked cake is to pipe vertical lines of buttercream on the sides using a no. 5 (10-mm) flat star tip (see Figure 18–2, page 502), piping the strips next to each other and making sure you cover the cardboard at the bottom at the same time; pipe from the bottom to the top. Another way is to leave about ¼ inch (6 mm) of space between the strips, then go back and fill the space in later with a series of small dots spaced evenly from top to bottom, the bottom dot covering the cardboard. Use the same plain tip to make the dots as you use to make the decoration on the tops of the cakes.

7. Even off any buttercream that sticks up above the edge on the top. Do the same on the lower edge of the cake, holding the spatula at a 45° angle against the cardboard. Decorate the top of the layers with a pearl pattern piped with a no. 3 (6-mm) plain tip.

8. When all of the layers are iced and decorated, place the bottom layer on the base made earlier, attaching it with loops of tape so it will not slide. Push the plastic pillars into the cake, spacing them evenly and placing them so that the next layer will fit securely on top. Stack the remaining layers with pillars in between in the same way. Decorate the cake with flowers.

Even though you could stack enough cakes to serve a wedding party of 400 to 500 guests if the layers were supported properly, it would be very expensive and is not really practical. A better way is to make a smaller cake for display and the cake-cutting ceremony, and to make up the remainder of the servings from sheet cakes made with the same flavors of sponge, filling, and buttercream. The sheet cakes can be cut and plated ahead of time and be ready to serve from the kitchen. This is also a good thing to suggest to a customer with a wedding party of 100 to 200 people who is trying to reduce the cost. A sheet cake will usually cut the per-person cost by about 60 percent, and if it is made of the same cake, the guests will never know the difference.

Naturally both the price and the number of servings you can get out of a cake depend on what kind of cake it is and who is serving it. Chocolate Truffle Cake with Raspberries, for example, can be cut into smaller slices than a light sponge cake. The following table works well for estimating the number of servings for various layers. To be even more accurate, you should also take into consideration what else is being served at the reception, whether it is just cake and champagne or a buffet dinner or hors d'oeuvres. Depending on these factors:

- an 18-inch (45-cm) cake will serve 40 to 50 guests
- a 16-inch (40-cm) cake will serve 30 to 40 guests
- a 14-inch (35-cm) cake will serve 25 to 30 guests
- a 12-inch (30-cm) cake will serve 15 to 20 guests
- a 10-inch (25-cm) cake will serve 10 to 15 guests
- an 8-inch (20-cm) cake will serve 8 to 10 guests

You usually cannot count the top tier (except on the bill), because it will probably be saved.

—NINETEEN—

Sauces and Fillings

Sauces
   Apricot Sauce
   Blueberry Sauce
   Caramel Sauce I
   Caramel Sauce II
   Cherry Sauce
   Cranberry Sauce
   Crème Fraîche
   Hot Fudge Sauce
   Hot or Cold Chocolate Sauce
   Kiwi Sauce
   Mango Sauce
   Mascarpone Sauce
   Mousseline Sauce
   Orange Sauce
   Persimmon Sauce
   Pineapple Sauce
   Plum Sauce

Raspberry Sauce
Romanoff Sauce
Strawberry Sauce
Sour Cream Mixture
   for Piping
Vanilla Custard Sauce
Fillings
   Cherry Filling
   Chocolate Cream
   Chunky Apple Filling
   Classic Bavarian Cream
   Crème Parisienne
   Ganache
   Lemon Cream
   Lemon Curd
   Mazarin Filling
   Pastry Cream
   Vanilla Bavarian Cream

*T*he old saying that a cook is judged by his or her sauces, originally said with savory sauces in mind, can be just as true in the pastry kitchen, and equally true for fillings. The sauce and filling can be as important as a pretty decoration on a cake. A refreshing red raspberry sauce with a dense slice of chocolate cake, rich caramel sauce on a warm apple tart, gooey fudge sauce on poached pears and vanilla ice cream, sauce sabayon with a liqueur soufflé, or strawberry sauce with sour cream hearts to garnish a Valentine dessert, are sauces that really make the dessert and turn it into something memorable.

Served on the side in a sauceboat, or presented on the plate and enhanced with a piped design, the sauce can add a tremendous amount to the presentation as well as to the flavor of the dessert. As discussed in Chapter 18, Decorations, the current fashion of making elaborate sauce paintings is extremely popular for both desserts and other courses. A particular sauce can also be used to change the feeling of a traditional dessert presentation and add more variety to your menu. For an exotic tropical presentation and a more sophisticated tone, try serving a mango or papaya sauce with a chocolate cake instead of the more mundane whipped cream or crème anglaise.

Although many sauces, especially those made with puréed fruit, are quickly prepared, it is much better to have a little left over than to run out in the middle of the service. Many sauces (and fillings) should always be on hand as part of your general *mise en place*.

Of course there is another old saying to keep in mind (para-phrased slightly): "As long as there is water in the tap, there is sauce on the menu."

As for fillings, what would a profiterole be without the Bavarian cream inside, or a bear claw without its nutty filling. And a layer of ganache or lemon curd can go a long way toward dressing up and flavoring many other pastries and petits fours. A rich, moist filling can also come to your rescue in saving a slightly overbaked or stale sponge (the emphasis here is on slightly — don't expect a miracle if the sponge is really finished).

As with sauces, different fillings can be used with the same shell to create a greater selection without increasing the work proportionately. Fill an assortment of tartlet shells with mazarin filling, ganache, pastry cream topped with fresh fruit, and caramel walnut filling. Garnish them appropriately, and you will have four entirely different pastries. If these fillings are kept on hand (along with a supply of short dough) this can be done with very little effort.

Sauces

Apricot Sauce

approximately 4 cups
(960 ml) sauce

2½ pounds (1 kg, 135 g)
    pitted fresh apricots
3 cups (720 ml) water
3 ounces (85 g) granulated sugar
2 tablespoons (16 g) cornstarch
2 tablespoons (30 ml) water

With such a variety of fresh fruit available from all over the world today, I am opposed to using fruit from a can just because a particular fruit is out of season. However, apricots are one of the few exceptions. Their season is too short to take full advantage of this delicious fruit, and because apricot sauce complements so many different desserts, it is welcome all year round.

1. Cut the apricots into quarters. Place in a saucepan with the first measurement of water and the sugar. Bring to a boil, then cook over medium heat until the fruit is soft. This will take approximately 10 minutes, depending on the ripeness of the fruit.

2. Strain the mixture, forcing as much of the flesh through the strainer as possible with the back of a spoon or ladle. Discard the contents of the strainer. Pour the sauce back into the saucepan.

3. Dissolve the cornstarch in the remaining water. Stir into the sauce. Bring the sauce back to a boil and cook for about 1 minute to remove the flavor of the cornstarch. Store the sauce covered in the refrigerator. If the sauce is too thick, thin with water to the desired consistency.

NOTE: The yield of this recipe will vary depending on the ripeness of the apricots.

Variation: Apricot Sauce from Canned Apricots

4 cups sauce (960 ml)

2½ pounds (1 kg, 135 g) strained apricots canned in syrup
2 cups (480 ml) liquid from canned apricots
2 tablespoons (16 g) cornstarch
2 tablespoons (30 ml) water

1. Follow the directions in the preceding recipe, replacing the first measurement of water with the apricot liquid, and reducing the cooking time in step 1 to 1 minute. If the sauce is too thick, thin with water to the desired consistency.

Blueberry Sauce

3 cups (720 ml) sauce

7 ounces (200 g) granulated sugar
1½ cups (360 ml) cranberry juice
1 tablespoon (15 ml) lime juice
2 tablespoons (16 g) cornstarch
3 tablespoons (45 ml) rum
1 dry pint (480 ml) blueberries

1. Place the sugar, cranberry juice, lime juice, cornstarch, and rum in a saucepan. Bring to a boil and cook for a few minutes.
2. Remove from the heat and stir in the blueberries. Let cool. Store covered in the refrigerator.

NOTE: Due to the large amount of pectin in blueberries, the sauce may set up too much. Reheat, stirring, until the sauce is liquid and smooth again, then adjust with water.

Caramel Sauce I

2½ cups (600 ml) sauce

1 pound (455 g) granulated sugar
1 teaspoon (5 ml) lemon juice
1½ cups (360 ml) water

1. Melt or caramelize the sugar and lemon juice to the desired color, following the procedure on page 488.
2. Remove the pan from the heat and carefully pour in the water. Stand back a little as you do this because the syrup may splatter. Stir to mix in the water.
3. Let the sauce cool completely, then add additional water, if necessary, to thin it to the proper consistency. You must wait until the sauce has cooled before judging the thickness because it will vary depending on the degree to which you caramelized the sugar.

Caramel Sauce II

2½ cups (600 ml) sauce

12 ounces (340 g) granulated
   sugar
2 tablespoons (30 ml) water
½ teaspoon (2.5 ml) lemon juice
1½ cups (360 ml) heavy cream
2 ounces (55 g) butter

This is a richer caramel sauce and is intended to be served hot. It will be quite thick when it has cooled. You can thin it with water to the desired consistency to serve cold or at room temperature, or you can use Caramel Sauce I, which is more appropriate for masking a plate, for example. Caramel Sauce II is perfect for serving with ice cream or tarts.

1. Melt and caramelize the sugar, water, and lemon juice to an amber color.

2. Remove the pan from the heat and add the heavy cream carefully. Stand back as you pour in the cream as the mixture may splatter. Stir to mix in the cream. If the sauce is not smooth, return to the heat and cook, stirring constantly, to remove any lumps.

3. Add the butter (with the pan off the heat). Keep stirring until the butter has melted and the sauce is smooth.

Cherry Sauce

2 cups (480 ml) sauce

1 pound (455 g) fresh cherries or
   sweet, canned cherries
8 ounces (225 g) granulated
   sugar, approximately
1½ cups (360 ml) red wine
grated zest from 1 lemon
2 tablespoons (16 g) cornstarch
1 teaspoon (5 ml) vanilla extract

1. Pit the cherries and place them in a saucepan together with the sugar, wine, and lemon zest. Bring to a boil and cook over medium heat until the cherries are soft (canned cherries will only need to cook about 5 minutes). Purée the mixture, then strain.

2. Dissolve the cornstarch in a small amount of the puréed liquid. Stir into the remainder. Bring to a boil and cook for a few seconds. Remove from the heat and add the vanilla extract. Cherry Sauce can be served hot or cold.

NOTE: I like to use bing cherries, when I can get them, because their dark skin gives the sauce a rich color. If you use canned cherries, strain out the syrup and reserve for another use, such as Black Forest Cake, or discard. You may want to adjust the amount of sugar depending on the type of cherries and wine used.

Cranberry Sauce

3 cups (720 ml) sauce

12 ounces (340 g) fresh or
   frozen cranberries
8 ounces (225 g) granulated sugar
2 cups (480 ml) water

1. Combine the cranberries, sugar, and water in a saucepan. Bring to a boil, then reduce the heat and simmer for 10 minutes. The cranberries should be soft and have popped open.

2. Remove from the heat. Immediately purée and strain. Bring back to a quick boil, then let cool.

3. Skim off any foam that forms on the surface. Store sauce covered in the refrigerator, but serve at room temperature. If the sauce is too thick after it has cooled, thin with water.

Crème Fraîche

2 cups (480 ml)

1 ounce (30 g) sour cream
2 cups (480 ml) heavy cream

1. Stir the sour cream into the heavy cream. Let stand at 80° to 90°F (26° to 32°C) for 24 hours. An oven with a pilot light, or the top of a stove with pilots, are possible places to maintain this temperature. Store covered in the refrigerator. Crème Fraîche will keep four to five days.
2. To thicken the cream, whip until you achieve the desired consistency.

Hot Fudge Sauce

6 cups (1 l, 440 ml) sauce

7 ounces (200 g) cocoa powder
8 ounces (225 g) brown sugar
8 ounces (225 g) granulated sugar
1¾ cups (420 ml) heavy cream
12 ounces (340 g) butter
½ teaspoon (3 g) salt

1. Thoroughly combine the cocoa powder, brown sugar, and granulated sugar.
2. Place the cream, butter and salt in a saucepan over low heat. Melt the butter in the cream and bring the mixture to scalding.
3. Whisk in the sugar and cocoa mixture gradually to avoid lumps. Cook over low heat, stirring constantly with the whisk, until the sugar has dissolved and the mixture is smooth. Serve immediately or keep warm over a hot water bath.

NOTE: This sauce must be served warm because it becomes much too thick when cold or even at room temperature. Reheat leftover sauce over simmering water.

Hot or Cold Chocolate Sauce

4 cups (960 ml) sauce

2 cups (480 ml) water
10 ounces (285 g) granulated sugar
½ cup (120 ml) glucose or light corn syrup
4 ounces (115 g) cocoa powder
10 ounces (285 g) melted dark chocolate

This is a versatile recipe which can be kept on hand to serve either hot or cold. It is best suited to garnish a dessert—a slice of cake, a pastry, or poached fruit, for example. If you serve the sauce as a main component of the dessert, most notably with ice cream, use Hot Fudge Sauce instead.

1. Combine the water, sugar, and glucose or corn syrup in a saucepan. Bring to a boil.
2. Add enough of the syrup to the cocoa powder to make a paste and stir it back into the remaining syrup.
3. Remove from the heat, add the melted chocolate, and stir until combined. If necessary, strain the sauce before serving.

NOTE: As with caramel sauce, chocolate sauce is much thinner when it is hot. If you plan to serve the chocolate sauce cold, let it cool to room temperature first, then add water if you need to thin it. If the sauce has been refrigerated, warm it up to room temperature before adjusting. The recipe makes a fairly thick sauce, ideal to cover a pear, for example, but it is usually too thick to mask a plate without adding water.

Chocolate Sauce for Piping

This sauce is used to pipe designs and decorate other sauces as part of many dessert presentations (see page 517). To make the most attractive designs and prevent the sauces from bleeding together, make the chocolate sauce the same consistency as the other sauce you are using. Adjust the chocolate sauce by adding water, to make it thinner, or melted chocolate, to thicken it.

Kiwi Sauce

*approximately 4 cups
(960 ml) sauce*

*3 tablespoons (27 g) unflavored
   gelatin powder
3½ cups (840 ml) kiwi juice
   (instructions follow)
12 ounces (340 g) granulated
   sugar, approximately*

You will need about 10 ripe kiwis to make the juice. Peel the fruit and process in a food processor for just a few seconds to ensure that you do not break too many of the black seeds; they can give the sauce a muddy appearance. Strain through a medium strainer, allowing some of the seeds to stay in the sauce.

1. Soften the gelatin in about ½ cup (120 ml) of the kiwi juice. Add the sugar to the remaining juice and heat the mixture to approximately 110°F (43°C).
2. Quickly whisk in the softened gelatin. Store covered. If the sauce is refrigerated, the gelatin will make the sauce set. Reheat it, stirring constantly, until liquid and smooth again.
NOTE: Since the kiwi fruit will lose most of its distinctive green color if heated to a boil, I prefer not to use cornstarch as a thickening agent in this recipe.

Mango Sauce

4 cups (960 ml) sauce

*3½ pounds (1 kg, 590 g)
   ripe mangos (5 to 6)
¼ cup (60 ml) lime juice,
   approximately
¼ cup (60 ml) orange juice,
   approximately*

1. Use only perfectly ripe mangos for this sauce. They should yield easily to light pressure and have a pleasant, sweet smell. Unfortunately, the ripe fruits are also extremely difficult to peel. To overcome this, slice off the two broader sides as close to the large flat seed as possible, and then scoop out the flesh from these halves. Discard the skin. Cut and scrape the remaining flesh away from the seed.
2. Place the mango pulp in a food processor along with the lime and orange juice. Purée; then strain out any stringy fibers using a fine-meshed strainer (*étamé*). Adjust the flavor and consistency with additional lime or orange juice as desired.
NOTE: If the sauce is not to be used within an hour or so, bring it to a quick boil to prevent the sauce from oxidizing and turning brown.

Mascarpone Sauce

about 4 cups (960 ml) sauce

1 pound, 5 ounces (595 g)
mascarpone cheese
at room temperature
3 tablespoons (45 ml)
amaretto liqueur
1¼ cups (300 ml) half-and-half,
approximately

1. Thoroughly combine the cheese, liqueur, and half-and-half, mixing until completely smooth.

2. Adjust the amount of cream as necessary to make the sauce thin enough to flow out when poured. Store covered in the refrigerator, but serve at room temperature.

Mousseline Sauce

about 6 cups (1 l, 440 ml) sauce

3 ounces (85 g) granulated sugar
5 egg yolks
⅓ cup (80 ml) boiling water
1 teaspoon (5 ml) vanilla extract
1½ cups (360 ml) heavy cream

1. Whip together the sugar and egg yolks just to combine. Whisk in the boiling water. Place the bowl over simmering water and thicken to ribbon stage, whipping constantly. Remove from the heat and whip until cool. Add the vanilla extract.

2. Whip the heavy cream until thickened to a sauce-like consistency. Combine with the yolk mixture. If needed, thin the sauce with a little heavy cream. Mousseline Sauce can be stored, covered, in the refrigerator for up to one week. It tends to become watery after one day, but whisking will bring it back to its original consistency.

NOTE: If you are serving Mousseline Sauce with a recipe that does not specify flavoring it with a liqueur or spirit, you may want to add ¼ cup (60 ml) per recipe.

Orange Sauce

4 cups (960 ml) sauce

4 cups (960 ml) fresh orange juice,
strained (10 to 12 oranges)
5 tablespoons (40 g) cornstarch
juice of half a lemon
6 ounces (170 g) granulated
sugar, approximately

1. Add enough orange juice to the cornstarch to make it liquid. Stir it into the remaining orange juice. Add the lemon juice and sugar. Adjust the taste by adding more or less sugar as needed, depending on the sweetness of the orange juice.

2. Heat to boiling in a stainless steel or other non-corrosive pan. Lower the heat and cook for 1 minute while stirring constantly. Let cool completely. If the sauce is too thick, thin with water. Store, covered, in the refrigerator.

NOTE: If the sauce sets to a jelly-like consistency, reheat it to thin. You can stretch the sauce by replacing part of the orange juice with water and sweetening it with sugar according to taste.

Bitter Orange Sauce

Follow the recipe for Orange Sauce with the following changes: cut the peel of half of the oranges into about six pieces each and add these to the juice. It is not necessary to strain the juice now, as directed. Follow the procedure for making the Orange Sauce, including the peels with the juice. Set the sauce aside to allow the peels to macerate for 30 minutes. Strain to remove the orange peel as well as any pits or sediment.

Persimmon Sauce

2 cups (480 ml) sauce

1¾ cups (420 ml) strained
    persimmon pulp
3 tablespoons (45 ml) lime juice
2 tablespoons (30 ml) orange juice
2 tablespoons (30 ml) honey

1. See the recipe for Persimmon Pudding on page 423 for information on how to process the persimmon pulp.
2. Combine the persimmon pulp, lime juice, orange juice, and honey. Thin with additional orange juice if desired.

Pineapple Sauce

2 cups (480 ml) sauce

2 medium-sized, fresh,
    ripe pineapples
2 tablespoons (16 g) cornstarch
6 ounces (170 g) granulated sugar
2 teaspoons (10 ml) lime juice
2 teaspoons (10 ml) light rum

1. Peel the pineapples and cut away the core. Measure 2 pounds (910 g) of pineapple flesh to use in the sauce. Set aside the remainder for another use.
2. Chop 3 ounces (85 g) of the pineapple to raisin-sized pieces. Reserve. Purée the remaining pineapple in a food processor, then strain into a saucepan.
3. Dissolve the cornstarch in a small amount of the pineapple purée, then stir it back into the remainder together with the chopped pineapple and the sugar.
4. Bring the mixture to a boil and cook over medium heat, stirring constantly, for about 1 minute.
5. Remove from the heat. Stir in the lime juice and rum. Cool, then store, covered, in the refrigerator.

Plum Sauce

4 cups (960 ml) sauce

2 pounds, 8 ounces (1 kg, 135 g)
    fresh pitted plums
    or
2 pounds (910 g) drained canned
    pitted plums
3 cups (720 ml) water or liquid
    from canned plums
6 ounces (170 g) granulated sugar
2 tablespoons (16 g) cornstarch

1. Santa Rosa or Casselman plums are a good choice when they are in season, but in any case use a red or purple variety of plum, which will give the sauce a pleasant pastel red color. Cut fresh plums into quarters.
2. Reserve 2 tablespoons (30 ml) of the water or canning liquid and place the plums in a saucepan with the remaining liquid and the sugar (if using canned fruit packed in syrup, omit the sugar). Bring to a boil and cook over medium heat until the fruit is soft enough to fall apart, approximately 15 minutes for fresh plums, 1 minute for canned.

3. Remove from the heat and strain, forcing as much of the pulp as possible through the strainer using the back of a spoon or a ladle. Discard the contents of the strainer.

4. Dissolve the cornstarch in the reserved liquid. Add to the sauce. Return the mixture to the saucepan and bring to a boil. Cook for 1 minute to remove the taste of the cornstarch. Serve hot or cold. Store covered in the refrigerator.

Raspberry Sauce

4 cups (960 ml) sauce

3 tablespoons (24 g) cornstarch
4 cups (960 ml) strained
*   raspberry purée*
granulated sugar

1. Place the cornstarch in a saucepan. Mix enough of the purée into the cornstarch to liquefy, then stir in the remaining purée.

2. Heat the sauce to simmering. Taste and add granulated sugar if needed, depending on the sweetness of the fruit.

3. Simmer the sauce for a few minutes. Cool and thin with water, if necessary. Store, covered, in the refrigerator.

Romanoff Sauce

4 cups (960 ml) sauce

3 cups (720 ml) heavy cream
1 cup (240 ml) sour cream

1. Mix the heavy cream with the sour cream and whip them together until the mixture has thickened to the consistency of molasses.

2. If the sauce is not to be used immediately, adjust the consistency at serving time by whipping the sauce to thicken it or adding additional heavy cream to thin it. Store the sauce in the refrigerator.

Strawberry Sauce

4 cups (960 ml) sauce

2 tablespoons (16 g) cornstarch
4 cups (960 ml) strained
*   strawberry purée*
granulated sugar

1. Place the cornstarch in a saucepan. Mix enough of the purée into the cornstarch to make it pourable, then stir in the remaining purée.

2. Heat the sauce to simmering. Add granulated sugar as needed, depending on the sweetness of the fruit.

3. Simmer the sauce for a few minutes. Cool and thin with water, if necessary. Store, covered, in the refrigerator.

NOTE: If the strawberries are not quite ripe, and therefore white inside, color the sauce with a small amount of raspberry juice or sauce. Only in the most dire case should you use a drop of red food coloring.

Sour Cream Mixture for Piping

heavy cream
sour cream

This is a much easier and quicker method than thickening the cream by whipping.

1. Gradually stir enough heavy cream into sour cream until the mixture is approximately the same consistency as the sauce you are decorating.

2. Pour into a piping bottle (see page 603). This mixture will keep for days in the refrigerator, but it may have to be thinned.

NOTE: The sour cream mixture and the sauce must have the same consistency for decorating. If the sour cream is too thick it will not blend with the sauce, but break up into pieces instead. If it is too thin, it will run into the sauce and you will not get clearly defined lines. The sauce, too, must be of the proper consistency to begin with: If it is too thin it cannot be decorated at all.

Vanilla Custard Sauce
(Crème Anglaise)

5½ cups (1 l, 320 ml) sauce

12 egg yolks
8 ounces (225 g) granulated sugar
1 quart (960 ml) half-and-half
1 vanilla bean, split
  or
1 tablespoon (15 ml) vanilla
  extract

Vanilla Custard Sauce is prepared using the same basic method that is used to make the custard for Vanilla Ice Cream. I use half-and-half, rather than milk, which is traditional, so that the chilled sauce can be frozen in a pinch to make ice cream. The resulting ice cream will not be quite as rich as usual but, as they say, "in a storm any port will do." In an emergency you can do the opposite and thaw Vanilla Ice Cream if you run out of Vanilla Custard Sauce (you will need to thin the ice cream a bit with some milk or half-and-half). The sauce tastes especially nice with apple or pear tarts, and can be flavored to complement many different desserts. Like any heated mixture containing eggs, Vanilla Custard Sauce is a perfect breeding ground for bacteria, so follow strict sanitary guidelines.

1. Combine the egg yolks and sugar in a mixing bowl. Whip until light and fluffy.

2. Bring the half-and-half to the scalding point with the vanilla bean, if used. Gradually pour the hot cream into the yolk mixture while stirring rapidly.

3. Place the mixture over simmering water and heat slowly, stirring constantly, until it is thick enough to coat the back of a spoon. (Be very careful not to get it hotter than 190°F (88°C) or it will curdle.)

4. Immediately pour the custard into another container and continue stirring for a minute or so. Remove the vanilla bean and save it for another use, or stir in the vanilla extract. Set the sauce aside to cool, stirring from time to time. Store, covered, in the refrigerator. The sauce will keep this way for up to one week.

NOTE: The sauce can be made up much quicker if you cook it directly over low heat. Of course, this is a little more tricky. Should you overheat and curdle the sauce, you can usually save it by adding 1 ounce (30 ml) heavy cream and processing it in a blender, providing the sauce has only curdled and not scorched.

Fillings

Cherry Filling

4 pounds, 4 ounces (1 kg, 935 g) filling

2 pounds (910 g) drained sweet canned cherries
3 cups (720 ml) liquid from canned cherries
Simple Syrup (page 7)
2 tablespoons (30 ml) raspberry juice
2 ounces (55 g) cornstarch
2 ounces (55 g) pectin powder
2 ounces (55 g) granulated sugar

1. Drain the juice from the cherries, pressing the cherries firmly without crushing them. The liquid must be completely drained off or the filling will be too runny. Measure the liquid; if there is not enough add Simple Syrup to make up the difference.
2. Add the raspberry juice to the cherry liquid. Dissolve the cornstarch in a small amount of this mixture before stirring into the remainder. Mix the pectin powder with the sugar. Blend into the cherry liquid mixture.
3. Bring the mixture to a boil, stirring constantly. Cook over medium heat until completely thickened, about 5 minutes.
4. Remove from the heat and add the drained cherries. Place a piece of baking paper directly on the surface to prevent a skin from forming as the filling cools. Store the filling, covered, in the refrigerator.

NOTE: The cornstarch will start to break down and the filling will become watery after a few days. To restore its original consistency, reheat to the scalding point, stirring constantly.

Variation: Fresh Cherry Filling

2 pounds (910 g) Bing or Lambert cherries
3 cups (720 ml) Poaching Syrup II (page 6)
2 tablespoons (30 ml) raspberry juice
¼ cup (60 ml) lemon juice
2 ounces (55 g) cornstarch
2 ounces (55 g) pectin powder

1. Wash, remove the stems, and pit the cherries.
2. Cook the cherries in poaching syrup until tender, 4 to 5 minutes. Strain, reserving the cherries and the syrup separately.
3. Combine the raspberry juice, lemon juice, cornstarch, and pectin powder, and stir to dissolve the cornstarch. Add this mixture to the reserved syrup.
4. Bring the mixture to a boil, stirring constantly. Cook over medium heat until completely thickened, about 5 minutes.
5. Remove from the heat and add the drained cherries. Place a piece of baking paper directly on the surface to prevent a skin from forming as the filling cools. Store the filling, covered, in the refrigerator.

Chocolate Cream

2 pounds, 6 ounces (1 kg, 80 g)
filling

3 pints (1 l, 440 ml) heavy cream
3 egg whites
7 ounces (200 g) melted
*   dark chocolate*
¼ cup (60 ml) Simple Syrup
*   (page 7)*
¼ cup (60 ml) water

1. Whip the cream with the egg whites until they become slightly thickened. Be careful: If you overwhip the cream it will break when you add the chocolate. (It can also break if the butterfat in the cream is too low; the egg whites help to stabilize the cream.)

2. Mix together the melted chocolate, simple syrup, and water. Heat the mixture to 130°F (54°C).

3. Place a small amount of the whipped cream mixture in a bowl and gradually add the chocolate mixture, whisking rapidly. Add the rest of the cream and mix in. If the chocolate cream seems runny, whip it to a firmer consistency.

Chunky Apple Filling

2 pounds, 12 ounces (1 kg, 250 g)
or 5 cups (1 l, 200 ml) filling

3 pounds (1 kg, 365 g) Granny
*   Smith, pippin, or Golden*
*   Delicious apples*
10 ounces (285 g) granulated
*   sugar, approximately*
¼ cup (60 ml) water
juice of half a lemon

1. Peel and core the apples. Chop approximately two-thirds of the apples into ½-inch (1.2-cm) pieces.

2. Place the chopped apples in a saucepan with the sugar, water, and lemon juice. Adjust the amount of sugar according to the tartness of the apples and your own taste. Stir to combine and cook over medium heat, stirring from time to time, until the mixture starts to thicken.

3. Chop the remaining apples into ¼-inch (6-mm) pieces and add them to the filling as it begins to thicken.

4. Continue cooking the filling until the apple chunks are soft and the filling has reached a jam-like consistency. Let cool at room temperature, then store, covered, in the refrigerator.

Classic Bavarian Cream

2 quarts (1 l, 920 ml), enough
for sixteen individual 4-ounce
(120-ml) or two 1-quart (960-ml)
charlotte molds

8 egg yolks
8 ounces (225 g) granulated sugar
2 tablespoons (18 g) unflavored
*   gelatin powder*
½ cup (120 ml) cold water
2 cups (480 ml) milk
1 vanilla bean, split or 1 teaspoon
*   (5 ml) vanilla extract*
2 cups (480 ml) heavy cream

1. Whip the egg yolks and sugar until light and fluffy. Reserve.

2. Soften the gelatin in cold water. Reserve.

3. Bring the milk to the scalding point with the vanilla bean, if used. Gradually pour the hot milk into the yolk mixture while whipping rapidly. Return the mixture to the heat, and bring back to the scalding point stirring constantly. Do not boil.

4. Remove from the heat and stir in the reserved gelatin. Set aside to cool at room temperature, stirring from time to time.

5. Whip the cream to soft peaks. Remove the vanilla bean from the custard and save for another use, or add the vanilla extract, if used. When the custard has cooled to body temperature, slowly stir it into the cream.

NOTE 1: As this filling cannot be reheated to soften, do not make it until you are ready to use it.

NOTE 2: Classic Bavarian Cream can also be served as a dessert by itself. Pour the filling into individual or large molds. After chilling, unmold and serve with fresh fruit and a fruit or chocolate sauce.

Classic Chocolate Bavarian Cream

Decrease the gelatin to 4 teaspoons (12 g) and add 8 ounces (225 g) melted dark chocolate when you stir in the gelatin.

Crème Parisienne (Chocolate Whipping Cream)

2 quarts (1 l, 920 ml) or
4 pounds, 8 ounces (2 kg, 45 g)

10 ounces (285 g) dark chocolate
1 quart (960 ml) heavy cream
¾ cup (180 ml) milk
3 ounces (85 g) granulated sugar

Crème Parisienne can be used for most of the recipes in this book that call for chocolate added to whipping cream, either as is or, if applicable, with gelatin added. This cream will not break (which happens when you add warm melted chocolate to whipped cream that is too low in butterfat) because its fat content has been increased by whipping the cream with the chocolate already added. Crème Parisienne must be made at least 12 hours before it is to be whipped (or it will not whip up), but it can be stored in the refrigerator unwhipped for up to one week and used as needed. This can be a real time-saver if, for example, you are filling Chocolate Eclairs or a similar pastry every day.

1. Chop the chocolate into small pieces and reserve.
2. Bring the cream, milk, and sugar to a boil in a saucepan. Remove from the heat and stir in the chopped chocolate. Continue to stir until the chocolate is completely dissolved. Cool and refrigerate for at least 12 hours before whipping.
3. To use, whip as you would whipping cream.

Ganache

6 pounds, 4 ounces (2 kg, 845 g)
ganache

8 egg yolks
8 ounces (225 g) granulated sugar
2 teaspoons (10 ml) vanilla extract
3 pounds, 8 ounces (1 kg, 590 g)
*   dark chocolate*
1 quart (960 ml) heavy cream

Ganache is a very rich chocolate paste that has many uses in the pastry kitchen. Ganache can be used warm as a glaze, to fill and decorate cakes or pastries, or to fill a basic truffle. The amount of chocolate in the recipe can be adjusted: For a firmer ganache, add more chocolate; for a softer ganache, decrease the amount. By not overworking the ganache when adding flavorings or softening it, you will preserve the rich, dark color. If you do want a lighter and fluffier ganache, whip in air by first softening the ganache over simmering water, then whipping at full speed for a few minutes.

1. Whip the egg yolks, sugar, and vanilla until light and fluffy.
2. Cut the chocolate into small pieces, place them in a saucepan, and add the cream. Heat to 150°F (65°C), stirring constantly.
3. Stir the hot cream mixture into the egg yolks and keep stirring for a minute or so to make sure the sugar is melted. If you plan to whip air into the ganache, keep stirring on low speed until it is cold, then whip it for a few minutes until it is light and fluffy.
4. Let the ganache cool and store it in airtight containers to use as needed. Ganache can be stored at room temperature for up to

one week. It should be refrigerated for longer storage.

NOTE: If a skin or crust forms on the top during storage, pour hot water on top of the ganache, let it stand for 1 minute, then pour the water off. If needed, ganache can be stored in the freezer for months. If the sugar has crystallized, or if all of the sugar was not dissolved in the first place, heat the ganache in a saucepan over low heat, stirring constantly, until all of the sugar crystals have dissolved, around 150°F (65°C).

Lemon Cream

2 quarts (1 l, 920 ml) filling

3½ cups (840 ml) lemon juice
½ cup (120 ml) orange juice
finely grated zest of 8 lemons
finely grated zest of 2 oranges
12 eggs
1 pound (455 g) granulated sugar
6 ounces (170 g) butter
¾ cup (180 ml) heavy cream

1. Combine the citrus juice and zest. Set aside.
2. Beat the eggs and sugar for a few seconds (just to combine) in a heavy saucepan made of stainless steel or another noncorrosive material; do not use aluminum. Add the juice and zest, then the butter and heavy cream.
3. Bring to the scalding point, stirring constantly, over medium heat; do not boil. Strain immediately. Use hot, as directed in individual recipes, or cool, then store, covered, in the refrigerator. Lemon cream can be stored for two to three weeks.

Lemon Curd

5 cups (1 l, 200 ml) filling

1½ cups (360 ml) lemon juice
finely grated zest of 8 lemons
8 eggs
1 pound, 8 ounces (680 g)
   granulated sugar
12 ounces (340 g) butter

Lemon curd makes an excellent flavoring or filling and can be used as a sauce when thinned with additional lemon juice or simple syrup. You will need approximately 8 medium-sized lemons for the juice in the recipe.

1. Combine the lemon juice and zest.
2. Beat the eggs and sugar together in a heavy stainless steel or other noncorrosive saucepan. Do not use aluminum. Add the lemon juice, zest, and butter.
3. Heat to boiling over low heat. Cook for a few seconds, stirring constantly, until the curd thickens. Strain immediately. Cool and use as needed. Lemon curd will keep for weeks stored, covered, in the refrigerator.

Mazarin Filling

4 pounds, 10 ounces
(2 kg, 105 g) filling

1 pound, 14 ounces (855 g)
  Almond Paste (page 4)
6 ounces (170 g) granulated sugar
14 ounces (400 g) softened butter
2½ cups (600 ml) eggs
3 ounces (85 g) bread flour

Mazarin filling, similar to frangipane, is an almond-based filling used in numerous European pastries and tarts. In addition to giving the paste a delicious flavor, the almonds absorb moisture, which helps baked goods with this filling stay fresh longer than average.

1. Place the almond paste and sugar in a bowl. Add the soft butter gradually while mixing on low speed with a paddle.

2. After all of the butter has been incorporated and the mixture is smooth, mix in the eggs a few at a time, then mix in the flour. Store the mazarin filling in the refrigerator. Bring to room temperature to soften, and stir until smooth before using.

NOTE: As with any uncooked filling that contains a large number of eggs, mazarin filling should be used right away to ensure the maximum volume in baked pastries.

Pastry Cream

6 pounds (2 kg, 730 g) custard

2 quarts (1 l, 920 ml) milk
2 vanilla beans, split
  or
2 teaspoons (10 ml) vanilla extract
5 ounces (140 g) cornstarch
1 pound (455 g) granulated sugar
1 teaspoon (5 g) salt
6 eggs

One-fourth Recipe

1 pound, 8 ounces (680 g) custard

1 pint (480 ml) milk
½ vanilla bean, split
  or
½ teaspoon (2.5 ml) vanilla
  extract
5 tablespoons (40 g) cornstarch
4 ounces (115 g) granulated sugar
¼ teaspoon (1 g) salt
2 eggs

Making pastry cream is one of the basic techniques that anyone involved with cooking (pastry shop or otherwise) should master, because pastry cream has so many applications. In an emergency, it can be thinned and used as a sauce; it is a base for soufflé; it is a filling and flavoring for cakes; and it can be used as a topping for Danish or other pastries. In the pastry kitchen, there should always be a supply of pastry cream in the refrigerator.

Since pastry cream is made with cornstarch, which stabilizes the eggs, there is no danger of overheating and curdling it as can happen, for example, with Vanilla Custard Sauce. Of course, you must still watch the heat and stir constantly to avoid burning it.

1. Place the milk and vanilla bean (if used) in a heavy-bottomed saucepan. Bring to a boil.

2. Keeping an eye on the milk, mix the cornstarch, sugar, and salt in a bowl using a whisk. Gradually add the eggs, and mix until smooth.

3. Slowly add about one-third of the hot milk to the egg mixture while whisking rapidly. Pour the tempered egg mixture back into the remaining milk.

4. Place over medium heat and cook, stirring constantly, until the mixture comes to a boil and thickens. Boil for a few seconds longer to make sure the raw starch taste has disappeared. Remove the vanilla bean, rinse and save it for another use, or add the vanilla extract.

5. Pour the cream into a bowl and cover with a piece of baking paper. When cooled, store in the refrigerator. If properly made and stored, pastry cream will keep fresh up to four days. However,

when it is that old it should only be used for pastries in which it will be baked.

NOTE: If the heat is too high or you are stirring too slow at the point when the pastry cream reaches a boil, it will lump. If this happens, pass it through a strainer immediately, before it cools.

Vanilla Bavarian Cream

approximately two pounds (910 g)

1½ cups (360 ml) heavy cream
½ teaspoon (2.5 ml) vanilla
   extract
1 pound, 4 ounces (570 g)
   Pastry Cream (page 569)
1 tablespoon (9 g) unflavored
   gelatin powder
¼ cup (60 ml) cold water

Although not a classic Bavarian cream, this is a time-saving version that uses pastry cream, a stock item in most pastry kitchens, as a prefabricated base. This eliminates the need for making a custard and waiting for it to cool. If you do not have pastry cream on hand you might want to make the Classic Bavarian Cream instead (see page 566). If you are making pastry cream specifically to use in this recipe, make it far enough in advance so that it is thoroughly chilled before you combine it with the whipped cream, or you will risk breaking the cream.

1. Whip the heavy cream and vanilla extract to stiff peaks. Fold into the pastry cream.

2. Soften the gelatin in cold water and heat to 110°F (43°C) to dissolve. Transfer one-third of the cream mixture to a separate bowl and rapidly stir in the gelatin. Still working quickly, stir into the remaining cream.

NOTE: If you are making Bavarian cream that is not all to be used at once, omit the gelatin and water. Store covered in the refrigerator.

Ingredients

Alcoholic Flavorings

Amaretto
A fruit-based liqueur from Italy. The primary flavor comes from sweet and bitter almonds.

Arrack
The fermented and distilled product of palm juice, raisins, and dates. Arrack has a very strong and distinctive aroma and is used in desserts and candies.

Brandy
Distilled from wine, brandy is classified by these labels: E—extra special, F—fine, M—mellow, O—old, P—pale, S—superior, V—very, and X—extra. V.S.O.P. means "very superior old pale."

Calvados
Apple brandy from France originating in the Normandy region. Known in America as applejack.

Chambord
A liqueur made from black raspberries and other fruits with herbs and honey.

Cognac
A type of brandy made in the vicinity of Cognac, a town in the Charente region of France.

Cointreau
A colorless French liqueur flavored with the peel of curaçao oranges and other oranges. For baking, it is interchangeable with Grand Marnier.

Crème de Cacao
A chocolate-flavored liqueur from France.

Crème de Cassis
A liqueur made from black currants.

Frangelico
An Italian liqueur derived primarily from hazelnuts, but flavored with berries and flowers as well.

Grand Marnier
A French liqueur made with oranges and aged cognac.

Kirschwasser
A colorless brandy distilled from the juice of a small black cherry found in the southern part of Germany. Also known as kirsch.

Madeira
A fortified sweet wine from the island of Madeira.

Maraschino
A liqueur made from the Amarasca cherry, it can be used as a substitute for kirschwasser.

Marsala
An Italian dessert wine originating from the Sicilian town Marsala.

Raspberry Brandy
A very strong, colorless brandy made from raspberries.

Rum
A spirit made from the fermented juice of the sugarcane; it is available, light or dark, in strengths up to 151 proof. Dark rum has a stronger flavor.

Whiskey
A spirit made from distilled grain, usually rye, corn, wheat, or barley.

Butter, Lard, and Margarine

Butter
A good quality butter is made up of at least 80 percent fat and not more than 15 percent water. The remaining 5 percent is mineral matter, such as salt and milk solids. Because of its low melting point and wonderful aroma, butter is indispensable in the making of first-rate pastries, especially those made with buttercream and puff paste. In hot climates, a small amount of margarine must be added to the butter to make it workable. Two types of butter are used in cooking and baking: salted and sweet. All of the recipes in this book use sweet butter, but salted butter can be substituted if the salt in the recipe is reduced by about ⅕ ounce (6 g) for every 1 pound (455 g) of butter. You cannot substitute salted butter, however, if there is little salt in the recipe or if the main ingredient is butter. Sweet butter should not be kept at room temperature for more than a day and should be stored in the refrigerator or freezer.

Clarified Butter
Clarified butter is butter with milk solids removed. It has a higher burning point than whole butter, which makes it preferable for frying. To clarify butter, melt it over low heat and let it bubble for a few minutes. Remove it from the heat and let it stand for about 10 minutes. Skim off all of the milk solids on top and carefully spoon or pour the clear butterfat into a clean container. Discard any residue in the bottom of the pan.

Lard

Lard is almost 100 percent refined pork fat. The highest quality lard is pork leaf fat; lard from other sources must be labeled "rendered pork fat." Lard is excellent for frying and is unbeatable for making flaky pie dough because of its elasticity and shortening power. It can be kept for months if stored covered in a cool place.

Margarine

Margarine is made up of about 80 percent fat, 18 percent water, and 2 percent salt (unless it is unsalted). There are two types of margarine: oleomargarine, which is made from beef and veal fat with vegetable and/or other oils added, and vegetable margarine, which was created as a substitute for butter and is usually made from corn or soybean oil. Oleomargarine is made primarily for the baking industry and has been developed to meet various demands of baking professionals. Some oleo-margarines are purposely made tough and with a high melting point; others cream well and are best in baked goods. If kept for a long time, margarine should be stored in a dark, dry place below 70°F (21°C).

Chocolate and Chocolate Products

Baker's Chocolate

Baker's chocolate is also referred to as non-temp chocolate or chocolate-flavored coating. The cocoa butter in this product has been replaced with other fats, making it very convenient to use. It does not need to be tempered, as does pure chocolate. Baker's chocolate is used for coating and for decorations. Do not confuse baker's chocolate with the unsweetened chocolate labeled "baking chocolate."

Cocoa Block

Cocoa block, baking chocolate, or chocolate liqueur is bitter or unsweetened chocolate. It is made from cocoa paste that has been finely ground and conched; the cocoa butter content should be at least 50 percent. Cocoa block is used as a flavoring and coloring agent for fillings, marzipan, mousses, and many other products; it is not eaten plain.

Cocoa Butter

Cocoa butter is fat extracted from cocoa paste using a hydraulic press. Its uses include thinning couverture, candy production, and coating marzipan figures to create a shine and to prevent them from drying out rapidly, plus noncooking uses, including the manufacture of cosmetic creams and lotions.

Cocoa Powder

Cocoa powder is the finely ground product of the pressed cake that remains after cocoa butter has been extracted from cocoa paste. It should contain a minimum of 20 percent fat. There are two types of cocoa powder: the so-called Dutch process, in which the powder is processed with an alkali giving it a smoother flavor and a bit darker color, and natural cocoa powder, which has not been treated and has a slight acid taste. Dutch process cocoa is easier to dissolve in liquid. Cocoa powder is used in candy production, decorating pastries and cakes, and flavoring and coloring cake batters and cookies.

Note: Baking soda is commonly used as part of the leavening agent in cakes and other batters that contain cocoa powder, because baking soda reacts with an acid. If you are using Dutch process cocoa powder, which is neutral and will not react with baking soda, substitute baking powder and double the measurement.

Couverture

Chocolate (dark or milk) with an increased cocoa butter content is commonly referred to as couverture, although this French word simply means "to coat" or "coating." The additional amount of cocoa butter varies with the manufacturer and the intended use, but the total fat content should be 30 to 40 percent. For coating candies and other items, a fat content of 35 percent is ideal; it should be slightly higher for molding.

Dark Chocolate

Dark chocolate is cocoa paste finely ground and conched, with the addition of sugar and vanilla; it should contain a minimum of 20 percent cocoa butter. Dark chocolate is used in fillings such as ganache and in a multitude of chocolate desserts.

Milk Chocolate

Milk chocolate must contain at least 15 percent milk solids, 3 to 4 percent of which should be milk fat. The total fat content must be at least 25 percent, and the maximum sugar content is 50 percent. Milk chocolate is used in much the same way as dark chocolate.

White Chocolate

White chocolate should be made up of at least 15 percent milk solids (3 to 4 percent of which should be milk fat), a minimum of 20 percent cocoa butter, and a maximum of 55 percent sugar. It is used primarily in the production of candies, but has become fashionable in mousses, ice creams, and cookies. It is not legal to label this as chocolate in the United States, since white chocolate does not contain any cocoa solids.

Cream and Milk

Cream

Cream is another name for the fat contained in whole milk. However, in modern dairies, instead of letting it settle on the surface on its own, it is skimmed off using a centrifugal method. Cream is produced and sold under many different names, mostly based on the fat content of the product. Most cream or cream-based products sold today have been pasteurized to destroy disease-producing bacteria, but even so, most ice cream recipes, for example, call for scalding the cream before proceeding just to make sure. This practice is left over from the days when pastry chefs got dairy products directly from the farmer.

Crème Fraîche

Crème fraîche is a cultured cream made by adding an acid-producing bacteria to pasteurized heavy cream. This produces a smooth, thick, yet pourable texture, and a slightly tangy taste.

Half-and-half

Half-and-half is a mixture of cream and whole milk containing between 10 and 18 percent butterfat.

Heavy Cream

Also called heavy whipping cream, this product should have at least 36 percent butterfat.

Light Cream

The butterfat content of light cream should be between 18 and 30 percent. This product is also known as coffee cream.

Manufacturing Cream

Not usually found in grocery stores, manufacturing cream is produced especially for the food industry. It is made with or without a stabilizer. Manufacturing cream should contain 40 percent butterfat which, together with the stabilizer, supposedly makes it possible to add a warm mixture, such as melted chocolate, to the cream without having it separate. Unfortunately pastry chefs have found out the hard way that this is not necessarily so, and I suspect that manufacturing cream sometimes comes out of the same spigot as heavy cream! In many of the recipes where whipped cream is added to a warm ingredient I add some egg white as a stabilizer as an extra precaution against separation.

Sour Cream

Sour cream must contain a minimum of 18 percent butterfat, and usually stabilizers and emulsifiers have been added. It is made commercially by adding a bacteria that produces lactic acid to pasteurized cream and then leaving the mixture to culture for about two days. Sour cream can also be made by adding vinegar to pasteurized cream and letting it curdle. This produces an acidified sour cream instead of the usual cultured.

Whipping Cream

This form of cream should have between 30 and 36 percent butterfat. It is sometimes called light whipping cream.

Milk

Milk, in addition to being a nourishing beverage, is one of the most frequently used ingredients in the bake shop. It contributes to the gluten structure in a bread dough and gives baked goods a nice crust, color, and flavor. Whole milk, fresh from the cow, contains almost 4 percent fat (usually referred to as butterfat) and 8 percent nonfat milk solids; the remaining 88 percent is water. When freshly drawn milk is left undisturbed for several hours the fat portion will rise to the surface where it can be skimmed off to use as heavy cream or to make butter. The remaining milk is very rich and would probably taste closer to what we know as half-and-half than the milk we are used to drinking. This raw milk, even if kept cold, has to be consumed within approximately 48 hours and cannot be sold because it has not been pasteurized.

Pasteurization is the process of heating milk to 160°F (71°C) and holding it at that temperature for 15 seconds, which kills harmful bacteria. Milk is usually homogenized after being pasteurized, to ensure that the milk fat is evenly distributed throughout and will not rise to the surface as previously described. Homogenization is essentially achieved by forcing the milk through tiny holes, breaking up the fat globules into small particles that remain dispersed throughout the liquid.

Milk is available for purchase in many varieties, the names of which, like cream, are based on the fat content of the product. Some of the names are confusing since different manufacturers and different states have their own particular names for certain grades. For example, extra-rich or premium milk has slightly more butterfat than regular whole milk and low-fat milk has a little more fat than skim or nonfat milk. Low-fat, skim, or nonfat milk should not be substituted for whole milk in a pastry recipe in most cases.

Buttermilk

Buttermilk is made from sweet (or sour) milk after it has been churned to remove the fat. Commercially produced buttermilk, called cultured buttermilk, is made today by adding a bacterial culture to pasteurized skim milk, which converts the milk sugar to lactic acid and gives the buttermilk its characteristic slightly tart taste. Buttermilk is used in pastry recipes containing baking soda, which reacts to its acidity to produce carbon dioxide gas.

Dry Milk or Milk Powder

Dry milk is produced when milk is rapidly evaporated by being forced through heated cylinders. Dry milk is usually made with skim milk, which gives it a very long shelf life and makes it an ideal substitute when it is impractical or impossible to get the fresh product. It is also used in some instances purely for the sake of convenience.

Evaporated and Condensed Milk

Evaporated milk is produced by heating whole milk to remove approximately 60 percent of the water content. It is then sterilized and canned. It can be reconstituted—made into whole milk again—by mixing it with an equal amount of water by volume. Condensed milk starts the same way, although it is usually not sterilized. It is also available as sweetened condensed milk, which contains 50 percent sugar.

Yogurt

Yogurt is made by adding a special bacteria to milk and holding it at a warm temperature, which causes the milk to ferment and coagulate, and produces a tangy flavor. Yogurt has a thick custard-like consistency and is eaten plain as well as flavored with berries or other fruits. It is used in the pastry kitchen to prepare reduced-calorie ice cream substitutes.

Eggs

Fresh Eggs

When eggs are called for in a recipe, usually the recipe is referring to eggs laid by domestic hens. However, eggs from turkeys, ostriches, or ducks can theoretically be used in baking; they are larger, but the basic composition is the same. Another variety of egg that is widely used is quail; they taste very much like chicken eggs and their petite size makes them popular for hors d'oeuvre preparations.

There is no nutritional or flavor difference between white and brown eggs; the color variations come from different breeds of hens, and the choice is just a matter of personal preference.

Eggs are one of the two structural materials in baking (flour is the other). The list of uses for eggs is endless: When eggs are combined with flour they create a framework that supports and traps the air in cake batters; egg whites are needed for meringues; eggs are used to thicken custards; egg wash is used to glaze breads and pastries. Eggs also contain a natural emulsifier that contributes to smoother batters and creams.

Eggs require very gentle cooking; they start to thicken at just 145°F (63°C). Desserts with eggs as the main ingredient, such as crème caramel, sauce anglaise, and zabaglione, are cooked over, or in, a water bath to protect them from too high a heat.

The average egg weighs about 2 ounces (55 g); the white is 1 ounce (28 g), the yolk is ⅔ ounce (20 g) and the shell is ¼ ounce (7 g). All of the recipes in this book use 2-ounce (55-g) eggs (graded as large). If you use eggs of a different size, adjust the number in the recipe accordingly. Eggs are graded for freshness and quality as AA, A, or B, and by size as jumbo, extra large, large, medium, small, and peewee.

Eggs are most commonly sold in the shell. The only reason for not buying eggs in this form is to save the time it takes to crack and empty the shell. Eggs are sold freshly cracked in some countries. Once cracked, however, whole eggs start to deteriorate and lose their whipping power very quickly. When cracked and separated, egg yolks start to form a skin almost immediately and must always be kept covered.

The shell of the egg is very porous, allowing the egg to absorb odors or flavors and to lose moisture, even before it has been cracked. Many commercially packaged eggs are coated with mineral oil to decrease moisture loss. It is essential to buy fresh eggs and keep them refrigerated; only those eggs needed for the day's work should be left at room temperature. Conversely, although fresh eggs are desirable, a *very* fresh egg, less than three days old, will not whip as high or increase sufficiently in volume during baking. If you are lucky enough to have a source for just-laid eggs, save them for your breakfast. You can determine the freshness of an egg by placing it in water mixed with 12 percent salt. If the egg is not more than a few days old it will sink to the bottom; if the egg floats to the top, it has spoiled.

Bad eggs are very rare these days due to improved methods of storage and inspection, but it is still a good idea when cracking a large number of eggs to crack a half dozen or so into a small container before emptying them into the big batch. In this way, should you encounter a rotten egg, the entire batch will not be wasted. An egg that is merely sour can be used as long as it is to be baked. Although it will not contribute as much to the volume, the smell and taste of the sour egg will disappear with the heat.

Frozen Eggs

Frozen eggs are an excellent substitute for fresh and are very convenient to use. Thaw them slowly at a temperature below 100°F (38°C) the day before you plan to use them (although you can place them under cold running water to thaw in an emergency). It is important to stir the eggs thoroughly before using them. Frozen egg whites and yolks can also be purchased separately.

Dehydrated Eggs

Eggs with the water removed are available in powdered form. They are used primarily by cake-mix and candy manufacturers, and are not practical for use in batters that need volume, such as yeast doughs, cakes, and some pastries. Dried egg whites are more widely used in the pastry shop, and with excellent results. These are especially useful when mixed with sugar and preservatives to make meringue powder. Dried egg yolks can be used to make egg wash. Dried eggs, unlike most dehydrated products, are very perishable and must be stored in the refrigerator or freezer tightly sealed.

Flour

Flour is the other of the two structural materials used in baking (eggs are the first), and, like eggs, flour is a vital ingredient in the bakery: it simply would be impossible to make breads or pastries without it. By law, flour must contain no more than 15 percent moisture when it is sold, but it can absorb more moisture if it is not stored in airtight containers. It is also possible for flour to dry out in high altitudes. These two factors are the reason you will often see, especially in bread recipes, a measurement such as 2½ to 3 pounds of flour; the amount required to reach a particular texture will vary with the amount of moisture in the flour.

Wheat Flours

Wheat flour, in a variety of different forms, is the flour used most often in the bakery. The wheat kernel is made up of three parts: the endosperm, where most of the starch is contained (85 percent); the germ or embryo, which is the inner core (2 percent); and the bran, which is the outer shell (13 percent). White flours are milled from the endosperm only. As different parts of the endosperm itself can be broken down into finer pieces than others, various grades of flour are produced from the same grain.

There are both "hard" and "soft" wheats. The hard wheats contain more of the proteins that will form gluten when the flour comes in contact with water and is kneaded. Flours made from hard wheats are used most often in making breads and in other yeast doughs. Soft wheat flour is used in combination with other flours in many recipes where a weaker gluten structure is desirable.

Bread Flour

Bread flour is a hard-wheat flour. It is very easy to dust into a thin film, making it ideal for rolling out and working with doughs. Bread flour is milled from wheat that is rich in protein. The wheat must be grown in areas with the appropriate amount of rainfall and in soil rich in nitrogen. Bread flour is pale yellow when first milled and turns off-white with aging. It feels slightly granular when rubbed between your fingers.

Cake Flour

Cake flour is made from soft wheat. The flour is chlorinated to further break down the strength of the gluten. It feels very smooth and can be pressed into a lump in your hand. The color is much whiter than bread flour. Because it contains less of the gluten-producing proteins, cake flour yields a more crumbly but lighter texture. It is used in making sponge cakes and other baked goods where a strong gluten structure is not desirable.

Pastry Flour

Pastry flour is another of the soft wheat flours. It is closer in color to bread flour, being off-white rather than true white like cake flour. It is slightly stronger in gluten than cake flour.

Whole Wheat Flour

Also known as graham flour, whole wheat flour is milled from the entire wheat kernel, including the germ and the bran; for this reason it is very nutritious. Whole wheat flour does not keep as long as white flour because of the fat contained in the wheat germ. Bread made from whole wheat flour is heavier than bread made with white flour, so most of the time a combination is used. Whole wheat bread dough takes less time to knead than bread made with white flour.

Rolled Wheat

Rolled wheat, also known as wheat flakes, looks much like rolled oats, although the flakes are darker and not quite as flat as oats. They are made by rolling whole wheat kernels flat while they are still soft. Rolled wheat is generally available in health or natural food stores.

Nonwheat Flours

In addition to the many varieties of wheat flour, we use flour milled from other plants as well. However, most bread recipes call for some wheat flour as well.

Barley Flour

This flour is seldom used in bread baking today, but in the past it was used extensively. To substitute barley flour for wheat flour, use half the amount by volume.

Buckwheat Flour

Buckwheat flour is made from the roasted seeds of the plant. Buckwheat is used most often in pancakes, especially in Eastern Europe for the popular buckwheat blini.

Corn Flour

Corn flour, not to be confused with cornstarch, is milled from either white or yellow corn. It is also produced as a by-product in the making of corn meal. This flour does not contain any gluten. (Cornmeal is made from coarsely ground dried corn. It is sprinkled on top of English muffins, sourdough breads, and bread sticks to give them a crunchy crust.)

Potato Flour

Potato flour is made from cooked, dried, ground potatoes. It is most frequently used as a thickening agent (in much the same way as cornstarch) rather than in baking.

Rye Flour

Rye flour is one of the best-tasting flours for making bread. It is divided into light, medium, and dark rye flours, as well as pumpernickel flour. As with wheat flour, these grades are determined by the part of the grain that the flour is milled from. The medium grade is the one most commonly used. Pumpernickel flour is made much the same way as whole wheat flour: it is milled from the entire rye grain including the bran. Rye flour is almost always mixed with some wheat flour to give it added gluten strength and rising power in bread baking. A small amount of vinegar added to rye bread dough will help to bring out the rye flavor.

Soy Flour

Soy flour is made from the soybean, rather than from a cereal grain. It is not commonly used in the pastry shop, but it is very nutritious and can be mixed with other flours in cakes for consumers on restricted diets.

Fruit

Apples

More than 20,000 varieties of apples are grown throughout the world, but only a dozen or so are sold commercially in the United States. Red Delicious, Golden Delicious, Rome Beauty, pippin, Jonathan, McIntosh, Stayman, Winesap, Gravenstein, and Northern Spy are commonly found on the market. Apples are generally classified as eating apples, cooking apples, or all-purpose apples. Good choices for cooking are pippin, Granny Smith, and Golden Delicious. All varieties of apples should be stored in a cool place or in the refrigerator. Apples are used in breakfast breads and pastries, tea cakes, apple charlotte, apple pies and tarts, and applesauce. In some recipes where the apples will be cooked into a filling, canned apples may be substituted for fresh. Apples are also used to make cider and brandy.

Apricots

Apricots are a stone fruit (drupe) and are part of the rose family, which includes, not surprisingly, peaches, plums, and nectarines. But it is surprising to note that this family also includes cherries, almonds, and coconuts. All have one seed (the kernel), which is enclosed in a stony endocarp called a pit. Almost all apricots sold in this country are grown in California. They are available fresh in the spring and summer months. Unfortunately, apricots are picked and shipped before they are ripe, as are peaches and plums, to protect them during transport. Ripe, plump, and juicy apricots simply would not travel very far without ending up bruised and damaged. Apricots are used in cakes, mousses, and fruit salads as well as in savory dishes. Apricot jam and apricot glaze are used extensively in the pastry shop. Dried apricots are often used in fruit cakes and tea breads. Apricot seeds are used to make a kernel paste that is similar to almond paste but has a bitter aftertaste. The most common varieties of apricot are Royal, Blenheim, and Tilton.

Bananas

Yellow bananas are the type most commonly used for eating plain and for baking. Bananas grow on huge trees in the heat of the tropics. Although we usually picture bunches of bananas hanging down from the stem, they actually grow with the bottoms of the fruit pointing up toward the sun. Bananas should be just ripe if used whole or in pieces in cakes or pastries, but very ripe bananas can be used in ice cream or tea cakes. Bananas are one of two fruits (pears are the other) that taste better when allowed to ripen off the tree. Therefore, bananas are shipped green, then ripened domestically in specially equipped warehouses. Costa Rica and Honduras rank as the two largest exporters of bananas to the United States. It is interesting to note that bananas are among the top three exports from such an unlikely place as Iceland. Here they are grown in greenhouses heated naturally by geysers that produce ideal humidity for the plants to thrive. Once bananas have ripened, store them in a cool place. Refrigerate only if absolutely necessary; the skin will turn brown but the flesh will not be affected. Bananas are available year-round.

Blackberries

Blackberries are available fresh through the summer and are also sold frozen or canned. Loganberries, boysenberries, and olallieberries are all hybrids of blackberries. Fresh berries are excellent for decorating and for use in fruit salads, tarts, and pies. Blackberries are very juicy and they make a delicious and attractive sauce when puréed. They are also made into jam. To keep fresh berries from becoming crushed and molding prematurely, store them in the refrigerator spread in a single layer on sheet pans. To freeze fresh berries, spread them in a single layer, without crowding, and place in the freezer until frozen solid. Package the frozen berries in airtight bags or storage containers.

Black Currants

These very small berries should not be confused with dried currants (which are a variety of grape). Black currants are rarely available fresh in this country; however, they are very popular in Scandinavia and other parts of Europe such as Germany and France. Black currants are always cooked before they are eaten as they are too bitter to eat raw. They are typically used in jams and are also used to make the French liqueur crème de cassis. Their dark color, which turns almost purple when mixed with other ingredients, gives cakes, mousses, or other desserts a very special look.

Blueberries

Blueberries grow wild in both Scandinavia and the United States. They are available fresh in the late spring and through the summer; they are also sold frozen and canned. Fresh blueberries are wonderful for adding color to fruit tarts and fruit salads. While not as desirable, frozen berries give a good result when used in muffins, tea cakes, pancakes, and other cooked products. Store or freeze blueberries as directed for blackberries; do *not* thaw frozen blueberries before adding them to batters.

Cantaloupes

Cantaloupes, also called muskmelons, are a member of the melon family and are only sold and eaten fresh. Cantaloupes are available all year as they are imported from Mexico throughout the winter. Cantaloupe flesh is very sweet and juicy and is used mostly in fruit salads in the pastry kitchen.

Cherries

Numerous varieties of cherries are grown all over the world. The most common sweet cherries for eating raw are Bing and Lambert. Bing cherries mature a few weeks before Lambert, and the Lambert is more elongated in shape, but both share the same rich flavor and dark, almost mahogany coloring. Royal Ann (also known as Golden Bing) is a light (white) fleshed sweet cherry, not as popular as it does not ship well. Its light skin shows even the slightest bruise. Sour cooking cherries include Montmorency, Morello, and the Amarasca cherry, which is used to make Maraschino liqueur. Cherries are used in pies, tarts, cake fillings, and of course cherries jubilee. Cherries do not keep well and should always be stored in the refrigerator and left whole (with the stem and pit). Once pitted they will start to deteriorate and spoil very quickly.

Coconuts

The coconut palm grows throughout the tempered part of the globe. It has been called the "tree of life" as it produces everything that is needed to sustain life: Ropes and fishing nets are made from the fibers surrounding the shell, the leaves are made into mats and used as roofing material, the trunk is used as timber, the coconut flesh and liquid are very nourishing, the shells can be used to make bowls, and the tiny shoots of the palm can be prepared and eaten as a vegetable.

Although the name suggests otherwise, the coconut is not a nut but a drupe (stone fruit) belonging to the same family as plums, apricots, and peaches. Each coconut palm contains about 20 nuts, which take approximately one year to ripen. Since the trees flower and bear fruit continuously, the fruits can be harvested all year round. In most grocery stores "fresh" coconut is sold with the thick leathery skin and fibrous coating removed. In choosing a whole coconut, pick one that feels heavy for its size. You should be able to hear a sloshing sound from the liquid inside when you shake it. Packaged coconut meat is available in many different forms: flaked, shredded, grated, and ground. Dried, very finely ground coconut is also called macaroon coconut. Macaroon coconut for use in the recipes in this book should be unsweetened. If you are able to find only sweetened coconut, you can remove most of the sugar by rinsing the coconut under running water. Pat it dry, then finish drying it in a low oven. Unsweetened coconut milk, exported mainly from Thailand, is available canned. It is usually sold in grocery stores specializing in Asian food products or in the oriental foods section of the supermarket.

Cranberries

Wild cranberry vines are indigenous to North America. Today most of the cranberries grown commercially come from Massachusetts. Cranberries are very tart and are almost always sweetened. They are used in tea cakes, muffins, sauces, and preserves. Their bright red color adds a festive touch to many holiday desserts. Fresh cranberries keep for weeks in the refrigerator and freeze very well with little loss of flavor or texture.

Dates

Dates are the fruit of the date palm, previously grown mostly in Iraq, but more recently in California. Dates are very sweet—almost half sugar. They are most often sold dried and are available whole or pitted. Dates can be stuffed with fondant or marzipan and glazed with sugar to serve on a petits fours tray. They are also used in nut breads and muffins.

Dried Currants

Also called currant raisins and sometimes simply currants, dried currants are not, as you might expect, made by drying fresh black or red currants. Dried currants look like small raisins and are indeed a dried seedless grape. Currants are frequently used in baking and are often used to decorate cookies, especially gingerbread figures. Zante currants are the most common variety.

Figs

Figs are sold and eaten both fresh and dried. The fig tree is a type of ficus cultivated in California and in the Mediterranean countries, particularly Turkey. Fresh figs are available from summer to early fall in varieties from whitish green to yellow to the purple, almost black, Black Mission figs. Fresh figs can be used in fruit salads, served with dessert cheeses, or baked with honey or syrup. Dried figs are used in tea cakes and candies.

Grapes

Grapes are one of the oldest cultivated fruits. In the United States most of the commercial crop is grown in California, including grapes produced for wine making. Grapes range in color from pale green to dark red, almost black. Popular varieties include Thompson Seedless, Red Flame, Concord, and Perlette. Grapes are used in fruit salads and on fruit tarts.

Honeydews

Honeydews are large, pale green melons with sweet, very juicy, light green flesh. They are used in the pastry kitchen in fruit salads and to make sorbet. Honeydews are shipped when they are hard (unripe) and then usually preripened before being sold. If the melon is very hard, leave it at room temperature for one or two days until it starts to soften slightly at the stem and bottom ends. Avoid honeydews that have a whitish tinge to the skin; they usually will never ripen fully. Honeydews are available throughout the year.

Kiwis

Kiwis are native to China and were originally known as Chinese gooseberries. The commercial crop was primarily exported from New Zealand until fairly recently when they began to be cultivated successfully in California. Kiwis are oval with fuzzy brown skin, bright green flesh and very small black seeds (which are eaten). Their colorful appearance has made them very popular in recent years for decorating. Kiwi fruit can be used in fruit salads, fruit tarts, sorbets, and sauces. A great way to peel kiwis and still retain their natural shape is to use an oval soup spoon. To work properly the fruit must be perfectly ripe. Cut off the top and bottom of the kiwi to make it the same length as the bowl of the spoon. Carefully (and gradually) insert the spoon between the skin and the flesh, pushing it through to the bottom of the spoon. Hold the kiwi in your palm and slide the spoon all the way around between the skin and the flesh. You will have a perfectly smooth kiwi with a minimum of wasted fruit.

Lemons

Lemons originated in India and are a member of the citrus family. Today they are grown in the Mediterranean, the United States, Canada, South

America, Asia, Australia, and Africa. Lemons, lemon juice, and lemon zest are all used frequently in dessert preparations as well as other types of cooking, as lemon enhances many flavors both sweet and savory. Lemon juice is used not only as a flavoring agent, but because of its acidic quality, it is also rubbed onto cut fruit to prevent oxidation (or it is used to make acidulated water for the same purpose). A few drops are used in caramelizing sugar to help prevent crystallization and premature darkening. Some lemon juice is added to the egg whites when whipping meringue to increase the volume, and lemon juice is worked into the butter block to make it more elastic in making puff pastry. As a flavoring, lemon juice is almost as widely used as vanilla and chocolate in the pastry kitchen. Lemons are used in lemon curd and other fillings, fruit sauces, doughs, cakes, cookies, mousses, candies, sorbets and ice creams, candied citrus peels, and pies. Soaking lemons in hot water for about an hour before juicing them will increase the amount of juice that can be extracted. Rolling the fruit firmly against the table will also help.

Limes

Limes are another member of the citrus family and are closely related to lemons. Limes are not used as extensively, but can be substituted for lemons in many cases. Because of its bright green color, lime zest is often used as a garnish.

Lingonberries

Lingonberries look and taste a bit like small cranberries. Lingonberry preserves are a very popular condiment in Scandinavia. Fresh lingonberries are not usually available in the United States, but the preserves are sold in most grocery stores. Lingonberries are used as a topping, in sauces, in parfaits, and in mousses. In Sweden (and in my home in the United States) lingonberry preserves are traditionally served with dinner as an accompaniment to mashed potatoes.

Litchis

The litchi (also spelled "lychee") is most popular in China where it is eaten as a fruit, often chilled in syrup, dried and sold as "litchi nuts," and cooked in meat dishes. The fruit grows in bunches; each litchi fruit is about the size of a small plum and is enclosed in a brittle, brownish red, bumpy skin. Inside is white flesh surrounding an inedible black pit. The flesh is juicy and has a sweet, almost perfumed, flavor and aroma. Fresh litchis are available in Asian markets in the summer, and can be stored in the refrigerator for several weeks or may be frozen. Canned litchis are available in some stores. Litchis can be used in mousses, charlottes, ice creams, and sauces.

Mangos

Mangos grow on evergreen trees in tropical climates. They are widely used in India for cooking in chutneys and curries, and to eat fresh. Different varieties of mango vary in color from yellow to green and red. When ripe, mangos have a very strong and sweet fragrance. They are available fresh from spring to late summer and are also available canned. Mangos have a large pit and are rather difficult to peel—the best way is to slice off the two broader sides as close to the large flat seed as possible, scoop out the flesh from these halves, and discard the skin. Mangos are used in fruit salads, as a garnish, in ice cream, and in sauces.

Nectarines

Nectarines are one of the oldest fruits and are said to have grown more than two thousand years ago. The early commercially grown nectarines were small, softened fast, and did not travel well. Newer varieties contain part "peach blood" from crossbreeding in an attempt to get a larger and firmer fruit. However, a nectarine is not, as many believe, a hairless peach, or a cross between a peach and a plum. Nectarines do share many characteristics of, and can in most cases be substituted for, peaches.

Oranges

Oranges are probably second only to apples in their popularity. They are the most commonly used member of the citrus family for eating and cooking, and their sweet juice is a typical breakfast beverage. Oranges are grown commercially in the United States in Florida, California, Texas, and Arizona. Fresh oranges are available year-round. The everbearing variety (like many other types of citrus) is one of the few fruits that flowers and bears ripe fruit at the same time. Oranges are used in many of the same dessert preparations as lemons. Blood oranges are a variety of orange with red flesh, juice, and rind. Their distinctive color is nice in sorbets, fruit salads, and sauces. Bitter oranges, such as the Seville, are used in marmalades and to make curaçao and Grand Marnier. Oranges (and many other fruits) are dipped in or sprayed with an edible wax to enhance their appearance and preserve freshness. Often an orange-colored vegetable dye is added to the wax. The colored wax is absolutely harmless and there is no need to wash it off before using the fruit.

Papayas

Papayas are a delicious tropical fruit, Mexican in origin, now grown in tropical climates all over the world. Their green skin turns yellow or orange when the fruit is ripe. Papayas are popular for breakfast and are used in ice cream, fruit salads, fruit tarts, and sauces. Papayas contain the enzyme papain which aids in digestion (in fact, papayas were named "the tree of health" in the Caribbean because the fruit is so beneficial to people with stomach problems). Because of this enzyme, papayas can also be used as a meat tenderizer, and for the same reason, raw papaya will inhibit gelatin from jelling.

Passion Fruits

Although the name makes this fruit sound like an aphrodisiac, passion fruit was given its name by Spanish missionaries who said the appearance of the flowers had a significance to the Crucifixion. Passion fruits are about the size of an egg and have a hard, wrinkled skin when the fruit is ripe. The skin, which is almost like a shell, is not eaten. The flesh consists mostly of seeds, which can be eaten, or the flesh can be forced through a sieve to extract the juice. Passion fruit can be used in ice creams, soufflés, sauces, and beverages. Passion fruits are native to Brazil but are also grown now in California, Hawaii, Florida, Africa, India, and New Zealand.

Peaches

Peaches, along with apricots and nectarines, are a stone fruit. There are both clingstone and freestone varieties. Red Haven is probably the most common peach sold. Peaches are very sweet and juicy when ripe, and are one of summer's favorite fruits for ice creams and cobblers. Peaches are also often used to make jam. They need a warm climate with no frost and are grown in both North and South America, Australia, Africa, and many parts of Europe. Unfortunately, tree-ripened peaches do not travel very well and the commercial crop is almost always picked and shipped hard and unripe. They will soften if left at room temperature, but the flavor is never as good as that of the tree-ripened variety.

Pears

Pears come in many sizes and colors from pale green to yellow, brown, and red. Some are best for cooking and others for eating raw. Popular varieties include Anjou, Bartlett, Bosc, Comice, and Seckel. One variety or another is available year-round. Pears are used in many desserts such as the well known pears belle hélène, as well as in tarts, charlottes, and ice creams, poached in wine, or served with cheese. Pears are also made into pear brandy and jam. Pears are harvested and shipped before they are ripe; the fruit actually develops a better flavor and texture if ripened off the tree. Pears served raw should be fully ripe. For baking and cooking, however, it is preferable to have them just a little underripe.

Persimmons

There are two varieties of persimmon found in the United States: Hachiya and Fuyu. Hachiya, the persimmon most commonly found in stores, has a slightly oblong shape and is pointed at the bottom. The Hachiya persimmon is very high in tannin and can be eaten only when fully ripe (the fruit should be almost jelly-like throughout). Instead of trying to peel the skin off the Hachiya, it is easier to cut it in half and use a spoon to scoop out the flesh; discard the stem, seeds, and skin. The smaller Fuyu persimmon is shaped like a tomato. It has very little tannin and can therefore be eaten before it is completely ripe and soft. This persimmon is easy to peel using a vegetable peeler. Both varieties are yellowish-orange in color and available during the winter months. Persimmons are used in many traditional holiday recipes, the most popular being persimmon pudding.

Pineapples

Pineapples are probably the most common and widely eaten tropical fruit. Like papayas, pineapples contain an enzyme beneficial to digestion. Fresh pineapples are available all year; canned pineapple and canned pineapple juice are also sold extensively. Pineapples are used in fruit salads, sorbets, tarts, and are delicious baked with rum and sugar. Candied pineapple is used in many fruitcake recipes.

Plums

There are so many varieties of plums (possibly up to two thousand) that sometimes even experts have trouble distinguishing them. It will be less bewildering if you keep in mind that there are two main categories:

Japanese and European. The Japanese varieties are medium to large and very juicy. They come in many different shades, of which only a few have a blueish or purple skin. Most of the European types of plum are blue or purple, usually smaller in size, round or oval, and have a firmer texture. In the United States about a dozen varieties are grown commercially. Plums are available from spring to early fall. Popular varieties include Santa Rosa, Casselman, Laroda, and Queen Ann. Prune plums are, as the name suggests, dried to make prunes. Plums are used in ice cream, cobblers, sauces, tarts, and fruit salads. Plums are also used to make brandy.

Raisins

Raisins are dried, seedless grapes. They are produced in abundance in California, almost exclusively from the Thompson Seedless grape. Raisins are used in tea cakes, muffins, breads, cookies, candies, fruitcakes, and compotes. For many recipes raisins should be soaked in water or spirits to plump them prior to use. This not only adds flavor, but makes the raisins easier to slice through, enabling you to make a clean cut in a cake or pastry. And if the raisins are to be frozen (in an ice cream, for example), soaking them in alcohol will prevent them from freezing rock-hard.

Raspberries

Raspberries originated in Asia and Europe and grow wild in many parts of the United States. Raspberries are very popular for decorating and garnishing cakes, pastries, and tarts because of their uniform petite size and bright red color (although there are also black raspberries, which are not very common, as well as a new hybrid golden raspberry). Raspberry sauce is used extensively in the pastry kitchen, and raspberries are also used in fruit salads, ice creams, and sorbets. Fresh raspberries, previously available only during the summer, are now available year-round due to imports from New Zealand and Chile. The prices of course are higher when the fruit is imported. Frozen raspberries may be used to make sauces and sorbets. Store or freeze raspberries following the instructions given for blackberries.

Red Currants

Red currants originated in Europe and are very popular in Scandinavia and Germany. They grow in bunches like grapes on large bushes and are harvested in the early fall. Red currants are not as tart as black currants and can therefore be eaten raw. Fresh red currants are very pretty and look great as a garnish and in fruit salads. Unfortunately, they are not widely available fresh in the United States. It is actually illegal to grow red currants in many parts of this country, as the plants can harbor a parasite that kills the white pine tree. Red currants are used to make red currant jelly, which is used in Cumberland sauce, to fill cakes and pastries, and to make a glaze for fruit tarts.

Rhubarb

Rhubarb is actually a vegetable; however, it is mentioned here as it is often used like a fruit in pies and other desserts. Rhubarb grows in stalks, looking something like overgrown red celery. Rhubarb is very tart and is almost always sweetened. It is quite juicy and will actually dissolve if overcooked. Rhubarb is used mostly in pies (sometimes combined with other fruits) and in cobblers.

Strawberries

Strawberries are one of the most popular fruits. The vines are found growing wild in many areas, but the berry grown commercially today is the result of much experimentation and crossbreeding. Strawberries are delicious served plain or with just a simple topping of cream and sugar. They are used in tarts, fruit salads, cakes, mousses, and strawberry shortcake. Fresh strawberries are available all year, although their flavor is at its peak in the summer. Frozen strawberries can be used in sauces and ice creams. Store or freeze strawberries as instructed for blackberries.

Tamarinds

Tamarinds, originally from the Asian and African rain forests, are cultivated today in the tropics and subtropics all over the world. Also known as sour dates, the tamarind pods, which have a reddish-brown hard shell and can grow up to 8 inches (20 cm) long, hang in clusters from the tall evergreen trees. The white flesh surrounding the black seeds turns light brown and dries up when the fruit is ripe. Tamarinds have a distinctive sweet-sour taste. Tamarinds can be obtained fresh beginning in late fall and into the winter. They are also available throughout the year, either dried or as a sticky paste, in many grocery stores specializing in Asian foods. In addition to being used in various frozen desserts, tamarinds are most often used in Asian cooking and in the preparation of curries.

Jellying Agents

Agar-agar

A natural vegetable substance extracted from Japanese seaweed, agar-agar can be purchased as a powder or in strips that look something like transparent noodles. It is odorless, colorless, and eight times stronger than gelatin. It is used when a very strong thickening agent is required: in some special meringues, pastries, jellies, and ice creams, for example.

Gelatin

Gelatin is derived from the bones and skins of animals. When dissolved, heated, and chilled, it has the ability to turn a liquid into solid. Unflavored gelatin is available in both powder and sheet (leaf) form. Either can be substituted in equal weights.

When a recipe calls for powdered gelatin, the amount of liquid used to soften and dissolve the gelatin is generally specified. This is usually cold water but might also be wine, for example. The gelatin is sprinkled over the liquid and left for a few minutes to soften; it is then possible to heat the mixture and dissolve the granules.

Most brands of sheet gelatin weigh $\frac{1}{10}$ ounce (3 g) per sheet. The gelatin sheets, like the powder, must also be softened in a liquid to be dissolved. However, they can be dissolved in virtually any amount of liquid as long as they are submerged. The amount of liquid need not be specified because as they soften, the sheets will always absorb the same amount: $1\frac{1}{2}$ ounces (45 ml) for every 9 grams (3 sheets). The sheets are removed once they are soft, without squeezing out the absorbed liquid. To substitute sheet gelatin in a recipe that calls for powdered, submerge the sheets in water, calculate the amount of liquid absorbed by each sheet, and figure that into your recipe. Then add the missing water to the gelatin sheets when you heat them to dissolve. For example: If the recipe instructs you to soften 2 tablespoons (18 g) of powdered gelatin in ½ cup (120 ml) of water, substitute six gelatin sheets (6 sheets at 3 grams each = 18 g), softened in enough water to cover. But, since you know they will have absorbed only 3 ounces (90 ml), add 1 ounce (30 ml) more water.

To substitute powdered gelatin in a recipe that calls for gelatin sheets, use an equal weight of powder dissolved in as much water as the sheets would have absorbed. For example: If the recipe uses 6 sheets of softened gelatin, you would substitute 18 g of powdered, softened in the amount of water that the sheets would have absorbed; in this case 3 ounces (90 ml).

After they are softened both types of gelatin must be heated until completely dissolved. However, they must never be boiled, as boiling reduces the strength of the gelatin, and causes a skin to form on the top.

Papayas, pineapple, and figs contain an enzyme when they are raw that inhibits the gelatin from setting; their presence in a recipe can adversely effect the outcome where gelatin is used. However, the enzyme is destroyed by cooking, so these fruits will gel normally if they are cooked first.

Gum Arabic

Gum arabic is produced by a species of the acacia tree. It will thicken or solidify a liquid in the same way as gelatin or gum tragacanth. Gum arabic is used primarily in marshmallows and other gummy candies or, mixed with water, as a glaze for cookies and pastries.

Gum Tragacanth

Gum tragacanth is collected from the stem of a plant found in the Middle East, either by gathering the natural runoff or by making cuts in the stem to help extract the juice. It is available dried, in flakes, or as a powder. The powder is most suitable for use in the pastry kitchen. When gum tragacanth is mixed with water, it will solidify the liquid much like gelatin.

Pectin

Pectin is naturally present in varying amounts in certain types of fruit. Apples, blueberries, cranberries, lingonberries, and most citrus fruits are particularly high in pectin. Pectin is used to thicken marmalades, jams, and jellies. Commercial pectin can be purchased in either powdered or liquid form. A glaze made from pectin is popular for use on fruit tarts and pastries in Europe, but generally a glaze made from apricot jam is substituted in this country, because pectin glaze is not readily available.

Leavening Agents

Ammonium Carbonate

Ammonium carbonate (or bicarbonate), also called hartshorn because it was originally produced from the hart's horns and hooves, is now made commercially and used mainly in cookies and short doughs to produce a longer-lasting crisp texture. It can also be used in pâte à choux to give it an extra puff, but can be used as a substitute for baking soda and baking powder only in cookies or doughs with very little moisture or in pastries baked at a high temperature. Ammonium carbonate reacts to heat, producing water, ammonia, and dioxide gas. It has a very strong odor that completely disappears above 140°F (60°C). It must always be stored in an airtight container or it will quickly evaporate. Ammonium carbonate is available from any bakery supply store. It can also be ordered from a chemist or local laboratory.

Baking Powder

Baking powder is composed of one part sodium bicarbonate and two parts baking acid (generally cream of tartar, or phosphates in the case of single-acting baking powder) plus a small amount of starch to keep it from caking. When baking powder comes in contact with liquid and heat, it releases carbon dioxide gas, which causes the batter to expand and rise. Single-acting baking powders react and release gas only when they come in contact with a liquid. This makes them impractical for use in some recipes. Double-acting baking powders, the type most commonly used and the type used in the recipes in this book, react to both liquid and heat. Double-acting baking powder gives you the advantage of being able to delay baking the product. Provided the correct amount has been used, baking powder will not leave an aftertaste, and should leave only small, even holes inside the baked dessert rather than large air pockets. Generally speaking, the softer and more fluid the batter is, the more the baking powder will react. At high altitudes the amount of baking powder called for in a recipe must be decreased; see page 614. Store baking powder, covered, in a cool place.

Cream of Tartar

Cream of tartar is a by-product of winemaking. Wine produces a crystallized sediment of basic tartar that is refined, bleached, and turned into a powder to produce the commercial cream of tartar used in baking. Cream of tartar is used in manufacturing baking powder; it is also used to inhibit crystallization in candies and syrups and to help stiffen egg whites for meringues.

Potash

Potash is a potassium compound that produces carbon dioxide when it comes in contact with an acid. It is an uncommon leavening agent, used mostly in cookies with spices and honey.

Sodium Bicarbonate

Sodium bicarbonate, or baking soda, has no leavening properties when used alone, but when combined with an acid it produces carbon dioxide gas to inflate batters in the same way as baking powder. Baking soda starts to release gas as soon as it comes into contact with moisture, so products in which it is used should be baked as soon as possible after mixing. (This is especially true if baking soda is not used in combination with baking powder.) In addition to acting as a leavening agent, bicarbonate of soda will darken the color of baked cakes and cookies, which can be an advantage in making gingerbread, for example. It will leave a strong alkaline flavor if too much is used, but in the case of gingerbread, the taste is overshadowed by the strong spices. Store sodium bicarbonate in an airtight container.

Yeast

Yeast is one of the most essential ingredients for the baker. It is a living microorganism, actually a fungus, which multiplies very quickly in the right temperature range (78° to 82°F, 26° to 28°C). In a bread dough, the yeast feeds on the sugars (both the actual sugar added to the dough and the sugar produced from the wheat starch in the flour), fermenting them and converting the sugars to carbon dioxide and alcohol. As the bread bakes, the carbon dioxide is trapped within the dough, causing the bread to rise; the alcohol evaporates during baking. Besides the yeast naturally present in the air, there are three types available commercially: fresh (or compressed) yeast, dry yeast, and brewer's yeast. As the name implies, this last product is used mainly in the production of wine and beer; only fresh and dry yeasts are used in baking. All of the recipes in this book use fresh yeast. To substitute dry yeast for fresh, reduce the amount called for in the recipe by half. Fresh yeast should have a pleasant smell (almost like apple), a cakey consistency, and should break with a clean edge. It can be kept up to two weeks in the refrigerator before it starts to lose its strength. Fresh yeast that is too old will be dry and crumbly and will begin to break down into a sticky, foul-smelling substance. To test yeast, dissolve a small amount in a mixture of ½ cup (120 ml) warm water, 2 teaspoons (10 g) of sugar, and 1 ounce (30 g) of flour: If the yeast is active it will expand and foam within 10 minutes. Fresh yeast can be frozen, but it will lose about 5 percent of its strength. Frozen yeast must be thawed very slowly and then used as soon as possible.

In working with yeast it is important to pay close attention to the temperature of the product. Yeast fermentation is damaged in temperatures above 115°F (46°C), and the yeast is killed at 145°F (63°C). Yeast fermentation is slowed but not damaged at temperatures below 65°F (19°C) and is nonexistent at 40°F (4°C) or lower. Mixing the yeast directly into large amounts of sugar or salt will also damage or actually kill it.

Nuts

All nuts have a high oil content and, once shelled, should be stored tightly closed in a dark, cool place or in the freezer.

Almonds

There are two types of almonds: sweet almonds, which are available in markets and are used for cooking and eating, and bitter almonds, which contain prussic acid (toxic except in small amounts) and are used for flavorings and extracts. Bitter almonds are not sold in the United States. Almonds are widely used in the pastry shop as an ingredient in numerous breads and cookies, as well as being used to decorate cakes, pastries, and Danish pastries. Almonds are available in a variety of forms: whole, sliced, slivered, or ground, and all of these can be purchased natural (skin on) or blanched (skin off). Almond extracts and flavorings are also widely used, and almonds are, of course, used to make almond paste and marzipan, two other important products in professional baking.

Apricot Kernels

The soft innermost part of the apricot pit, the kernel, is used to make a paste similar to almond paste. Although it has an almond-like flavor, apricot kernel paste has a strong, bitter aftertaste.

Chestnuts

Chestnuts can be purchased fresh in the shell or canned in a puréed or glacéed form. They are also made into chestnut flour. Chestnuts must be cooked before they are eaten. To remove the shell from fresh chestnuts, cut a small X on the flat side of the shell, and either roast them at 375°F (190°C) for 10 to 15 minutes or cook them in boiling water for 5 to 15 minutes, depending on whether or not the chestnuts will be given any further cooking. Chestnuts are easiest to peel while still warm. Sweetened chestnut purée is used alone as a filling and to flavor buttercream; whole candied chestnuts can be used to decorate cakes; chopped candied chestnuts can be added to candies and ice creams. Because fresh chestnuts are available in the winter months, chestnuts are often used in holiday desserts.

Hazelnuts

Hazelnuts, also known as filberts, are grown throughout Europe; Turkey and Italy are the largest producers. Their distinctive flavor is much improved by toasting, which is also the best way to remove the nuts' skin. After toasting, let cool slightly, then rub the nuts between your hands. As much of the thin brown skin as possible should be removed before using the nuts. Hazelnuts are used in cakes, cookies, candies, and pastries; finely ground hazelnuts are used in linzer dough and in place of flour in some tortes. They are also used to make hazelnut paste, an important flavoring agent.

Macadamia Nuts

Macadamia nuts, grown mostly in Hawaii, have a delicious buttery flavor good in cookies and ice cream where their taste is not overshadowed by the other ingredients. Because the shells are very difficult to crack, the nuts are almost always sold shelled and usually roasted as well. If you are able to find only roasted and salted nuts, thoroughly blanch and dry the nuts before using them in dessert recipes. Macadamia nuts can be substituted for other nuts in some recipes to give a dessert a tropical feeling.

Pecans

Pecans (as well as walnuts) are indigenous to North America, and both are a type of hickory. Pecans are generally purchased, already shelled, in halves or pieces. They are more expensive than most other varieties of nuts and are especially suitable for decorative purposes. Pecans are used in some candies and breakfast pastries and, of course, the American favorite, pecan pie.

Pine Nuts

Known as pignola in Italy, pine nuts are the edible seed of the stone pine. Their rich flavor is increased by light toasting. Pine nuts are not used as much in baking as they are in other types of cooking. They are popular in savory dishes from Italy and the Mediterranean and are also used in Chinese preparations. Because pine nuts are quite high in oil and turn rancid very quickly, they should always be stored in the refrigerator or freezer. Pine nuts are good in cookies, and their petite, uniform size makes them attractive as a decoration on cakes as well.

Pistachios

Pistachios are popular for their distinctive green color and are usually used as a garnish on petits fours or candies and, of course, to make pistachio ice cream. Pistachios need hot, dry summers and cold winters. Iran and Turkey are the major producers. The nuts have two shells: a red outer shell that is removed before packing and a thin inner shell, beneath which a thin skin surrounds the nuts. To show off the nut's color to its fullest, remove the skin by blanching the nuts in boiling water, then pinching them between your fingers or rubbing them in a towel. Adding a pinch of salt to the water will also help to heighten the green color.

Walnuts

Walnuts are second only to almonds in their numerous uses in baking. Walnuts are used in many types of breakfast pastries and muffins, cookies, breads, brownies, ice creams, and tortes. Walnuts are always purchased shelled for use in commercial production, and are available in halves for decorating, or in broken pieces at a less expensive price. Because of their high oil content, it is difficult to grind walnuts without turning them into a paste. Grinding them with some of the granulated sugar in a recipe will help to alleviate this problem. Also because of the oil, it is preferable not to chop the nuts in a food processor; chop them by hand with a sharp knife instead. Be sure to store shelled walnuts in the refrigerator or freezer.

Sweeteners

Sugar and other sweeteners play many roles in baking, the most obvious one being to add a sweet flavor. But sugar also helps to give baked goods an attractive brown color, serves as a nutriment for yeast, makes doughs more tender, and, to some extent, acts as a preservative in the finished product. As described below, sugar and other sweeteners are available in numerous forms.

AA Confectioners' Sugar

AA confectioners' sugar, not to be confused with powdered sugar, is a granulated sugar with large crystals and few impurities. It is used, often in combination with sliced almonds, to decorate and glaze many Danish pastries. It is also excellent to use in boiling and caramelizing sugar.

Brown or Golden Sugar

Brown sugar is beet or cane sugar that is not fully refined. It contains molasses and many more impurities than granulated sugar. A mixture of granulated sugar and molasses can be used as a substitute for brown sugar in most recipes. Brown sugar is available to the professional in a variety of grades from light to dark brown; the darker sugars have more impurities and a more bitter taste. Brown sugar contains a great deal of moisture and must be stored in airtight containers to keep it from hardening. If the sugar should become hard or lumpy, sprinkle a few drops of water lightly on top and warm it in a low oven, or place a slice of apple or bread in the sugar bin to add moisture.

Castor Sugar

Castor sugar is a granulated sugar which has been ground finer than regular table sugar, but not as fine as powdered sugar. It is actually the British equivalent of American powdered sugar. Castor sugar is used when a sugar that will dissolve very quickly is needed.

Corn Syrup

Corn syrup is made from cornstarch that has been treated with enzymes to convert it to more simple compounds. It is used mostly in making candies and for sugar boiling because it keeps other sugars from crystallizing. Corn syrup is also valuable for its ability to retain moisture in baked goods, and it is added to marzipan to improve elasticity. Corn syrup is available in both light and dark forms; the dark syrup contains added caramel color and flavorings and is not used as extensively. Although it is a liquid, a large amount of corn syrup or glucose is more easily (and less messily) measured by weight, by weighing it on top of one of the other ingredients in the recipe.

Glucose

Glucose is also made from starch and is used for the same purposes as corn syrup. Glucose is sometimes labeled as thick or heavy corn syrup. It is not quite as fluid as corn syrup, and, for the most part, the two are interchangeable.

Golden Syrup

Golden syrup is a by-product of sugar manufacturing that is refined to a greater extent than molasses. When the sugar, after many boilings, stops yielding crystals, the remaining syrup is clarified by filtering and reduced. Golden syrup also goes through a decolorizing process which gives it a milder flavor. It is composed of sucrose, dextrose, levulose, and a small amount of water. It is used in breads, cookies, and cakes.

Granulated Sugar

White granulated sugar is the most commonly used sugar variety and is what is meant when a recipe simply calls for sugar. It is produced for both cooking and table use. Granulated sugar is made from either sugar beets or sugarcane, and both varieties are slightly more than 99 percent pure sucrose. Granulated sugar is perfect for making cakes because the sugar granules are the right size for incorporating the proper amount of air into cake batters, and will melt and dissolve at the required speed and temperature during baking.

Honey

Honey comes from a natural source: It is the nectar collected by bees and deposited in their honeycomb. In addition to its sweetening power, honey also imparts the flavor of the flowers from which it was gathered. Honey is produced in nearly every country in the world. Popular varieties include orange blossom honey from Spain, California, and Mexico; sunflower honey from Greece, Turkey, and Russia; rosemary honey produced in the Mediterranean countries; and clover honey, which is the honey most commonly used in America. The color of the honey will vary widely depending on the source. Honey is available in three forms: comb honey, still in its waxy capsules; chunk honey, which contains both the filtered, extracted honey and a piece of the honeycomb; and extracted honey, the type most familiar for cooking and table use. Honey adds moisture to baked goods and gives a soft chewy texture to cakes and cookies. It will crystallize when stored for even short periods of time but is easy to liquify by heating.

Invert Sugar

A chemically processed heavy syrup, sweeter than sugar, that will not crystallize. It is used mostly in icings and flavorings.

Loaf and Cube Sugar

Sugar cubes are made by pressing damp, granulated sugar into molds, drying it, then cutting it into the desired shapes. Loaf sugar is used to make sugar sculptures.

Malt Sugar or Syrup

Malt sugar is extracted from sprouted barley that has been dried and ground. It is used in yeast breads. Diastatic malt contains diastase, an enzyme that breaks down starch into sugars, which in turn provide food for the yeast during fermentation. Diastatic malt should not be used in products with a long fermentation, however, as too much of the starch will be broken down. Nondiastatic malt is processed using a higher temperature, which kills the diastase. When malt syrup or malt sugar is called for in the recipes in this book, you should use the nondiastatic formula. Malt sugar caramelizes at low temperatures and has a very distinctive taste. It is also excellent for retaining moisture in baked goods.

Maple Syrup

Made by boiling the sap of maple trees, this syrup has a wonderful rich flavor. It can be used in the pastry kitchen to make candies, to flavor ice cream, to make dessert sauces, and of course, as is traditional in the United States, to top pancakes. The syrup is graded by color; the darker the syrup, the stronger the flavor. Maple syrup should be refrigerated after opening.

Molasses

Molasses is produced in the first stages of refining raw sugar. Used in breads and cakes, it adds a unique flavor and improves the shelf life. Molasses is available in three grades: light, dark, and blackstrap molasses. The grades are produced from the first, second, and third sugar boilings respectively. Molasses may be labeled as sulfured or unsulfured, depending on whether or not sulfur was used in the sugar-refining procedure.

Powdered Sugar

Also called confectioners' sugar, this sugar is produced by grinding granulated sugar to a powder. Starch is usually added to prevent caking or lumping. Powdered sugar is used mostly for uncooked icings, decorating, and in some meringues.

Tartaric Acid

Some tartaric acid is naturally present in most fruits, but the commercial product is extracted from grapes. Despite the somewhat poisonous-sounding name, tartaric acid is used for a number of purposes in cooking. Cream of tartar is made from it, and it is found in baking powder and ammonium carbonate. When used in sorbets and fruit desserts, it brings out the fruit flavor. It can be used whenever acidulated water or citric acid is called for (providing of course that the citrus flavor is not a necessary addition). Tartaric acid is not usually available in grocery stores but can be purchased or ordered from a drugstore; it is inexpensive and lasts a very long time. Tartaric acid also acts as the catalyst for pectin glaze.

Tartaric Acid Solution
Mix ½ cup (120 ml) hot water and 4 ounces (115 g) tartaric acid until all of the granules are dissolved. Pour the liquid into a drop bottle.

Thickeners

Arrowroot
Arrowroot is the powdered root of a plant called *Maranta arundinacea*, grown in the Caribbean. It is used to thicken glazes, fruit fillings, and puddings. Unlike cornstarch, arrowroot is not broken down by the acid in fresh fruits. Arrowroot thickens at a lower temperature than either cornstarch or flour, which is beneficial when you need to thicken products that should not boil.

Cornstarch
Cornstarch is a fine, white powder derived from corn. It is used to thicken fruit fillings, glazes, and sauces. It becomes transparent once it has gelatinized, making it preferable to flour for maintaining bright colors and a more attractive appearance. To keep cornstarch from lumping, you must dissolve it in a cold liquid before adding it to any hot mixture. It will gelatinize at temperatures above 170°F (77°C), and will leave an unpleasant taste if it is not cooked long enough. Cornstarch is also added to sponge and cake batters to dilute the gluten strength of the flour because it is close to 100 percent starch.

Potato Starch
Potato starch can be substituted for cornstarch, often with better results. It gelatinizes at 176°F (81°C), leaves no unpleasant taste, and, when used as a thickener, will not break down and get watery the next day as cornstarch tends to do. It can also be used to reduce the gluten strength of flour.

Tapioca Starch
Tapioca starch is derived from the root of the South American plant cassava. It is used in the same way as arrowroot, cornstarch, and potato starch, but is preferable for products that are to be frozen as it will not break down when thawed. Pearl tapioca consists of small balls of dried tapioca starch and is used to make tapioca pudding, a custard-like dessert made without eggs.

Vanilla

Vanilla, sometimes called "the orchid of flavor," is the most widely used flavoring agent in the pastry kitchen. Its uses are endless because its taste complements just about any other flavor, and will improve many of them. Vanilla also has the distinction of being more expensive than any other flavoring or spice, with the exception of saffron. The expense is due in a large part to the fact that it can take up to one year, from blossom to cured vanilla bean, to produce a product of the highest quality.

Vanilla is the fruit of a tropical vine which is part of the orchid family. It requires a humid tropical climate and thrives around the equator from sea level to around 2,000 feet. The vine grows wild, climbing to the top of the tallest trees in the jungle. But as long as the vines can continue to grow upward they will not flower. For this reason the vines of *Vanilla planifolia*, or fragrance, the species most widely used for commercial cultivation, are pruned regularly and bent into loops to keep the beans within easy reach of the workers.

Clusters of buds are produced on the vines taking many weeks to develop into orchids, which then bloom from early morning to late afternoon. If the flowers are not pollinated they will drop from the plant by the early evening. Although a healthy vine will produce up to 1,000 flowers, only about 10 percent would be pollinated naturally. When grown commercially the flowers are therefore always hand-pollinated and, in the process, thinned to guarantee a good-quality bean. After pollination the flowers develop into long, thin, cylindrical-shaped green beans which can reach a length of up to 12 inches (30 cm), although the more common size is around 8 inches (20 cm). The beans are ready for harvest after approximately 8 months.

There are different ways of curing the bean once it is harvested. The most common and ideal is to let the sun finish the ripening process. After a few days of storage the beans are spread out on blankets and left in the sun for several hours. The blankets are then folded over to cover the beans for the rest of the day, then wrapped around them and stored in airtight containers to sweat all night. This procedure is repeated for about two weeks until the beans have turned from green to dark brown. In the last step the beans are spread out on mats to dry every day for about two months. They are then stored indoors until they are dry enough to be packed and shipped.

According to history, the Spaniards stole vanilla cuttings from Mexico and planted them on the island of Madagascar. Madagascar had a monopoly on the crop for hundreds of years and today is, together with Mexico, the major producer of vanilla. The same species (sometimes referred to as bourbon vanilla from the name of one of the Madagascar islands) is grown in both Mexico and Madagascar. Tahiti is also an important growing area, producing a sweeter and more flowery-tasting bean.

Equipment

Adjustable Frame

A 2-inch-high (5-cm) frame, usually placed around a baking pan, that adjusts to different widths and lengths.

Adjustable Ring

A 2-inch-high (5-cm) ring that typically adjusts from 6½ inches (16.2 cm) to 14 inches (35 cm) in diameter. It is used to hold a filling while it sets and is useful for making odd-size cakes.

Baba Mold

A small thimble-shaped baking form used for making baba au rum pastries. The forms are usually made of aluminum and measure 2¼ inches (5.6 cm) high, 2½ inches (6.2 cm) across the top, and 2 inches (5 cm) across the bottom. (The traditional baba forms used in Europe are slightly taller and narrower, but they are not readily available in this country.)

Baguette Form

A baking pan used for baguettes. It is made of several long half-spheres joined together side-by-side. The pans produce round loaves, rather than loaves that are flat on one side. Some baguette forms are made of perforated metal to allow air to circulate around the loaves.

Bain-marie

A hot water bath used to protect delicate foods from heat that is too intense. A bain-marie is used in any of three ways: When food is to be placed over the hot water on the stove (such as with a double boiler) to cook a delicate sauce or to melt chocolate; to keep cooked foods warm until serving, as in a steam table; or when the container holding the food is placed in the water to bake custards or other desserts in the oven, to provide them with constant, even heat and protect them from overcooking.

Baker's Rack
A metal rack available in several sizes that holds 8 to 24 full-sized sheet pans. The racks are indispensable in a professional kitchen: Stationary racks are used for storage and for holding items during preparation, saving table space; portable racks are used for unloading deliveries and transporting goods to and from the walk-in, the work area, or the retail area. The rolling racks are available with locking wheels, and some models have adjustable shelves that can be raised to hold higher products.

Baking Paper
Also called parchment paper or silicon-coated paper, baking paper is a specially treated nonstick paper that is used extensively in pastry and cake baking. It is available in two thicknesses; the thicker paper can be used more than once.

Balloon Whisk
A whisk with a round (balloon) shape at the end. It is especially useful for incorporating the maximum amount of air into a batter.

Baumé Thermometer
An instrument, also known as a saccharometer, used to determine the density of a liquid. It is a thin glass tube with a graduated scale that ranges from 0° to 50° Baumé. It is adjusted with weights at the bottom to read 0° BE in water that is 58°F (15°C). The weights also allow the saccharometer to remain in a vertical position in liquid. (See page 615 for further information.)

Bear-Claw Cutter
A round cutter attached to a handle that has multiple blades and can be rolled along the edge of a Danish dough to cut the slits for bear claw pastries.

Brioche Pan
A round, fluted metal baking form with slanted sides. The small individual molds are 3¼ inches (8.1 cm) across the top, 1½ inches (3.7 cm) wide on the bottom, and 1¼ inches (3.1 cm) high; larger forms are available in several sizes. In addition to being used for baking brioche, the pans can be used for charlottes and custards.

Bundt Pan
A tube-shaped cake pan that is rounded at the bottom and has a decorative pattern on the sides; this pan is very similar to a gugelhupf pan.

Cake Decorating Turntable
A rotating round disk on a heavy base, usually 4¾ inches (11.8 cm) high. The disk can be rotated with one hand while applying decorations or buttercream to a cake.

Cake Rack or Cake Cooler
A cake rack looks like a grill and is designed so that air can circulate under, and also around, cooling breads or cakes. It is handy for icing pastries as well if a sheet is placed under the rack to collect the runoff.

Cardboard Cake Rounds

These sturdy cardboard sheets are available in several round sizes, as well as square and rectangular sizes that are designed to hold cakes baked in standard half- or full-sized sheet pans. The cardboard is coated on one side. The larger sizes are available in either single or double thickness; the thicker style is preferable because the sheets will lie flat. Finished cakes are placed on the sheets, in combination with a doily, to transport them from the bakery. The cardboard is also used to support cake layers or short dough cake-bottoms, making it much easier to move them during assembly and decorating.

Charlotte Mold

A metal form used to make charlottes. The forms vary in size, but the classic style is plain (not fluted), round, and flat on the bottom, with slightly slanted sides.

Chinois

A rigid, cone-shaped strainer with a fine mesh; also known as a China cap. In the pastry kitchen it is used to strain sauces or custards.

Chocolate Mold

A hollow mold used for making chocolate figures. The molds are made of two pieces that can be clamped together leaving a hole in the bottom to add melted chocolate. The molds can be made of plastic or metal and come in numerous sizes and special shapes such as animals, Santas, and Easter eggs. (See page 458 for information on using chocolate molds.)

Citrus Stripper

A small hand tool used to cut long, thin strips of citrus zest. The tool has a notch in the blade to remove the peel in uniform pieces, and can also be used to make decorative patterns on vegetables or to score the skin on cucumbers.

Comb Scraper or Cake Comb

A plastic or metal scraper with a fluted or serrated edge. It is used to make a pattern in the icing of cakes or pastries.

Deep-Frying Thermometer

A thermometer specifically designed to read the temperature of hot fat for deep frying.

Dipping Fork

A small fork, also known as a tempering fork, typically with two to four prongs, but also available with different shapes on the end, such as circles or ovals, designed to hold various shapes of candies. It is used for dipping pastries and candies into chocolate or icing.

Docker or Pricker

A tool that has spikes to prick doughs, eliminating air bubbles and preventing the dough from rising too much during baking. On one style the spikes protrude from a tube-shaped base attached to a handle, so it can easily be rolled over a large sheet of dough.

Dowel

A wooden pin usually 2 inches (5 cm) thick and 18 inches (45 cm) long. A dowel is used to roll out small pieces of dough that would be too delicate for a heavier rolling pin. A slightly longer and thinner dowel is useful to transfer rolled sheets of dough, or as a guide to cut straight lines.

Drum Sieve

A circular wire strainer with straight sides about 4 inches (10 cm) high, usually with a wooden frame around the top edge. The mesh is available in various sizes. The sieve is used to sift flour, powdered sugar, or nuts.

Eggs-in-Aspic Form

An oval metal form, 3¼ inches long and 2½ inches wide at the top (8.1 × 6.2 cm), with sloping sides making it slightly narrower at the bottom. The form is primarily used in the *Garde Manger* kitchen for the dish it was named for, but is nice for molding custards and charlottes as well.

Étamé

A cone-shaped strainer with a soft, very fine mesh.

False-Bottom Tart Pan

A tart pan with sides 1 inch (2.5 cm) high and a removable bottom. The most common size measures 11 inches (27.5 cm) in diameter. The pans are used for custard-based tarts and quiches that cannot be inverted to unmold.

Fixative Syringe

A hand tool used to apply color to finished pieces in sugar work. Also known as a hand sprayer. The syringe consists of two tubes, one slightly longer and thinner than the other, connected by a hinge. The tubes are bent at a 90° angle when the tool is in use; they fold flat for storage. The liquid coloring is sprayed (blown) on the sugar by submerging one end of the tool in the color and placing the other in your mouth. By blowing air into the syringe the color is sprayed in a very fine mist.

Flan Ring

A thin metal circle about 1 inch (2.5 cm) high that comes in various sizes. It is used to bake tarts.

Guéridon

A small serving cart on casters that is used in restaurants to cook food at the table. The carts have one or two burners and are used most often for flambé work.

Gugelhupf Pan

A tube pan with a rounded bottom and a decorative pattern on the sides. The typical size has just over a 1-quart (960-ml) capacity. It is used to bake gugelhupf, a type of coffee cake.

Hotel Pan

A stainless steel pan that comes in different sizes and depths. The pan has a lip all around so that it can be placed on top of a basin of hot water (steam table) to keep food warm. Hotel pans are also useful for marinating and storing food, and for baking custards and soufflés in a water bath.

Loaf Pan
A rectangular metal baking form. Also known as a bread pan, loaf pans are used for breads, pound cakes, fruit cakes, and molding frozen desserts in the pastry kitchen. A standard pan is 5 inches (12.5 cm) wide across the top, 9 inches (22.5 cm) long, and 3 inches (7.5 cm) high.

Marzipan Modeling Tools
A set of five or more hand tools about 5 inches (12.5 cm) long, used to mark and form marzipan figures. The ends of the tools have a blunt, round, pointed, or engraved surface to make the various imprints.

Mazarin Form
A small, round baking form with slanted sides, typically 2½ inches (6.2 cm) in diameter on top, 1½ inches (3.7 cm) on the bottom, and 1¼ inches (3.1 cm) high.

Melon Baller
A hand tool with hollow half-spheres on either end used to scoop out fruit into uniform balls. This tool can also be used to make small, elegant chocolate curls.

Metal Bars
Aluminum bars available in varying widths and lengths. Two bars can be used as a guide to roll out candies and special doughs to a precise thickness; four bars can be used to hold a liquid such as boiled sugar or candy filling within a small area, or in a certain shape, while it is setting up. A typical bar is 18 inches (45 cm) long and ¾ inch (20 mm) thick on all sides.

Muffin Pan
A metal baking pan with deep indentations or cups to hold and shape muffins as they bake. Pans for professional use come in a standard full-sheet-pan size holding three dozen muffins, 2¾ inches (6.8 cm) in diameter, and a smaller size holding two dozen muffins.

Multiple Pastry Wheel
A tool with four or five pastry wheels connected, so that multiple strips of dough can be cut quickly. The wheels are adjustable.

Pastry Bag
A cone-shaped plastic, nylon, or cloth bag that comes in lengths from 7 inches (17.5 cm) to over 20 inches (50 cm). When fitted with a piping tip, or pastry tip, it is used to pipe out batters and doughs. (See page 501 for information on using a pastry bag for decorating.)

Pastry Brush
Small flat brushes used to apply a glaze, chocolate, or melted butter. Larger brushes are used to remove excess flour when rolling doughs. The brushes should be made with natural bristles rather than nylon.

Pastry Cutters or Cookie Cutters
Professional pastry or cookie cutters come in round, oval, square, star, and heart shapes in sets of graduating sizes, in plain or fluted styles. Other cookie cutters, for both professional and home use, are available in a multitude of shapes and sizes for special occasions and specific recipes.

Pastry Wheel
A sharp, round disk attached to a handle so that it can roll. Also known as a pizza cutter, it comes fluted or plain and is used to cut dough.

Perforated Sheet Pan
A metal baking sheet with tiny holes used to promote a crisp crust and ensure proper baking on the bottom of breads and rolls baked in a rack oven. The pans are used without baking paper and should be completely dry or the product will stick. The pans are not used in regular shelf-type ovens because the product would overbrown on the bottom.

Pie Weights
Small metal or ceramic pellets used to weigh down a dough or crust to prevent it from expanding too much. Dried beans are a common substitute.

Pincers
A hand tool with two flat, springy arms that have a fluted pattern on the edges. Pincers are available in different widths and shapes, and are used for decorating the edges of pie crusts or to pinch a design on marzipan.

Piping Bag
A small paper cone, approximately 5 inches (12.5 cm) long, used for precise and delicate decorations and held by the fingers only. (See page 505 for instructions on making a piping bag.)

Piping Bottle
A small plastic squeeze bottle with a narrow opening used in decorating. (See page 517 for more information.)

Piping Tip
Also known as a pastry tip, a piping tip is a small metal or plastic hollow cone that is fitted into a pastry bag. The tips come in many shapes and sizes. The most standard styles are either plain, giving a smooth edge, or are star-shaped, which makes a fluted pattern. Other tips are available for specific uses such as filling pastries or making buttercream decorations.

Plastic Strips
Flexible heavyweight sheets of plastic cut to the desired size for use in making chocolate containers or lining the sides of forms for chilled desserts. (The plastic strips are not ovenproof like baking paper and cannot be used as a substitute if the product is to be baked.)

Pots de Crème Forms
Small ceramic forms with tight-fitting lids used to bake and serve individual portions of custard. The lids have a small hole to allow steam to escape.

Proof Box
A cabinet or room in which heat and humidity are controlled to create the correct environment for proofing a yeast dough.

Rack Oven
A large convection oven holding one to four baker's racks at a time. The ovens are very expensive but save time by producing a large quantity of evenly browned breads and rolls at once. The ovens come with racks

specifically designed to fit that oven. The rack is rolled into the oven and locked onto an arm that rotates the rack during baking. Each rack holds about 15 full-size sheet pans. Rack ovens are usually equipped with steam injectors. Since the sheet pans do not come in contact with the bottom of the oven, as they would in a shelf oven, it is necessary to use perforated sheet pans so the product will brown on the bottom.

Ramekins
Shallow earthenware dishes in which single portions (e.g., individual soufflés) are baked and served. They are also used to mold chilled desserts. The most common size measures about 3 inches (7.5 cm) across and 1½ inches (3.7 cm) high, and holds 5 ounces (180 ml).

Rectangular Fluted Pan
A metal baking pan generally used for tea cakes. The pans are rectangular on the top but slope down to a rounded, fluted design on the bottom. The typical size is 10 × 4¾ inches (25 × 12 cm) and 2 inches (5 cm) high. They are known in Germany as *rehrücken* or saddle-of-venison pans.

Salamander
A broiler with the heat source at the top, or a hot metal plate that is used to brown or caramelize food.

Savarin Form
A small, doughnut-shaped baking form. Its sizes vary, but a useful size is 3½ inches (8.7 cm) in diameter, 1 inch (2.5 cm) deep, with a 1¼-inch (3.1-cm) hole. Savarin forms are used for making individual servings of savarins, as the name suggests, but can also be used for many other pastries and desserts.

Sheet Pan
A metal baking sheet used in professional kitchens. The pan measures 24 × 16 inches (60 × 40 cm) and has 1-inch (2.5-cm) sides. Half-sheet pans are 16 × 12 inches (40 × 30 cm) and will fit the home oven.

Skimmer
A flat, finely meshed (or with small holes) strainer attached to a handle, used to remove dirt or scum from a boiling liquid, to poach, and to deep fry.

Small Swedish Pancakes Pan (Plättiron)
A round cast-iron skillet measuring 9 to 10 inches (22.5 to 25 cm) in diameter. The skillet has five to seven 2½- to 3-inch (6.2- to 7.5-cm) round depressions to form pancakes as they are cooking.

Springform Pan
A baking pan with removable sides, used mostly for baking cheesecakes. A clamp tightens the sides against the bottom.

Steam Injector

A device available on some commercial ovens that sends steam into the oven while baking. The steam creates a moist environment that prevents a crust from forming too quickly on breads or rolls. The result is a thinner crust with a very crisp texture. The steam also makes breads and rolls shiny, much like egg wash. (See page 47 for more information.)

Sugar Pan

An unlined copper pan made especially for cooking sugar. The acidity of the copper causes some of the sugar to break down into invert sugar, which is more resistant to crystallization. The sugar will also cook faster in this type of pan. A sugar pan has a small spout to make it easy to pour out the boiled sugar.

Sugar Thermometer

A thermometer specifically designed to measure the temperature of boiled sugar. Some have the names of the various sugar stages printed next to the corresponding temperatures.

Tart Pan

A metal baking pan available in many shapes and sizes. The most frequently used tart pan is round, 11 inches (27.5 cm) in diameter, and 1 inch (2.5 cm) deep, but tarts are also made in square or rectangular shapes. Tart pans can be one solid piece or two pieces; the latter, called "false-bottom pans," simplify removal of the baked tart. The pans have straight, usually fluted, sides.

Tartlet Pans

Pans used for making small, individual tarts that are usually filled with fruit or custard. Tartlet pans can be plain or fluted.

Template

A guide used to create a desired shape. A template is sometimes used as a stencil to form a batter or paste. It can also mask part of a product when applying a decoration; sifting powdered sugar over a doily on top of a cake, for example, uses a template in this way.

Tread Rolling Pin

A decorating tool that creates a pattern of fine parallel lines when rolled over a sheet of dough or marzipan.

Waffle Rolling Pin

A decorating tool shaped like a very thin rolling pin, about 13 inches (32.5 cm) long and 1 inch (2.5 cm) in diameter. The surface of the roller resembles a waffle iron and creates a decorative waffle pattern when rolled over dough. It is often used on marzipan.

Zester

A hand tool used to cut the zest (the colored part of the rind without the white pith) from citrus fruits. About the size of a paring knife, the zester has five small holes at the end to remove the skin in small threads.

Conversion and Equivalency Tables

The Metric System

Accuracy of measurement is essential to achieve a good result in the pastry shop. Ingredients are therefore almost always weighed, or "scaled," to use the professional term. The few exceptions are eggs, milk, and water; for convenience, these are usually measured by volume at the rate of 1 pint to 1 pound, 1 liter to 1 kilogram, or, for a small quantity of eggs, by number. The system of measurement used in the United States is highly complicated and confusing compared to the simple metric system used just about everywhere else in the world. In the U.S. system, the number of increments in any given unit of measure is arbitrarily broken down into numbers that have no correlation to each other. For example: there are 12 inches in 1 foot, 32 ounces in 1 quart, 4 quarts in 1 gallon, 3 teaspoons in 1 tablespoon, and so on. Adding to the confusion is that ounces are used to measure both liquids by volume and solids by weight; so if you see the measurement "6 ounces of melted chocolate," you do not really know if this means to weigh the ingredient or measure it in a cup. The metric system, on the other hand, is divided into four basic units, one for each type of measurement:

- **Degree Celsius** is the unit used to measure temperature. The freezing point is 0°C and the boiling point is at 100°C. Degree Celsius is abbreviated as °C throughout the text.
- **Meter** is the unit used to measure length and is divided into increments of centimeters and millimeters.

> 10 millimeters = 1 centimeter
> 100 centimeters = 1 meter

Meters, centimeters, and millimeters are abbreviated as m, cm, and mm, respectively, throughout the text.

- **Liter** is the unit used to measure volume. A liter is divided into deciliters, centiliters, and milliliters.

10 milliliters = 1 centiliter
10 centiliters = 1 deciliter
10 deciliters = 1 liter

Liters, deciliters, centiliters, and milliliters are abbreviated as l, dl, cl, and ml, respectively, throughout the text.
- **Kilogram** is the unit used to measure weight.

1 kilo = 10 hertograms
1 hertogram = 100 grams

The measurement of hertogram is rarely used in this country and the kilo is instead divided into 1,000 grams. Kilograms are abbreviated as kg and grams as g throughout the text.

The following approximate equivalents will give you a feeling for the size of various metric units:

- 1 kilo is slightly over 2 pounds
- 1 liter is just over 1 quart
- 1 deciliter is a little bit less than ½ cup
- 1 centiliter is about 2 tablespoons
- 1 meter is just over 3 feet

Larger or smaller units in the metric system are always made by multiplying in increments of 10, making it a more precise system and much less confusing once you understand the principles. Nevertheless, many people who did not grow up using this method are reluctant to learn it and think it will be difficult to understand. Reading that there are 28.35 grams to 1 ounce looks intimidating, but actually it shows how the metric system can give you a much more accurate measurement. When measuring any ingredient by weight that is less than 1 ounce, use the gram weight for a precise measurement.

The equivalency tables in this chapter have been used to convert the measurements in this book and provide both the U.S. and metric measurements for all ingredients in the recipes. However, they do not precisely follow the conversion ratio; instead the tables have been rounded off to the nearest even number. For example, 1 ounce has been rounded up to 30 grams rather than 28.35, which is the actual equivalent; 2 ounces has been rounded down to 55 grams instead of 56.7 grams, and so on. As the weight increases, every third ounce is calculated at 25 grams rather than 30, to keep the table from becoming too far away from the exact metric equivalent. Here are the precise measurements for converting the various types of measure.

Precise Metric Equivalents

Length	1 inch	25.4 mm
	1 centimeter	0.39 inches
	1 meter	39.4 inches
Volume	1 ounce	29.57 milliliters
	1 cup	2 dl, 3 cl, 7 ml (237 ml)
	1 quart	9 dl, 4 cl, 6 ml (946 ml)
	1 milliliter	0.034 fluid ounce
	1 liter	33.8 fluid ounces
Weight	1 ounce	28.35 grams
	1 pound	454 grams
	1 gram	0.035 ounce
	1 kilogram	2.2 pounds

Precise Metric Conversions

Length	*To convert:*	*Multiply by:*
	inches into millimeters	25.4
	inches into centimeters	2.54
	millimeters into inches	0.03937
	centimeters into inches	0.3937
	meters into inches	39.3701
Volume	*To convert:*	*Multiply by:*
	quarts into liters	0.946
	pints into liters	0.473
	quarts into millileters	946
	millileters into ounces	0.0338
	liters into quarts	1.05625
	millileters into pints	0.0021125
	liters into pints	2.1125
	liters into ounces	33.8
Weight	*To convert:*	*Multiply by:*
	ounces into grams	28.35
	grams into ounces	0.03527
	kilograms into pounds	2.2046

In the tables that follow metric amounts have been rounded to the nearest even number. These conversions should be close enough for most purposes.

Metric and U.S. Equivalents: Volume

U.S.	Metric	U.S.	Metric
½ teaspoon	2.5 ml	20 ounces (2½ cups)	600 ml (6 dl)
1 teaspoon	5 ml	21 ounces	630 ml (6 dl, 3 cl)
1 tablespoon	15 ml (1 cl, 5 ml)	22 ounces	660 ml (6 dl, 6 cl)
1 ounce	30 ml (3 cl)	23 ounces	690 ml (6 dl, 9 cl)
2 ounces (¼ cup)	60 ml (6 cl)	24 ounces (3 cups)	720 ml (7 dl, 2 cl)
3 ounces	90 ml (9 cl)	25 ounces	750 ml (7 dl, 5 cl)
4 ounces (½ cup)	120 ml (1 dl, 2 cl)	26 ounces	780 ml (7 dl, 8 cl)
5 ounces	150 ml (1 dl, 5 cl)	27 ounces	810 ml (8 dl, 1 cl)
6 ounces (¾ cup)	180 ml (1 dl, 8 cl)	28 ounces (3½ cups)	840 ml (8 dl, 4 cl)
7 ounces	210 ml (2 dl, 1 cl)	29 ounces	870 ml (8 dl, 7 cl)
8 ounces (1 cup)	240 ml (2 dl, 4 cl)	30 ounces	900 ml (9 dl)
9 ounces	270 ml (2 dl, 7 cl)	31 ounces	930 ml (9 dl, 3 cl)
10 ounces	300 ml (3 dl)	32 ounces (1 quart)	960 ml (9 dl, 6 cl)
11 ounces	330 ml (3 dl, 3 cl)	33 ounces	990 ml (9 dl, 9 cl)
12 ounces (1½ cups)	360 ml (3 dl, 6 cl)	34 ounces	1 l, 20 ml
13 ounces	390 ml (3 dl, 9 cl)	35 ounces	1 l, 50 ml
14 ounces	420 ml (4 dl, 2 cl)	36 ounces (4½ cups)	1 l, 80 ml
15 ounces	450 ml (4 dl, 5 cl)	37 ounces	1 l, 110 ml
16 ounces (1 pint)	480 ml (4 dl, 8 cl)	38 ounces	1 l, 140 ml
17 ounces	510 ml (5 dl, 1 cl)	39 ounces	1 l, 170 ml
18 ounces	540 ml (5 dl, 4 cl)	40 ounces (5 cups)	1 l, 200 ml
19 ounces	570 ml (5 dl, 7 cl)		

U. S. Volume Equivalents

3 teaspoons	= 1 tablespoon
2 tablespoons	= 1 ounce
8 ounces	= 1 cup
2 cups	= 1 pint
2 pints	= 1 quart
4 quarts	= 1 gallon

Metric and U.S. Equivalents: Weight

U.S.	Metric	U.S.	Metric
½ ounce	15 g	39 ounces (2 pounds, 7 ounces)	1 kg, 110 g
1 ounce	30 g	40 ounces (2 pounds, 8 ounces)	1 kg, 135 g
1½ ounces	40 g	41 ounces (2 pounds, 9 ounces)	1 kg, 165 g
2 ounces	55 g	42 ounces (2 pounds, 10 ounces)	1 kg, 195 g
2½ ounces	70 g	43 ounces (2 pounds, 11 ounces)	1 kg, 220 g
3 ounces	85 g	44 ounces (2 pounds, 12 ounces)	1 kg, 250 g
3½ ounces	100 g	45 ounces (2 pounds, 13 ounces)	1 kg, 280 g
4 ounces	115 g	46 ounces (2 pounds, 14 ounces)	1 kg, 310 g
5 ounces	140 g	47 ounces (2 pounds, 15 ounces)	1 kg, 340 g
6 ounces	170 g	48 ounces (3 pounds)	1 kg, 365 g
7 ounces	200 g	49 ounces (3 pounds, 1 ounce)	1 kg, 395 g
8 ounces	225 g	50 ounces (3 pounds, 2 ounces)	1 kg, 420 g
9 ounces	255 g	51 ounces (3 pounds, 3 ounces)	1 kg, 450 g
10 ounces	285 g	52 ounces (3 pounds, 4 ounces)	1 kg, 480 g
11 ounces	310 g	53 ounces (3 pounds, 5 ounces)	1 kg, 505 g
12 ounces	340 g	54 ounces (3 pounds, 6 ounces)	1 kg, 535 g
13 ounces	370 g	55 ounces (3 pounds, 7 ounces)	1 kg, 565 g
14 ounces	400 g	56 ounces (3 pounds, 8 ounces)	1 kg, 590 g
15 ounces	430 g	57 ounces (3 pounds, 9 ounces)	1 kg, 620 g
16 ounces (1 pound)	455 g	58 ounces (3 pounds, 10 ounces)	1 kg, 650 g
17 ounces (1 pound, 1 ounce)	485 g	59 ounces (3 pounds, 11 ounces)	1 kg, 675 g
18 ounces (1 pound, 2 ounces)	510 g	60 ounces (3 pounds, 12 ounces)	1 kg, 705 g
19 ounces (1 pound, 3 ounces)	540 g	61 ounces (3 pounds, 13 ounces)	1 kg, 735 g
20 ounces (1 pound, 4 ounces)	570 g	62 ounces (3 pounds, 14 ounces)	1 kg, 765 g
21 ounces (1 pound, 5 ounces)	595 g	63 ounces (3 pounds, 15 ounces)	1 kg, 795 g
22 ounces (1 pound, 6 ounces)	625 g	64 ounces (4 pounds)	1 kg, 820 g
23 ounces (1 pound, 7 ounces)	655 g	65 ounces (4 pounds, 1 ounce)	1 kg, 850 g
24 ounces (1 pound, 8 ounces)	680 g	66 ounces (4 pounds, 2 ounces)	1 kg, 875 g
25 ounces (1 pound, 9 ounces)	710 g	67 ounces (4 pounds, 3 ounces)	1 kg, 905 g
26 ounces (1 pound, 10 ounces)	740 g	68 ounces (4 pounds, 4 ounces)	1 kg, 935 g
27 ounces (1 pound, 11 ounces)	765 g	69 ounces (4 pounds, 5 ounces)	1 kg, 960 g
28 ounces (1 pound, 12 ounces)	795 g	70 ounces (4 pounds, 6 ounces)	1 kg, 990 g
29 ounces (1 pound, 13 ounces)	825 g	71 ounces (4 pounds, 7 ounces)	2 kg, 20 g
30 ounces (1 pound, 14 ounces)	855 g	72 ounces (4 pounds, 8 ounces)	2 kg, 45 g
31 ounces (1 pound, 15 ounces)	885 g	73 ounces (4 pounds, 9 ounces)	2 kg, 75 g
32 ounces (2 pounds)	910 g	74 ounces (4 pounds, 10 ounces)	2 kg, 105 g
33 ounces (2 pounds, 1 ounce)	940 g	75 ounces (4 pounds, 11 ounces)	2 kg, 130 g
34 ounces (2 pounds, 2 ounces)	970 g	76 ounces (4 pounds, 12 ounces)	2 kg, 160 g
35 ounces (2 pounds, 3 ounces)	1 kg (1,000 g)	77 ounces (4 pounds, 13 ounces)	2 kg, 190 g
36 ounces (2 pounds, 4 ounces)	1 kg, 25 g	78 ounces (4 pounds, 14 ounces)	2 kg, 220 g
37 ounces (2 pounds, 5 ounces)	1 kg, 50 g	79 ounces (4 pounds, 15 ounces)	2 kg, 250 g
38 ounces (2 pounds, 6 ounces)	1 kg, 80 g	80 ounces (5 pounds)	2 kg, 275 g

Metric and U.S. Equivalents: Length

U.S.	Metric	U.S.	Metric
¹⁄₁₆ inch	2 mm	5½ inches	13.7 cm
⅛ inch	3 mm	6 inches	15 cm
³⁄₁₆ inch	5 mm	6½ inches	16.2 cm
¼ inch	6 mm	7 inches	17.5 cm
⅜ inch	9 mm	7½ inches	18.7 cm
½ inch	1.2 cm	8 inches	20 cm
¾ inch	2 cm	8½ inches	21.2 cm
1 inch	2.5 cm	9 inches	22.5 cm
1¼ inches	3.1 cm	9½ inches	23.7 cm
1½ inches	3.7 cm	10 inches	25 cm
1¾ inches	4.5 cm	11 inches	27.5 cm
2 inches	5 cm	12 inches (1 foot)	30 cm
2½ inches	6.2 cm	18 inches (1½ feet)	45 cm
3 inches	7.5 cm	24 inches (2 feet)	60 cm
3½ inches	8.7 cm	30 inches (2½ feet)	75 cm
4 inches	10 cm	36 inches (3 feet)	90 cm
4½ inches	11.2 cm	40 inches	1 meter
5 inches	12.5 cm		

Temperature Conversions

Fahrenheit	Celsius	Fahrenheit	Celsius
32°F	0°C (freezing point)	240°F	115°C
40°F	4°C (yeast is dormant)	245°F	118°C (sugar syrup for Italian Meringue)
50°F	10°C		
60°F	16°C	250°F	122°C
70°F	21°C	260°F	127°C
80°F	26°C (ideal temperature for yeast to multiply)	270°F	132°C
		280°F	138°C
90°F	32°C (working temperature for couverture)	290°F	143°C
		300°F	149°C
100°F	38°C (working temperature for baker's chocolate and fondant)	310°F	155°C
		320°F	160°C (sugar starts to caramelize)
110°F	43°C	330°F	166°C
120°F	49°C	340°F	170°C
130°F	54°C	350°F	175°C
140°F	60°C	360°F	183°C
145°F	63°C (yeast is killed)	370°F	188°C
150°F	65°C	380°F	193°C
160°F	71°C	390°F	199°C
170°F	77°C	400°F	205°C
180°F	82°C	410°F	210°C
190°F	88°C	420°F	216°C
200°F	94°C	430°F	222°C
210°F	99°C	440°F	226°C
212°F	100°C (water boils at sea level)	450°F	230°C
220°F	104°C	500°F	260°C
230°F	110°C		

To Convert Celsius to Fahrenheit   Multiply by 9, divide by 5 (Celsius × 9/5), then add 32.
Example: 190°C × 9/5 = 342 + 32 = 374°F.

To Convert Fahrenheit to Celsius   Subtract 32, multiply by 5, then divide by 9 (Fahrenheit × 5/9).
Example: 400°F − 32 = 368 × 5/9 = 204.4°C.

Volume Equivalents of Commonly Used Products

1 pint water	1 pound
7 egg whites (average size)	1 cup
4 eggs (average size)	1 cup
16 eggs (average size)	1 quart
12 egg yolks (average size)	1 cup
1 pound sliced almonds	6 cups (loosely packed)
1 pound bread flour (unsifted)	4 cups
1 pound cake flour (unsifted)	4⅓ cups
1 pound butter	2 cups
1 pound granulated sugar	2¼ cups
1 pound powdered sugar	4 cups
1 pound brown sugar	2⅔ cups
1 pound cocoa powder	4¾ cups

Gram Weights of Commonly Used Products

Item	Grams per Teaspoon	Grams per Tablespoon
ammonium carbonate	3.5	10
baking powder	4	12
baking soda	4	12
ground cinnamon	1.5	5
cocoa powder	2.5	8
cornstarch	2.5	8
cream of tartar	2	6
granulated sugar	5	15
ground spices (except cinnamon)	2	6
malt sugar	3	9
mocha paste	4	12
powdered gelatin	3	9
powdered sugar	3	9
salt	5	15

High-Altitude Adjustments for Cake Baking

Since most recipes are developed for use at sea level (including those in this book), when baking at higher altitudes where the atmospheric pressure is much lower you must make some adjustments to produce a satisfactory result. Although some experimental baking has to be done to convert a sea-level recipe to a particular local condition and altitude, certain manufacturers supply the rate of adjustment for some of their products.

At high altitudes the lower air pressure causes water to boil at a higher temperature. Thus, more evaporation takes place while a cake is baking. This results in insufficient moisture to fully gelatinize the starch, which in turn weakens the structure. The lower air pressure also causes the batter to rise higher; however, it later collapses due to the lack of stabilizing starches.

It is necessary to make adjustments with cake baking starting at altitudes from around 2,500 feet (760 meters). In general the changes consist of

- reducing the amount of baking powder or baking soda;
- reducing the amount of sugar;
- increasing the amount of liquid, sometimes with additional eggs, egg whites, or yolks;
- increasing the flour; and
- using a higher baking temperature.

These changes apply to a greater degree as the altitude gets higher. Although these changes help to protect the shape and consistency of the cake, they reduce its quality and flavor.

Adjustments for specific ingredients are as follows.

Leavening Agents

Baking powder or soda, and any other substitute that reacts with heat, must be reduced by 20 percent starting at 2,500 feet (760 meters) and gradually be reduced up to 60 percent at 7,500 feet (2,280 meters). For example, if the recipe calls for 10 ounces (285 g) of baking powder, only 4 ounces (115 g) should be used at 7,500 feet (2,280 meters). In a dark cake or muffin recipe that calls for both baking powder and baking soda together with buttermilk, it is best to change to sweet milk, and use baking powder only (add the two amounts together) to save having to convert both leavening agents.

Eggs

At 2,500 feet (760 meters), add 3 percent more whole eggs, egg whites, or egg yolks. Progressively increase the number of eggs until, at 7,500 feet (2,280 meters) you are adding 15 percent more eggs. For example, if your recipe calls for 36 ounces (1 kg) of eggs (which is 1 quart or 960 ml), you must use an additional 5¼ ounces (145 g) at the 7,500-foot (2,280-meter) level.

Flour

Beginning at 3,000 feet (915 meters), add 3 percent more flour, gradually increasing the amount up to 10 percent more at 8,000 feet (2,440 meters). For example, if the recipe calls for 40 ounces (1 kg, 135 g) of flour, you should use 1¼ ounces (35 g) more at 3,000 feet (915 meters).

Oven

Starting at 3,500 feet (1,065 meters), increase the baking temperature by 25 percent. For example, if your recipe says to bake at 400°F (205°C), you should increase the temperature to 500°F (260°C) at 3,500 feet (1,065 meters). The baking time should remain the same as at sea level, but take care not to bake any longer than necessary to prevent the rapid evaporation that takes place at high altitudes.

Storage

Everything dries quicker in thin air, so, to assume maximum moisture and freshness, cakes should be removed from the pans, wrapped in plastic, and stored in the refrigerator as soon as they have cooled. It is actually preferable not to keep any sponges in stock at high altitudes; instead make them up as you need them.

Baumé Scale

A French chemist, Antoine Baumé, perfected the saccharometer, an instrument used to determine the density of a liquid. The saccharometer is a thin glass tube with a graduated scale that ranges from 0° to 50° BE. The weights at the bottom of the saccharometer are precisely adjusted by the manufacturer so that it will read 0° BE when placed in water that is 58°F (15°C). Before using the instrument for the first time, it is a good idea to test it, and, if necessary, compensate for any discrepancy, plus or minus, when using. The weights at the bottom also allow the instrument to remain vertical in a liquid. To use, a high narrow container, preferably a laboratory glass, must be filled with enough liquid to float the saccharometer. The scale is read at the point where the instrument meets the surface of the liquid. For example, if the saccharometer settles at 28° BE, the density of the solution is 1.28 which means that 1 liter (33 ounces) of the solution will weigh 1 kg, 280 g (2 pounds, 13 ounces). The following table gives the Baumé readings for certain percentages of sugar solutions when measured at room temperature (65°F/19°C). When measured hot, the BE is 3° lower.

Baumé Readings for 2 Cups (480 ml) Water

Granulated Sugar	Baumé at Room Temperature
5 ounces (140 g)	14° (sorbet syrup)
6 ounces (170 g)	15°
7 ounces (200 g)	17°
8 ounces (225 g)	18° (baba syrup)
10 ounces (285 g)	21° (candied citrus peel syrup)
12 ounces (340 g)	25°
14 ounces (400 g)	27°
1 pound (455 g)	28° (simple syrup)
1 pound, 2 ounces (510 g)	29°
1 pound, 4 ounces (570 g)	31°
1 pound, 6 ounces (625 g)	32°
1 pound, 8 ounces (680g)	33°
1 pound, 10 ounces (740 g)	34°
1 pound, 12 ounces (795 g)	35° (liqueur candies)

Sugar Boiling Conversions

Sugar conversion tables in ten different cookbooks can give ten different temperatures and almost as many names to describe the same stage. Some charts have 14 separate stages—which really can make your head spin! All of these names and stages are, in a way, misleading, and unrealistic for use by anyone who doesn't have years of experience. For example, by the time you have tested and determined that the sugar is at the crack stage, it has probably already reached hard crack. The point is not what a particular stage is called and how to test for it, but what temperature you want the sugar. I suggest you rely on an accurate sugar thermometer rather than your poor index finger and ignore all the different names.

Special thermometers for boiling sugar are calibrated according to the temperature range needed. Professional thermometers have a wire screen that protects the glass and should be stored hanging up, using the handle that is part of this screen. Although Centigrade is used more and more for measuring sugar in European countries, I have included the old Réaumur system here because it is still part of the scale on professional European thermometers.

Sugar Boiling Conversions

Stage	Fahrenheit	Celsius	Réaumur	Testing Procedure
Thread	215°–230°	102°–110°	82°–88°	Pull a little sugar between your thumb and index finger; shorter or longer threads will form depending on the temperature. (Pinch and open your fingers quickly to cool the sugar and prevent burns.)
Soft Ball	240°	115°	92°	Put your index finger in ice-cold water, dip it very quickly into the hot syrup and immediately plunge it back into the ice water. The sugar will fall off your finger and you will be able to roll it into a ball.
Firm Ball	245°	118°	94°	Same as for soft ball stage but the ball will be harder.
Hard Ball	250°–260°	122°–127°	97°–101°	Same as for soft ball stage but the sugar will be more resistant to forming a ball.
Small Crack	265°–270°	130°–132°	104°–105°	Dip your finger into water and sugar as for soft ball test; the sugar cannot be formed and will show small cracks.
Crack	275°–280°	135°–138°	108°–110°	Same as for small crack stage, except that the sugar will break apart.
Hard Crack	295°–310°	146°–155°	116°–123°	Test as for soft ball stage; the sugar will shatter in the ice water.
Caramel	320°	160°	128°	To test: Check the color. Sugar turns from amber to golden brown to light brown.

Index

AA confectioners' sugar, 593
Adjustable frame, 598
Adjustable ring, 598
Agar-agar, 588
Alcoholic flavorings, 571–572
Almond (s), 591
  Chocolate Snow Hearts, 414
  Cinnamon Stars, 416
  Cocoa Almond Sponge, 163
  Doubles, 247
  Kirschwasser Rings, 237
  Lemon-Almond Tartlets, 238
  Macaroon Cookies, 123
  Mazarin Filling, 569
  Mazarins, 241
  Noisette Rings, 242
  Orange Almond Filling, 100
  Paste, 4
  Polynées, 253
  Sponge, 162–163
  Tart Holladaise, 155
  Truffles, 225
Amaretto, 571
  Chocolate Trifle, 319
Ammonium carbonate, 589–590
Apple (s), 580
  Chunky Apple Filling, 566
  Cinnamon Cake, 166
  Cinnamon Filling, 307
  Cobbler with Apples and Ginger,
    276–277
  Cointreau Tart with Apple, Pear or
    Rhubarb, 148
  Fruit Waffles, 235
  Jam with Calvados, 281
  Mazarins, 225–226
  -Pecan Buttermilk Muffins, 114–115
  Rum Charlotte, 306–307
  Strudel, Austrian Style, 272
    German Style, 273–274
  Tart Parisienne, 145
  Tart Tatin, 155–156
  Turnovers, 82
  Wine Cake, 175–177
Apricot (s), 580
  Bavarois, 308
  Cream Cake, 177
  Glaze, 526
  Kernels, 592
  Sauce, 556
  Souffle. See Blueberry Souffle
  Whipped Cream, 178
Arrack, 571
Arrowroot, 596

Baba (s)
  Dough, 292
  Mold, 598
  Rum, 291–292

Baguette form, 598
Baguettes, 48
Bain-marie, 598
Baked Alaska, 335–336
Baked Bananas with Banana-Tofu Ice
  Cream, 382–383
Baked Chocolate Sheet, 324
Baked Figs with Honey-Vanilla Frozen
  Yogurt, 373
Baker's chocolate, 442, 573
Baker's rack, 599
Baking at high altitudes, adjustments for,
  613–615
Baking paper, 599
Baking powder, 590
Baking soda. See Sodium bicarbonate
Balloon whisk, 599
Banana (s), 580–581
  Baked Bananas with Banana-Tofu Ice
    Cream, 382–383
  Chocolate Mousse Cake with, 194
  Macaroon, 239–240
  Muffins, 115
  Poppy Seed Ice Cream, 356
  Tea Cake, 167
  -Tofu Ice Cream, 383
Basic Bombe Mixture, 368
Basic Doughs, 13–14
  Cobbler Topping, 277
  Cocoa Short Dough, 31
  Hazelnut Short Dough, 32
  Linzer Dough, 14
  Pâte à Choux, 15–16
  Pie Dough, 17
  Pizza Dough, 18
  Puff Paste, 19–23
  Quick Puff Paste, 23
  Salt Dough, 28
  Short Dough, 31
  Unbaked Salt Dough, 29
  Weaver's Dough, 36
  Whole Wheat Weaver's Dough, 36
Basketweave pattern, 502
Baumé scale, 615
Baumé thermometer, 599
Bavarian Rum Cream, 206
Bavarois, 306
  Apricot, 308
  Charente, 310
  Lychee, 395
  Pear, 311–312
  Persimmon, 420
  White Chocolate, with Macadamia and
    Pistachio Nuts, 312
Bear-claw cutter, 599
Bear Claws, 106–107
Beignets. See Plum Fritters
Berliners, 83–84
Beurre noisette, 87

Biscotti, 124
Biscuit Viennoise, 163
Bitter Orange Sauce, 561
Blackberry (ies), 581
  Cake, 214
  Meringue Tartlets, 336–337
Black Currant (s), 581
  Cake, 179–181
  Glaze, 180
  Mousse, 180
  Purèe, 180
  Souffle. See Blueberry Souffle
Black Forest Cake, 181–182
  Meringue, 345–346
Blood Orange
  Sauce, 385
  Sorbet, 385
  Sorbet in Magnolia Cookie Shells, 383
Blueberry (ies), 581
  Fruit Barrels, 284–286
  Ginger Muffins, 115
  Sauce, 557
  Souffle, 326
Boiled Sugar
  Basic Recipe, 469
  Method I, 470
  Method II, 470–471
Bombe (s), 355, 367
  Aboukir, 368
  Basic Bombe Mixture, 368
  Bourdaloue, 369
  Ceylon, 369
  Monarch, 370
Braided Stollen, 405
Braided White Bread, 49–53
Bran
  Honey-Bran Muffins, 117
  Oat Bran–Yogurt Muffins, 118
Brandy, 571
  Brandied Whipped Cream, 424
  Bread Pudding, 313
  Pretzels, 247
Bread baking
  history of, 45
  sponge method in, 46
  straight dough method in, 46
  steam, to create in, 48
  yeast in, 45
Bread (s). See also Breakfast Breads; Rolls
  Baguettes, 48
  Basket, 37–43
  Braided Loaves, 50–53
    Two-String Braid, 51
    Three-String Braid, 52
    Four-String Braid, 52
    Five-String Braid, 52
    Six-String Braid, 52
    Seven-String Braid, 52
    Eight-String Braid, 53

Bread, Braided Loaves (*cont.*)
Star Braid, 56–59
Braided Stollen, 405
Braided White, 49–53
Brioche, 85–86
Butter Wheat, 59
Christmas Stollen, 406
Crisp, 68
Farmer's Rye Rings, 60
Garlic, 60–61
Italian Easter, 62
Joggar, 63
Knäckebröd, 74
loaves, to form, 48
Onion-Walnut, 64
Potato, 65
Pre-dough, 77
Raisin, 66
Rosemary, 67
Russian Rolled-Wheat, 68–69
San Francisco Sourdough Loaves, 71
Star Braid, 56–59
Sticks, 76
Swedish Orange Rye, 72
Swedish Peasant, 73
Swedish Peasant Rings, 73
Swedish Spice, 410
Swedish Thin, 74
Triestine, 411
Bread Pudding, Brandy, 313
Breakfast, breads and pastries for, 81–82
Breakfast Breads. *See also* Breakfast Pastries;
    Coffee Cakes
Apple-Pecan Buttermilk Muffins,
    114–115
Banana Muffins, 115
Blueberry Ginger Muffins, 115
Brioche, 85–86
Chocolate Chip Muffins, 116
Chocolate Honey Muffins, 116–117
Croissants, 94–96
English Muffins, 97–98
Honey-Bran Muffins, 117
Lucia Buns, 407–408
Oat Bran-Yogurt Muffins, 118
Persimmon Muffins, 119
Pumpkin Muffins, 118–119
Zucchini-Walnut Muffins, 119
Breakfast Pastries. *See also* Breakfast Breads;
    Coffee Cakes; Muffins
Apple Turnovers, 82
Bear Claws, 106–107
Berliners, 83–84
Butter Gipfels, 87–88
Butterhorns, 108
Cherry Cross-Over Strip, 89–90
Choux Surprise, 91
Cinnamon Knots, 92
Cinnamon Swirls, 92
Danish Cinnamon Wreath, 108–109
Danish Twists, 109–110
    Cherry Twists, 110
    Figure Eights, 110
    Singles, 110
Envelopes, 111
Hungarian Chocolate Twists, 99–100
Klenäter, 84
Mayor's Wreath, 112
Puff Paste Diamonds, 100–102
Raisin Snails, 112–113

Sister's Pull-Apart Coffee Cake, 113
Sugar Buns, 114
Swedish Breakfast Spirals, 102–103
Sweet Pig's Head, 409
Twisted Loaves and Wreaths, 93–94
Wales Surprise, 91
Brioche, 85–86
Brioche pan, 599
Brown sugar, 593
Brownies, Raisin, 139
Brysselkex Cookies, 124–126
    Checkerboard, 126
    Dough, 124
    Marble, 125
    Vanilla, 124
Boiled Sugar
    Basic Recipe, 469
    Method I, 470
    Method II, 470–471
Bouchées, 27–28
Búche de Nöel. See Yule Logs
Budapest Swirls, 274–275
Bundt pan, 599
Butter, 572
Butter and Flour Mixture, 4
Butter Gipfels, 87–88
Butter Wheat Bread, 59
Buttercream, 500
    Basketweave pattern for, 502
    Chocolate, 501
    Pearl and shell patterns for, 504
    Praline, 343
    Roses, 503–504
    Rosettes, 504
    Vanilla, 501
Butterhorns, 108

Cake Batters. *See* Sponge Cakes
Cake comb. *See* Comb scraper
Cake decorating turntable, 599
Cake rack or cake cooler, 599
Cake(s), Decorated, 173–175. *See also* Tea
    Cakes; Sponge Cakes
Apple Wine, 175–177
Apricot Cream, 177
Black Currant, 179–181
Black Forest, 181–182
Blackberry, 214
Caramel, 183
Carrot, 184
Cheesecake, 185
Chestnut, 413–414
Chestnut Puzzle, 187–189
Chestnut Rum Torte, 412–413
Chocolate and Frangelico Mousse,
    190–191
Chocolate Decadence, 192
Chocolate Hazelnut, 193
Chocolate Mousse Cake with Banana,
    194
Chocolate Truffle Cake with Raspberries,
    195–196
Coconut Cake Hawaii, 196–197
Cranberry Mousse, 181
Florentine Torte, 416–418
Fruit, 418–419
Gâteau Arabe, 338–339
Gâteau au Diplomate, 198
Gâteau Istanbul, 199
Gâteau Lugano, 200

Gâteau Malakoff, 201–202
Gâteau Moka Carrousel, 202–204
Gâteau Saint-Honoré, 204–206
Harlequin, 206
Ice Cream Cake Jamaica, 339–340
Kiwi Mousse, 220
Lemon Chiffon, 207–208
Meringue Black Forest, 345–346
Pariser Chocolate, 208
Persimmon Cream Slices, 421–423
Poppy Seed, 209
Princess, 210–211
Queen of Sheba, 211–212
Raspberry, 212–214
Sacher Torte, 214
Sicilian Macaroon, 215–216
Strawberry Kirsch, 216–218
Swedish Chocolate, 218
Tropical Mousse, 219–220
Wedding Cake Assembly and
    Decorations, 549–553
White-Chocolate Pumpkin Cheesecake,
    220
Cake-Bottoms, Short Dough, 32
Calvados, 571
Apple Jam with, 281
Custard, 145
Whipped Cream, 281
Wine Filling, 177
Candied Citrus Peels, 520–521
    Quick Method for, 521
Candies, 460
    Dark Truffles, 464
    Fig Logs, 460
    Gianduja, 461
    Gianduja Bites, 461
    Glazed Fruit, 489–490
    Light Truffles, 465
    Mimosa, 462
    Nougat Montélimar, 462–463
    Orange Moons, 463
    Pistachio Slices, 464
    White Truffles, 465
Cantalopes, 581
Caramel
    Cake, 183
    Cream, 183
    Crème Caramel with Ginger, 313
    Filling, 157
    Ice Cream, 356
    Ice Cream in a Cage, 356–358
    Mimosa, 462
    Sauce I, 557
    Sauce II, 558
    Small Pear Tartlets with Caramel Sauce,
        294–295
    Walnut-Caramel Tart, 156–157
    -Walnut Tartlets, 269
Caramelized Almonds, Hazelnuts, Walnuts
    and Pecans, 488–489
Caramelized Pineapple Barbados, 386
Caramelized Pineapple with Coconut Ice
    Cream, 386
Caramelized Sugar, 487
    Dry Method, 488
    with Water, 488
Cardboard cake rounds, 600
Carrot Cake, 184
Carrot Sponge, 184
Castor sugar, 594

Chambord, 571
Champagne Sorbet, 365
Charente Bavarois, 310
Charlotte (s), 305
    Apple Rum, 306–307
    Charente, 308–309
    Classic Charlotte Royal, 395
    Lychee Charlotte Royal, 394–395
    Mold, 600
    Pear, 310–311
    Persimmon, 420–421
    Russe, 309
Checkerboard Brysselkex, 126
Cheese Souffle, 10
Cheese Straws, 11
Cheesecake (s), 185
    Lingonberry Cheese Pudding, 315–316
    New York-Style, 186
    White-Chocolate Pumpkin, 220
Cherry (ies), 581–582
    Black Forest Cake, 181–182
    Clafoutis with, 147
    Cross-Over Strip, 89–90
    Filling, 565
    Jubilee, 374
    Sauce, 558
    Twists, 110
Chestnut (s), 592
    Cake, 413–414
    Purée, 412–413
    Puzzle Cake, 187–189
    Rum Filling, 414
    Rum Torte, 412–413
Chinois, 600
Chocolate, 439–443, 573–574
    Amaretto-Chocolate Trifle, 319
    Baked Chocolate Sheet, 324
    Baker's chocolate, 442, 573
    Biscuit, 163
    Buttercream, 501
    Butterfly Ornaments, 455
    Casting or Painting, 456–457
    Chip Cookies, 127
    Chip Muffins, 116
    Chunky White-Chocolate Chip Cookies, 127
    Cigars. *See* Curls
    Circles, 445–447
    Classic Chocolate Bavarian Cream, 567
    Cocoa Almond Sponge, 163
    Cocoa block, 573
    Cocoa butter, 573
    Cocoa Cuts, 128
    Cocoa Dobosh Sponge, 164
    Cocoa Painting, 457–458
    Cocoa powder, 573
    Cognac Cream, 195
    Couverture, 440, 574
    -Covered Pretzels, 247
    Cream, 566
    Crème Parisienne, 567
    Crisp Cake, 167
    Curls, 444–445
    Cut-outs, 445–447
    Dark chocolate, 574
    Dark Chocolate Cream, 191
    Dark Chocolate Filling, 325
    Dark Truffles, 464
    Decadence, 192
    Double-Chocolate Indulgence, 130

Eclairs, 226–227
Figurines, 449–454
and Frangelico Mousse Cake, 190–191
Ganache, 567–568
Gianduja, 461
Gianduja Bites, 461
Glaze, 526
Gugelhupf, 168
Harlequin Cake, 206
Harlequin Souffle, 329
Hazelnut Cake, 193
Hazelnut-Chocolate Biscuit, 164
Hollow Chocolate Figures Using Molds, 458–459
Honey Muffins, 116–117
Hot Fudge Sauce, 559
Hot or Cold Chocolate Sauce, 559
Ice Cream, 358
Ladyfingers, 135
Leaves, 447–448
Light Truffles, 465
Macaroons, 227–228
Meringue Landeck, 349
Milk chocolate, 574
Milk Chocolate Filling, 325
Mimosa, 462
Modeling Chocolate, 449
Mold, 600
Molding Chocolate Strips, 459
Mousse Cake with Banana, 194
Mousse in Chocolate Teardrops, 320–321
Orange Moons, 463
Orange Truffle Strips, 242–243
Pariser Chocolate Cake, 208
Pine Nut Tart, 146
Piping Chocolate, 449
Pistachio Slices, 464
Pots de Crème, 319
Production chart, 441
Queen of Sheba Cake, 211–212
Raisin Brownies, 139
Rectangles, 445–447
Roses, 449
Roulade, 427
Rum Pudding, 314
Sauce for Piping, 560
Shavings, 448
Snow Hearts, 414
Souffle, 329
Sponge Cake, 162
Squares, 445–447
Streaking, 455
Swedish Chocolate Cake, 218
Tempering, 442–443
Triangles (decoration), 445–447
Triangles (pastry), 228–230
Triple Chocolate Terrine, 324–325
Truffle Cake with Raspberries, 195–196
Tulips, 546–548
White chocolate, 442, 574
White Chocolate Bavarois with
    Macadamia and Pistachio Nuts, 312
White Chocolate Filling, 325
White Truffles, 465
Yule Logs, 425–427
Choux Surprise, 91
Christmas Cookie Ornaments, 414–415
Christmas Desserts
    Chestnut Cake, 413–414

Chestnut Rum Torte, 412–413
Cranberry Mousse Cake, 181
Florentine Torte, 416–418
Fruit Cake, 418–419
Persimmon Charlotte, 420–421
Persimmon Cream Slices, 421–423
Persimmon Pudding, 423–424
Yule Logs, 425–427
Christmas Stollen, 406
Chunky Apple Filling, 566
Chunky White-Chocolate Chip Cookies, 127
Cinnamon
    Apple Cinnamon Cake, 166
    Apple Cinnamon Filling, 307
    Cobbler with Peaches and, 278
    Knots, 92
    Stars, 416
    Sugar, 4
    Swirls, 92
Citrons, 231
Citrus
    Candied Citrus Peels, 520–521
        Quick Method, 521
    Citrus stripper, 600
Clafoutis with Cherries, 147
Classic Bavarian Cream, 566
Classic Charlotte Royal, 395
Classic Chocolate Bavarian Cream, 567
Classic (French) Puff Paste, 21–23
Classic Napoleons, 263
Cobbler
    Topping, 277
    with Apples and Ginger, 276–277
    with Peaches and Cinnamon, 278
    with Rhubarb and Honey, 278
Cocoa
    Almond Sponge, 163
    Block, 573
    Butter, 573
    Cuts, 128
    Dobosh Sponge, 164
    Painting, 457–458
    Powder, 440, 573
    Short Dough, 31
    Strassburger Cookies, 141
Coconut, 582
    Cake Hawaii, 196–197
    Cream Filling, 197
    fresh coconut, to open, 359
    Fresh-Coconut Ice Cream, 359
    Macaroons, 129
    Quick Coconut Ice Cream, 359
Coffee Cakes. *See also* Breakfast Breads;
        Breakfast Pastries
    Danish Cinnamon Wreath, 108–109
    Gugelhupf, 98
    Mayor's Wreath, 112
    Sister's Pull Apart Coffee Cake, 113
Coffee Reduction, 5
Cognac, 571
    Chocolate Cognac Cream, 195
Cointreau, 571
    Custard, 148
    Pear Sauce, 401
    Tart with Apple, Pear, or Rhubarb, 148
Cold Sabayon, 398
Colomba Pasquale. *See* Italian Easter Bread
Comb scraper or cake comb, 600
Confectioner's sugar. *See* Powdered sugar

Conversion and equivalency tables, 606–616
Cookie cutters. *See* Pastry cutters
Cookies, 121–122
    Almond Doubles, 247
    Almond Macaroon, 123
    Biscotti, 124
    Brandy Pretzels, 247
    Brysselkex, 124–126
    Chocolate Chip, 127
    Chocolate-Covered Pretzels, 247
    Chocolate Crescent, 200
    Chocolate-Filled Macadamia Morsels, 248
    Chocolate Ladyfingers, 135
    Chocolate Snow Hearts, 414
    Christmas Cookie Ornaments, 414–415
    Chunky White-Chocolate Chip, 127
    Cinnamon Stars, 416
    Cocoa Cuts, 128
    Cocoa Strassburger, 141
    Coconut Macaroons, 129
    Double-Chocolate Indulgence, 130
    Florentinas, 130–131
    Gingerbread, 419
    Gingersnaps, 132
    Hazelnut Butter, 132–133
    Hazelnut Cuts, 248
    Hazelnut Flowers, 249
    Hazelnut Squares, 133
    Hiede Sand, 133–134
    Ladyfingers, 134
    Lemon-Butter Cookie Dough, 415
    Macadamia Nut, 135
    Miniature Palm Leaves, 250
    Oat Flakes, 135
    Orange Macaroons, 136
    Palm Leaves, 136–137
    Peanut Butter, 138
    Pine Nut, 135
    Pirouettes, 138–139
    Raisin Brownies, 139
    Raisin Oatmeal, 139
    Raspberry Cut-outs, 251
    Raspberry Turnovers, 140
    Short Dough, 35
    Spritz Rings, 140
    Strassburger, 141
    Strawberry Hearts, 251
Cornstarch, 596
Corn syrup, 594
    measuring, 7
Coupe (s), 335, 370
    Bavaria, 370
    Belle Hélène, 371
    Hawaii, 371
    Niçoise, 371
    Sweden, 373
Couverture, 440, 574
Crackers
    Bread Sticks, 76
    Knäckebröd, 74
    Swedish Thin Bread, 74
    Swedish Whole-Grain Crisp Rolls, 78
    Wheat Crisp Rolls, 79
Cranberry (ies), 582
    Mousse Cake, 181
    Purée, 181
    Sauce, 558
Cream, 574

Chantilly, 343
Crème Fraîche, 559, 574
half-and-half, 575
Horns, 232–233
light, 575
manufacturing, 575
sour, 575
whipping, 575
Cream Cheese
    Filling, 184
    Filling for Danish, 106
Cream of tartar, 590
Crème Anglaise. *See* Vanilla Custard Sauce
Crème Brûlée, 314–315
Crème Caramel with Ginger, 313
Crème de cacao, 571
Crème de cassis, 571
Crème Fraîche, 559, 574
Crème Parisienne, 567
Crepe (s), 388–389
    Souffle, 327
    Suzette, 279–280
    Vienna, 387
    Lemon Chiffon Pouches, 393
Crisp Bread, 68
Crisp Waffles, 280–281
Croissants, 94–96
    Ham and/or Cheese, 9
Cupid's Treasure Chest, 331–332
Currants, dried, 583. *See also* Black currants; Red currants
Custards, 305
    Amaretto-Chocolate Trifle, 319
    Brandy Bread Pudding, 313
    Calvados, 145
    Chocolate Pots de Crème, 319
    Chocolate Rum Pudding, 314
    Cointreau, 148
    Crème Brûlée, 314–315
    Crème Caramel with Ginger, 313
    Lingonberry Cheese Pudding, 315–316
    Riz à la Malta, 317
    Riz Impératrice, 317
    Trifle with Fresh Fruit, 318–319
    Vanilla Pots de Crème, 319

Danish Fillings
    Cream Cheese, 106
    Danish Filling I, 105
    Danish Filling II, 106
Danish Pastries
    Bear Claws, 106–107
    Butterhorns, 108
    Cinnamon Wreath, 108–109
    Envelopes, 111
    Mayor's Wreath, 112
    Pastry Dough, 104–105
    Raisin Snails, 112–113
    Sister's Pull-Apart Coffee Cake, 113
    Sugar Buns, 114
    Twists, 109–110
Dark chocolate, 574
Dark Chocolate Cream, 191
Dark Chocolate Filling, 325
Dark Truffles, 464
Dates, 582
Decorating, 498
    with fondant, 523–524
    glazing or icing with fondant, 524–525
    Paste, Hippen, 527

Modified, 546
Paste, Macaroon, 123
with a pastry bag, 501–502
with a piping bag, 505–506
piping designs for special-occasion cakes, 506–516
piping gel, 506
with sauces, 517–519
tracing onto marzipan, 531
Wedding Cake Assembly and Decorations, 549–553
Decorations
    Buttercream
        Basketweave Pattern, 502
        Roses, 503–504
        Pearl and Shell Patterns, 504
        Rosettes, 504
    Candied Citrus Peels, 520–521
        Quick Method, 521
    Caramelized Almonds, Hazelnuts, Walnuts and Pecans, 488–489
    Chocolate
        Butterfly ornaments, 455
        Cocoa painting, 457–458
        Curls, 444–445
        Cut-outs, 445–447
        Figurines, 449–454
        Hollow Chocolate Figures Using Molds, 458–459
        Leaves, 447–448
        Modeling, 449
        Molding Chocolate Strips, 459
        Roses, 449
        Shavings, 448
        Streaking, 455
    Fondant Ornaments, 523
    Marzipan
        Angel, 532–533
        Bear, 534–536
        Carrots, 185
        Coffee Beans, 204
        Easter Bunny, 536–537
        Easter Chicken, 538–539
        Oranges, 243
        Pig, 539–540
        Roses and Leaves, 541–544
    Pâte à Choux for, 545
    Royal Icing, 528–529
    Sugar
        Glazed Fruit, 489–490
        Gum Paste with Gum Tragacanth, 491
        Nougat, 492
        Nougatine Crunch, 493
        Pastillage, 493–494
        Pulled Sugar Bow with Ribbons, 476–478
        Pulled Sugar Rose, 474–476
        Rock, 494–495
        Spun, 495–497
        Tulips, 546–548
Decorative Doughs
    Salt, 28
    Unbaked Salt, 29
    Weaver's, 36
    Whole Wheat Weaver's, 36
Deep-frying thermometer, 600
Desserts. *See* Christmas Desserts; Frozen Desserts; Meringue Desserts; Light Desserts
Diplomats, 233

Dipping fork, 600
Dobosh Sponge, 164
  Cocoa, 164
Docker or pricker, 600
Double-Chocolate Indulgence, 130
Double Loops, 53–54
Double turn, 22–23
Dough (s). *See* Basic Doughs; Decorative
  Doughs; Specific names
Dowel, 601
Drum sieve, 601

Eclairs, Chocolate, 226–227
Egg (s), 576–578
  -in-Aspic Form, 601
  Wash, 5
  Wash for Spraying, 5
  Yolk Wash, 5
English Muffins, 97–98
Envelopes, 111
Equipment, 598–605
Étamé, 601

False-bottom tart pan, 601
Farmer's Rye Rings, 60
Fig (s), 583
  Baked Figs with Honey-Vanilla Frozen
    Yogurt, 373
  Logs, 460
  Tart, 152
Filling (s)
  Apple Cinnamon, 307
  Apple Jam with Calvados, 281
  Apricot Whipped Cream, 178
  Bavarian Rum Cream, 206
  Black Currant Mousse, 180
  Calvados Custard, 145
  Calvados Wine, 177
  Caramel, 157
  Caramel Cream, 183
  Charente Bavarois, 310
  Cherry, 565
    Fresh, 565
  Chestnut Rum, 414
  Chocolate Cognac Cream, 195
  Chocolate Cream, 566
  Chunky Apple, 566
  Classic Bavarian Cream, 566
  Classic Chocolate Bavarian Cream, 567
  Coconut Cream, 197
  Cointreau Custard, 148
  Cream Chantilly, 343
  Cream Cheese, 184
    for Danish, 106
  Crème Parisienne, 567
  Danish Filling I, 105
  Danish Filling II, 106
  Dark Chocolate, 325
  Dark Chocolate Cream, 191
  Frangelico Cream, 191
  Ganache, 567–568
  Hazelnut Cream, 200
  Hazelnut Nougat Cream, 237
  Kirsch Whipped Cream, 218
  Lemon Cream, 568
  Lemon Curd, 568
  Macaroon-Maraschino Whipped Cream,
    216
  Maraschino Cream, 202
  Mazarin, 569

Milk Chocolate, 325
Mocha Cream, 349
Mocha Whipped Cream, 204
Nougat Butter, 199
Orange Almond, 100
Passion Fruit Mousse, 220
Pastry Cream, 569–570
Pear Bavarois, 311–312
Pecan, 151
Persimmon, 423
Praline Buttercream, 343
Raspberry Cream, 214
Raspberry Mousse, 338
Rum Ball, 256
Rum Parfait, 340
Tamarind Parfait, 303
Trier, 265
Triple Chocolate, 325
Vanilla Bavarian Cream, 570
White Chocolate, 325
White Chocolate Mousse, 207
Fixative syringe, 601
Flan ring, 601
Fleurons, 24
Florentina (s), 130–131
  Batter, 131
  Cones with Seasonal Fruit, 282–283
  Noisettes, 283
  Peach Ice Cream in Florentina Baskets,
    361–362
  Surprise, 234
Florentine Torte, 416–418
Flour, 578–580
Fondant, 521–522
  Decorating with, 523
  Glazing or icing with, 524–525
Frangelico, 572
  Chocolate and Frangelico Mousse Cake,
    190–191
  Cream, 191
French Bread. *See* Baguettes
French Meringue, 333
Fresh-Coconut Ice Cream, 359
Fresh Strawberries with Champagne
    Sabayon, 389
Fritter Batter, 288
Fritters
  with Fresh Berries, 288
  Plum, 286–288
Frozen Desserts
  Baked Alaska, 335–336
  Baked Figs with Honey-Vanilla Frozen
    Yogurt, 373
  Blood Orange Sorbet in Magnolia
    Cookie Shells, 383–385
  Bombe Aboukir, 368
  Bombe Bourdaloue, 369
  Bombe Ceylon, 369
  Bombe Monarch, 370
  Caramel Ice Cream in a Cage, 356–358
  Caramelized Pineapple Barbados, 386
  Champagne Sorbet, 365
  Cherries Jubilee, 374
  Coupe Bavaria, 370
  Coupe Belle Hélène, 371
  Coupe Hawaii, 371
  Coupe Niçoise, 371
  Coupe Sweden, 373
  Frozen Hazelnut Coffee Mousse,
    375

Frozen Raspberry Mousse with
    Meringues, 337–338
Fruit-flavored Frozen Yogurt, 387
Ginger Soufflé Glacé, 375–377
Honey-Vanilla Frozen Yogurt, 386
Ice Cream Cake Jamaica, 339–340
Individual Baked Alaskas, 336
Lingonberry Parfait, 377
Macadamia Nut Ice Cream, 360
Medley of Sorbets in Tulips, 378
Meringue Glacé Chantilly, 351
Meringue Glacé Leda, 346–348
Papaya Ice Cream, 360
Peach Ice Cream in Florentina Baskets,
    361–362
Poached Pears with Ginger Ice Cream
    and Two Sauces, 378–379
Vacherin with Plum Ice Cream,
    350–351
Fruit, 580–588. *See also* Specific names
  Barrels, 284–286
  Cake, 418–419
  -flavored Frozen Yogurt, 387
  Florentina Cones with Seasonal,
    282–283
  Glazed, 489–490
  Puff Pastry with Fruit and Champagne
    Sabayon, 288–289
  Tartlets, 234–235
  Trifle with Fresh, 318–319
  Valentines, 389–391
  Waffles, 235
  Winter Fruit Compote, 400–401

Ganache, 567–568
Garlic Bread, 60–61
Gâteau. *See also* Cakes, Decorated
  Arabe, 338–339
  au Diplomate, 198
  Istanbul, 199
  Lugano, 200
  Malakoff, 201–202
  Moka Carrousel, 202–204
  Saint-Honoré, 204–206
Gelatin, 588–589
  in cake fillings, 174–175
Gianduja, 461
  Bites, 461
Ginger
  Blueberry Ginger Muffins, 115
  Cobbler with Apples and, 276–277
  Crème Caramel with, 313
  Poached Pears with Ginger Ice Cream
    and Two Sauces, 378–379
  Soufflé Glacé, 375–377
Gingerbread
  Cookies, 419
  Houses, 427–437
  Muffins (variation), 169
  Soft Gingerbread Cake, 169
  Sponge, 422
Gingersnaps, 132
Glazed Fruit, 489–490
Glaze (s)
  Apricot, 526
  Black Currant, 180
  Chocolate, 526
  Lemon, 208
  Passion Fruit Jelly, 219
  Pectin, 526–527

Glaze (s) (*cont.*)
    Red Currant, 527
Glazing or Icing with Fondant, 524–525
Glucose, 594
    measuring, 7
Golden sugar. *See* Brown sugar
Golden syrup, 594
Gougères (Cheese Puffs), 11
Grand Marnier, 572
    Soufflé, 327–328
Granulated sugar, 594
Grapes, 583
Gugelhupf, 98
    Chocolate, 168
    pan, 601
Guéridon, 601
Gum arabic, 589
Gum tragacanth, 589
    Gum Paste with, 491

Ham and/or Cheese Croissants, 9
Harlequin Cake, 206
Harlequin Soufflé, 329
Hazelnut (s), 592
    Butter Cookies, 132–133
    -Chocolate Biscuit, 164
    Chocolate Hazelnut Cake, 193
    Cream, 200
    Cuts, 248
    Florentina Noisettes, 283
    Flowers, 249
    Frozen Hazelnut Coffee Mousse, 375
    Japonaise, 341
    Meringue Noisette, 334
    Nougat Butter, 199
    Nougat Cream, 237
    Nougat Slices, 236–237
    Paste, 6
    Short Dough, 32
    Squares, 133
    Streusel, 8
    Swedish Hazelnut Tart, 154
Heide Sand Cookies, 133–134
High altitude adjustments for cake baking,
    613–615
Hippen Decorating Paste, 527
    Coupe Hawaii, 371
    Meringue Glacé Leda, 346–348
    Modified, 546
Hollow Chocolate Figures Using Molds,
    458–459
Honey, 594–595
    -Bran Muffins, 117
    -Vanilla Frozen Yogurt, 386
Honeydew (s), 583
    Melon Sorbet, 366
Hors d'oeuvres
    Cheese Straws, 11
    Gougères (Cheese Puffs), 11
    Ham and/or Cheese Croissants, 9
Hot Cross Buns, 67
Hot Fudge Sauce, 559
Hot or Cold Chocolate Sauce, 559
Hotel pan, 601
Hungarian Chocolate Twists, 99–100

Ice Cream, 353–355. *See also* Bombes;
    Coupes; Frozen Desserts
    Baked Alaska, 335–336
    Banana Poppy Seed, 356

Banana-Tofu, 383
Cake Jamaica, 339–340
Caramel, 356
Caramel Ice Cream in a Cage, 356–358
Cherries Jubilee, 374
Chocolate, 358
Fresh-Coconut, 359
Individual Baked Alaskas, 336
Macadamia Nut, 360
Mango, 360
Meringue Glacé Chantilly, 351
Meringue Glacé Leda, 346–348
Papaya, 360
Peach, 361
Peach Ice Cream in Florentina Baskets,
    361–362
Pistachio, 362–363
Plum, 363
Poached Pears with Ginger Ice Cream
    and Two Sauces, 378–379
Quick Coconut, 359
Strawberry, 364
Vacherin with Plum, 350–351
Vanilla, 364
White-Chocolate, 365
White-Chocolate Ice Cream with Ginger,
    364–365
Icing (s)
    Chocolate Buttercream, 501
    Fondant, 521–522
    Praline Buttercream, 343
    Royal, 528–529
    Simple, 529
    Vanilla Buttercream, 501
Individual Baked Alaskas, 336
Ingredients, 571–597
Invert sugar, 595
Italian Easter Bread, 62
Italian Meringue, 333

Japonaise, 341
    Batter, 333
Jellying agents, 588–589
Joggar Bread, 63

Kaiser Rolls, 76
Kirschwasser, 572
    Kirsch Whipped Cream, 218
    Rings, 237
    Strawberry Kirsch Cake, 216–218
Kiwi (s), 583
    Mousse Cake, 220
    Sauce, 560
    Tart, 149
Klenäter, 84
Knäckebröd, 74
Knots, 53

Ladyfingers, 134
    Chocolate, 135
Lard, 573
    in pie dough, 17
Leavening agents, 589–591
Lemon (s), 583–584
    -Almond Tartlets, 238
    -Butter Cookie Dough, 415
    Chiffon Cake, 207–208
    Chiffon Pouches, 393
    Citrons, 231
    Cream, 568

Curd, 568
    Glaze, 208
    Raspberry-Lemon Tart, 151
Light Desserts, 381–382
    Baked Bananas with Banana-Tofu Ice
        Cream, 382–383
    Banana-Tofu Ice Cream, 383
    Blood Orange Sorbet in Magnolia
        Cookie Shells, 383–385
    Caramelized Pineapple Barbados, 386
    Crepes Vienna, 387
    Fresh Strawberries with Champagne
        Sabayon, 389
    Fruit-flavored Frozen Yogurt, 387
    Fruit Valentines, 389–391
    Honey-Vanilla Frozen Yogurt, 386
    Lemon Chiffon Pouches, 393
    Lychee Charlotte Royal, 394–395
    Orange Gratin, 396–397
    Pears California, 397
    Sabayon, 398
    Salzburger Soufflé, 398–399
    Strawberry-Peach Yogurt Creams, 400
    Winter Fruit Compote, 400–401
    Zinfandel Poached Pears, 401
Light Truffles, 465
Lime (s), 584
    Strawberry-Lime Sauce, 281
Lingonberry (ies), 584
    Cake, 168
    Cheese Pudding, 315–316
    Parfait, 377
Linzer Dough, 14
Linzer Tartlets, 238
Liqueur Soufflés, 328
Litchi. *See* Lychee
Loaf pan, 602
Loaf sugar, 595
Lucia Buns, 407–408
Lychee (s), 584
    Bavarois, 395
    Charlotte Royal, 394–395

Macadamia Nut (s), 592
    Chocolate-Filled Macadamia Morsels,
        248
    Cookies, 135
    Ice Cream, 360
    White Chocolate Bavarois with
        Macadamia and Pistachio Nuts, 312
Macaroon (s)
    Almond Macaroon Cookies, 123
    Bananas, 239–240
    Candies, 249–250
    Chocolate, 227–228
    Coconut, 129
    Decorating Paste, 123
    -Maraschino Whipped Cream, 216
    Orange, 136
    Sicilian Macaroon Cake, 215–216
    Vanilla, 268
Madeira, 572
Malt sugar or syrup, 595
Mandarin (s)
    Sorbet, 366
    Tart with Armagnac, 149
Mango (s), 584–585
    Ice Cream, 360
    Sauce, 560
Maple syrup, 595

Maraschino, 572
  Cream, 202
Marble Brysselkex, 125
Margarine, 573
Maria Puffs, 300
Marjolaine, 342–343
Marsala, 572
Marzipan, 529–532
  Angel, 532–533
  Bear, 534–536
  Carrots, 185
  Coffee Beans, 204
  Easter Bunny, 536–537
  Easter Chicken, 538–539
  modeling tools, 602
  Oranges, 243
  Pig, 539–540
  Roses and leaves, 541–544
Mascarpone Sauce, 561
Mayor's Wreath, 112
Mazarin (s), 241
  Apple, 225–226
  Filling, 569
  Form, 602
Medley or Sorbets in Tulips, 378
Melon baller, 602
Meringue, 331–332
  Baked Alaska, 335–336
  Basic
    French, 333
    Italian, 333
    Japonaise Batter, 333
    Noisette, 334
    Nut, 343
    Swiss, 334
  Baskets with Raspberries, 344–345
  Black Forest Cake, 345–346
  Blackberry Meringue Tartlets, 336–337
  Budapest Swirls, 274–275
  Chocolate Meringue Landeck, 349
  Frozen Raspberry Mousse with, 337–338
  Fruit Valentines, 389–391
  Gâteau Arabe, 338–339
  Glacé Chantilly, 351
  Glacé Leda, 346–348
  Hazelnut Cuts, 248
  Ice Cream Cake Jamaica, 339–340
  Individual Baked Alaskas, 336
  Japonaise, 341
  Landeck, 348–349
  Marjolaine, 342–343
  Mocha, 350
  Rhubarb Meringue Tart, 153
  Vacherin with Plum Ice Cream, 350–351
Metal bars, 602
Metric System, 606–612
  metric and U.S. equivalents:
    length, 611
    temperature, 612
    volume, 609
    weight, 610
  precise metric equivalents and conversions, 608
Milk, 575–576
  buttermilk, 576
  dry or milk powder, 576
  evaporated and condensed, 576
Milk chocolate, 574

Milk Chocolate Filling, 325
Milk Rolls, 54–55
Mimosa, 462
Miniature Palm Leaves, 250
Mise en place, use in professional kitchen, 3
Mocha Cream, 349
Mocha Meringues, 350
Mocha Whipped Cream, 204
Modeling Chocolate, 449
Modified Hippen Decorating Paste, 546
Molasses, 595
Molding Chocolate Strips, 459
Mousseline Sauce, 561
Mousse (s), 305
  Black Currant, 180
  Chocolate Mousse in Chocolate Teardrops, 320–321
  Cupid's Treasure Chest, 321–322
  Frozen Hazelnut Coffee, 375
  Frozen Raspberry Mousse with Meringues, 337–338
  Raspberry White Chocolate, 323
  Triple Chocolate Terrine, 324–325
Muffins. See Breakfast Breads
Muffin pan, 602
Multiple pastry wheel, 602

Napoleons
  Classic, 263
  Swedish, 262
Nectarines, 585
Noisette Rings, 242
Nougat, 492
  Butter, 199
  Montélimar, 462–463
Nougatine Crunch, 493
Nut Meringue, 343

Oat Bran-Yogurt Muffins, 118
Oat Flakes, 135
Onion-Walnut Bread, 64
Orange (s), 585
  Almond Filling, 100
  Bitter Orange Sauce, 561
  Blood Orange Sauce, 385
  Blood Orange Sorbet, 385
  Blood Orange Sorbet in Magnolia Cookie Shells, 383–385
  Budapest Swirls, 274
  Grand Marnier Souffle, 327–328
  Gratin, 396–397
  Macaroons, 136
  Moons, 463
  Sauce, 561
  Sorbet, 366
  Swedish Orange Rye Bread, 72
  Syrup, 293
  to cut segments of, 276
  Truffle Strips, 242–243
  Walnut-Orange Tartlets, 268
Othellos, 244

Palm Leaves, 136–137
  Miniature, 250
Panettone (Italian Easter Bread), 62
  Toasted Panettone with Mascarpone Sauce, 300
Pancakes, Small Swedish, 296–297
Papaya (s), 585

Ice Cream, 360
Parfaits, 354
Pariser Chocolate Cake, 208
Pariser Waffles, 236
Passion Fruit (s), 585
  Jelly, 219
  Mousse Filling, 220
Pastillage, 493–494
Pastries, Individual, 223–224. See also Breakfast Pastries
  Almond Doubles, 247
  Almond Truffles, 225
  Apple Mazarins, 225–226
  Blackberry Meringue Tartlets, 336
  Brandy Pretzels, 247
  Caramel-Walnut Tartlets, 269
  Chocolate-Covered Pretzels, 247
  Chocolate Eclairs, 226–227
  Chocolate-Filled Macadamia Morsels, 248
  Chocolate Macaroons, 227–228
  Chocolate Meringue Landeck, 349
  Chocolate Roulade, 427
  Chocolate Triangles, 228–230
  Citrons, 231
  Classic Napoleons, 263
  Cream Horns, 232–233
  Diplomats, 233
  Florentina Surprise, 234
  Fruit Tartlets, 234–235
  Fruit Waffles, 235
  Hazelnut Cuts, 248
  Hazelnut Flowers, 249
  Hazelnut Nougat Slices, 236–237
  Japonaise, 341
  Kirschwasser Rings, 237
  Lemon-Almond Tartlets, 238
  Linzer Tartlets, 238
  Macaroon Bananas, 239–240
  Macaroon Candies, 249–250
  Maria Puffs, 300
  Marjolaine, 342
  Mazarins, 241
  Meringue Baskets with Raspberries, 344
  Meringue Landeck, 348–349
  Miniature Palm Leaves, 250
  Mocha Meringues, 350
  Noisette Rings, 242
  Orange Truffle Strips, 242–243
  Othellos, 244
  Pariser Waffles, 236
  Persimmon Cream Slices, 421–423
  Petits Fours, 244–246
  Polynées, 253
  Porcupines, 257
  Pretzels, 253–254
  Raspberry Cut-outs, 251
  Rum Balls, 254–256
  Rum-Chocolate Spools, 258
  Small Princess Pastries, 259
  Strawberry Hearts, 251
  Streusel Kuchen, 260
  Swans, 260–261
  Swedish Napoleons, 262–263
  Tosca, 266–267
  Triangles, 264
  Trier Squares, 264–265
  Vanilla Macaroons, 268
  Vienna Petits Fours, 252
  Walnut-Orange Tartlets, 268

Pastry bag, 602
  decorating with, 501–502
Pastry brush, 602
Pastry Cream, 569–570
Pastry cutters or cookie cutters, 602
Pastry wheel, 603
Pâte à Choux, 14, 15–16
  Chocolate Eclairs, 226–227
  Choux Surprise, 91
  for Decoration, 545
  Gougères (Cheese Puffs), 11
  Maria Puffs, 300
  Swans, 260–261
  Swans for Restaurant Service, 262
  Swedish Profiteroles, 299–300
Peach (s), 586
  Cobbler with Peaches and Cinnamon,
    278
  Ice Cream, 361
  Ice Cream in Florentina Baskets,
    361–362
  Strawberry-Peach Yogurt Creams, 400
Peanut Butter Cookies, 138
Pear (s), 586
  Bavarois, 311–312
  California, 397
  Charlotte, 310–311
  Cointreau Pear Sauce, 401
  Cointreau Tart with Apple, Pear, or
    Rhubarb, 148
  Poached Pears with Ginger Ice Cream
    and Two Sauces, 378–379
  Small Pear Tartlets with Caramel Sauce,
    294–295
  Zinfandel Poached, 401
Peasant Breads
  Farmer's Rye Rings, 60
  Russian Rolled-Wheat Bread, 68–69
  Swedish Peasant Bread, 73
  Swedish Peasant Rings, 73
Pecan (s), 592
  Apple-Pecan Buttermilk Muffins,
    114–115
  Filling, 151
  -Raisin Souffle, 329
  -Whiskey Tart, 150–151
Pectin, 589
  Glaze, 526
Perforated sheet pan, 603
Persimmon (s), 423–424, 586
  Bavarois, 420
  Charlotte, 420–421
  Cream Slices, 421–423
  Filling, 423
  Muffins, 119
  Pudding, 423–424
  Sauce, 562
Petits Fours, 244–246
Petits Fours Sec, 246–247
  Almond Doubles, 247
  Brandy Pretzels, 247
  Chocolate-Covered Pretzels, 247
  Chocolate-Filled Macadamia Morsels,
    248
  Hazelnut Cuts, 248
  Hazelnut Flowers, 249
  Macaroon Candies, 249–250
  Miniature Palm Leaves, 250
  Raspberry Cut-outs, 251
  Strawberry Hearts, 251

Vienna Petits Fours, 252
Pie (s), 143–144
  Dough, 17
  fluted edge, to make, 17–18
  Pumpkin or Sweet Potato, 424–425
  weights, 603
Pincers, 603
Pine Nut (s), 592–593
  Chocolate Pine Nut Tart, 146
  Cookies, 135
Pineapple (s), 586
  Caramelized Pineapple Barbados, 386
  Caramelized Pineapple with Coconut Ice
    Cream, 386
  Sauce, 562
Piping bag, 603
  instructions to make, 505–506
Piping bottle, 603
Piping Chocolate, 449
Piping designs for special-occasion cakes,
    506–516
Piping gel, 506
Piping tip, 603
Pirouettes, 138–139
Pistachio (s), 593
  Ice Cream, 362–363
  Slices, 464
Pizza Dough, 18
Plastic strips, 603
Plättar. See Small Swedish Pancakes
Plättiron. See Small Swedish Pancakes pan
Plum (s), 586–587
  Fritters, 286–288
  Ice Cream, 363
  Sauce, 562–563
  Souffle. *See* Blueberry Souffle
  Vacherin with Plum Ice Cream,
    350–351
Poached Fruit, 6
Poached Pears
  with Ginger Ice Cream and Two Sauces,
    378–379
  Zinfandel, 401
Poaching Syrup I, 6
Poaching Syrup II, 6
Polynées, 253
Poppy Seed
  Banana Poppy Seed Ice Cream, 356
  Cake, 209
  Cake Base, 210
Porcupines, 257
Potash, 590
Potato Bread, 65
Potato starch, 596
Pots de Crème
  Chocolate, 319
  forms, 603
  Vanilla, 319
Powdered sugar, 595
Praline, 7
  Buttercream, 343
  Paste, 7
Pre-dough, 77
  in bread baking, 46
Pretzels, 253–254
Pricker. *See* Docker
Princess Cake, 210–211
Profiteroles
  Maria Puffs, 300
  Swedish, 299

Proof box, 47, 603
Puff Paste, 13, 19–20
  Apple Turnovers, 82
  Bouchées, 27–28
  Cherry Cross-over Strip, 89–90
  Choux Surprise, 91
  Classic (French), 21–23
  Classic Napoleons, 263
  Cream Horns, 232–233
  Diamonds, 100–102
  double turn for, 22–23
  Fleurons, 24
  Fruit Waffles, 235
  Gâteau Saint-Honoré, 204–206
  Miniature Palm Leaves, 250
  Pariser Waffles, 236
  Pretzels, 253–254
  Palm Leaves, 136–137
  Quick, 23
  Swedish Napoleons, 262–263
  Tart Tatin, 155–156
  Vol-au-Vent, 25–26
  Wales Surprise, 91
  with Fruit and Champagne Sabayon,
    288–289
Pumpkin
  Muffins, 118–119
  or Sweet Potato Pie, 424–425
  White-Chocolate Pumpkin Cheesecake,
    220

Queen of Sheba Cake, 211–212
  Cake Base, 212
Quiche Lorraine, 10
Quick Coconut Ice Cream, 359
Quick Method for Candied Citrus Peels,
    521
Quick Puff Paste, 23
Quick Vanilla Sugar, 406

Rack oven, 603
Raisin (s), 587
  Bread, 66
  Brownies, 139
  Cake, 169
  Muffins, 169
  Oatmeal Cookies, 139
  Pecan-Raisin Souffle, 329
  Snails, 112–113
Ramekins, 604
Raspberry (ies), 587
  Brandy, 572
  Cake, 212–214
  Chocolate Truffle Cake with, 195–196
  Cream, 214
  Cupid's Treasure Chest, 321
  Cut-outs, 251
  Frozen Raspberry Mousse with
    Meringues, 337–338
  -Lemon Tart, 151
  Meringue Baskets with, 344–345
  Mousse Filling, 338
  Sauce, 563
  Sorbet, 366–367
  Turnovers, 140
  Wafers, 289–291
  -White Chocolate Mousse, 323
Rectangular fluted pan, 604
Red Currant (s), 587
  Glaze, 527

Rhubarb, 587–588
Cobbler with Rhubarb and Honey, 278
Cointreau Tart with Apple, Pear, or
    Rhubarb, 148
Meringue Tart, 153
Strawberry-Rhubarb Tart, 152–153
Rice Pudding. See Riz à la Malta; Riz
    Impératrice
Rising, amounts for breads and rolls, 47
Riz à la Malta, 317
Riz Impératrice, 317
Rock sugar, 494–495
Rolled-wheat, 579
Russian Rolled-Wheat Bread, 68–69
Rolls, 74
Bread Sticks, 76
Dinner (variation), 409–410
Double Loops, 53–54
forming, 75
Hot Cross Buns, 67
Kaiser, 76
Knots, 53
Milk, 54–55
Onion-Walnut, 64
Pre-dough, 77
Rustica, 77
Swedish Whole-Grain Crisp, 78
Tessiner, 79
Twists, 54
Wheat Crisp, 79
Romanoff Sauce, 563
Rosemary Bread, 67
Roulade
Batter, 170
Chocolate, 427
Swedish Jam Roll, 170
Yule Logs, 425–427
Royal Icing, 528–529
Rum, 572
Apple Rum Charlotte, 306–307
Babas, 291–292
Ball Filling, 256
Balls, 254–256
Chocolate Rum Pudding, 314
-Chocolate Spools, 258
Parfait, 340
Syrup, 292
Russian Rolled-Wheat Bread, 68–69
Rustica, 77
Rye Bread (s)
Farmer's Rye Rings, 60
Swedish Orange, 72

Sabayon, 398
Fresh Strawberries with Champagne,
    389
Puff Pastry with Fruit and Champagne,
    288–289
Saccharometer. See Baumé thermometer
Sacher Biscuit, 215
Sacher Torte, 214–215
Salamander, 604
Salt Dough, 28
Salzburger Soufflé, 398–399
San Francisco Sourdough Loaves, 71
Sauce(s), 555–556
Apricot, 556
    from Canned Apricots, 557
Bitter Orange, 561
Blood Orange, 385

Blueberry, 557
Brandied Whipped Cream, 424
Calvados Whipped Cream, 281
Caramel I, 557
Caramel II, 558
Cherry, 558
Chocolate Sauce for Piping, 560
Cointreau Pear, 401
Cranberry, 558
Crème Fraîche, 559
decorating with, 517–519
Hot Fudge, 559
Hot or Cold Chocolate, 559
Kiwi, 560
Mango, 560
Mascarpone, 561
Mousseline, 561
Orange, 561
Orange Syrup, 293
Persimmon, 562
Pineapple , 562
Plum, 562–563
Raspberry, 563
Romanoff, 563
Rum Syrup, 292
Sour Cream Mixture for Piping, 564
Strawberry-Lime, 281
Strawberry, 563
Vanilla Custard, 564–565
Savarin form, 604
Savarins, 292
Savory Recipes, 9–11
Sheet pan, 604
Short Dough, 13, 29–31
Cake-Bottoms, 32
Cocoa, 31
Cookies, 35
Hazelnut, 32
lining tart pans with, 33
Pretzels, 253–254
Raspberry Turnovers, 140
Sicilian Macaroon Cake, 215
Simple Icing, 529
Simple Syrup, 7
Single turn, 96–97
Sister's Pull-Apart Coffee Cake, 113
Skimmer, 604
Small Pear Tartlets with Caramel Sauce,
    294–295
Small Princess Pastries, 259
Small Swedish Pancakes, 296–297
Small Swedish Pancakes pan, 604
Sodium bicarbonate, 574, 590–591
Soft Gingerbread Cake, 169
Sorbet, 354
Blood Orange, 385
Blood Orange Sorbet in Magnolia
    Cookie Shells, 383–385
Champagne, 365
Honeydew Melon, 366
Mandarin, 366
Medley of Sorbets in Tulips, 378
Orange, 366
Raspberry, 366–367
Soufflé Glacé, Ginger, 375–377
Souffle (s), 306
Apricot. See Blueberry
Black Currant. See Blueberry
Blueberry, 326
Cheese, 10

Chocolate, 329
Crepe, 327
Grand Marnier, 327–328
Harlequin, 329
Liqueur, 328
Pecan-Raisin, 329
Plum. See Blueberry
Sour Cream Mixture for Piping, 564
Sourdough Bread, 69–70
San Francisco Sourdough Loaves, 71
Sourdough Starter, 69–70
Sponge Cakes and Other Cake Batters,
    159–161
Almond Sponge, 162–163
Baked Chocolate Sheet, 324
Biscuit Viennoise, 163
Carrot Sponge, 184
Chocolate Biscuit, 163
Chocolate Sponge Cake, 162
Cocoa Almond Sponge, 163
Cocoa Dobosh Sponge, 164
to cut and move layers of, 174
Dobosh Sponge, 164
Gingerbread Sponge, 422
Hazelnut-Chocolate Biscuit, 164
Othello Batter, 244
Poppy Seed Cake Base, 210
Queen of Sheba Cake Base, 212
Roulade Batter, 170
Sacher Biscuit, 215
Sponge Cake, 161–162
Vanilla Butter Cake, 165
Sponge method in bread baking, 46
Springform pan, 604
Spritz Rings, 140
Spun Sugar, 495–497
Star Braid, 56–59
Steam injectors, 47, 605
Steam oven, 47
steam, to create in bread baking, 48
Stollen
Braided, 405
Christmas, 406
Strassburger Cookies, 141
Strawberry (ies), 588
Fresh Strawberries with Champagne
    Sabayon, 389
Hearts, 251
Ice Cream, 364
Kirsch Cake, 216–218
-Lime Sauce, 281
-Peach Yogurt Creams, 400
Pyramids, 297–299
-Rhubarb Tart, 152–153
Sauce, 563
Streusel Kuchen, 260
Streusel Topping, 8
Strudel
Apple Strudel, Austrian Style, 272
Apple Strudel, German Style, 273–274
Sugar, 467–469, 593–595
Baumé readings for, 615
Blown, 473–474, 478–479
Boiled Sugar Basic Recipe, 469
Boiled Sugar Conversions, 615–616
Boiled Sugar Method I, 470
Boiled Sugar Method II, 470–471
Caramelized, 487
Dry Method, 488
with Water, 488

Sugar (*cont.*)
  Caramelized Almonds, Hazelnuts,
    Walnuts and Pecans, 488–489
  Cast, 479–487
    metal forms for, 487
    templates for, 480–482
  colors in working with 471–472
  Gum Paste with Gum Tragacanth, 491
  Nougat, 492
  Nougatine Crunch, 493
  pan, 605
  Pastillage, 493–494
  Pulled, 473–474
    Rose, 474–476
    Sugar Bow with Ribbons, 476–478
  Rock, 494–495
  Simple Syrup, 7
  Spun, 495–497
  Syrup, 20° Baumé, 521
  thermometer, 605
  workbox, 478
Sugar Buns, 114
Swans, 260–261
Swedish
  Breakfast Spirals, 102–103
  Chocolate Cake, 218
  Hazelnut Tart, 154
  Jam Roll, 170
  Napoleons, 262–263
  Orange Rye Bread, 72
  Peasant Bread, 73
  Peasant Rings, 73
  Profiteroles, 299–300
  Spice Bread, 410
  Thin Bread, 74
  Whole-Grain Crisp Rolls, 78
Sweeteners, 593–595. *See also* Sugar;
  Specific sweeteners
Sweet Pig's Head, 409
Sweet Potato
  Pumpkin or Sweet Potato Pie, 424–425
Swiss Meringue, 334

Tamarind (s), 588
  Parfait, 303
  Tropical Surprise Packages, 301–303
Tapioca starch, 596
Tart pan, 605
Tart Shells
  lining with short dough, 33
  prebaking or baking blind, 33, 143
Tartaric acid, 595–596
  Solution, 596
Tartlet pans, 605
Tartlets
  Blackberry Meringue, 336–337
  Caramel-Walnut, 269
  Fruit, 234–235
  Lemon-Almond, 238
  Linzer, 238
  Small Pear Tartlets with Caramel Sauce,
    294–295
  Walnut-Orange, 268
Tart (s), 143–144
  Apple Tart Parisienne, 145
  Chocolate Pine Nut, 146
  Clafoutis with Cherries, 147

Cointreau Tart with Apple, Pear, or
    Rhubarb, 148
  Fig, 152
  Hollandaise, 155
  Kiwi, 149
  Mandarin Tart with Armagnac, 149
  Pecan-Whiskey, 150–151
  Raspberry-Lemon, 151
  Rhubarb Meringue, 153
  Strawberry-Rhubarb, 152–153
  Swedish Hazelnut, 154
  Tatin, 155–156
  Walnut-Caramel, 156–157
Tea Cakes, 165–166
  Apple Cinnamon Cake, 166
  Banana, 167
  Chocolate Crisp Cake, 167
  Chocolate Gugelhupf, 168
  Lingonberry Cake, 168
  Raisin Cake, 169
  Soft Gingerbread Cake, 169
  Swedish Jam Roll, 170
  Tiger Cake, 171
Temperature conversions, 612
Tempering chocolate, 442–443
  seeding, 443
  tabliering, 442
Tempering fork. *See* Dipping fork
Template, 605
Tessiner Rolls, 79
Thermometers
  Baumé, 599
  deep-frying, 600
  sugar, 605
Thickeners, 596
Tiger Cake, 171
Toasted Panettone with Mascarpone Sauce,
    300
Tosca, 266–267
Tread rolling pin, 605
Triangles, 264
Trier Filling, 265
Trier Squares, 264–265
Triestine Bread, 411
Trifle
  Amaretto-Chocolate, 319
  with Fresh Fruit, 318–319
Triple Chocolate Terrine, 324–325
Tropical Mousse Cake, 219–220
Tropical Surprise Packages, 301–303
Truffles, 464–465
Tulips
  Blood Orange Sorbet in Magnolia
    Cookie Shells, 383–385
  Champagne Sorbet, 365
  Chocolate, 546–548
  Fruit Barrels, 284–286
  Macadamia Nut Ice Cream, 360
  Medley of Sorbets in, 378
  Papaya Ice Cream, 360
  Vanilla, 546–548
Twisted Loaves and Wreaths, 93–94
Twists, 54

Unbaked Salt Dough, 29

Vacherin with Plum Ice Cream, 350–351

Vanilla, 596–597
  Bavarian Cream, 570
  beans, storage of, 8
  Brysselkex, 124
  Butter Cake, 165
  Buttercream, 501
  Custard Sauce, 564–565
  Extract, 8
  Ice Cream, 364
  Macaroons, 268
  Pots de Crème, 319
  Sugar, 8
    Quick 406
  Tulips, 546–548
Vienna Petits Fours, 252
Vol-au-Vent, 25–26
Vörtbröd. See Swedish Spice Bread

Waffle rolling pin, 605
Waffles, Crisp, 280–281
Wales Surprise, 91
Walnut (s), 593
  Caramel-Walnut Tartlets, 269
  Onion-Walnut Bread, 64
  Walnut-Caramel Tart, 156–157
  Walnut-Orange Tartlets, 268
  Zucchini-Walnut Muffins, 119
Wedding Cake Assembly and Decorations,
    549–553
Wheat Crisp Rolls, 79
Wheat flours, 578–579
Whiskey, 572
  Pecan-Whiskey Tart, 150–151
White Chocolate, 442, 574
  Bavarois with Macadamia and Pistachio
    Nuts, 312
  Chunky White-Chocolate-Chip Cookies,
    127
  Filling, 325
  Ice Cream, 365
  Ice Cream with Ginger, 364–365
  Mousse Filling, 207
  Pumpkin Cheesecake, 220
  Raspberry–White Chocolate Mousse,
    323
  Triple Chocolate Terrine, 324
  White Truffles, 465
Whole Wheat Weaver's Dough, 36
Winerbrod, 81
Winter Fruit Compote, 400–401

Yeast, 591
  doughs, using salt and sugar in, 45
  fermentation, 46
Yogurt, 576
  Baked Figs with Honey-Vanilla Frozen
    Yogurt, 373
  Fruit-flavored Frozen, 387
  Honey-Vanilla Frozen, 386
  Strawberry-Peach Yogurt Creams, 400
Yule Logs, 425–427

Zabaglione. See Sabayon
Zester, 605
Zinfandel Poached Pears, 401
Zucchini-Walnut Muffins, 119